# The Tokyo War Crimes Tribunal

Like its Nuremberg counterpart, the Tokyo Trial was foundational in the field of international law. However, until now, the persistent notion of "victor's justice" in the existing historical literature has made it difficult to treat it as such. David Cohen and Yuma Totani seek to redress this by cutting through persistent orthodoxies and ideologies that have plagued the trial. Instead they present it simply as a judicial process, and in so doing reveal its enduring importance for international jurisprudence. A wide range of primary sources are considered, including court transcripts, court exhibits, the majority judgment, and five separate concurring and dissenting opinions. The authors also provide comparative analysis of the Allied trials at Nuremberg, resulting in a comprehensive and empirically grounded study of the trial. The Tokyo Tribunal was a watershed moment in the history of the Asia-Pacific region. This groundbreaking study reveals it is of continuing relevance today.

DAVID COHEN directs the WSD Handa Center for Human Rights and International Justice at Stanford University (formerly the War Crimes Studies Center at University of California, Berkeley, where Cohen taught for thirty-five years before moving the Center to Stanford in 2013). He publishes on international criminal law, transitional justice, human rights, classics, and comparative legal history, while also directing human rights, rule of law, and accountability projects in South and Southeast Asia and Africa.

YUMA TOTANI is a historian of modern Japan and presently teaches at the University of Hawaii. Her research interests are in World War II and war crimes trials in Asia and the Pacific. She is the author of *The Tokyo War Crimes Trial* (2008) and *Justice in Asia and the Pacific Region, 1945–1952* (2015). She has received various fellowships, including a National Fellowship from the Hoover Institution (2016), the Frederick Burkhardt Residential Fellowship (2012), and the Abe Fellowship (2011).

# The Tokyo War Crimes Tribunal
*Law, History, and Jurisprudence*

David Cohen
*Stanford University*

Yuma Totani
*University of Hawaii*

# CAMBRIDGE
## UNIVERSITY PRESS

University Printing House, Cambridge CB2 8BS, United Kingdom

One Liberty Plaza, 20th Floor, New York, NY 10006, USA

477 Williamstown Road, Port Melbourne, VIC 3207, Australia

314–321, 3rd Floor, Plot 3, Splendor Forum, Jasola District Centre,
New Delhi – 110025, India

79 Anson Road, #06-04/06, Singapore 079906

Cambridge University Press is part of the University of Cambridge.

It furthers the University's mission by disseminating knowledge in the pursuit of education, learning, and research at the highest international levels of excellence.

www.cambridge.org
Information on this title: www.cambridge.org/9781107119703
DOI: 10.1017/9781316348659

© David Cohen and Yuman Totani 2018

This publication is in copyright. Subject to statutory exception and to the provisions of relevant collective licensing agreements, no reproduction of any part may take place without the written permission of Cambridge University Press.

First published 2018

*A catalogue record for this publication is available from the British Library.*

ISBN 978-1-107-11970-3 Hardback

Cambridge University Press has no responsibility for the persistence or accuracy of URLs for external or third-party internet websites referred to in this publication and does not guarantee that any content on such websites is, or will remain, accurate or appropriate.

# Contents

| | |
|---|---|
| *Acknowledgments* | *page* ix |
| *Note to the Reader on Translation, Sources, and Citation* | xi |

| | |
|---|---|
| Introduction | 1 |
|    Aims and Methods | 1 |
|    The Relevant Legal Framework | 6 |
|    Historiographical Overview | 11 |
|    Chapter Overview | 22 |

## Part I  The Allied War Crimes Policy, the Indictment, and Court Proceedings

| | |
|---|---|
| 1  The Framework of the Trial | 29 |
|   1.1  From War to Peace | 29 |
|   1.2  Planning for the Trial of Far Eastern War Criminals | 36 |
|   1.3  A Chronological Overview of the Tokyo Trial | 44 |
|   1.4  Rules of Procedure | 53 |
|   1.5  Types of Evidence Collected | 61 |
| 2  Charges of Crimes against Peace | 69 |
|   2.1  Counts and Appendices in the Indictment | 70 |
|   2.2  The Legal Argument of the Prosecution | 86 |
|   2.3  The Legal Argument by the Defense | 94 |
| 3  The Japanese System of Government | 101 |
|   3.1  The Prosecution's Initial Presentation | 103 |
|   3.2  Evidence during the Court Proceedings | 120 |
|   3.3  The Prosecution's Final Argument during the Summation | 135 |
|   3.4  Conclusion | 141 |
| 4  Individual Roles in the Making of the War, and the Overall Conspiracy | 143 |
|   4.1  "Obtaining Control of Manchuria" | 147 |
|   4.2  "The Expansion of Control and Domination from Manchuria to the Rest of China" | 161 |

vi    Contents

|  |  |  |
|---|---|---|
| 4.3 | "Internal and External Preparation for Aggressive War in Asia and in the Pacific" | 175 |
| 4.4 | "Expansion of Aggression to the Rest of East Asia and the Southwest Pacific" | 178 |

## 5  Counts on Murder, War Crimes, and Crimes against Humanity — 188

| 5.1 | Counts on Conventional War Crimes | 193 |
|---|---|---|
| 5.2 | Implications of Appendices D and E in the Indictment | 200 |

## 6  Accountability for War Crimes — 203

| 6.1 | Challenges and Methods of Proof | 204 |
|---|---|---|
| 6.2 | The Prosecution's Case | 208 |
| 6.3 | The Defense Case on China | 225 |
| 6.4 | The Defense Case on the Pacific Region | 236 |
| 6.5 | The Prosecution's Summation on Government Responsibility | 250 |

## Part II  The Law and Jurisprudence of the Judgments and Separate Opinions

## 7  The Majority Judgment: Crimes against Peace — 255

| 7.1 | Introduction | 255 |
|---|---|---|
| 7.2 | Chapter II of the Majority Judgment and the Law of Crimes against Peace | 261 |
| 7.3 | Chapter III of the Judgment and the Framework of International Treaty Law | 270 |
| 7.4 | Chapters IV–VIII of the Judgment: The Master Conspiracy Narrative | 271 |
| 7.5 | Chapter IX: Findings | 292 |
| 7.6 | The Verdicts | 296 |

## 8  An Alternative Perspective on Accountability for Crimes against Peace: The Two Webb Judgments — 305

| 8.1 | Introduction | 305 |
|---|---|---|
| 8.2 | The Law of the Tribunal | 309 |
| 8.3 | Individual Factual Findings and Verdicts on Crimes against Peace | 318 |

## 9  The Majority Judgment on War Crimes — 339

| 9.1 | Introduction | 339 |
|---|---|---|
| 9.2 | Standards of Responsibility in Chapter II of the Judgment | 340 |
| 9.3 | Standards of Responsibility and Factual Findings in Chapter VIII | 349 |
| 9.4 | Standards of Responsibility in the Individual Verdicts | 355 |

## 10  An Alternative Tokyo Judgment: The Draft Webb Judgment on War Crimes — 370

| 10.1 | Issues and Context | 370 |
|---|---|---|
| 10.2 | Individual Cases | 375 |
| 10.3 | Conclusion | 389 |

## 11  The Dissenting Opinions of Justices Bernard and Roeling — 391

| 11.1 | Bernard's Dissent | 391 |
|---|---|---|
| 11.2 | Roeling's Dissent | 402 |

Contents vii

| 12 Pal's "Judgment," or Dissenting Opinion, on Crimes against Peace | 431 |
|---|---|
| 12.1 Introduction | 431 |
| 12.2 Preliminary Overview | 437 |
| 12.3 The Crime of Aggressive War | 439 |
| 12.4 The Conspiracy Charges | 452 |
| 13 Pal's Treatment of War Crimes Charges | 459 |
| 13.1 Introduction | 459 |
| 13.2 War Crimes against Civilian Populations | 462 |
| 13.3 Crimes against Prisoners of War | 476 |
| 14 The Concurring Opinions of Justices Webb and Jaranilla | 496 |
| 14.1 Jaranilla's Concurring Opinion | 496 |
| 14.2 Webb's Separate Opinion | 509 |
| Conclusion | 513 |
| *References* | 523 |
| *Index* | 535 |

# Acknowledgments

This book is the result of many years of research and collaboration by the coauthors. During this time we have both presented papers and attended conferences in many countries where we have discussed our ideas with colleagues. In our conversations with other researchers engaged with World War II war crimes trials we have also learned a great deal from hearing their views and, of course, reading their scholarship. It would be tedious to list all of these individuals but our interlocutors know who they are and will perhaps forgive us for acknowledging them collectively rather than individually. We have benefited enormously from being part of the growing group of scholars in the United States, Europe and Asia who have turned their attention to World War II war crimes trials in general and the Tokyo Trial in particular. It has also been particularly heartening to see the emergence over the past decade of a group of younger scholars who are pursuing this field with energy and commitment. We are also grateful to them for having engaged with us in their research and collaborative activities.

# Note to the Reader on Translation, Sources, and Citation

## I Transliteration, Ranks and Titles, and Translation

All Japanese personal and place names are transliterated in accordance with the standard style romanization. However, different types of romanization may appear in historical documents, such as Konoye Fumimaro instead of Konoe Fumimaro, Tojo Hideki instead of Tōjō Hideki, Kempeitai (military police force) instead of Kenpeitai, and so on. The former type of romanization is retained when providing direct quotes from historical documents. Most Chinese personal and place names are transliterated in accordance with the internationally accepted pinyin system of romanization. However, exceptions are made for those names that are better known with alternative romanization, such as Chiang Kai-shek instead of Jiang Jieshi, and Manchukuo instead of Manzhouguo. Japanese and Chinese names are given in the traditional manner throughout this book, that is, the family name precedes the personal name. The Western names that carry an umlaut (¨) are romanized in conformity with the transliteration practice in English, such as Roeling instead of Röling, and Weizsaecker instead of Weizsäcker.

When referring to individuals with ranks or titles, the highest rank or title retained at the end of hostilities is indicated at the first appearance of the name, such as "Baron Wakatsuki Reijirō," "Lieutenant General Kawabe Torashirō," "General Douglas MacArthur," and so on. It is dropped thereafter (i.e., "Wakatsuki," "Kawabe," "MacArthur," and so on). However, reference to wartime ranks and titles of certain individuals may be repeated if needed for clarification.

The Japanese word *rikugunshō* – which was the administrative branch of the Imperial Japanese Army – commonly appears in English-language historical documents as "War Ministry," but it is a misnomer. This book will use instead the "Ministry of the Army" for the sake of accuracy, alongside the "Ministry of the Navy," which is the English translation of *kaigunshō*, the administrative branch of the Imperial Japanese Navy. Similarly, the minister, the vice minister, ministry officials, and ministerial documents of *rikugunshō* are translated throughout this book as "army minister," "vice army minister," "army-ministry

xi

xii  Note to the Reader on Translation, Sources, and Citation

officials," and "army-ministry documents." Exceptions apply, however, in the case of direct quotes from those historical documents where the terms "War Ministry," "war minister," "vice war minister," etc. are used. The translation of the navy side will appear as "navy minister," "vice navy minister," "navy-ministry officials," and "navy-ministry documents."

The operational commands of the Imperial Japanese Army and Navy were known as *sanbō honbu* ("General Staff") and *kaigun gunreibu* ("Navy Operational Command," renamed in 1933 as *gunreibu* [Operational Command]) respectively. This book will translate these terms as "Army General Staff" and "Navy General Staff" to reflect the actual functions of these two command organs.

## II About the Records of Trials

Various editions of the record of the Tokyo Trial in print, digital format, microfilm, and microfiche are currently available. The National Diet Library at Tokyo, Japan, hosts large collections of the trial record and related documents that have been collected from the National Archives and Records Administration (NARA) at College Park, Maryland; the Australian War Memorial, Canberra; and various other archival repositories in Japan, such as the Japanese Supreme Court, the Japanese Ministry of Legal Affairs, the Asahi Newspaper Company, the University of Tokyo, Waseda University, and Ritsumeikan University. Some of the Diet Library's holdings have been digitized and made accessible online, including the transcripts of court proceedings and the judicial decisions of the Tokyo Tribunal (www.ndl.go.jp/index.html). The Japan Center for Asian Historical Records (JACAR) of the National Archives of Japan hosts at its website a complete set of the digital version of the transcripts of court proceedings and court exhibits, in both English and Japanese (www.jacar.go.jp/index.html). The International Criminal Court Legal Tools Database similarly hosts at its website the English-language transcripts of court proceedings and court exhibits, but the uploaded court exhibits are an incomplete set (www.icc-cpi.int/en_menus/icc/Pages/defaut/aspx). While none of these digital sources are text-searchable, the Database of the Tokyo Trials Literature at Shanghai Jiao Tong University Press carries text-searchable English-language transcripts of court proceedings (www.tokyotrial.cn). This collection will be expanded to include English-language court exhibits, the Japanese-language trial record, and the Chinese translation of the same, in text-searchable format.

At the present time when digital databases of the Tokyo Trial are being developed worldwide in the foregoing manner, print editions of the trial record remain highly valuable. The ones that are indispensable to researchers are R. John Pritchard and Sonia Magbanua Zaide (eds.), *The Tokyo War Crimes Trial*, 22 vols. (1981) and its companion five-volume index and guide, R. John Pritchard, Sonia Magbanua Zaide, and Donald Cameron Watt (eds.), *The Tokyo*

II   About the Records of Trials

*War Crimes Trial: The Comprehensive Index and Guide to the Proceedings of the International Military Tribunal for the Far East in Five Volumes* (1981–87); Neil Boister and Robert Cryer (eds.), *Documents on the Tokyo International Military Tribunal: Charter, Indictment, and Judgments* (2008); and *Kyokutō kokusai gunji saiban sokkiroki* [Transcripts of court proceedings of the International Military Tribunal for the Far East], 10 vols. (1968). This book uses a combination of these varied digital and print editions.

There are various editions of the record of the International Military Tribunal at Nuremberg (1945–46) and the twelve Subsequent Proceedings at the Nuremberg Military Tribunals under Control Council Law No. 10 (1946–49), also in print, digital format, microfilm, and microfiche. This book will make use of the following published editions: *Trial of the Major War Criminals before the International Military Tribunal: Nuremberg, 14 November 1945–1 October 1946*, 42 vols. (1947–49); and *Trials of War Criminals before the Nuernberg Military Tribunals Under Control Council Law No. 10, October 1946–April 1949*, 15 vols. (1949–53). These publications have been digitized and are made available at the website of the Military Legal Resources at the Library of Congress (www.loc.gov/rr/frd/Military_Law/Nuremberg_trials.html).

The official record of the Trial of General Yamashita Tomoyuki at the US military commission at Manila ("Yamashita Trial," October–December 1945) comprises the following three sources: (1) the transcripts of court proceedings; (2) the decision of the US military commission at Manila; and (3) the review decision on the case by the reviewing authority, General Douglas MacArthur of the US Army. These records need to be distinguished from the summary of the Yamashita Trial as it appears in the United Nations War Crimes Commission's *Law Reports of Trial of War Criminals*, vol. IV (1948), or the United States Supreme Court's decision *in re Yamashita* on the habeas corpus motion (1946), since, despite the commonplace practice, these latter two sources are not part of the official record of the Yamashita Trial. This book will treat these sources accordingly. At present, the transcripts of court proceedings, the decision of the US military commission, and the review decision are available in hardcopy and on microfilm. They are housed at the National Archives and Records Administration (NARA) at College Park, Maryland, as well as various archival sites internationally.

The official records of contemporary trials at the international criminal tribunals and hybrid courts are available at their respective official websites: Extraordinary Chambers in the Courts of Cambodia (https://eccc.gov.kh/en); the International Criminal Tribunal for the Former Yugoslavia (www.icty.org/); the Special Court for Sierra Leone, the Residual Special Court for Sierra Leone (http://rscsl.org/); and the United Nations Mechanism for International Criminal Tribunals, the Legacy Website of the International Criminal Tribunal for Rwanda

xiv    Note to the Reader on Translation, Sources, and Citation

(http://unictr.unmict.org/). Elements of these trial records are referred to both in the text and in notes by case numbers or other official names attributed to them, such as "Case File 002/19-09-2007-ECCC/SC," "*Prosecutor* v. *Tadic*, Case IT-94-1-A," "International Criminal Tribunal for the former Yugoslavia, Rules of Procedure and Evidence," etc.

Legal documents and case law from the body of US criminal law literature are referred to in the notes according to the convention, such as "*Gideon* v. *Wainwright* 372 US 335."

## III    Abbreviations and Citations in Notes and in the Text

When page numbers in the transcripts of court proceedings are referred to in this book, they are preceded by the prefix "T." When citing a court exhibit, the exhibit number will be preceded by prefix "PX" in the case of the prosecution's court exhibit, and "DX" in the case of the defense court exhibit. For instance, "PX257, T3453-4" means Prosecution Exhibit No. 257, pages 3453–4 in the transcripts of court proceedings.

To increase efficiency in citation practices, this book adopts certain special abbreviations for oft-cited sources. In Part I, the word "*Documents*" is used in notes when referring to Boister and Cryer (eds.), *Documents on the Tokyo International Military Tribunal: Charter, Indictment, and Judgments*. In Part II, further short citations and abbreviations are applied when referring to judicial opinions contained in the same publication. The decision by the majority justices is referred to as the "Majority judgment" in the text, and "MJ" in the notes. Separate opinions by Justices Henri Bernard, Delfin Jaranilla, Radhabinod Pal, and B. V. A. Roeling are referred to in the text as "Bernard's dissenting opinion," "Jaranilla's concurring opinion," "Pal's dissenting opinion," and "Roeling's dissenting opinion," and in the notes as "Bernard Opinion," "Jaranilla Opinion," "Pal Opinion," and "Roeling Opinion," respectively.

With regard to the judicial opinions by the president of the tribunal, Justice Sir William F. Webb, there are two versions that will be discussed throughout this book. One is his draft judgment, which is never published, but which is deposited at the Australian War Memorial (ref. no. 3DRL/2481), and the other is a much shorter text that Webb provided as his concurring separate opinion, and which is included in *Documents on the Tokyo International Military Tribunal*. Throughout this book, the former will be referred to as "Webb's draft judgment," or "The President's Judgment," and will be abbreviated in the notes as TPJ. The latter will be referred to as "Webb Separate Opinion" in notes.

Similarly, records of the International Military Tribunal at Nuremberg and the twelve Subsequent Proceedings at Nuremberg under Control Council Law No. 10 will be referred to in abbreviated form. The terms, "IMT Charter,"

III  Abbreviations and Citations in Notes and in the Text                    xv

"IMT indictment," and "IMT judgment" are used both in the text. Sometimes, the IMT judgment is indicated as the "IMT Nuremberg judgment" so as to distinguish it from the judgments arising from the twelve Subsequent Proceedings, or "Nuremberg judgment" to distinguish it from the Tokyo judgment. The IMT trial record we utilize is contained in Volume 1 of *Trial of the Major War Criminals before the International Military Tribunal: Nuremberg*.

As for the Nuremberg Military Tribunals that heard the twelve Subsequent Proceedings, we utilize the official *trials of war criminals before the Nuernberg military tribunals under control council law no. 10, October 1946–April 1949*. 15 vols. The cases are abbreviated collectively as NMT in notes and in the text, and the judgments of individual cases as "Medical Case" and "Milch Case" (both contained in Volume 2); "Justice Case" (in Volume 3); "Einsatzgruppen Case" (in Volume 4); "RuSHA Case" and "Pohl Case" (both contained in Volume 5); "Flick Case" and "Hostages Case" (both contained in Volume 6); "Ministries Case" (in Volume 7); "Farben Case" (in Volume 8); "Krupp Case" (in Volume 9); and "High Command Case" (in Volume 11). For instance, "High Command Case, 512–15," means the judgment of the High Command Case, pages 512–15 (in Volume 11 of *Trials of War Criminals Before the Nuernberg Military Tribunals Under Control Council Law No. 10*).

Abbreviated forms are also used in notes when citing other sources and secondary literature, such as "Reel, *The Case of General Yamashita*," instead of "A. Frank Reel, *The Case of General Yamashita* (Chicago: University of Chicago Press, 1949)." The full citation information is provided in the list of References at the end of this book.

# Introduction

### Aims and Methods

This book aims to fill a gap in the voluminous literature on the proceedings before the International Military Tribunal for the Far East (IMTFE, "Tokyo Trial," or "Tokyo Tribunal"). As will be elaborated below, several generations of Japanese scholars have contributed to what can be considered a major field of historical study focused on the Tokyo Trial. This literature, despite the intensity of its research, has focused far more on the political context of the trial, on the individual accused or other personalities, and on historical and ideological controversies concerning the war and what Japanese scholars term "war responsibility [*sensō sekinin*]" than on the substantive legal content of the proceedings. Early attempts by Western scholars to write about the trial, such as those of Richard Minear or Arnold Brackman, were either ideologically colored by contemporary political preoccupations or largely descriptive of the historical background of the creation and operation of the tribunal. Pursuing other agendas, they also did not engage in legal analysis of the substance of the proceedings. Much of the ensuing English-language scholarship followed these two paths or focused upon specific individuals, such as the Indian Justice, Radhabinod Pal. On the whole, it is fair to say, the volume and depth of Japanese scholarship on the Tokyo Tribunal dwarfs that produced by Western scholars and, unfortunately, the bulk of the Western scholarship has largely ignored the research of their Japanese colleagues, which will be reviewed below.

Apart from the characteristics just noted, what is striking about both the Japanese- and English-language scholarly traditions is the relative paucity of legal analysis of the trial process as a whole. By this we mean systematic analysis of all of the major constituents of the proceedings, that is, the way in which the prosecution and defense developed their respective case strategies, supported them through their arguments and the introduction of evidence, and focused them for the judges through their opening and closing statements. The other major constituent, of course, has to do with the way in which the judges managed the trial process, deliberated amongst themselves on legal and procedural issues, and reached factual findings and legal conclusions as reflected in their internal memoranda and, ultimately, embodied in the judgment of the tribunal and the five separate opinions appended to it. Our basic argument is that an assessment of the trial before the IMTFE as *a judicial process* demands a comprehensive analysis of *all* of these constituent elements. To date there has been no such comprehensive juristic assessment and this is the gap we aim to fill.[1]

Attempting such an assessment faces several challenges. The first is the sheer volume of the relevant primary sources: 52,000 pages of trial transcript, hundreds of exhibits and affidavits introduced into evidence, voluminous internal memoranda of the judges and records of the prosecution, and, not least, the six opinions of the judges that take up 1355 closely printed pages. Of these, the majority judgment setting out the findings and reasoning of the tribunal alone comprises 558 printed pages, primarily of detailed factual analysis, and the dissenting opinion of Justice Pal is even longer at 616 pages. Apart from the poor organization, density, and obscurity of argument of these two opinions, scholarship has been handicapped because until recently the complete juridical opinions of the IMTFE had never been brought together and published in an authoritative edition. The seminal work of Neil Boister and Robert Cryer (eds.), *The Tokyo International Military Tribunal: Documents on the Tokyo International Military Tribunal: Charter, Indictment, and Judgments* (2008), has corrected that shortcoming by publishing the official version of the majority judgment and five separate opinions, together with the indictment and other key documents, together in one massive volume.

In assessing the performance of the prosecution, defense, and judges as reflected in the trial record, we address an array of highly controversial questions that have arisen in the scholarship and public discussions on the Tokyo Trial. As we are well aware that our book challenges many of the orthodoxies that have informed these controversies we have adopted a methodology that eschews "anecdotal" commentary and criticism based upon a few selected references to the trial record. Because of the political and ideologically charged context of the Asia-Pacific War (1931–45) in which many discussions of the Tokyo Trial have implicitly or explicitly been located, we have adopted a dual strategy for dealing with the challenges that such a context represents for research that revises received wisdom, whether that of the right or that of the left.

First, we offer no account of the larger political and historical questions of the rights and wrongs of the war, such as whether Japan was in fact waging a war in self-defense because of the threat of communism from China, whether the colonial system of the Western Powers justified Japanese expansion by

---

[1] By far the most important English language work assessing the judicial aspects of the IMTFE and putting its overall proceedings in the context of applicable legal standards is the major account of Boister and Cryer, *The Tokyo International Military Tribunal*.

military means, whether the Nanjing Massacre actually took place or how many victims were murdered there, whether the United States was justified in its campaign of firebombing of Japanese cities and its use of the atomic bomb at the end of the war, whether Foreign Minister Hirota Kōki was an innocent martyr, etc. While these and many other such questions may all be interesting and important historical issues, offering an opinion on them is not relevant to assessing the work of the judges at Tokyo in arriving at their various legal conclusions. What is relevant instead, is what evidence was brought before the court, how the prosecution and defense dealt with that evidence in making their respective cases, and how the judges, in reference to that evidence, justified the legal conclusions they reached in their various opinions. To state the obvious, the judges did not have the benefit of the last seventy years of historical research and debate on World War II in Asia and the Pacific and they could not take cognizance of evidence that was not before the court. In other words, our task is to assess the substantive legal performance of the judicial process based upon the trial record and no more. While, as will be seen, some of our conclusions are highly critical of some participants in the proceedings, the criticisms are based solely upon what these individuals said and wrote within their respective roles as judges, prosecutors, and defense counsel.

The second part of our strategy for dealing with the controversial context in which the trial has so often been viewed is to base our conclusions upon systematic, in-depth analysis of the major components of the proceedings. Because it is impossible to examine every aspect of a trial process that took up two and a half years and produced a massive corpus of trial records we have instead focused in-depth on essential elements of the trial in the following manner. We trace the evolution of the prosecution case first through detailed examination of how the prosecution initially prepared their case and presented it in the indictment and their opening statement to the court. We then analyze how the prosecution case changed in response to the evidentiary and other challenges that arose during the proceedings, as reflected most clearly in their lengthy closing statement. We consider the evolution of the defense case as the defense responded to the evidence and arguments of the prosecution. Finally, we provide detailed analysis of the legal basis, factual analysis, and arguments that inform the majority opinion, taking up two full chapters with a discussion of the way in which the majority reached their conclusions on crimes against peace and on war crimes. Each of the five separate opinions receives similar detailed consideration of the reasoning and evidentiary findings on which their respective conclusions rest. Only through such a systematic approach, we maintain, can one fairly assess the juristic quality of the work of the judges and prosecution. The analysis that implements this approach, in turn, is based upon a set of criteria for judicial performance against which the conclusions of the judges can fairly be measured.

Following this approach, our book revises much of the existing understanding of the Tokyo Trial and presents a substantially new basis for understanding the work of the prosecution, defense, and judges. We argue that close consideration of the prosecution strategy prompts reassessment both of the nature of the prosecution's case and the way in which the change in their case strategy strongly impacted the majority judgment. In regard to the assessments of the judgment and separate opinions, our analysis produces a new and firmly grounded critique of the majority judgment as a final written decision of the tribunal as well as a clearer perspective on the nature and shortcomings of the separate opinions, and particularly those of justices Henri Bernard, Pal, and B. V. A. Roeling.

A further and crucially important component of our contribution to newly assessing the trial is provided by two chapters devoted to analysis of the unpublished judgment of the president of the tribunal, Sir William F. Webb. Webb, as will be seen in detail later, wrote a judgment of more than 600 pages of typescript which he proposed as the judgment of the tribunal. When a majority of judges, for reasons discussed in subsequent chapters, refused to accept this draft judgment Webb set it aside and wrote a brief concurring opinion. Webb's draft judgment, we argue, provides an important new perspective for evaluating both the evidentiary record and legal basis on which all of the judges based their opinions as well as providing a vastly better account of the justification for convictions than the poorly argued and poorly written majority judgment was able to do.

As noted above, we are aware of the challenges in producing a more definitive and systematic account of the legal content of the trial than has yet been available. Apart from the sheer volume of the trial record, much of the evidence was introduced not in the form of viva voce testimony but rather affidavits and other written documents in great quantity. The contents of these evidentiary submissions are often not reflected in the trial transcript for reasons that will become apparent in subsequent chapters. Yet, it is essential for analyzing the weight of the prosecution and defense case, as well as the evidentiary basis of the judicial opinions, to take account of the full scope of evidence the parties introduced in various forms. Most of the existing scholarship has failed to do so.

This task is further complicated by the necessity of being able to evaluate Japanese primary sources in their original language as well as taking into account the mountain of Japanese scholarship that is virtually unknown to most Western scholars. Our book integrates these important Japanese contributions along with Western scholarship. On both the Western and Japanese sides much of the scholarship – though with a few notable exceptions – has been produced by historians who have lacked both knowledge of the body of law applied at Tokyo and an understanding of the nature of an international criminal trial and

Aims and Methods 5

the criteria by which it should be assessed. This kind of knowledge is particularly essential for analysis of the majority judgment and separate opinions and evaluation of the work of the tribunal. For example, the dissenting opinion of Justice Pal has been lionized as the focal point of right wing revisionism in Japan and elsewhere, largely out of sympathy for its anti-imperialist and anti-colonial stance rather than its juristic quality. While its more than 600 pages are replete with interminable and repetitive quotations from international law treatises and articles, these alone do not establish the soundness of Pal's legal arguments. For this reason it is important to analyze his opinion, as well as the others, systematically *as a legal opinion*. This has never been comprehensively done before, which explains the rather inordinate length of the chapters on Pal.

In short, lack of systematic attention, preoccupation with historical, political, and ideological issues extraneous to the trial, and too often a lack of careful legal analysis, have produced a body of scholarship in which, apart from a few notable exceptions, scant attention has been paid to substantive quality of the body of legal opinions that on the one hand justified the verdicts and on the other hand attacked them.[2] Addressing this gap in the scholarship requires systematic analysis of the judgment, separate opinions, and Webb's draft judgment rather than conclusory, unsystematic, or ill-founded assessments.

Another shortcoming that reflects unsystematic methodologies in both some of the scholarly literature and in some of the separate opinions has to do with the scope of the jurisdiction of the tribunal. It is vital to remember that when Japan attacked Pearl Harbor and other targets in Southeast Asia in December 1941 its forces had already been fighting an ever-growing and, by 1937 massive, war in China since 1931. As we will see, more of the majority judgment focuses on the period 1928–41 than on the Pacific War (1941–5). Yet some accounts neglect to consider the ten years of war in China preceding the outbreak of the Pacific War and the decisive role consideration of that conflict played in the judges' (with the exception of Pal's) understanding of the aggressive war charges and the process by which the Japanese government ultimately decided to broaden the war at the end of 1941. Our account aims to redress this imbalance through a more comprehensive account of the way the prosecution made its case and how the judges responded in their respective opinions.

Finally, most of the scholars writing about the IMTFE from either the Japanese or the Western side have not viewed the Tokyo Trial in the context of other post-World War II war crimes trials. In particular, they have not placed the Tokyo Trial in the context of its Western counterpart, the International Military Tribunal (IMT), or Nuremberg Tribunal, which ended its work in 1946

---

[2] One of the most notable of those exceptions is Boister and Cryer's landmark *The Tokyo International Military Tribunal*, as well as some of the articles noted in chapters below that have focused on specific legal issues or aspects of particular opinions.

and thus provided what the judges at Tokyo regarded as an authoritative model for the IMTFE, both courts operating on substantially the same legal basis. Scholars of the Tokyo Trial have also seldom referenced the twelve Nuremberg subsequent proceedings which are of fundamental jurisprudential importance and were taking place at the same time as the Tokyo Trial and drew considerable attention among the international legal community. Features of the Tokyo Trial which have appeared anomalous to scholars of Japanese history were often in fact the standard procedures which informed the trials at Nuremberg and reflected the procedural standards of that epoch. Our study, accordingly, also aims to view the Tokyo Tribunal in the context of the other trials taking place contemporaneously, and in particular those at Nuremberg, to show the impact of those trials on the Tokyo proceedings as well as to highlight some of the important contrasts between them. We maintain that the work of both tribunals must be judged by the same standards.

## The Relevant Legal Framework

How, then, do we evaluate the trial before the Tokyo Tribunal as a judicial process? We might take as a starting point the standard articulated by the judges in the High Command Case in the Nuremberg subsequent proceedings, the leading WWII case on the responsibility of military commanders for war crimes and crimes against humanity. The judges referenced the standard to which they were duty bound and that same standard applies to Tokyo, as it does to any tribunal worthy of the name:

The first [point] is that this Tribunal was created to administer the law. It is not a manifestation of the political power of the victorious belligerents which is quite a different thing. The second is that the fact that the defendants are alien enemies is to be resolutely kept out of mind. The third is that considerations of policy are not to influence a disposition of the questions presented.[3]

These principles enumerated by the judge of the High Command Case embody the most fundamental principles of judicial ethics and fair trials rights: that judges are bound by the law and they apply the law to the case before them with independence and impartiality. They are not agents of the policies of the governments of their national jurisdictions and they must observe the presumption of innocence despite the fact that the accused were enemies until the cessation of hostilities. These are the standards by which the performance of the judges at both Nuremberg and Tokyo must be measured. Further, what follows from these principles is that the judges are bound to take into account all the

---

[3] High Command Case, 484.

evidence before them without preference to either party. They must base their judgment upon factual findings that reflect a fair weighing of all of the evidence and arguments of both the prosecution and defense. They must apply a clearly articulated legal standard to those factual findings and reach legal conclusions that are based upon the findings and are reached according to the burden of proof upon the prosecution to prove its case beyond a reasonable doubt. These, as amplified in subsequent chapters in greater detail, are the criteria we apply in assessing the majority judgment and the separate opinions. It has perhaps too often been neglected, especially in reference to Justice Pal, that dissenting judges are equally bound by these standards and to the oath of office they have sworn upon accepting their appointment.

In considering the standard of guaranteeing a fair trial through impartial and independent judges we must also consider one of the challenges to impartiality and independence that is implicit in one of the most frequent criticisms of the Tokyo Tribunal, that of so-called "victor's justice." A section below will consider in greater detail how that criticism has manifested itself in Japanese and Western scholarship, but here it is appropriate to reflect on that concept from a conceptual standpoint and more specifically how it bears upon the standards for assessing a judicial proceeding.

We may begin by noting that in the post-war decades the criticism of victor's justice was directed at both Nuremberg and Tokyo, as well as at the Allied various national war crimes programs more generally. The charges of victor's justice in regard to Nuremberg may be put into perspective by considering that on December 13, 1946 the General Assembly of the United Nations unanimously adopted a resolution affirming the "principles of international law by the Charter of the Nuremberg Tribunal and the judgment of the Tribunal."[4] Those "Nuremberg Principles" continue to command respect today as an important reference point in the development of international law and have provided the foundation for the newly established International Nuremberg Principles Academy at the courthouse in Nuremberg where the IMT and subsequent proceedings took place. The IMTFE had barely been established when the General Assembly adopted the Nuremberg principles, but it must be remembered that both tribunals were founded upon these principles and shared the same legal framework as European and Asian counterparts. Given the affirmation of the work of the Nuremberg Tribunal by the General Assembly, what was meant by charging that the IMT had only applied "victor's justice"?

In fact, charges of victor's justice plagued the legacy of Nuremberg in the post-war period until a new generation of German politicians, jurists, and scholars decided that the Nuremberg Trials were a point of pride as the foundation of modern international law rather than the blemish that many scholars

---

[4] Quotation from GA 95 (1) December 13, 1946.

in previous generations, more closely connected to the past, had considered them to be.⁵ As noted earlier, the Nuremberg courtroom building has now been made into a museum and the German government established the Nuremberg Academy to carry forth the foundational legacy of Nuremberg through training and education of judges from around the world.

In Japan and among some Western commentators, on the other hand, victor's justice continues today to be a label that is widely used to condemn and dismiss the Tokyo Trial as a mere sham proceeding. Given that the Nuremberg and Tokyo Trials operated under essentially the same Charter and legal framework, and reached very similar conclusions in regard to the basic issues of jurisprudence and the guilt of the accused, this discrepancy in reception is somewhat puzzling. Despite the fact that the authoritative judgment of the Nuremberg IMT was handed down long before that of the Tokyo Tribunal, and that the Tokyo Tribunal closely followed the legal pathways set out by the IMT, those who reject the legitimacy of the Tokyo Tribunal often do not consider that their criticisms may apply with equal force to Nuremberg, or to the affirmation of the Nuremberg Principles by the UN General Assembly. It is also striking that Japanese scholars who reject the IMTFE on the grounds of victor's justice have been supported by many American scholars of modern Japan whereas that is much less the case in regard to Nuremberg.

Our book repeatedly references the Nuremberg judgment for two reasons; firstly because the IMT was the coequal European counterpart of the IMTFE and the judges of the Tokyo Tribunal drew upon it extensively. Indeed, the majority and Webb considered it authoritative and followed its holdings on the most important jurisdictional issues. Secondly, we argue that the same critical criteria should be applied to both tribunals and call into question whether some critics who reject the Tokyo judgment's findings on aggressive war, for example, would have been prepared to reject Nuremberg's application of the same legal principles to convict Nazi war leaders of aggression.

Another striking feature of many dismissals of the IMTFE as victor's justice is that they are formulated in a blanket and typically un-nuanced manner, and do not clearly define what that term means. It has become a sort of label that is often uncritically applied as if its applicability is self-evident. As noted above, the critics of the Tokyo Trial seldom consider Nuremberg, and reject it on

---

⁵ On the transformation of attitudes in the German legal profession in the 1990s, see Mouralis, "The Rejection of International Criminal Law in Germany after the Second World War." A sense of the shift in the attitudes of leading German scholars of the immediate post-war generation, and the recognition of the foundational importance of Nuremberg, is conveyed by the very title of an article Hans-Heinrich Jescheck, a dominant figure in German criminal law jurisprudence, published 52 years later on the importance of the Nuremberg legacy: "The General Principles of International Law as Set Out in Nuremberg, as mirrored in the ICC Statute." Jescheck, of course, had himself been one of the immediate post-war critics of the trial, as evidenced by his *Habilitationschrift*.

similar grounds. This is indicative of a double standard in that Nuremberg and Tokyo operated under essentially the same Charter and legal framework, were both composed only of victor nations, and both conducted the trials in essentially the same manner and with the same rules of evidence. Moreover, one can argue that the Tokyo Tribunal was far more broadly based and representative than that of Nuremberg because it consisted of eleven nations rather than four, including India, China, and the Philippines. If the charge that there was no crime of aggression prior to WWII is applied to the Japan's initiation of war with her neighbors, the same is true of Germany's aggression. Yet how many of the critics of the IMTFE would be equally ready to dismiss the legitimacy of the Nuremberg Trial of the major German war criminals in the same way they attack Tokyo? In other words, ignoring the judgment and jurisprudence of the IMT, and of the Nuremberg subsequent proceedings, has made it easier for critics to treat Tokyo as sui generis and an aberration.

There are at least four main senses in which one may criticize and dismiss a trial as merely "the justice of the victor" as, for example, Pal does.[6] On the one hand one may criticize Nuremberg and Tokyo as a matter of principle because they did not, for example, include or consist entirely of judges from neutral states. This criticism does not imply any defect in the *conduct* of the trial, that is the fairness of the proceedings themselves, but is rather a formal objection to the constitution of a court that was not more broadly representative of the international community.[7] In the case of both "neutral" judges or those who actually sat at Tokyo, one would equally have to inquire as to whether they acted with competence, fairness, and impartiality.

It is obvious that both Nuremberg and Tokyo were constituted by the victorious nations and it was always acknowledged by the Allied Powers that the establishment of both tribunals followed from the Moscow and Potsdam Declarations and from their status as victors to whom Germany and Japan had unconditionally surrendered. In order to render such considerations as substantive rather than formal criticisms, one would have to show that the judges conducted the trial and reached conclusions in a manner that was not independent and impartial. We will apply these criteria to consideration of the majority judgment and separate opinions and will argue that if anything, it is two of the dissenting judges whose independence or impartiality must be called into question.

Apart from the manner in which a tribunal is constituted one may also object that its legal basis has been created or defined by the victors. Thus, one may

---

[6] See, for instance, Pal Opinion, 1424, where he dismissed the trial as the "interest of the stronger."
[7] Of course we know today that neither Switzerland nor Sweden were in reality completely neutral, let alone Portugal and Spain who supported the Nazi regime. Many South American countries were also implicated in one way or an other with parties to the conflict.

reject the legal basis of the charges against the accused, for example, that the crimes instantiated in the Charter and charged in the indictment were ex post facto laws, not having existed at the time the alleged crimes were committed. Here the core notion is that the victors have unfairly applied new legal standards, not recognized at the time of the commission of the crimes, in order to punish the defeated nation's leaders under color of law. This is indeed a serious matter as it is a basic principle of legality, and one clearly recognized by the judges at Nuremberg and Tokyo, that conviction on the basis of acts that were not a crime when they were committed is unjust and illegitimate. We will consider in some detail the way in which the prosecution, defense, and the majority and other judges dealt with this issue.

One may also allege as victor's justice the way in which the trial was conducted, that is, its inherent fairness as a judicial proceeding. For example, one may argue that there was no opportunity to prepare a defense, that the defendants were not provided with competent counsel and did not have an opportunity to challenge the prosecution's witnesses, or that verdicts were not based upon the evidence. We will also examine these issues in some detail, in particular the question of whether the various opinions of the judges were based upon the evidence and applied consistently the standard of proof beyond a reasonable doubt.

Finally, one may claim victor's justice as a delegitimizing ground on the basis that the trial was in reality not a trial but a political stage-managed show. Here the essential claims are that such a "show trial" is in its very essence political rather than legal, that there has been no real consideration of evidence, that the judges and participants were mere puppets of other forces, and that the judges handed down a verdict that had been determined by external political authorities. Examples of such political show trials from the World War II era might be the Soviet trial in Kharkov in 1943, the German trials before the infamous Volksgericht (People's Court) of the July 20 conspirators against Hitler, the American trial of General Yamashita before a military commission in Manila, or the Japanese Army's trials of American flight crew, such as the trial of the "Doolittle Flyers," held in Shanghai in August 1942, where there were no defense counsel, no opportunity for the accused to defend themselves, and where the verdicts and penalties had been predetermined by Tokyo. We will also consider these issues, but, as will become apparent, the extensive internal memoranda of the judges – debating legal and procedural issues, considering the evidence on various charges, and discussing the appropriate legal standards – indicate that whatever one may think of its shortcomings it was no politically staged show trial and, hence, not victor's justice in that sense. Indeed, the most clearly documented cases of political interference applied to the dissenting judge, Roeling, and to the way in which all the parties, judges, prosecution, and defense, treated the sensitive matter of the exclusion of Emperor Hirohito from the ranks of the accused.

Critics of the Tokyo Trial, as opposed to the German scholars who challenged Nuremberg through their academic writings from the 1950s onwards, tend to conflate all four of these grounds without any careful analytical distinction or demonstration based on careful examination of the legal issues involved.[8] This is especially true of Japanese right-wing rejections of the trial and the casual dismissals by some American scholars. German critics, until the reversal of the past two decades or so, focused almost exclusively on the second point, that is the legitimacy of the charge of crimes against peace. They, like critics of Tokyo, typically ignored the fact that there were no grounds for rejecting the war crimes charges because they were clearly established by the Hague Conventions, to which Japan and Germany had acceded, and were also firmly established in international customary law.[9]

## Historiographical Overview

### Initial Receptions in Japan

The Tokyo Trial commenced at the time when the ordinary Japanese people were still reeling from the effects of war and almost total urban devastation, coping with homelessness, poverty, hunger, and the loss of family members, friends, and neighbors. Under those circumstances, it might be that they had neither the time nor the luxury to take an interest in the day-to-day proceedings at the Tokyo Trial. However, contemporary news reporting points to broad-based popular awareness that the Tokyo Trial was an important showcase for the Allied authorities of the ongoing demilitarization and democratization effort in Japan, or, as one might call it, an integral part of the Allied implementation of "transitional justice" in post-conflict Japanese state and society.[10] Such an understanding was keenly shared among legal scholars, political scientists, and historians at major Japanese research institutions, as

---

[8] See, as exemplary of this German line of scholarship, the post-war work of Hans Heinrich Jescheck, one of the foremost German criminal law scholars of the post-WWII era and founding director of the Max Planck Institute for Comparative Criminal Law in Freiburg. Jescheck wrote his *Habilitationschrift* as a doctrinally focused criticism of the legal basis of Nuremberg, which certainly did not hurt the trajectory of his stellar career. The published version of his Habilitation is *Die Verantwortlichkeit der Staatsorgane nach Voelkerstrafrecht*. Jescheck's criticisms focused largely upon the ex post facto nature of the criminalization of aggressive war.

[9] In a conversation in 2003 between David Cohen and the Emeritus Director of one of the foremost academic institutions for the study of international law in Germany the subject of Nuremberg came up. The former director immediately stated that the trial was of fundamental political importance but of course it was legally illegitimate because it applied ex post facto laws. When confronted with the reply that there was nothing "ex post facto" about conventional war crimes, he replied, "Yes, that's true. We always forget about those charges."

[10] See, for instance, Yokota, "Sekai no shinpan".

some of their contemporaneous commentaries on the Tokyo Trial, as discussed later, show.[11]

It is notable that some of the leading Japanese legal authorities in the immediate post-war period rejected the claim of "victor's justice" based upon the ex post facto nature of the charges of aggressive war. Yokota Kisaburō, a professor of international law at Tokyo Imperial University (the predecessor of the University of Tokyo) and later chief justice of the Japanese Supreme Court (1960–6), recognized the Tokyo Trial as a path-breaking event, where suspected war criminals were prosecuted not only on charges of the violation of laws and customs of war but also the planning and waging of aggressive war. He regarded this type of prosecutorial effort to be valid, based on his view that an international tribunal had legitimate legal grounds to adjudicate on the criminality or otherwise of the war, and to determine the attribution of individual guilt and punishment. The ex post facto criticism, he held, must be rejected, since such a criticism attacked the deficiencies of international law on technical grounds while glossing over the substantive issues in criminal allegations.[12] Yokota's opinion was echoed in contemporary articles written by Kainō Michitaka, another member of the law faculty at Tokyo Imperial University. He, too, rejected the ex post facto criticism by arguing that the main issue here was for the judges to adjudicate on the substance of alleged offenses, based on the interpretation of law and fact. Moreover, Kainō pointed out that the ex post facto criticism should be invalidated in light of the Nuremberg judgment, which ruled that "the maxim *nullum crimen sine lege* is not a limitation of sovereignty, but is in general a principle of justice."[13]

Dandō Shigemitsu, yet another member of the law faculty at Tokyo Imperial University with the area of specialization in criminal law, who also served as a judge of the Supreme Court in later years (1974–83), advanced similar views. He maintained that the body of international law had been evolving for some time, from adhering to the primacy of state sovereignty to incorporating the "global citizenship law [*sekai shimin hō*]." As a result, those individuals

---

[11] For more discussion on the historiography of the Tokyo Trial, see Totani, *The Tokyo War Crimes Trial*, chapters 8 and 9, and the concluding chapter; and Totani, "Zhanfan shenpan yanjiu de lishi yiyi." See also Sumitani, "Sensō hanzai saiban ron, sensō sekinin ron no dōkō." For comprehensive lists of book-length publications on the Tokyo Trial, see Nichigai Associates, ed., *Taiheiyō sensō tosho mokuroku 45/94*, 545–9; and *Taiheiyō sensō tosho mokuroku: 2005–15*, 498–504. For a guide to English sources and publications on the Tokyo Trial, see Welch, ed., *The Tokyo Trial*.

[12] Yokota's major publications concerning the Tokyo Trial include the following: Yokota, *Sensō hanzai ron*, "Tōkyō hanketsu to jiei ron"; and "Sekai no shinpan."

[13] Kainō, "Sensō saiban no hōritsu riron." 23. The quoted passage in the Nuremberg judgment can be found in *Trial of the Major War Criminals Before the International Military Tribunal*, vol. 1, 219. Kainō's other major publications concerning the Tokyo Trial are "Hōtei gijutsu," "Kyokutō saiban," and "Kyokutō saiban."

Historiographical Overview 13

who committed certain types of offenses, such as piracy, counterfeiting, and trafficking of women and children, became subject to criminal prosecution under international law.[14] It was in the context of this historical development in international law that, in Dandō's opinion, ex post facto criticism at the Tokyo Trial must be rejected, and instead allow prosecution of those who abused power to commit crimes against citizens of the international community. He deemed crimes against peace to be one such category of offense for which there should be individual accountability.

Quite apart from the legal questions surrounding the charges of crimes against peace, Dandō also wrote approvingly of court practices at the Tokyo Trial, where, unlike the prewar and wartime Japanese justice system, the rights of the defense were recognized. Disregard of defense rights "has become the talk of the time now past [*ima dewa kore mo mukashi gatari*]," so Dandō reminisced. He especially commended a group of American lawyers who were seen as discharging their professional duty as defense counsel in earnest, regardless of the fact that their clients were the nationals of their former foe.[15] Uchida Rikizō, a professor at Tokyo Imperial University with expertise in Anglo-American law, concurred with Dandō's opinion. Uchida recognized superior court practices of Anglo-American law, and deemed the Tokyo Trial a "practical lesson [*jitsubutsu kyōiku*]" of exemplary court practices.[16] Moreover, he observed that, unlike the existing Japanese justice system, the presumption of innocence applied at the Tokyo Trial, as well as the requirement that the prosecution meet the burden of proof to establish the guilt of the accused. He wrote, "Here rests the pride of Anglo-American law that, if one were to put it in extreme terms, is prepared to save ninety-nine guilty ones in order to save one innocent man."[17]

Commentaries by contemporary trial observers thus centered on assessing the historical significance of the legal concept of crimes against peace and the introduction of Anglo-American court practices in Japan. Commentaries on jurisprudence, meanwhile, were limited, although a few took a moment to illuminate the path-breaking nature of the theory of "cabinet liability" that applied at the Tokyo Trial. Yokota was one such contemporary trial observer. He wrote in his book, *Sensō hanzairon* [A treatise on war crimes] (published in 1947; the expanded edition in 1949), that, according to the decision of the Tokyo Tribunal, members of the Cabinet were jointly held accountable if they failed to discharge the duty of protecting prisoners of war and civilian internees, either on account of negligence or by knowing inaction.[18] Another trial observer, Irie

---

[14] Dandō, "Sensō hanzai no rironteki kaibō," 164–5.
[15] Ibid., 183.
[16] Uchida, "Kyokutō saiban no hōrironteki igi," 24.
[17] Ibid., 30.
[18] Yokota, *Sensō hanzai ron*, 297–8.

14     Introduction

Keishirō, similarly discussed the same theory of liability in his article, "Tōkyō hanketsu no yōryō to sono shōkai" [A summary and explanation of the Tokyo judgment] (1949). He remarked that this theory "did not limit the responsibility of the proper treatment of prisoners of war to administrative organs or their staff that were directly in charge, but also extended the responsibility to cabinet members." In Irie's opinion, the conviction of certain accused – such as Koiso Kuniaki (prime minister, 1944–5), Shigemitsu Mamoru (foreign minister, 1943–5), and Hirota Kōki (foreign minister, 1937–8) – were "extremely important," since they "expanded the horizon of personal responsibility [*sekinin no jinteki genkai o hirogeta*]."[19]

The first generation of Japanese trial observers, in this manner, offered brief yet incisive commentaries on a range of topics on law and jurisprudence arising from the Tokyo Trial. The kind of reasoned assessments that they advanced, however, appeared to gain little traction in Japanese society. They also failed to inspire the next generation of researchers to inquire further into the law and jurisprudence of the Tokyo Trial.[20] What came to characterize the post-trial Japanese debates and research trends instead was to draw upon popularly held views that the Tokyo Trial was "victor's justice," i.e. a trial where victor nations dispensed justice in an unfair, unilateral manner to further their political goals alone. In time, two distinct strands of victor's-justice criticism took root in Japan, and *these* came to define the parameters of the Japanese debates and research trends on the Tokyo Trial.

### Two "Victor's Justice" Perspectives

One of the two strands of victor's-justice criticism has its origin in the court proceedings at the Tokyo Trial itself, where the defense disputed the legitimacy of the Tokyo Tribunal on the grounds that the victor nations applied new laws retroactively. The defense especially took issue with the concept of crimes against peace. It argued that the existing body of international law did not recognize the planning, preparation, initiation, or waging of aggressive war, or the participation in a common plan to carry out those acts, as constituting

---

[19] Irie, "Tōkyō hanketsu no yōryō to sono shōkai," 39–40.
[20] A few exceptions would be Ōnuma Yasuaki and Fujita Hisakazu, although their respective takes on the studies of international law are quite different. Ōnuma adopts a "realist" position, so to speak, in his analysis of the Tokyo Trial, as he brings to light the political import in the historical formation of the concept of crimes against peace. See Ōnuma, *Sensō sekinin josetsu*. Fujita, meanwhile, is focused on the contributions of the legal principles applied at the Nuremberg and Tokyo Trials in the historical development of international humanitarian law. See Fujita, *Sensō hanzai to wa nani ka*, and "Tōkyō saiban no konnichiteki imi." See also Fujita, *Kokusai jindō hō*. Okuhara Toshio is another legal scholar who produced a substantive research piece on the Tokyo Trial (focusing on the doctrine of criminal conspiracy). See Okuhara, "Tōkyō saiban ni okeru kyōdō bōgi riron."

international offenses. The defense also rejected the applicability of the principle of individual criminal liability on the grounds of the sanctity of the Acts of State doctrine. If the Tokyo Tribunal were to allow the application of ex post facto law nonetheless, the defense would argue that to be tantamount to a unilateral imposition of "victor's justice." As we will discuss in Part II, this type of critiquing of the law was a potent defense strategy, since the opinion was divided in the legal community those days as to the legal effect of existing international treaties, conventions, and agreements concerning aggressive war. Such jurisdictional challenges are typical of international criminal proceedings today, and were made with great force by the defense at Nuremberg as well. In the context of defeated Japan following World War II, the defense's argument had the merit of being sufficiently straightforward for the general public to comprehend it readily, and to use it as a convenient reason to reject the Tokyo Tribunal's finding that Japan committed the crime of aggression.

The victor's-justice criticism advanced by the defense might not have gained the kind of enduring popularity that it did in Japan in later decades, however, had it not been for the dissemination of the dissenting opinion by Justice Pal, the member of the Tokyo Tribunal from India. The decision of the eleven-member Tokyo Tribunal, as we shall see in this book, was split between the majority judgment of eight justices, two separate concurring opinions, and three separate dissenting opinions. Of these opinions, the one written by the Indian member stood out for its certain peculiarities. First, it concluded that none of the twenty-five accused was guilty of any of the charges leveled against them, even though the majority judgment and the two concurring and two dissenting opinions all provided extensive legal and factual reasoning that supported guilty verdicts. Second, Pal based his not-guilty verdicts on rejecting the prosecution's case in its entirety while siding almost completely with the defense case. In fact, Pal advanced an out-and-out rejection of not just the prosecution's case, but rather the whole edifice of international law. In his long and complicated discourse, he charged in part that international law historically had been, and continued to be, nothing but a tool for the "haves" in the West to entrench their domination over the "have-nots" in the non-Western world. He appeared to reason that, since Japan was not one of the originators of this particular international law system, the Japanese accused at the Tokyo Trial should be spared of being judged by it, and instead be set free. (For in-depth discussion of Pal's dissenting opinion, see Chapters 12 and 13.)

Pal's dissenting opinion unsurprisingly found an enthusiastic audience in Japan where the sentiments of victimhood to Western imperialism were prevalent. Such sentiments had arisen in Japan since the time of Commodore Matthew Perry's opening of Japan (1854), if not earlier, and were kept alive, capped by the latest collective experiences of American bombing campaigns against the Japanese homeland (1944–5), ensuing defeat and unconditional

16    Introduction

surrender to the Allied Powers (August 1945), and the prolonged Allied military occupation of Japan (1945–52). The popular sentiments of victimhood, of course, conveniently overlooked the concurrent history of Japanese colonialism, imperialism, aggression, and atrocity to which the people of neighboring countries in Asia and the Pacific fell victim.

Copies of Pal's dissenting opinion came to circulate shortly after the end of the Allied military occupation, and they still do in Japan today. Different versions of abridged and full texts of the dissenting opinion in Japanese translation are presently available. A wide variety of commentaries that celebrate Pal's dissenting opinion as "Pal's judgment" have come into print as well.[21] Justice Pal himself helped fire up the Japanese veneration of his legacy. Upon invitation from Pal enthusiasts, he visited Japan three times in 1952, 1953, and 1966. He traveled across Japan to tout his dissenting opinion as the *only* authoritative judicial decision to arise from the Tokyo Trial. He also spent his time in Japan meeting with bereaved families of convicted war criminals while giving lectures on law, world peace, and Greater Asianism.[22] It is worth noting that the actual judgment of the Tokyo Tribunal, meanwhile, failed to receive the same level of recognition, let alone enthusiasm, in Japanese society. The full text of the majority judgment appeared in print just once (in 1949), and extracts from the majority judgment were introduced to the public only sporadically in subsequent decades.[23] The result, inevitably, was that the Japanese public were able to gain no more than a cursory understanding of the substance of the Tokyo judgment and the trial itself.

Pal's dissenting opinion found a receptive audience in an unlikely place as well: the United States. The one to introduce the dissenting opinion to the American public was Richard Minear in his *Victor's Justice: The Tokyo War Crimes Trial* (1971). This book was meant to be a monograph on the Tokyo Trial, but its primary concern was to offer criticism of the United States'

---

[21] Publications on Pal and his dissenting opinion are indeed numerous. To limit to listing those editions of Pal's dissenting opinion that have gained wide circulation in Japan, the following ones are particularly noteworthy: Tanaka, ed., *Pāru hakase jutsu, shinri no sabaki, Nihon muzai ron*; Tanaka, *Pāru hakase no Nihon muzai ron*; Pal, *Zen'yaku, Nihon muzairon*; and Tōkyō saiban kenkyūkai, ed., *Kyōdō kenkyū*.

[22] For a path-breaking biography of Pal and his impact on the Japanese discourse on the Tokyo Trial, see Nakazato, *Nationalist Mythology in Postwar Japan*. See also Totani, *Tokyo War Crimes Trial*, chapter 8.

[23] The Tokyo Tribunal published the Japanese translation of the entirety of the majority judgment and the five separate opinions upon the conclusion of the Tokyo proceeding, in 1948, although it is not clear how widely it was distributed. One copy is deposited at the National Diet Library, and its digitized version can be viewed and downloaded from its website. For the Japanese translation of the full text of the majority judgment, published in 1949, see *Tōkyō saiban hanketsu*. Excerpts of the majority judgment, the full text of Pal's dissenting opinion, and parts of four other separate opinions, are reproduced in Asahi shinbun hōtei kishadan, ed., *Tōkyō saiban*. The Japanese-language transcripts of court proceedings, which were published in 1968, contain the majority judgment. See *Kyokutō kokusai gunji saiban sokkiroki*, vol. 10.

disastrous entanglement in the Vietnam War. Minear posited that the Tokyo Trial was an early manifestation of the self-righteous foreign policy of the United States vis-à-vis Asia in the cold-war era, and he read this line of interpretation into the analysis of the Tokyo Trial. What is more, he found in Pal's dissenting opinion the voice he was looking for, and used it extensively to advance his critique of America's Asia policy. Uninformed by balanced legal analysis, Minear's *Victor's Justice*, in this regard, is more a polemical, advocacy piece than an empirical inquiry into the Tokyo Trial. It nevertheless found a sympathetic audience in the West, and came to define English-language scholarship on the Tokyo Trial in the ensuing decades.

As Pal's dissenting opinion came to influence the public perceptions of the Tokyo Trial in Japan and in the West, another strand of victor's-justice criticism took shape among the new generation of Japanese historians who began researching the Tokyo Trial in the late 1970s. Their victor's-justice criticism was distinct from the one above, since they did not focus on the charges or the legal standards applied at the Tokyo Trial. They were also not particularly interested in analyzing the legal or factual findings of the Tokyo Tribunal either. What did concern them was to find out why the Allied authorities put on trial the individuals they did while not doing so with others, and why the Allied authorities chose certain types of war crimes for prosecution while overlooking the other ones. Based on their research, the new generation of historians came to the conclusion that the Allied prosecutorial priorities were politically motivated, and that justice rendered at the Tokyo Trial, consequently, was highly unsatisfactory.

Their complaints were many, and clearly reflected the political currents of the time. The Allied Powers decided not to prosecute Emperor Hirohito, so it was pointed out, and numerous other suspected war criminals who ought to have been tried were similarly set free, such as the members of Unit 731, the infamous bacteriological warfare unit of the Imperial Japanese Army. It was also charged that the Western colonial powers represented at the Tokyo Trial were sympathetic to Japan as a colonial power, and that, because of this bias, they neglected to make a full inquiry into Japanese war crimes against the Asian people, and especially the crimes targeted at the people of colonial Korea and Taiwan. Furthermore, sexism allegedly led the Allied authorities to overlook the prosecution of sexual violence against women. It was argued, too, that there was no accountability with respect to the American use of atomic bombs against Hiroshima and Nagasaki, which the new generation of Japanese historians invariably deemed a war crime.[24]

---

[24] It might be noted that this was a generation of historians who came of age during the height of the student activism and anti-war movements of the 1960s, and that they had a natural intellectual inclination to embrace the cause of justice, including the one at the Tokyo Trial. For the general

18   Introduction

The new strand of victor's-justice criticism faced several problems. For instance, it became clear from further research that the Allied prosecutors actually documented the Japanese crimes against the Asian people extensively, and that some of the Japanese accused at the Tokyo Trial were convicted of those crimes.[25] Similarly, it was soon revealed that substantial evidence on sexual violence was admitted at the Tokyo Trial, including documentation of abduction and forced prostitution of women. Some of the accused were convicted in connection with mass rape. Furthermore, there arose theoretical problems in expecting the Tokyo Trial, which had a specific prosecutorial mandate, to serve as a venue for addressing a wider range of historical wrongs by Japan and its former foes.

It was Awaya Kentarō, a professor of history at Rikkyō University, who breathed new life into the studies of the Tokyo Trial by grounding studies of the trial research based upon new archival materials. He brought to light voluminous internal records of the prosecution, which he discovered during his research at the US National Archives and Records Administration, records which at that point had largely been ignored by Western researchers as well. He used these sources to illuminate behind-the-scenes dealings among the Allied prosecutors in determining the prosecutorial priorities, and especially matters concerning the treatment of Emperor Hirohito as a war criminal.[26] Awaya continued to explore archives in the United States and elsewhere well into the 1990s, and he also encouraged the next generation of historians to do the same, i.e. to use new sources to shed light on little-known backstories of the Tokyo Trial.

---

tone and the substance of the second strand of victor's-justice criticism, see Awaya, *Tōkyō saiban ron*. To see how the two contrasting strands of victor's-justice perspective have come to define the Japanese debates on the Tokyo Trial, see Hosoya, Andō, and Ōnuma, eds., *Kokusai shinpojiumu*. This publication is available in English as well. Hosoya, et al. *The Tokyo War Crimes Trial*. See also Ōnuma, *Tōkyō saiban kara sengo sekinin no shisō e*; and Ajia minshū hōtei junbikai, ed., *Toinaosu Tōkyō saiban*.

[25] See, for instance, Kajii's "Tōkyō saiban ni okeru 'BC-kyū hanzai' tsuikyū." This article was considered unique in the studies of the Tokyo Trial in the 1990s, since the author took the trouble of delving into the transcripts of court proceedings to illuminate the hitherto-overlooked scope of the prosecution's documentation on war crimes.

[26] Awaya published his new findings in a series of articles in *Asahi jānaru* in 1984–5. These articles were later complied and published as Awaya, *Tōkyō saiban e no michi* in 2006, and an expanded edition in 2013. A new line of inquiry that Awaya pursued regarding the Allied treatment of Emperor Hirohito is developed further by other scholars. See, especially, Yoshida, *Shōwa tennō no shūsenshi*. There are numerous Japanese-language publications that investigate the circumstances leading to the Allied decision not to prosecute Emperor Hirohito as a war criminal. A path-breaking piece on this topic in the earlier years is Takeda, *Tennō kan no sōkoku*. This publication is available in English as well. Takeda, *The Dual-Image of the Japanes Emperor*. There is also a comprehensive Japanese-language source book concerning the Allied post-war policies concerning the retention of the person and the institution of the Japanese emperor. See *Shiryō Nihon senryō: 1. Tennōsei*.

Awaya's research initiatives greatly energized the studies of post-WWII Allied war crimes trials, and new lines of research have developed since. One of the important scholarly achievements to be made from the new research initiatives was Higurashi Yoshinobu's *Tōkyō saiban no kokusai kankei: kokusai seiji ni okeru kenryoku to kihan* [International Relations of the Tokyo Trial: Power and Norm in International Politics] (2002). This mammoth monograph of 708 pages built on Awaya's source analysis and research methods, but it also broadened significantly the breadth of primary source materials to include voluminous diplomatic papers, government records, and internal memos of the Tokyo Tribunal that Higurashi collected from archives in Australia, Great Britain, and the United States as well as Japan. As its title suggests, the main thrust of this monograph is to treat the Tokyo Trial as a microcosm of international politics of the post-WWII era, and to illuminate competition, rivalry, and partnership among the victor nations over the redefinition of the world order as manifested inside and outside the courtroom.[27]

The new research initiatives in Japan as represented by Awaya and Higurashi characteristically adopted international politics as an analytical lens, and emphasized the importance of exploring behind-the-scenes stories for developing a new historical understanding of the Tokyo Trial. This type of research proved highly effective in identifying the hitherto little-known political dealings among the eleven participating Allied nations, which, in turn, shaped the legacy of the Tokyo Trial. The new lines of inquiry had one major downside, however. They tended to emphasize the importance of exploring political problems of the Tokyo Trial while neglecting to do the same with regard to law and jurisprudence. Indeed, little effort was made by Awaya or Higurashi to address some of the most fundamental questions of criminal trials, such as: What theories of liability applied at the Tokyo Trial? How did the prosecution establish the link between the accused and the documented instances of war crimes? How did the prosecution meet its burden of proof? What was the defense strategy in grappling with the prosecution's case? Did the defense succeed in raising a reasonable doubt about the prosecution's evidence, and if yes, which part and how? Above all, what legal and factual findings did the Tokyo Tribunal make? How did the judges weigh evidence, and what standards of liability did they apply? Such questions about the legal substance of the trial and the legal foundation of the judges' respective opinions are largely absent in their research.

It is noteworthy, in this connection, that although under Awaya's editorial supervision many volumes of the prosecution's internal records were compiled

---

[27] Higurashi's publications are many. His path-breaking research pieces in the early years include the following: Higurashi, "Kyokutō kokusai gunji saibansho kōseikoku no jōken," and "Paru hanketsu saikō." For more recent work, see Higurashi, *Tōkyō saiban*.

20   Introduction

and published, a similar undertaking did not occur with respect to the record of the Tokyo Trial itself.[28] It is true that the full Japanese translation of the majority judgment was published as early as in 1949, and that the complete Japanese-language transcripts of court proceedings came to print in 1968 as well. However, these published sources remained under-utilized due to limited circulation of finding aids, indexes, and guides.[29] The fact that these problems were left unresolved during the resurgence of the studies of the Tokyo Trial points to the prevailing notion in Japan that the analysis of law and jurisprudence was of limited importance for advancing our understanding of the Tokyo Trial.[30]

*The Research Environment in Western Academia*

The research environment in the West, by contrast, took on a different outlook. The studies of the Tokyo Trial were comparatively tempered,[31] but important steps were taken in the 1970s and the 1980s to improve the accessibility of the trial record. Two individuals deserve special credit in this regard. One of them is Justice Roeling, the Dutch member of the Tokyo Tribunal, and one of the three justices who wrote dissenting opinions. Roeling's relationship with the Tokyo Tribunal was a complicated one because, as we shall see in Part II, he produced a dissenting opinion of contradictory quality after an unsuccessful

---

[28] See *Kokusai kensatsu kyoku (IPS) jinmon chōsho*, 52 vols.; *Tōkyō saiban e no michi*, 5 vols.; *Tōkyō saiban shiryō: Kido Kōichi jinmon chōsho*; *Tōkyō saiban shiryō: Tanaka Ryūkichi jinmon chōsho*; and *Tōkyō saiban to kokusai kensatsu kyoku*, 5 vols.

[29] Shortly after the Tokyo Trial, the Asahi Newspaper and the Institute of Social Science at the University of Tokyo separately developed indexes and guides to the record of the Tokyo Trial. It appears that they printed only a limited number of their indexes and guides. A copy of each has been deposited at the National Diet Library at Tokyo, Japan. See *Kyokutō kokusai gunji saiban kiroku mokuroku*, 3 vols.; and, *Kyokutō kokusai gunji saiban kiroku*. For more information about published and unpublished finding aids, visit the website of the National Diet Library at www.rnavi.ndl.go.jp/kensei/entry/IMTFE.php and see also Sumitani, Utsumi, and Akazawa, "Tōkyō saiban, BC-kyū sensō hanzai, sensō sekinin kankei shuyō bunken mokuroku," appendix (28 pages), p. 2. For a Japanese-language narrative summary of the Tokyo proceedings, published in 2010, see Matsumoto, ed., *Tōkyō saiban shinri yōmoku*.

[30] The body of scholarship by Fujita Hisakatsu is an exception in this regard, as it sheds light on the substantive aspects of the law applied at the Tokyo Trial and assesses its contribution to the historical development of international humanitarian law. See Fujita, "Tōkyō saiban no konnichiteki imi."

[31] There are nevertheless noteworthy book-length publications on the Tokyo Trial in the West contemporaneously. They include: Brackman, *The Other Nuremberg*; Harries, *Sheathing the Sword*; and Maga, *Judgment at Tokyo*. Picchigallo, *The Japanese on Trial*, helped establish the context of the Tokyo Trial by providing a detailed overview of the Allied war crimes program in the Asia-Pacific region. Russell, *The Knights of Bushido*, also deserves attention. It is written by a legal officer of the British Army with an insider knowledge of the Allied war crimes operations, and it makes extensive use of the record of the Tokyo Trial to reconstruct the history of Japanese aggression and atrocity. For a comprehensive bibliographical guide to English-language sources and publications on the Tokyo Trial, see Welch, ed., *The Tokyo Trial*.

attempt to reconcile conflicting legal and political views between himself and the Dutch Government.[32] Even so, Roeling in his old age appears to have moved beyond this uncomfortable past. He at least came to attach sufficient importance to the legacy of the Tokyo Trial to undertake the publication in 1977 of the entirety of the majority judgment and the five separate concurring and dissenting opinions.

Another individual to be credited for improving research environment in the West is R. John Pritchard and his associates. Their undertaking was much broader and more ambitious in scope than the one by Roeling, since not only did they clean and reproduce in facsimile the entirety of the English-language transcripts of court proceedings and all of the judicial decisions of the Tokyo Tribunal, but they also developed a set of comprehensive tools to enable researchers to explore the voluminous trial record efficiently and systematically. The transcripts they reproduced are admittedly hard to read, since four pages worth of text are accommodated each per single page to make it possible to fit some 52,000 pages into 22 over-size volumes. However, the set of innovative indexes and guides that they developed – which are available in five additional over-size volumes – are thorough and eminently reliable.[33] The sources prepared by Roeling and Pritchard became indispensable to consequent researchers on the Tokyo Trial.[34] The publication of Neil Boister and Robert Cryer's *Documents on the Tokyo International Military Tribunal: Charter, Indictment, and Judgments* (2008) constitutes another major development that contributed to the improvement of the research environment of the Tokyo Trial.

*Summary*

To sum up, debates and research on the Tokyo Trial within and outside Japan have taken a curious historical trajectory. The first generation of trial observers offered perceptive comments, but they failed to capture the imagination of

---

[32] On Roeling's complicated relationship with the Tokyo Tribunal and with the Dutch Government, see Van Poelgeest, *Tōkyō saiban to Oranda*. This book was originally published as Van Poelgeest, *Nederland en het Tribunaal van Tokio*. There are indications that Roeling made personal efforts to burnish his legacy as a Tokyo Trial judge later in his life. For more insights into this matter, see Roeling's retrospective accounts of the Tokyo Trial in Röling and Cassese, *The Tokyo Trial and Beyond*. See also Hosoya et al., eds., *The Tokyo War Crimes Trial*, 125–34.

[33] *The Tokyo War Crimes Trial*, 22 vols.; and *The Tokyo War Crimes Trial: The Comprehensive Index and Guide to the Proceedings of the International Military Tribunal for the Far East in Five Volumes*, 5 vols. The reproduced transcripts also include the majority judgment, the five separate concurring and dissenting opinions, and records of proceedings in chambers, as well as the Bill of Indictment, the Charter of the Tokyo Tribunal, the rules of procedure, and other essential official and unofficial records of the trial.

[34] Various other print and online versions of the trial record are presently available. For more information, see *Note to the Reader on Translation, Sources, and Citations*.

22     Introduction

the Japanese people regarding the possibilities and promises of international criminal justice. What has come to dominate the postwar assessments of the trial was an often ill-defined or conceptually ungrounded notion of "victor's justice," which effectively denied that the Tokyo Trial had substantive contributions to the field of international law.[35]

## Chapter Overview

To carry out the agenda outlined erlier we have divided our book into two sections dealing with the trial proceedings and the judgment and opinions of the judges respectively. Part I, "The Allied War Crimes Policy, the Indictment, and the Court Proceedings," considers the legal framework of the trial from Allied policy decisions about the shape of the tribunal to the reflection of those policies in the indictment prepared by the International Prosecution Section of the IMTFE. The framing of the indictment played a vital role in defining the charges against the accused but also caused considerable confusion because of the infelicitous multiplication of counts, most of which were ultimately dismissed by the majority opinion.

Chapter 1 provides background on the creation of the tribunal and the formulation of Allied war crimes policy in preparation for the IMTFE. Chapter 2 take up the charges regarding crimes against peace and aggressive war which, as at Nuremberg, constituted the main focus of the prosecution's case. This sets the stage for consideration of the similar preoccupation with charges of aggressive war that also characterizes the majority judgment and the separate opinion. War crimes, as we will see, represented a secondary concern. In this vein Chapter 2 provides a detailed analysis of both the indictment, particularly on charges related to aggressive war, and the principal theory of liability, conspiracy, on which it and the prosecution case was based. It then turns to an analysis of the legal arguments by the prosecution and defense in regard to the nature and legitimacy of these charges and the prosecution's theory of the case

---

[35] Study of the legal substance of the Tokyo Trial was invigorated by research conducted by the parties and chambers at the International Criminal Tribunal for the former Yugoslavia (ICTY) and the International Criminal Tribunal for Rwanda (ICTR) in the 1990s. Resumption of international criminal proceedings at these tribunals prompted the practitioners of international criminal law to review post-WWII war crimes trials, including the Tokyo Trial, in search for law and jurisprudence relevant to the present cases. New lines of inquiry into the Tokyo Trial began against this historical backdrop. David Cohen, "Beyond Nuremberg: Individual Responsibility for War Crimes" (1999), was the first to conduct a systematic analysis of theories of individual responsibility that applied at the Yamashita Trial (1945), the Tokyo Trial, and the Nuremberg Trials. Other new studies about the history and law of the Tokyo Trial ensued, which include, but are not limited to: Boister and Cryer, *The Tokyo International Military Tribunal*; Futamura, *War Crimes Tribunals and Transitional Justice*; Osten, "Tōkyō saiban ni okeru hanzai kōsei yōken no saihō"; Tanaka, McCormack, and Simpson, eds. *Beyond Victor's Justice?*; Totani, *The Tokyo War Crimes Trial*; Udagawa, "Tōkyō saiban to Nihon kaigun."

based upon conspiracy doctrine. An understanding of both the charges in the indictment and the prosecution's theory of liability to link the accused to the crimes charged is essential for understanding both the course of the proceedings and the conclusions reached in the judgment and the separate opinions. It must always be kept in mind that the task of the judges is limited to assessing the evidence on the charges in the indictment and only the crimes alleged there. Some commentators without a background in law, and particularly in the nature of proceedings before an international criminal tribunal of the WWII era, have sometimes not viewed the trial process through this lens. Although obvious, it is worth stating clearly at this point what the respective roles of the participants in the IMTFE were. The job of the prosecution was to frame the charges in an indictment, provide a theory of liability to apply to the accused in light of the evidence that they were required to put before the judges, and then to prove each element of each of the charges beyond a reasonable doubt. The task of the defense was to create a reasonable doubt either by challenging the evidence put forward by the prosecution or by advancing evidence and alternative theories of their own. As we will see, the defense at times chose not to challenge essential elements of the prosecution's case. Finally, the role of the judges was, as outlined earlier, to impartially assess the evidence that supported or challenged each of the 55 counts in the indictment against the accused and justify their ultimate conclusions in a reasoned decision. The chapters in Part I analyze how the defense and the prosecution pursued their respective tasks. Part II assesses the manner in which the judges fulfilled, or failed to fulfil, their mandated role.

Chapter 3 addresses one of the most fundamental and most fraught issues that confronted the parties and the tribunal: the structure of the Japanese government and policy making institutions from 1928 to 1945, the period under consideration for the tribunal. This issue is fraught both because of the complexity of the Japanese institutional and quasi-institutional structures for formulating policy, making policy decisions, and implementing those decisions. It is also fraught because those structures evolved continuously during the relevant seventeen-year period and particularly in response to emerging and shifting challenges in the conflicts first with China and Russia and then in the broader war from 1941. This issue is fundamental and absolutely central to an assessment of the proceedings because the structures of authority and system of policy formation constituted the necessary basis for the judges' analysis of the roles, responsibility, and legal liability of each of the accused. Here it must also be remembered that the task of the judges was not to assess the liability of the accused as a collective but rather as each individual based upon their roles, words, and deeds in relation to the charges against each of them individually. As the account in Part I will show, the prosecution's understanding and account of the Japanese system of government changed quite radically from the beginning to the end of the trial. It was then the job of the judges, as will be seen in Part II, to determine what, if anything, the prosecution had actually succeeded in proving beyond a reasonable doubt.

Chapter 4 follows on from Chapter 3 by taking up an equally vital element of the prosecution and defense cases: the roles of specific individuals within the structures of authority and the flow of actual events and decisions that led to and continually broadened the Japanese scope of Japanese military activity from the acquisition and incorporation of Manchuria in 1931 as the puppet entity of Manchukuo (1932–45) to the establishment, however temporary, of an empire that stretched from the borders of Australia to northern China and from the borders of India to Alaska. It was not enough for the prosecution to argue that the acquisition of this empire was criminal, the burden was upon the prosecution alone to show even if it was criminal that each of the accused could be held criminally accountable for what they said and did in their respective positions in the government or armed forces.

Chapters 5 and 6 may be considered together as they both focus upon the war crimes charges, which, although not at the forefront of the tribunal's attention, provided the basis for convicting many of the accused for crimes that could not be considered ex post facto because of their well-established nature in international conventional and customary law.[36] Chapter 5 considers the somewhat complicated formulation of the war crimes in the indictment and their legal basis, while Chapter 6 provides an analysis of the prosecution's case in attempting to prove these charges. Such proof required, it must be recalled, not just establishment that the alleged crimes actually occurred as charged but also, and equally importantly, proof of the linkage of each of the accused charged with these crimes to their commission. The chapter also considers the defense case in attempting to refute the evidence and arguments advanced by the prosecution.

Part II builds upon the analysis in Part I by considering what the judges made of the case presented to them by the parties over the 24 months of trial proceedings. We must again recall that the case was framed for the judges by the parties and they were obligated to base their conclusions solely upon the evidence before them and through application of the burden of proof beyond a reasonable doubt. Part II takes up the judgment and separate opinions in some

---

[36] We may perhaps note here that international law, unlike most domestic legal regimes, has a dual basis. On the one hand, international conventions, such as the Hague Conventions of 1907 and the 1929 Geneva conventions, provided a statutory or "conventional" series of legal obligation for the states that had ratified and acceded to those instruments. On the other hand, international law recognizes as universally binding on all nations certain norms which have established themselves, through recognition and practice, as part of what was during that period referred to as "the laws and customs of war."

depth, focusing upon the analysis and reasoning on which conclusions were based and upon the quality of that analysis and legal reasoning.

Chapter 7 considers the majority judgment on crimes against peace. As these charges take up the bulk of the judgment over many hundreds of pages our account cannot cover every aspect of the judgment, but it subjects the core of the judgment on crimes against peace to detailed critical analysis. The chapter in particular focuses upon the way in which the narrative structure of the judgment's treatment of crimes against peace operates to obscure the role of specific individuals and inhibits systematic analysis of the evidence against each of them. As will be seen, this has much to do with the way in which the judges adopted the prosecution's theory of an overarching conspiracy and the account of the Japanese governmental structures in the prosecution's closing statement (which is analyzed in detail in Part I).

Chapter 8 provides a counterpoint to the majority's treatment of crimes against peace by considering the draft judgment of the tribunal's president, Justice Webb. Webb provides a very different and far more incisive account of the evidence on crimes against peace. More importantly, he provides what the majority judgment fails almost completely to do: he assesses in great detail the specific evidence advanced on each of the accused in regard to the individual charges against them.

Chapter 9 turns to an assessment of the majority's treatment of the war crimes charged in the indictment. Here the crucial issue beyond establishing the occurrence of these crimes was how they could be linked to the accused. This provided both the prosecution and the tribunal with a major challenge, because such crimes were committed by Japanese forces across the reach of the entire empire in every theater in which they either fought or occupied territory. How could these crimes against civilians and prisoners of war be linked to individuals far away in Tokyo or regional headquarters? What was required here was a theory of liability and account of the structures of policymaking on the basis of which such linkages could be established. The chapter analyzes how the majority attempted to meet this challenge and the way in which they succeeded or failed in applying that standard systematically to justify convictions against specific accused. Chapter 10 again provides a counterpoint in considering Webb's draft judgment. It shows how Webb succeeded where the majority failed, that is, in providing, for the most part, a nuanced analysis of the evidence against individuals accused on which their liability for specific war crimes might be predicated. Consideration of Webb's draft judgment is vital to an understanding of the trial because it organizes and analyzes the evidence before the tribunal in a far sounder manner than the majority judgment or any of the separate opinions. This evidence was, in fact, before the tribunal and we must consider Webb's account of it in assessing to what extent specific charges against specific accused could be justified on the basis of the evidence available to the judges. We conclude that had the majority accepted Webb's judgment our view of the Tokyo Tribunal would be very different.

Chapters 11–14 focus on the separate dissenting and concurring opinions of Justices Bernard, Roeling, Jaranilla, Webb, and Pal. While much has been written about the dissents of Pal and Roeling, systematic analysis of the evidence and legal arguments on which their dissents are based has been relatively rare. The challenges in analyzing the vast, ill-organized and meandering judgment of Pal have already been noted, and Chapters 12 and 13 take up this challenge in assessing his treatment of the charges on crimes against peace and war crimes, respectively. These chapters also consider the nature of Pal's dissent, what he sought to accomplish, and the extent to which his aims were compatible with the standards of judicial conduct outlined earlier. The dissenting opinion of Roeling has often been praised but an analysis of its legal content calls into question both the coherence of its argument, which is fraught with contradictions, and his conduct as a judge in relation to these same standards of judicial conduct. Chapter 11 analyzes Roleing's dissent in some depth and compares it with the interesting and often neglected dissenting opinion of Justice Bernard. Finally, Chapter 14 considers the arguments advanced by Justices Jaranilla and Webb in their concurring opinions and particularly their views on the controversial issue of Emperor Hirohito's responsibility and their implicit and explicit commentary on the dissents of Justice Pal.

In sum, Part II, building upon the essential foundation of Part I, presents a comprehensive account of the totality of the various opinions put forward by the judges of the IMTFE. We argue that it only such an account, informed both by detailed analysis of the legal content of the opinions and consideration of the internal memoranda of the judges, that can provide a solid basis for assessing the quality of the process of reaching judgment at Tokyo.

*Part I*

The Allied War Crimes Policy, the Indictment, and Court Proceedings

# 1  The Framework of the Trial

Any inquiry into post–World War II Allied war crimes prosecutions must begin with reviewing the unique political and military circumstances under which the war was brought to an end and the resultant Allied policies defining the postwar treatment of Axis war criminals. This chapter will start with a brief account of the last stretch of the war that culminated in defeat and surrender of the Axis Powers. Of particular significance are a series of Allied Powers' wartime statements concerning war crimes policies, the Allied demand for immediate surrender of Japan as made in the Potsdam Proclamation of July 26, 1945, and diplomatic exchanges between the Allied Powers and the Imperial Government of Japan in August 1945 regarding the future status of the Japanese emperor in the eventuality of Japan's acceptance of surrender. The remainder of this chapter will then take up several basic issues framing the Tokyo Trial, namely: (1) the Allied policy decisions concerning the trial of Far Eastern war criminals, including the one relating to Emperor Hirohito (1901–89; r. 1926–89); (2) a chronological overview of the Tokyo Trial; (3) applicable rules of procedure; and (4) types of evidence used at the trial. This chapter thus provides the foundational information for the analysis of the Tokyo Trial in the ensuing chapters.

## 1.1  From War to Peace

The Allied Powers in the South Pacific, led by the American and Australian armed forces, fought grueling battles against the Japanese by sea, land, and air in 1942 and 1943 in order to stem Japan's further advance in this theater of operations.[1] The Central Pacific Drive that ultimately brought Japan to her knees commenced in the fall of 1943. Shortly after the bloody Battle of Tarawa (November 20–23, 1943), the leaders of the United States of America, the National Government of the Republic of China, and Great Britain met at Cairo to agree on a common policy regarding the future military operations

---

[1] There are numerous books on the war in the South Pacific, including American, Australian, and Japanese official war histories series. For a thoughtful thematic analysis, see Bergerud, *Touched with Fire*.

against Japan. In their joint declaration, the three powers set forth their collective resolve "to bring unrelenting pressure against their brutal enemies" and "to restrain and punish the aggression of Japan," thus making public their intention to mete out punishment to Japan for carrying out aggressive war. The same declaration at Cairo showed that the three powers were also determined to strip Japan of territories taken from China since the time of the Sino-Japanese War (1894–5) and that, moreover, "mindful of the enslavement of the people of Korea, are determined that in due course Korea shall become free and independent."[2]

One month prior to the declaration at Cairo, leaders of the three powers and those of the Union of the Soviet Socialist Republics met in Moscow, where they issued a separate, four-power declaration on their war aims relative to the fight against Nazi Germany and Imperial Japan. The declaration articulated the four powers' joint resolve to continue hostilities against the Axis Powers until the latter laid down their arms "on the basis of unconditional surrender." This condition for the cessation of hostilities played an important role in the implementation of Allied war crimes policy through the creation of international criminal tribunals to try Axis war leaders.

This Moscow Declaration of 1943 also issued a warning that German war criminals would be "sent back to the countries in which their abominable deeds were done in order that they may be judged and punished according to the laws of these liberated countries and of free governments which will be erected therein." Looking ahead to the creation of what would become the Nuremberg Tribunal, the Moscow Declaration further provided that this policy would be "without prejudice to the case of German criminals whose offenses have no particular geographical localization and who will be punished by joint decision of the government of the Allies."[3] Following up on implementing the Moscow Declaration, Great Britain, the United States, and nine European governments-in-exile established in London the United Nations War Crimes Commission (UNWCC, 1943–8) and began collecting evidence of German-perpetrated atrocities. The commission initially limited its investigation to war crimes in the European theater, but soon expanded to accommodate war crimes in the Far East.[4]

---

[2] *Documents*, 71.
[3] Moscow Conference, Avalon Project website.
[4] By the Declaration of St. James's, of January 13, 1942, nine European governments-in-exile committed to pursuing judicial actions against German war criminals. The United Nations War Crimes Commission served as an inter-governmental organizational platform to pursue the mission of the Declaration. (The Soviet Union had no part in the commission.) For more information, see United Nations War Crimes Commission, comp., *History of the United Nations War Crimes Commission and the Development of the Laws of War*.

## 1.1 From War to Peace

In the intervening months, Nazi Germany – Japan's key ally since the conclusion of the Anti-Comintern Pact in November 1936 and the Tripartite Pact in September 1940 – was already on the defensive on the Eastern Front in the face of tremendous industrial and military capabilities unleashed by the Stalinist Soviet Union. The German forces were repulsed at Moscow by the first month of 1942; the German Sixth Army under command of Field Marshal Friedrich Paulus capitulated to the Soviet Red Army at Stalingrad on February 2, 1943; and Adolf Hitler's desperate effort to change the tide of war at the Battle of Kursk in the middle of 1943 ended in failure. In 1944 the Soviet forces broke the siege of Leningrad and began the series of offensives that led to the collapse of the German front and to the final drive on Berlin in the spring of 1945. In the face of these events, the German people awoke to the reality that the promised Thousand Year Reich was now lost and ultimate defeat was inevitable, culminating in the Battle of Berlin and German capitulation in April–May 1945.[5]

With surrender of Germany in hand, the Allied Powers now focused on defeating the remaining Axis Power in the Far East. Apart from the initiation of hostilities against the United States and Great Britain in December 1941, the Empire of Japan had been fighting a long, drawn-out war against China since 1931. Although American and British histories of World War II in the Asia-Pacific theaters typically pay scant attention to the China theater, more than 2.5 million Japanese ground troops were still deployed in China throughout 1941–5, although without clear military victory or defeat for either side in sight. By 1945 this was more than double the number of Japanese troops engaged in all other theaters of operation.[6]

With Allied Powers' continuing success in the Central Pacific "island hopping" campaign, the Allied invasion of the Japanese homeland became imminent. Saipan, a prewar Japanese colonial territory, had fallen in July 1944. This made it possible for the US military to begin relentless air campaigns against Japan by deploying sorties of a new-generation long-range bomber, the B-29. Iwo Jima fell in March 1945, thereafter serving as B-29's emergency landing base and also a critical airfield for shorter-range escort fighters. The use of B-29 for massive low-altitude incendiary bombings from March 1945 wreaked havoc on fifty-one Japanese cities, the worst instance of destruction being the

---

[5] Publications on World War II in Europe are countless. For accessible and informative narrative accounts of the German war on the Eastern Front, see Beevor, *Stalingrad*, and, *The Fall of Berlin, 1945*.

[6] The ground troops of the Imperial Japanese Army in the Pacific region certainly increased over time, from the initial number of about 155,000 in December 1941 to 810,000 in August 1945. However, the vast majority of the army's ground forces remained in China, including some of the best trained at the Soviet–Manchukuo borders in preparation for the war against the Soviet Union. For more information about the distribution of Imperial Japanese Army's ground forces, see Yamada, *Gunbi kakuchō no kindaishi*, 167.

air raid against Tokyo on March 6, which resulted in more than 80,000 deaths and 1 million homeless overnight.[7]

The Battle of Okinawa, in preparation for the future invasion of Kyūshū, began at the start of April 1945 and brought about enormous casualties on both sides over the course of more than two and a half months of fighting. The dead included numerous Okinawan civilians, who were either caught in crossfire or made to join the battles as youth recruits and nurses. Not an insignificant number of Okinawan civilians were driven to mass suicide, as the Japanese military compelled them to choose "honorable death" instead of the disgrace of surrender.[8]

It was against this backdrop of horrendous death and destruction in and around Japan that the leaders of three major Allied Powers in this theater – China, Great Britain, and the United States – issued a joint declaration during the meeting at Potsdam in occupied Germany, on July 26, 1945. The declaration read that "Japan shall be given an opportunity to end this war," while the Allied Powers were "poised to strike the final blows upon Japan" and prepared to prosecute the war "until she [Japan] ceases to resist." Making a pointed remark on the ramifications of German defeat, the three powers conveyed to Japan the following ominous warning:

The result of the futile and senseless German resistance to the might of the aroused free peoples of the world stands forth in awful clarity as an example to the people of Japan. The might that now converges on Japan is immeasurably greater than that which, when applied to the resisting Nazis, necessarily laid waste to the lands, the industry and the method of life of the whole German people. The full application of our military power, backed by our resolve, *will* mean the inevitable and complete destruction of the Japanese armed forces and just as inevitably the utter devastation of the Japanese homeland.[9] (emphasis in the original)

The three powers declared that now was the time for Japan to "follow the path of reason." The option otherwise would be facing the onslaught of Allied military attacks, and that would mean total annihilation not only of the Japanese

---

[7] Publications on World War II–era air campaigns are numerous. For a detailed study of the use of B-29 in the Pacific theater, see, for instance, Werrell, *Blankets of Fire*. For the prehistory of strategic bombing campaigns (as carried out in Europe), see Overy, *The Bombers and the Bombs*.

[8] According to studies by Hayashi Hirofumi, the Japanese army forces garrisoned in various parts of Okinawa expressly urged those civilians under their control to commit suicide and, at some places, they distributed hand grenades to facilitate the civilian mass suicide. The Japanese communities in the Marianas, the Philippines, and Manchuria died or were killed *en masse* in similar coercive circumstances. For more information, see Hayashi, *Okinawa sen to minshū*; *Okinawa sen*; and *Okinawa sen ga toumono*. The Japanese-language literature on death, destruction, and atrocities meted out against the people of Okinawa by the Japanese military is plentiful. See the classic Okinawa taimusu sha, ed., *Tetsu no bōfū*.

[9] Proclamation Defining Terms for Japanese Surrender, in *The Department of State Bulletin*, vol. 13, nos. 314–40 (July–December 1945), 137.

armed forces but also of the Japanese homeland. "Following are our terms," the declaration read, while stressing once again the urgency of the matter. "We will not deviate from them. There are no alternatives. We shall brook no delay."

The terms of the Potsdam Declaration encompassed comprehensive policies on the demilitarization of Japan, which included to disband the Japanese armed forces, to dismantle war industries, and to break up the Japanese empire as had been forewarned in the Cairo Declaration. Destroying all war potential in Japan, it was remarked, was *not* to be construed as the Allied intention that "the Japanese people shall be enslaved as a race or destroyed as a nation." However, militarists would be purged, and "stern justice shall be meted out to all war criminals, including those who have visited cruelties upon our prisoners."[10] Post-surrender Japan would fall under Allied military control, but the occupation forces would be withdrawn "as soon as these objectives have been accomplished and there has been established in accordance with the freely expressed will of the Japanese people a peacefully inclined and responsible government." The declaration concluded with the reiteration of the demand that the Government of Japan "proclaim now the unconditional surrender of all Japanese armed forces" or, failing that, "the alternative for Japan is prompt and utter destruction."[11]

Despite the ominous warning of imminent destruction of the homeland in the case of the failure to surrender promptly, no reply was forthcoming. Prime Minister Suzuki Kantarō held on July 28 a press conference, whereupon he indicated that his government regarded the Potsdam Declaration as a mere restatement of the Cairo Declaration and hence meriting little consideration. He stated that the Japanese government's position, accordingly, was "killing in silence [*mokusatsu*]," i.e. to ignore the joint declaration, and to continue with the prosecution of the war.[12] Just about two weeks later, on August 6, B-29 bomber *Enola Gay* took off from Tinian and dropped an atomic bomb on Hiroshima. Another B-29 flew out on August 9 to drop a second on Nagasaki.[13] In-between the unleashing of two atomic bombs, the Soviet Union on August 8 declared war on Japan in fulfillment of the promise that Josef Stalin had previously made to his American and British counterparts during their joint conference at Yalta, back in February 1945. The agreement was that, "in two or three months after Germany has surrendered and the war in Europe is terminated, the Soviet Union shall enter into war against Japan on the side of the Allies."[14]

---

[10] Ibid., 137–8.
[11] Ibid., 138.
[12] Bōeichō bōei kenshūjo senshishitsu, *Senshi sōsho: Daihon'ei rikugunbu*, vol. 10, 389.
[13] For a judicious account of the sequence of events that culminated in the US deployment of atomic bombs and the ensuing surrender negotiations, see Frank, *Downfall*.
[14] The Yalta Conference, Avalon Project website. The Soviet Union had been briefly at war with Japan twice earlier, in 1938 and 1939, when the Japanese army stationed in Manchukuo

Massive Soviet armed forces rolled into the territory of the Japanese-controlled state of Manchukuo (1932–45) in northeastern China, as well as into Japanese territories of Southern Sakhalin and Kuril Islands, and closed in on Hokkaidō. A number of Japanese conscripts and colonists in Manchukuo died or were killed during the military takeover, while others were captured and later packed off to Siberia for forced labor.

On August 10, 1945, the Japanese government at last intimated to the US government, by way of the Swiss Minister in Japan, its readiness to accept the Potsdam terms, but with a qualification. The Japanese government specified that the acceptance of Potsdam terms was premised on "the understanding that the said declaration does not comprise any demand which prejudices the prerogatives of His Majesty [the Emperor of Japan] as a Sovereign Ruler." In other words, the reply did not accept unconditional surrender. The Japanese offer of surrender with this qualification received an immediate Allied reply. Dated August 11, and transmitted by the US government on behalf of the Four Powers (now including the Soviet Union), the reply made no reference to the qualification for protecting the Japanese emperor. Instead, it read that "from the moment of surrender the authority of the Emperor and the Japanese Government to rule the state *shall be subject to* the Supreme Commander for the Allied Powers who will take such steps *as he deems proper* to effectuate the surrender terms" (emphasis added).

The reply also stated that the Japanese emperor would be "required to authorize and ensure the signature by the Government of Japan and the Japanese Imperial General Headquarters of the surrender terms necessary to carry out the provisions of the Potsdam Declaration." He would be required to order all of the Japanese armed forces "wherever located to cease active operations and to surrender their arms" and to "issue such other orders as the Supreme Commander [for the Allied Powers] may require to give effect to the surrender terms." As for the ultimate form of the Japanese government, the Allied Powers reiterated that the matter would be determined by the freely expressed will of the Japanese people, "in accordance with the Potsdam Declaration."[15]

The Four-Power reply did not elicit an immediate response from the Japanese government, which spent additional two days to deliberate its readiness or otherwise to accept the Potsdam Declaration. A conclusive reply was finally returned to the Swiss Minister on August 14, to be forwarded to the Allied Powers. The Japanese reply read, "His Majesty the Emperor has issued an Imperial rescript regarding Japan's acceptance of the provisions of

---

instigated border conflict. The two countries concluded a neutrality pact in April 1941, and maintained an uneasy peace since. The Soviet government informed Japan in April 1945 its intention to abrogate this pact, however, and it adhered to the Potsdam Declaration upon declaration of war against Japan on August 8, 1945.

[15] *The Department of State Bulletin*, vol. 13, nos. 314–40 (July–December 1945), 206.

the Potsdam declaration." The Emperor was now prepared to fulfill all the requirements specified in the Four-Power reply, namely, "to authorize and ensure the signature" on the Instrument of Surrender; "to issue his commands" to the entire Japanese armed forces to cease military operations and disarm; and "to issue any other orders" as the Supreme Commander for the Allied Powers may require. In transmitting this message to the US government, the Swiss Minister added a note, remarking that "I deem this reply a full acceptance of the unconditional surrender of Japan," since "*in this reply there is no qualification*"[16] (emphasis added).

The formal surrender ceremony took place some two weeks later, on September 2, 1945, on *USS Missouri* at Tokyo Bay. Shigemitsu Mamoru and General Umezu Yoshijirō, representing the Government of Japan and the Imperial Headquarters respectively, participated in the ceremony along with a small Japanese delegation. The Allied side was headed by General Douglas MacArthur, formerly Commander of the US Army Forces in the Far East (1941–2) and subsequently the Supreme Commander for the Allied Forces in the South West Pacific Area (1942–5), who was then appointed by the US President Harry S. Truman to serve as the Supreme Commander for the Allied Powers (SCAP, 1945–51).[17] Representatives of nine other Allied Nations also attended the ceremony in order to countersign the surrender document. Hundreds of Allied servicemen and commissioned officers, too, lined the decks of *Missouri* to become witness to this historic event.

Emperor Hirohito alone was conspicuous for being absent, but this was expected. The Allied requirement was that he gave authorization to his subordinates to affix their signatures on the surrender document, and not that he signed it himself. This arrangement was made apparently on the British government's recommendation. At the time of Japan's surrender overture back in August, the British government urged the United States that the Japanese emperor be required to *authorize* the signing but not to do the signing himself,

---

[16] The Japanese reply in full read:

1. His Majesty the Emperor has issued an Imperial rescript regarding Japan's acceptance of the provisions of the Potsdam declaration. 2. His Majesty the Emperor is prepared to authorize and ensure the signature by his Government and the Imperial General Headquarters of the necessary terms for carrying out the provisions of the Potsdam declaration. His Majesty is also prepared to issue his command to all the military, naval, and air authorities of Japan and all the forces under their control wherever located to cease active operations, to surrender arms and to issue such other orders as may be required by the Supreme Commander of the Allied Forces for the execution of the above-mentioned terms.

*The Department of State Bulletin*, vol. 13, nos. 314–40 (July–December 1945), 255.

[17] MacArthur's responsibility as Supreme Commander was reaffirmed when the leaders of the United States, Great Britain, the Soviet Union, and China met in Moscow in December 1945. The Moscow Agreement read, "The Supreme Commander shall issue all orders for the implementation of the terms of surrender, the occupation and control of Japan and directives supplementary thereto." *Documents*, 73.

so that he could be used to "secure the immediate surrender of Japanese in all outlying areas and thereby save American, British and Allied lives." This was a recommendation made not only by the newly elected British Prime Minister, Clement Atlee, but also his predecessor, Winston Churchill, who held that "using the Mikado will save the lives in outlying areas."[18] The British proposal had the support of the US government, as the final wording of the Four-Power reply indicates. It will be seen that the Allied Powers continued to make use of the Japanese emperor for advancing their strategic goals in post-surrender Japan, even if it could mean prioritizing the establishment of peace while compromising the pursuit of justice and accountability.[19]

## 1.2   Planning for the Trial of Far Eastern War Criminals

In the wake of V-J Day, the responsibility of developing the actual policies regarding the implementation of the Potsdam terms fell on the US government, due partly to disproportionate military contributions that the United States had come to make in winning the final battles, and due partly to the preponderance of the US armed forces in the Allied occupation of Japan. The Allied policy concerning the trial of Japanese war criminals also originated in the US government. On October 2, 1945, the State-War-Navy Coordinating Committee (SWNCC) – which served as the highest inter-departmental policymaking body within the US government – approved a comprehensive policy document on the Allied war crimes program. The main part of the document – known

---

[18] The Ambassador in the United Kingdom (Winant) to the Secretary of State, August 11, 1945, in *Foreign Relations of the United States,* 1945, vol. VI, 628–9. *Foreign Relations of the Unites States* will be referred to as *FRUS* hereafter. This publication series can be read online at the website of the Office of Historian of the US Department of State.

[19] That it was the US and British intention from the beginning to use the Emperor as a tool for their political aims is made clear in the exchanges in August 1945 between these two governments. See *FRUS,* 1945, vol. VI, 626, 628–9, 631–2, 646–7, 651–2. See also *Documents on Australian Foreign Policy, 1937–1949, Vol. VIII: 1945,* document nos. 135-6, 148–9, 171, 173, 176–9, 181–2, 187, 189, 191, 195, 198, 254, 266, 403, 421, and 427. This publication can be viewed at the website of the Department of Foreign Affairs and Trade of the Australian government. In a cablegram dated August 12, 1945, British Prime Minister Atlee offered to Australian Prime Minister J. B. Chifley a similar justification about the substance of the Four-Power reply: (pp. 329–30). The Australian government replied the same day, "In view of the terms of message to the Japanese Government and of the Potsdam declaration, we take it that culpability and trial of the Emperor for war crimes will remain a question for determination by the Allied authorities subsequent to surrender. We would be glad of your confirmation of this as a matter of urgency" (p. 330). The British government replied affirmatively to this query, as its cablegram, dated August 17, 1945, read as follows:

> Statements in question do not in themselves prejudice question of the treatment to be given to Emperor Hirohito, which will be a matter for consideration by the Allied Powers. We consider, however, that it would be a capital political error to indict him as a war criminal. *We desire to limit commitment in manpower and other resources by using Imperial Throne as an instrument for the control of the Japanese people*, and indictment of present occupant would in our view be most unwise. (emphasis added, p. 350)

## 1.2 Planning for the Trial of Far Eastern War Criminals

as "SWNCC 57/3," and titled, "Policy of the United States in Regard to the Apprehension and Punishment of War Criminals in the Far East" – set forth the types of offense to be investigated and to be tried by the Allied authorities. It also outlined the responsibilities of the Supreme Commander for the Allied Powers in identifying, investigating, apprehending, and trying war criminals, as well as the responsibilities of other Allied military commanders for carrying out war crimes investigations and trials at former theaters of war.

The US policy envisioned a two-track war crimes program in the Far East. One track consisted of the trials of Far Eastern war criminals at special international military courts, which would be appointed by the Supreme Commander. The other track consisted of the trials of war criminals at special national military courts, which would be appointed by the military commander of any of the Allied Nations or Italy in occupied or recovered territories in the Asia-Pacific region. There was to be a division of labor of sorts, therefore, between the Supreme Commander and other Allied military authorities. The power of the latter was somewhat restricted, however, as they were limited to handling "war criminals not held or requested by the Supreme Commander for trial by an international military court or tribunal."[20]

The US policy document made no particular temporal requirement, but it recommended that the offenses in the Far East "in general, should have been committed since, or in the period immediately preceding the Mukden incident of September 18, 1931," viz. the start of the Japanese invasion of Manchuria in northeastern China.[21] This recommendation reflected the opinion of the United Nations War Crimes Commission, first articulated in early 1945 by its Far Eastern and Pacific Sub-Commission, that this commission "should not limit its investigation to war crimes committed after a particular date, and that each case should be considered on its own merits."[22]

The types of offenses for which apprehension and trial were to be carried out were stipulated as follows:

1. The term "war crimes" as used herein, includes:

    A. Planning, preparation, initiation, or waging of a war of aggression or a war in violation of international treaties, agreements or assurances, or participation in a common plan or conspiracy for the accomplishment of any of the foregoing.
    B. Violation of the laws and customs of war. Such violations shall include but not be limited to murder, ill-treatment or deportation to slave labor

---

[20] *FRUS*, 1945, vol. VI, 931.
[21] Ibid., 933.
[22] Ibid., 928. The Far Eastern and Pacific Sub-Commission was established at the Provisional Government of China at Chongqing.

38    The Framework of the Trial

or for any other purpose of civilian population of, or in, occupied territory, murder or ill-treatment of prisoners of war or internees or persons on the seas or elsewhere, improper treatment of hostages, plunder of public or private property, wanton destruction of cities, towns or villages or devastation not justified by military necessity.

C. Murder, extermination, enslavement, deportation, and other inhumane acts committed against any civilian population, before or during the war of persecutions on political, racial, or religious grounds in execution of or in connection with any crime defined herein whether or not in violation of the domestic law or the country where perpetrated.[23]

These three categories of offense had already been recognized in the Charter of the International Military Tribunal at Nuremberg ("IMT Charter" hereafter) as appended to the London Agreement of August 8, 1945, and referred to as crimes against peace, war crimes, and crimes against humanity, respectively.[24] Among policymakers in the Asia-Pacific region, these three offenses came to be known also as Classes 1.A., 1.B., and 1.C. offenses – or simply Classes A, B, and C – on account of the numbering convention adopted in the US policy document above.

A military directive that contained the foregoing policy was promptly transmitted from the US Joint Chiefs of Staff (JCS) to the Supreme Commander for the Allied Powers for implementation. By the JCS directive, the Supreme Commander was ordered to "take all practicable measures to identify, investigate, apprehend and detain all persons whom you suspect of having committed war crimes as defined in paragraph 1, subparagraphs B and C above." At the same time, the Supreme Commander "will similarly apprehend and detain the persons deemed to be liable under paragraph 1.A. above." The Supreme Commander was further empowered to appoint "special international military courts" at his own discretion, but not the ones for the trial of Class 1.A. offenses (i.e. crimes against peace). For the establishment of the courts for the latter purpose, the Supreme Commander was ordered to wait "until further authorization by the Joint Chiefs of Staff."[25] The JCS directive made a requirement of further authorization presumably to allow the US government a sufficient time to carry out negotiations with other Allies through diplomatic channels before formally committing to establishing in the Far East another Nuremberg-type international criminal tribunal.[26]

---

[23] Ibid., 932.
[24] Friedman, ed., *The Law of War*, 883–93.
[25] *FRUS,* 1945, vol. VI, 934.
[26] For related discussion, see Totani, *The Tokyo War Crimes Trial,* chapter 1. For the US policy on war crimes prosecutions of German war criminals, see Taylor, *The Anatomy of the Nuremberg Trials,* chapters 2–4.

1.2 Planning for the Trial of Far Eastern War Criminals 39

The above restriction aside, the JCS imposed another limit on the Supreme Commander's authority. It concerned the treatment of the Japanese emperor. The final segment of the JCS directive contained the following order:

> You [SCAP] will take no action against the Emperor as a war criminal pending receipt of a special directive concerning his treatment.[27]

A separate message from the Joint Chiefs of Staff, dated November 29, 1945, clarified the purport of the order. This was not to be construed as the granting of immunity to the emperor from war crimes prosecution, but rather a temporary withholding of action in consideration for the need to establish peace and security in the occupied territory. The relevant part in the message read:

> As you know, the subject of whether Hirohito is eventually to be tried as a war criminal is of great interest to the US. The US Government's position is that Hirohito is not immune from arrest, trial and punishment as a war criminal. It may be assumed that when it appears that the occupation can proceed satisfactorily without him, the question of his trial will be raised. It may also be assumed that if such a proposal will serve a purpose, it may be raised by one or more of our Allies.[28]

In light of the US policy as explained above, the Joint Chiefs of Staff instructed the Supreme Commander to begin collecting evidence against the Japanese emperor without delay, since "any decision not to try him should be made in the light of all available facts."[29]

The foregoing JCS directive and instructions did not appear to elicit much enthusiasm on the part of the Supreme Commander, however, who not only took no action to collect evidence against Emperor Hirohito, but also made it clear of his opposition to any plan of his trial. He returned to the Joint Chiefs of Staff on January 25, 1946 a recommendation that criminal actions against the Emperor be not considered. In his message, MacArthur expressed grave doubts that the trial of the Emperor was advisable, the reason being that "great changes must be made in occupational plan" in such an eventuality. He pointed out that the Emperor was still recognized as the unifying symbol of Japan, and that his trial would "unquestionably cause a tremendous convulsion among the Japanese people, the repercussions of which cannot be over-estimated." He further warned his military superiors in Washington that not only did the Japanese people continue to revere the Emperor, but they also *"believe rightly or wrongly that the Potsdam agreements were intended to maintain him as*

---

[27] *FRUS*, 1945, vol. VI, 936.
[28] State-War-Navy Coordinating Committee, Treatment of the Person of Hirohito, Emperor of Japan, October 29, 1945, T1205 (microfilm), roll 6, RG 353, National Archives and Records Administration. NARA hereafter.
[29] Ibid.

*the emperor of Japan*" (emphasis added). Such a belief having become so widespread, the Japanese people would likely "regard Allied action to the contrary as the greatest betrayal in their history and the hatreds and resentments engendered by this thought will unquestionably last for all measurable time."[30] These words of warning did not lead to any change with the JCS directive, however, which remained binding on the Supreme Commander.[31]

In the intervening weeks the Supreme Commander declared, on January 19, 1946, the establishment of an international military tribunal in Tokyo. This action capped the diplomatic negotiations that the US government had been carrying out with the individual Allied governments behind the scenes, to agree on the basic organizational framework of the Far Eastern Class 1.A. tribunal. It was generally agreed that the model at the International Military Tribunal at Nuremberg would be followed, but that the Supreme Commander would be entrusted with the preparatory work for the sake of expediting the process. With the US assurances on equitable representation of all participating countries, the US government and its Allied counterparts agreed to have the Supreme Commander proceed with the Class A case.

The Charter of the International Military Tribunal for the Far East ("IMTFE Charter" hereafter), which was promulgated the same day, set out the three types of offenses that had been recognized in the IMT Charter and repeated in the US policy document, SWNCC 57/3, as coming within the jurisdiction of the new tribunal at Tokyo ("IMTFE," "Tokyo Tribunal," or "Tribunal" hereafter). Of the three types of offenses, crimes against peace were identified in the IMTFE Charter as the core prosecutorial concern by way of the insertion of the following passage in one provision:

The Tribunal shall have the power to try and punish Far Eastern war criminals who as individuals or as members of organizations are charged with offenses *which include Crimes against Peace*.[32] (emphasis added)

As will be seen in subsequent chapters, this particular passage in the IMTFE Charter was interpreted as requiring the prosecuting agency to prioritize the charges of crimes against peace while the remaining two categories of offenses – war crimes and crimes against humanity – might be treated as being

---

[30] General of the Army Douglas MacArthur to the chief of staff, United States Army (Eisenhower), January 25, 1946, in *FRUS*, 1946, vol. VIII, 397.

[31] It is known that MacArthur's aid contacted Emperor Hirohito to have him prepare an apologia about his wartime leadership. This document – discovered in the 1980s and commonly referred to as "Emperor Shōwa's Monologue" – is believed to have been completed in April 1946, in anticipation of Hirohito being called to the stand as a witness or an accused at the Tokyo Trial. For the full text of the emperor's personal account of the war, see Terasaki, *Shōwa tennō dokuhakuroku*.

[32] Article 5 of the IMTFE Charter. *Documents*, 8.

## 1.2 Planning for the Trial of Far Eastern War Criminals

of secondary concern.³³ The prosecution prepared its case accordingly, which, as we will see, impacted the nature of the findings made during the court proceedings and in the final decisions of the Tokyo Tribunal.

The IMTFE Charter followed the IMT model in regard to the applicable principles of liability, although there were a few modifications. One notable change is that all the provisions concerning criminal liability based on membership in criminal organizations (Articles 9, 10, and 11 in the IMT Charter) were omitted in the IMTFE Charter. Consequently, the prosecution made no effort to name any particular organ of government or nationalist organization as an accused.³⁴ Another notable change can be found in the provisions of individual responsibility that were carried over from the IMT Charter to the IMTFE Charter. The IMT Charter provided that:

Article 7. The official position of defendants, whether as Heads of State or responsible officials in Government Departments, shall not be considered as freeing them from responsibility or mitigating punishment.

Article 8. The fact that the Defendant acted pursuant to order of his Government or of a superior shall not free him from responsibility, but may be considered in mitigation of punishment if the Tribunal determines that justice so requires.³⁵

In the case of the IMTFE Charter, these two were combined, and read the same way except for the omission of the phrase, "Heads of States":

Article 6. Responsibility of accused. Neither the official position, at any time, of an accused, nor the fact that an accused acted pursuant to order of his government or of a superior shall, of itself, be sufficient to free such accused from responsibility for any crime with which he is charged, but such circumstances may be considered in mitigation of punishment if the Tribunal determines that justice so requires.³⁶

In all likelihood, the framers of the IMTFE Charter omitted "Heads of State" out of consideration for the politically delicate nature of addressing the issues of imperial culpability in Japan.³⁷ This omission did not compromise

---

³³ Under the US policy document (SWNCC 57/3), the prosecuting agency at the Tokyo Trial was instructed to prioritize the investigation and trial of Far Eastern war criminals on crimes against peace, as it read, "This agency should attach importance to the investigation of the evidence that offenses of the type described in paragraph 1.A. above have been committed." *FRUS*, 1945, vol. VI, 930.

³⁴ Friedman, ed., *Law of War*, 887–8. At the IMT trial of major German war criminals, the German Cabinet, the Nazi Party leadership corps, Gestapo, and so on, were named as accused, along with Hermann Goering and twenty-three other individuals.

³⁵ Ibid., 887.

³⁶ *Documents*, 8.

³⁷ Those who drew up the IMTFE Charter were a handful of American lawyers, who came to Japan to form the core group of the new international prosecuting agency at Tokyo, and also to serve as special legal counsel for the Supreme Commander on matters of war crimes trials.

the principle of individual responsibility, however, since Article 6 in the IMTFE Charter was still worded as to reject that any person would be exempt from liability for international offenses on account of his or her official position.

A few months later on April 3, 1946, the Far Eastern Commission (FEC, 1945–52) deliberated for approval the US policy document (SWNCC 57/3). This commission had been established upon the initiative of the US government at the end of 1945, so that it would function as the highest-level inter-Allied body to "formulate the policies, principles, and standards in conformity with which the fulfillment by Japan of its obligations under the Terms of Surrender may be accomplished."[38] The members of the Far Eastern Commission unanimously adopted the US policy the same day on April 3, although they made a few modifications to impose certain limits on the scope of the Supreme Commander's authority.

The revised version – which was retitled as "FEC 007/3: Policy in Regard to the Apprehension, Trial and Punishment of War Criminals in the Far East" – set out the Supreme Commander as being vested with the power to prescribe rules of procedure for international military courts "subject to consultation with the representatives of those governments [i.e. member states of the Far Eastern Commission]," and to approve, reduce or otherwise alter any sentences imposed by international military courts "after consultation with the Allied Council for Japan [an inter-Allied advisory body of the Supreme Commander] and the Representatives in Japan of the other powers, members of the Far Eastern Commission."[39] With these modifications, FEC 007/3 instituted a system by which the individual Allied Powers would have opportunities to review the procedure and the outcomes of the Class A war crimes proceedings.

The Far Eastern Commission also discussed at the same meeting its policy regarding the treatment of Emperor Hirohito. For several months prior to April 3, 1946, the Allied governments had been debating the question of whether or not to put Hirohito on trial. The Government of Australia, for one, had insisted since the time of Japanese surrender that the trial of the Emperor was a prerequisite for achieving peace and justice in the Asia-Pacific region. However, Great Britain and the United States opposed the Australian advocacy, and resisted strenuously the latter's attempt to have UNWCC name him as a major war criminal.[40] It was in this context that the member states of the Far Eastern Commission deliberated what policy it should adopt on the issues of imperial culpability.

---

As provided in SWNCC 57/3 *"This agency should advise the Supreme Commander and other Military commanders for the Allies on matters relating to war crimes"* (emphasis added). *FRUS*, 1945, vol. VI, 930.
[38] Blakeslee, *The Far Eastern Commission*, 17.
[39] *FRUS*, 1946, vol. VIII, 425.
[40] See Totani, *The Tokyo War Crimes Trial*, chapter 2.

of secondary concern.³³ The prosecution prepared its case accordingly, which, as we will see, impacted the nature of the findings made during the court proceedings and in the final decisions of the Tokyo Tribunal.

The IMTFE Charter followed the IMT model in regard to the applicable principles of liability, although there were a few modifications. One notable change is that all the provisions concerning criminal liability based on membership in criminal organizations (Articles 9, 10, and 11 in the IMT Charter) were omitted in the IMTFE Charter. Consequently, the prosecution made no effort to name any particular organ of government or nationalist organization as an accused.³⁴ Another notable change can be found in the provisions of individual responsibility that were carried over from the IMT Charter to the IMTFE Charter. The IMT Charter provided that:

Article 7. The official position of defendants, whether as Heads of State or responsible officials in Government Departments, shall not be considered as freeing them from responsibility or mitigating punishment.

Article 8. The fact that the Defendant acted pursuant to order of his Government or of a superior shall not free him from responsibility, but may be considered in mitigation of punishment if the Tribunal determines that justice so requires.³⁵

In the case of the IMTFE Charter, these two were combined, and read the same way except for the omission of the phrase, "Heads of States":

Article 6. Responsibility of accused. Neither the official position, at any time, of an accused, nor the fact that an accused acted pursuant to order of his government or of a superior shall, of itself, be sufficient to free such accused from responsibility for any crime with which he is charged, but such circumstances may be considered in mitigation of punishment if the Tribunal determines that justice so requires.³⁶

In all likelihood, the framers of the IMTFE Charter omitted "Heads of State" out of consideration for the politically delicate nature of addressing the issues of imperial culpability in Japan.³⁷ This omission did not compromise

---

³³ Under the US policy document (SWNCC 57/3), the prosecuting agency at the Tokyo Trial was instructed to prioritize the investigation and trial of Far Eastern war criminals on crimes against peace, as it read, "This agency should attach importance to the investigation of the evidence that offenses of the type described in paragraph 1.A. above have been committed." *FRUS*, 1945, vol. VI, 930.

³⁴ Friedman, ed., *Law of War*, 887–8. At the IMT trial of major German war criminals, the German Cabinet, the Nazi Party leadership corps, Gestapo, and so on, were named as accused, along with Hermann Goering and twenty-three other individuals.

³⁵ Ibid., 887.

³⁶ *Documents*, 8.

³⁷ Those who drew up the IMTFE Charter were a handful of American lawyers, who came to Japan to form the core group of the new international prosecuting agency at Tokyo, and also to serve as special legal counsel for the Supreme Commander on matters of war crimes trials.

the principle of individual responsibility, however, since Article 6 in the IMTFE Charter was still worded as to reject that any person would be exempt from liability for international offenses on account of his or her official position.

A few months later on April 3, 1946, the Far Eastern Commission (FEC, 1945–52) deliberated for approval the US policy document (SWNCC 57/3). This commission had been established upon the initiative of the US government at the end of 1945, so that it would function as the highest-level inter-Allied body to "formulate the policies, principles, and standards in conformity with which the fulfillment by Japan of its obligations under the Terms of Surrender may be accomplished."[38] The members of the Far Eastern Commission unanimously adopted the US policy the same day on April 3, although they made a few modifications to impose certain limits on the scope of the Supreme Commander's authority.

The revised version – which was retitled as "FEC 007/3: Policy in Regard to the Apprehension, Trial and Punishment of War Criminals in the Far East" – set out the Supreme Commander as being vested with the power to prescribe rules of procedure for international military courts "subject to consultation with the representatives of those governments [i.e. member states of the Far Eastern Commission]," and to approve, reduce or otherwise alter any sentences imposed by international military courts "after consultation with the Allied Council for Japan [an inter-Allied advisory body of the Supreme Commander] and the Representatives in Japan of the other powers, members of the Far Eastern Commission."[39] With these modifications, FEC 007/3 instituted a system by which the individual Allied Powers would have opportunities to review the procedure and the outcomes of the Class A war crimes proceedings.

The Far Eastern Commission also discussed at the same meeting its policy regarding the treatment of Emperor Hirohito. For several months prior to April 3, 1946, the Allied governments had been debating the question of whether or not to put Hirohito on trial. The Government of Australia, for one, had insisted since the time of Japanese surrender that the trial of the Emperor was a prerequisite for achieving peace and justice in the Asia-Pacific region. However, Great Britain and the United States opposed the Australian advocacy, and resisted strenuously the latter's attempt to have UNWCC name him as a major war criminal.[40] It was in this context that the member states of the Far Eastern Commission deliberated what policy it should adopt on the issues of imperial culpability.

---

As provided in SWNCC 57/3 *"This agency should advise the Supreme Commander and other Military commanders for the Allies on matters relating to war crimes"* (emphasis added). *FRUS*, 1945, vol. VI, 930.
[38] Blakeslee, *The Far Eastern Commission*, 17.
[39] *FRUS*, 1946, vol. VIII, 425.
[40] See Totani, *The Tokyo War Crimes Trial*, chapter 2.

## 1.2 Planning for the Trial of Far Eastern War Criminals

The record of the meeting shows that Sir Carl Berendsen, member from New Zealand, initiated the discussion by making the following remark:

In the directive issued to General MacArthur there is an instruction to him not to take any action on the Emperor without further directive. In terms of this document [FEC 007/3], any government representatives of this table can indict a war criminal for trial. I should like to have it understood that I have no grief for the Emperor – I believe he is a war criminal of the deepest dye – but I should like it understood that no action will be taken against the Emperor without a further directive, that that is still the understanding.

Major General Frank R. McCoy, member from the United States and chairman of the Far Eastern Commission, offered an immediate affirmative reply, stating, "There will be no change in that respect. He's governed by a general directive."[41] By this remark, McCloy appeared to be referring to the JCS directive that Berendsen mentioned (since no other general directive had been issued to MacArthur regarding the treatment of the emperor as a war criminal.) An off-the-record discussion ensued. The minutes of the meeting do not show what further remarks McCloy might have made, or what opinions other members might have expressed. Instead, it is tersely recorded that the Far Eastern Commission then approved FEC 007/3, "with the understanding that the directive to be forwarded by the US Government to the Supreme Commander would be so worded as to exempt the Japanese Emperor from indictment as a war criminal without direct authorization."[42] No new directive was issued, however, which meant that the previous JCS directive, "You take no action against the Emperor as a war criminal pending receipt of a special directive concerning his treatment," remained binding on the Supreme Commander, now, as an integral part of the FEC war crimes policy.

What is to be made of the foregoing decision? The dominant interpretation in the existing scholarship is that FEC 007/3 should be construed as a formal policy decision by the Allied Powers to grant Emperor Hirohito immunity from war crimes prosecution. This clearly is a misreading, as the exact wording of the policy document undercuts the viability of such an interpretation. The Far Eastern Commission certainly decided to exempt him from indictment at the time, in the absence of a policy directive otherwise. But the qualifier, "pending receipt of a special directive concerning his treatment," indicates that the Allies retained the leverage that the continuing threat of prosecution gave them. That being said, however, none of the member states made a formal request with

---

[41] Far Eastern Commission. Transcript of Seventh Meeting of the Far Eastern Commission, Held in Main Conference Room 2516 Massachusetts Avenue, N. W., Wednesday, April 3, 1946, in file titled, "F.E.C. Verbatim Transcript of Meetings 1–10," Box 1/Entry 1067/RG 43, NARA.
[42] *FRUS,* 1946, vol. VIII, 428.

44    The Framework of the Trial

the Far Eastern Commission for his trial later on.⁴³ Consequently, no special directive on the matter was ever issued by the Far Eastern Commission to either MacArthur or his successor, General Matthew Ridgway (SCAP, 1951–2).

The fact remains, in any event, that due to the Allied decision that he was more useful to their postwar plans for Japan if he was not tried and convicted, Emperor Hirohito was not one of the accused at the IMTFE trial. He was never called to the stand as a witness either. It will be seen in subsequent chapters that the absence of Emperor Hirohito in the courtroom put great strains on the prosecution's case, since the prosecution attempted to make up for this particular shortcoming by either downplaying or denying the Emperor's role in the making of the war. Such attempts fell flat, however, as the evidence simply contradicted such claims. What is more, the absence of Emperor Hirohito in the indictment put strains on the Tokyo Tribunal as well. It will be seen in Part II of this book that most justices were reluctant to address the Emperor's culpability squarely, presumably out of consideration for its political sensitivity. The president of the tribunal, Justice Sir William F. Webb, and the French member, Justice Henri Bernard, were exceptions. Webb, in particular, directly addressed the issues of imperial responsibility by treating it an essential element for determining the guilt of the accused.

## 1.3    A Chronological Overview of the Tokyo Trial

The courtroom of the International Military Tribunal for the Far East was constructed inside the former Japanese military academy at Ichigaya, located outside the northern moat of the Imperial Palace in central Tokyo. This building had housed the Ministry of the Army and the Army General Staff during the war years. Contemporary observers duly noted the symbolic significance of using the Ichigaya academy for the trial of major Japanese war criminals. Justice E. H. Northcroft, the New Zealand member of the Tokyo Tribunal, commented that "there is an element of imaginative justice in using this very place."⁴⁴ A lead Japanese defense lawyer, Kiyose Ichirō, grudgingly remarked, too, that the victor nations were using this building to "make an example" of the Japanese military establishment.⁴⁵

---

[43] It is worth noting that the member states of the Far Eastern Commission continued to speculate on the future trial of the emperor after the adoption of FEC 007/3, and that the Soviet government went so far as to float one such proposal through diplomatic channels as late as in 1950. Arguably, the Allied governments would not have contemplated the possibility of the emperor's trial if the Far Eastern Commission had adopted a formal decision to grant him immunity. See Totani, *The Tokyo War Crimes Trial*, chapter 2.

[44] *Documents on New Zealand External Relations*, 1521.

[45] Kiyose, *Hiroku Tōkyō saiban*, 46.

1.3  A Chronological Overview of the Tokyo Trial    45

Each of eleven countries that participated in the Tokyo Trial provided a judge, a prosecutor, and supporting staff.[46] The prosecution unit was formally known as the International Prosecution Section (IPS, also referred to as "the prosecution" throughout this book). It was made up initially of a small group of thirty-nine American lawyers and staff members, who arrived in Tokyo in early December of 1945. Representatives of ten other Allied Nations arrived in February 1946 or later months. The International Prosecution Section grew into a multinational force of around 500 at a high point of the trial, although still much smaller than their Nuremberg counterparts.[47]

Joseph B. Keenan, formerly director of the Criminal Division of the US Justice Department and an assistant to the US Attorney General, was appointed to serve as chief of counsel for the International Prosecution Section. His leadership role was a limited one, however, as he turned out to be "an exceedingly incompetent lawyer."[48] He was known for his fondness for publicity and addiction to drinking. These problems, coupled with his prolonged absences from Tokyo and his lack of a grasp of actual prosecutorial work, were the subject of constant complaints among the members of the International Prosecution Section. The Japanese accused, too, remarked disapprovingly on the chief prosecutor's poor courtroom performance. Two of the accused, Kido Kōichi and Shigemitsu Mamoru, recorded in their respective prison diaries contemporaneously their impressions of Keenan as "lacking preparation [*mu-junbi*]," being in "want of study [*benkyō busoku*]," "wide of the mark [*mato ga hazure*]," and so on. Shigemitsu also suspected one day that alcohol might be interfering with Keenan's courtroom performance, as the chief prosecutor was seen as "repeating the same questions as if a drunkard" when cross-examining Kido.[49] What saved the International Prosecution Section from poor leadership and disunity was the willingness of other members to make up for the chief prosecutor's shortcomings. Several of the American assistant prosecutors, and other

---

[46] The four participating countries at Nuremberg had the equal right to appoint a judge, an alternate, and a chief prosecutor each. (See Articles 2–4, IMT Charter.) The same arrangement was not replicated at Tokyo. The power of appointment was instead entrusted with a single authority, the Supreme Commander for the Allied Power, who had the power to establish the tribunal and the prosecuting agency, as well as to appoint one chief prosecutor (instead of multiple chief prosecutors, which was the case at IMT).

[47] The American team at Nuremberg alone numbered 654 staff. See Jackson, *Report of Robert H. Jackson United States Representative to the International Conference on Military Trials*, 433. According to the data of the International Prosecution Section at the Tokyo Trial, the total number of prosecution staff at its high point was 509. This included seventy-two Allied attorneys and 232 Japanese staff. As for defense counsel, there were 404 in total, which comprised forty-six Allied nationals (including twenty-five American attorneys) and 358 Japanese staff (including seventy-nine Japanese attorneys). *Tōkyō saiban to kokusai kensatsu kyoku*, vol. 5, 322.

[48] This is a remark made by Justice Northcroft. *Documents of New Zealand External Relations*, 1612.

[49] Shigemitsu, *Sugamo nikki*, 281, 325; Kido, *Kido Kōichi nikki, Tōkyō saibanki*, 447.

Allied prosecutors who joined the International Prosecution Section to serve as associate prosecutors, deserve credit for their patience, professionalism, and teamwork.[50]

The defense counsel (also referred to as "the defense" throughout this book) comprised individuals of mixed talents and backgrounds, including several dozen Japanese who had little or no prior training in law, but many of whom came to serve because they were the individual accused's trusted friends, family members, wartime colleagues, or former subordinate officials.[51] This decision by Japanese defendants to choose counsel with little experience in criminal defense inevitably meant that they were at a disadvantage in relation to experienced prosecutors. It benefitted the accused, however, that about two-dozen American lawyers joined the defense team as well. They were added to address concern expressed by the Japanese government about "the difficulty of leaving the matter of defense solely to Japanese counsel ... since the procedure before this tribunal would differ so sharply from the ordinary civil or criminal practice in Japan."[52]

The role of American defense lawyers was therefore to assist their Japanese counterparts with technical aspects of the trial. Such was at least the understanding of G. C. Williams, who explained to his client (accused Hoshino Naoki) that "the American defense counsel were sent here as advisors only," and "my principal duty is to advise on matters of law and procedure, since this is predominantly Western and Anglo-American Tribunal."[53] In reality, however, American defense lawyers assumed a far greater role than mere advising. They were usually the ones who effectively represented the interests of individual accused in the courtroom, taking charge of making arguments, raising objections, filing motions, and carrying out direct examinations and cross-examinations of witnesses. A handful of Japanese defense lawyers did the same, but the vast majority of Japanese members in the defense team assumed little more than a supporting role on account of their limited experience in criminal trials. The right of accused persons to choose their own defense counsel, recognized as a fundamental fair trial right, necessarily implies the risk that an accused person may choose counsel of limited or no competence. This is not a unique feature of the Tokyo Trial, for there have been numerous such examples in the proceedings of contemporary international tribunals.

---

[50] For complete listing of key members in the International Prosecution Section, see *The Tokyo War Crimes Trial: The Comprehensive Index and Guide*, vol. 5.

[51] Shimanouchi, *Tōkyō saiban*, 30–1.

[52] Memorandum Re: Conference with Mr. Ohta, Liaison Officer, Japanese Government, Concerning Trial of War Criminals, February 15, 1946, M1668, Roll 10, NARA. For complete listing of defense counsel, see *The Tokyo War Crimes Trial: The Comprehensive Index and Guide*, vol. 5.

[53] Memorandum from G.C. Williams to Messrs. Fujii and Migita, February 12, 1947, MSS 78–4, Box 1, Arthur J. Morris Law Library, University of Virginia.

1.3   A Chronological Overview of the Tokyo Trial                                          47

The Japanese accused and defense lawyers at first took a guarded attitude toward American lawyers, whom they thought could not be trusted because they were the nationals of the former enemy country. The initial wariness dissipated quickly, however, as the American lawyers were seen as conducting themselves with dedication and professionalism.[54] During a government-conducted interview in 1964, Kido remarked that "I don't know whether it was out of their business-mindedness or love of Japan, but American lawyers genuinely stood by the accused and did very well." He also observed that "the trial would have ended in a huge mess [*mecha-kucha*] had the Japanese lawyers been left alone, without any idea of how to deal with such a large volume of evidentiary materials."[55] Another accused, Hoshino, similarly remarked approvingly of the service rendered by American counsel, and especially C. G. Williams, the lawyer assigned to him. When Williams completed the defense work and was about to depart for the United States for good, Hoshino presented him with a letter of gratitude. "Difficulties you confronted [in preparation of Hoshino's case] were beyond description," the letter read, and despite tremendous challenges, "you devoted all your energy, put much effort into my defense, and finally in the last two days in the courtroom synthesized the results of the effort and completed brilliantly the submission of evidence on my behalf." Recalling the visual impression of Williams making the final argument in the courtroom, Hoshino wrote, "your crisp appearance [*sassō taru sugata*] is seared in my eyes, which I will not forget for a long time."[56]

Other participants in the Tokyo Trial, too, recognized the merit of having American lawyers in defense counsel but were less enthusiastic. For instance, Justice Northcroft was prepared to say that providing additional legal assistance to Japanese accused was "proper," but he found that the American lawyers "behaved in the most unseemly fashion, being constantly on their feet with the most unmeritorious, technical, and for the most part stupid, objections and protests to almost every words that was said."[57] From the defense perspective, however, this meant that they were doing their job in serving, in their view, the interests of their clients.

R. H. Quilliam, associate prosecutor from New Zealand, was not impressed either, as he observed that defense counsel "consistently wastes time, and one

---

[54] In post-trial interviews, former members of Japanese defense counsel comment frequently on exemplary conduct of American defense lawyers. See, for instance, "Kyokutō kokusai gunji saiban bengonin Shiobara Tokisaburō shi kara no chōshusho," Kaikō bunko, Yasukuni Shrine; and "Bengonin, Tōkyō saiban, bengonin kara no chōshusho", H-11-Hōmu Series, no. 6826, National Archives of Japan.
[55] Kido, *Kido Kōichi nikki, Tōkyō saibanki*, 447.
[56] Letter from Hoshino Naoki to G.C. Williams, September 25, 1947, MSS 78-4, Box 1, Arthur J. Morris Law Library, University of Virginia.
[57] *Documents on New Zealand External Relations*, 1612–13.

is forced to the conclusion that this is a deliberate policy."[58] The defense lawyers' conduct also invited caustic remarks from Justice Webb, the President of the Tokyo Tribunal and the member from Australia. He once remarked, "What are we to do with the defense, conducted by able lawyers, if they repeatedly disregard our rulings and if, as a result of our insisting upon our rulings being given effect to, the defense case is brought to a standstill?" He went on to observe that, "By repeatedly doing that they could prevent this Court, if this Court were foolish enough to allow them to do so, from ever reaching a verdict."[59] These stern words from the president of the tribunal notwithstanding, delays resulting from motions and objections – from both the prosecution and the defense – remained frequent throughout the court proceedings. The amount of leeway allowed to defense and prosecution in making motions and objections remains an issue of trial management at all international criminal tribunals, because it inherently involves balancing the requirement of expeditious proceedings against the right of the accused to a fair trial.

Some one hundred individuals had been identified as suspected "Class 1.A." war criminals in the immediate months following the surrender ceremony in September 1945. The named suspects, including a handful of foreign nationals, were placed either under house arrest or in the US Army's custody at Sugamo Prison (within a short drive to and from Ichigaya), or detained by the British military authorities in Southeast Asia. Of these, the International Prosecution Section chose twenty-eight Japanese individuals for trial. They were made up of a "representative group" of those whom the prosecution deemed to have "played vital roles in Japan's program of aggression," i.e. the commission of Class 1.A. offenses.[60] Most had held key positions in the policy-making circles, but a minority of the accused had served as second-tier or lower-ranking members of Japanese government or military establishment, during all or part of the war years. One accused, Ōkawa Shūmei, alone was a non-state, non-military actor. His case was dropped, however, upon the Tribunal's decision that he was mentally unfit to stand trial. Two other accused fell out of the Tribunal's consideration, too, as they died of illnesses in the early months of the trial (Admiral Nagano Osami, chief of the Navy General Staff, 1941–4; and Matsuoka Yōsuke, foreign minister, 1940–1).

The indictment against the original group of twenty-eight was formally lodged on Monday, April 29, 1946, whereupon Justice Webb set the date of

---

[58] Ibid., 1598.
[59] T24247.
[60] Horwitz, "The Tokyo Trial," 496. For an authoritative account regarding the prosecution's selection of prospective defendants, see Awaya, *Tōkyō saiban e no michi*. The IPS notion of "representative" was quite different than that of the IMT, which encompassed accused from most key branches of government, military, Nazi party, economy, propaganda, etc.

1.3  A Chronological Overview of the Tokyo Trial                                   49

arraignment to be May 3.⁶¹ But the actual arraignment did not take place until a week later on May 6, as two full days – May 3 and 4 – were spent on reading out the indictment.⁶² A possibility of further delay emerged when the defense challenged Webb's qualification to serve on the Tribunal. It was pointed out that Webb had investigated in the period of 1943–5 Japanese war crimes in the South Pacific on behalf of the Government of Australia.⁶³ The Tribunal dismissed the defense challenge, however, on the ground that the Tribunal was vested with no power to unseat any of its own members.⁶⁴ As had been the case at Nuremberg, further defense motions that challenged the jurisdiction of the Tribunal were similarly dismissed. No explanation was given at this point, but the Tribunal declared that the reasoning would be offered "later."⁶⁵ (The Tribunal gave its reasoning considerably late, when delivering its judgment in November 1948.) The plea of not guilty was then entered by the individual accused. With the arraignment completed, the historic trial of major Japanese war criminals – remembered in Japan since as *Tōkyō saiban* ("The Tokyo Trial") – began. The Tokyo Tribunal thereafter convened daily from Monday through Friday, except holidays and during the court's adjournments.⁶⁶

The case by the prosecution commenced on June 3, 1946, and continued until January 24, 1947. The prosecution presented the evidentiary materials for its case in fifteen separate "phases." These phases were designed to document various facets of the Japanese planning, preparation, initiation, or waging of war, or participation in a common plan to commit the foregoing acts. Some phases were set aside for documenting aspects of Japanese wartime atrocities. When the prosecution had concluded its case the defense filed motions for dismissal of the charges. Five days were spent by the prosecution and the defense to argue against and for the motions. The Tribunal denied all motions.

---

[61] For a concise statement of the timeline of the Tokyo proceedings, see the opening segment of the IMTFE judgment. *Documents*, 71–2. For a detailed narrative summary, see "Narrative Summary of the Proceedings," in *The Tokyo War Crimes Trial: The Comprehensive Index and Guide*, vol. 3.

[62] Five appendices in the Indictment were not read in court.

[63] For Webb's wartime and postwar services as chief war crimes investigator for the Government of Australia, see Sissons, "Australian War Crimes Trials and Investigations (1942–1951)." A brief account of the "Webb Commissions," papers relating to Justice Webb, and guides to archival materials can be found at the website of the Australian War Memorial. The Australian War Memorial hereafter is referred to as AWM.

[64] T98.

[65] T319. The substance of the defense's challenges and the Tribunal's reasons for dismissal are summarized in the majority judgment. See *Documents,* 79–82. Further defense motions challenging the jurisdiction of the tribunal were made after the defendants entered their plea, between May 13 and 15, 1946.

[66] The holidays were January 1 and 2, July 4, November 11, and December 25. The daily schedule of the court proceedings was usually that the Tribunal convened at 9:30 a.m. and adjourned at 4:00 p.m., with a lunchtime recess between 12:00 p.m. and 1:30 p.m.

## The Framework of the Trial

The defense case commenced after a three-week recess, on February 24, 1947. The defense organized its case to form six separate "divisions." The presentation generally corresponded to the prosecution's except the last "division," which was set aside for individual accused to testify on their behalf as well as to present additional evidentiary materials. (Nine accused chose not to take the witness stand.[67]) The defense rested its case on January 12, 1948. The prosecution's rebuttal and the defense's surrebuttal ensued between January 12 and February 10, followed by the prosecution's summation, the defense's summation, and the prosecution's reply. The summations were major presentations of the respective cases and, reflecting the massive scope of the trial, lasted for a little over two months, from February 11 to April 16. The prosecution and the defense went at length in detailing their summations also because of repeated instructions by Justice Webb that they provide "every bit of evidence upon which they relied and their supporting arguments."[68] After completion of the summations the Tribunal adjourned to consider its judgment.

In total, the amount of evidence presented to the court was massive. "In all 4,335 exhibits were admitted in evidence, 419 witnesses testified in court, 779 witnesses gave evidence in depositions and affidavits, and the transcript of the proceedings convers 48,412 pages," according to the summary provided by the Tribunal.[69] The volume of evidence before the Tribunal significantly exceeded that at Nuremberg where the tribunal heard only ninety-four witnesses (thirty-three for the prosecution and sixty-one for the defense), received only 143 witness statements in written form (all for the defense), and also had "approximately" 4,000 exhibits entered into evidence.[70] In all, the Tokyo Trial consumed two years from the time of the filing of the indictment to the last day of summations, more than twice as long as its Nuremberg counterpart. The Tribunal took an additional one-half year to deliberate and draft the final decisions.

The court reconvened on November 4, 1948 to deliver its findings, verdicts, and sentences. The voice of Justice Webb reverberated throughout the courtroom for seven full days (on November 4, 5, 8–12), as he read the entirety of the judgment himself while ten other judges remained seated quietly.

---

[67] The ones who chose not to take the witness stand consisted of five former army generals (Dohihara, Hata, Kimura, Satō, and Umezu), and four former ministers of state (Hoshino, Hiranuma, Hirota, and Shigemitsu).

[68] Webb left the following remark in a memorandum, dated January 8, 1948, from him to an American member, Myron Cramer: "From time to time during the trial I asked the prosecution and Defense Counsel to plan in their final advances or summations every bit of evidence upon which they relied and their supporting arguments." AWM 3DRL 2481.

[69] *Documents*, 76.

[70] See Jackson, *Report of Robert H. Jackson United States Representative to the International Conference on Military Trials*, 433.

## 1.3 A Chronological Overview of the Tokyo Trial

The decision of the Tokyo Tribunal was split between the majority opinion of eight justices ("majority judgment" hereafter), three dissenting opinions, and two concurring opinions. "The Member for India dissents from the Majority Judgment and has filed a statement of his reasons for such dissent," so Justice Webb announced right before the sentencing, and "the members for France and the Netherlands dissent as to part only from the Majority Judgment and have filed statements of their reasons for such dissents." The member for the Philippines, too, submitted a separate opinion, although his was concurring with the majority justices (also referred to as "the majority" hereafter). Webb himself filed another: "Generally, I share the view of the majority as to facts," he states, and "in most matters the majority judgment is to the same effect as mine." However, he produced a separate opinion to express his own reasoning "for upholding the Charter [of the Tribunal] and the jurisdiction of the Tribunal and of some general considerations that influenced me in deciding on the sentences."[71]

While not read in the courtroom, the text of his separate opinion revealed that Webb had originally prepared a 658-page draft judgment ("Webb's draft judgment" or "The President's Judgment" hereafter), because he had found himself "unable to agree with a majority of the Tribunal." He withdrew it at the end of the day, however, stating, somewhat disingenuously, that he found the majority judgment to be "to the same effect as mine" after all.[72] As will be seen, the majority had refused to accept Webb's draft judgment, and Webb's proposed judgment actually had little in common with which the majority drafting committee in the end produced. The vast difference in quality of the two judgments raises the question as to why, in fact, Webb withdrew his draft judgment. This question will be explored in Part II.

The defense had made a prior request that the separate opinions be read in open court, but Justice Webb informed them when delivering the majority's decision that the request was denied. That said, he assured that all the separate opinions would be included in the official record of the Tokyo Trial, and that they would become "available to the Supreme Commander [for the Allied Powers], to the Defense Counsel and to others who may be concerned."[73] The majority judgment – which was adopted as the judgment of the Tokyo Tribunal (also referred to as the "Tokyo judgment," the "IMTFE judgment," or, at times,

---

[71] *Documents*, 626. The justices who joined the majority opinion are the following: Myron C. Cramer (the United States), Delfin Jaranilla (Philippines), Mei Ruao (China), E. S. McDougall (Canada), E. H. Northcroft (New Zealand), Lord Patrick (Great Britain), Sir William F. Webb (Australia), and Ivan M. Zaryanov (USSR). The three dissenting justices are Henri Bernard (France), Radhabinod Pal (India), and B. V. A. Roeling (Netherlands). For the career profile of individual justices, see *Documents*, lii–lvi.
[72] Ibid., 631.
[73] Ibid., 626.

the "judgment" hereafter) – found all the accused guilty of one or more counts of the indictment. Seven were sentenced to death by hanging, while all others, except two, were sentenced to life in prison. At Nuremberg twelve of the nineteen convicted were sentenced to death by hanging. The two with lesser penalties were Shigemitsu Mamoru (seven years) and Tōgō Shigenori (twenty years). Both had served as foreign ministers during the war years (Shigemitsu, 1943–5; Tōgō, 1941–2 and 1945).

The Tokyo Trial came to its formal conclusion on November 12, 1948, with the handing down of the sentences. The remaining task for the Allied Powers was to have the confirming authority review, confirm, and carry out the Tribunal's decision. Accordingly, the judgment was transmitted to the Supreme Commander, who promptly reviewed the case and announced his position, on November 24, 1948. "No duty I have ever been called upon to perform in a long public service replete with many bitter, lonely and forlorn assignments and responsibilities is so utterly repugnant to me as that of reviewing the sentences of the Japanese War Criminal defendants adjudged by the International Military Tribunal for the Far East," so MacArthur declared. The conclusion he reached was that, "under the principles and procedures prescribed in full detailed by the Allied Powers concerned, I can find nothing of technical commission or omission in the incidents of the trial itself of sufficient import to warrant my intervention in the judgments which have been rendered."[74] Thus satisfied with the decision of the Tribunal, he confirmed all of the verdicts and sentences. From the standpoint of fair trial rights, one may question the advisability of having the authority who convened the Tribunal and oversaw the operations of the prosecution also be the only reviewing authority (as at Nuremberg there was no appeal from the verdicts of the Tribunal). Indeed, the lack of any detailed consideration in his brief review of any of the legal or factual issues in contention in the trial also indicates the limitations of MacArthur as a juridical authority for review of the verdicts and sentences.

The carrying out of the sentences did not occur immediately, however, since defense counsel for several accused applied to the US Supreme Court for leave to file petitions for writs of habeas corpus.[75] The Supreme Court heard the argument for the Japanese accused over three days in mid-December 1948, and concluded that it had no jurisdiction over the case. The pertinent part in the decision read that the Tokyo Tribunal was "not a tribunal

---

[74] Ibid., 70.
[75] Defense counsel was following the examples of General Yamashita Tomoyuki and Lieutenant General Honma Masaharu, who had been convicted of war crimes by the US military commission at Manila (October 1945–February 1946), and whose defense counsel unsuccessfully sought from the US Supreme Court habeas corpus protection. For discussion of the two cases, see Totani, *Justice in Asia and the Pacific Region, 1945–1952*, chapter 1.

of the United States, and the courts of the United States have no power or authority to review, affirm, set aside, or annul the judgments and sentences imposed by it on these petitioners, all of whom are residents and citizens of Japan."[76]

The seven death sentences were carried out within days of this decision by the US Supreme Court, on the early morning of December 23, 1948. As for other convicted Class A war criminals, they were kept at the Sugamo Prison in Tokyo – their original place of detention – to serve their sentences. Five of them died of illnesses while in prison.[77] All others were released on parole later, in the period between 1955 and 1956, owing to successful efforts by the Government of Japan in negotiating with the former Allied governments. Shigemitsu alone enjoyed an early release, in 1950, and returned to public service shortly thereafter, which included his reappointment as foreign minister (1954–6).[78] A few followed Shigemitsu's path, but most sought a new career in the private sector or chose life in retirement.

## 1.4  Rules of Procedure

One hallmark of the Tokyo Trial arose from the decision to follow the model provided by IMT in ensuring to the accused a full range of fair-trial protections. Specific rules for safeguarding the fairness of the proceeding were set out in the IMTFE Charter (dated January 19, 1946, and amended April 26, 1946[79]), and "The Rules of Procedure of the International Military Tribunal for the Far East" (dated April 25, 1946, with further amendments on

---

[76] *Hirota* v. *MacArthur*, 338 US 197 (1949). Argued December 16–17, 1948, and decided December 20, 1948.

[77] The ones who died in prison are Hiranuma, Tōgō, Umezu, Koiso, and Shiratori.

[78] The Treaty of Peace, signed at San Francisco on September 8, 1951, contained the following provision regarding the obligations of the Japanese government on the handling of the judgments of Allied war crimes trials:

> Article 11. Japan accepts the judgments of the International Military Tribunal for the Far East and of other Allied War Crimes Courts both within and outside Japan, and will carry out the sentences imposed thereby upon Japanese nationals imprisoned in Japan. The power to grant clemency, to reduce sentences and to parole with respect to such prisoners may not be exercised except on the decision of the Government or Governments which imposed the sentence in each instance, and on recommendation of Japan. In the case of persons sentenced by the International Military Tribunal for the Far East, such power may not be exercised except on the decision of a majority of the Governments represented on the Tribunal, and on the recommendation of Japan.

For an authoritative account of the release of war criminals convicted at the Tokyo Trial, see Higurashi, *Tōkyō saiban*, chapter 7.

[79] The amendment was made to increase the number of judges to serve on the tribunal from nine to eleven, so that new nominations from India and the Philippines could be accommodated ("Article 2. Members"). *Documents*, 7, 73.

May 20, 1946, and August 16, 1946[80]; "IMTFE Rules of Procedure" hereafter). The IMTFE Charter articulated the foundational rules concerning the constitution, jurisdiction, and conduct of the Tribunal, fair-trial protection for the accused, admissibility of evidence, and general procedural rules. The IMTFE Rules of Procedure, meanwhile, amplified the basic provisions set out in the IMTFE Charter by offering more detailed guidelines about the handling of witnesses, documentary evidence, and other matters.

In addition to rules contained in the IMTFE Charter and the IMTFE Rules of Procedure, the Tokyo Tribunal made a number of other rules while the trial was in session, in order to address new problems and challenges that arose from the actual court proceedings. Some were decided during the formal sessions in the courtroom, while others during informal conferences in Chambers among the members of the Tribunal, the prosecution, and the defense.[81] Certain of the rulings were issued in the form of court orders, but most were recorded as they were made, directly into the transcripts of court proceedings or the record of proceedings in Chambers. The Tribunal never published a document that compiled comprehensively all of the new rulings.

The International Prosecution Section, however, compiled what it considered to be "the more important rules of the IMTFE," and produced a 274-page reference material, titled, "IPS Document No. 0006: Rulings of the International Military Tribunal for the Far East" (undated, compiled probably in mid-1947; "IPS Document No. 0006" hereafter).[82] This document arranges numerous court rulings under seventeen separate topics, with numbers and short headnotes. It quotes each ruling verbatim from the trial transcripts or the record of proceedings in Chambers, alongside bulk quotes of arguments made by the prosecution and the defense, and explanatory remarks made by the president of the tribunal regarding the rationale behind each ruling. These three documents – the IMTFE Charter, the IMTFE Rules of Procedure, and the IPS Document No. 0006 – are essential for the understanding of how the

---

[80] Amendments were made to Rule 6 (b) to expand its scope. Court Papers No. 66 (May 20, 1946), No. 301 (July 22, 1946), and No. 368 (August 16, 1946). Amended Rule 6 (b) read, in pertinent part, as follows:

> Except as otherwise provided by the Tribunal, (1) A copy of every document intended to be aduced in evidence by the prosecution or the defense will be delivered to the accused concerned or his counsel or to the prosecution, as the case may be, and also to the officer in charge of the Language Section of the Secretariat of the Tribunal, not less than twenty-four hours before such document is to be tendered in evidence. Every such copy shall have plainly marked thereon the part or parts upon which the prosecution or the defense, as the case may be, intends to rely ... T918, roll 1, NARA, accessible also at the National Diet Library at Tokyo, Japan, with the call number CIM-1. For the list of applications and court orders regarding the waiver of Rule 6 (b) (1), see "Index to the Court Docket" (pp. 9–12, 115–18) in *The Tokyo War Crimes Trial: The Comprehensive Index and Guide*, vol. 4.

[81] Records of proceedings in Chambers are reproduced in *The Tokyo War Crimes Trial*, vol. 22.
[82] This document is reproduced in *The Tokyo War Crimes Trial: The Comprehensive Index and Guide*, vol. 4.

principle of fair and expeditious proceedings was applied at the Tokyo Trial, not only in form but also in practice. It can be said, however, that some critiques of the fairness of the Tokyo proceedings have not focused systematic attention on these documents and the way they were applied in court.

One section in the IMTFE Charter, titled, "III. Fair Trial for Accused," is where the basic principles of fairness are articulated. Six types of fair-trial protection are listed. They are namely: (1) that the indictment "shall consist of a plain, concise, and adequate statement of each offense charge," whose copy and any amendment "shall be furnished, in adequate time for defense ... in a language understood by the accused"; (2) that the trial "shall be conducted in English and language of the accused," which would include provision of "translations of documents and other papers ... as needed and requested"; (3) that an accused had the right to be represented by counsel, either of his own choosing or, in the case a defendant did not have counsel of his choosing, by the Tribunal's designation; (4) that an accused "shall have the right ... to conduct his defense, including the right to examine any witnesses"; (5) that an accused "may apply in writing to the Tribunal for the production of witnesses or of documents"; and (6) that an accused may file "motions, applications, or other requests" prior to trial, in which case they "shall be made in writing and filed with the General Secretary of the Tribunal for action by the Tribunal."[83] The Tribunal thus recognized the basic fair trial rights prevalent in that era, or going beyond them.[84]

The right of the accused to conduct their own defense was not without restriction, however, as the Tribunal was empowered by the same Charter to take necessary steps to confine the proceedings "strictly to an expeditious hearing of the issues raised by the charges," and "to prevent any action which would cause any unreasonable delay and rule out irrelevant issues and statements of any kind whatsoever" (Article 12). As noted above, this tension between expeditious trial management and the right of the defense to a fair trial continues to inform international criminal proceedings.[85]

In regard to the admission of evidence, following Nuremberg, the IMTFE Charter gave the Tribunal broad authority in determining the admissibility of evidence. "The Tribunal shall not be bound by technical rules of evidence," the relevant provision read, and the Tribunal "shall adopt and apply to the greatest possible extent expeditious and non-technical procedures, and shall admit any

---

[83] *Documents*, 9.
[84] In the United States, for example, the right to counsel even when an accused cannot afford one was only recognized as a fundamental right applicable to the states in 1963 in *Gideon v. Wainwright* 372 US 335.
[85] See, for example, Article 20 of the Statute of the International Criminal Tribunal for the former Yugoslavia: "The Trial Chambers shall ensure that a trial is fair and expeditious." See also most recently the extensive defense challenges to the fairness of the proceedings because of limitations on witnesses and cross-examination at the Khmer Rouge Tribunal. See the Judgment of the Supreme Court Chamber of the Extraordinary Chambers in the Courts of Cambodia of November 23, 2016, Case 002 (Case File 002/19-09-2007-ECCC/SC), pp. 9–36, 62–97, 126–38.

evidence which it deems to have probative value" (Article 13). This approach of Nuremberg and the IMTFE set the general standard for evidence which is still applied today in international criminal proceedings: "A Chamber may admit any relevant evidence which it deems to have probative value."[86]

The IMTFE Charter listed five types of evidence as admissible at the Tokyo Trial. They are as follows: (1) documents that appeared to the Tribunal as having been signed or issued by any officer, department, agency, or member of the armed forces of any government even if there was no authentication or proof; (2) reports that appeared to the Tribunal as having been signed or issued by members of the International Committee of the Red Cross, other medical professions, investigators, and intelligence; (3) affidavits, depositions, and other signed statements; (4) diaries, letters, and the like, which the Tribunal deemed "to contain information relating to the charge"; and (5) copies of documents or other secondary evidence of documents, "if the original is not immediately available."[87] During the Tokyo Trial, the prosecution and the defense frequently disputed the admissibility or otherwise of various exhibits proposed for introduction into evidence. On those occasions, the Tribunal deliberated the merits of each case while referring back to the IMTFE Charter, where it read that the Tribunal was not bound by technical rules of evidence.[88]

The record of the Tokyo Trial indicates that, of the six fair-trial protections as set out under "III. Fair Trial for Accused" in the IMTFE Charter, the Tribunal went to great lengths to ensure the safeguarding of the right of accused to have the hearing in their own language, though with mixed results. The Tokyo Trial proceeded bilingually, using English and Japanese. This proved to be a challenging task, as the Tribunal complained that "the need to have every word spoken in Court translated from English into Japanese, or vice versa, had at least doubled the length of the proceedings." Much of the interpretation had to be carried out consecutively instead of simultaneously, due to the complexity of translating between the two highly dissimilar languages and the fact that electronic simultaneous translation systems were in their infancy at the time. "Translation cannot be made from the one language into the other with the speed and certainty which can be attained in translating one Western speech into another," the Tribunal observed, and literal translation proved "impossible." What was possible, as the Tribunal found out, amounted to little more than paraphrasing, which is distinct from interpretation. But then, "experts in both languages will often differ as to the *correct paraphrase*"[89] (emphasis added).

---

[86] International Criminal Tribunal for the former Yugoslavia, Rules of Procedure and Evidence Art. 89 C.
[87] *Documents*, 10.
[88] For concrete instances of dispute over admissibility of evidence, see IPS Document No. 0006, from page VII-1 through page VII-77.
[89] *Documents*, 77.

## 1.4 Rules of Procedure

The Tribunal set up a Language Arbitration Board to address this problem, but, as shown in Kayoko Takeda's *Interpreting the Tokyo War Crimes Tribunal* (2008), its effectiveness was mixed, and the quality of court interpretation varied throughout the trial. Despite great advances in simultaneous interpretation in general, the quality of interpretation remains an unresolved issue in international criminal proceedings today, particularly where non-Western languages are involved, as in Cambodia, East Timor, Rwanda, and Sierra Leone.

IPS Document No. 0006 shows that the Tokyo Tribunal resorted to various other measures to tackle the difficulties in safeguarding the right of the accused to have the trial conducted in their own language and also in ensuring the expeditious court proceedings. One of the additional steps taken was to allow the use of affidavit evidence in lieu of oral direct examination when a non-native speaker of English took the stand to testify. This decision, adopted upon the prosecution's proposal as early as June 1946 (i.e. shortly after the start of the prosecution's case), had the merit of expediting the court proceedings, because the witnesses' testimony would be taken and translated in advance, and it would be read out in the courtroom alongside the reading of the Japanese original, hence allowing "simultaneous" interpretation, of sorts, to occur in the courtroom.

That said, the decision to allow the use of affidavit evidence was made with great reluctance at first. In the words of Justice Webb, "we [the judges] are making a big concession here, perhaps not without misgivings." There was concern that, when preparing the affidavit, the deponent would give statements in response to "a number of leading questions which we would not allow if he were examined in court." Even so, the Tribunal decided to try out this new method with the understanding that the use of affidavit evidence would be followed by "a high standard of cross examination, or a high standard of answers in cross-examination."[90] This latter point dealt with the most problematic aspect of affidavit testimony, the right of confrontation of witnesses, where the affiant did not appear before the court.

The Tribunal's initial skepticism dissipated with the progress of the trial, as Justice Webb made the following remark a year later:

> The insistence by the Tribunal on affidavits by the defense witnesses cannot prejudice a fair trial of the accused. On the contrary, it gives an advantage to the accused, and we know it if you [defense counsel] don't. There is no jury here. The deponents will take the box and be subject to cross-examination and re-examination. All that will happen will be that the witness will give his examination, his direct examination or the evidence therein, after careful consideration and that direct examination will be simultaneously broadcast. The only change involved will be to the advantage of the accused.[91]

---

[90] IPS Document No. 0006, page I-2.
[91] Ibid., I-5.

58    The Framework of the Trial

It was nevertheless decided that the use of affidavit evidence applied only to non-native speakers of English, and not to American or other witnesses from the English-speaking countries. The Tribunal insisted on oral direct evidence, at least with English speakers, apparently because of the enduring notion that the principle of fair trial required it, and insofar as it would not unduly protract the court proceedings. The Tribunal was quite blunt in expressing its displeasure, then, when an English-speaking witness showed signs of having "a lot to say" and of taking up an inordinate amount of time. The Tribunal suggested that counsel should consider using affidavit evidence instead in such eventualities.[92] (As for non-native speakers who were fluent in English, the Tribunal had them use affidavit evidence in lieu of oral direct evidence.[93])

Another new ruling to ensure a fair and expeditious hearing concerned the translation and introduction of documentary evidence relating to war crimes. Before presenting evidence of war crimes relative to the Pacific theater, the prosecution requested the Tribunal to allow it to adopt an abridged form of presentation for the sake of saving time and resources. There were two concrete proposals in the request. One was that the prosecution be required to furnish the Japanese-language translation of *excerpts* of evidentiary documents, and not the Japanese translation of the documents in their entirety.

A massive amount of evidence on war crimes was at the prosecution's disposal by then, the vast majority of which was written in English. They had to be translated into Japanese for use at the Tokyo Trial, for which the prosecution had neither sufficient time nor resources. Alan S. Mansfield, associate prosecutor from Australia and the one in charge of presenting evidence on war crimes in the Pacific theater, explained to the Tribunal that the prosecution would have to undertake an inordinate amount of work if it were to translate every single word in the evidentiary materials. He thus stated: "If it is possible to be ready in time to have some of these documents from which excerpts are being used – one document runs into forty pages; we are only using one page from it. That will have to be translated into Japanese and that will take forty days for one person."[94]

Another component of the prosecution's request was that it be permitted to use a synopsis of court exhibits when introducing them, and to read out the synopsis in the main, and not the court exhibits themselves. A synopsis would contain a brief summary of each exhibit, stated in a sentence or two, instead of going into the details of offense.

The advantage of the prosecution's two-prong proposal regarding the preparation of evidence was clear. On the one hand, it would enable the prosecution

---

[92] Ibid., I-6.
[93] Ibid., from page I-2 through page I-8.
[94] Ibid., I-9.

## 1.4 Rules of Procedure

to introduce its vast corpus of evidentiary materials in their entirety, without being required to translate every single page in them, and without unduly delaying the court proceedings. On the other hand, the rights of the accused remained protected to the extent that the accused would receive the Japanese translation of the excerpts of the prosecution's court exhibits, as well as the English-language original of the entirety of the same exhibits. The danger in regard to the rights of the accused, of course, was that other parts of the same document might contain material that was either potentially exculpatory or that contradicted the excerpted portion. Presumably American defense counsel could have dealt with this, but it nonetheless created a disadvantage for the Japanese defense counsel.

After deliberating the matter, the Tribunal approved the prosecution's proposal. The method of presentation, as Justice Webb summarized, would be as follows:

Then you [the prosecution] intend to serve on the defense in English a copy of the affidavit in full, a copy of the excerpt, and a copy of the synopsis; and in Japanese a copy of the excerpt and a copy of the synopsis. The defense, in those circumstances, would be at liberty to draw to the Court's attention anything in the affidavit which does not appear in the excerpt or in the synopsis. They would be that by tendering the part omitted upon which they would rely, and would do it in the course of giving evidence for the defense. In that way, every particle of the affidavit would be drawn to the Court's attention.[95]

Mansfield had previously speculated that the International Prosecution Section would need at least ten weeks to present its evidence on war crimes for the Pacific theater, and, "If a complete historical record of atrocities were presented, the phase would be probably last twelve months."[96] Thanks to the Tribunal's approval of the new method of presentation, however, his team was able to complete its presentation in just six weeks. But whether this gain in efficiency was offset by other considerations is another matter.

The abridged presentation of evidence on war crimes indeed brought certain disadvantages. For one, it relied on the judges to examine the evidence in full that was not presented in court. As will be seen in Part II, the judges divided up the war crimes case into different components and it is clear that not all of the judges had gone through all of the evidence contained in the full documentary record whose abbreviated form had been presented in court. As indicated by the speed with which the prosecution completed this phase of its case, it also inevitably limited the testing of the evidence in open court.

---

[95] Ibid.
[96] Memorandum from Justice Mansfield to Chief of Counsel (Keenan), (B) and (C) Offenses, November 5, 1946, A1067/1, UN46//WC/15, NAA.

Beyond these considerations connected to the quality of the in-court proceedings, the abbreviation of the case on war crimes limited the opportunity for the public to learn the full scope of the exhibits, since the prosecution usually confined itself to reading in the courtroom the synopses and, on occasion, some short excerpts. What is more, the brisk method of presentation had the effect of understating in the eyes of the Japanese public the importance of war crimes charges against the major Japanese war criminals. Perhaps most significantly, as will be seen in Part II, the brevity of the prosecution's case on war crimes impacted the majority judgment which adopted a similarly abbreviated format for consideration of these charges against the Accused.

IPS Document No. 0006 shows that there is yet another important additional ruling with which the Tribunal sought to strike a balance between safeguarding the right of the accused and ensuring expeditious court proceedings. Concern was aired from early on that the very large group of accused would complicate the process of examining and cross-examining witnesses, with a likely outcome of a prolonged court hearing. "If each accused exercises his right to cross-examine witnesses, there would be twenty-eight cross-examinations," as Justice Webb remarked.[97] The prosecution and the defense shared this concern, and conferred with each other to work out a solution. They formally presented to the Tribunal a joint proposal that contained a detailed guideline as to how the examination and cross-examination of witnesses should be regulated. Specifics of the joint proposal are documented in the record of the proceedings in Chambers (dated March 4, 1947), and also reproduced in the IPS Document No. 0006. Despite its length, it is worth quoting in full, as it shows how the prosecution, the defense, and the Tribunal worked together to overcome pressing practical problems in realizing fair and expeditious court proceedings. The joint proposal set out the following five-point guideline:

1. During the presentation of the general phase of the defense case, without the special permission of the Tribunal, not more than one counsel for the accused shall examine a witness in chief on the matters then being presented. Upon the completion of this examination, counsel for the individual accused may examine the witness on matters which specifically and particularly concern his client to the extent only that they have not been covered in the preceding examination. Such counsel shall state at the beginning of his examination that the examination is direct.
2. Upon completion of all direct examination, if the witness has given evidence against the interest of any accused, counsel for such accused may cross-examine the witness. If in the course of a cross-examination by counsel for the accused, adverse testimony against any of the accused is

---

[97] IPS Document No. 0006, page III-5.

1.5 Types of Evidence Collected          61

adduced, counsel for such accused shall, prior to the cross-examination by the prosecution, cross-examine or further cross-examine the witness. A defense counsel cross-examining a witness shall announce his intention so to do at the beginning of his examination.

3. After all cross-examination by counsel for the accused shall have been completed, counsel for the prosecution shall cross-examine. Without the special permission of the Tribunal not more than one prosecuting counsel shall cross-examine.
4. Upon completion of cross examination by the prosecution, counsel for any accused regarding whom new testimony has been given in the course of the prosecution cross-examination may further cross-examine the witness.
5. Upon the completion of all cross-examination, without the special permission of the Tribunal, redirect examination shall be conducted by the counsel who conducted the general direct examination. Other counsel for individual accused may examine a witness on redirect examination only on matters specifically relating to his client and not covered by the general redirect examination.[98]

The day after receiving the joint proposal, the Tribunal agreed that it should be put to use to see if it could work. In the words of Webb, "We have decided to give a trial to the rules agreed upon by the prosecution and the defense." He explained that the judges did have some misgivings as to how adequate this new system of direct- and cross-examinations would be, but remarked that the Tribunal was willing to give it a try, since "we are sure we will have the cooperation of the prosecution and the defense in endeavoring to make them work successfully."[99] The subsequent record of court proceedings shows that the prosecution and the defense indeed lived up to the expectation of the Tribunal, allowing the new rules to attain practical relevance for the duration of the trial. This episode illustrates that, regardless of oft-raised criticisms about the defense's obstructionism and delaying tactics, the Tokyo Tribunal could actually count on the cooperation of both the prosecution and the defense to carry out the trial in a fair and expeditious manner.

## 1.5 Types of Evidence Collected

It became known to the Allied authorities shortly after commencing the military occupation of Japan that the Japanese authorities took advantage of the two-week hiatus between the acceptance of Potsdam terms on August 14, 1945, and the formal surrender ceremony on September 2, 1945, to destroy

[98] Ibid.
[99] Ibid.

government and military records *en masse* to prevent them from falling into Allied hands.[100] Those Japanese army and navy forces responsible for episodes of war crimes at outlying areas, too, lost little time in destroying incriminating evidence or simply fleeing prior to the arrival of Allied war crimes investigators. But how extensive or systematic, exactly, were the Japanese efforts to obstruct the Allied war crimes investigation? Which documents and how much of them were destroyed? The scope of government-led document destruction indeed became a subject of inquiry at the Tokyo Trial, although for the limited purpose of ascertaining as to why certain documents mentioned in some witnesses' testimony could not be produced.

The record of the trial shows that the Ministry of Foreign Affairs was among the first to carry out large-scale document destruction at the war's end, in anticipation of imminent Allied land invasion. Isono Yūzō, a defense witness and formerly chief of the Archive Section of the Secretariat of the Ministry of Foreign Affairs (1945–6), testified that the "chiefs of secretariat sections or bureau chiefs" held urgent meetings in the last week of June 1945, whereupon they "decided to burn papers of comparatively recent dates which in our opinion at that time more of a confidential character." The types of records destroyed were "[a]ll originals, copies and drafts of top secret, secret and coded telegrams, letters, messages and other communications, memoranda of conversations and opinions and manuscripts."[101] Part of the foreign-ministry records was kept in safe areas in Saitama Prefecture. They, too, were destroyed the same week. The witness could not say how thoroughly the document destruction was carried out, as "the work was done in such a rush, and was done so haphazardly, that there were some documents burned which should not have been burned and others which were not burned which should have been burned." He added that some of the ministerial records had been lost during a fire that caught the foreign-ministry building on January 7, 1942. In addition, "the Foreign Office was almost totally destroyed" as a result of the US air campaigns that were repeated against Tokyo, on May 23–4, 1945.[102]

Lieutenant General Kawabe Torashirō, a defense witness and a former senior officer of the Army General Staff in the Army Department of the Imperial Headquarters (IHQ), gave testimony concerning the fate of the records in possession of the Army General Staff. He confirmed that the Army General Staff destroyed a large quantity of its records at the war's end, namely,

---

[100] This state of affairs stood in contrast with the last war days in Nazi Germany, where the invading Allied forces overran the German homeland and allowed little time for large-scale document destruction to occur. For studies of document destruction by the Japanese authorities at the war's end, see Yoshida, "Gunji kankei shiryō no sengoshi" and "Haisen go ni okeru kōbunsho no shōkyaku to intoku."

[101] T22761, 22774.

[102] T22764, 22777–8.

## 1.5 Types of Evidence Collected 63

"documents relating to strategic plans" and "operational plans." Kawabe went on to explain that "other reports, intelligence reports and originals of telegrams sent" were destroyed. Army regulations required that such records be burned periodically "as soon as they had been disposed of."[103] When the prosecution questioned whether or not the Army General Staff destroyed "only those documents which will be harmful if they fell into the hands of the Allies," Kawabe denied it. He explained that the main goal had been "to burn all documents of a military nature, and we did not have in mind anything as to whether there would be – as to whether a military tribunal of this nature would be convened or not in the future." He was of the opinion that those documents which might have been "helpful to Japan and to the accused" were likely to have been burned, unintentionally that is, as well as those documents which might have served the opposite purpose.[104]

The Ministry of the Army appears to have followed a similar course of actions, as the prosecution's evidence indicates. Dated August 14, 1945, and issued by the adjutant general of the army minister, a telegram addressed to army units at theaters of war contained the instruction that "the confidential documents held by every troop should be destroyed by fire immediately."[105] This appears to be a general order to destroy all the confidential documents, which might be construed as steps ordinarily taken by the armies facing imminent invasion by the enemy forces. Yet the prosecution's case also contained a different kind of army-ministry instruction, issued on August 20, 1945, whose purpose unequivocally was protecting Japanese war criminals. Notated as a Military Top-Secret document, it read as follows:

Personnel who mistreated prisoners of war and internees or who are held in extremely bad sentiment by them are permitted to take care of it by immediately transferring or by fleeing without trace. Moreover, documents which would be unfavorable for us in the hands of the enemy are to be treated in the same way as secret documents and destroyed when finished with.[106]

This particular document was sent from the chief of Prisoner-of-War Camps, Tokyo, to practically all Japanese armed forces across the theaters of war, being addressed to "Korean Army, Taiwan Army, Kwantung (Manchuria) Army, North China Area Army, Hong Kong," and repeated to "Korea, Taiwan, Mukden, Borneo, North China, Hong Kong, Thailand, Malaya, Java. Each POW Camp Commanding Officer."[107]

---

[103] T22006–7.
[104] T22010.
[105] PX 2000, T14700.
[106] PX 2011, T14718–9.
[107] Ibid., T14719.

An investigation report that the International Prosecution Section separately produced for internal use, dated July 21, 1947, confirmed that a system-wide effort to destroy documents was indeed carried out, but that it was done in a hasty, haphazard manner. The report read that "on the 14th or 15th of August 1945 a conference was held by the vice-ministers of the various ministries in which it was decided to burn all documents which should not fall into the hands of the enemy." This decision met a counter-order *not* to destroy documents within days, however, causing much confusion among the ministries concerned. The author of the report observed that burning documents before the arrival of enemy forces "may be considered a normal procedure," and that the Japanese action, in this regard, need not be construed as a deliberate effort to obstruct the Allied war crimes investigations. That said, the same report also reached the conclusion that the Japanese authorities issued certain orders to destroy documents, whose aim was to protect war criminals.[108] Based on this report and other oral and documentary evidence from the trial record as above, it is possible to say that document destruction was carried out extensively, but that the actual damage done was of a mixed character and that many documents did survive.

The pretrial internal records of the International Prosecution Section show that the Allied authorities failed to take full advantage of those surviving documents due to several missteps on their part.[109] To begin with, the Allied occupation forces did not place guards on the Japanese government buildings or confiscate the Japanese records in the immediate days following the surrender ceremony. An internal report of the International Prosecution Section, dated January 22, 1946, reveals that Allied personnel were, in fact, positively prohibited from having "access to any government files or could interview any person connected with the Jap[anese] government," unless they submitted requests "in writing" to the Japanese Liaison Office (which facilitated communication between the Allied occupation forces and the Government of Japan). Such requests were rarely made initially, and "no evidence was collected or specifically searched for bearing on the case against major war criminals." In Europe, on the other hand, American war crimes investigators entered towns together with the frontline troops to seize Nazi records before they could be destroyed. On this basis the American prosecution team decided to base its case largely upon the German government's own documents.

---

[108] Special Studies #17, Burned and Destroyed Japanese Documents, July 21, 1947, M1668, roll 17, NARA.

[109] Some of the pretrial records of the International Prosecution Section have been published on microfilm by NARA. The core records relating to policy decisions of the prosecuting agency have been reprinted and published in book format as well. For the latter, see *Tōkyō saiban e no michi*, 5 vols. All the original is available at NARA.

1.5 Types of Evidence Collected

The core group of the International Prosecution Section – i.e. the American prosecution team – arrived in early December 1945, and only then did the occupation authorities "order the Emperor to sign a pass entitling us [war crimes investigators] to go into any government department and interview and look at records."[110] Having obtained such a pass, however, the International Prosecution Section stopped short of taking full advantage of it. From the start, the American prosecution team devoted its resources to investigating Class 1.A. offenses, i.e. crimes against peace, on the understanding that the mandate of the International Prosecution Section was to prosecute Japanese war criminals primarily for this category of offense, and secondarily for war crimes and crimes against humanity.[111] The American prosecution team did not mean to ignore the importance of war crimes and crimes against humanity, but it decided from early on to leave the study of Classes 1.B. and 1.C. with other Allied prosecutors, whom they believed to be "most interested" in those latter types of offenses.[112]

The first of these other Allied prosecutors reached Tokyo in the second half of February 1946, from Australia, Canada, Great Britain, and New Zealand. The prosecutors from China, France, India, the Netherlands, the Philippines, and the Soviet Union arrived with some delays, in the period between March and May. The associate prosecutors from British Commonwealth countries greatly helped expedite the preparation of the indictment, but it turned out that neither they nor other Allied prosecutors had much to contribute in terms of staff, resources, or evidentiary materials. The New Zealand associate prosecutor, Quilliam, took note of this shortcoming among the latecomers:

One of the difficulties in settling the form of the Indictment has been the late arrival here of the Dutch, French, Russian and Philippines prosecutors, coupled with the somewhat remarkable lack of information in their possession (excepting in the case of the Russian) and in the possession of the Chinese prosecutor.

He further observed that, "as late as the 21st instant [April 1946] the Dutch, French, and Chinese prosecutors left by air for Batavia, French Indo-China

---

[110] Memorandum of Staff Meeting, December 10, 1945, *Tōkyō saiban e no michi*, vol. 1; and, Memorandum to Mr. J. B. Keenan from Lieutenant Colonel B. E. Sackett, Investigation, Progress Report, January 22, 1946, M1668, roll 16, NARA.

[111] Preliminary Report to the Supreme Commander of the Allied Powers by Joseph B. Keenan (draft), December 14, 1945, M1668, roll 16, NARA; Assignment Chart. Preparation of Trial Brief of Facts and memoranda from Joseph B. Keenan to individual work groups about assignment instructions, December 28, 1945, M1668, roll 1, NARA; and Memorandum from Lieutenant Colonel B. E. Sackett to Mr. J.B. Keenan, Investigation Division, Progress Report, January 22, 1946, M1668, roll 16, NARA.

[112] Memorandum from J. W. Brabner-Smith to Mr. Keenan, Assignment of Associate Counsel, February 4, 1946, M1668, roll 2, NARA; Memorandum from Chief of Counsel to All the Staff, Assignments, Groups "H" and "I," February 12, 1946, M1668, roll 1, NARA.

and China respectively in order to endeavor to obtain evidence in respect to their parts of the case."[113] The Bill of Indictment was already completed by then, and was lodged with the Tribunal about a week later (on April 29). These travels – whose main goal was to collect evidence on war crimes – could not be expected to contribute to the development of charges, which were already finalized. Those Allied prosecutors who remained in Tokyo likely made little progress in exploring the Japanese records either, as they did not read Japanese.

What sorts of evidence, then, did the International Prosecution Section manage to secure? One can learn from the record of the Tokyo Trial that the prosecution actually succeeded in sifting through various Japanese records, with assistance from Japanese informants and translators, insofar as the charges of crimes against peace were concerned. The evidentiary materials that the prosecution obtained in connection with Class 1.A. offenses would fall under the following seven categories: (1) Japanese legal documents that showed the organization, functions, and workings of the government; (2) records and minutes of meetings of key decision-making organs, such as the cabinet, the Privy Council, the Imperial Diet, and various highest-level policymaking conferences; (3) records generated by the Japanese government ministries, and their outposts overseas, such as consul-generals and ambassadors; (4) documents generated by the high-command organs at Tokyo and military headquarters of overseas Japanese armed forces; (5) documents generated by the Ministry of Imperial Household; (6) Japanese and foreign newspaper reporting; and (7) diaries, memoirs, and other semi-official journals by high-ranking government officials.

Of these varying categories of evidence, the last one took on a unique role in the making of the prosecution's case, and especially two journals kept by top advisors to Emperor Hirohito. One of them was *Kido nikki* (*The Kido Diary* hereafter). Its author was Marquis Kido Kōichi, formerly a high official of the Ministry of Imperial Household, which included his service as Lord Keeper of the Privy Seal (1940–5). Kido voluntarily turned over his journal to the Allied war crimes investigators at the end of 1945, with the hope that it would help defend his case and also protect Emperor Hirohito from war crimes prosecution.[114] The prosecution thereafter put *The Kido Diary* to active use for developing its case on crimes against peace. Another journal that carried great weight in the prosecution's case was *Saionji-Harada nikki* (*The Saionji-Harada Memoirs* hereafter). Its author was Baron Harada Kumao, who served as a personal secretary to Prince Saionji Kinmochi, the last surviving *genrō* ("elder statesman") with the responsibility to render advice to the Emperor for

---

[113] *Document on New Zealand External Relations*, 1562.
[114] For the circumstances of Kido's turning over of his diary and related matters in pretrial Allied war crimes investigations, see Awaya, *Tōkyō saiban e no michi*, vol. 1, 100–48.

1.5 Types of Evidence Collected                                                67

life. The two diaries offered in great detail the words and deeds of numerous high-ranking Japanese government officials, military officers, and members of the imperial court, who individually advised Emperor Hirohito on wide-ranging matters, including those concerning decisions on war and peace.

Probative value and admissibility of these documents were argued at length during the Tokyo Trial. The Tribunal ultimately concluded that they were admissible as having probative value for the following reasons:

> KIDO's voluminous diary is a contemporary record covering the period from 1930 to 1945 of the transactions of KIDO with important personages in his position as secretary of the Lord Keeper of the Privy Seal, State Minister and later as confidential adviser to the Emperor while holding the Office of the Lord Keeper of the Privy Seal. Having regard to these circumstances we regard it as a document of importance. Another document or series of documents of importance are the Saionji-Harada Memoirs. These have been the subject of severe criticism by the defense, not unnaturally; as they contain passages the defense consider embarrassing. We are of opinion that the criticism are not well founded and have attached more importance to these records than the defense desired us to do. The special position of Prince Saionji as the last of the Genro provoked full and candid disclosure to him through his secretary Harada. Harada's long period of service to the Genro in this special task of obtaining information from the very highest functionaries of the Government and the Army and Navy is a test of his reliability and discretion.[115]

It will be seen in subsequent chapters that these two documents proved to a double-edged sword for the prosecution. They contained incriminating evidence not only against the individual accused but also against Emperor Hirohito, whom the prosecution could not name as a suspected war criminal because of the political decision at the highest level of the Allied governments.

As regards evidence on war crimes, the International Prosecution Section acquired sources mostly in the English language. Surprisingly, the prosecution does not appear to have tried investigating the Japanese government's military records in any thoroughgoing manner. This may have to do with the difficulties in translating all of the available Japanese-language evidentiary documents in order to make them available to the prosecution in a timely manner.[116]

The types of evidence that the prosecution assembled generally fall under the following six categories: (1) affidavits, statements, and depositions that were taken from victims, witnesses, and perpetrators of atrocity, and as transcribed

---

[115] *Documents*, 78–9.
[116] The Allied prosecutors certainly could hire Japanese interpreters and translators insofar as their resources permitted. However, most of those interpreters and translators who acted as the eyes and ears of prosecutors probably lacked the ability to carry out the essential forensic tasks needed for the trial, namely, to search, to sift through, to identify, and to isolate useful evidentiary materials among the sea of Japanese government records, with the insight of a criminal investigator and/or a prosecutor.

in English; (2) records of contemporaneous Allied war crimes investigations and trials, also written in English; (3) the English-language translation of Allied intelligence reports, including confiscated Japanese military records; (4) diplomatic records that documented the Allied governments' formal protests regarding the Japanese mistreatment of prisoners of war and other Allied nationals under Japanese control, also available in English; (5) records of postwar Allied interrogations of individual accused, transcribed in English; and (6) a small selection of army-ministry records concerning the Japanese prisoner-of-war administration, which were written in Japanese.

Many of these evidentiary materials could help prove the broad geographical distribution and recurrence of war crimes in Japanese-occupied territories, but they rarely contained affirmative proof of criminal orders or authorizations by the individual accused. How, then, was the prosecution going to establish the guilt of accused for war crimes using these evidentiary materials? We shall address this question in Chapters 5 and 6. Before turning to those matters, however, it is necessary to examine the central focus of the prosecution's case: crimes against peace.

## 2  Charges of Crimes against Peace

The preceding chapter has shown that crimes against peace (Class A offenses) took the center stage in the IMTFE trial of major Japanese war criminals. Although the nature of the charges as set out in the indictment is well known, there has been much less analysis of some of the doctrinal questions arising from the way in which the charges of crimes against peace were interpreted and addressed by the prosecution, the defense counsel, and the judges. What, for example, were the theories of liability on which the prosecution built its case for aggressive war? How did the prosecution apply the doctrine of criminal conspiracy – a controversial legal concept that had been introduced in the IMT Charter and repeated in the IMTFE Charter – in establishing the guilt of the Japanese accused? How did the defense respond to the prosecution's theory of the case? What strategy did the defense counsel adopt and what doctrinal issues did they raise both to challenge the jurisdiction of the tribunal and to attack the prosecution's case?

This chapter addresses such questions by exploring the core legal arguments made and the strategies adopted by the prosecution and the defense during the Tokyo Trial. This is a necessary preliminary to assessment of the majority judgment and separate opinions in later chapters. It is also a task that is seldom addressed in the literature on the IMTFE judgment and separate opinions, though to fully understand the prosecution and defense cases that the judges were responding to is indispensable. The judgment and opinions are often treated in a vacuum but in Tokyo, as in all international criminal trials, the judges both depended upon the evidence submitted by the parties and largely responded to the case as presented by the prosecution. Accordingly, a firm grasp of the challenges both the defense and the prosecution faced and how they responded to those challenges can provide the foundation for assessment of the final decisions of the judges. Having established the legal basis of the prosecution here, Chapters 3 and 4 will consider the evidence advanced to prove that case beyond reasonable doubt.

This chapter is divided into three sections. The first section explores the scope of the charges as set out in the Bill of Indictment. The main task in this section is to determine how the prosecution interpreted the applicable law when formulating the counts of crimes against peace. This section also explores four of the five appendices that are included in the Bill of Indictment, as they contain important legal and factual details on which the prosecution grounded its case for crimes against peace. The second section turns to the transcripts of the IMTFE court proceedings to trace the way in which the prosecution developed its argument, and the third section does the same with respect to the defense.

A main analytical focus of this chapter is to identify the significant influence of the Nuremberg Trial in defining the parameters of the legal arguments for crimes against peace as made at the Tokyo Trial. The judgment at Nuremberg ("IMT judgment" hereafter) was handed down on October 1, 1946, five months after the start of the Tokyo Trial. We will see that the legal holdings of the IMT judgment were extensively referenced during the summations at Tokyo (February–April 1948), although the prosecution and the defense did so in contrasting manners, and in support of their respective interpretations of the laws.

The IMT judgment also impacted the judges' final decisions at the Tokyo Tribunal, as will be seen in Part II. For now, it suffices to note that the judges at the Tokyo Trial essentially followed the lead of their Nuremberg brethren on crimes against peace and the jurisdiction of the tribunal. This was not the case, however, for two of the three dissenting judges, Pal and Roeling, from India and the Netherlands, respectively. These two justices implicitly or explicitly rejected the key legal holdings of the IMT and were highly skeptical of the legality of *any* international prosecutions for crimes against peace. Their interpretation of legal issues thus generally followed those advanced by the defense. This chapter will accordingly highlight some of those defense's contentions that subsequently figured prominently in the two dissenting opinions.

## 2.1 Counts and Appendices in the Indictment

The Bill of Indictment ("indictment" or "IMTFE indictment" hereafter) is a closely typed 46-page document that contains a preamble, concise statements of the charges in fifty-five separate counts, and five appendices. The appendices are important for understanding the approach of the prosecution and they comprise the following: a list of particulars of principal matters and events relative to the charges of crimes against peace (Appendix A); a list of treaties violated by Japan relative to the charges of crimes against peace (Appendix B); a list of assurances, made and violated by Japan, also relative to the charges of crimes against peace (Appendix C); a list of treaties and assurances violated by Japan relative to war crimes, and particulars of beaches of laws and customs of war (Appendix D); and a statement of the principle of individual responsibility,

## 2.1 Counts and Appendices in the Indictment

a list of key policymaking meetings prior to the outbreak of the Pacific War, and short biographies of individual defendants (Appendix E).[1]

Of these various components in the indictment, the decision to include a preamble was controversial at first, as some members of the prosecution expressed concern that its propagandistic tone made it unfitting for judicial proceedings. According to the associate prosecutor from New Zealand, Quilliam, the preamble being proposed was objectionable because it amounted to "a comprehensive indictment of the Japanese in picturesque and extravagant loose language." Associate prosecutors from the Philippines and the Soviet Union advocated its inclusion, however, and the matter was settled when the chief prosecutor, Keenan, urged compromise in favor of the Soviet and Philippine position.[2] The preamble, however, should not be dismissed as an insignificant propaganda piece, because some of its language materially influenced the ways in which the majority drafted the judgment of the tribunal.[3]

In contrast to the four counts in the Nuremberg indictment, which were set out in great factual detail, the prosecution at Tokyo created an unwieldy document encompassing fifty-five counts. As we will see the judges, who were obliged to make specific findings and conclusions on each of them, struggled with the plethora of counts and ultimately dismissed many of them. The more focused approach of the indictment at Nuremberg would have assisted in better management of the case for the judges, the defense, and the prosecution itself.

The Tokyo indictment encompassed the fifty-five counts within three groupings: crimes against peace (Group One); murder (Group Two); and conventional war crimes and crimes against humanity (Group Three). Counts that came within Group One can be further subdivided into four separate categories according to the types of offense for which the accused were held liable: participation in a common plan or conspiracy (Counts 1–5); planning and preparation of specific aggressive wars (Counts 6–17); initiation of aggressive war (Counts 18–26); and waging of specific aggressive wars (Counts 27–36). Each of these counts articulated concisely the particulars of the offense, along with the names of individuals accused, the time and location of the offense, and particular treaties and assurances that were violated. This chapter will explore

---

[1] A reprint of the original Bill of Indictment can be found in, *The Tokyo War Crimes Trial*, vol. 1. Also available at the Website of the Harry S. Truman Library & Museum. https://www.trumanlibrary.org/whistlestop/study_collections/nuremberg/documents/index.php?documentid=18-2&pagenumber=1. Accessed July 5, 2018.

[2] *Documents on New Zealand External Relations*, 1560–1.

[3] The opening segment of the preamble in the indictment foreshadows the majority judgment and reads as follows: "In the years hereinafter referred to in this indictment the internal and foreign policies of Japan were *dominated and directed by a criminal militaristic clique*, and such policies were the cause of serious world troubles, aggressive wars, and great damage to the interests of peace-loving peoples, as well as the interests of the Japanese people themselves" (emphasis added). *Documents*, 16–17.

these thirty-six counts and four appendices that directly related to the counts of crimes against peace (Appendices A–C, E). The remaining groups of offenses and the appendix will be discussed in Chapter 5.

The counts on crimes against peace, by and large, were worded in such a way as to follow the definition of crimes against peace as set out in Article 5 of the IMTFE Charter, which read in part:

Article 5. Jurisdiction Over Persons and Offenses ...
The following acts, or any of them, are crimes coming within the jurisdiction of the tribunal for which there shall be individual responsibility:

(a) Crimes against peace: Namely, the planning, preparation, initiation or waging of a declared or undeclared war of aggression or a war in violation of international law, treaties, agreements or assurances, or participation in a common plan or conspiracy for the accomplishment of any of the foregoing.
(b) ...
(c) ...

Leaders, organizers, instigators and accomplices participating in the formulation or execution of a common plan or conspiracy to commit any of the foregoing crimes are responsible for all acts performed by any person in execution of such plan.[4]

The prosecution deduced from Article 5 four distinct types of offenses as coming within the category of crimes against peace: (1) planning and preparation of aggressive war; (2) initiation of aggressive war; (3) waging of aggressive war; and (4) participation in a common plan or conspiracy for the accomplishment of any of the foregoing acts. Furthermore, the prosecution treated the final paragraph in Article 5 as articulating the theory of liability applicable to the charges of conspiracy.

### 2.1.1 The Conspiracy Theory

Article 5 provided for the liability of anyone who served as a leader, organizer, instigator, or accomplice in either the formulation or the implementation of a conspiracy to commit any of the crimes charged in the indictment. This meant, as the Charter specified, that such persons could be held accountable for "all acts" of any person who participated in the carrying out of the conspiracy.

---

[4] The original of the IMTFE Charter as reprinted in Pritchard's *Tokyo War Crimes Trial*, vol. 1, shows the sentence starting with "Leaders, organizers, instigators" to form a separate, independent paragraph. But the version reproduced in Boister and Cryer's *Documents on the Tokyo International Military tribunal* indicates the same sentence as part of Article 5(c). It is not clear which version is correct. To somewhat confound the matter, it is worth noting that, during the summation, the prosecution urged the tribunal to regard this sentence as "applicable to all parts of Article 5," even though "*it is printed in our Charter continuously and not as a separate paragraph*" (emphasis added). T39051.

This cast the net very wide because it meant that, for example, an accused who had been involved in the formulation of policies that led to war could be held accountable for the criminal conduct of any person who participated in that war. The prosecution replicated the same wording in each conspiracy count of the indictment.[5]

Conspiracy counts were the core part of the prosecution's theory of the case at both the IMT and IMTFE trials, although there are some differences in how they were incorporated in the respective bills of indictment. What is striking is the fact that although the judges at Nuremberg rejected the prosecution's allegation of a single overarching conspiracy, the Tokyo prosecution team nonetheless proceeded with this strategy. In a sense they were correct to do so, because unlike their Nuremberg counterparts the majority judges at the IMTFE wholeheartedly embraced this theory, with consequences that Chapters 7–10 will explore later.

One of the notable differences between the conspiracy theories at Nuremberg and Tokyo appears from the way in which the Nuremberg prosecutors developed a single, all-encompassing count of conspiracy, which "involved the commission of Crimes against Peace, War Crimes, and Crimes against Humanity" (Count 1 of the indictment at the IMT; the "IMT indictment" hereafter). The International Prosecution Section at Tokyo, by contrast, developed multiple conspiracy counts in connection with different types of offenses, namely, five counts pertaining to crimes against peace (Counts 1–5), three on murder (Counts 37–38, and 44), and one on war crimes and crimes against humanity (Count 53).[6] The prosecutors at both trials employed the doctrine of criminal conspiracy as their central focus because conspiracy doctrine, like its modern counterpart of "joint criminal enterprise," offered a convenient way of encompassing a wide variety of actors who assumed different roles and contributed in different ways to conduct ranging over vast geographical areas and a time span of seventeen years (in the case at Tokyo).[7] Rather than having to prove

---

[5] The prosecution offered during the summation a seven-point account of the theory of liability under the law of conspiracy, which reads in part:

> 1. That the crime of conspiracy is complete with the agreement by two or more to commit a crime against the security of the State, whether in fact it is committed or any active steps are taken for the purpose or not. (In some American States an 'overt act' is by statute required, but may be of a slight nature.) …
>
> 5. That planning and preparation by one person to commit a crime is not by itself a crime, unless it amounts at least to an attempt. T39038-9.

[6] For the IMT indictment, see *Trial of the Major War Criminals before the International Military Tribunal*, vol. 1, 27–92.

[7] Joint criminal enterprise, or JCE as it is commonly known, became the primary mode of liability charged at the International Criminal Tribunal for the former Yugoslavia following its "invention" in the Tadic Appeals judgment of that tribunal. Other tribunals, though not all, have also

the precise connection of each accused to each crime charged, under the prosecution's version of the conspiracy doctrine the prosecution would only have to prove that an individual was a conspirator and that the alleged crimes were "in execution" of the conspiracy.

The decision to use the doctrine of criminal conspiracy was successful only in part, however, as the Nuremberg Tribunal deemed it inapplicable to offenses other than crimes against peace and even there, as noted earlier, rejected the prosecution's allegation of a single overarching conspiracy embracing all of the accused. The Tokyo Tribunal similarly rejected the applicability of conspiracy to crimes other than crimes against peace, but the International Prosecution Section was successful in convincing the judges of a grand conspiracy to wage wars of aggression, spanning the years 1928–45.

The Nuremberg Tribunal, however, interpreted the meaning of conspiracy narrowly, so that it would amount to no more than the *planning* of aggressive war and, unlike the IMTFE judges, required affirmative proof that the individual accused participated in concrete episodes of war planning. The Nuremberg decision on the conspiracy count is significant because, as Chapter 7 will show, it highlights the more individuated approach to liability adopted there in comparison with the use of the conspiracy doctrine in the majority judgment at Tokyo. In order to understand fully the legal framework of the trial and judgment at Tokyo we must further examine in some detail all of the counts under Group One and the related appendices in the IMTFE indictment. We begin with Count 1 as the core of the case, centered on the prosecution's theory of a grand conspiracy encompassing all of the accused.

Count 1 sets out what the International Prosecution Section referred to as "a general over-all conspiracy," covering "not only the whole period but all the various phases [of the war,] which subsequently developed although their details might not in the beginning have been foreseen." The position of the prosecution was that, if the Tokyo Tribunal established a single overall conspiracy as charged in Count 1, it would become "unnecessary to consider separately Counts 2–5 inclusive" in which those various phases of the war were articulated. Alternatively, the tribunal might find that there were multiple common plans or conspiracies as charged in these latter four counts, instead of a single, overall conspiracy as set out in the first count. In that case, the tribunal could disregard Count 1 and upheld instead Counts 2–5.[8] Count 1 and Counts 2–5, in this manner, contained overlapping charges and were designed to be in

---

robustly employed this doctrine precisely because of its flexibility in encompassing the broad array of actors who may play many different roles in state-organized criminality. See *Prosecutor v. Tadic*, Case IT-94-1-A, Appeals Chamber judgment of July 15, 1999, pp. 78–105.

[8] T39048–9.

complementary relationship. What, then, were the exact allegations made in these counts?

The opening segment of every conspiracy count in Group One made a common statement about the types of individuals alleged to be accountable, the temporal dimension of the charge, and the applicable theory of liability. It thus read:

All the defendants together with divers other persons, between the 1st January, 1928, and the 2nd September, 1945, participated as leaders, organizers, instigators, or accomplices in the formation or execution of a common plan or conspiracy, and are responsible for all acts performed by themselves or by any person in execution of such plan.[9]

A new paragraph immediately followed the one above in each of the five counts, to explain the substance of "a common plan of conspiracy." In the case of Count 1, the second paragraph read as follows:

The object of such plan or conspiracy was that Japan should secure military, naval, political and economic domination of East Asia and of the Pacific and Indian Oceans, and of all countries and islands therein and bordering thereon and for that purpose should alone or in combination with other countries having similar objective, or who could be included or coerced to join therein, wage declared or undeclared war or wars of aggression, and war or wars in violation of international law, treaties, agreements and assurances, against any country or countries which might oppose that purpose.[10]

This paragraph is somewhat long and convoluted, but what it essentially does is to articulate two interrelated allegations under the conspiracy charge: (1) that a common plan or conspiracy had the object to "secure military, naval, political and economic domination of East Asia and of the Pacific and Indian Oceans, and of all countries and islands therein and bordering thereon," and (2) that a common plan or conspiracy involved the acts of "wag[ing] declared or undeclared war or wars of aggression, and war or wars in violation of international law, treaties, agreements and assurances, against any country or countries which might oppose that purpose."

The very same construction was repeated in the remainder of conspiracy counts in Group One. Thus it was charged in the first paragraph in each of them that, "All the defendants together with divers other persons, between the January 1st, 1928, and the September 2nd, 1945, participated as leaders, organizers, instigators, or accomplices in the formation or execution of a common plan or conspiracy, and are responsible for all acts performed by themselves or by any person in execution of such plan." The paragraph to follow read that the

---

[9] *Documents*, 18.
[10] Ibid.

object of a common plan or conspiracy was to secure military, naval, political, and economic domination of the northeastern provinces in China – i.e., roughly the region of Manchuria – and, for that purpose, to wage aggressive war against China (Count 2). The same formulation applied in regard to war against China for the domination of all China (Count 3), and war against the Soviet Union, France, Portugal, the Netherlands, Thailand, and the Anglo-American Powers (Count 4). Count 5 went beyond specific national boundaries and broadly alleged a conspiracy to secure military, naval, political, and economic domination of the whole world by the Axis Powers.[11]

Some members of the International Prosecution Section aired concerns before the start of the Tokyo Trial about the adequacy of the foregoing construction of conspiracy counts. The main critic was Lieutenant Colonel John W. Brabner-Smith, an American member and a special assistant to the chief prosecutor, Keenan. He pointed out in a memorandum, dated April 14, 1946, that the way in which the indictment was drawn up was "objectionable," in part because it failed to make "a plain, concise and adequate statement of each offense charged" as required by the IMTFE Charter (Article 9). Moreover, the five conspiracy counts in the indictment alleged such offenses "which are not crimes under the charter," in the sense that "the only act of conspiracy for which punishment can be imposed is the conspiracy of planning, preparing, initiating or waging of wars."[12] He was concerned that the Japanese accused would deny having ever contemplated the alleged objects, and that such denial might undercut the prosecution's case. The following scenario, in his opinion, was very likely during the trial:

The alleging of acts which it is not necessary to prove; i.e., the plan to secure domination of East Asia, Manchuria, etc., increases trial difficulties. It enables the defendants to bring in evidence immaterial to the crime for which they can be punished; i.e., evidence that their object was not to gain economic, etc., domination of any country. For instance, many Japanese have asserted from time to time [during the war] that the object of Japan was to awaken a spiritual consciousness in the Far East; others have said that the object was to bring together peoples of the same fundamental characteristics. *This evidence is immaterial if they are charged only with conspiring to wage war.*[13] (emphasis added)

---

[11] The scope of the object stated in Count 5 is geographically broader than the one in Count 1 (i.e., to secure the Axis Powers' domination of "the whole world" in Count 5, as opposed to Japan's domination of the Asia-Pacific region in Count 1). However, the prosecution still treated Count 5 as a subset of the overall conspiracy in Count 1, presumably because the formalization of the Axis Alliance did not materialize until September 1940, that is, at the beginning of the fourth quarter of the period of the alleged overall conspiracy.

[12] Memorandum from Lieutenant Colonel Brabner-Smith to Chief of Counsel, April 14, 1946, p. 2, M1668, roll 9, NARA. Reproduced in *Tōkyō saiban e no michi*, vol. 4, 344–6.

[13] Ibid.

Brabner-Smith feared that this type of defense tactic was likely, and urged that the prosecution take steps to prevent it from occurring. Furthermore, he also expressed skepticism that alleging conspiracy in alternative forms was necessary. The charge in the five counts was basically the same, he noted, and the only justification for retaining them would be to make it possible to state the different objects of a common plan or conspiracy. He reiterated that the object of conspiracy was "completely immaterial to the issue – whether the accused conspired to wage, etc. war." He added that the equivalent count in the IMT indictment simply read, "the common plan or conspiracy embraced the commission of Crimes against Peace, in that the defendants planned, prepared, initiated, and waged wars of aggression."[14] He, with good reason, saw it best to follow this example.

Internal records of the International Prosecution Section indicate that some other members were sympathetic to Brabner-Smith's objections, but that they were unable to force change. When this issue was raised, the New Zealand associate prosecutor, Quilliam, expressed his "regret that this matter was not discussed at length before the Committees which considered the indictment." He urged that it be taken up directly with Arthur S. Comyns-Carr, associate prosecutor from Great Britain. Comyns-Car had been appointed by Keenan on February 28, 1946 to serve as chairman of the Executive Committee of the International Prosecution Section, which acted as the central decision-making body. All associate prosecutors and the chief prosecutor's assistants also became members of the Executive Committee. Comyns-Carr took a leading part in expediting the preparatory work, including drawing up the indictment. Quilliam suggested that Comyns-Carr was the one who "drafted this language," but that he "may not be fully aware of the objections which have been expressed to alleging the main conspiracy in this form."[15] Frank S. Tavenner, Jr., an American member on the executive committee (and later serving as acting chief prosecutor at the time of Keenan's prolonged absences), accordingly requested that Comyns-Carr convene a meeting of the Executive Committee to consider the matter. But the British prosecutor did not welcome any last-minute changes. He reasoned that the indictment had already been approved by all the associate prosecutors, and that he "saw no purpose" in presenting it afresh to the Executive Committee.[16] No changes were thus made.

---

[14] Ibid.
[15] Memorandum from Lieutenant Colonel Brabner-Smith to Mr. Arthur Comyns Carr, April 19, 1946, M1668, roll 9, NARA. This memorandum is reproduced in *Tōkyō saiban e no michi*, vol. 4, 359. For the formation regarding the establishment of the executive committee, see ibid., vol. 4, 173. The constitution of the committee in charge of drafting the indictment preceded the formation of the executive committee, on February 15, 1946. See ibid., vol. 3, 148.
[16] Memorandum, from Frank S. Tavenner, Jr., to Hon. Joseph B. Keenan, Chief of Counsel, April 18, 1946, p. 2, M1668, roll 9, NARA.

Under those circumstances, it must have come as no surprise for the prosecution when Brabner-Smith's fear materialized during the court proceedings, as exemplified in the strategies of defense counsel. Kiyose Ichirō, a Japanese defense lawyer, contended at the start of the defense's opening statement on February 24, 1947 that Japan throughout modern times had prided herself to be the standard-bearer of "racial equality" and "progress of humankind," and that it was erroneous to charge the accused with having had the object of securing Japan's military, naval, political, or economic domination of China, the Asia-Pacific region, or the world.[17] He asserted that the foreign-policy slogans of wartime Japan – "All The World Under One Roof" (*hakkō ichiu*), "Greater East Asia Co-Prosperity Sphere" (*dai-Tōa kyōeiken*), "Imperial Way" (*kōdō*), and so on – were merely the Japanese ways of expressing universal values of mankind, such as the principles of equality, fraternity, and common good. The Japanese foreign-policy views under these slogans, therefore, should be understood as "just the opposite to the idea of militarism and despotism."[18]

Uzawa Sōmei, another defense lawyer, went further. He delivered an opening speech during the summation for the defense a year later, whereupon he expounded on the Japanese traditional concept of "Kingly Way" (*ōdō*) while drawing upon a few Japanese ancient texts, such as "The Chronicle of Japan" (*Nihon shoki*, completed in 720) and the "Seventeen-Article Constitution" (compiled in 602). The gist of his argument was that Japan had its own time-honored tradition of upholding the ideals of justice, responsibility, and peace, and that Japan continued to live up to these ideals well into the modern times. Uzawa denied any validity in the allegations of the Japanese pursuit of territorial conquest, reasoning that such a pursuit was simply incompatible with Japan's own traditional political philosophy. Steeped in abstraction and largely immaterial to the case at the Tokyo Trial, however, Uzawa's speech predictably elicited little enthusiasm from the tribunal. Justice Webb dryly remarked at its end, "Have you completed what you have to say?"[19]

The justice from India alone appears to have taken a great liking to Uzawa's discourse. There is anecdotal evidence that Justice Pal visited the defense counsel's room afterwards to express his personal appreciation. He was quoted as saying, "You don't know how sad I have been to find your defense counselors spending most of their time discussing international law and never touching upon Eastern philosophy. You made me very glad today."[20] If true, Pal's conversation with defense counsel represents a serious violation of judicial

[17] T17019.
[18] T17028.
[19] T42109.
[20] Nakazato, *Nationalist Mythology in Postwar Japan*, 21. The original of this quote (rendered in Japanese) can be found in Sugawara, *Tōkyō saiban no shōtai*, 242.

## 2.1 Counts and Appendices in the Indictment

ethics, as judges are strictly forbidden from speaking to either defense counsel or prosecutors about any aspect of the case before them, and particularly during the trial proceedings. In addition, Pal indicated his favorable view of the conduct of one of the parties, which is a further and even more serious breach of the fundamental duty of impartiality.[21] As we will see in Chapters 12 and 13, however, Pal's disregard for basic judicial ethics in this matter hardly comes as a surprise.

### 2.1.2 The Other Counts on Crimes against Peace

The remainder of counts on crimes against peace in the IMTFE indictment articulated the substantive offenses of crimes against peace, i.e., the planning, preparation, initiation, and waging of aggressive war. These counts were constructed to follow faithfully the definition in the IMTFE Charter and, in that regard, contain far fewer phraseological complications than those in the conspiracy counts. That said, one technical feature deserves attention. As indicated earlier, the prosecution developed as many as twenty-one counts on the planning, preparation, initiation, and waging of aggressive war, when it could have simply followed the example of the IMT indictment by developing a single count.[22]

Developing multiple counts might have had the benefit of clarifying specific charges that the prosecution meant to level against each accused, but it also presented problems of trial management to the judges. As the majority judgment later noted, "In all there are 55 counts in the indictment charged against the 25 defendants ... In respect to Crimes against Peace alone there are for consideration no less than 756 separate charges." The majority did appreciate the logic behind the multiplication of counts by stating, "This situation springs from the adoption by the prosecution of the common practice of charging all matters upon which guilt is indicated by the evidence it proposes to adduce even though some of the charges are cumulative or alternative."[23] Even so, the majority found the number of counts too unwieldy to serve any practical purpose. The majority accordingly dismissed those counts that they deemed to be duplicating the charges, as well as those that they found to have fallen

---

[21] On the applicable international standards of judicial conduct see, for example, the "Bangalore Principles of Judicial Conduct" (2002), Articles 1.2, 2.1, 2.4, 4.3 and 5.3, available online.

[22] A brisk summary of the remaining counts in Group One may be given as follows. It was charged in the indictment that all the Japanese accused were responsible for the "planning and preparation" of aggressive war against China, the United States, Great Britain, Australia, New Zealand, Canada, India, the Philippines, the Netherlands, France, Thailand and the Soviet Union (Counts 6–17). Certain named defendants were also charged that they were responsible for the "initiation" or "waging" of aggressive war against specified countries (initiation in Counts 19–26, waging in Counts 27–36).

[23] *Documents*, 85.

outside the tribunal's jurisdiction.[24] In the end, of the fifty-five counts of the indictment only ten counts survived the judges' scrutiny, eight of which pertained to crimes against peace. The judges effectively consolidated the charges into seven counts, one for each country in regard to which the defendants were alleged to have waged aggressive war, and the overall conspiracy count (Count 1).[25] Justice Webb alone took a different path in his draft judgment, weighing the merits of each count of crimes against peace instead of streamlining the counts the way the majority did.[26]

### 2.1.3 The Appendices to the Indictment

While the counts under Group One articulated the offenses of crimes against peace in a concise and bare-bones manner, four appendices to the indictment provided more details on points of both law and fact in support of the charges on crimes against peace. It is important to appreciate the role of these appendices as clarifying and amplifying the focus of the prosecution, which had been reflected in the indictment only in very abbreviated form. Appendix A offered a narrative summary of principal events and occurrences relating to the charges of crimes against peace, under ten separate headings. The main function of this appendix was to cover the factual ground of the charges. Specifics of events and occurrences need not detain us, for what is important to recognize is that Appendix A set out the narrative framework for the prosecution's subsequent presentation of evidence in the courtroom.

Appendix B gave a list of numerous excerpts from a total of twenty-three international treaties, conventions, agreements, and so on, including the Covenant of the League of Nations (1920–45), all of which related to crimes against peace. These, as will be seen in Chapter 7, were taken up by the majority judgment, albeit in a form which contributed little in substance to the judgment. Of the enumerated instruments, the interpretation of two particular treaties became hotly contested during the Tokyo Trial. The first of these was the General Treaty for Renunciation of War as an Instrument of National Policy, better known as the Pact of Paris or the Kellogg-Briand Pact, signed in Paris on August 27, 1928. This Pact formed the central point of contention in both Nuremberg and Tokyo on the crucial issue of the status of aggressive war under prevailing international law during the period under the jurisdiction of

---

[24] Ibid., 84–6.
[25] The seven counts on the waging of aggressive war encompassed China (Count 27), the United States, including the Philippines (Count 29), the British Commonwealth of Nations (Count 31), the Netherlands (Count 32), France (Count 33), the Soviet Union (Count 35), and the Mongolian People's Republic and the Soviet Union (Count 36).
[26] For the majority decision, see *Documents*, 84–5, 527–30, 594–7. See Chapter 8 for analysis of Webb's draft judgment.

## 2.1 Counts and Appendices in the Indictment

the IMT and IMTFE. The Pact condemned recourse to war as a means for solving international disputes, but fell short of stating explicitly that the planning and waging of war of any kind constituted an international crime for which individuals could be held accountable:

Article 1. The High Contracting Parties solemnly declare in the names of their respective peoples that they condemn recourse to war for the solution of international controversies, and renounce it as an instrument of national policy in their relations with one another.
Article 2. The High Contracting Parties agree that the settlement or solution of all disputes or conflicts of whatever nature or of whatever origin they may be, which may arise among them, shall never be solved except by pacific means.[27]

Imperial Japan as well as Germany were signatories to the Pact, along with sixty-one other states, comprising almost all members of the League of Nations. The interpretation of the import of the Pact became a central focus of dispute between the prosecution and the defense at the Tokyo Trial, as it had at Nuremberg. Unlike Nuremberg, where the four judges were unanimous in their agreement that the Pact outlawed aggressive war, in Tokyo, as we shall see, the interpretation of the Pact formed a focal point for dissent among the eleven judges.

Another treaty whose legal effect gave rise to dispute was the Treaty between the United States of America, the British Commonwealth of Nations, Belgium, China, France, Italy, Japan, the Netherlands, and Portugal. Commonly known as the Nine-Power Treaty, it was signed in Washington, DC, on February 6, 1922. The conclusion of this treaty was a landmark event in international relations of the post–World War I era, since it added another layer to the international peace mechanism being introduced by the League of Nations while also setting out a fresh legal framework for effectuating a system of multilateral conflict resolution, especially for the Asia-Pacific region. The underlying idea was for the signatories to enable the young Republic of China a sufficient opportunity to grapple with internal divisions and conflicts in the aftermath of the overthrow of the Qing Dynasty in 1911. Because the Japanese war in China (1931–45) played such a dominant role in the majority judgment, it is important to understand the significance of the Nine-Power Treaty, which provided that:

Article 1. The Contracting Powers, other than China, agree:

1. To respect the sovereignty, the independence, and the territorial and administrative integrity of China;
2. To provide the fullest and most unembarrassed opportunity to China to develop and maintain for herself an effective and stable Government;

[27] *Documents*, 53.

3. To use their influence for the purpose of effectually establishing and maintaining the principle of equal opportunity for the commerce and industry of all nations throughout the territory of China;
4. To refrain from taking advantage of conditions in China in order to seek special rights or privileges which would abridge the rights of subjects or citizens of friendly States, and from countenancing action inimical to the security of such States.[28]

Through these provisions, the nine signatories, including Japan, agreed that the political stability of China was essential for establishing a new legal order in the Far East. It became a point of major contention at the Tokyo Trial as to how the Japanese accused could reconcile the difference between their stated adherence to the Nine-Power Treaty on the one hand, and, on the other, their wartime advocacy of Japan's economic, political, and military aggression in China.

Appendix C reinforced the Japanese commitments expressed in the Nine-Power Treaty by enumerating further official assurances to foreign governments regarding promoting international peace. Eight of the listed Japanese assurances pertained to China, and the prosecution sought to establish that Japan broke all of its treaty commitments and violated its repeated express assurances not to pursue territorial conquest in China. Proving Japanese aggressive intentions in China was at the core of the prosecution's case, and demonstrating the continuing discrepancy between official assurances on the one hand and actual conduct on the other provided the means of proving the ongoing conspiracy alleged in the indictment. The list of eight official assurances aimed to demonstrate that continuous pattern of deceit implicit in Japan's China policy:

1. September 25th, 1931: That Japan had no territorial designs in Manchuria.
2. November 25th, 1931: That there was no truth in the report of a Japanese advance on Chinchow [Jinzhou, in northeastern China].
3. December 22nd, 1931: That Chinese sovereignty would be accepted and that the open door policy would be maintained.
4. January 5th, 1933: That Japan had no territorial ambitions south of the Great Wall of China.
5. April 25th, 1934: That Japan had no intention whatsoever of seeking special privileges in China, of encroaching upon the territorial and administrative integrity of China, or of creating difficulties for the bona fide trade of other countries with China.
6. August 15th, 1937: That Japan harbored no territorial designs on China and would spare no efforts in safeguarding foreign interests and rights in China.

---

[28] Ibid., 51.

2.1 Counts and Appendices in the Indictment 83

7. September 1937: That Japan had peaceful intentions and a lack of territorial designs in North China.
8. February 17th, 1939: That Japan had no territorial designs in China and that the occupation would not go beyond military necessity.[29]

Looking beyond the war in China, the prosecution also enumerated the pattern of assurances concerning Japan's relationships with the Axis Powers in Europe and the Western Powers in the Asia-Pacific region. The prosecution case aimed to establish that Japan violated each of these assurances offered to foreign governments:

9. August 26th, 1939: That Japan had decided to abandon any further negotiations with Germany and Italy relative to closer relations under the Anti-Comintern Pact.
10. April 15th, 1940: That Japan had no plans nor purpose to attack the Netherlands East Indies.
11. May 16th, 1940: That Japan had no plans nor purpose to attack the Netherlands East Indies.
12. March 24th, 1941: That under no circumstances would Japan attack the United States of America, Great Britain or the Netherlands East Indies.
13. July 8th, 1941: That Japan had not so far considered the possibility of fighting the Union of Soviet Socialist Republics.
14. July 10th, 1941: That Japan contemplated no action against French Indo-China.
15. December 5th, 1941: That troop movements in French Indo-China were precautionary measures.[30]

Throughout the Tokyo Trial the prosecution invoked these violated assurances to prove that deceit was the primary tool by which the Japanese government conducted its foreign relations and thereby sought to realize the aims of the conspiracy.

Finally, Appendix E contained three additional sets of theoretical and factual elaborations of charges in the indictment. Two of these compel our attention: (1) a statement on the principle of individual responsibility, and (2) a list of key policymaking meetings of the Japanese government prior to the outbreak of the Pacific War.[31]

The first section is important because it articulates the prosecution's theory of individual responsibility that would apply to all the "non-conspiracy" counts in the indictment, that is, the substantive counts of crimes against peace (Counts 6–36), those on murder (Counts 39–43, 45–52), and those on war crimes and

[29] Ibid., 56.
[30] Ibid.
[31] The third section in Appendix E merely provides brief biographies of the accused.

crimes against humanity (Counts 54–55). This statement thus reveals the prosecution's strategy for linking all of the accused in their disparate roles to the wide range of crimes alleged in the indictment. Our ensuing analysis will consider to what extent the prosecution was in fact able to establish individual responsibility on this basis through the presentation of their case. The opening segment of Appendix E provides:

> Statement of Individual Responsibility for Crimes Set Out in the Indictment.
>
> The statements hereinafter set forth following the name of each individual defendant constitute matters upon which the prosecution will reply inter alia as establishing individual responsibility of the defendants.
>
> It is charged against each of the defendants that *he used the power and prestige of the position which he held and his personal influence* in such a manner that he promoted and carried out the offences set out in each Count of this indictment in which his name appears.
>
> It is charged against each of the defendants that during the periods hereinafter set out against his name *he was one of those responsible for all the acts and omissions of the various Governments of which he was member*, and of the various civil, military [army] or naval organizations *in which he held a position of authority*.[32] (emphasis added)

Under the principle of individual responsibility as set out above, it would be necessary for the prosecution to prove the following elements beyond reasonable doubt: (1) that the accused held a *position of authority in the government*; (2) that the accused used the *power* and *prestige* derived from such a position, or his or her *personal influence*; (3) that the accused enabled the commission of offenses as charged in the indictment; and (4) that the accused did so knowingly or intentionally.

The second provision of the theory of responsibility in the quote above is sweeping in its scope. In providing that each of the accused was responsible "for *all* the acts and omissions of the various Governments of *which he was member*," the prosecution appears to be proposing a theory of collective responsibility that operates independently of a demonstration of a connection to particular criminal policies or conduct. Indeed, it is difficult to see the difference in impact between this theory of individual responsibility for the non-conspiracy charges and the conspiracy counts of the indictment. In each case, all of the accused are, in the prosecution's view, to be held liable for all the criminal acts and policies of the government or military organization of which they were a member. Chapters 4, 5, and 6 will discuss what these key terms in the theory of individual responsibility – "power," "prestige," "individual influence," and "member" – exactly meant, as the prosecution sought to apply it to actual cases.

---

[32] Ibid., 62–3.

2.1  Counts and Appendices in the Indictment                    85

The second section in Appendix E relates to the prosecution's strategy for establishing the responsibility of the accused. This section enumerates fourteen key policymaking meetings held in 1941, which culminated in the Japanese decision to wage war against the United States, the British Commonwealth of Nations, and the Netherlands:

1. June 25th, 1941 (Liaison)
2. June 26th, 1941 (Liaison)
3. June 27th, 1941 (Liaison)
4. June 28th, 1941 (Liaison)
5. June 30th, 1941 (Supreme War Council)
6. July 2nd, 1941 (Imperial)
7. August 7th, 1941 (Thought Control Council)
8. August 22nd, 1941 (Cabinet)
9. September 6th, 1941 (Imperial)
10. October 17th, 1941 (Ex-Premiers)
11. November 28th, 1941 (Liaison)
12. November 29th, 1941 (Ex-Premiers)
13. December 1st, 1941 (Imperial)
14. December 1st, 1941 (Cabinet)[33]

The words shown in parentheses denote different types of high-level governmental organs at which decisions on Japan's war policies allegedly were made. Conflicting evidence and arguments were advanced during the trial as to the actual policymaking authority of these organs and the cabinet. These conflicts were by no means resolved by the majority judgment, which instead rather sidestepped the issue. It was crucial to the prosecution's case to establish the dynamics of policy- and decision-making authority, an issue that will be explored in depth in Chapters 3 and 4. What was also essential for the prosecution was to connect specific individuals to the key meetings where policies were actually formulated and relevant decisions made.

As an indicator of the prosecution's initial strategy to establish the crucial connection of individuals to policies, this list of key meetings represents a curious addition in the Bill of Indictment. It is especially striking that there appears to be no consistent logic as to what has been included or excluded. For instance, the above list contains *some* of the most important, highest-level policymaking meetings relating to the Japanese decision to go to war against the United States, *but not all of them*. Moreover, the list fails to include any of the critical, highest-level policymaking meetings relating to the Japanese decision to wage war against *China*. This list lost much of its purpose by the end of the trial in any event, because the prosecution corrected these omissions

[33] Ibid., 63.

as it developed its case. The shortcomings of this list reveal the incompleteness of the prosecution's understanding of the evidence at the pretrial phase, while the broad sweep of its proposed theory of individual responsibility indicates a strategy designed to compensate for the potential inability to link specific individuals accused to specific criminal policies and conduct. What needs to be elaborated further, then, is how the prosecution actually developed its case from the pretrial phase to its Opening Statement and onward through the evidentiary phase to its final summation in its Closing Statement.

## 2.2 The Legal Argument of the Prosecution

As had been the case at the IMT trial, one major point of legal controversy arising from the IMTFE trial was the question of whether or not the Allied Powers had the authority to try and punish the leaders of the Japanese government and military on the charges of crimes against peace. The prosecution generally held that the question was a nonissue, based on its position that, "Long before the occurrence of the acts complained of in this indictment, aggressive warfare had been condemned as illegal."[34] The prosecution also grounded its position on the precedent of the Nuremberg Trial, asserting that the IMTFE Charter was "conclusive as to the composition and jurisdiction of the tribunal," and "merely declaratory of international law."[35]

### 2.2.1 *The Potsdam Declaration and the London Charter*

The prosecution argued that the legality of the Allied Powers to promulgate the IMTFE Charter was also not in doubt since the IMTFE Charter "derive[d] its authority" from the Instrument of Surrender of September 2, 1945 and other joint declarations that the Allied Powers had made previously.[36] The prosecution argued that the Cairo Declaration of November 27, 1943 set out that the war aim of the Allied Powers was "to restrain and *punish the aggression* of Japan," and the Potsdam Declaration eighteen months later on July 26, 1945 stated that "*stern justice shall be meted out to all war criminals*, including those who have visited cruelties upon our [Allied] prisoners"[37] (emphasis added).

The prosecution also invoked the Allied Powers' promulgation of the London Agreement to establish the IMT at Nuremberg, on August 8, 1945, two weeks after the Potsdam Declaration. The IMT Charter, as appended to the London Agreement, set out crimes against peace as one of the three categories

---

[34] T415.
[35] T39002.
[36] T39000.
[37] The Cairo Conference, Avalon Project Web site; *Documents*, 1–2.

2.2 The Legal Argument of the Prosecution                                      87

of international offense over which the IMT would have jurisdiction.[38] Japan communicated its acceptance of Potsdam terms to the Allied Powers about a week later, on August 14, 1945, and the Japanese surrender was formalized at the ceremony in Tokyo two weeks later. As the prosecution pointed out, the Japanese government thereafter became responsible "to issue *whatever orders and take whatever action may be required* by the Supreme Commander for the Allied Powers or by any other designated representative of the Allied Powers *for the purpose of giving effect to that Declaration*"[39] (emphasis added). Given these declarations and the sequence of events leading to the Japanese surrender, the prosecution argued that the Allied authorities were justified to define "war criminals" as including those who were responsible not only for committing war crimes but also for aggressive war.

The prosecution also argued that the Japanese leaders, including Emperor Hirohito, likely had the same understanding in these last days of the war of the import of the Potsdam Declaration and the consequences of Japan's unconditional surrender. The entry for August 10, 1945 of *The Kido Diary* recorded Hirohito stating to Kido that "I could not bear the sight ... of those responsible for war [*sensō sekininsha*] being punished ... but I think that now is the time to bear the unbearable."[40]

### 2.2.2 The Authority of Nuremberg: Crimes against Peace

Based on this interpretation of the relevant legal documents, the prosecution urged that the Tokyo Tribunal "make an authoritative decision on this matter," and drew the tribunal's attention to the fact that the judgment of the Nuremberg Tribunal was already available. In its judgment, the Nuremberg Tribunal had produced an independent section, titled, "The Law of the Charter," to articulate in full its position on the law of crimes against peace.[41] The prosecution read out the relevant segment in bulk during its summation, in order to signal its significance for the Tokyo Trial.[42]

As Chapter 7 will show, the majority judgment followed the prosecution's argument and fully accepted the authority of Nuremberg on the status of crimes against peace. It is interesting to note, however, that when the prosecution read out the "Law of the Charter" section of the IMT judgment they omitted the initial four paragraphs. In these paragraphs the Nuremberg Tribunal indicated

---

[38] Article 6 of the IMT Charter, Friedman, ed., *Law of War*, vol. 1, 887.
[39] *Documents*, 3.
[40] T39001. The defense countered the prosecution's take interpretation, asserting that the Japanese term, *sensō sekininsha*, "did not prior to the armistice necessarily mean 'persons responsible for war' but equally meant 'persons responsible in the course of war.'" (T42233).
[41] *Trial of the Major War Criminal before the International Military Tribunal*, vol. 1, 218.
[42] T39003–13.

its conclusive opinion on the right of the victor nations to exercise their "sovereign legislative authority" in creating the IMT Charter, and the legality of the Charter under international law. We will see later that the defense discussed these omitted paragraphs to challenge the authority of victor nations and the legality of the IMTFE Charter.

Turning to what the prosecution did read to the tribunal from the IMT judgment, they began with a quotation of the passage where the Nuremberg Tribunal addressed the criticism of retroactive application of the law, a criticism raised first at Nuremberg and then repeated at Tokyo. The Nuremberg Tribunal flatly rejected the criticism, for the reason that the prohibition of ex post facto law applied only insofar as it helped further the cause of justice:

> In the first place, it is to be observed that the maxim nullum crimen sine lege ["no crime without law"] is not a limitation of sovereignty, but is in general a principle of justice. To assert that it is unjust to punish those who in defiance of treaties and assurances have attacked neighboring states without warning is obviously untrue, for in such circumstances the attacker must know that he is doing wrong, and so far from it being unjust to punish him, it would be unjust if his wrong were allowed to go unpunished.[43]

The Nuremberg Tribunal maintained that the German accused, or at least some of them, must have been aware that international treaties outlawed the recourse to war for the settlement of international disputes, and that their pursuit of the plans of invasion and aggression were acts committed in open defiance of international law. "On this view of the case alone, it would appear that the maxim has no application to the present facts."[44] As we will see, the majority judgment at Tokyo simply followed the lead of Nuremberg, relying on its authority.

In the passage quoted by the prosecution at the Tokyo Trial, the Nuremberg Tribunal further expressed confidence that the legal effect of the Pact of Paris was in no doubt either:

> In the opinion of the tribunal, the solemn renunciation of war as an instrument of national policy necessarily involves the proposition that such a war is *illegal* in international law; and that those who plan and wage such a war, with its inevitable and terrible consequences, are committing a *crime* in so doing.[45] (emphasis added)

The prosecution employed this passage to show that although the Nuremberg Tribunal acknowledged that the Pact of Paris contained no express provision to criminalize the wars waged in violation of the Pact, it nonetheless concluded

---

[43] T39003.
[44] T39004.
[45] T39006.

## 2.2 The Legal Argument of the Prosecution

that the absence of express provisions should not deprive the Pact of having a legal effect. Here the quoted passage based its argument on analogy to the undisputed criminality of violations of the 1907 Hague Conventions, despite the fact that they, like the Pact of Paris, contained no express provisions to establish criminal liability for violations.

In response to the position of the defense, the passages quoted by the prosecution also aimed to demonstrate that the Nuremberg judgment emphasized the inherently evolutionary nature of international law:

The law of war is to be found not only in treaties, but in the customs and practices which gradually obtained universal recognition, and from the general principles of justice applied by jurists and practiced by military courts. This law is not static, but by continual adaptation follows the needs of a changing world. Indeed, in many cases treaties do no more than express and define for more accurate reference the principles of law already existing.[46]

On this basis, the Nuremberg Tribunal had pointed out that the Pact of Paris was signed by many countries *not* in a vacuum, but that it capped multiyear, multilateral efforts, culminating in the Pact of Paris, to "reinforce the construction ... that to resort to a war of aggression is not merely illegal, but is criminal."[47]

As we will see, this contention was the focal point of disagreement between the majority and Webb on the one hand and Bernard, Pal, and Roeling on the other. That is, did the development of international law in the interwar years result in the establishment of an international customary law norm criminalizing aggressive war?[48] Chapters 7, 8, 11, and 12 will take up this central issue on the status of crimes against peace. What is important to note here is that the prosecution based its argument on this issue on the authority of the Nuremberg judgment. The majority, as we will see, also embraced this strategy in formulating its own legal conclusions.

### 2.2.3 The Authority of Nuremberg: Individual Criminal Responsibility

The Tokyo Prosecution also faced a challenge from the defense as to whether the principle of individual criminal responsibility should apply to government

---

[46] T39008.
[47] T39011.
[48] Unlike domestic law, international law has two major sources of law: international conventions and treaties on the one hand, and customary law that reflects the universal or near universal practices of nations on the other. International customary law is binding on all states, unlike convention or treaty law which is only binding on those states who ratified and acceded to the instrument (unless the convention is so widely adopted so as to become part of international customary law).

officials for violations of the laws of war. Here again, the prosecution's strategy was to invoke the authority of Nuremberg and quote the words of the IMT judgment. The defense at the IMT trial had disputed the applicability of individual responsibility on the grounds that no person was subject to criminal liability for "acts of state," and that the principle of state sovereignty remained inviolable. The Nuremberg Tribunal summarily rejected the so-called Act of State doctrine,[49] and the defense argument in words quoted by the Tokyo Prosecution on the same issue:

> It was submitted that international law is concerned with the action of sovereign States, and provides no punishment for individuals; and further, that where the act in question is an act of state, those who carry it out are not personally responsible, but are protected by the doctrine of the sovereignty of the State. In the opinion of the tribunal, both these submissions must be rejected. *That international law imposes duties and liabilities upon individuals as well as upon States has long been recognised.*[50] (emphasis added)

The Nuremberg Tribunal followed the statement above with five additional short paragraphs to elaborate its position on the principle of individual responsibility, and with reference to relevant provisions in the IMT Charter (Articles 7 and 8). The prosecution at the Tokyo Trial omitted to read these paragraphs, however, possibly to avoid an awkward position of discussing the issues of imperial culpability (to the extent that Article 7 of the IMT Charter identified "heads of state" as being subject to the principle of individual responsibility).

The prosecution at the Tokyo Trial generally relied on the argument that the judgment of the Nuremberg Tribunal applied *in toto* to the case against the Japanese accused, and that no further discussion concerning the legality of the law of crimes against peace or of the principle of individual criminal responsibility for violations of international law was thus necessary. The majority of the judges were apparently persuaded by the prosecution's argument.

The prosecution also faced two further challenges from the defense that arose from the court proceedings in regard to crimes against peace. One concerned the right of self-defense, and the other, the doctrine of criminal conspiracy.

### 2.2.4 Wars of Self-Defense

In response to the defense argument that Japan had only asserted the right of a sovereign state to act in self-defense, the prosecution maintained that the right

---

[49] IMT judgment, 222–3. This passage uses the rejection of the Act of State doctrine to develop the watershed principle of individual responsibility for international crimes.
[50] T39012.

## 2.2 The Legal Argument of the Prosecution

of self-defense was untouched by the Pact of Paris, but that the war waged in the name of self-defense was subject to a third-power arbitration to determine its legality. The prosecution again was quick to point out that its view had the backing of the Nuremberg Tribunal's decision where a similar defense argument had been made:

> It was further argued [by the German accused] that Germany alone could decide, in accordance with the reservations made by many of the Signatory Powers at the time of the conclusion of the Briand-Kellogg Pact, whether preventive action was a necessity, and that in making her decision her judgment was conclusive. But whether action taken under the claim of self-defense was in fact aggressive or defensive must ultimately *be subject to investigation and adjudicated* if international law is ever to be enforced.[51] (emphasis added)

Here the Tokyo Prosecution went beyond mere quotation of the Nuremberg judgment and pointed out that that the leading authority on international law, L. Oppenheim's *International Law: A Treatise, Vol. 2: Disputes, War and Neutrality*, ed. H. Lauterpacht, 6th edn (1940), articulated the same view. Oppenheim's treatise – from which the prosecution quoted at length – did not deny that every state had the right to decide whether or not it was confronted with such danger as to justify an act in self-defense. However, Oppenheim also stated that "elementary principles of interpretation preclude a construction which gives to a State resorting to an alleged war in self-defense the right of ultimate determination." Furthermore, while the Pact of Paris contained "no obligation to submit the disputed question of self-defense to a judicial decision," the legality of recourse to force in self-defense was "in each particular case a proper subject for impartial determination by judicial or other bodies."[52]

In light of these views expressed by the Nuremberg Tribunal and Oppenheim's *International Law*, the prosecution maintained that it was entirely proper for the Tokyo Tribunal to adjudicate the legality of the wars Japan had waged and for which the defense claimed it had done so in the name of self-defense. The prosecution added that the right of "self-defense" should be understood as meaning the right to use force in self-defense in the face of "a reasonably anticipated armed attack," and *not* in response to "'encirclement'[,] either military or still less economic even if it existed."[53] By this remark, the prosecution was urging the tribunal to reject the assertions repeatedly made by the defense during the court proceedings that Japan's use of force was justified in the face of the "ABCD" encirclement, i.e., economic boycott, trade embargo, and freezing

---

[51] T39022–3; IMT judgment, 208.
[52] T39024–5. For the original, see Oppenheim, *International Law*, 6th edn, vol. 2, 155.
[53] T39025.

of Japanese assets by American, British, Chinese, and Dutch Powers. As will be seen in Part II, all the justices at the Tokyo Trial rejected the defense's contention of self-defense, except Justice Pal. He alone maintained that economic encirclement justified Japan to have a bona fide belief that she faced menacing circumstances, and to wage war in self-defense.

### 2.2.5 The Applicability of Conspiracy Doctrine in International Law

Because the theory of an overarching conspiracy was the foundation of the prosecution's case, and because it was essentially a legal doctrine unique to the Anglo-American criminal law, the prosecution aimed to establish its legitimacy, especially to members of the tribunal for whom it was likely unfamiliar. The argument by the prosecution had two main components.

First, the prosecution discussed conspiracy as a *category* of criminal offense, and made a case that conspiracy as a criminal offense already had broad recognition in the criminal laws of many countries, including Japan. The prosecution argued that this state of affairs justified applying the concept of conspiracy as a criminal offense in the field of international law as well. It further argued that "a conspiracy to disturb the peace of the world ... is so closely analogous in the international sphere to the conspiracy against the security of the state in the municipal sphere." The prosecution held that, in both form and substance, it was therefore entirely appropriate to draw parallels and to recognize conspiracy as a practical legal concept under international law.[54]

Second, the prosecution treated the doctrine of criminal conspiracy as *a mode of liability*, and offered a set of practical guidelines as to how the judges might apply it to determine the guilt of individual accused. The following "tests of guilt" were provided during the summation in order to provide the judges with standards to apply, by which an individual accused should be convicted if one of these three sets of circumstances could be satisfied:

1. Counts as to which *there is direct evidence of participation* by the individual *in the actual commission of the offense*, whether as to the whole, or in the case of a continuing offense, part of its duration ...
2. Counts as to which *there is no such evidence* but the event occurred or the conduct continued after the individual is *proved to have become a party to the conspiracy*. The offense was within the scope of that conspiracy, and *there is no evidence of objection by him* ...

---

[54] T39039. As will be seen in Chapter 11, Justice Roeling's dissenting opinion also relied on an analogy to the security of the state.

3. Counts similar to the last named in all respects *except that there is some evidence accepted by the tribunal of his disagreement with the action*, the subject of the Count.[55] (emphasis added)

These so-called tests of guilt are troubling in several respects. First of all, they do not make clear what mental element the prosecution must prove in order to establish liability under each of the three "tests." In regard to the second "test," it is not even clear if the accused must share the criminal intent of the conspirators or have knowledge of the criminal conduct for which he is to be held liable after joining the conspiracy. The second "test" also grounds liability on an omission to object where there is no evidence that the accused had actual knowledge of the crimes or had engaged in any general conduct in furtherance of the conspiracy. This test neglects what American criminal law terms the "overt act" requirement and the mens rea requirement (mental element or state of mind), which in the case of conspiracy doctrine require that the prosecution must prove some act of participation in or in furtherance of the conspiracy and must also prove that the accused shares the criminal purpose of the conspiracy and agrees with other persons to further that purpose.[56] In regard to disagreement, as provided in the third "test," from a doctrinal standpoint the relevant question is whether the accused left the conspiracy, not whether they might have expressed some disagreement with a particular act that was part of the implementation of the criminal aims of the conspiracy.

On the last of the three tests of guilt, the prosecution appears to have contradicted its own criteria in explaining that an accused would not be absolved of responsibility even if there were evidence of disagreement, provided that "he was in office at the time, allowed his scruples to be overruled, and continued in office." What the third "test" thus in reality required was complete disavowal of the conspiracy and withdrawal, "by resigning, or still more effectively if he was a cabinet minister, by refusing either to agree or resign, in which case the whole cabinet would have to resign and the war might thus have been prevented."[57]

The analysis of the majority judgment in Part II will consider to what extent the judges made use of these criteria in their individual verdicts. What appears clear, however, is that the prosecution proposed to the judges a theory of conspiracy that could encompass any government official who did not resign from office or bring about the fall of the cabinet in protest.

---

[55] T39052–3.
[56] See Model Penal Code Section 5.03.1 and 5.03.5. Available online.
[57] T39057–8.

94    Charges of Crimes against Peace

## 2.3    The Legal Argument by the Defense

The defense generally held that the law of crimes against peace was not an established legal principle and that under the principle of *nullem crimen sine lege* no accused, therefore, should be convicted of this category of offense. The defense contention was multifaceted, but the core issue aimed to challenge the authority of victorious Allied Powers to create the IMTFE Charter. On the one hand, the defense agreed that the Allied Powers in the European theater had the right to promulgate a Charter, and to hold German war criminals accountable for the launching of aggressive war. On other hand, the defense questioned whether or not the victor nations could do the same in the case of Japanese accused, for the stated reason that Japan surrendered only *conditionally*, which presumably put limits on the victor nations' authority. In light of the Allied demand of unconditional surrender, to which we have seen Japan acceded, what exactly did the defense mean by the Japanese conditional surrender?

To clarify its interpretive position, the defense during the summation first discussed the opening segment of "The Law of the Charter" in the IMT judgment, where the Nuremberg Tribunal remarked on the authority of victorious Allied Powers in the European theater. One passage in the opening segment, as referenced by the defense, read:

> The making of the Charter was the exercise of the sovereign legislative power by the countries to which the German Reich unconditionally surrendered; and the undoubted right of these countries to legislate for the occupied territories has been recognised by the civilised world.[58]

The defense readily agreed that this passage aptly stated the authority of victor nations insofar as their relationship with defeated Germany was concerned. "The German Government ceased to exist in May 1945, through conquest by the Allies," the defense maintained, and the Allied Powers thereafter could "exercise rights of sovereignty in the territories over which they had complete control." The rights of sovereignty the Allied Powers assumed, in the defense's understanding, were of an unlimited character, so that the victor nations could "govern the country in whatever way they pleased," and "if they liked, behave as an absolute monarch like Louis XIV." With regard specifically to the treatment of suspected German war criminals, the Allied Powers could "set up a tribunal to punish those persons they disfavored by laying down an ex-post-facto law," or even "disposed of them by executive action without any trial at all"[59] (underline in the original). It would follow that it

[58] T42116.
[59] T42116–7.

## 2.3 The Legal Argument by the Defense

was well within the victor nations' sovereign legislative authority to promulgate the IMT Charter and to punish the German war criminals in whichever manner they desired.

In so arguing, the defense appear to overlook the other remark by the Nuremberg Tribunal in the same opening segment of "The Law of the Charter," which was this: "it is ... not strictly necessary to consider whether and to what extent aggressive war was a crime before the execution of the London Agreement," since the IMT Charter was *"not an arbitrary exercise of power on the part of the victorious nations, but* in the view of the tribunal ... *it is the expression of international law existing at the time of its creation*; and to that extent is itself a contribution to international law" (emphasis added). The Nuremberg Tribunal did detail its opinion on the law of crimes against peace in the judgment, but *not* because it believed the legality of the IMT Charter was in question, but rather because it recognized "the great importance of the questions of law involved."[60]

The defense at the Tokyo Trial ignored the former part ("not an arbitrary exercise of power on the part of the victorious nations") but highlighted the latter ("it is ... not strictly necessary to consider whether and to what extent aggressive war was a crime before the execution of the London Agreement") to assert that the IMT Charter was definitely an expression of the victor nations' arbitrary exercise of the sovereign legislative power and ex post facto law, and that the Nuremberg Tribunal for this reason had no obligation to produce a reasoned opinion on anything. The Nuremberg Tribunal did produce a reasoned opinion, but the defense at the Tokyo Trial treated it as merely "a sort of <u>obiter dictum</u>, a display of learning which was not strictly necessary for the judgment itself"[61] (underline in the original).

If the circumstances of German surrender were as described earlier, the defense contended that the situation of Japanese surrender was an "entirely different" affair. The sequence of events leading to the termination of the war was described in the defense summation as follows:

Unlike Germany, Japan was not at the time of its surrender overrun by the Allied forces. The Japanese mainland was still unoccupied and *Japan was then in a position to offer strenuous armed resistance for some time to come, necessarily involving losses to the Allied forces*. The Japanese government contented in such circumstances to accept the peace offer of the Allies, the "terms" of which are laid down in the Potsdam Declaration. The Instrument of Surrender formally and expressly referred to the terms of that Declaration.[62] (emphasis added)

---

[60] IMT judgment, 218–19.
[61] T42117.
[62] T42118.

96  Charges of Crimes against Peace

In this statement, the defense portrayed Japan at the time of its initial surrender overture on August 10, 1945 as still retaining substantial military capabilities as well as a firm resolve to inflict further damage on the Allied armed forces, that is, in the eventuality of the latter's land invasion of the Japanese homeland. The defense recognized that Japan did accept surrender within four days, but that the acceptance was made by way of agreeing to the "terms" of surrender – or the "conditions" of surrender, as the defense would like to call it – as set out in the Potsdam Declaration. The conditional nature of Japanese surrender, so the defense argument went, denied the victorious Allied Powers the right to assume sovereign legislative authority vis-à-vis defeated Japan. The victors and the vanquished instead were bound by the Potsdam "terms," which were reaffirmed by the Instrument of Surrender.

The defense, somewhat ingeniously, maintained that the Allied Powers and Japan accordingly became "contracting parties." Japan was certainly "duty-bound to perform all the demands made by the Allies within those limits," so the defense agreed, but she also retained "the right to insist that those limits shall not be overridden" by the victor nations that signed the surrender document.[63] *This presumption of contractual relations* was key to the defense's position disputing the legality of the IMTFE Charter.

It is worth noting in this connection that, back in early September 1945, US President Truman transmitted to the Supreme Commander for the Allied Powers, General MacArthur, an express instruction that the Allied Powers were committed to respect the Potsdam terms *not* because they were bound by any contractual agreement with Japan, but purely because it was the Allied *policy* to do so. The relevant segment in the instruction read as follows:

1. The authority of the Emperor and the Japanese government to rule the State is subordinate to you as Supreme Commander for the Allied Powers. You will exercise your authority as you deem proper to carry out our mission. Our relations with Japan *do not rest on a contractual basis*, but on an unconditional surrender ...
2. ...
3. The statement of intentions contained in the Potsdam Declaration will be given full effect. *It will not be given effect, however, because we consider ourselves bound in a contractual relationship with Japan as a result of that document.* It will be respected and given effect because the Potsdam Declaration forms a part of our *policy* stated in good faith with relation to Japan and with relation to peace and security in the Far East.[64] (emphasis added)

[63] T42119.
[64] *The Department of State Bulletin*, vol. 13, nos. 314–40 (July–December 1945), 480.

## 2.3 The Legal Argument by the Defense

This presidential instruction to the Supreme Commander, dated September 6, 1945, was published contemporaneously in *The Department of State Bulletin*. In all likelihood, the Government of Japan was alerted to its contents, if not informed directly by the Supreme Commander. That instruction, moreover, followed the provisions of the terms of surrender to which the Japanese government agreed.

The defense's presumption of a contractual relationship between the victorious Allied Powers and vanquished Japan set the baseline for the next line of defense argument regarding the legality of the IMTFE Charter and, more specifically, the law of crimes against peace. The defense held that "war crimes" as set out in the Potsdam Declaration should be understood as meaning *conventional* war crimes for all intents and purposes, i.e., "violations of certain recognized rules regarding warfare committed by members of the armed forces and other persons, including the ill-treatment of prisoners of war, all hostilities in arms committed by individuals who are not members of the armed forces, espionage and war treason, and marauding acts."[65] This argument, as we will see, had persuasive power for some of the dissenting opinions.

The IMT Charter, which was promulgated in the weeks after the Potsdam Declaration, certainly identified crimes against peace, war crimes, and crimes against humanity as categories of international offenses for which the Axis leaders would be tried. However, the defense saw no reason as to why the law set out in the IMT Charter should be carried over to the IMTFE Charter in its entirety. The defense held that doing so "deviated from the natural interpretation of the [Potsdam] Declaration."[66] The IMT Charter, in the defense's opinion, was a product of the victor nations' arbitrary exercise of power, and it applied only to defeated Germany. The defense thus somehow maintained – in the face of the reality of total defeat – that Japan, unlike Germany, had not been defeated by the Allies.

The defense, meanwhile, did acknowledge that the Pact of Paris condemned the recourse to war as a means of solving international disputes, but downplayed its legal implications by characterizing it as "nothing but *a pious expression of the will to peace*"[67] (emphasis added). This expression also found resonance in the dissenting opinion of Justice Roeling, as discussed later as well as in Chapter 11.

---

[65] T42121. The relevant provision in the Potsdam Declaration read as follows. "We do not intend that the Japanese shall be enslaved as a race or destroyed as a nation, but stern justice shall be meted out to all war criminals, including those who have visited cruelties upon our prisoners." *Documents*, 1–2. The defense held that the passage, "including those who have visited cruelties upon our prisoners of war," should be understood as a qualifier that *limited* the scope of Allied prosecutions to conventional war crimes. T42122.
[66] T42123.
[67] T42156.

The defense also attacked the jurisprudence of the most influential contemporary authorities on international law, whose views flatly contradicted the defense position. They hyperbolically belittled the importance of Oppenheim's *International Law*, castigating it as a "personal view of a text-writer."[68] The defense went on to denigrate the opinion of Lord Wright by charging that he wrote "not as a judge, but as an advocate."[69] Lord Wright was a prominent Australian jurist who served as chairman of the United Nations War Crimes Commission (1945–6). His seminal article, "War Crimes and International Law," in *International Law Review* (1946), affirmed that aggressive war constituted a criminal offense under international law. The record of the trial shows that the last of these remarks met the displeasure of Justice Webb, who interjected, "Apparently Lord Wright is a partisan. That is your view. But the people you quote as favoring your views are not partisans. [That is also your view.]"[70] The defense subsequently retracted its remarks in which it attacked the integrity of Lord Wright.[71]

It is instructive to note that the defense's position of the Pact of Paris as a mere expression of pacifist sentiments resonated with two justices on the Tokyo Tribunal, Roeling and Pal. As early as March 1947, Roeling privately expressed to Webb his skeptical views of the legal effect of the Pact, describing it as "*merely an expression of a pacific mood*" (emphasis added). As will be discussed in Chapter 11, Roeling did come around to accept the law of crimes against peace in the end, but he did so not on account of the Pact – whose legal effect he continued to reject – but on the basis of entirely novel extra-legal reasoning of his own. Pal took a more radical position. He was dismissive not only of the legal effect of the Pact but also of the entire body of international law, which he condemned as a political tool for the Western imperial powers to perpetuate their domination and subjugation of the non-Western world (see Chapter 12).

The defense at the Tokyo Trial had further objections to the application of the law of crimes against peace even if one were to accept the proposition that aggressive war as an international crime was an established legal concept. The defense's objections boil down to the following five points: (1) that the right of self-defense remained untouched by the Pact of Paris; (2) that the signatories of the Pact had no intention to allow a third power or a tribunal to adjudicate on the legality of the war waged in the name of self-defense; (3) that aggressive war lacked a clear definition to serve as a practical legal concept; (4) that, under international law, there was no individual responsibility for acts of state;

---

[68] T42241.
[69] T42177.
[70] T42178.
[71] T42195.

## 2.3 The Legal Argument by the Defense

and (5) that there was no legal ground on which to allow the application of the doctrine of criminal conspiracy under international law. The contention by the defense on each of these five points was long and detailed. Of these, the ones concerning the application of the doctrine of criminal conspiracy deserves attention, as the defense appears to have put to good use the decision made by the Nuremberg Tribunal.

The defense generally held that the doctrine of criminal conspiracy should not have been introduced at all, because it was "a peculiar product of English legal history,"[72] and because using this doctrine was tantamount to "going back to the collective responsibility which prevailed in the tribal age of mankind."[73] The defense also faulted the prosecution's broad interpretation of the meaning of conspiracy, by which matters extraneous to the core issue of the charge – such as the "objects" of conspiracy – were brought against the accused. The defense pointed out that, according to the IMTFE Charter, "the crime alleged or described in the charter is the planning, preparation, initiation or waging of a war in violation of international law."[74]

The defense went on to bring to the Tokyo Tribunal's attention that the Nuremberg Tribunal, too, was skeptical about the adequacy of the doctrine of criminal conspiracy as a theory of liability. A relevant segment in the IMT judgment, which the defense quoted in full (as shown below), brought out that, as a matter of fact, the Nuremberg Tribunal rejected a single, overarching conspiracy embracing all of the accused. The judges at Nuremberg instead construed "conspiracy" as meaning no more than war *planning*:

> The prosecution says, in effect, that any significant participation in the affairs of the Nazi Party or Government is evidence of a participation in a conspiracy that is in itself criminal. Conspiracy is not defined in the charter. *But in the opinion of the tribunal the conspiracy must be clearly outlined in its criminal purpose.* It must not be too far removed from the time of decision and of action. The planning, to be criminal, must not rest merely on the declarations of a Party programme, such as are found in the twenty-five points of the Nazi Party, announced in 1920, or the political affirmations expressed in *Mein Kampf* in later years. The tribunal must examine whether a concrete plan to wage war existed, and determine the participants in that concrete plan.[75] (emphasis added)

Based on the foregoing ruling, the Nuremberg Tribunal held that affirmative proof of participation in specific war-planning conferences would be required in order to convict the accused under the count of conspiracy. This essentially

---

[72] T42136.
[73] T42137.
[74] T43013–4.
[75] T43014.

negated the legal importance of conspiracy as a central tool for the prosecution and as a mode of liability.

The defense at the Tokyo Trial asked that, if the decision of the Nuremberg Tribunal on conspiracy should determine the applicability of that doctrine for the IMT, "What is the extent of the 'concrete plan to wage war' *for the purpose of this trial?*"[76] (emphasis added). By this remark, the defense suggested to the Tokyo Tribunal that the all-embracing single conspiracy should be rejected in light of the Nuremberg decision. It is fair to say that the defense here made a valid point. As will be seen in Part II, however, the defense failed to convince the majority. It was only Justice Webb's draft judgment that affirmed the IMT decision and rejected the majority's interpretation of the doctrine.

---

[76] Ibid.

# 3  The Japanese System of Government

The analysis of the indictment in the preceding chapter has shown that two different theories of liability supported the various charges of crimes against peace, murder, war crimes, and crimes against humanity. One of them was the doctrine of criminal conspiracy, and the other was the principle of individual responsibility as set out in Appendix E. In adopting the latter, the prosecution effectively took upon itself the task of explaining to the Tokyo Tribunal the system of government in wartime Japan, whose comprehension was essential for the tribunal to make its findings on the non-conspiracy counts. This was going to be a complex task to fulfill for the prosecution, however, since modern Japanese governmental institutions were comparatively recent inventions that underwent phases of test, evolution, and transformation, particularly under the pressures of the war years, growing to form a complicated political structure. This chapter will address the way in which the prosecution grappled with this challenge, analyzing the strategy which the prosecution developed to persuade the tribunal of its view of the governmental structures of decision-making relevant to the charges against the accused.

The daunting nature of this challenge, especially given linguistic and other barriers that limited their direct access to the documentary record, should not be underestimated. No prosecuting agency could be expected to develop a ready grasp of the Japanese political system in less than five months of pretrial war crimes investigation. What is more, to treat the Japanese government as a subject of inquiry was still a relatively novel endeavor in the field of social sciences. This put the International Prosecution Section in the unlikely, and unintended, historical position of being a pioneer in the academic field.

The voluminous oral and documentary evidence that the prosecution amassed indeed became the foundational sources for the future study of the institutional history of Imperial Japan. Historians in subsequent decades took full advantage of this resource to seek answers to the same questions that the International Prosecution Section had posed at the Tokyo Trial. How was the wartime Japanese government organized? What sorts of power did individual members of the government derive from those offices they had held during the war years? It was essential for the prosecution to pose these questions and to answer them in a way that would prove the accountability of the accused beyond a reasonable doubt by showing the role each defendant played in formulating and implementing the policies that formed the basis of the charges.

The foregoing state of affairs with the Allied war crimes investigation has an important bearing on our analysis of the Tokyo Trial, since it compels us to consider how the case evolved over time as the prosecution gained greater experience in handling evidentiary materials and greater familiarity with their content during the court proceedings.

The record of the trial proceedings shows that the prosecution at the outset had an incomplete understanding of the organization of the Japanese government, and that its comprehension sharpened as numerous witnesses were examined against the massive corpus of documents admitted into evidence. What has not been adequately analyzed in the literature on the Tokyo Trial is the way the prosecution's understanding of the Japanese system of government that emerged during the court proceedings became significantly more complex than the one the prosecution initially presented in its opening statement. What has also not been sufficiently recognized, moreover, is that in the last days of the trial the prosecution contradictorily turned its back on the complex picture of the Japanese government that it had so painstakingly painted. What the prosecution did instead was to present to the tribunal a far more reductive version of the system of government, which reflected only in part what the admitted evidence had shown, but which was apparently designed to appeal to the judges as a simple, practical tool for determining the guilt of individual accused. Analysis of the majority judgment in Part II will indicate the success of this strategy.

This chapter will trace this evolution of the case and why the prosecution changed course so radically at the end of the trial. The pages to follow explore the prosecution's case in three different phases of the court proceedings: (1) the presentation of the theory of the case at the beginning of the trial; (2) the evidentiary proceedings of the prosecution and defense cases; and (3) the summary of the evidence in the closing phase as it reflects the concluding theory of the case.

It is striking that the defense offered no alternative concept of government to compete with that presented by the prosecution. What the defense did do was to limit its task to responding to the prosecution's case in a piecemeal fashion, namely, challenging specific evidentiary materials when they directly related to individual accused. For this reason, this chapter cannot provide a comprehensive account of a defense theory of the structures of decision-making and responsibility in the Japanese government. We instead will discuss parts of the defense evidence insofar as they added to, or contested, the prosecution's case in any material way.

## 3.1 The Prosecution's Initial Presentation

### 3.1.1 *The Constitution and Related Laws*

"What I will have to say is not controversial and is based almost in its entirety upon the laws and ordinances which had already been received in evidence in this case," so remarked Brigadier Henry G. Nolan, the associate prosecutor from Canada. Over the course of three days in mid-June of 1946, he and an American assistant prosecutor, Solis Horwitz, took charge of presenting the very first phase of the prosecution's case under the heading, "The Constitutional Organization of Japan."[1] Their chief task was to offer a concise, two-part presentation on how the modern Japanese government was organized since its inception, and how it came to function in more recent decades, and especially during the years covered by the indictment. Their presentation was built on thirty-two sets of basic laws of Japan that had just been admitted into evidence, namely, the Japanese Constitution of the Empire of Japan (1889; "Meiji Constitution" or "Constitution" hereafter),[2] four dozen or so imperial ordinances and other laws that defined the establishment, organization, functions, and responsibilities of various branches of government (dates of documents ranging between 1885 and 1942), the National General Mobilization Law (1939), and the revised Peace Preservation Law (1941).[3] The prosecution's aim in this phase was to present "a picture, imperfect thought it may be, of the governmental structure of Japan," so that it would be able to help "expedite the proceedings and be of interest to all counsel engaged in the trial," as well as to "be of assistance to the tribunal in coming to a conclusion upon some of the issues which will ultimately present themselves for determination."[4]

The picture thus presented was indeed a rough sketch, and some information was duplicative, causing redundancies in the two-part presentation. One can, however, reasonably say that a fair balance of essential information and minimal interpretation characterized this phase of the prosecution's case. A large part of the narrative account was focused on enumerating government organs, outlining their formal functions, and cross-referencing them with provisions contained in corresponding imperial ordinances and laws. The prosecution at times brought to the tribunal's attention some interpretive issues concerning the jurisdiction and responsibility of key organs. On such occasions, the prosecution drew upon the constitutional provisions themselves, relevant imperial ordinances, and written commentaries by Japanese constitutional-law experts,

---

[1] T518.
[2] "Meiji" is the reign title of Emperor Mutsuhito, the first modern emperor of Japan (r. 1868–1912). The reign titles of three subsequent modern emperors are: Taishō (1912–26), Shōwa (1926–89), and Heisei.
[3] T503–7 (1989–2019).
[4] T518.

so that there would be just enough material to shed light on the prosecution's understanding of the prevailing interpretive positions in the Japanese legal texts. In this section, we will offer a critical summary of the main points made in this initial presentation.

As the prosecution aptly noted at the outset, the modern Japanese government was built around an ancient indigenous political institution whose original formation traced back to the "officially recognized year of the founding of the Japanese Empire in 660 B.C.,"[5] that is, in the mythical age of gods and goddesses as related in the ancient chronicles of Japan, *Kojiki* and *Nihon shoki* (completed in the eighth century). The ancient institution in question – that is, the institution of the emperor – survived to the modern era and was given a new life under the Meiji Constitution. The formal structure of modern Japanese government was modeled on various examples in the Western world, so that "the basic law or Constitution is essentially Prussian in origin, the structure of the law-making bodies is patterned on those of England, and the system of local government is similar to that of France's Third Republic."[6] The Meiji Constitution, however, retained the indigenous institution of the emperor in the name of the restoration of the tradition of imperial rule.

As presented by the prosecution, the preamble of the Meiji Constitution gave a narrative justification for the formal establishment of the emperor-centered government.[7] In brief, it claimed that the emperor inherited the right of sovereignty from his imperial ancestors in lineal, unbroken succession since time immemorial, and that this right of sovereignty was to be bequeathed to his descendants in lineal succession indefinitely. Two of the initial articles in, "Chapter 1. The Emperor," in the Meiji Constitution accordingly set out the following two fundamental principles regarding the establishment of imperial rule:

Article 1. The Empire of Japan shall be reigned over and governed by a line of Emperors unbroken for ages eternal.
Article 3. The Emperor is sacred and inviolable.

More than a dozen articles ensued in the same chapter, detailing the substance of the power that the emperor assumed, and the manner in which he was entitled to exercise it. The articles to which the prosecution drew special attention of the Tokyo Tribunal pertained to the emperor's monopoly of power to make laws, to exercise executive power, to command and control the national armed forces, and to make decisions on foreign policies, including matters of war and peace. Some of the main provisions referred to by the prosecution

[5] Ibid.
[6] T522.
[7] PX86, introduced at T505.

make clear the considerable extent of the emperor's constitutional authority in areas relevant to the proceedings:

Article 4. The Emperor is the head of the Empire, combining in Himself the rights of sovereignty, and exercises them, according to the provisions of the present Constitution.
　Article 6. The Emperor gives sanction to laws, and orders them to be promulgated and executed.
　Article 11. The Emperor has the supreme command of the Army and Navy.
　Article 12. The Emperor determines the organization and peace standing of the Army and Navy.
　Article 13. The Emperor declares war, makes peace, and concludes treaties.[8]

These and other articles in the first chapter of the Meiji Constitution were important for the case at the Tokyo Trial, since they set the necessary legal foundation for the prosecution to advance the *next* line of analysis that, while undoubtedly concentrated in the emperor, the power of government was not acted upon by the emperor alone but exercised through the medium of the institutions of government.

The prosecution focused in particular on documenting the establishment, organization, and functions of a wide range of executive, legislative, and advisory organs, i.e. the Cabinet, the Privy Council, the Imperial Diet, ministries of state, and military high-command organs, as well as numerous subordinate boards, councils, bureaus, sections, and so on, of these various government organs. The prosecution also enumerated the offices, aides, and advisory organs that came within the Imperial House (or the "Imperial Household"). The state of Manchukuo (1932–45) was briefly touched upon, too, whose key government positions were held by the Japanese technocrats and military personnel throughout the war. The main goal of the prosecution in detailing these various political and military institutions in the Government of the Empire of Japan was to show that the individuals serving in them were subject to the principle of accountability by the law of Japan, by reason of being assigned a role in the emperor's exercise of his power.

### 3.1.2　The Formal Structure of Governmental Institutions

That said, it was not easy for the prosecution to present a picture of the organization of the Japanese government in a manner that would be readily accessible for the Tokyo Tribunal. The Meiji Constitution posed one problem. A quick survey of this document must have revealed to the prosecution that the Meiji Constitution was not designed to detail the structure of the Japanese

---

[8] PX68, introduced at T503.

government. Its main consideration was rather to establish the principle of imperial sovereignty so as to consolidate the state power, and additionally to offer provisions regarding the rights and duties of imperial subjects. Needless to say, such a document presented problems in relation to the complete absence of Emperor Hirohito from the proceedings, whether as witness or defendant.

The prosecution indicated its full appreciation of the particular political import of the Meiji Constitution in its historical context. There was a "dual purpose" in this document, so the prosecution pointed out, one being meeting the "popular clamor for representative institution," and the other, "perpetuating and fortifying the centralized and autocratic governmental structure which its framers, the Meiji leaders believed necessary for the continued existence and development of Japan in the modern world."[9] By this, the prosecution was referring to the volatile political situations in Japan in the 1880s, when the young government in the wake of the imperial restoration (known as the "Meiji Restoration," 1868), the civil war (known as the "Boshin War," 1867–9), and a series of armed rebellions in the 1870s (the worst instance of which being the Satsuma Rebellion, 1877), faced further challenges in controlling the so-called Freedom and People's Rights Movement led by numerous powerful political dissidents.

Such being the case, a lot of things were left out of the Meiji Constitution while a lot of others were included, for the sake of justifying imperial rule and of allowing a limited degree of popular participation in the national government. The gaps in the Constitution presented difficulties for the prosecution in using this document to explain the de facto structure of authority in Japan during the period relevant to the charges before the tribunal. Apart from 17 articles concerning the sovereignty of the Emperor, 15 on the rights and duties of the imperial subjects, and 33 on the legislative authority of the Japanese Imperial Diet, not much else was stipulated. Not a single article was included in the Constitution concerning the Cabinet, ministries of state, or military high-command organs, even though they had already come to function in the 1880s as indispensable parts of the formal structure of the modern Japanese government.

These were not the only significant gaps. The Imperial Household, the Privy Council, state ministers, and the judiciary were included in the Constitution but not treated in any detail. Because these institutions were instead grounded in numerous imperial ordinances and laws, in order to get a full picture of the formal structure of the Japanese government the prosecution was compelled to explicate the relation of these laws to the Meiji Constitution.

### 3.1.3 Informal Advisory Organs

Beyond these complexities, in presenting its case the prosecution had to explain to the Tokyo Tribunal two additional peculiarities about the manner in which

[9] T638.

the Japanese system of government had been set up. One was the existence of various informal organs that influenced the workings of the formal structure of government. The prosecution referred to them as "extra-constitutional" bodies, or alternatively, "the bodies and offices of administrative power which are 'unseen'."[10] These informal organs came into being over the course of the formation of the modern Japanese government, presumably by custom – or "by force of tradition," as the prosecution put it – to render advice to the emperor in his exercising of the right of sovereignty.[11]

In the absence of written laws, it was no easy task for the prosecution to define clearly the power vested in each of the various informal organs. To deal with this issue, the prosecution pointed out that all of these unseen organs carried outsized prestige on account of the lineage, ranks, titles, or other marks of honor, including membership by birth in the royal family.

The Board of Marshals and Fleet Admirals (*gunsei-fu*, established in 1898) was one such informal advisory organ, and the Supreme War Council (*gunji sangi-in*, established in 1903) was another. Both organs, as the prosecution noted, had as their core members "the Princes of the Royal Blood and the highest army and naval officers." The chiefs of the Army General Staff and the Navy General Staff, the army and navy ministers, and any other generals and admirals who were nominated by the emperor himself, were also formal members of the Supreme War Council, and they rendered advice to the emperor in such capacity.[12] The chief aide-de-camp to the emperor was yet another unseen advisory organ. A full general, who did not hold an office in the high-command organs concurrently, usually served in this position. According to the prosecution, "All military memorials and requests for audiences with the Throne are submitted through him and all Imperial orders for the army and the navy are transmitted by him."[13]

In addition to this already formidably complex array of informal bodies, the informal imperial advisory organ *par excellence* was the *genrō* ("elder statesmen"). The *genrō* refers to a handful of founding fathers of Meiji-era Japan, including Itō Hirobumi, who served as imperial advisors for life. An extra-legal institution both in name and in substance, the *genrō* navigated freely through the formal structure of the government, and exerted tremendous influence over the successive emperors behind the scenes as well. Somewhat contradictorily, however, the *genrō* put to use their extraordinary prestige, charisma, and life experience to make themselves the bedrock of the Japanese constitutional order. The *genrō* as an institution died out when the last of its kind, Prince Saionji Kinmochi (1849–1940), passed away. This transition also underscores the vital

---

[10] T523.
[11] Ibid.
[12] T524, 671–2.
[13] T674.

point that the structures of authority were by no means static in the almost two decades falling under the jurisdiction of the tribunal. In order to accurately portray the actual dynamics of policy formation and decision making authority in regard to specific events charged in the indictment, the prosecution thus had to not only map out the roles of these formal and informal institutions but also the way in which patterns of power, influence, and authority shifted over time.

The prosecution pointed out that, with the fading of the *genrō*, alternative advisory organs rose to fill in the power vacuum. One was the Lord Keeper of the Privy Seal (*naidaijin*), one of the two top officials in the Inner Court of the Imperial Household,[14] which was an imperial advisory organ in its own right. Another was the *jūshin* ("senior statesmen"), which was made up of ex-prime ministers, and which was formally convoked in July 1940.[15] The Lord Keeper absorbed one of the *genrō*'s customary prerogatives of nominating to the emperor the successive prime ministers, in consultation with the *jūshin*. The Lord Keeper and the *jūshin* rendered other types of advice to the emperor as well, in their respective advisory capacities.[16] (The prosecution did not discuss the Lord Keeper's advisory role in any length at the initial stage of the Tokyo Trial, but this matter received much greater attention later on, in connection with the accused Kido Kōichi, who served as the Lord Keeper of the Privy Seal in 1940–5.)

### 3.1.4 Another Informal Advisory Organ: Wartime Liaison Bodies

The second institutional peculiarity that the prosecution had to explain to the tribunal was that, in addition to informal imperial advisory organs as outlined earlier, another category of advisory organs came into being during the period covered by the indictment, prompted by the exigencies of coordinating Japan's

---

[14] The prosecution explained that the Imperial Household Officers comprised the Outer Court (headed by the minister of the Imperial Household) and the Inner Court (the first office of which was headed by the grand chamberlain, acting as the emperor's adjucant; and the second office headed by the Lord Keeper of the Privy Seal). T674–5. For imperial ordinances concerning the organization of the Imperial House, the Ministry of the Imperial Household, and the Office of the Lord Keeper of the Privy Seal, see PX69, PX94, and PX95, introduced at T503–6.

[15] T679.

[16] According to the PX95 (Imperial Ordinance on the Organization of the Lord Keeper of the Privy Seal's Office), it was the responsibility of the Office of the Lord Keeperto "keep custody of the Privy Seal and the Great Seal, and take charge of affairs concerning Imperial Rescripts, Imperial Messages, and other documents of the Inner Court [of the Imperial Household]" (Article 1) as well as regularly assisting the emperor (Article 2). The substance of the Lord Keeper's advisory role was undefined in the imperial ordinance. The meaning of "regularly assist [*jōji hohitsu*]" in Article 2 became a point of controversy during the defense phase. In a 1964 interview, Kido described his advisory role as having been very broad indeed, with "no limits, subsuming all affairs of government and command." Kido, *Kido nikki, Tōkyō saibanki*, 450, 453. For recent scholarship on the Lord Keeper of the Privy Seal, see Chadani, *Shōwa senzenki no kyūchū seiryoku to seiji*.

far flung war efforts. They were what the prosecution referred to as "liaison bodies."[17] The evidence admitted at the Tokyo Trial (which is explored in the next section and in Chapter 4) shows that liaison bodies served as *superstructures* of sorts in relation to the *formal* structure of government. They made policy decisions over and above the cabinet, and their decisions were binding. This function of the liaison bodies was significant for assessing the accountability of the many accused who had served in the cabinet because, as we will see, the majority judgment tended to focus narrowly on the cabinet as a locus of authority.

The liaison bodies did not assume any formal executive authority, and their policy decisions had to be brought back to formal government organs (such as the Cabinet, or the military high-command organs if the decisions pertained to military matters), so that the latter would deliberate, approve, and take executive action, as required by the law, to formalize the policy decisions. If the executive actions pertained to the exercising of the right of sovereignty, they then had to be presented to the emperor for his formal sanction. This last step may be unnecessary, however, in the case of the emperor having personally presided over the meeting of the liaison body at which a policy decision appertaining to the exercising of the right of sovereignty was adopted.[18] Needless to say, establishing beyond a reasonable doubt the responsibility of individual accused persons in specific roles for specific policies, decisions, or events within this institutional maze was no easy task. In Part II we will see how the majority and the other judges dealt with such a challenge, but here we examine further the way in which the prosecution attempted to outline the key role of these liaison bodies in relation to the other mechanisms of policy formulation.

The prosecution explained that the basic idea of liaison bodies was to enable the formal structure of government to negotiate the "areas of divided jurisdiction," "areas of jurisdiction which have not been assigned to any constitution organ whatsoever," and "areas of conflicting and overlapping jurisdiction."[19] These kinds of issues of coordination naturally became particularly acute as the scope of the war effort broadened from 1937 onward. Resolving inter-organ disputes, in turn, enabled the government to act in coordinated manners under unified policies. It was important for the prosecution's case to explain to the Tokyo Tribunal the important function of liaison bodies, since

---

[17] T679.
[18] According to the Japanese official war history series, *Senshi sōsho*, "if a decision was made at the conference in the presence of the Emperor, it goes without saying that it received the sanction of the Emperor on the spot and also that it carried far greater weight from the standpoint of the national policy decisionmaking, and therefore, it was customary to refer to the Conference in the Presence of the Emperor the deliberation of those decisions on important national policies." Bōeichō bōei kensyūjo senshishitsu, ed., *Senshi sōsho: Daihon'ei rikugunbu dai-Tōa sensō kaisen keii*, vol. 1, 435.
[19] T643–4.

many of the accused had taken part in the meetings of these bodies as regular members and made decisions on war policies, *as well as* holding offices in the formal structure of government.

The prosecution's narrative account informed the judges that "liaison bodies" at their inception were not exactly super-government organs that made decisions over and above the Cabinet, but more like "summit meetings" of key cabinet members. To summarize the explanation by the prosecution, it became customary in the 1930s for the prime minister, the foreign minister, the army minister, and the navy minister to hold meetings among themselves, for the purpose of adjusting differences and generating unanimous policies on affairs of the state. Their meetings came to be known as the "Four Minister Conference," or when joined by the finance minister, the "Five Minister Conference."[20] To meet the requirements of wartime decision making, a much more robust liaison body was convened after the outbreak of full-scale hostilities between Japan and China in July 1937. This necessitated the liaison activities to occur beyond the confines of the Cabinet. According to the prosecution, "With the intensification of the situation following the outbreak of the China War in 1937, the need for a device to coordinate the activities of the ministers of state and the high command in their overlapping spheres of authority became readily apparent."

The new liaison body was referred to as the "Liaison Conference" (*renraku kaigi*).[21] It comprised key members of the Cabinet and the Imperial Headquarters (IHQ). The former was represented by the prime minister, the foreign minister, the army minister, the navy minister, the home minister, and a selection of their subordinate officials, such as the chief cabinet secretary, the president of the Planning Board (a top cabinet official under direct control of the prime minister), the director of the Military Affairs Bureau of the Ministry of the Army, and the director of the Naval Affairs Bureau of the Ministry of the Navy (subordinate officials of the army and navy ministers respectively). The IHQ side was represented by the chiefs of the Army General Staff and the Navy General Staff, and the vice army and navy chiefs.[22]

The prosecution maintained that the Liaison Conference met frequently, and on rare occasions was convened in the presence of the emperor as well. In the latter case, the conference was referred to as the "Imperial Conference" (*gozen kaigi*).[23] The prosecution explained that, while there were no constitutional provisions, laws, or ordinances regarding the convening of a meeting with the emperor present, this practice had historical roots "for hundreds of years," and it "continued to function as the organ for reconciling the conflicts

---

[20] T679–80.
[21] The "Liaison Conference" is the abbreviation of the "Liaison Conference between the Imperial Headquarters and the Government."
[22] T680.
[23] *Gozen kaigi* in literal translation would be "Conference in the Presence of the Throne."

arising from the division of authority in various spheres" well into the modern times. The composition of the Imperial Conference could vary, although when it met during 1940 and 1941, participants were the same as those in the Liaison Conference, plus the finance minister and the president of the Privy Council.[24] The prosecution stressed the unique importance of the Imperial Conference by repeating that it was convened "only under the gravest conditions to determine matters of gravest policy," and it "did not meet at regular intervals but only at times of grave national importance."[25] This interpretation provided a basis for arguing that those accused who attended such meetings were participating in the most important policy making instrument in wartime Japan and, hence, could be held accountable for the consequences of decisions made.

According to the prosecution, the general procedure followed by policy formulation in the year leading up to December 7, 1941 was that a subject or a plan to be presented at the Imperial Conference was first deliberated at the Liaison Conference. Subsequently, "Ordinarily, in practice, no formal decision was made at the time of the [imperial] conference, but the consensus of the conference is made [sic] the formal decision of the Cabinet."[26] In other words, the general procedure was for the differences of opinion between the Cabinet and the IHQ to be resolved at the Liaison Conference first, which would then receive the emperor's sanction at the Imperial Conference. The decision would then be returned to the Cabinet for adoption. Explaining further the relationship between the Liaison Conference and the Imperial Conference, the prosecution offered the following remark:

In as much as the personnel of these meetings was, with the exception of the Emperor, practically indentical with the personnel of the Conference before the Throne hereafter discussed, and since liaison conferences always preceded Conferences before the Throne, *the decisions reached in the liaison conference were of the utmost importance in relation to the decision of the mere formal conference.*[27] (emphasis added)

In the statement above it is not clear whether the prosecution presented the function of the Imperial Conference as little more than rubber-stamping what transpired at the Liaison Conference. Given the prosecution's concurrent assertion that the Imperial Conference met "only under the gravest of conditions to determine matters of gravest policy," the apparent ambiguity could also reflect an interpretation that the Liaison Conference was the indispensable preliminary policy formulation step required before decisions were made at the highest level. In this case, the prosecution may have intended to show that *both*

[24] T682.
[25] T681–2.
[26] T683.
[27] T680–1.

those who participated in the Liaison Conference, *and* those who attended the Imperial Conference, could all be held accountable for what transpired at those meetings. We will explore some evidentiary materials relating to this matter in the second and third sections of this chapter in order to elucidate further the exact interpretive position of the prosecution on this important question of accountability.

In addition to the functions of the two bodies just considered, the prosecution also mentioned two further liaison organs that were formed as the Pacific War progressed to its ultimate and disastrous conclusion for Japan. The first was the "Conference for the Supreme Direction of the War" (*saikō sensō shidō kaigi*, created in August 1944), which, however, was "in fact the old liaison conference under a new name."[28] The fact that a new liaison body was formed later in the war suggests that the earlier one – the Liaison Conference – lost its efficacy at some point over the course of the Pacific War. Another liaison body, the Imperial Headquarters Conference (*daihon'ei kaigi*), came into being at the start of April 1945. The prosecution argued that, "when, during the course of the war, the Liaison Conference and the Conference for the Supreme Direction of the War failed to adequately meet the problems involved, the premier began attending meetings of Imperial Headquarters but without participating in strategic or tactical matters."[29] No further information was offered regarding the latter of these two liaison bodies. We will explore evidence relating to these two liaison bodies in the second section of this chapter.

When introducing these liaison bodies to the Tokyo Tribunal, the prosecution limited its task to enumerating them, just enough for the tribunal to acquire basic information about their organization and functions. Meanwhile, the prosecution did provide details of various formal government organs and especially the functions and responsibilities of the Imperial Diet, the Privy Council, and the Cabinet. For now, let us trace the main points that the prosecution brought out relative to these formal organs of the government.

### 3.1.5    *The Role of the Imperial Diet*

The Imperial Diet was a national deliberative assembly whose constitutional responsibility was to serve as the primary imperial advisory organ on legislative matters. The relevant provision thus read, "The Emperor exercises the legislative power *with the consent of the Imperial Diet*" (Article 5 of the Meiji Constitution; emphasis added). The Imperial Diet comprised some 400 members in the House or Peers, and another 466 in the House of Representatives. Men of means and privilege served the former, on account of lineage, peerage,

---

[28] T681.
[29] Ibid.

wealth, or individual nomination by the emperor, while members of various political parties, who were elected by popular votes, served in the latter.[30]

The formal importance of the Imperial Diet appears from the fact that as much as 43.5 percent of the provisions in the Meiji Constitution was devoted to defining its authority. The prosecution's analysis of these provisions, however, showed that the Meiji Constitution was designed as much to empower the national deliberative assembly as to undercut it. The legislative power was vested in the emperor alone to begin with, and the Imperial Diet was required to hold the formal session for mere three months annually. The Privy Council and the Cabinet had the power to exercise legislative authority when the Imperial Diet was not in session, by way of initiating, drawing up, deliberating, and/or issuing imperial ordinances and imperial rescripts. These two organs also had the power to make changes, approve, or disapprove of the laws passed by the Diet, thereby maintaining relative superiority to the latter on legislative matters. To further diminish its authority, the Diet had no power whatsoever to touch on the Imperial Household Law, nor was it allowed to have any direct part in policy decisions concerning war, peace, or treaties. The ability of the Diet to control the government expenditure was limited, too, as certain budgetary matters were kept outside the purview of the Diet.[31]

All in all, the prosecution brought out that the Imperial Diet was a prominent institutional feature in the Imperial government of Japan, but that its legislative authority was limited as well as precarious. In light of its view of the de facto limited power of the Imperial Diet, the prosecution largely omitted that institution from its account of wartime decision making. Such an interpretation, of course, operated to focus attention on the role of the accused.

This is not to say that, from a historical standpoint, the Imperial Diet should be understood as a pacifically minded body. There was no shortage of military hard-liners among some 800-plus lawmakers in Japan the 1930s and the 1940s. They exerted considerable influence over the administration, as they used the Diet sessions as a public platform to shame those political leaders who advocated peace and diplomacy. The cabinet decision in mid-January of 1938 to launch a full-scale war against China – which we will discuss in depth in Chapter 4 – is one example where the hawkish lawmakers – who were supported by the hawkish Japanese public – compelled the administration to stiffen its attitude and hastened it to abandon the Sino-Japanese peace negotiations. Since the accused, on the whole, were not members of the Diet but rather participants in the various formal and informal institutions discussed above, it was natural for the prosecution to minimize attention on the Diet and

---

[30] T556–7. For relevant constitutional provisions and other laws relating to the Imperial Diet, see PX68, PX81, and PX92, introduced at T503–5.

[31] T661–3.

focus instead on the key policy-making bodies where decisions relevant to the charges were made. As indicated in our introductory chapter, the prosecution's task, as that of the tribunal, was to prove the responsibility of specific individuals within the Japanese government, not to indict the Japanese state as a whole or to provide an historical account of its functioning.

### 3.1.6 The Privy Council

The Privy Council is what the prosecution described as "the supreme advisory body to the Emperor."[32] It consisted of the president, the vice president, and twenty-five councilors. All of them were appointed by the emperor to serve in the Privy Council for life. In addition to the core members, those state ministers who comprised the Cabinet served as ex-officio members of the Privy Council, and princes of royal blood could also take formal part. There were, therefore, some 40–50 members who regularly participated in deliberations and voted on the Privy Council's decisions. According to the prosecution, the emperor "sometimes attended as an auditor." The principle of majority vote applied in decision-making, and minority votes, along with their opinions, were recorded.[33]

From the prosecution's perspective, it was important to establish the actual influence of the Privy Council. If it was a largely honorific or passive body, it would be of relatively little importance for the charges against the accused. Indeed, the relevant provision in the Meiji Constitution suggests that the Privy Council's advisory capacity was fundamentally a "passive" one, in that the Privy Council was not to render advice to the emperor at its own initiative, but only when expressly requested by the emperor to do so. The relevant imperial ordinance thus read, "The Privy Councillors shall, in accordance with the provisions for the organization of the Privy Council, deliberate upon important matters of State, when they have been consulted by the Emperor."[34] It still held true, however, that the Privy Council was vested with broad, though delimited, legislative and executive authority.[35] According to the prosecution, the Privy Council as an institution evolved over time, and "in recent decades it has come to resemble a 'Third Chamber' with broad supervisory powers over the executive in both foreign and domestic matters."[36] The characterization of the Privy Council as a "Third Chamber" was used against one accused who played a significant role in the war against China: Baron Hiranuma Kiichirō.

---

[32] T640.
[33] T553, 663.
[34] Article 56 of the Imperial Ordinance Concerning the Organization of the Privy Council, PX 83, introduced at T505.
[35] T551–3.
[36] T640.

## 3.1 The Prosecution's Initial Presentation 113

wealth, or individual nomination by the emperor, while members of various political parties, who were elected by popular votes, served in the latter.[30]

The formal importance of the Imperial Diet appears from the fact that as much as 43.5 percent of the provisions in the Meiji Constitution was devoted to defining its authority. The prosecution's analysis of these provisions, however, showed that the Meiji Constitution was designed as much to empower the national deliberative assembly as to undercut it. The legislative power was vested in the emperor alone to begin with, and the Imperial Diet was required to hold the formal session for mere three months annually. The Privy Council and the Cabinet had the power to exercise legislative authority when the Imperial Diet was not in session, by way of initiating, drawing up, deliberating, and/or issuing imperial ordinances and imperial rescripts. These two organs also had the power to make changes, approve, or disapprove of the laws passed by the Diet, thereby maintaining relative superiority to the latter on legislative matters. To further diminish its authority, the Diet had no power whatsoever to touch on the Imperial Household Law, nor was it allowed to have any direct part in policy decisions concerning war, peace, or treaties. The ability of the Diet to control the government expenditure was limited, too, as certain budgetary matters were kept outside the purview of the Diet.[31]

All in all, the prosecution brought out that the Imperial Diet was a prominent institutional feature in the Imperial government of Japan, but that its legislative authority was limited as well as precarious. In light of its view of the de facto limited power of the Imperial Diet, the prosecution largely omitted that institution from its account of wartime decision making. Such an interpretation, of course, operated to focus attention on the role of the accused.

This is not to say that, from a historical standpoint, the Imperial Diet should be understood as a pacifically minded body. There was no shortage of military hard-liners among some 800-plus lawmakers in Japan the 1930s and the 1940s. They exerted considerable influence over the administration, as they used the Diet sessions as a public platform to shame those political leaders who advocated peace and diplomacy. The cabinet decision in mid-January of 1938 to launch a full-scale war against China – which we will discuss in depth in Chapter 4 – is one example where the hawkish lawmakers – who were supported by the hawkish Japanese public – compelled the administration to stiffen its attitude and hastened it to abandon the Sino-Japanese peace negotiations. Since the accused, on the whole, were not members of the Diet but rather participants in the various formal and informal institutions discussed above, it was natural for the prosecution to minimize attention on the Diet and

---

[30] T556–7. For relevant constitutional provisions and other laws relating to the Imperial Diet, see PX68, PX81, and PX92, introduced at T503–5.
[31] T661–3.

focus instead on the key policy-making bodies where decisions relevant to the charges were made. As indicated in our introductory chapter, the prosecution's task, as that of the tribunal, was to prove the responsibility of specific individuals within the Japanese government, not to indict the Japanese state as a whole or to provide an historical account of its functioning.

### 3.1.6 The Privy Council

The Privy Council is what the prosecution described as "the supreme advisory body to the Emperor."[32] It consisted of the president, the vice president, and twenty-five councilors. All of them were appointed by the emperor to serve in the Privy Council for life. In addition to the core members, those state ministers who comprised the Cabinet served as ex-officio members of the Privy Council, and princes of royal blood could also take formal part. There were, therefore, some 40–50 members who regularly participated in deliberations and voted on the Privy Council's decisions. According to the prosecution, the emperor "sometimes attended as an auditor." The principle of majority vote applied in decision-making, and minority votes, along with their opinions, were recorded.[33]

From the prosecution's perspective, it was important to establish the actual influence of the Privy Council. If it was a largely honorific or passive body, it would be of relatively little importance for the charges against the accused. Indeed, the relevant provision in the Meiji Constitution suggests that the Privy Council's advisory capacity was fundamentally a "passive" one, in that the Privy Council was not to render advice to the emperor at its own initiative, but only when expressly requested by the emperor to do so. The relevant imperial ordinance thus read, "The Privy Councillors shall, in accordance with the provisions for the organization of the Privy Council, deliberate upon important matters of State, when they have been consulted by the Emperor."[34] It still held true, however, that the Privy Council was vested with broad, though delimited, legislative and executive authority.[35] According to the prosecution, the Privy Council as an institution evolved over time, and "in recent decades it has come to resemble a 'Third Chamber' with broad supervisory powers over the executive in both foreign and domestic matters."[36] The characterization of the Privy Council as a "Third Chamber" was used against one accused who played a significant role in the war against China: Baron Hiranuma Kiichirō.

---

[32] T640.
[33] T553, 663.
[34] Article 56 of the Imperial Ordinance Concerning the Organization of the Privy Council, PX 83, introduced at T505.
[35] T551–3.
[36] T640.

3.1 The Prosecution's Initial Presentation 115

He had served as vice-president (1931–6) and president (1936–9, 1945) of the Privy Council.[37]

### 3.1.7 The Crucial Role of the Cabinet

Of the three government organs that came under the prosecution's scrutiny, the cabinet was arguably the most complicated piece to clarify as to its organization, power, and responsibility. It was also of key importance because one of the central theories of liability apparently applied in the majority judgment was that of cabinet responsibility for both crimes against peace and war crimes. Anticipating the discussion of the majority judgment in later chapters, it is thus crucial to clarify the position that the prosecution took on the role and authority of the Cabinet and the way in which they sought to assign responsibility to its members for criminal policies of the Japanese government.

One complication in assessing the role of the cabinet arose from the Meiji Constitution itself, where there was not a single word articulated about the cabinet, regardless of the fact that the cabinet system had been introduced in 1885, and had continued to serve as the chief executive organ of the Japanese government since. The prosecution recognized this oddity as it stated, "It is to be observed that except by inference, the Cabinet is not mentioned in the Constitution."[38]

What the Constitution did recognize was the "ministers of state." State ministers were those who served as chiefs of various ministries with specialized areas of competence, and who concurrently held membership in the Cabinet. The Meiji Constitution somehow failed to mention this latter institutional requirement of state ministers (i.e. to belong to the Cabinet). The Constitution contained a single article about the state ministers, which read as follows:

Article 55. The respective Ministers of State shall give their advice to the Emperor, and be responsible for it.
(2) All Laws, Imperial Ordinance, and Imperial Rescript of whatever kind, that relate to the affairs of the States, require the countersignature of a Minister of State.[39]

---

[37] The defense disputed the adequacy of the prosecution's portrayal of the Privy Council as the "Third Chamber," arguing that "the Prosecution is under a grave misapprehension regarding the true scope of the authority of the Privy Council and have consequently greatly exaggerated and overrated its political importance." (T43862). The recent scholarship on the institutional history of the Privy Council shows that the Privy Council did grow to function as a Third Chamber of sorts in relation to the Imperial Diet in the 1920s, but that its political power waned in the 1930s. It is also pointed out that, while Hiranuma grew to be an influential figure in the policymaking circles, it was not so much because of his formal position in the Privy Council as his personal charisma. For more discussion, see Yui, ed., *Sūmitsuin no kenkyū*.
[38] T530.
[39] PX 68.

116    The Japanese System of Government

The article above gives a concise statement as to what every state minister was empowered to do and what he was to be held responsible for, but it is silent about the power or responsibility of ministers *as members of the Cabinet*. Provisions pertaining to the organization, functions, and responsibility of the Cabinet were available elsewhere, however, in imperial ordinances that were issued at the time of the promulgation of the Constitution and afterwards. It was these that the prosecution introduced to the tribunal.[40]

The Imperial Ordinance Concerning the Cabinet Organization (1889) defined the Cabinet at the initial formation as comprising thirteen state ministers. The number slightly increased over time on account of the creation of new ministries and the appointment of "ministers without portfolio."[41] The procedural rules of the Cabinet were not set out in the imperial ordinance. According to the prosecution, however, the general practice was that "voting on questions is rare[,] and differences of opinion are either compromised in the cabinet meeting or the final decision is left to the Prime Minister and only one decision or opinion is made public."[42] In other words, the Cabinet customarily avoided divisive discourse at its meetings and focused instead on reaching consensus, while it also recognized the power of the chief minister to have the final say. The principle of the prime minister's relative superiority vis-à-vis the entire Cabinet was, in fact, stipulated in the imperial ordinance, as we will see shortly. This fact was highly relevant to those accused, such as Hirota, Hiranuma, Tōjō, and others who had served in this position.

It was also crucial to an understanding of the dynamics of Japan's wartime decision making that unlike the Privy Council, the Cabinet as a permanent government organ was subject to a recurring cycle of dissolution and reconstitution. "As in other countries, Cabinets fell in Japan for a number of reasons," the prosecution explained, and the reasons of the cabinet downfalls included "opposition from the military; opposition from the House of Peers or House of Representatives; opposition from the Privy Council; defeat in the elections; public opinion and the death of the Prime Minister."[43] The cabinet downfall was an important subject of further inquiry in the prosecution's presentation. As we will see shortly, any cabinet's reluctance to accede to demands of the military, for example, could be overcome by bringing about the dissolution of that body.

The Imperial Ordinance Concerning the Cabinet Organization stipulated that the Cabinet assumed a wide range of legislative and executive authority. The specific provisions that the prosecution brought to the tribunal's attention

---

[40] T530. For imperial ordinances concerning the cabinet, see PX 70, PX73, PX96, and PX97, introduced at T503–6.
[41] See PX70, PX73, and PX97.
[42] T545.
[43] Ibid.

included the Cabinet's power to deliberate matters pertaining to drafts of laws, treaties, imperial ordinances relating organization and regulation of government offices, and expenditures outside the annual budget; and inter-ministerial disputes. Furthermore, "any important matters connected with the affairs in charge of various Ministries and having relation to the higher administration shall also be submitted for deliberation by the Cabinet Council."[44] In other words, the Cabinet could deliberate on practically any matter insofar as the Cabinet as a whole or the individual ministers deemed them important.

On the prosecution's account, the primary responsibility of the Cabinet was to render advice to the emperor in its official capacity – in this case as the chief executive organ. An important issue in relating this responsibility to particular Cabinet members arose, however, in regard to the relation of the prime minister to the Cabinet's other members. Thus, instead of charging all the members of the Cabinet with the responsibility of advising the emperor, the imperial ordinance singled out the prime minister as the one to act on behalf of the Cabinet in serving the emperor:

Article 2. The Prime Minister stands at the head of the Ministers of State, *reports affairs of State to the Sovereign,* and in compliance with Imperial instructions, maintains the co-ordination of the various branches of the Administration.
Article 3. The Prime Minister, should an occasion seem sufficiently important to demand such a course, has competence to suspend dispositions made or orders issued by the Administration, *pending Imperial sanction.*[45] (emphasis added)

The first of the two provisions above made it the duty of the prime minister to represent the ministers of state and report the affairs of state to the emperor. In the second, the prime minister was given the power to override the orders issued by his administration when necessary, provided that the emperor sanctioned him to do so. One can deduce from these provisions that, in his advisory capacity to the emperor, the prime minister maintained relative superiority vis-à-vis the rest of the cabinet members, and that he may thus be considered as being *chiefly* responsible for the cabinet's advisory role. But how did this relate to the responsibility of the rest of the members? Were they considered as having any share of responsibility for the cabinet's advising of the emperor?

In its initial presentation, the prosecution took a moment to consider these exact questions. Instead of advancing its own interpretive position, however, the prosecution referred to Itō Hirobumi's *Commentaries on the Constitution of the Empire of Japan* to establish the authoritative opinion of the framer of the Meiji Constitution. Evidently, Itō had given some thoughts on the prime minister's standing in the cabinet, and on the issues of the responsibility of

[44] T533.
[45] PX70.

cabinet members. In the passages relied upon by the prosecution, Itō remarked that the purpose of instituting the prime minister was "to give weight to the functions of the Ministers of State and to impress upon them a higher sense of their responsibility and, on the other, to maintain the unity of the Cabinet and to avoid all complications and variances therein."[46] He therefore recognized the relative importance of the prime minister for the effective workings of the Cabinet. Significantly, Itō also paid heed to Article 55 of the constitution in maintaining that the state ministers should be "severally [sic] held responsible for the matters within their respective competency." It would follow that "there is no joint responsibility among them in regard to such matters" relating to individual ministerial competence. That said, Itō went on to recognize that important matters that might concern all the state ministers could arise, on which the prime minister might like to consult them. In that case, Itō would not hesitate to say that "it would of course be proper for the Cabinet to assume joint responsibility."[47] The extent to which the responsibility of the Cabinet was collective or individual would prove to be a critical issue for the Tokyo Tribunal in reaching judgment.

Based on the foregoing opinion of Itō, the prosecution tentatively drew the following conclusion about the principles of responsibility under the Japanese law, on which the Japanese cabinet may have operated:

> Thus, I submit, it may be said that ITO contemplated individual responsibility for cabinet ministers for matters pertaining to their respective departments, joint responsibility for general matters, and responsibility of the Premier for both types of decisions.[48]

The prosecution also referred to another expert on the Meiji political system, Ozaki Yukio (1859–1954) whose view they regarded as having an important bearing on the present discussion:

> For acts done by the head of a department of state of his own volition and not by virtue of resolutions passed in the Cabinet, the Minister concerned alone is responsible, while for acts done pursuant of resolutions passed in the Cabinet, all the Ministers are conjointly responsible.[49]

It is striking that having cited these authorities, the prosecution made no suggestion as to how their opinions should inform the case they were presenting. It is clear, however, that the prosecution considered them to be sufficiently pertinent to merit the attention of the tribunal, apparently leaving it to the judges to decide how such principles should be applied to the accused.

[46] T531.
[47] T575.
[48] T576.
[49] Ibid.

## 3.1 The Prosecution's Initial Presentation

Having dealt with these major organs of government there was yet another important institutional feature that the prosecution wished to bring to the attention of the tribunal. This concerned the relative autonomy of the army and navy ministers within the Cabinet, and the two ministers' relative superiority to other ministers in accessing the emperor. This feature was also closely related to the issue of the dissolution of Cabinets pointed out earlier.

The prosecution had informed the tribunal at the outset of its presentation that all the ministers of state were "appointed by the Emperor on the advice of the Prime Minister."[50] This remark was later qualified, however, as the prosecution restated that the prime minister did not have the power to name the army or navy ministers. "These two Ministers are nominated by their respective services," the prosecution explained, and "[n]o civilian has ever held the posts." In other words, the army and navy services reserved the right to nominate the army and navy ministers respectively, and to do so from among their own men. This practice evidently had been in place since the start of the Meiji constitutional order, as Itō justified this practice in an 1891 report to Emperor Meiji, explaining that its purpose was "to maintain Imperial prerogatives as well as military prestige and to place the supreme military and naval command beyond parliamentary interference and party politics."[51]

The Imperial Ordinance Concerning the Cabinet Organization, meanwhile, contained the following provision that recognized the army and navy ministers' privileged access to the emperor:

Article 7. Such matters as concern military secrets and military orders and are reported to the Emperor, unless referred to the Cabinet by the Emperor, shall be reported to the Prime Minister by the Minister of War and the Minister of the Navy.[52]

The prosecution pointed out that every minister had the right to access to the emperor, but that because of the provision above, "the right of the war [army] and navy ministers to approach the Throne is greater than that of other ministers and is coequal with that of the Prime Minister."[53] These three ministers were the only ones in the Cabinet who were authorized to gain information on military secrets and orders, and to discuss them with the emperor.

The prosecution maintained that the guaranteeing of a privileged position for the army and navy ministers in the foregoing manners made the Cabinet vulnerable to the influence of the army and navy services, and that it became one of the main causes of the cabinet downfalls. The army and navy ministers

---

[50] T530.
[51] T546. For written laws regarding the requirement to nominate the army and navy ministers from military personnel, see PX93, T506.
[52] T665.
[53] T664.

could make or break the Cabinet "by failing to appoint a war minister or a navy minister," "by compelling the war or navy ministers ... to resign," or "through the use of the right to direct access to the Throne ... to obtain the establishment of policy which is contrary to the opinions of the Premier and the other members of his cabinet."[54]

These institutional features that, in practice, enabled the army and navy ministers to override or ignore the opinion of other Cabinet members obviously had an important bearing not only upon their responsibility but also upon that of the other ministers. Should the Cabinet as a whole be held responsible even when its decisions were de facto subordinated to the approval or disapproval of the military services? Should the prime minister alone be held responsible even though he had no power to choose the army or navy minister? The prosecution did not rely on further opinions by the Japanese legal experts to answer such questions, but they did introduce evidentiary materials that addressed them.

## 3.2   Evidence during the Court Proceedings

In the course of the trial proceedings both the prosecution and the defense presented voluminous oral and documentary evidence that illuminated the workings of the Japanese system of government. In their respective efforts to prove or disprove the charges made against the individual accused, the parties disputed numerous points, especially on interpretive issues of power, duty, and responsibility.

Despite their differences, however, one remarkable and surprising area of consensus emerged during the proceedings: The two parties fundamentally agreed about the essential features of the Japanese government as had been set out by the initial presentation of the prosecution. The points of agreement included four essential aspects of the structure of responsibility among the various formal and informal institutions of governance: (1) the inviolability of the principle of imperial sovereignty; (2) the indispensability of the formal structures of government for exercising the emperor's sovereign power; (3) the indispensability also of the informal advisory organs in the functioning of the formal structures; and (4) the significance of the emergence of liaison bodies during the war years, which formed a superstructure to make policy decisions over and above the formal structure of the government. Needless to say, such agreement should have made it easier for the tribunal to determine the criteria for assessment of the liability of the individual accused. Part II will consider to what extent the judges understood and exploited the significance of an uncontested account of the interconnected functioning of the key governmental institutions and bodies.

---

[54]   T666–7.

## 3.2 Evidence during the Court Proceedings

### 3.2.1 The Military and the Cabinet

Beyond this foundational agreement, the defense also did not contest the prosecution's portrayal of the institutional peculiarities of the Japanese cabinet, including the Cabinet's vulnerability to the military ministers' intransigence. Whether defense counsel for the accused who held such key military roles fully understood the way in which the failure to contest these points could provide a basis for inculpating their clients remains an open question.

What is clear, however, is the significance of the relative autonomy of the army and navy ministers as it came to be documented during the court proceedings. Their autonomy in relation to the civilian members of the Cabinet raises the question afresh as to the adequacy of legal theories that the responsibility for the acts of the Cabinet rested either with the entire membership of the Cabinet, or with the prime minister alone. Indeed, prosecution evidence showed that the institutional history of Japan during the war years was basically a chronicle of the rapid turnover of the Cabinet, which was caused by no small measure the military ministers' refusal to cooperate except where the Cabinet gave in to their demands on war-related policy matters. The impact of the military's grip on the levers of government appears clear enough from the historical narrative of the majority judgment, even though the majority failed to fully analyze its legal significance.

For instance, the prosecution presented entries from *The Kido Diary* showing that there was a rumor in mid-August 1939 of the army's plan yet again to bring down the cabinet that had only been formed a half-year earlier. The army service had been advocating the conclusion of a Germany-Japan military alliance and had been mounting pressure on the cabinet to accelerate the negotiation. Kido, then serving as welfare minister, recorded in his diary that he tried to dissuade Army Minister General Itagaki Seishirō from resigning, by remarking that "if the Army and the Navy are permitted to continue to back one another, and the Emperor should order the formation of a new Cabinet, it is certain that it would be impossible to form one."[55] The Cabinet nonetheless fell in a matter of days, although not because the army minister resigned. It was rather because the German government reneged on its prior commitment to the Anti-Comintern Pact with Japan (signed in 1936), by concluding the German-Soviet Non-Aggression Pact. (The German invasion of Poland began a week later.) Prime Minister Hiranuma Kiichirō, who himself had supported the Germany–Japan military alliance enthusiastically, took responsibility for this foreign-policy blunder, and promptly resigned.

As the prosecution showed, two cabinets rose and fell in rapid succession in the coming year. The second of these two cabinets fell on July 21, 1940,

---

[55] PX2271, T16238–9.

because, in this case, Army Minister General Hata Shunroku resigned. *The Kido Diary* recorded the words of lamentation that ex-premier Hiranuma expressed at that time, which read, "It is a bad example that the Cabinet should fall on account of the War Minister's resignation, and it is regrettable that we have often had such examples."[56]

The army intransigence did not go unchecked, however, when Hata approached Emperor Hirohito in person to recommend the next army minister. This met the displeasure of the Emperor, who considered that Hata's action was "out of order" and that the "procedure was wrong." Emperor Hirohito had just appointed as next Prime Minister Prince Konoe Fumimaro (1891–1945), the scion of the aristocratic clan of Konoe, and formerly prime minister of Japan ("First Konoe Cabinet," 1937–9). By this appointment, Konoe became empowered to nominate the members of the next Cabinet. Kido, by then serving as the Lord Keeper of the Privy Seal, recorded in his diary that he was "impressed with the reasonableness of the emperor's opinion," and advised Hata to coordinate his action with Konoe.[57]

This particular sequence of events confirmed one of the institutional features of the cabinet that the prosecution had brought out at the start of the trial, namely, that the military services had the freedom to give or withhold their men to be represented in the Cabinet. Consequently, the military services were able to retain autonomy vis-à-vis the cabinet and to determine the fate of any government. In these instances cited, the prosecution showed how the army used its power of nomination to bring down the Cabinet repeatedly so as to determine policy, causing grave concern among the top civilian officials about the proper functioning of the government. Emperor Hirohito's displeasure with Hata's procedural violation did not appear to help prevent the army ministers from causing the make or break of the Cabinet.

### 3.2.2 The Military and the Foreign Ministry

The evidence presented by the prosecution confirmed that the military services repeatedly took advantage of their unique position of autonomy in the Cabinet to advance their policies. On this basis, the prosecution was able to demonstrate how this tool became particularly potent during the war years because of the concurrent, broader trend of the military's institutional encroachment within and outside the cabinet organization. Evidence showed that the army was especially adept at developing new institutional platforms for the purpose of advancing the army agenda concerning the Japanese-controlled territories in China. Evidence further showed that the army's aggressive effort

---

[56] PX532, T6251–2.
[57] Ibid., 6266–7.

## 3.2 Evidence during the Court Proceedings

to consolidate its influence within the formal structure of government put the army establishment in direct jurisdictional conflict with the foreign service. It was left to the judges to determine how such conflicts in particular, and the military's role in general, impacted assessments of responsibility. As we will see, how this issue was determined could be crucial in conclusions about the responsibility of accused such as Hirota, who happened to be foreign minister during the Nanjing Massacre.

The rivalry between the army and foreign services had been implied in the prosecution's initial presentation, but it was never fully elucidated. The prosecution during the trial proceedings, however, addressed the jurisdictional battles between the army and the Ministry of Foreign Affairs more fully, arguably because this particular institutional problem touched many of the individual accused. The defense presented much evidence on the same, too, whose substance generally agreed with the prosecution's case, and which shed further light on the conflict between the two services during the war years. Let us examine the area where evidence by the two parties intersected.

The majority of accused had been former high-ranking members of the Ministry of Foreign Affairs, the Ministry of the Army, or the Kwantung Army (the Japanese army garrisoned in the leased territory of Kwantung in southern Manchuria, chiefly responsible for the invasion of Manchuria in 1931 and the establishment of Manchukuo in 1932).[58] Oral evidence by accused Tōgō Shigenori (testifying on his own behalf) is noteworthy in this regard, since its content almost entirely focused on chronicling the battles that the foreign service had fought against the army service during the entire period covered by the indictment, in its effort to preserve the integrity of the Ministry of Foreign Affairs as the chief organ entrusted with the foreign affairs of the Japanese government.

According to a comprehensive investigative report concerning the Japanese invasion of Manchuria that the League of Nations generated in 1932, introduced into evidence by the prosecution, rivalry between the army and foreign services had existed well before the start of the Japanese invasion of Manchuria, over the control of the Kwantung leased territory.[59] Tōgō's testimony confirmed this state of affairs, and he further showed that the army's institutional encroachment into the jurisdiction of the Ministry of Foreign Affairs took a new turn with the establishment in 1934 of the Manchurian Affairs Bureau (*tai-Man jimu kyoku*). This bureau was one of many new boards, bureaus, councils, and committees that were created as part of the cabinet organization during

---

[58] The Kwantung Leased Territory was one of the territorial gains that Japan had made as a result of victory in the Russo-Japanese War, 1904–5.
[59] PX59 (Lytton Report), introduced at T502.

the war years, and came under the prime minister's jurisdiction.[60] This board "concerned matters arising in connection with Manchuria and the Kwantung Leased Territory," according to the initial presentation by the prosecution.[61] Further evidence by the defense brought out that this bureau also assumed the power to supervise the commander of the Kwantung Army, who concurrently served as Japanese ambassador to the Government of Manchukuo. There did not seem to be much civilian oversight with the Manchurian Affairs Bureau, since the army minister was the one to hold its directorship.[62] Tōgō testified that "Manchurian affairs had in the main been confided for many years to the Taiman jimukyoku (Manchurian Affairs Board)," and added that he himself had "nothing to do with this body." Tōgō served as chief of the European-Asiatic Bureau of the Ministry of Foreign Affairs in 1934–7. He went on to recount at the Tokyo Trial that the Ministry of Foreign Affairs as a whole had little part in Japan-Manchukuo relations, other than maintaining the Japanese embassy and consulates in the region and carrying out negotiation with the Soviet Union on matters pertaining to Manchukuo. "The post of Ambassador was held ex officio by the Commander-in-Chief of the Kwantung Army," he stated, "and the Foreign Ministry of course did not control him."[63]

General Minami Jirō, an accused and formerly commander of the Kwantung Army (1934–6), confirmed during the defense phase that the army had full control over the Manchurian affairs by way of the Kwantung Army Commander, who "on behalf of Japan exercise[d] absolute control over the military and diplomatic affairs of Manchukuo."[64] Hoshino Naoki, another accused and formerly chief of the General Affairs Board of the Government of Manchukuo (1938–40), recalled during the pretrial interrogation (whose record was presented as prosecution evidence) that there was "a very close connection" between the Kwantung Army and the Government of Manchukuo, and that policies of the Manchurian government "represented pretty much the opinion of the [Kwantung] Army."[65]

It was perhaps inevitable that as the war in China intensified the military's role in this theater of operations would come to overshadow that of the Ministry of Foreign Affairs. The evidence led by the prosecution, on the creation of the new China Affairs Board (*kōa-in*; lit. "the Asia Development Board"),[66] further illustrated this point. The China Affairs Board was established

---

[60] The prosecution explained the main organs to come under control at T536–43. See PX451 for the imperial ordinance concerning the Manchurian Affairs Bureau, T5112.
[61] T540.
[62] PX452-A, T5116.
[63] DX3647, T35748–9.
[64] T19963.
[65] PX454, T5166–7.
[66] PX455 (the imperial ordinance concerning the China Affairs Board), introduced at T5183.

in December 1938, i.e. one year after the fall of the capital of the chiang kai-shek government at Nanjing. The China Affairs Board was theoretically a subordinate organ of the Cabinet, but the composition of the board members made it more like its extension. The prime minister served ex-officio as president of the board, while the finance minister, the foreign minister, the army minister, and navy minister jointly served as vice-presidents.[67] According to Tōgō's testimony, this board took charge of "all political, economic, and cultural and other business of China (excluding Manchuria's)," and "it had its agencies at various places in China, and negotiations with regional regimes in China were its affairs."[68] By "regional regimes in China," Tōgō was referring to several "autonomous" governments that Japan helped establish in north and central China in the 1930s, by way of military conquest, inducement, and collaboration with local political and military strongmen. The new autonomous governments included the Japanese-sponsored Government of the Republic of China with Chiang Kai-shek's rival, Wang Jingwei, as president (1940–5). Tōgō held that the establishment of the China Affairs Board "opened a new and major phase of China relations," since "its purpose was frankly that of removing from the Foreign Ministry control, so far as concerned China matters, the normal functions of foreign office."[69]

Tōgō elaborated on this point by explaining that this Board was created at the time when his ministry's "liberal attitude toward other countries" came under attack by "militarists." Under those circumstances, the role of the Ministry of Foreign Affairs relative to China became limited to "diplomacy in the narrowest sense," that is, to maintain formal diplomatic relations with the wang jingwei government and to fulfill consular business, such as ensuring the protection of Japanese nationals in China.[70] In other words, in this major theater of operations the military supplanted the foreign ministry in substantive matters.

As the Pacific War developed, this trend of military domination of foreign affairs continued. The two cabinet organs discussed in the preceding paragraphs were abolished and integrated into a new ministry in November 1942, known as the Ministry of Greater East Asia (*dai-Tōa shō*). The initiative to establish this new ministry came from the army, specifically from Lieutenant General Suzuki Teiichi, who was then serving as president of the Planning Board (1941–3). The Planning Board, too, had been set up in the wake of the start of all-out war against China in 1937, and was placed under control of

---

[67] T542–3.
[68] DX3647, T35747–8.
[69] Ibid. According to Horiba's *Shina jihen senso shidōshi*, p. 239, the purpose of the China Affairs Board actually was to empower the Five Minister Conference to check the army domination on Japan's dealing with China affairs.
[70] DX3647, T35747–8.

the prime minister to render him advice "so as to avoid conflicts and to adjust all matters amongst the various ministries."[71]

The establishment of the Ministry of Greater East Asia involved the absorption of the Ministry of Overseas Affairs (which had been in charge of the affairs of Japanese colonial territories overseas), and incorporation also of some functions of the Ministry of Foreign Affairs.[72] Tōgō revealed to the Tokyo Tribunal that the plan of the new ministry met with strenuous resistance from the members of the Ministry of Foreign Affairs and himself in particular, since they firmly believed that the new ministry "would in practice remove from the Foreign Ministry the essential part of the diplomacy of Japan, thus impairing the unity of Japanese diplomacy, and would injure the pride as independent nations of the other countries in Greater East Asia, with the result that it would become impossible for Japan to maintain friendly cooperation with them."[73] Tōgō admitted that he ultimately backed down, however, under the threat of the military forcing a Cabinet change in order to get its way. Shortly after, the then navy minister, Admiral Shimada Shigetarō, advised Tōgō that "a change of cabinet was not desired by the [Imperial] Court," Tōgō tendered his resignation, out of a "desire not to cause annoyance to the Emperor by further complicating the matter."[74] General Tōjō Hideki, who supported Suzuki's proposal in his capacity as prime minister (1941–4) and concurrently army minister (1940–4), promptly filled the position of foreign minister to ensure the continuation of the Cabinet, and turned over the position to Tōgō's successor in a matter of two weeks.[75]

This sequence of events, as brought out by the prosecution and by the defense in the evidentiary phases, brings to light two matters that had been implied but not fully elucidated in the prosecution's initial presentation. First, it showed that the formal structure of the government evolved in various directions to meet new institutional needs, demands, and interests that arose from Japan's military conquest overseas. In this example, one can see that the cabinet organization expanded significantly in the 1930s in a manner that allowed the army to have new institutional platforms for influencing the government policies on

---

[71] T538. See PX71 for the imperial ordinance concerning the Planning Board.

[72] See PX 90 for the imperial ordinance concerning the Greater East Asia Ministry, introduced at T505.

[73] DX3647, T35757.

[74] Ibid., T35760–1. Yamamoto Kumaichi, formerly director of the East Asia Bureau of the Ministry of Foreign Affairs, recalled that the then foreign minister and the rest of staff were "unanimously opposed to the establishment of the new ministry and as a result both the minister, Mr. TOGO, and the Vice-Minister, Mr. NISHI, took responsibility and resigned from their positions." (T18051–2).

[75] Tani Masayuki, a career diplomat and a foreign-ministry official, was formally appointed to serve as foreign minister on September 17, 1942.

3.2 Evidence during the Court Proceedings 127

China, and that the expansion culminated in the creation of the Ministry of Greater East Asia.

Second, the expansion of the army's role in managing the affairs of China was achieved by cutting into the integrity of the Japanese foreign service. It is possible that Tōgō testified in a self-serving manner, since he had much to gain by showing to the tribunal that the power of his ministry incrementally eroded.[76] However, documentary evidence was unambiguous that the Ministry of Foreign Affairs did lose part of its diplomatic prerogatives due to the army's institutional encroachment. That being said, it would be hasty if one were to assume that the army's increased influence in the government explained Japan's pursuit of pro-war policies. The record of the trial shows that civilian leaders of government were at times the ones to advocate extreme pro-war positions while members of military services might recommend peace and diplomacy. One such example will be examined in Chapter 4, in connection with the Imperial Conference on January 11, 1938.

### 3.2.3 The Development of the Liaison Bodies

Let us turn to evidence pertaining to liaison bodies. As was the case with the Cabinet, there was little dispute between the prosecution and the defense as to the basic institutional features of liaison bodies, including their origins, compositions, functions, and purposes. Both sides accepted it as factual that various forms of inter-minister conferences were convened in the 1930s – i.e. the "Four Minister Conference" and the "Five Minister Conference" – whereby the prime minister, the army minister, and the navy minister met as the core members (and joined by the finance minister as needed) with the purpose of resolving inter-ministerial differences and developing unified policies on a wide range of issues.

The prosecution and the defense also agreed that new liaison bodies were activated as the war intensified in the period between 1937 and 1945. They both acknowledged that the Liaison Conference was convened for the first time toward the end of 1937; the Imperial Conference at the start of the following year; the Conference for the Supreme Direction of the War in August 1944; and the Imperial Headquarters Conference in April 1945. These liaison bodies had a common purpose, namely, to facilitate the deliberations on the affairs of state between the members of the Cabinet and those of the Imperial Headquarters, and to enable them to agree on unified national policies. One might again query to what extent the defense was cognizant of the

---

[76] According to the Japanese official war history series, *Senshi sōsho*, Tōgō actually worked in harmony with his army and navy colleagues, at least, in his early days as foreign minister. *Senshi sōsho: Daihon'ei rikugunbu Daitōa sensō kaisen keii*, vol. 5, 174–5, 189–190, 448, 433–5.

potential consequences of failing to challenge the prosecution's presentation of the important role which the liaison bodies played. Was the defense not aware that their failure to offer an alternative account might have serious implications for the potential liability of the accused who participated in the bodies? After all, the prosecution was here building a foundation for arguing that the individual accused who had such roles played a central part in policy formulation.

Because of the potential importance of these liaison bodies for assessing accountability, we may inquire further as to the details of the prosecution's evidence on why it was necessary to convene multiple of liaison bodies during the war years. The prosecution led evidence to show that the Liaison Conference convened for the first time about five months after the outbreak of the Lukouchiao Incident of July 7, 1937, for the purpose of adjusting views between the Cabinet and the Imperial Headquarters and of generating unified policies on the ever-escalating armed conflict in China. The Liaison Conference appeared to have become temporarily inactive after January 1938, but it met increasingly frequently in 1941 to function as the de facto highest policymaking body of the government. The prosecution introduced evidence garnered from wartime Japanese newspaper reports to demonstrate that the Liaison Conference met as many as thirty-five times in the period between January and July 1941.[77] Participation of individual defendants in these frequent meetings during crucial months when preparations for the Pacific War were being made could be highly relevant for the charges of planning or initiating aggressive war, or for the conspiracy count of the indictment.

To support its case, the prosecution could also draw upon evidence from defense witnesses. For example, a former foreign-minister official, Yamamoto Kumaichi, revealed that the Liaison Conference met daily between October 23 and November 2, 1941, and five or six more times between November 6 and 29 the same year, immediately preceding the attack on Pearl Harbor and British and Dutch installations in Southeast Asia. Yamamoto himself attended all of the meetings of the Liaison Conference in his capacity as a subordinate official of Foreign Minister Tōgō in late 1941. He testified that the meetings "continued until all views of the members present were completely agreed, and after that all the members present signed the draft decided upon."[78] This testimony was also potentially highly inculpatory by indicating that the Liaison Conference operated on a consensus basis with formal signature approval by all participants of decisions taken. Based on the frequency of the meetings and the thoroughgoing nature of the deliberation process, the prosecution could claim

---

[77] PX1103, introduced at T10051.
[78] DX3444, T33017–8. Yamamoto served as director of the East Asia Bureau of the Ministry of Foreign Affairs (1940–2) and concurrently director of the America Bureau (1941–2).

that it had demonstrated beyond a reasonable doubt that, by those months on the eve of the Pearl Harbor attack, the Liaison Conference had become an indispensable part of the policymaking process of the Japanese government. It may be appropriate to recall here that in regard to aggressive war charges at Nuremberg, the standard applied by the IMT was not the official, de iure, position but rather focused on de facto participation in the inner policy circle.

The liaison activities between the Cabinet and the Imperial Headquarters by way of the Liaison Conference presumably continued after the start of the Pacific War, but documentation after December 7 is limited in the record of the Tokyo Trial. For purposes of the prosecution, establishing the role of specific institutions and individuals in the planning, preparation, initiation, and waging of aggressive war, as well as participation in the conspiracy to do the same, would have been sufficient. From this perspective, then, it is not surprising that little evidence was introduced on the role of this body after 1941. It is less clear, however, as to why the prosecution omitted to present further evidence concerning two other liaison bodies that had emerged in the last year of the war – the Conference for the Supreme Direction of the War, and the Imperial Headquarters Conference. A few accused had served in these liaison bodies, such as General Koiso Kuniaki (prime minister, 1944–5) and Shigemitsu Mamoru (1943–5).

The defense, for its part, sought to underplay the significance of these latter two liaison bodies. For instance, Tanaka Takeo, a key defense witness and formerly chief cabinet secretary of the Koiso Cabinet, stressed the powerlessness of Prime Minister Koiso, who is said to have met with strenuous resistance from the IHQ members when he attempted to discuss military matters at the Conference for the Supreme Direction of the War. According to Tanaka, Koiso became so exasperated by the IHQ's refusal that he requested Emperor Hirohito to issue an imperial order authorizing the prime minister to attend in person the separate conference of the Imperial Headquarters. This request was granted, and the Imperial Headquarters Conference involving the prime minister's presence was formally convened.[79]

From the standpoint of the prosecution's case, perhaps the most important aspect of Tanaka's testimony indicated that these institutional innovations did not give Koiso a stronger voice in regard to military strategy, as "the authority of the Premier was confined to being informed of the condition of operations and tactics and he was not vested with the authority to set forth his view and to have a share in the discussions in the conference on operations and tactics."[80] According to Tanaka, the only way for Prime Minister Koiso to have had frank and open discussions of war situations with his military colleagues

---

[79] DX3390, T32536–9.
[80] Ibid., T32538–9.

in the IHQ would have been for him to "return to active service and hold the additional portfolio of War Minister." As we will see, it is in regard to such situations that a clear definition of the standard of responsibility is crucial. Was mere participation in such bodies enough to ground liability for possible criminal consequences of decisions made there or was it necessary that a participant could influence the outcome or had personally advocated for or approved decisions made?

The sequence of events leading from the establishment of one liaison body to another during the Koiso Cabinet brings out two institutional features of liaison bodies that the prosecution's initial presentation had implied but never fully explicated. First, while functioning as the highest policymaking bodies, none of the liaison bodies was vested with the authority to deliberate the operational aspects of the war. The members of the Imperial Headquarters kept to themselves that prerogative.[81] Second, the episode above warns us against assuming that military men represented on the Cabinet on the one hand, and the high-command organs on the other, always acted in concert. This point is also significant for the prosecution's theory, adopted by the majority, of a monolithic, overarching conspiracy that embraced all of the accused. In Koiso's case above, the Imperial Headquarters refused to cooperate with the Cabinet, even though one of their own – an army general in this case – was heading it. We will see in Chapter 4 further evidence that division of the army from within was not uncommon, thus warning the judges against assuming the Japanese "army" as constituting a monolithic institution.

### 3.2.4 The Imperial Conference and the Role of the Emperor

The record of the trial proceedings shows that the Imperial Conference was distinct from the rest of the liaison bodies, in that the sheer presence of the emperor gave the decisions at the conference a heightened level of authority and prestige. Moreover, decisions at the Imperial Conference were invariably treated as conclusive and irrevocable, that is, unless the emperor himself reversed the decisions (which could and did occur). A full list of the meetings was not generated during the Tokyo Trial, but it was clear that the Imperial Conference met rarely and only for making decisions on matters of gravity.[82]

---

[81] For the imperial military ordinance concerning the IHQ, see PX80, introduced at T504. The IHQ sometimes convened its own conference in the presence of the emperor. This "imperial conference," as one might call it, should not be confused with the "Imperial Conference," viz. the Liaison Conference held in the presence of the emperor. For more information, see Yamada, *Shōwa tennōno gunji shisō to senryaku*.

[82] It is known from the existing historical literature that the Imperial Conference was convened fifteen times in total, in the period between 1938 and 1945. For more information about the Imperial Conference, see Yamada, *Shōwa tennō no gunji shisō to senryaku*, 106–8.

## 3.2 Evidence during the Court Proceedings 131

Establishing participation in this body would thus be important for the prosecution in building its case against individual accused.

The prosecution presented in evidence voluminous oral and documentary evidence that documented the proceedings and decisions of the Imperial Conference, and so did the defense. From the standpoint of defining responsibility for crimes charged, the questions to be asked when reviewing this evidence is: what was the essential function of the Imperial Conference? Was it merely rubber-stamping of the decisions that had been previously made at the Liaison Conference, or were the outcomes of its sessions the de facto ultimate policy decision? In regard to the decisions on launching the Pacific War in December 1941, such questions were crucial to the charges of planning and initiating aggressive war.

The prosecution's initial presentation was ambiguous and set forth conflicting interpretations. To what extent, then, did the prosecution succeed in resolving this ambiguity through the further evidence introduced during the court proceedings?

What emerges from examination of the trial record is striking in its clarity and significance. Evidence presented by *both* the prosecution and the defense indicated the Imperial Conference was far from a "rubber-stamp," and that neither Emperor Hirohito nor his advisors believed it to be so. Instead, the evidence demonstrated that the Imperial Conference was a dynamic policy-making organ where Emperor Hirohito participated in the meetings in order to give his sanction on matters of utmost importance *in a manner appropriate to each given occasion*. This conclusion has obvious relevance for the liability of those accused who participated in the Conference and also underscores the central role of Emperor Hirohito himself. The question of how his authoritative presence at these meetings, given his absence in the defendants' dock, would impact decisions about the liability of other accused was thus framed for the judges by such testimony. Part II will examine how different judges used or ignored such evidence in reaching their legal conclusions.

The evidence showed that while Hirohito adopted reticence as a preferred mode of participation in the initial meetings, he later replaced it with an express, interventionist mode, so that he could lead and command the meetings. A prosecution's exhibit, titled "Records Concerning the Imperial Conferences" (a document provided by the Ministry of Imperial Household), sheds light on the circumstances that led Hirohito to initially choose the mode of reticence. This document showed that on January 10, 1938 the Emperor received a petition from the government for the Liaison Conference to be convened in his presence. This request set off a debate within the inner circle of imperial advisors as to how the Emperor should conduct himself at such a meeting. The ones who injected themselves in the internal debates at this instance were Admiral Prince Fushimi (1875–1946), a member of the royal family, who at the time served as chief of the Navy General Staff; Prince Saionji Kinmochi, the last *genrō*; Baron Harada Kumao, the personal secretary of Saionji; Baron Yuasa Kurahei, the Lord Keeper of the Privy Seal; and Prince Konoe Fumimaro, then serving as prime minister:

Prior to this [the meeting of the Imperial Conference], His Imperial Highness Prince Chief of the Naval General Staff made an offer that it was desirable that his Majesty also ask a few questions or the like, because, according to his experience hitherto at the Imperial Conferences, there was no one who dared to speak and no word by His Majesty, so that the Conference was extremely difficult to conduct. However, as Prince SAIONJI was long since so prudent about His Majesty's speech, Lord Keeper of the Privy Seal told Baron HARADA ... to hear the opinion of the elder statesman once, and added that he, the Lord Keeper, was of the opinion that His Majesty's speech might be admissible unless it was included in a final decision. [Harada subsequently returned Saionji's reply] that the elder statesman was also of the same opinion as Lord Keeper of the Privy Seal, that is, he meant that *he didn't want to fix responsibility upon His Majesty* and that he regarded other questions admissible.[83] (emphasis added)

It is significant that although the four imperial advisors were favorably inclined to Emperor Hirohito taking some proactive part in the deliberation process of the Imperial Conference, they were also reluctant for the Emperor to be seen as personally accountable for decisions made at the meeting.

The four advisors did not have to dwell on this conundrum for long, however, as Prime Minister Konoe later approached the Lord Keeper with a suggestion. Konoe's basic idea was that "there would be no need of His Majesty's speech, since he [Konoe] was going to bring a plan, whose most part was already decided, and only it would be formally decided before the Throne."[84] In other words, what the prime minister wanted from the Imperial Conference was the Emperor's sheer presence, which would give the Liaison Conference's decision the weight of imperial sanction. The Imperial Conference was duly convened the following day, where "the Emperor made not a single remark," as the record of the meeting indicated.[85] What this explanation leaves unresolved is under what circumstances the plan "was already decided."

The precedent set at the first meeting of the Imperial Conference was generally adhered to at subsequent meetings. However, there was at least one occasion when Emperor Hirohito used one of his advisors to pose questions in his behalf, and also articulated his own sentiments of displeasure about the substance of the meeting in a brief yet pointed manner. (See Chapter 4 for more detail.) More significantly, further evidence showed that Emperor Hirohito broke with the mode of reticence on the last days of the Pacific War, and instead

[83] PX3264, T29838–9.
[84] Ibid., T29839.
[85] Ibid., T29841.

## 3.2 Evidence during the Court Proceedings

injected himself in the meetings of the Imperial Conference to issue expressly his command. Kido Kōichi's testimony in the courtroom and segments from *The Kido Diary* (which were presented by the defense) help shed light on this transformation in the dynamics of the Imperial Conference.

In the excerpted diary entries and court testimony below, Kido is seen serving as the Lord Keeper of the Privy Seal, being daily in contact in the first half of August 1945 with Emperor Hirohito on the one hand, and with a full range of imperial advisors on the other hand, including the prime minister, other cabinet members, the president of the Privy Council, the *jūshin* (ex-premiers), the emperor's chief aid-de-camp, and members of the royal family. The trial record shows that Kido did not attend the meetings of liaison bodies himself, but that he was always kept informed of their contents when having separate meetings with the prime minister or when Emperor Hirohito received him in audience.

From Kido's courtroom testimony and *The Kido Diary*, one can learn that a highly volatile situation prevailed among members of various imperial advisory organs in the last week of the war, between August 9 and 14, 1945. The pressing question was whether or not to accept the Potsdam Declaration in the wake of the atomic bombings of Hiroshima and Nagasaki and the Soviet entry in the war against Japan. To generate a unified policy on the matter, the Conference for the Supreme Direction of the War convened in the morning of August 9. The decision it adopted was to accept the Potsdam Declaration, but with four conditions attached: "(1) Preservation of the Imperial House; (2) Withdrawal of the Japanese troops on Japan's own initiative; (3) Those responsible for the war be dealt with by the Japanese Government; (4) No guarantee occupation be carried out."[86]

Neither Emperor Hirohito nor his key advisor, Kido, supported the decision of the Conference for the Supreme Direction of the War, because they feared that the Allied Powers would construe the Japanese demands of these four conditions as refusal to surrender. It was against this backdrop that, just before the midnight on the same day, the Imperial Conference convened to deliberate the decision reached by the Liaison Conference. The relevant segment in *The Kido Diary* describes the gist of the meeting:

The Imperial Conference was held in the presence of His Majesty in the room attached to his library from 11:50 P.M. August 9, to 2:20 A.M. August 10, when it was decided to accept the Potsdam Declaration on the sole condition of reaffirmation of the Emperor's sovereignty and the Imperial House, the draft plan prepared by the Foreign Minister, *thanks to His Majesty's decision.*[87] (emphasis added)

---

[86] DX3340, T31175.
[87] Ibid., T31177.

Although *The Kido Diary* does not contain the details of the deliberation, it is apparent that, after spending more than two hours on deliberation, Emperor Hirohito rejected the decision already reached by the Liaison Conference, and delivered instead his own. He directed his government to accept the Potsdam Declaration on one condition only, viz. on the condition that the emperor's sovereign power and the imperial court would be preserved.[88]

The Japanese peace offer with one condition attached was duly transmitted to the US government on August 10, and the Allied reply was returned to the Japanese government in the morning of August 12. As already seen in Chapter 1, the Allied reply made no reference to protecting the emperor or the imperial court, but it simply stated that the authority of the emperor and the Japanese government "shall be subject to the Supreme Commander for the Allied Powers," and that, "The ultimate form of government of Japan shall, in accordance with the Potsdam Declaration, be established by the freely expressed will of the Japanese people."[89] According to Kido's testimony, this reply led to considerable dissension among key military and civilian officials, particularly because of resistance to the consequences of entrusting the future form of the Japanese government to the freely expressed will of the Japanese people. They feared that it would mean the dismantling of the imperial institution, a prospect they were not prepared to accept. The opposition from opponents was too strong for the premier to convene another meeting of the Conference for the Supreme Direction of the War.[90]

What ultimately broke this deadlock was the direct intervention of the Emperor. According to Kido, this state of affairs led Lord Keeper Kido and Prime Minister Suzuki Kantarō to petition Emperor Hirohito jointly that he "not only convoke a joint Imperial conference of the cabinet ministers and the component members of the Supreme Council for Direction of War, but to *command* the termination of the war and drafting of an Imperial Rescript, terminating the war"[91] (emphasis added). Kido gave the following summary in his testimony as to what ensued:

As the result, His Majesty convoked a joint Imperial conference of the cabinet ministers and the component members of the Supreme Council for Direction of War for 10:30 a.m. As it was, however, the joint Imperial conference got under way in the presence of the Emperor in the room attached to His Majesty's library at about 11:00 a.m. *when it was finally decided to terminate the Pacific War.*[92] (emphasis added)

---

[88] The Japanese original of Kido's affidavit reads that it was "by the sacred decision [*seidan*], it was decided to accept the Potsdam Declaration with the sole condition of the recognition of the sovereign power of the Emperor of the Imperial Court [*kōshitsu tennō tōchi taiken no kakunin nomi o jōken toshi*]." See *Kyokutō kokusai gunji saiban sokkiroki*, vol. 7, 187.
[89] See *Department of State Bulletin*, vol. xiii, nos. 314–40 (July–December 1945), 206.
[90] DX3340, T31184–90.
[91] Ibid., T31190.
[92] Ibid., T31191.

What is notable in this episode is that the liaison body – whose decision regarding conditions of surrender had been overruled by the Emperor just two days ago – ceased to fulfill its liaison function entirely, since the division among its core members became irreconcilable.[93] Emperor Hirohito thus made his decision without the advice from the liaison body, commanding unilaterally that the war be terminated.

The foregoing episodes bring to light two important institutional characteristics of the Imperial Conference that the prosecution either failed to address or portrayed in a conflicting manner at its initial presentation. First, it can be seen that the Imperial Conference was a far more dynamic institution than the prosecution had suggested, where the Emperor made policy decisions in various manners that he and his aides judged to be befitting in the given circumstances. Reticence was surely one mode of participation that Emperor Hirohito adopted under certain circumstances, but he also adopted an activist mode as well, expressly acting on his authority under different circumstances.

Second, the trial record shows that the connection between the Imperial Conference and liaison bodies was far more tenuous than the prosecution had initially suggested. Evidence indicates that it certainly would be erroneous to characterize the Imperial Conference as a venue for mere rubber-stamping. The prosecution had once remarked that, "Inasmuch as the personnel of these meetings was, with the exception of the Emperor, practically identical with the personnel of the Conference before the Throne hereafter discussed, and since liaison conferences always preceded Conferences before the Throne, the decisions reached in the liaison conference were of the utmost importance *in relation to the decision of the mere formal conference*"[94] (emphasis added). It can be fairly said that this statement is not supported by the evidence. Above all, the defense showed that there were actually such occasions when the Imperial Conference rejected the decisions of the Liaison Conference and that, if necessary, it made decisions without the convening of any liaison body.

## 3.3   The Prosecution's Final Argument during the Summation

"We should be unwarranted in assuming that the Japanese governmental structure was like that of other nations, particularly the western nations, and it would be unsafe for us to proceed upon that assumption," so Solis Horwitz remarked, as he took to the lectern to offer the summation by the prosecution on the organization of the wartime Japanese government. He emphasized

---

[93] According to the Japanese official war history series, *Senshi sōsho*, a "Meeting by the Members of the Conference for the Supreme Direction of the War" was convened on August 13. Participants in this meeting were presumably the same as the regular members of the Conference for the Supreme Direction of the War, but this meeting was to be distinguished from the formal meeting of the Conference. *Senshi sōsho: Daihon'ei rikugunbu*, vol. 10, 487, 492–4.

[94] T680–1.

the importance of taking into account the uniqueness of the Japanese system of government by further stating, "The evidence shows that while there were many surface points of similarity, there were many variants of gravest importance from the usual basic governmental structure."[95]

What, then, were the "many variants of gravest importance" that the prosecution wished to highlight afresh in the last days of the court proceedings? As it turned out, the prosecution chose to ignore most of the important points of variation that it had so painstakingly laid out during the trial, and instead presented to the tribunal a far more reductive vision of the Japanese system of government. Why did the prosecution choose this path? In the final section of this chapter, we will trace the prosecution's summation to seek an answer for this question.

The first striking point is that the prosecution appropriately shifted attention from the structures of governmental authority as a whole to the role of the individual accused within those structures. The prosecution began its summation by restating that its case was focused on those Japanese individuals who had been "engaged in the task of formulating Japan's aggressive policy." By this the prosecution did not limit its discussion to those accused that had been party to the formulation of aggressive policy in their official capacities alone. Some, for sure, were officeholders with formal authority to make national policies, but others were not. The prosecution also pointed out that none of the accused had held just one position, but rather multiple positions, both within and outside the government, during the seventeen-year period covered by the indictment. With the foregoing points in mind, the prosecution offered a general theory of policymaking dynamics for the tribunal's consideration, so that it might be used as an analytical tool to sort out the complex picture of interlocking officeholders and non-officeholders that influenced the formulation of national policies.

In the newly offered analytical tool, the prosecution identified three categories of individuals involved in the policymaking process of the government and, hence, to be held accountable for their conduct: "(1) Those defendants who had the ultimate duty or responsibility for policy formulation fixed by the law of Japan; (2) those defendants, who although they do not have the ultimate duty or responsibility, had the duty or responsibility for policy formulation in a subordinate or intermediate capacity fixed by the law of Japan; and (3) those defendants, who although they had no duty or responsibility fixed by the law of Japan, had by their acts and statements placed themselves on the policy-making level and are therefore chargeable with responsibility in fact."[96]

Elaborating the first category, the prosecution stated that it comprised those individuals who had been "members of a policy-making body or were the

---

[95] T40550–1.
[96] T40542–3.

### 3.3 The Prosecution's Final Argument during the Summation          137

policy-making head of some main branch of the Japanese government structure." The prosecution maintained that this category of individuals should be held accountable not only for having exercised the power derived from their respective official positions, but also for having "permit[ted] someone else to exercise that power." On the latter point, the prosecution offered the following explanatory remark:

> If a member of a policy-making body delegates his power to one or more of the other members of the body either expressly or impliedly [sic], he is liable for the decision of those other members in the same way as if he had personally participated in the decision.[97]

In other words, the prosecution held that the first category of individuals should be liable for decisions made by a policymaking body on account of de jure *membership,* as well as for decisions resulting from their own actions while serving as a member in a policymaking body. The prosecution immediately qualified its assertion, however, stating that a person in a policymaking body could be absolved if he or she "expressly repudiates the decisions made by them [other members of the same policymaking body]."[98]

This first category of individuals was to be held accountable also for acts of their subordinates, because, in the opinion of the prosecution, "The law imposes the ultimate responsibility upon him, and unless the decision is reversed by him, he must be deemed to have acquiesced in to have sanctioned it." The same principle should apply to the armed forces, so the prosecution maintained, where a commander may delegate his power to subordinate officers for "purposes of administrative efficiency," while he was still the one with "ultimate responsibility."[99]

Treating the first category of individuals as being primarily responsible did not lead the prosecution to take a lenient view of the subordinate officials, as the prosecution stated: "There is, unfortunately, a tendency in modern political thinking to overlook the importance of this intermediate group in the formulation of government policy and to impose sole liability upon the persons with ultimate responsibility." The prosecution pointed out that those in the intermediate positions were usually the ones to formulate the policies, and that the policies thus formulated were often adopted as the formal government policies. Those individuals who took part in their subordinate or intermediary capacity, in this regard, were "actual participants," and they could be technically understood as "instigators and accomplices."[100]

---

[97] T40544.
[98] T40544–5.
[99] T40545.
[100] T40548.

As for the third category of individuals, the prosecution described them as having no formal authority whatsoever to take part in policy formulation, but as having injected themselves into the policymaking process regardless. They comprised various government officials without policymaking authority and non-state actors, such as "pressure groups and the trusted confidents of the responsible official," who resorted to "threats, unlawful inducements and acts of unlawful force which bring about the adoption of a specific policy." The prosecution considered this category of individuals as being equally responsible for the formulation of aggressive policy, "at least as instigators and accomplices."[101]

Equipped with a three-tier conception of policymaking dynamics as above, the prosecution next revisited the evidence concerning the organization of the wartime Japanese government. The very first thing the prosecution did was to recapitulate the findings relating to the institution of the emperor. "According to the Constitution of Japan in force during the period covered by this proceeding," the prosecution recalled the Meiji Constitution, "all powers of government were vested in the Emperor of Japan." Having made this point, however, the prosecution quickly discounted its importance by stating that "the defendants themselves, in so far as they have touched upon the problem, have asserted that the Emperor acted only upon the advice of his advisers." The prosecution referred, in particular, to the testimony by two accused, Kido and Tōjō, in which it had been asserted that Emperor Hirohito acted on advice only. The prosecution had the following observation to make about their testimony:

Whether this testimony can be considered, unless qualified, as an exact statement of Japanese constitutional law, or whether the matter, instead of involving a question of lack of power, merely represented the actual practice followed of accepting the decisions of the advisers is *immaterial to this proceeding*. The net effect of accepting either view is the same.[102] (emphasis added)

In this statement, the prosecution indicated to the tribunal that it regarded the issue of imperial culpability as requiring no particular scrutiny because it was "immaterial to this proceeding." The prosecution was content simply to accept the logical outcome of the defense contention, i.e. to attribute responsibility for formulating aggressive-war policies to those individuals who "*have elected to place ultimate responsibility upon themselves*"[103] (emphasis added). This of course reflected a political decision to shield the Emperor from inculpatory evidence so as to justify the decision not to include him among the accused. As was seen in the previous section, however, there was ample evidence to

[101] T40549–50.
[102] T40551.
[103] T40552.

## 3.3 The Prosecution's Final Argument during the Summation

show that Emperor Hirohito substantively participated, both directly and indirectly, in the policymaking process and could indeed function as the ultimate authority on war and peace.

Despite intention to the contrary, the segments in Kido's and Tōjō's testimony that the prosecution made direct reference to highlighted the emperor's agency.[104] In the case of Kido, the transcripts of the court proceedings show that Kido went to great lengths to portray Emperor Hirohito as a man of peace, but he appears to have gone too far in doing so. Specifically, Kido, in insisting on Emperor Hirohito's commitment to peace, unwittingly drew the tribunal's attention to the fact that, when appointing Tōjō as next prime minister on October 18, 1941, Emperor Hirohito directed the new premier to return to "carte blanche" the war policy that the Imperial Conference had adopted back on September 6, 1941, and to review afresh all the available options before finalizing the decision to wage war against the United States.[105] Kido might have thought that this type of testimony would help impress the judges with Hirohito as a peacefully inclined sovereign. That was not how Justice Webb looked at it, however, as he immediately interjected, "Where did he get that authority?"[106] In reply, Kido offered the following explanation:

WITNESS [Kido]: In this instance the wishes and desires of His Majesty were conveyed to the Prime Minister, and the cabinet over which this Prime Minister presided subjected the matter to the re-examination. Such a measure was not to be found at all even in the MEIJI era [1868–1912], and in this instance can be considered to be a rather advanced step that was taken.[107]

In this reply, Kido appears to try downplaying the significance of Emperor Hirohito's carte blanche order. Even so, he failed to answer Justice Webb's question as to where from, exactly, the Emperor derived such a sweeping authority with which he struck down the joint policy decision of his government and the IHQ, as already adopted in own presence.

The segment that the prosecution referred to in Tōjō's testimony also tended to show that Emperor Hirohito was the one in charge rather than the one being controlled, regardless of Tōjō's repeated claim that the emperor "had no free choice" and "was not in the position to reject the recommendation and advice of the Cabinet and the High Command."[108] What undercut Tōjō's claim was that, in his zeal to express his reverence for Emperor Hirohito, Tōjō blurted out on one occasion that "there is no Japanese subject who would go against the will of

[104] T40551.
[105] T31380.
[106] Ibid.
[107] Ibid.
[108] T36383.

His Majesty; more particularly, among high officials of the Japanese government or of Japan." This statement caught the immediate attention of Justice Webb, who interjected, "Well, you know the implications from that reply."[109] Webb, reflecting the stated position of the Australian government as well as his own convictions, was acutely attuned to the responsibility of the Emperor and immediately focused on the import of such evidence.

There is anecdotal evidence that, alarmed by the clear implications of Tōjō's remark, the chief prosecutor, Keenan, privately conferred with defense counsel afterwards, and arranged for a "redirect" in the courtroom next day in order to get Tōjō to alter his testimony.[110] If he in fact did consult with defense counsel in this manner it was the grossest breach or prosecutorial ethics and fair trial procedures. The following day, Tōjō backpedaled somewhat, stating, "It may not have been according to his will, but it is a fact that because of my advice and because of the advice given by the High Command the Emperor consented, though reluctantly, to the war."[111] Tōjō seemed to downplay the significance of his statement the day before, but he did not go so far as to deny its validity.

The prosecution during the summation chose to paper over those damning statements by Kido and Tōjō, and tried to move onto addressing the responsibility of imperial advisors alone. Oddly enough, given the breadth of its presentation of evidence on the complex structure of Japanese policy formation, the prosecution singled out the Cabinet, the Supreme Command, the Privy Council, and the Lord Keeper of the Privy Seal as the *sole* policymaking bodies that required the tribunal's immediate attention. Other policymaking bodies that the prosecution had documented during the court proceedings were nowhere to be found in its final presentation. The prosecution also omitted to recall the complex workings of the wartime Japanese government, with the exception of offering the following brief remark concerning the Liaison Conference and the Imperial Conference:

Since both the cabinet and the Supreme Command had overlapping authority with respect to the determination of national policy, to coordinate the functions of the two groups the Liaison Conference and the Imperial Conference were used for that purpose. The Liaison Conference was usually made up of the officials of the cabinet, having the chief responsibility, both ultimate and intermediate, for the formulation of policy, and members of the Supreme Command. The accused maintain that this body had no power

---

[109] T36521.
[110] "Moto kyokutō kokusai gunji saiban bengonin Shiobara Tokisaburō shi kara no chōshusho (dai-1-kai)" [The record of the inteview (no. 1) of Mr. Shiobara Tokisaburō, formerly defense lawyer at the International Military Tribunal for the Far East], in "Inoue Tadao shiryō, kyokutō kokusai gunji saiban kankei chōshusho shiryō" [Sources of Inoue Tadao, Sources of the records of interviews pertaining to the International Military Tribunal for the Far East], Senkō bunko, Yasukuni Shrine.
[111] T36780.

to decide anything, but that its decisions had to be implemented by subsequent action of the cabinet and the Supreme Command. This is of course an immaterial matter, for there is no evidence that any final decision of either the Liaison Conference or the more formal Imperial Conference was not carried out by either the cabinet or the Supreme Command within the respective spheres. The decisions invariably became the national policy of Japan. This was the sole purpose of the conferences.[112]

There are three observations to be made about the remark above. First, the prosecution recognized the Liaison Conference and the Imperial Conference as the highest policymaking *venues*, but showed reluctance to recognize them as the highest policymaking *bodies* to which one could attribute the ultimate duty or responsibility of formulating national policies. The prosecution instead referred back to the cabinet and the military high-command organs, and identified the members of *these organs* as ultimately responsible for the formulation of national policies. Such an assertion had the effect of downplaying the significance of liaison bodies as the super-structure of the Japanese government, where, as voluminous evidentiary materials had shown, policy decisions were made over and above the cabinet and the military high-command organs.

Second, the prosecution failed to mention two additional liaison bodies convened in 1944 and 1945, thereby doubly downplaying the significance of liaison bodies as a critical institutional innovation in the functioning of the Japanese government during the war years. Third and finally, the prosecution retained the phraseology of the "*more formal* Imperial Conference" in the remark above, regardless of evidence that invalidated the notion of the Imperial Conference as a government organ of mere formality. The above remark, in this regard, had the effect of the prosecution advancing an assertion *not supported by the trial record* concerning the power, authority, and prestige assumed and exercised by the Imperial Conference.

## 3.4 Conclusion

Why did the prosecution summarize the Japanese system of government and attribution of responsibility the way it did? It falls within the realm of speculation, but the decision to exempt Emperor Hirohito from the trial might well have put the prosecution in an awkward position, to say the least, and this particular problem might have forced the prosecution to behave in a contradictory manner. On the one hand, the prosecution appeared not to want to address the issues of imperial culpability at all, given the fact that the prosecutorial work had been constrained from the start by a highest-level policy decision of the Allied governments, not to name Hirohito as a major war criminal.

[112] T40562–3.

(See Chapter 1.) On the other hand, the prosecution must have been aware from early on that the intrinsic structure and workings of the modern Japanese government made it impossible not to address the issues of imperial culpability.

The prosecution's initial presentation on the Japanese system of government is a testament to such awareness. The prosecution's predicament likely deepened as further evidence was introduced during the court proceedings, both by the prosecution and the defense, which showed beyond any reasonable doubt that the institution of the emperor was the ultimate decision-making body of the Imperial government of Japan *both in name and in fact*. That evidence also highlighted the crucial role of the Imperial Conference and the subordinate but also crucially important significance of other liaison bodies. To make things complicated for both the prosecution and for the defense, the evidence was incriminatory also for the *person* of the emperor, Hirohito, as well as the institution of the emperor. In a word, the prosecution likely found itself caught in a difficult, if not impossible, position, from the standpoint of justice and accountability, to defend the Allied policy decision not to prosecute Emperor Hirohito. The implications of this predicament, as we shall see in Part II, were made clear enough by Justices Webb and Bernard in particular, while being totally ignored by the majority judgment.

This particular predicament of the prosecution became even more pronounced when additional evidence was introduced during the court proceedings concerning the cases of individual accused. The admitted evidence was inculpatory not only to the accused themselves, but often to Emperor Hirohito, as we shall now see in Chapter 4.

# 4 Individual Roles in the Making of the War, and the Overall Conspiracy

The preceding chapter has explored some segments of the trial record that shed light on how the powers of decision-making were shared among various branches of the wartime Japanese government. This exploration has brought out critical evidentiary materials upon which the judges could later draw to determine the nature of the *power*, *prestige*, and *influence* that individual accused acquired during the period covered by the indictment. The present chapter follows up on the previous one, as it delves into other evidentiary materials before the tribunal concerning how those individuals who had a share of government power *exercised* it. This chapter explores the prosecution and defense evidence on the charges of crimes against peace. Chapter 6 addresses the case on war crimes.

Before we proceed, let us briefly review the thirty-six counts of crimes against peace in the indictment. We have already seen that there were five counts of conspiracy (Counts 1–5) and thirty-one counts on substantive offenses (Counts 6–36). Count 1 constituted the centerpiece of the prosecution's case on crimes against peace, as it alleged the existence of a single, overarching conspiracy that embraced all of the accused, and that subsumed most of the allegations made in Counts 2–36. To recap, it was alleged that all the accused in the period between January 1, 1928 and September 2, 1945 participated in the formulation of a common plan or conspiracy, whose object was to secure Japan's military, naval, economic, and political domination of East Asia and the Pacific and Indian Oceans, and all other countries and the islands therein and bordering thereon, and waged wars of aggression in pursuit of the object (Count 1). The prosecution posited that either a single, overarching conspiracy as alleged in Count 1 could be proven or, alternatively, separate conspiracies with overlapping objects against specified countries as set out in Counts 2–5. The remainder of the counts on crimes against peace charged the accused with planning, preparing, initiating, or waging aggressive war against specified countries. This chapter argues that the prosecution's evidence tended to prove many of these counts on aggressive war but not Count 1. Nonetheless, as Chapter 7 will argue, the prosecution's repeated assertions that a single, overarching

143

conspiracy did exist, and that each accused participated in its formulation and execution, had a major impact on the shape of the Majority Judgment.

The main difficulty for the prosecution seems to have been that it elected to emulate the prosecution's strategy at Nuremberg, in which a single, overarching conspiracy embracing all of the accused had taken center stage. This model turned out to be ill-fitting with the Japanese case (and, in October 1946, the Nuremberg Tribunal rejected it in the judgment). The prosecution at the Tokyo Trial admitted this problem. The chief prosecutor, Keenan, acknowledged it when delivering the opening statement on June 4, 1946:

Although we charge that each of these accused was party to the progressive conspiracy alleged in this indictment and that they were acting in concert to commit the other offense alleged, *the evidence will not show that they were a united band who were in agreement with one another*, as was the case among the German conspirators. On the contrary, there appear to have been *sharp differences of opinion between them and fierce rivalries*, upon matters some of which are, and some of which may not be relevant to these charges.[1] (emphasis added)

Keenan went on to state that there was "another cause of dissention among some of these accused, namely, a *three-cornered struggle for power within Japan between the Army, the Navy and the civilians; each group being further divided by factions and rivalries within itself*"[2] (emphasis added). In other words, the case being made at the Tokyo Trial was that of deeply divided leadership, replete with rivalry, factionalism, and competition. Despite this telling admission, the prosecution developed the theory of the overarching conspiracy and – as will be seen in Chapter 7 – it was accepted by the majority judges even though their judgment implicitly reveals just the division and conflicts alluded to by Keenan.

The prosecution's case as presented in the ensuing months did not betray the chief prosecutor's forewarning, nor did the defense case. In a word, there was ample evidence that the Japanese leadership was deeply fractured, and made policy decisions on grave affairs of the state in a haphazard manner throughout the war years. Although there were repeated attempts within the Japanese government to resolve internal differences and to strengthen its unity, the shifting alliances and divisions were never fully overcome. The exact intents and purposes of Japanese accused in adopting pro-war policies in the 1930s and the early 1940s were a subject of intense contestation between the prosecution and the defense. It is, at any rate, of fundamental importance for assessing the prosecution's evidence and the judges' opinions

---

[1] T471. The chief prosecutor was mistaken to describe the German accused at the Nuremberg Trial as forming a "united band." They, in fact, did not form a united band.
[2] T472.

that the revelations of deep division were undisputed and of sufficient nature to undercut the theory of a single, overarching conspiracy.

To make things further complicated for the prosecution, as noted in Chapter 2, the Nuremberg Tribunal interpreted the meaning of conspiracy so narrowly that it lost any substantive importance: a conspiracy under crimes against peace would be construed as no different from war *planning*. The Nuremberg Tribunal accordingly required that, to convict an accused under the count of conspiracy, there must be proof of the accused's participation in actual high-level conferences whereby a concrete plan of war was adopted. If the conspiracy charge that was the core of the American prosecution team's case against Nazi war criminals fell flat like this, would the Tokyo Prosecution's theory meet a similar fate? Keenan had already stated that the Japanese accused did not even form "a united band," but instead had "sharp differences of opinion between them and fierce rivalries," which was compounded by a "three-cornered struggle for power." In light of the Nuremberg judgment, if the prosecution's evidence supported these initial observations, one might assume that the prosecution's chances of success in convincing the judges with its case on conspiracy were indeed slim. As we will see in Chapter 7, however, the majority of the judges at Tokyo were a different lot than their Nuremberg brethren.

By the time of the Nuremberg judgment, the prosecution at the Tokyo Trial had already completed much of its presentation on crimes against peace. The prosecution chose to hold its ground and continued to assert that it had proved a single, overarching conspiracy as alleged in Count 1. When Keenan took the lectern to deliver the opening statement for the summation, on February 11, 1948, he acknowledged afresh the prosecution's challenges but downplayed their significance. Admitting first that the Japanese leadership was divided, he stated, "One of the difficulties in relation to the analysis of this conspiracy is that it was of such breadth of scope that it is difficult to conceive of its being undertaken by a group of human beings." He went on to assert, however, that every critical event was "coldly calculated, planned for and put into execution." Moreover, "at no time during the entire course of the conspiracy did any of the accused differ from others on the fundamental object of the conspiracy itself." He did not deny that differences existed among the accused, but he brushed aside their importance by contending that the differences "arose from the fact that certain defendants desired at certain times to *hasten* the course of the conspiracy while others *urged waiting* a little longer until the time fixed by the basic plan had arrived"[3] (emphasis added). In other words, he held that the *timing* of the war was the only major point of disagreement among the accused, who otherwise were united by the "fundamental object of the

[3] T38973.

conspiracy itself." We will see that the lack of clarity and consistency in defining the "fundamental object of the conspiracy" played an important role in the Majority Judgment's application of the doctrine in convicting the accused on these charges.

Despite Keenan's attempts to explain away the contradiction revealed by the prosecution's own evidence, his statement was further contradicted by a four-part presentation in which the members of the prosecution took turns to summarize the factual findings to be made from the prosecution's and defense evidence concerning crimes against peace.[4] They, too, downplayed the significance of differences among the accused, insisting that the differences were mainly a matter of *timing*, and that they were resolved over time as the accused gradually secured domination of the government in pursuit of their common object. But the very evidence they referred to showed otherwise. Disagreements were recurrent and often of a fundamental nature, and there was no single overarching and continuing agreement among them as required by the conspiracy doctrine. What the prosecution's four-part summation did show was that three political considerations helped bring together this otherwise fractured lot, namely: fear of leadership disunity from within, fear of political challenges from without, and the individual and collective desire to preserve political power. But these political considerations that sufficed to move the war effort forward despite internal conflicts and repeated shifts in direction did not appear to provide the basis for concluding beyond reasonable doubt the existence of the overarching conspiracy that embraced every single one of the accused.

The prosecution's summation on cases for individual accused that followed the four-part presentation, too, tended to confirm the chronic division of the Japanese leadership from within. This further had the effect of undermining the effort by the prosecution to explain the role of each individual accused as a co-conspirator in a single grand conspiracy.[5]

The defense, for its part, had denied throughout the proceedings that the alleged conspiracies had ever existed. In its detailed summation of general factual matters and of individual cases, the defense reiterated its position, and asserted that each accused made decisions on national policies in pursuit of his official duties and on his firm convictions of Japan's lawful acts in self-defense.[6] What is more, the defense repeated that the Japanese wartime leadership was divided throughout the period covered by the indictment, and

---

[4] The prosecution's summation on crimes against peace was prepared along the line to support a single, overarching conspiracy as alleged in Count 1. No separate summations on Counts 2–5 or Counts 6–36 were given for the stated reason that it would be "wholly repetitious" (T39984).
[5] For the prosecution's summation of individual cases, see T40568–42075.
[6] For the defense summation on general factual matters relating to crimes against peace, see T41515–616, and 42696–43263. For the defense summation on individual cases (including factual matters relating to war crimes), see T43263–48109.

that such division made it impossible for them to act in concert in accordance with the alleged conspiracy. The defense case, in short, was substantially the same as the prosecution's, since both accepted the existence of fundamental divisions at the policy level.

An understanding of the tensions between the charge of a single, overarching conspiracy and the rest of counts of crimes against peace is critical for our analysis of the judges' decisions on conspiracy in Part II. As we will see, the application of conspiracy doctrine proved to be a major point of contention and notwithstanding the inherent problems in the prosecution's case as outlined earlier, the majority accepted the theory of a single, overarching conspiracy *in toto* and upheld Count 1. To confound the matter further, the majority dismissed all of the substantive counts on war planning and preparation (Counts 6–17) and also all the counts on the war initiation (Counts 18–26) for the reason that they duplicated the charges. What this effectively meant, as will be elaborated in Part II, was that the majority chose to make decisions on individual cases by relying almost entirely on the doctrine of criminal conspiracy while declining to make findings on the basis of the principle of individual responsibility for planning, waging, or initiating aggressive war.[7]

In reviewing the evidence that was introduced on conspiracy, the headings of the four-part summation by the prosecution may usefully serve as an analytical guide in the present chapter. The four are: (I) "Obtaining Control of Manchuria"; (II) "The Expansion of Control and Domination from Manchuria to the Rest of China"; (III) "Internal and External Preparation for Aggressive War in Asia and in the Pacific"; and (IV) "Expansion of Aggression to the Rest of East Asia and the Southwest Pacific."[8] The summation by the defense will not be a subject of direct inquiry in this chapter, since the main concern here is to bring to light the internal contradiction of the prosecution's case that subsequently impacted how the eleven justices made their respective findings on the conspiracy counts. However, we will discuss the defense case as incorporated in the prosecution's summation to show how the prosecution interpreted the defense evidence for its own purposes.

## 4.1 "Obtaining Control of Manchuria"[9]

Since the prosecution alleged that the overarching conspiracy began in 1928, it was critical to its case to prove that from that time the conspirators intended to wrest control of Manchuria from China by force. The position of the Japanese

---

[7] Justice Webb's draft judgment alone weighed the evidence against individual accused relating to almost all of the counts on crimes against peace, which he concluded was not proven. See Chapter 8 for more detail.

[8] The prosecution's four-part summation on conspiracy can be found at T39061–976.

[9] For the prosecution's summation on Part I ("Obtaining Control of Manchuria"), see T39061–190.

government and, hence the defense, had a very different interpretation of the so-called Manchurian "Incident."[10] How, then, did the prosecution set out to prove its interpretation of events beyond a reasonable doubt?

The prosecution's summation of the Manchurian phase began by establishing the framework of international law to which Japan was bound. It was essential, in the prosecution's view, to establish that Japan had not only acquired Manchuria by force, itself an illegal act under the Charter, but in doing so it had also violated its international treaty obligations.

### 4.1.1 Japan's Rights and International Obligations

The prosecution began with a summary of Japan's treaty obligations relating to China, including those arising from the Nine-Power Treaty and the Pact of Paris, as well as a brief historical overview of the Japanese acquisition of lease rights associated with the "Kwantung Territory" (*kantō shū*), the southern part of the Liaodong Peninsula in the region of Manchuria in northeastern China.[11] The prosecution's summation drew extensively upon a 148-page comprehensive investigative report on the Japanese invasion of Manchuria, completed by a special Commission of Inquiry of the League of Nations in September 1932 ("Lytton Report").[12] This document provided important support to the prosecution's case and had been introduced as a prosecution exhibit at the start of the Tokyo Trial. Other reports and resolutions adopted by the League of Nations, too, were subsequently introduced in evidence, along with various diplomatic papers and Japanese government records. Utilizing these documents from the League of Nations buttressed the prosecution's claims concerning Japan's disregard for and violation of international law and treaty obligations.

In addition to documentary evidence, the prosecution presented in-court testimony from a number of American, Chinese, and Japanese political leaders and other types of witnesses. They included Henry Pu Yi, the last emperor of Qing China and the head of the Japanese-controlled government of Manchukuo (1932–45), as well as former members of the Japanese Cabinet before or during the invasion of Manchuria, such as Baron Wakatsuki Reijirō (prime minister, 1931), Baron Shidehara Kijūrō (foreign minister, 1929–31), and Baron Admiral Okada Keisuke (navy minister, 1927–9).

The Lytton report played an important role for the prosecution in documenting the prior developments that provided the context in which the military takeover of Manchuria should be understood. This was crucial for alleging

---

[10] For discussion of the Japanese use of the term, "incident [*jihen*]," see Chapter 6 under Section 6.2.2.
[11] T39062–77.
[12] The Lytton Report was admitted as PX57 at T502.

### 4.1 "Obtaining Control of Manchuria"

that the conspiracy had begun long before the "Incident" that precipitated an international crisis. By referring afresh to the Lytton Report during the summation, the prosecution reminded the Tokyo Tribunal of the uniquely troubled territorial situations of southern Manchuria on the eve of the Manchurian Incident of September 18, 1931. The report showed that Japan had come to exercise "practically full sovereign rights" over this strategically important piece of land in Liaodong Peninsula since the transfer of its lease from Imperial Russia after the Russo-Japanese War (1904–5).[13] The lease period was initially 25 years, but it was extended to be 99 years by Japan's imposition of the Twenty-One Demands on the young Republic of China in 1915. The prosecution also reminded the Tribunal that, according to the Lytton Report, Japan had endeavored to counter the rising tide of Chinese nationalism in the 1920s by claiming "a special position in Manchuria, a claim which later grew into Japan's averment that Manchuria was the lifeline of Japan." It was also asserted by the Japanese in those years that "China was menacing Japan's national defense."[14] This, of course, was an essential element of the defense case and had to be disproved by the prosecution.

#### 4.1.2 Assassination of Zhang Tsolin, and Further Unrest from Within and Without

Drawing upon the court testimony by key witnesses, the prosecution further reviewed the precarious situations of Japanese domestic politics on the eve of the Manchurian Incident. The Japanese government under the leadership of the then prime minister, Baron General Tanaka Giichi (1927–9), had sought to strike a balance between the Japanese claim of special interests in Manchuria on the one hand, and the Chinese people's pursuit of national unity on the other. Tanaka was known for adopting the so-called Positive Policy, which aimed at countering China's nationalism and expanding Japan's rights in Manchuria by collaborating with Zhang Tsolin, military governor of Manchuria. However, the prosecution pointed out that the Tanaka Cabinet was confronted with the recalcitrant Kwantung Army (*Kantō gun*) – the Japanese armed forces garrisoned in the Kwantung Territory – which "had become dissatisfied with the TANAKA policy of collaboration and desired to use force to occupy Manchuria, and that a clique of its officers had planned and plotted the murder" of Zhang Tsolin. The assassination did take place in 1928, in the form of railway explosion on the Southern Manchurian Railway.[15]

---

[13] T39070.
[14] T39074–5.
[15] T39079–80.

These conflicting aims in Manchuria from 1928 represented the beginning of the account of the various divisions and internal machinations within Japanese institutions that informed the subsequent course of events in China and beyond. That the Kwantung Army plotted and carried out the assassination was generally known at the time, and the prosecution's summation referenced a testimony by the then navy minister, Okada, that Emperor Hirohito desired "strong disciplinary action with respect to the army" in the wake of the assassination. However, Premier Tanaka could not do anything about it because there was "such strong opposition on the part of the [Army] General Staff and other army officers."[16] Failing to fulfill the Emperor's desire for enforcing military discipline, the Tanaka Cabinet took responsibility and resigned. As discussed in Chapter 3, such events vividly illustrated the continuing pattern of conflict between and within military and governmental institutions.

Building its case to prove the overarching conspiracy alleged in Count 1, the prosecution maintained that the assassination of Zhang was "of the utmost importance" since it was "the first overt action in the conspiracy to carry out the object of the conspiracy" and "the first overt act by the Army to project itself into the formulation of government policy."[17] In other words, this particular episode was presented as the starting point of the execution of the overall conspiracy. The prosecution also asserted that the "conspirators" in those years regarded the duly-established Government of Japan as "one serious obstacle to the easy accomplishment of the conspiracy," and that they "conceived of and proceeded to execute a plan for seizing the government."[18] By the word "conspirators," the prosecution at this stage was referring not to all of the accused but to specific individuals in the Kwantung Army, and their civilian and military sympathizers, who engaged in political agitations, propaganda, and military actions in pursuit of the shared vision of Manchurian takeover.

The prosecution went on to recapitulate how the named and unnamed "conspirators" worked together to gain control of the Japanese government, while also continuing their activities overseas with their pursuit of establishing control over Manchuria. The prosecution also showed how the alleged conspirators were prepared to use violent means to achieve these ends, even against their own political officials. Domestic political agitations, for example, culminated in the assassination attempt of Prime Minister Hamaguchi Osachi in November 1930, and a foiled coup attempt in March 1931 (known as the "March Incident" [*sangatsu jiken*]).

The next Cabinet under the leadership of Wakatsuki (April–December 1931) found no peace either, as the prosecution introduced evidence that its so-called

[16] PX175, T1819.
[17] T39081.
[18] T39091.

4.1 "Obtaining Control of Manchuria" 151

Friendly Policy (commonly known as the "Shidehara Diplomacy") seeking to maintain the status quo with China was even less popular among the army. Moreover, the Wakatsuki Cabinet received disturbing information regarding the Kwantung Army's plots and schemes in Manchuria, suggesting that something ominous was about to happen. The prosecution especially brought to the tribunal's attention a segment of court testimony by the former foreign minister, Shidehara, who had testified that, on the eve of the Manchurian invasion, "I received confidential reports and information that the Kwantung Army was engaged in amassing troops and bringing up ammunition and material for some military purpose, and knew from such reports that action of some kind was contemplated by the military clique."[19] This and other pieces of information prompted Shidehara to take up the matter directly with the army minister, General Minami Jirō (an accused), so that the army authorities would take necessary steps to prevent the Kwantung Army from taking any unauthorized actions.

### 4.1.3 The Manchurian Incident, September 18, 1931

It was against this backdrop of tense Sino-Japanese relations, the resort to plots and murderous violence by dissidents within the military, and the volatile domestic political climate from the late 1920s that the prosecution undertook to review the circumstances of the Japanese invasion of Manchuria. The prosecution's main goal was to make a case that this phase (including the 1928 assassination of Zhang Tsolin) constituted the "very beginning of the conspiracy," and that some of the accused were the "original conspirators," whose ultimate object already was to secure Japan's domination of East Asia and the Pacific and Indian Oceans, and all countries and islands therein and bordering thereon, as alleged in Count 1.[20] The prosecution also aimed at showing that the conspirators put pressure on the central government to issue authorization, after-the-fact, of the Kwantung Army's plan of the military takeover of Manchuria, and that they succeeded in doing so shortly after the fall of the Wakatsuki Cabinet. The question for us to ask is, did the evidence support these allegations?

The trial records shows that the prosecution certainly asserted the existence of the conspiracy within the meaning of Count 1, but that the evidence failed to support it.[21] That said, the prosecution did have evidence to show that certain

---

[19] PX156, T1324 and 1333.
[20] This phrase, "original conspirators," appears in the prosecution's summation on the case against Dohihara (T40617), and the phrase, "the very beginning of the conspiracy," is used in the prosecution's summation of the case against Itagaki (T40985).
[21] Some accused such as Ōkawa and Hashimoto had published prophetic writings and speeches in which they envisioned Japan's future military confrontation with the West. Some of these were

individual officers in the Kwantung Army and their sympathizers participated in a common plan to achieve the military takeover of Manchuria (i.e. a conspiracy within the meaning of Count 2), and that they resorted to the use of force in pursuit of their common plan. The evidence also revealed that the following sequence of events had occurred: (1) that the central government failed to take control of the Kwantung Army; (2) that the failure caused the fall of the Wakatsuki Cabinet; and (3) that the ensuing cabinet revised the government policy and came to give full support to the Kwantung Army's scheme of Manchurian takeover. How did the evidence explain this policy shift, if not by the theory of an overall conspiracy as alleged in Count 1? To consider this question we may reconstruct the government responses following the Manchurian invasion in September 1931, as documented in the prosecution's summation.

The Kwantung Army's invasion of Manchuria began on the night of September 18, 1931. A light explosion occurred at around 10 o'clock in the evening, near the train station at Mukden (present-day Shenyang) of the Southern Manchurian Railway in the leased territory. Claiming that the Japanese armed forces came under attack from the Chinese, General Itagaki Seishirō (an accused), then a colonel and a staff officer, acted as a stand-in for the absent commander of the Kwantung Army, and promptly took control of the Special Service Organ – which the prosecution alleged to have functioned as the communication hub of the Kwantung Army – to direct massive mobilization of the troops.[22] Morishima Morito, a prosecution witness and formerly first assistant to the consul general at Mukden, testified that he was immediately summoned to the Kwantung Army headquarters, whereupon Morishima repeatedly advised Itagaki to seek peaceful settlement. However, Itagaki replied that the Army would not tolerate civilian officials' interfering with the "right of military command."[23]

Wakatsuki Reijirō, a prosecution witness and formerly prime minister of Japan at the time of the Kwantung Army invasion, also took the witness stand

---

introduced in evidence by the prosecution as proof of conspiracy, but the Nuremberg Tribunal expressly rejected this type of evidence.

[22] Itagaki testified that the Special Service Organ "had a telegraph – [a] code[d] telegram form and not everybody having this form; and so, if there was any need to send a coded military telegram, it was necessary to call up the Special Service Organ." T30353.

[23] PX245, T3021. Itagaki gave a similar reply to Consul General Hayashi Kyūjirō, when they spoke over the phone in the immediate hours of the invasion. According to Hayashi's contemporaneous telegram addressed to Foreign Minister Shidehara, and dated September 19, 1931, "In view of the fact that there have been several requests from the Chinese side to settle the Incident amicably, I telephoned Staff Officer ITAGAKI that … it would be essential at this juncture to endeavor not to aggrandize the Incident unnecessarily and to arrange to settle the Incident through diplomatic channels. However, the said staff Officer replied that, as it was a matter of concerning the prestige of the State and of the Army, … the Army's policy was that, as the Chinese Army had attacked our troops it had to be dealt with thoroughly." PX2193, T15735–6.

### 4.1 "Obtaining Control of Manchuria" 153

to testify on the initial responses of his government. The Cabinet, he recounted, held an extraordinary meeting on September 19 where Army Minister Minami reported that the "Chinese troops had fired on Japanese troops at Mukden and their fire had been returned." Wakatsuki went on to testify that, "At this time it was the unanimous sense of the Cabinet that these operations in Manchuria must cease immediately." Army Minister Minami is said to have expressed that he was of the same opinion, and "agreed to put this Cabinet policy into effect with the Army at once."[24] The Cabinet decision contemporaneously received the backing from Emperor Hirohito as well. Kido Kōichi (an accused), then serving as chief secretary to the Lord Keeper of the Privy Seal and concurrently as an advisor to the Imperial Household, wrote in *The Kido Diary* that the Emperor "expressed satisfaction and approval to the prime minister and the Minister of War for the governmental policy to strive not to extend further the Manchurian Incident."[25]

Illustrating the prosecution's claim that the army sympathizers of the Kwantung Army intended to achieve their aims regardless of the government's and Emperor's policy, Wakatsuki's further testimony indicated that Army Minister Minami actually had no inclination to implement the Cabinet's decision:

However, day after day expansion continued and I, the Prime Minister, had various conferences with the aforesaid War Minister, General MINAMI. I was shown maps daily on which the aforesaid General MINAMI would show by a line a boundary which the Army in Manchuria would not go beyond and almost daily this boundary line was ignored and further expansion was reported by always with assurances that this was the final move.[26]

Minami's indifference to the cabinet's decision appears to have reflected the general attitude of the army establishment. According to *The Kido Diary*, the army was "indignant" that Emperor Hirohito was persuaded "by his personal attendants" into endorsing the non-expansion policy. Alarmed by the army authorities' resentments, Hirohito's aides decided that "the Emperor had better not say anything further about the Manchurian policy, unless he is necessitated to do so," nor should Prince Saionji – the last surviving *genrō* – travel to Tokyo unless the situation changed, since "the Army harbors antipathy" against him.[27]

These records documenting the initial reactions of cabinet members, Emperor Hirohito, and his immediate circle of advisors are important, since they support the prosecution's key contention concerning the continuing ascendance

---

[24] PX162, T1554, and 1556.
[25] PX179, T1938.
[26] PX162, T1556.
[27] PX179, T1938–9.

of the military, a conclusion which was taken over wholesale by the Majority Judgment. This testimony by key figures also reveals grave concerns and conflicted sentiments that these individuals contemporaneously had expressed as to how best to respond to the unfolding military crisis in Manchuria. It is clear that few leaders in the central government – except perhaps those in the army establishment – approved the Kwantung Army's initiatives, but that there appears to have been a general sense of helplessness in the face of the army hard-liners' determination. As Wakatsuki's testimony indicated, he as prime minister could do little but to look on, while Army Minister Minami reported to him day after day about the breach of the new boundary line in Manchuria with the express promise that "this was the final move." *The Kido Diary* also points to consensus within the imperial court not to take too strong a stance against the army, lest the latter be provoked and cause an attempt to harm the imperial advisors. In this way, the occasional resort to assassinations apparently succeeded in intimidating fearful civilian and imperial officials.

According to the prosecution's summation, it further became known in those early days that the Korea Army (the Japanese armed forces stationed in colonial Korea) sent into Manchuria reinforcement troops, without obtaining prior authorization from the central government. The fact that Lieutenant General Hayashi Senjūrō, commander of the Korea Army, took an independent action was confirmed in the testimony of Lieutenant General Kawabe Torashirō, a defense witness and formerly a member of the Operations Section of the Army General Staff at the time of the Manchurian invasion. He testified that the Army General Staff issued an express order to Hayashi not to meddle with the Manchurian situation, but that Hayashi disobeyed and had his army join the fray on September 21, 1931, claiming that military aid was urgently needed by the Kwantung Army.[28] This reveals a dynamic of conflict within the military establishment itself, setting a pattern that would be repeated throughout the war years.

Under these circumstances, the Cabinet apparently felt it was left with little choice but to accept what the Korea Army asserted, and it approved after-the-fact the defraying of the Korea Army's expenses. According to Wakatsuki's testimony, he promptly informed Emperor Hirohito of this decision. The chief of the Army General Staff – that is, General Prince Kan'in (1865–1945) of the royal family – similarly sought the imperial sanction for the Korea Army's military operation, which the Emperor granted.[29] The accused Minami confirmed the occurrence of this sequence of events: "The Prime Minister immediately reported the affair to the Emperor, the Chief of the General Staff following suit,

---

[28] DX2408, T19412–4.
[29] T1564–5.

and the Imperial Order for the crossing of the border was communicated to the Korean Army [Korea Army] by the Chief of the Army General Staff."[30]

The above sequence of events, as documented by both the prosecution and the defense, is significant as it cast further doubt on the validity of the overall conspiracy charge. Moreover, it shows that the ones having difficulty in controlling the overseas Japanese armed forces were not just the civilian leaders of the government. The army high-command organ, too, had a hard time, as its servicemen in overseas territories openly disregarded if not disobeyed its orders. The question unanswered by the evidence, however, is whether the pattern of "reluctant" after-the-fact acquiescence in the violation of policies and orders provided a convenient means for higher-level officials to avoid taking responsibility for conduct which they in fact condoned or supported.

The record of the trial shows that the disobedience of overseas armed forces was not limited to matters pertaining to military operations. According to testimony by accused Minami, the Wakatsuki Cabinet decided as early as September 21, 1931 not to allow the establishment of any military administration in occupied territory in Manchuria, and expressly prohibited the participation of Japanese persons in the establishment of a new government in the occupied territory. These decisions were transmitted within five days as orders to the Japanese consulates in China and to the Kwantung Army.[31] The evidence showed, however, that the Kwantung Army failed to comply. General Honjō Shigeru (the commander of the Kwantung Army) appointed a staff officer, General Dohihara Kenji (an accused), then a colonel, to serve as mayor of Mukden in the month following the invasion, and subsequently dispatched him to Tianjin to spirit away Pu Yi, so that the latter could be used as a nominal head of the new government being formed by the Kwantung Army in Manchuria.

A telegram in evidence, from Kuwashima Kazue, Consul General at Tianjin, to Foreign Minister Shidehara, dated November 3, 1931, indicates that plotters of the Manchurian invasion were determined to pursue their action to its logical end – namely, to establish a new state in Manchuria – even in open defiance of the central government. Dohihara is said to have broached to the consulate staff at Tianjin that, in the case of the government disapproval, "the Kwantung Army might separate from the government."[32] This statement, recorded contemporaneously in the internal communication of the Japanese diplomatic services, reveals both internal conflicts and the grievous state of military discipline within the officer corps of the Imperial Japanese Army, in which mid-level officers such as Itagaki and Dohihara had no compunction

---

[30] T19783.
[31] DX2435, T19783; and T19878.
[32] PX290, T4368.

in taking action against their own government. This issue of discipline within the army is also relevant, as we shall see in Chapter 6, for responsibility for the war crimes charged against the accused.

### 4.1.4 International and Domestic Repercussions of the Manchurian Incident

The Lytton Report, as referenced by the prosecution, recounted that the League of Nations received an appeal from the Government of the Republic of China requesting that, in accordance with Article 11 of the Covenant of the League of Nations, it "take immediate steps to prevent the further development of a situation endangering the peace of nations."[33] After preliminary deliberations and initial resolutions to address the evolving crisis, the League unanimously adopted, on December 10, 1931, a resolution that called on Japan and China for restraint and withdrawal of troops, and for cooperation of all parties concerned to facilitate an investigation, which would be carried out by a five-member Commission of Inquiry. What came to be known as the "Lytton Commission" (led by Lord Lytton of Great Britain) assumed the responsibility "to study on the spot and to report to the Council on any circumstances, which, affecting international relations, threaten to disturb peace between China and Japan, or the good understanding between them upon which peace depends."[34]

The evidence indicated that the Government of Japan, in reply, agreed to the League's call for restraint and proposal for the establishment of a Commission of Inquiry. The Japanese government nevertheless indicated that its acceptance of the League's resolution was "based on the understanding" that it was "not intended to preclude the Japanese forces from taking such action as might be necessary to provide directly for the protection for the lives and property of the Japanese subjects against the activity of *bandits and lawless elements* rampant in various parts of Manchuria"[35] (emphasis added).

This reply is interesting because it demonstrates a tacit acceptance of the norm against aggressive war. The Japanese reply is phrased so as to preserve the right of legitimate self-defense and to characterize Japanese military action in Manchuria as falling only within its ambit. This right of self-defense as the *sole* justification for the use of force is the basic norm, now enshrined in Article 51

---

[33] PX57, T1693.
[34] Ibid., T1698.
[35] Ibid., T2252. The characterization of the Chinese forces as "bandits" reflects an intention to trigger the right of self-defense by implicitly characterizing the Chinese government as incapable of protection Japanese lives against these "lawless" elements. This is an age-old strategy employed, for example in the French war in Algeria, to deny that an armed conflict under international legal criteria is taking place as opposed to a legitimate security action against criminal groups that have no standing in international law.

of the Charter of the United Nations, that at the time of the Manchurian crisis already informed the League of Nations' Charter and the Kellogg-Briand Pact of 1928. It is important to underscore this point when considering the dissenting opinions, such as that of Justice Pal, that question both the existence of and Japan's acknowledgment of international legal norms in the use of force. Indeed, the entire justification of Japan's conduct in the Manchurian "Incident" was to argue that it was only acting in self-defense and was thus respecting established international norms. It is perhaps also worth recalling that Hitler used exactly the same fraudulent device in justifying the invasion of Poland on September 1, 1939: The German forces staged an attack against themselves so that they could then tell the world that the invasion that precipitated World War II was only an act of self-defense.

The reply of the Japanese government also shows that the Wakatsuki Cabinet sought to display to the international community the unity of his government and its respect for the international normative system when, internally, it struggled to take control of rebels within the Army. The days of the Wakatsuki Cabinet were numbered by then, as the latest foiled coup attempt by the sympathizers of Manchurian takeover (known as the "October Incident" [*jūgatsu jiken*]) shook its confidence in continuing to lead the government. Wakatsuki eventually resigned, on December 12, 1931, taking responsibility for his failure to establish control over the army's actions in Manchuria.[36]

The trial record shows that the imperial court moved to reorient itself in dealing with the ongoing crisis in Manchuria shortly after the fall of the Wakatsuki Cabinet. According to the entry in *The Kido Diary*, dated January 11, 1932, Colonel Itagaki of the Kwantung Army was allowed personal audience with Emperor Hirohito. Itagaki used this occasion to explain "the situation concerning the progress of campaign against *soldier bandit forces* in Manchuria and Mongolia as well as the progress in establishing a new state in Manchuria" (emphasis added). He went on to outline a proposal then under consideration regarding the establishment of a new state, Manchukuo (lit. "the Manchurian State"). The plan included that a new ruler would be installed to head the Manchukuoan state and that the Japanese army would be responsible for the defense of Manchukuo. This latter point again reflects the attempt to characterize the situation as one of lawful self-defense in the face of the supposed inability of the Chinese government to maintain the order and security necessary on the one hand to protect Japanese citizens and property against rampant lawlessness and, on the other hand, to constitute a state. In other words, the use of force was justified as self-defense and the establishment of a puppet state justified by maintaining that the Chinese were unable to provide

[36] T1557.

158    Individual Roles in the Making of War

the requirements of political order and hence Japan was only legitimately filling a vacuum by creating a state where none existed.

Itagaki also proposed that the Japanese "would participate in the management of a new state as high government officials and such Japanese becoming Manchurian officials would be invited to become Manchurian subjects." With regard to this last point, Itagaki added that new rules and regulations may be necessary to facilitate "the naturalization and dual certificate of nationality." Kido recorded in the diary his great surprise to learn the Kwantung Army officer's bold plan. He wrote, "Hearing this from ITAGAKI[,] I was rather astonished to find that there are [sic] a wide difference between my 'head' and that of theirs."[37]

### 4.1.5    The Establishment of Manchukuo

The wide gap with Itagaki that surprised Kido may not have been unbridgeable, however, as the prosecution pointed out that Itagaki's audience with Emperor Hirohito signaled "a marked change in the Japanese government policy, and the Cabinet took for itself the power to regulate the business of Manchuria."[38] According to admissions made during his pretrial interrogations, the next army minister, General Araki Sadao (an accused), initiated new policies by which the Cabinet agreed to support the Kwantung Army's continued military campaigns to take control of four northeastern provinces of China (then under control of Marshal Zhang Xueliang, the son of Zhang Tsolin), and to recognize Manchukuo as a state independent of China.[39]

When taking the witness stand during the court proceedings, Araki explained that his government, "after careful consideration of the matter, decided to follow the views of the Foreign Office, which suggested that the new state was the result of an internal split of an independent nation and that recognition of such state which acquired its legal independence would not in any way infringe international law."[40] The readiness of the Japanese government to accede to the military fait accompli engineered by the army and embrace Manchukuo as a new political reality was further evidenced in a series of cabinet resolutions presented by the prosecution, which set out new economic, political, diplomatic, and administrative details regarding the formal establishment of Manchukuo. The series of events culminated in the signing of the Japan-Manchukuo Protocol, on September 15, 1932.[41] A pattern was in this manner

---

[37] PX2191, T15732.
[38] T39153–4.
[39] PX188, T2217–23; PX229, T2899–900.
[40] DX3161, T28150.
[41] PX440, Japan-Manchukuo Protocol, T5033–5. By this protocol, the Japanese government "recognized that Manchukuo, in accordance with the free will of its inhabitants, has organized

## 4.1 "Obtaining Control of Manchuria" 159

established whereby the Cabinet and the imperial court acceded to new realities created in the field by the Army. This not only allowed the military to drive foreign policy but also provided a convenient mechanism whereby government and court officials and could deny having any responsibility for the military's actions.

The prosecution's evidence also revealed, however, that the about-face in the government policy regarding Manchuria made some officials uneasy. The minutes of the extraordinary meeting of the Privy Council, held in the presence of Emperor Hirohito two days prior to the promulgation of the Japan-Manchukuo Protocol, helps bring out the conflicted sentiments within the Japanese leadership circles. Baron Hiranuma Kiichirō (an accused) in his capacity as vice chairman of the Privy Council and concurrently as chairman of the Judging Committee of the Privy Council, explained to the Council members the purpose and significance of the proposed Japan-Manchukuo Protocol and other existing Japan-Manchukuo bilateral agreements.[42] Thereupon one councilor, Okada Ryōhei, expressed concern that the Protocol might constitute Japan's breach of international obligations. He was especially worried that Japan might be violating the Pact of Paris and the Nine-Power Treaty. In making his point, he suggested that countries such as the United States "might say that it would be all right if MANCHUKUO had become independent by the free will of his own people, but that it was a violation of the said Pact and a disregard of CHINA's sovereignty for JAPAN to assist and proclaim this independence."[43] This disagreement over Japanese policy in Manchuria thus also reflects a fundamental division in Japanese leadership circles over Japan's obligations under international law in the eyes of the international community.

Given the likelihood of such objections from other governments, Councilor Okada suggested that it would be prudent if "sufficient study and preparations would be made beforehand."[44] Discussions ensued on this and various other points raised by the councilors, during which individual members of the cabinet present made assurances that there was no ground for concern. Okada did

---

and established itself as an independent State." The following two clauses were set out in the protocol as the fundamentals of Japan-Manchukuo relations: "1. Manchukuo shall confirm and respect ... all rights and interest possessed by Japan or her subjects within the territory of Manchukuo by virtue of Sino-Japanese treaties, agreements or other arrangements or of Sino-Japanese contracts, private as well as public. 2. Japan and Manchukuo, recognizing that any threat to the territory or to the peace and order of either of the High Contracting Parties constitutes at the same time a threat to the safety and existence of the other, agree to cooperate in the maintenance of their national security; it being understood that such Japanese forces as may be necessary for this purpose shall be stationed in Manchukuo." For a series of resolutions adopted by the Japanese Cabinet concerning Manchukuo, see PX222–5 (T2817–33) and PX233–4 (T2925–36).

[42] PX241, T2972–82.
[43] Ibid., T2983.
[44] Ibid., T2987.

not appear entirely convinced, as he continued to express his misgivings. When the president of the Privy Council wrapped up the discussion and asked to take the vote, however, all of the participants, including Okada, voted in favor of signing the Japan-Manchukuo Protocol.[45] No explanation is recorded in the minutes regarding the unanimity of the decision. However, given the policy reorientation signaled by the imperial court back in January 1932, and given the personal presence of Emperor Hirohito at the extraordinary meeting of the Privy Council that day, it was likely difficult, if not impossible, for Okada or any other skeptics to continue expressing their reservations.[46] The prosecution's evidence thus succeeded in showing the gradual erosion of respect for international norms and international opinion in the face of seizing opportunities for Japanese expansion under the pressures of consensus decision-making.

The prosecution could now establish that members of the Japanese government, in this manner, quickly transitioned from being the critics of the Kwantung Army's unauthorized aggressive actions to being their full supporters. What the prosecution's summation shows is that they did so *not* in pursuit of a common object as alleged in Count 1, but rather in their collective efforts to reestablish control over the army and, eventually, to embrace the gains made by the invasion. We will see that turning a blind eye to the problem of military disobedience while publicly endorsing military gains became the preferred mode of leadership in Japan hereafter. This leadership style, in turn, cut into the ability of the central authorities to take effective control over other episodes of insubordination, or to maintain the unity of the government as Japan's involvement in China continued to deepen and developed eventually into a full-scale war of conquest.[47]

---

[45] Ibid., T2994. A comprehensive record of the Privy Council's meetings has been compiled and published in Japanese. See *Sūmitsuin kaigi gijiroku*, 96 vols. The record of the meeting relative to the Japan-Manchukuo Protocol is included in vol. 71, 115–131. For an analysis of the Privy Council's involvement in foreign-policy decisions, see Katō, "Sūmitsu-in to gaikō: 'Daiseishijun no fu' no genkai."

[46] According to Yamada's *Shōwa tennō no gunji shisō to senryaku*, Emperor Hirohito disapproved of the overseas armies' unauthorized actions, but that he was not opposed to the actual gains made in Manchuria. The Emperor himself confirmed that he was unconcerned in those years about the implications of the Manchurian Incident. He remarked in his 1946 retrospective account of the war that, "since Manchuria was a backwoods [*Manshū wa inaka*], it wasn't a big deal if an incident occurred [*jiken ga okotte mo taishita koto nai*]. I was worried, however, that the occurrence of the incident in Tianjin and Beijing [in 1937] might culminate in the interference of the Anglo-American Powers and our [military] confrontation." Terasaki, *Shōwa tennō dokuhakuroku*, 35.

[47] Two of the plotters of the Manchurian invasion, Colonel Itagaki and Colonel Dohihara, were promoted to the rank of a major general in the wake of the invasion, on August 8, 1932, and on April 11, 1932, respectively. Itagaki and Dohihara were promoted to the rank of a full general, on July 7, 1941, and April 28, 1941, respectively.

## 4.2 "The Expansion of Control and Domination from Manchuria to the Rest of China"

The second of the prosecution's four-part summation covered the Sino-Japanese relations in the period between 1933 and 1945.[48] The main task of the prosecution in this part was twofold. First, the prosecution aimed at showing that the overall conspiracy, whose ultimate object was to secure Japan's domination in the Asia-Pacific region, and which allegedly had been conceived and set in motion by the "original conspirators" since 1928, gained official endorsement of the central government in the form of a policy document, the "Basic Principle of National Policy," adopted on August 7, 1936, by the Five Minister Conference under the leadership of Prime Minister Hirota Kōki (an accused). The prosecution treated this policy document – which we will examine shortly – as an unequivocal statement of the Japanese government's commitment to pursue a conspiracy within the meaning of Count 1.

Second, the prosecution aimed at documenting how the "original conspirators" and those who joined in the second half of the 1930s united in pursuit of the next phase of the conspiracy, that is, to achieve Japan's military, naval, economic, and political domination of China (i.e. within the meaning of Count 3). To that end, the prosecution traced the Japanese-sponsored separatist movements starting in the mid-1930s on the one hand, and the resumption of Sino-Japanese armed conflict since the Lukouchiao Incident on July 7, 1937 on the other. The latter event culminated in the decision of the central government in January 1938 that Japan would continue waging war against China with the goal of destroying the Republic of China. The question for us to ask once again is, did the prosecution's case support these allegations that were premised upon the existence of a single, overarching conspiracy?

### 4.2.1 The Tangku Truce and Beyond

The prosecution first pointed out that the Japanese military conquest of four northeastern provinces in China came to an end with the signing of a truce between China and Japan on May 31, 1933 ("Tangku Truce"[49]). By this truce, the two countries agreed to set up a demilitarized area in northeastern Hebei (or "Hopei") Province, i.e. the area of strategic importance between the Japanese-sponsored state of Manchukuo in the northern perimeter, and the municipalities of Beiping (or "Peiping," present-day Beijing) and Tianjin in the southern perimeter. The prosecution treated the Tangku Truce as a critical

---

[48] For the prosecution's summation of Part II ("The Expansion of Control and Domination from Manchuria to the Rest of China"), see T39191–325.
[49] PX193, T2272–4.

event in its case at the Tokyo Trial, since this was to be understood as the point where "the conspirators had completed the first step in their conspiracy and had secured complete military domination of Manchuria." The prosecution further contended that the demilitarized zone and its adjacent areas in the wake of the Tangku Truce became the next scenes of the conspirators' armed actions and political intrigues, whose object was to cause the "disintegration of China and the destruction of Chinese Nationalist Government, [which is] an essential prerequisite for the successful achievement of the aims of the conspirators."[50]

Factual matters relating to the Japanese military activities following the Tangku Truce were uncontroversial, as the prosecution and the defense generally agreed that the overseas Japanese armed forces continued to take the lead in defining the central government's policies on China. The importance of this acquiescence of the defense in this characterization of the dynamics of political decision-making should be underscored and borne in mind when considering the way in which the various judges' opinions characterized the development of Japanese policy toward the conflict with China. The lack of defense contestation of course made it easier for the prosecution to make its case beyond a reasonable doubt.

The evidence before the tribunal particularly brought out the following facts: (1) that the demilitarized zone was broadened in the wake of the Tangku Truce, as the Kwantung Army and the China Garrison Army[51] made demands in mid-1935 for concluding two additional bilateral agreements with their Chinese counterparts[52]; (2) that these Japanese armies in North China promoted the "autonomous movements" in demilitarized zones thereafter, viz. creating new self-governing bodies that would separate from the Republic of China; (3) that the fresh armed skirmishes in the outskirts of Beiping on July 7, 1937 (known as the "Lukouchiao Incident"), were carried out by the China Garrison Army without the central government's prior authorization; and (4) that the theater of war broadened rapidly in the wake of the Lukouchiao Incident, with the Japanese armed forces taking control of major Chinese cities in North and Central China – including Beiping, Tianjin, Shanghai, and Nanjing – within a half-year. In other words, the consequences of the pattern

---

[50] T39191.

[51] The China Garrison Army was another Japanese army, garrisoned in Tianjin on account of the Boxer Protocol and its supplementary agreement in 1901–2. For the Boxer Protocol and related documents, see PX247, T3312–14; and DX2483–4, T20592–602. The Kwantung Army as of 1934 comprised 3 divisions, 1 armored brigade, 3 independent guard units, and an air unit carrying 70 airplanes. The approximate troop strength was 50,000. The China Garrison Army was a much smaller corps, expanding to only 5,774 troops by June 10, 1936. See *Senshi sōsho: Shina jihen rikugun sakusen*, vol. 1, 30–31, and 72.

[52] The two post-Tangku agreements were the "Ho-Umezu Agreement," concluded on June 10, 1935, and the "Ching-Dohihara Agreement," concluded on June 27, 1935.

previously alluded to of civilian acquiescence and de facto leadership by the forces in the field were making themselves felt as the military's continually expanding actions inevitably led to the achievement of their goal of an outright war of conquest against the Chinese state. What remains to be seen, however, is how the judgment of the Tribunal would assess the responsibility of those high-level government officials who appeared to be so passive in the face of military leadership.

As for the central government's responses to the unfolding political and military situations in China in the post-Tangku period, the prosecution and the defense were again in agreement with respect to important aspects of the case. The two parties agreed: (1) that the central government promptly gave its endorsement to the actions of overseas Japanese armed forces, both before and after the Lukouchiao Incident; (2) that the central government adopted military defeat of the Republic of China as its formal policy in the wake the fall of Nanjing in December 1937; and (3) that the policy to continue waging war against China remained in place until the termination of hostilities on September 2, 1945. The failure of the defense to contest these allegations of the prosecution (except from making repeated assertions that Japan acted in self-defense) is puzzling, in that they provided the legitimate basis for the tribunal to consider them as established facts upon which the judges could make legal findings in regard to the culpability of the accused. Under the international legal framework applied through the IMTFE Charter, all the judges would have to find was that Japanese military action in China did not constitute legitimate self-defense in order for them to conclude that all three of the uncontested actions enumerated above were criminal and provided a basis for conviction for planning, preparing, initiating, or waging aggressive war of those officials who actively participated in any of the three categories. In this regard, such individuals could be held accountable for their individual conduct.

What was not supported by the either side of evidence, meanwhile, was the prosecution's allegation that the "conspirators" adopted pro-war policies because of their commitment to a common plan or conspiracy as alleged in Count 1. The evidence rather indicates that the central government was divided as to how to meet the new crises in China since the Lukouchiao Incident, and that it made a series of conflicting decisions in a stop-gap manner to address the unfolding crises. What is more, the evidence brought to light that the Japanese government continued to grapple with the following three types of political challenge from within, both before and after the Lukouchiao Incident: (1) disobedience and coup attempts by dissidents in military services; (2) the rise of military hard-liners among civilian government leaders; and (3) the need to suppress internal dissent to strengthen the unity of the government.

### 4.2.2 The Hirota Cabinet's "Basic Principle of National Policy," August 7, 1936

With respect to the first of three domestic political problems pointed to above, one can learn from the trial record that the Japanese government was shaken by yet another coup attempt in late February of 1936 (known as the "February 26 Incident" [*ni-ni-roku jiken*]). The seriousness of these military challenges to civilian authority is made clear by the testimony of a prosecution witness, the then prime minister, Admiral Okada Keisuke, who recounted how Tokyo came under siege for three and a half days through the actions of 1,400 diehard imperial loyalists, led by twenty-two young army officers. Several of Emperor Hirohito's trusted senior advisors, all prominent political figures, were shot to death or mortally wounded during the siege.[53] Premier Okada, having "barely escaped death," could no longer serve in his official capacity.[54] The rebels were brought under control in a short while, and the main culprits were sternly punished.[55] However, the unprecedented scale of violence of the February 26 incident put great pressure on the next Cabinet to exercise firm leadership, so that it could restore the power of the government. The formation of the new government, as the evidence showed, had fateful consequences for the development of China policy.

The mandate to form the new Cabinet fell on Hirota Kōki, a career diplomat and formerly foreign minister of two previous Cabinets. The prosecution's evidence showed that as prime minister, Hirota chose to work closely with military ministers to forge a united front and to strengthen the unity of the government in the aftermath of the military insurrection. From the standpoint of the prosecution's case and of the course of events in China, of fundamental importance was Hirota's initiative that resulted in the "Basic Principle of National Policy," referred to above. Hirota tellingly negotiated this policy document first with the army and navy ministers, and it was subsequently adopted at the Five Minister Conference on August 7, 1937.

---

[53] The dead included the Lord Keeper of the Privy Seal and a former prime minister, Viscount Saitō Makoto, and the then finance minister, Viscount Takahashi Korekiyo. Among the wounded were the former Lord Keeper, Count Makino Nobuaki, the grand chamberlain and aid to Emperor Hirohito, and Baron Admiral Suzuki Kantarō. Prime Minister Okada was little hurt, but Navy Captain Matsuo Denzō, who was Okada's secretary and brother-in-law, was killed as the assassins mistook him as Okada himself. PX175, T1831–2.

[54] The rebels occupied the prime minister's residence, the metropolitan police building, the Imperial Diet building, the offices of the Ministries of Home Affairs and the Army, and the Army General Staff building. Ibid., T1831.

[55] The February 26 Incident was brought to an end promptly when Emperor Hirohito, greatly enraged by the murder of his most trusted advisors, denied the rebels any recognition as imperial loyalists, and indicated to the chief aid-de-camp, General Honjō Shigeru, that he himself was prepared to take command of the Imperial Guards Division to lead the punitive expedition against them. Honjō, *Honjō nikki*, 275–6.

This new formulation of national policy carried great weight in the prosecution's case, as its adoption both set the course that would lead to an ever-expanding war and on the prosecution's view elevated the original conspiracy that had been planned and implemented since 1928 to the level of the formal policy of the Japanese government. However, the actual substance of the "Basic Principle of the National Policy" fell far short of stating the object of conspiracy or the plan of war within the meaning of Count 1. It rather articulated the attempt of the Hirota Cabinet to accommodate varying demands and interests of competing stakeholders from within. As shown below, it celebrated a shared vision of the Empire of Japan as the hegemon of East Asia by affirming the legitimacy of Manchukuo, and by sanctioning expansion by diplomatic means and military preparedness ostensibly to counter the menace of Russia (i.e. the erstwhile enemy of the Imperial Japanese Army) on the one hand, and Great Britain and the United States (i.e. two major naval powers in the Pacific region, rivaling the Imperial Japanese Navy) on the other.[56] The entirety of the policy reads as follows:

Basic Principle of National Policy

The basic principle of governing the state is to realize the ideal of the founding of the Empire, which means to solidify, based on righteousness, the national foundation inwardly and prosper outwardly, making the Empire both in name and reality a stabilizing power in East Asia, thus securing peace in East Asia, and contributing to the well-being and happiness of the whole world.

In view of the situation in and out of the Empire, the fundamental national policy to be established by the Empire is to secure the position of the Empire on the East Asia Continent by dint of diplomatic policy and national defense, mutually dependent on each other, as well as to advance and develop the Empire toward the South Seas. The basic principles are as follows:

1. It is the realization of the Imperial way to correct dominating policies of the power and to share mutual happiness according to the real spirit of co-existence and co-prosperity. This should be our consistent guiding principle for our outward developing policy.
2. We should replete our national defense and military preparations, which are necessary to secure peace for the nation, protect its development, and to ensure the position of the Empire, which should be a stabilizing power in East Asia.
3. The fundamental principles of our continental policy are as follows: a sound development and accomplishment of Manchoukuo [sic]; intensification of national defence of Japan and Manchoukuo in order to eradicate the Soviet menace in the north and at the same time to prepare against Britain and America; and realization of a close cooperation among Japan, Manchoukuo and China for our economic development. In carrying out these policies, we should be careful to have friendly relations with other countries.[57]

---

[56] For the history leading to the Hirota Cabinet's adoption of the Basic Principle of National Policy, see *Senshi sōsho: Daihon'ei rikugunbu*, vol. 1, 370–92.
[57] PX216, introduced at T2720, and read in part at T2727–8.

During the summation, the prosecution argued that four core principles could be deduced from the basic principle above, which, in turn, proved the Hirota Cabinet's policy-level commitment to the grand conspiracy within the meaning of Count 1. The four core principles were namely:

(1) the attaining of the object and end of the conspiracy was made the fundamental national policy of Japan; (2) the object of the national policy and the conspiracy was to be attained, if possible, through diplomatic means with military assistance; (3) if diplomacy failed, the object was to be achieved by war – euphemistically called national defense – against all obstacles; and (4) the Japanese nation, its people and its economy were to be prepared for and geared towards war.[58]

When assessed against the actual text of the basic principle, however, it is clear that the prosecution deduced these four principles from its own theory of the single, overarching conspiracy as alleged in Count 1, and not the basic principle itself. We will see that, regardless, the prosecution referred to the Hirota Cabinet's basic principle repeatedly for the remainder of the four-part summation, treating it as the critical evidence in support of the prosecution's case of conspiracy. As we will also see, interpretation of the Basic National Policy Principle played an important role in the deliberations of the judges as reflected in the majority and separate opinions.

### 4.2.3   The Lukouchiao Incident, July 7, 1937

The prosecution's presentation with respect to the latter two of three domestic political problems in the 1930s reflects the dynamics of translation of the foregoing national-policy document into the policy realities of the ongoing conflict in China. Indeed, the prosecution's case provides the basis for assessing what the various ambiguous terms, such as "national defense" of securing "the position of the Empire on the East Asia continent," actually meant. The trial record shows that the fresh outbreak of armed conflict on July 7, 1937, followed by a series of successful military campaigns that culminated in the capture of Nanjing on December 13, 1937, greatly boosted the confidence of the civilian government leaders in the impending defeat of the Republic of China, and in the prospect of Japan's rise as the hegemon of East Asia, both in name and in fact. These situations emboldened these leaders to advocate a far more radical pro-war policy against China than their predecessors had done.

The trial record also shows, however, how shifting and complex the process of policy formulation could be, again calling into question the very theory of an overarching conspiracy that the prosecution was advocating. In apparent

---

[58] T39220.

## 4.2 "The Expansion Domination from Manchuria China"

contradiction to their previous machinations, the newly emergent extreme pro-war stance of civilian leaders now alarmed the senior members of the Army General Staff, who believed that escalating the Sino-Japanese armed conflict at this stage was counterproductive and inadvisable. But it was the turn of the military to accede to the leadership of the civilian government. The Army General Staff ultimately backed down, as it came under tremendous pressure to show due respect to foreign-policy expertise and discernment of the highest executive organ of the government (i.e. the Cabinet), or risk the cabinet downfall and be held responsible for it. Apart from the fact that it was now the civilian leadership that, against the counsel of the military strategists, set the course leading to an ever-expanding war, the Cabinet in the wake of the Lukouchiao Incident boldly cut into the high-command organ's prerogative of making decisions on military matters. This development upended the inherent institutional feature of the Japanese government that accorded the military services relative autonomy and superiority vis-à-vis the Cabinet (as explored in Chapter 3). For now, let us trace the sequence of events, as documented in the prosecution's summation, which led to the dramatic confrontation between the Army General Staff and the cabinet, a confrontation that ultimately determined the course of war with China.

A fresh episode of armed conflict broke out on the night of July 7, 1937, at Lukouchiao in the vicinity of Beiping, over the course of a night maneuver that the China Garrison Army carried out that evening. Horinouchi Kensuke, a defense witness and formerly vice foreign minister at the time of the Lukouchioao Incident, testified that the Cabinet under the leadership of Prime Minister Konoe ("First Konoe Cabinet," June 1937–January 1939) held an extraordinary session on July 9, 1937, whereupon it was decided "to hold fast to the policy to arrest the spread of the disturbance and to seek a prompt, local settlement on the matter."[59] However, the same Cabinet approved on July 11, the proposal from the Army General Staff that two brigades from the Kwantung Army, one division from the Korea Army, and three divisions from Japan be dispatched as reinforcements in the Beiping-Tianjin area.[60]

It is not fully explained in the trial record as to why the Konoe Cabinet adopted these contradictory policies in the window of mere three days, but there are indications that conflicting sentiments existed among the cabinet members as to whether to disapprove or endorse the latest military development in North China from the standpoint of national prestige and gains. The then foreign minister, Hirota, for one, is shown to have vacillated between the two contradictory policies in those days. According to testimony by Horinouchi, Foreign Minister Hirota conferred with three subordinate officials (including

---

[59] DX3260, T29685.
[60] DX2582, T21986.

the witness himself) prior to the July 11, cabinet meeting, whereupon "it was decided that the [army] proposal should be opposed." However, Hirota later returned to inform them that he actually "consented to this decision [on reinforcements] with reservations that the dispatch of troops-should be exclusively for the purpose of protecting the Japanese residents and securing the safety of the North China Stationary Force itself which was comparatively small in strength."[61] Horinouchi offered no satisfactory explanation as to why Hirota changed his position. Instead, he asserted that Foreign Minister Hirota was a pacifist at heart and that he worked very hard to seek pacific solutions to the conflict. Yet we will see shortly that, by the year's end, Hirota emerged as a leading proponent of war against China, and the one who compelled the Army General Staff to withdraw its recommendations for negotiated settlement.[62]

### 4.2.4 The Escalation of the Sino-Japanese Armed Conflict

The Japanese government eventually offered to China a truce on August 5, 1937, that is, shortly after Beiping came under Japanese military control. The Japanese demands at this point focused on firming up the territorial gains made directly from the Lukouchiao Incident.[63] However, the start of another episode of armed conflict in Shanghai on August 13 brought the truce negotiation to naught, and the Konoe Cabinet reverted to escalating the conflict.

A dramatic increase of military reinforcements ensued, and as many as fifteen divisions in total were sent into China in the period between July and October 1937.[64] The Imperial Japanese Navy also began deploying its naval and air power with the goal to disable the Chinese supplies in the coastal areas and inflict damage "on the ports and the cities of the interior," according to a contemporary report made by the League of Nations and introduced into evidence.[65]

---

[61] DX3260, T29687 and 29678.
[62] Ishii Itarō, formerly director of the East Asia Bureau and one of the top three foreign-ministry officials with whom Hirota conferred regarding the policy on the Lukouchiao Incident, related this episode somewhat differently in his postwar memoir. According to Ishii, the Ministry of the Army was internally divided in those days, and those who desired non-expansion of the conflict requested behind the scenes that Foreign Minister Hirota reject the army proposal on reinforcement at the July 11 cabinet meeting. Ishii recalled being greatly angered not only by the irresponsible attitude of the army authorities, but also by the failure of Hirota to stand firmly against the army demand for reinforcement. Ishii, *Gaikōkan no isshō*, 272. Ishi also recorded in his wartime diary his disgust at Hirota's readiness to bend his principles and to please pro-war colleagues in the Cabinet. See Ishii, *Ishii Itarō nikki*, 167–8.
[63] The demands comprised (1) that unfortified zones be established in the Beiping-Tianjin area; (2) that there would be no annexation of territories; and (3) that there would be no demand for indemnities. DX3260, T29692.
[64] DX2488, T20685.
[65] PX58, T3306.

4.2 "The Expansion Domination from Manchuria China" 169

In November 1937, the Imperial Headquarters was established and placed under direct command of Emperor Hirohito, thereby bringing the army and navy high-command organs to a war footing.[66] The Chinese government similarly prepared for an all-out war. According to Lieutenant General Tanaka Shin'ichi, a defense witness and formerly a staff officer of the Army General Staff at the time of the Lukouchiao Incident, he acquired knowledge that "the Chinese had established headquarters on August 15th, made Chiang Kai-Shek Supreme Commander of all the land, sea and air forces[,] and divided the whole country into four war zones ... and that general mobilization was ordered on the same day."[67] In short, Japan and China entered a state of de facto war in a little over one month since the Lukouchiao Incident. The conflict continued to escalate into a full war of conquest for the remainder of the year. The city of Shanghai fell in late November, and Nanjing – the capital of the Republic of China – fell on December 13. The capital cities of Chahar, Hebei, Suiyuan, Shansi, Zhejiang, and Shandong Provinces, too, fell under Japanese military control by the end of the year.[68]

These dramatic military achievements of the Japanese armed forces appear to have boosted the Japanese people's national pride tremendously. Horinouchi testified that the capture of Nanjing, in particular, "had considerably stiffened the general feelings of the Japanese public towards China."[69] It was under those circumstances of aroused popular nationalist sentiments, in late 1937, that the Government of Japan accepted the German offer to mediate the Sino-Japanese peace negotiation. Success of the peace talk was bleak, however, as the record of the trial indicates that the members of the Cabinet had little desire to end the hostilities, unless China relented and granted Japan significant concessions that would essentially destroy its national sovereignty.

### 4.2.5 The Sino-Japanese Peace Negotiation: Division from Within

The peace negotiations began in earnest in early December of 1937, when the German ambassador in Japan, Herbert von Dirksen, inquired as to whether or not Japan was prepared to use as the baseline a peace offer it had made back on August 5 (i.e. the offer of truce following the fall of Beiping). Horinouchi testified that Foreign Minister Hirota, in response, had his subordinate official confer with the army and navy counterparts, and "it was made clear that both the army and the navy had no objection to the peace terms of the

---

[66] For the imperial ordinance on the Imperial Headquarters, see PX80, introduced at T504. The exhibit is dated November 11, 1939, but the correct year of the issuance of this ordinance is 1937.
[67] DX2488, T20700.
[68] PX254, T3430.
[69] DX3260, T29702.

170   Individual Roles in the Making of War

August plan."⁷⁰ That said, Hirota indicated to the German ambassador that the final word of approval was still required from his government. Hirota later relayed to Dirksen a peace offer that was significantly modified from the August 5 version. The original text of the new peace offer was not presented in evidence, but the prosecution and the defense generally agreed that the main points of the new offer contained the following elements:

1. China shall abandon her pro-communist and anti-Japanese policies, and collaborate with both Japan and Japanese domination. When in an anti-communist policy.
2. Demilitarized areas shall be established in necessary regions, and special organs (wide-scale free government system) shall be set up in the said areas.
3. A close economic treaty shall be conducted among the three nations, Japan, Manchukuo, and China.
4. China shall make necessary reparations.⁷¹

It is apparent that, unlike the August 5 offer, the revised Japanese peace offer set out broadly defined terms regarding demilitarized zones, reparations, and China-Japan-Manchukuo relations. These terms most likely reflected the desire of the Japanese cabinet to make as much gain as possible from the latest military achievements on the ground. That being said, these exacting terms that would result in the de facto demise of China as a sovereign nation controlling its own territory and political destiny, became highly controversial when deliberated among the top officials of the central government authorities.

The Army General Staff, for one, was positively opposed to making these demands, apparently aware that the Chinese government would not accede to its own downfall and the dismantling of the Chinese state, and would thus feel compelled to continue the armed struggle against Japanese domination. When the members of the Cabinet and the Imperial Headquarters were summoned to convene the Liaison Conference on December 20, 1937, the vice army chief, Lieutenant General Tada Hayao, expressed serious concern over "the domestic tendency which was likely to become too aggressive," and suggested that "the conditions of truce were so aggressive that they might impair future diplomatic relations between Japan and China."⁷² Yet these words of caution from the vice army chief merely elicited puzzlement from the members of the Cabinet. Kido testified that Prime Minister Konoe, who was unable to comprehend the Army General Staff's intent, asked Kido (then serving as education minister) to have a word with the army side in private to find out what was going on. Explaining

---

⁷⁰ PX3260, T29701.
⁷¹ PX270, T3619–20. See also DX3260, T29702–3.
⁷² PX3265, T29856–7. The chief of the Army General Staff at the time was Prince Kan'in of the royal family.

his own mental state at that time, Kido informed the Tokyo Tribunal that he himself "failed to fully understand ... that the army had made a firm determination to bring about peace at all costs."[73]

These accounts point to a perception gap between the civilian and military members of the government about the significance of military developments since the Lukouchiao Incident. The civilian members of the government apparently regarded the renewed Sino-Japanese armed conflict as offering a welcome opportunity for making substantial gains from China, while the latter feared that an unprincipled pursuit of military conquest was contrary to Japan's national interests. What the army, with its better grasp of military realities, seemingly realized was that Japan was not likely to win a prolonged conflict in China and that the best outcome would be Chinese capitulation to acceptable peace terms. This prognosis of an unlikely all-out military victory proved to be correct. It is ironic that it was the civilian officials who, flushed with success and positive popular sentiment, now advocated for continuing the war until a successful conclusion. This shift in stance as documented by the prosecution as well as by the defense was, of course, critical in establishing for the tribunal the responsibility of the Cabinet for charges related to aggression against China.

### 4.2.6  The Policy Decision at the Imperial Conference, January 11, 1938

In the context of these events, the first of the Imperial Conferences was then convened, on January 11, 1938, whereupon "The Fundamental Policy for the Disposition of the China Incident" was adopted. In the policy document, it was prefaced that the formation of "an axis for peace of the Orient in cooperation with Manchukuo and China" was the core principle of the Empire of Japan, and it went on to set out two possible courses of action that Japan would pursue as a solution to the Sino-Japanese armed conflict. The two options as produced in the trial provided that:

1. If the present Chinese Central Government shall reconsider at this juncture and sincerely ask for reconciliation, we will negotiate with them in accordance with the conditions of the Negotiations for Peace between Japan and China as indicated on the attached sheet ...
2. If the present Chinese Central Government does not ask for reconciliation, the Empire will not wholly depend upon the settlement of the Incident by taking them as her opponent, but will assist the formation of the new Chinese Government, with which to negotiate on adjusting the mutual relationship, and to cooperate to establish the regenerated New China.

---

[73] DX3340, T30836.

172    Individual Roles in the Making of War

> As for the present Chinese Central Government, the Empire *shall be determined to annihilate them*, or take measures to absorb them under the new central government.[74] (emphasis added)

By setting out these two options, the Imperial Conference made it a formal policy that China be given the opportunity to accept the exacting Japanese peace terms or, failing that, be annihilated or, alternatively – and in reality the same – be "absorbed" into a new government to be set up in China with the Japanese assistance, i.e. a Japanese puppet government as in Manchukuo. It is not clear from the record of the Imperial Conference as to how the recommendations of the Army General Staff were reflected in "The Fundamental Policy for the Disposition of the China Incident," if at all. What one can know from other evidence (as discussed below) is that the Army General Staff and the Cabinet remained deeply divided regarding the advisability of the war, and that the division resurfaced when the Liaison Conference met four days later.

The prosecution introduced further evidence documenting the reply from the Chinese government, which reached Foreign Minister Hirota via German Ambassador Dirksen, on January 13, 1938. The reply did not accept or reject the Japanese peace offer, but instead requested further clarification. The Japanese terms were "rather too broad in scope," the Chinese government was said to have maintained, and it therefore desired to be "apprized of the nature and content of the newly submitted conditions in order to make a careful examination and reach a definite decision."[75] Hirota's reaction to the Chinese reply is documented in a telegram dispatched from Dirksen to German Foreign Minister Konstantin von Neurath, dated January 14, 1938 (presented as a prosecution's exhibit). The pertinent part reads as follows:

I have handed over to the Foreign Minister [Hirota] the text of the declaration given by the Chinese Foreign Minister to Ambassador TRAUTMANN [in China].

HIROTA was very angry at the meaningless Chinese declaration, considered it as mere evasion and remarked that the Chinese had all the necessary bases in order to say yes or no. Finally, it was China who was beaten and who must ask for peace, and not Japan, who had to give information continually.[76]

According to the same telegram, Dirksen attempted to talk Hirota into seeing the reasonableness of the Chinese request, pointing out that China had been informed only of four basic principles of the Japanese peace offer. Accordingly, "I advised him, either to stipulate the details of these declarations or to announce agreement that they would be now communicated to the

---

[74] PX3264, T29845. For details of the peace terms, see ibid., T29847–50.
[75] PX486-B, T5984.
[76] PX486-C, T5987.

4.2 "The Expansion Domination from Manchuria China"          173

Chinese as official statements of the Japanese Government." Hirota reportedly replied that he would have to consult the Cabinet, and assured that he would return his government's reply speedily.[77]

One can learn from the trial record that Hirota did bring to the Cabinet's attention the reply from China immediately, but not to discuss the details of the peace terms. Rather, he merely recommended that the peace negotiation be terminated. According to court testimony by Kido, "the Foreign Minister informed his cabinet colleagues of his conclusion that no bona fides could be discerned on the Chinese side," because the Chinese reply was "such a dilatory nature at this late stage." The other members of the Cabinet accepted the foreign minister's recommendation, and resolved the same day "not to deal with the Kuomin [Guomindang] government any more and instead establish peace in the Orient in cooperation with a new China in anticipation of the formation of a new Chinese Administration."[78] In plain language, the Cabinet resolved to abandon peace negotiations and seek military victory as the means to establish its own chosen government in China.

### 4.2.7   The Cabinet-Army Confrontation at the Liaison Conference, January 15, 1938

An excerpt presented by the prosecution from *The Saionji-Harada Memoirs* reveals that the Cabinet's decision was made hastily and in disregard of a previous decision to wait for China's final reply until January 15, and that the Army General Staff criticized the Cabinet's rushed decision when the Liaison Conference reconvened the same day (i.e. January 15). The pertinent segment in *The Saionji-Harada Memoirs* cited by the prosecution recounted that, "the Army General Staff Headquarters was out and out in favor of ending the hostilities with China even if only a day sooner *and of making preparations against the Soviet*, and this was its greatest desire and concern." Tada went so far as to propose that the matter be "submitted to His Imperial Majesty's judgment before a decision is made"[79] (emphasis added).

These passages reveal that the Army General Staff, in light of the fact that the defeat of China was by no means imminent, was consumed with concern over ensuring Japan's military preparedness to face *the Russians* – who had been Japan's principal regional rival since the time of the Russo-Japanese War, if not earlier. Having failed to gain a swift victory in China, they now desired to make peace with China as quickly as possible *precisely for this reason,*

---

[77] Ibid., T5988.
[78] DX3340, T30838–9. The guomindang government refers to the Government of China under the leadership of the Chinese Nationalist Party ("*guomindang*"), headed by Chiang Kai-shek.
[79] PX3789-A, T37722.

that is, so as to refocus military preparation in what would result in the 1939 invasion of the Soviet Union and the crushing defeat of the Japanese military at Nomonhan.

The executive branch of the government expressed no sympathy with the Army General Staff's geostrategic considerations and objections. *The Saionji-Harada Memoirs* shows that during the meeting on January 15, Hirota countered Tada by asserting that the Imperial Conference had already made its decision back on January 11, and that, therefore, there was "no alternative but to proceed with our alternate plan." By this, he meant that Japan should proceed with the decision to destroy the Republic of China militarily. The navy minister, Admiral Yonai Mitsumasa, backed Hirota and exerted additional pressure: "Does that mean that the Army General Staff Headquarters does not have confidence in the Government? If so, it means that either the Army General Staff Headquarters or the Cabinet must resign en masse as a result of opposition between the two." This particular remark by the navy minister apparently hit Tada hard. He backed down in the end, reasoning that, "To have a change in the government at the present time is not wise. The General Staff Headquarters has confidence in the Government and will concur with the decision it makes." Subsequently, Emperor Hirohito received Prime Minister Konoe in audience, whereupon Konoe made a "complete report of the proceedings."[80]

The foregoing sequence of events, as documented in the prosecution's evidence, brings to light the deep schism that emerged between the army high command and the Cabinet on fundamental policy issues regarding the ultimate issues of war or peace in Sino-Japanese relations. Equally important, it showed that, unlike the situation during the Manchurian Incident in the earlier years, the Cabinet was the one to advocate war, while the Army General Staff unsuccessfully advised for peace. Such evidence goes to support the prosecution's argument of the responsibility of the Cabinet yet at the same time undercuts their theory of the overall conspiracy as alleged in Count 1.

The prosecution appears to have recognized this incoherence in their position and in their summation downplayed the significance of the foregoing episodes: "The speed with which the area of fighting was expanding and the momentum of the movement which was taking Japan deeper and deeper into the heart of China presented a serious problem to the conspirators." The summation further observed that, "The action was going ahead too fast, and it had

---

[80] Ibid., T37723. According to the Japanese official war history series, *Senshi sōsho*, the cabinet picked January 15 as the final deadline for China's reply to preempt the annual session of the Imperial Diet, which was scheduled to begin on January 20. Adopting a hardline position presumably helped the cabinet avoid possible criticisms from lawmakers for being soft on China. *Senshi sōsho: Daihon'ei rikugunbu*, vol. 1, 526. Tada'a strenuous opposition to the cabinet's decision is said to have caused the discontinuation of the Liaison Conference for a while.

4.3 "Internal External Preparation Aggressive War in Asia Pacific" 175

got beyond their control."[81] In other words, the prosecution tried to paper over the inconvenient revelations about the division between the Cabinet and the Army General Staff, insisting that differences between them were all about the *timing* of the conspiracy rather than calling into question the existence of the grand conspiracy itself. As they concluded,

The feeling on the part of the army did not represent any abandonment of the object of the conspiracy. It meant only that the military men, *with their knowledge of strategy, tactics and the needs of warfare*, felt it better to consolidate the position in North China, to stop the warfare, and to prepare adequately against the contingencies of conflicts with third powers before advancing the area of aggression further.[82] (emphasis added)

What the prosecution ignores in the remark above is that, *precisely because of their deep knowledge of military strategy and warfare*, members of the Army General Staff saw the dangers posed by the pro-war policy of the central government leading Lieutenant General Tada to express strenuous opposition on their behalf, although ultimately unsuccessfully.

## 4.3 "Internal and External Preparation for Aggressive War in Asia and in the Pacific"

In framing the next part of their summation on the conspiracy charges the prosecution returned to the import of the basic national policy decision as defining "the ultimate objective of the conspiracy."[83] Pursuing the implementation of this policy, the conspirators "entered into a program of preparing Japan for war in every possible way."[84] The aim of this part was to review voluminous evidentiary materials pertaining to Japan's domestic and external preparation for the war in the second half of the 1930s and at the start of the 1940s, allegedly in pursuit of the grand conspiracy within the meaning of Count 1. The Hirota Cabinet's Basic Principle figured prominently in this context, as the prosecution treated it as the official war-policy blueprint according to which the Japanese government took concrete preparatory steps toward realizing the object of conspiracy.

The prosecution divided this part of the summation into two sections. The first section, "The Preparation of the Japanese Nation for War," detailed the expansion of Japan's war economy, war industries, and strategic and tactical preparations for the war by the Japanese army and navy in the period

---

[81] T39250–1.
[82] T39264.
[83] For the prosecution's summation on Part III ("Internal and External Preparation for Aggressive War in Asia and in the Pacific"), see T39326–517.
[84] T39326–7.

between 1936 and 1941. The second section, "The Alliances with the Axis for Preparation for Aggressive War," traced Japan's initiatives of seeking military alliance with Germany and Italy, which culminated in the conclusion of the Tripartite Pact on September 26, 1940.[85]

Documenting these two facets of Japan's war preparation was relatively straightforward for the prosecution, given the availability of a wealth of documentary evidence and witnesses. However, the prosecution once again fell short of substantiating the existence of the grand conspiracy as alleged in Count 1. As before, the prosecution made the assertion that a single, overarching conspiracy existed, but the evidence they submitted plainly failed to support it. Instead, the evidence brought out the recurrence of divisions and disagreements among the members of the Japanese government concerning the nation's foreign-policy directions and objects. When we turn to the Majority Judgment in Chapters 7 and 8 we will see that it is informed by this same incoherence as to the nature of the alleged conspiracy.

### 4.3.1 *Insubordination of Diplomatic Officials*

Differences of opinion within the Japanese policy leadership were particularly pronounced on the advisability of pursuing a comprehensive German-Japanese military alliance. Achieving clarity on this issue was important for the prosecution because alliance with Germany was charged in the indictment and played an important role in the prosecution's theory of the conspiracy. The evidence led by the prosecution pointed to a broad-based reluctance among the Japanese leaders in the late-1930s to expand the alliance with Nazi Germany since they were aware that it could mean risking war with Great Britain and the United States. The complexities of Japan's relations with Nazi Germany were partly to blame for as many as three Cabinets to rise and fall in rapid succession in 1939–40. The challenge for the prosecution was to explain the connection of the accused to these events, and particularly to the fear of risking war with the great powers, as part of the alleged overarching conspiracy.

The trial record indicates that the prosecution had great difficulty in presenting a coherent account of Japan's foreign-policy directions and objects in the second half of the 1930s, since it meant handling the evidence of two recalcitrant accused, both Japanese officials, who had been posted overseas in that period: Lieutenant General Ōshima Hiroshi and Shiratori Toshio. Ōshima had served as resident attaché to the Japanese embassy in Germany (1934–8), and Envoy Extraordinary and Ambassador Plenipotentiary in Germany (1938–9, 1940–5), while Shiratori, a career diplomat, had served as Envoy Extraordinary and Ambassador Plenipotentiary in Italy (1938–40). Both individuals were

---

[85] The first section of Part III can be found at T39326–445, and the second section at T39446–517.

## 4.3 "Internal External Preparation Aggressive War in Asia Pacific" 177

shown to have developed close ties with their counterparts in their respective host countries, and both made great personal efforts to represent *these* countries' interests rather than Japan's. For example, they shared secret information regarding the Japanese government's negotiation plans and tactics, and freely offered advice as to how best to respond to incoming Japanese diplomatic communications, thereby assisting Germany and Italy in maintaining an upper hand in negotiating the military alliance with Japan. The question for the prosecution, of course, was how the actions of these two accused could be consistent with the theory of a monolithic conspiracy to which they were charged with being a party.

During the summation, the prosecution could hardly conceal its bafflement with these individuals' unethical conduct that bordered on treason. Commenting on one such instance the prosecution remarked that, "It is rather difficult to follow OSHIMA's justification of his commitment to Germany in excess of the desires of his government." The trial transcript indicates the prosecution's quandary as to how to handle this type of evidence, which could have served to discredit the charges of conspiracy.[86] Resorting to downplaying the significance of Ōshima's conduct, they explained to the Tribunals that,

This conflict between OSHIMA and the other conspirators, of course, *does not establish that there was no conspiracy*. Here again, there is another conflict between the various conspirators as to the proper *timing* of a particular act in furtherance of the conspiracy.[87] (emphasis added)

As the prosecution well knew, however, their own evidence contradicted this assertion. Indeed, the prosecution conceded the shortcoming of its interpretive position by immediately adding, "However, they did differ at that particular time as to the *scope* of the alliance"[88] (emphasis added). This is itself and understatement for what was at stake was whether or not Japan should enter into such an alliance at all.

It is also striking that bafflement at the disobedience of these overseas Japanese diplomats was also shared among the senior members of the wartime Japanese government, again pointing up the important divisions within the alleged conspiracy. Another excerpt from *The Saionji-Harada Memoirs* presented by the prosecution shows that the Army General Staff was troubled by the fact that one of their men, Ōshima, was not following orders from the central government despite his official position as an ambassador. They expressly instructed Ōshima in early 1939 to correct his behavior and reminded him that "the supreme authority of diplomacy is vested in the Emperor," and that "it

---

[86] T39472.
[87] T39473.
[88] Ibid.

is not desirable to forget one's position and always do as Germany says by saying that he is of the same opinion." Insofar as the Army General Staff was concerned, it had "no intention of infringing upon the diplomatic prerogative of the Emperor," nor does it have any plan to "pay any attention to the present-day Rightist because they are a most outrageous lot."[89]

### 4.4 "Expansion of Aggression to the Rest of East Asia and the Southwest Pacific"

In the final segment of the four-part summation on the conspiracy, the prosecution reviewed evidence concerning Japan's relations with the Western Powers to support its argument as to how the Japanese initiation of war in the broader areas of the Asia-Pacific region fit into the theory of a single, overarching conspiracy.[90] The prosecution reiterated the importance of the Hirota Cabinet's Basic Principle of National Policy, which it treated as affirmative proof of the existence of conspiracy within the meaning of Count 1. The opening segment of the fourth part thus declared:

The plan of 1936 to secure a steady footing on the Asiatic Continent and to advance to the South Seas for the purpose of building Japan's New Order in Greater East Asia and the all-out preparation for war in excess of the need occasioned by the hostilities in China make it apparent that Japan's plans for expansion did not stop at the borders of China. The conspiratorial plans envisioned not only domination of the vast domain of China but also domination of the rest of East Asia and of the Southwest Pacific.[91]

By reading into the 1936 Basic Principle a common plan or conspiracy whose object was to dominate all of East Asia and the Southwest Pacific, the prosecution laid the groundwork to prove that since 1936 Japan had affirmatively put herself onto a collision course with all the Western Powers that opposed her pursuit of the object of conspiracy. According to the prosecution, Japan came to identify two types of obstacles in this process. One of them was the Soviet Union, the erstwhile enemy of Imperial Japan, and the other, some other Western Powers and "particularly Britain, the United States, France and Holland."[92] The prosecution argued that Japan, or rather, the "conspirators," chose the path of military confrontation with these countries by their single-minded pursuit of the grand conspiracy within the meaning of Count 1.

---

[89] PX3795-A, T37766–7.
[90] For the prosecution's summation of Part IV ("Expansion of Aggression to the Rest of East Asia and the Southwest Pacific"), see T39518–976.
[91] T39518.
[92] Ibid.

## 4.4 "Expansion of Aggression Rest of East Asia Southwest Pacific" 179

This final part of the prosecution's summation on conspiracy was divided into two sections. The first section, "Aggression against the Western Powers," reconstructed Japan's relations during the war years with French Indochina, Great Britain, the Dutch East Indies, and the United States, focusing on: (1) US-Japan relations since the outbreak of the Manchurian Incident in 1931 through the end of 1938, during which Japan met repeated condemnations from the US government for her progressive breach of the post-WWI treaty system in relation to China; (2) Japan's military occupation of northern and southern French Indochina in July 1940 and in August 1941, respectively, following the fall of France to Nazi Germany; (3) trade negotiations between Japan and the Dutch East Indies in the second half of 1940 and the start of 1941, during which Japan unsuccessfully sought preferential access to raw materials produced in the Dutch colonies in Southeast Asia; (4) US-Japan diplomatic talks throughout 1941, during which the two countries unsuccessfully negotiated an agreement concerning Japan's military obligations under the Tripartite Pact and her war policies on China, among other disputed issues; (5) a series of meetings held by the Japanese Cabinet, the Liaison Conference, the Imperial Conference, and the *jūshin* (ex-premiers) in the second half of 1941, during which the Japanese leaders firmed up their decision to go to war against Great Britain, the Netherlands, and the United States; and (6) wartime Japanese programs on the construction of the so-called Greater East Asia Co-Prosperity Sphere, following the initiation of the Pacific War.[93]

The second section of this final part of the summation, "Aggression against the Soviet Union," focused exclusively on reviewing evidence concerning the Soviet-Japan relations. This section turned out to be a long and detailed affair, as the Soviet prosecutor did not limit his task to summarizing the evidence pertaining to the Lake Khasan Incident in 1938 and the Nomonhan Incident in 1939 (two instances of large-scale armed conflict at the borders of Manchukuo, which are itemized in Counts 25, 26, 35, and 36) but also documenting other Japanese military activities in Manchuria bordering Russia since before the Russo-Japanese War through the end of World War II.[94]

As has been the case with the previous three parts of the prosecution's summation on conspiracy, the evidence discussed in the fourth part was devoid of proof in support of the grand conspiracy within the meaning of Count 1. What the evidence showed instead was the recurrent problem of overseas Japanese armed forces' insubordination (that is, in the case of the two instances of border warfare with the Soviet Union).[95] As for the decision to go to war with the

---

[93] The first section of Part IV can be found at T39519–735.
[94] The second section of Part IV can be found at T39736–974.
[95] According to *The Saionji-Harada Memoirs*, the army insubordination relating to Nomonhan caused Emperor Hirohito to rebuke the Army Minister Itagaki and the army chief, General Prince Kan'in, by saying, "There are frequent instances where a sneaky method was used, quite

180    Individual Roles in the Making of War

Western Powers in the Pacific region, the evidence brought to light not only the continuing problem of division and disunity among the members of the central Japanese government, but also a sense of *bewilderment* that they now confronted the imminent possibility of war with the United States.

Many of those who served in the central government in 1941 had risen to power by denouncing the post-WWI treaty system, by endorsing the policy that aimed at destroying militarily the Republic of China, and by advocating the establishment of Japan's autarky in Greater Asia even at the future risk of war with the Anglo-American Powers. They had gone so far as to take concrete steps to prepare the Japanese nation for the eventuality of the war in the Pacific. However, the trial record shows that many, though not all, of them were unprepared to shoulder the heavy responsibility of starting such a war *in fact*, and that they made a desperate effort throughout 1941 to reconcile the difference between their unbending pro-war rhetoric and policies on the one hand, and their personal desire to avoid war, especially with the United States, on the other hand. Reflecting the deep divisions over this fundamental decision for war or peace, they did manage to resolve the contradictions of their foreign-policy stance eventually, by the end of 1941. Their final decision was to go to war after all, which they deemed the only foreign-policy option they could unanimously agree on. The process by which that decision was arrived at, as presented by the prosecution (shown below), hardly seems to support the theory of an overarching conspiracy. As we will see in Chapter 7, however, despite its shortcomings it was sufficient to persuade the majority judges. For now, let us look at how the sequence of events by which the Japanese leaders finalized their decision reflects the divisive nature of policy formation in favor of war.

### 4.4.1    The Decision to Go to War, Adopted at the Imperial Conference, September 6, 1941

The trial record shows that the Japanese government leaders deliberated in earnest the possibility of war against Great Britain, the Netherlands, and the United States in the summer of 1941. The war against China had entered a stalemate long before then, partly because of the Western Powers' decisions to provide wide-ranging military and financial aid to the chiang kai-shek government, and partly because of the imposition of economic sanctions against Japan. The sanctions started in 1939 with the US abrogation of the trade

---

improper for my army disobeying the orders from the central authorities and deciding on the judgment of the authorities on the spot, such as: The case of Liutiaokou in the Manchurian Incident and the actions at the Marco Polo Bridge at the beginning of this Incident [the China Incident]." The Emperor then turned to Itagaki, stating, "Hereafter, you must not move one soldier without my command!" The army minister and the army chief reportedly retreated from the audience "with trepidation." PX3793-A, T37756–7.

4.4 "Expansion of Aggression Rest of East Asia Southwest Pacific" 181

embargo (following the Japanese occupation of northern French Indochina), which culminated in the freezing of Japanese assets and oil embargo by the three powers in the summer of 1941. It was in this context that Japan formally initiated bilateral negotiations with the United States and sought to break out of the tightening economic encirclement. Negotiations did not take Japan very far, however, as the United States would not be persuaded into accepting Japan's claim of her free hand in China or that of autarky in Greater Asia in the name of Japan's "living sphere [*seikatsu-ken*]," a phrase eerily reminiscent of Nazi Germany's justification of the need for "Lebensraum" (literally "living space").[96]

One can learn from the trial record that, seeing little sign of success in diplomatic talks with the United States, the Imperial Conference met on September 6, 1941 to determine Japan's next step. The prosecution introduced into evidence the summary of the Imperial Conference's resolution according to which the following three steps were formally approved:

1. In order to secure self-existence and self-defense, Japan, with a determination for a war with the United States (Britain and the Netherlands), will have completed her preparations by the end of October.
2. Meanwhile, in pace with the above, Japan will strive for the fulfillment of her demands through diplomatic measures with the United States and Britain …
3. If, through the above negotiations, our demands have no hope of fulfillment by the beginning of October, we shall immediately determine to wage war against the United States (Britain and the Netherlands).[97]

By the decision above, it became Japan's formal policy not to continue US-Japanese negotiations indefinitely, but to resort to opening hostilities in the eventuality of no success with diplomacy by early October.

Further evidence by the prosecution and the defense shows that these decisions produced considerable controversy within policy circles. Emperor

---

[96] In one of the instructions he transmitted to the Japanese ambassador in charge of the US-Japan negotiations at Washington DC, dated February 7, 1941, Foreign Minister Matsuoka (an accused), wrote, "I believe that America should not meddle in the 'living sphere' of other powers, but be awakened to her original responsibility or mission towards the peace of the world, and devote herself towards breaking the present world crisis." PX1009, T9657. In another instruction, Matsuoka wrote that, "Putting aside such an ideal [of *Hakkōichiu*, Eight Corners under One Roof] and taking up questions of daily affairs, our country is finding it necessary to find a way to settle the problems of both self-supporting and self-sufficiency in Greater East Asia. Are these ideals or desires of Japan unjust and unreasonable, when one considers the position of the U.S.A., dominating as she does the whole Western hemisphere, besides extending her influence over both the Atlantic and the Pacific Oceans? *Surely the U.S.A. can allow thus much to Japan?*" (emphasis added). PX1008, T9645–6.

[97] PX588, introduced at T6566. The segment quoted in the text appears in pp. 4–5 of the exhibit (not read into the record).

Hirohito, for one, supported it only half-heartedly, and, as shown below, he invalidated it when the Cabinet subsequently failed to take the next executive action as required by the September 6 resolution. According to Kido's court testimony and *The Kido Diary*, the main problem was that Hirohito had been dissatisfied with poor advising rendered by the chief minister of the Cabinet and the army and navy chiefs of the Imperial Headquarters. The day prior to the September 6 meeting, he peppered Prime Minister Konoe with many questions on military strategies in the case of war against the United States, but he found Konoe unable to answer any of them. The premier merely "petitioned His Majesty to summon the Chiefs of Staff to the Army and Navy."[98] The army and navy chiefs were duly summoned the same day, but their presence was equally dissatisfying for the Emperor. Kido recorded the gist of the meeting in *The Kido Diary* as follows:

At this time Prince KONOYE told me His Majesty put various questions to them, including that put to Marshal SUGIYAMA, Chief of Staff of the Army as to when the projected southern campaign would be terminated. The Chief of Staff of the Army replied to the Emperor that he expected that the campaign would be terminated in a short period of time. Whereupon, His Majesty reprimanded Marshal SUGIYAMA, reminding him that he said a similar thing at the outbreak of the China Affair, which was not yet settled. The Marshal pleaded that there was a difference between the two, China being a continent, while the southern area mostly consisted of islands. But even his pleading would not persuade His Majesty to approve of his contention.[99]

The chief of the Navy General Staff, Admiral Nagano Osami, reportedly impressed Emperor Hirohito with the urgency of the proposed war by stating that, "If things go on as they are, we shall steadily lose the game, but there will be a hope of recovery if a drastic operation is undergone." Konoe came under further questioning regarding the forthcoming resolution of the Imperial Conference. Emperor Hirohito reportedly asked as to "why diplomatic negotiation was not placed first."[100] The premier, in reply, assured him that diplomacy was his government's priority. By introducing this evidence, both the prosecution and the defense, however unintentionally, also made clear that Hirohito

---

[98] DX3340, T30950.

[99] Ibid., T30951. This episode is related somewhat differently in Konoe's personal recollections of the war, published posthumously as *Heiwa e no doryoku*, 86–7. It reads that Emperor Hirohito questioned General Sugiyama at the meeting about the army chief's views on the prospect of the war in the Pacific region, stating, "You were the army minister at the time of the outbreak of the China Incident. You said to me at that time that the Incident would be over in just about two months, but the China Incident has not come to an end despite the passage of four years by now." Sugiyama is said to have replied that military operations in China did not progress as intended, because "the hinterland of China turned out to be vast." This explanation caused Hirohito to state, "If the hinterland of China is vast, the Pacific Ocean is even more vast. On what grounds do you estimate [the length of the war in the Pacific region] to be three months?"

[100] DX3340, T30951–2.

4.4 "Expansion of Aggression Rest of East Asia Southwest Pacific"    183

was far from a passive participant but rather played an active and vital role in policy decision-making.

When the Imperial Conference met on September 6, Hirohito had some of the same questions posed to participants by way of the president of the Privy Council, Baron Hara Yoshimichi. *The Kido Diary* shows that no satisfactory answers, however, were forthcoming this time either. This state of affairs was unsatisfactory for the Emperor, who, at the close of the meeting, "declared that it was regrettable that the Supreme War command did not give any reply." Expressing his displeasure, Hirohito then "emphasized that wholehearted efforts should be made in the conduct of diplomatic negotiations with the United States."[101]

It should come as no surprise, then, that Emperor had the September 6 resolution nullified soon after the Konoe Cabinet failed to act on it and resigned abruptly, on October 16, 1941. According to undated private notes by Konoe (titled, "Facts Pertaining to the Resignation of the Third Konoye Cabinet," and presented by the prosecution in evidence[102]), Konoe came under tremendous pressure from the then army minister, General Tōjō Hideki (an accused), to follow through the September 6 resolution when the October deadline came and went. Konoe noted that the Navy declined to take any initiative on the matter, having "no will to fight, but couldn't say so herself."[103] Deeming the entire matter deadlocked, and the September 6 resolution impossible to implement, Konoe stepped down. In his letter of resignation to the Emperor, introduced into evidence by the prosecution, Konoe pleaded that he already felt burdened by a sense of "much responsibility ever since the outbreak of the China Incident." By this, he was referring to the fact that his Cabinet (i.e. the First Konoe Cabinet, 1937–9) was the one to adopt the policy to wage war against the chiang kai-shek government with the goal to annihilate it, only to get bogged down in the conflict. Konoe informed the Emperor that he was unprepared at present "to endure plunging the nation again into a titanic war the outcome of which cannot be forecast when even the China Incident has not yet been settled."[104]

The developments just detailed are important because they make clear the implausibility of regarding the accused as a group of conspirators united by a criminal agreement which they had unwaveringly pursued since at least 1936. The path to war was littered with disputes, shifts in position, shifting alliances, and obstacles that had to be overcome. Even in these final months before the

---

[101] PX1135, T10216.
[102] Konoe committed suicide by taking poison shortly after he was named as a major war crimes suspect in December 1945. Some of his private notes that he left behind were presented in evidence at the Tokyo Trial.
[103] PX1148, T10263.
[104] Ibid., T10286.

decision to launch the Pacific War it is apparent how fraught the process was, casting serious doubt on the validity of the prosecution's theory that a single, overarching conspiracy as alleged in Count 1 determined the course of Japan's foreign policy in 1941.

### 4.4.2 The Decision to Go to War Again, Adopted at the Imperial Conference, November 5, 1941

The prosecution evidence showed how, in the crucial months before December 1941, despite the doubts and misgivings of various individuals a consensus to go to war emerged. *The Kido Diary*, as cited by the prosecution, recounts that Emperor Hirohito summoned Army Minister Tōjō shortly after Konoe's resignation, and gave him the mandate to form the next Cabinet. Given Tōjō's track record, it must have been clear to the Emperor and his personal advisors that he was unlikely to work for peace. Regardless, Kido reportedly met with Tōjō at the ante-room afterwards to deliver a separate instruction from the Emperor that the army and the navy should strive to cooperate, and that, "In deciding the fundamental policy of our country[,] we need not necessarily follow the decisions of the Council in the Imperial presence on the 6th of September, but should study carefully conditions both at home and abroad."[105] Tōjō confirmed the occurrence of this episode, as he testified that he received the "Back to Blank Paper [a clean slate] Message of the Emperor."[106]

The record of the trial is insufficient to establish conclusively the exact purpose of Emperor Hirohito or his aides in the imperial court in issuing Tōjō a clean-slate order. What the trial record shows is that the Tōjō Cabinet met no imperial displeasure when it decided to go to war after all. The Imperial Conference adopted the decision when it met on November 5, 1941.[107] The resolution read in part as follows:

When it is recognized that the Japanese-American negotiation comes to an end and warfare is inevitable (imagined to be after November 25, probably), we inform Germany (Italy), without delay, Japan has an intention to open hostilities against the U.S.A. and Britain before long as soon as the preparation will be completed.[108]

The US-Japan negotiations did reach a final impasse over conditions set by the US government for a peaceful settlement of the conflict in a note signed by

---

[105] PX1154, T10292.
[106] DX3655, T36309.
[107] Hirohito at least spoke highly of Tōjō in his 1946 retrospective account of the war, commending that Tōjō worked very hard to fulfill the imperial will. Terasaki, *Shōwa tennō dokuhakuroku*, 68–9, 88–9.
[108] PX1169, T10333–4.

4.4 "Expansion of Aggression Rest of East Asia Southwest Pacific"   185

Secretary of State Cordell Hull (known as the "Hull Note," dated November 26, 1941.[109]) According to the trial record, members of the Japanese Cabinet invariably regarded the Hull Note as "tantamount to ultimatum," leaving them with no other option but to act on the November 5 resolution.[110] Speaking of his own mental state at the time, the then foreign minister, Tōgō, testified that the "very existence of the Japanese nation was at stake, and I was compelled to agree that we must wage war, whatever the prospects, unless America would reconsider."[111]

Whatever disunity had gone before, and whatever personal misgivings many of the participants still harbored as to the prospects for success, a consensus finally coalesced for war. While the prosecution's account of this process might have been sufficient to prove that in deciding for war the Cabinet and other participants made themselves potentially accountable for initiating the war, the difficulty in achieving this consensus undermines the thesis of linear and inexorable development of a conspiracy that began in 1928.

### 4.4.3 The Decision to Go to War Once Again, Adopted at the Imperial Conference, December 1, 1941

The actual commencement of the war did not occur in the immediately ensuing days however, since Emperor Hirohito and his aides believed that some stage-setting was necessary prior to the Emperor's formal sanctioning of the war. According to *The Kido Diary*, "It would not be a good policy to plunge into a war merely by reason of the fact that the month of November had expired, and if we did so, the unification of public opinion would be very difficult."[112]

---

[109] PX1245-I, T10815–23. Dated November 26, 1941, the US proposal, signed off by the Secretary of State Cordell Hull, urged that the two countries address afresh their "conflict with the fundamental principles," and he made several concrete recommendations. Steps that the Hull Note recommended comprised the following: (1) conclusion of a multilateral nonaggression pact of China; (2) respect of French Indochina's territorial integrity; (3) Japan's withdrawal of "all military, naval, air and police forces from China and Indochina"; (4) recognition of no other government but the chiang kai-shek government as the legitimate government of China; (5) multilateral surrender of all of the existing extraterritorial rights in China; and (6) relaxing of economic sanctions against Japan, starting with the removal of the freezing of assets.

[110] Testimony by Shimada Shigetarō, T34729. Tōgō similarly testified that, "Ignoring all past progress and areas of agreement in the negotiations, the United States had served upon us what we viewed as an ultimatum containing demands far in excess of the strongest positions theretofore taken." DX3647, T35706. The then finance minister, Kaya, testified that the Hull Note was "a big blow to all," and, deeming any settlement with the United States impossible, "a decision to wage war in self defense was inevitable." DX3337, T30656.

[111] DX3647, T35710.

[112] PX1181, T10390. It appears that this passage was later re-translated for the sake of accuracy. A new translation is hand-written on the same page in the transcripts of proceedings.

A special joint meeting between the members of the Cabinet and the *jūshin* (ex-premiers) was duly convened in the presence of Emperor Hirohito.[113]

The results of this meeting were far from what was intended by the conveners. As a majority of ex-premiers in attendance had varying degrees of misgivings about the advisability of the war, the decision was again opened to debate. *The Kido Diary* records the variety of views that were expressed.

Wakatsuki, to start with, had doubts about his nation's "material power" to endure the war. He could agree that the war ought to be fought "to the last" if for the sake of national defense. However, he maintained that "we should avoid the war if we intended to realize our ideals such as the 'Asiatic Co-prosperity Sphere' or 'the stabilizing of power in Asia,' because such a war would be very dangerous." Admiral Okada shared Wakatsuki's concern, as he, too, had "grave doubts as to our supply capacity in regard to war materials." Hiranuma, on the other hand, concurred with Wakatsuki's remark about the Japanese people's spiritual strength, but he recommended some beefing up of their spiritual strength by way of "further measures to awaken patriotic sentiment." Konoe, for his part, expressed both despair and hope, as he remarked that "there would be no need to resort to a hasty war just because of the rupture of the negotiations." Konoe's opinion found support from Hirota, who remarked that "we should be able to seize an opportunity to solve the pending problems between the two countries even after the commencement of hostilities, if we were sincere enough in our diplomatic efforts." Another navy ex-premier, Admiral Yonai, took an ambivalent position, stating that "we should be careful not to lose what little we possess by trying to avoid becoming poorer by the inches." Two other ex-premiers – General Abe Genki and General Hayashi Senjūrō – alone supported the decision to go to war.[114]

Meanwhile, Prince Takamatsu (1905–87), one of three younger brothers of Emperor Hirohito and a naval officer himself, privately spoke to Hirohito. Takamatsu informed that "the Navy's hands were full and it appeared that they wished to avoid a Japanese-American war."[115]

Despite these misgivings, however, the Imperial Conference convened on December 1 and decided for war. According to *The Kido Diary*, varying reservations expressed by the *jūshin*, and the information of the navy's lack of desire to fight, caused the Emperor to summon the navy minister and the navy chief on November 30 to ascertain the "true intention of the Navy." After the private meeting with them went satisfactorily for him, Hirohito summoned Kido and

---

[113] The ones who participated to represent the government side were Tōjō, Navy Minister Shimada, Foreign Minister Tōgō, Finance Minister Kaya, and the president of the Planning Board, Suzuki. See DX3655, T36365.
[114] PX1196, T10452–4. Kido repeated the same during his direct examination, DX3340, T31040–4.
[115] PX1198, T10468.

## 4.4 "Expansion of Aggression Rest of East Asia Southwest Pacific" 187

"ordered as follows: The navy minister and the chief of the naval general staff have answered my question about the previous matter with considerable confidence, so instruct the Premier to proceed as planned."[116]

What are we to make of the foregoing sequence of events leading to the final decision to go to the war on December 1, 1941, as documented in the record of the trial? The record indicates that the Japanese government leaders in Fall 1941 looked to the prospect of "a titanic war the outcome of which cannot be forecast" with trepidation, but that they were too caught up in their own inflexible pro-war policy to recommend an alternative path. For them, conceding to American demands on China was simply unthinkable. What got them to this point, however, was not the smooth unfolding of a conspiracy initiated in 1928 as alleged in the indictment. For sure, the prosecution's case as reviewed thus far provided substantial evidence of the participation of specific accused in planning and initiating the war through their policy decisions. But what is far from clear was whether the evidence presented was also sufficient to prove beyond a reasonable doubt that those accused who did engage in planning and initiating the broader conflict did so through a conspiracy begun in 1928, or even in 1936 (during the Hirota Cabinet) for that matter. Making a determination on this crucial issue fell to the judges. Chapters 7–14 will explore how the Majority Judgment, the five separate opinions, and the draft judgment by the president of the tribunal, Justice Webb, sought to resolve this crucial issue.

---

[116] Ibid. The corrected translation of this exhibit was reintroduced at T12480–1. Kido explained during his direct examination that "the Emperor's instructions were to proceed with the Imperial Conference, not the war." DX3340, T31047. Tōjō attested to the same effect, as he testified that he received a phone call from Kido the same evening, notifying that "the Emperor allowed the Imperial Conference to be held on 1 December as slated." DX3655, T36371. This particular piece of evidence in *The Kido Diary* was taken up in Bernard Opinion, 677.

# 5 Counts on Murder, War Crimes, and Crimes against Humanity

We have seen in preceding chapters that prosecuting the Axis leaders for crimes against peace had been the top priority at both Nuremberg and Tokyo. The defense teams in both instances attempted to discredit the legitimacy of these charges and, more generally, the trials as a whole, on the basis of the alleged ex post facto nature of the crime. The defense challenges were ultimately rejected in the final decisions of the two tribunals. They did, however, impact the popular perceptions of the trials in postwar Germany and Japan, giving rise to the enduring notion that their wartime leaders were unjustly punished – or to draw upon the popular parlance – that they were subjected to "victor's justice."

What has attracted far less attention from the critics, meanwhile, yet is hardly insignificant from the standpoint of the historical development of international criminal law, is the fact that the same accused were also prosecuted on the basis of well-established international norms defining conventional war crimes. Perhaps unsurprisingly, the defense attacks on the charges of war crimes at both Nuremberg and Tokyo were somewhat tempered, as defense counsel moved away from ex post facto criticisms (which were inapplicable) and instead contested the finer points of methods of proof, modes of liability, and required elements of proof. What, then, was the exact nature of the charges made against the accused that the defense at the Tokyo Trial took issue with? What legal theories on war crimes were applied and contested? The purpose of this chapter is to address these questions by exploring the relevant segments in the trial record, laying the necessary groundwork for our subsequent analysis of the judges' decisions on these charges. Evidence on factual matters of war crimes will be discussed in Chapter 6.

A main analytical focus of this chapter is to compare and contrast the charges concerning the Axis Powers' atrocities as made at the Nuremberg and Tokyo Trials. The pages to follow will show that the IMT and IMTFE indictments had little in common when it came to counts on war crimes, and that the final decision on these charges in the majority judgment was also unlike that of the Nuremberg judgment. Differences between the two trials are most pronounced in the following three regards.

First, when developing counts other than crimes against peace, the prosecution at the Tokyo Trial looked *beyond* Nuremberg and sought the relevant precedents elsewhere and, in particular, in the trial of General Yamashita Tomoyuki (October–December 1945; "Yamashita Trial" or "Yamashita Case" hereafter). The Yamashita Trial was the first of 87 war crimes trials that the US Army held at a special military commission established in Manila (1945–7) and the first major US war crimes trial completed in the aftermath of WWII.

Yamashita had served as commander-in-chief of the 14th Area Army that fought against the US armed forces in the Philippines in the last year of the war. He was tried and convicted of war crimes on the legal basis of a particular formulation of the doctrine of command responsibility. The conviction of Yamashita was widely cited internationally, and its influence on the Tokyo Trial appears from the IMTFE indictment which replicated some of the key wordings in the charge that had been made against Yamashita. This indicates that the prosecution at the Tokyo Trial elected to build its war crimes case mainly on the precedent arising from the Yamashita Trial and not that of the Nuremberg Trial.[1] That said, to complicate the matter somewhat, the prosecution also injected its own distinct theory of liability when drawing up the indictment, and combined it with the formulation of the doctrine of command responsibility that was articulated in the indictment of Yamashita.[2] Consequently, the theories of liability relating to war crimes in the IMTFE indictment became highly complex and quite unlike those of any other WWII trial. Adding to this complication, the majority judgment of the Tokyo Tribunal also drew upon the decision made by the US military commission at the Yamashita Trial and, at the same time, injected their own distinct interpretive twist. As a result, the jurisprudence on war crimes in the Tokyo judgment bears the mark of multiple influences and became extremely complex, if not opaque.

The second notable dissimilarity between the IMT and IMTFE indictments concerning the war crimes counts arises from the Tokyo prosecution's decision

---

[1] For discussion of the link between the Tokyo Trial and the Yamashita Trial from the standpoint of jurisprudence, see Cohen, "Beyond Nuremberg," and "The Historiography of the Historical Foundations of Theories of Responsibility in International Criminal Law." For a detailed overview of the Yamashita Trial, see "Case No. 21. Trial of General Tomoyuki Yamashita," in United Nations War Crimes Commission, *Law Reports of the Trials of War Criminals*, Vol. IV. For the Yamashita Trial and its impact on the Allied war crimes trials in the Asia-Pacific region in subsequent years, see Totani, *Justice in Asia and the Pacific Region, 1945–1952*.

[2] For the full record of the Yamashita Trial, see "Records of Trials of Accused Japanese War Criminals Tried at Manila, Philippines, by a Military Commission Convened by the Commanding General of the United States Army in the Western Pacific, 1945–1947," M1727, rolls 29–33, NARA. Note that this microfilm publication does not include court exhibits or the decision of the US military commission. A copy of the decision may be located at various archival sites, including one deposited at the Hoover Library and Archives titled, "Preliminary Inventory to the United States. Army. Forces in the Western Pacific. Military Commission Records, 1945–1946," collection number XX191.

to include murder under the rubric of crimes against peace as well as within the category of war crimes and crimes against humanity. As Counts 37 and 38 of the crimes against peace section of the indictment provided, the accused conspired,

> unlawfully to kill and murder the persons described below, *by initiating unlawful hostilities* against the United States of America, the Commonwealth of the Philippines, the British Commonwealth of Nations, the Kingdom of the Netherlands and the Kingdom of Thailand, and *unlawfully ordering, causing and permitting* the armed forces of Japan to attack the territory, ships and airplanes of the said nations or some of them.[3] (emphasis added)

The Nuremberg indictment, as one would expect, followed standard international law doctrine and treated murder only as a war crime or crime against humanity. The strategy elected by the Tokyo prosecution found no favor with the judges who explicitly rejected all of the counts encompassing murder under crimes against peace. What explains the formulation of the indictment put forward by the prosecution?

The rationale behind the linkage of murder and crimes against peace is clear, albeit mistaken. As the majority judgment held, "It was argued that the waging of aggressive war was unlawful and involved unlawful killing, which is murder. From this it was submitted further that a conspiracy to wage war unlawfully was a conspiracy to also commit murder."[4] Finding this logic unpersuasive and without foundation, the majority concluded that, "There is no specification of the crime of conspiracy to commit murder by the waging of aggressive war or otherwise."[5] While the Nuremberg judgment also rejected conspiracy to commit war crimes, they were not faced with an indictment that used conspiracy to link murder to aggressive war. At Tokyo, the majority thus dismissed Counts 37, 38, and 44–53 of the indictment.

What may explain the puzzling position taken by the Tokyo prosecution in comparison with their brethren at Nuremberg is the untoward influence of General MacArthur, the Supreme Commander for the Allied Powers. Indeed, there is anecdotal evidence that the prosecution adopted this strategy in response to suggestions made by him.

Internal records of the prosecution show that, shortly after its establishment in December 1945, MacArthur conveyed to the newly appointed chief prosecutor, Keenan, his personal "reluctance to bring the trial on any theory that would be offensive to the ex post facto principle," and urged the latter to consider punishing the Japanese war criminals for murder.[6] MacArthur further advised

---
[3] *Documents*, 27–8.
[4] MJ 85.
[5] Ibid.
[6] Notes for Meeting with Secretary of War, January 5, 1946, p. 1, M1668, roll 2, NARA.

that deaths resulting from the attack on Pearl Harbor might well be classified as murder "on the grounds that such a surprise attack without declaration of war amounted to murder."[7] This position, of course, confuses the legality of a war, ius ad bellum, with the legality of the conduct of hostilities, ius in bello.[8] The prosecution, nonetheless, was amenable to MacArthur's suggestions, as seen immediately above.[9] MacArthur's suggestion found its way into the indictment as Count 39, which also served as the model for Counts 40–3. Count 39 alleged that the accused,

By ordering, causing, and permitting the armed forces of Japan to attack the territory of the United States of American with which nation Japan was then at peace, at Pearly Harbor ... unlawfully killed and murdered Admiral Kidd and about 4000 other members of the naval and military forces of the United States.[10]

The incoherence of this part of the indictment connecting murder to crimes against peace is further highlighted by the shift in focus in Count 44. Whereas the preceding counts had directly linked the charges of murder to the illegal initiation of hostilities, Count 44 adopted an approach that was directly duplicative of the conventional war crimes charges that followed in the next section of the indictment. Thus, Count 44 alleged that the accused had conspired "to procure and permit the murder on a wholesale scale of prisoners of war ... in ruthless pursuit of victory in the unlawful wars in which Japan was ... engaged."[11]

Murdering prisoners of war was well established in conventional and customary international law as a paradigmatic war crime. Why then was it necessary to allege it as a crime against peace when it properly fell under the ensuing section on war crimes? It was, to say the least, a novel approach to argue that murdering prisoners of war was illegal *because* the murders occurred during an unlawful war. Mistreatment of prisoners of war was a war crime

---

[7] Minutes of Eleventh Meeting of Executive Committee, March 27, 1946, p. 2, MSS 78–3, box number, University of Virginia Law Library.

[8] See Roeling's discussion of the fallacy in the prosecution's approach which he formulates as: "According to the prosecution, these killings are a crime against peace because 'murder is a necessary consequence of aggressive war.'" Referring to the prosecution's argument that this position follows "general principles" of international law, Roeling rightly concludes, "In my opinion the prosecution is wrong here." Memo to Webb of February 5, 1948, AWM 3DRL 2481/20 4.

[9] See e.g., the introductory paragraph of the counts on murder: "The following Counts charge the crimes of murder, and conspiracy to murder, being acts for which it is charged that the persons named and each of them are individually responsible, being at the same time Crimes against Peace, Conventional War Crimes, and Crimes against Humanity contrary to all the paragraphs of Article 5 of the said Charter, to International Law, and to the domestic laws of all the countries where committed, including Japan, or to one or more of them." This formulation appears designed to ward off accusations of ex post facto charges. *Documents*, 27.

[10] Ibid., 29.

[11] Ibid., 29–30.

regardless of the legality of the war. It was not a crime against peace. Count 44 thus again confuses the basic categories of ius in bello and ius ad bellum. Given these irregularities in the construction of the murder counts, it was no surprise when the defense criticized them as ill-conceived and ill-defined.[12] Paradoxically, MacArthur and the prosecution were apparently unaware that the construction of the murder as crimes against peace counts of the indictment directly contradicted the Supreme Commander's advice that murder counts be adopted specifically to avoid the criticism that such charges were based upon ex post facto norms.

The other salient point revealed here is the inappropriate influence of MacArthur upon a prosecution that should have defended the principal of prosecutorial independence against such interference. Beyond this, as MacArthur also constituted himself as the sole reviewing authority for the convictions entered by the Tribunal it was an egregious breach of judicial ethics for the reviewing authority to be communicating with, let alone advising and instructing, the prosecution.

The third notable dissimilarity between the IMT and IMTFE indictments has to do with the treatment of the law pertaining to crimes against humanity. The IMT Charter and the IMTFE Charter stipulated crimes against humanity as one of the three categories of chargeable offenses, and the IMT indictment duly contained an independent count on crimes against humanity (Count 4). It was charged that the German accused were accountable for "murder, extermination, enslavement, deportation, and other inhumane acts committed against civilian populations before and during the war," and "persecution on political, racial, and religious grounds *in execution of and in connection with the common plan mentioned in count one*" (emphasis added). The highlighted phrase aimed to avoid the problem of applying an ex post facto norm by requiring a nexus of the alleged crimes against humanity to the commission of either war crimes or crimes against peace. That is, this provision made it a requirement that the alleged crimes against humanity be committed after the outbreak of hostilities. In the case of the IMTFE indictment, it merely referenced the law of crimes against humanity *as supplementary* to the making of the counts on murder (Counts 37–52) and conventional war crimes (Count 53–55). It contained no independent count on crimes against humanity. Why did the prosecution at the Tokyo Trial choose this path?

Internal records of the prosecution indicates this feature of the IMTFE indictment as reflecting the prosecution's decision, adopted one month prior the start of the Tokyo Trial, that "actually this Section has no cases falling only under Class C [crimes against humanity], but that all of the cases against the

---

[12] For the defense's argument questioning the validity of murder counts, see T42196-201, 42251–5, 42341–9.

proposed defendants come under murder counts or Class B – conventional war crimes." The prosecution further agreed that the indictment might still make reference to crimes against humanity, although only for the limited purpose of using it as an "additional means of showing that the Court has jurisdiction to try 'plain' charges of murder."[13] Although from a legal standpoint the meaning of this formulation is far from clear, it appears that the prosecution decided to invoke the legal concept of crimes against humanity merely to cover the charges of murder and war crimes, and not to make any specific case of crimes against humanity. Such a usage of the concept of crimes against humanity appears conceptually incoherent and deviated from its original purpose. The members of the prosecution were likely aware of the deviation, as they were familiar with the IMT Charter and the IMT indictment. Still, they may have settled the matter the way they did due to the lack of intellectual resources to make a sounder formulation of charges of crimes against humanity.

In regard to the formulation of both the crimes against humanity charges as well as the linkage of murder to conspiracy to wage aggressive war, the lack of knowledge of international law on the part of the indictment drafting team is apparent. On the whole, the Tokyo indictment is a puzzling and confused document, especially in comparison with its counterpart at Nuremberg. The majority judges chose to follow Nuremberg closely in their treatment of the law of the Charter, and the prosecution would have been well advised to have followed a similar path. The interference of MacArthur with the legal formulation of the charges is also deeply troubling. MacArthur, plainly no expert in criminal law of international law, exercised a heavy hand on the conduct of both judges and prosecutors in the Yamashita Case and the result was a kangaroo court that has been well-characterized as sanctioning judicial murder.[14] In the case of the formulation of the IMTFE indictment, his interference did not add to the coherence of the indictment and, as we have seen, sixteen counts of the indictment dealing with murder were accordingly dismissed by the majority.

Having focused on these shortcomings of the indictment, the remainder of this chapter will turn to the charges of conventional war crimes that framed the prosecution's case and influenced the majority judgment's approach.

## 5.1 Counts on Conventional War Crimes

The IMTFE indictment treats war crimes under the heading "Group Three: Conventional War Crimes and Crimes against Humanity" (Counts 53–55). Counts 54 and 55 provide the basis for the war crimes convictions rendered

---

[13] Minutes of Fourteenth Meeting of Executive Committee, April 4, 1946, p. 2. MSS no. 78-3, Box no. 2. Virginia Law Library.
[14] For detail of the Yamashita Trial, see Reel, *The Case of General Yamashita*, Ryan, *Yamashita's Ghost*; and Totani, *Justice in Asia and the Pacific Region, 1945–1952*, chapter 1.

in the majority judgment. According to the introductory segment of this group, the charges arose from "conventional War Crimes and Crimes against Humanity, being acts for which it is charged that the persons named and each of them are individually responsible, in accordance with Article 5 and particularly Article 5(b) and (c) of the Charter of the International Military Tribunal for the Far East, and in accordance with International Law, or either of them."[15] The relevant part of the IMTFE Charter defined the conventional war crimes and crimes against humanity referred to in this passage:

Article 5. Jurisdiction Over Persons and Offenses.

(a) ...
(b) Conventional War Crimes: Namely, violations of the laws or customs of war;
(c) Crimes against Humanity: Namely, murder, extermination, enslavement, deportation, and other inhumane acts, before or during the war, or persecutions on political or racial grounds in execution of or in connection with any crime within the jurisdiction of the Tribunal, whether or not in violation of the domestic law of the country where perpetrated.[16]

The actual charges made under Counts 53–55 were limited to conventional war crimes alone. As indicated earlier, crimes against humanity were effectively discarded by the prosecution as it admitted during the summation, limiting its application of Counts 53–55 to war crimes.[17]

To highlight the way in which the Tokyo prosecution formulated and applied the war crimes charges, it may be useful again to compare the treatment of war crimes at the Nuremberg Trial. The IMT indictment contained a single count on war crimes, whose construction was fairly straightforward. The initial segment of the relevant count read as follows:

Count 3. All the defendants committed War Crimes between 1 September 1939 and 8 May 1945, in Germany and in all those countries and territories occupied by the German Armed Forces since 1 September 1939, and in Austria, Czechoslovakia, and Italy, and on the High Seas.[18]

The ensuing two paragraphs specified that the accused were charged with a conspiracy to commit war crimes in their conduct of hostilities and their treatment of prisoners of war and occupied territories. These initial brief paragraphs were accompanied by a lengthy and detailed statement of particulars of specific charges, taking up some 7,900 words. The particulars of offense appeared under ten separate subheadings, and each subheading contained short

---

[15] *Documents*, 32.
[16] Ibid., 8.
[17] T39992.
[18] Count 1 of the IMT indictment included the charge of conspiracy to commit war crimes.

## 5.1 Counts on Conventional War Crimes

narrative descriptions of offenses and lists of specific instances of war crimes with relevant dates, locations, types of offense, and numbers of victims. Some entries also carried tables and statistical data. The nature of "commission" of war crimes by the individual German accused was elaborated in Appendix A of the IMT indictment (which is titled, "Statement of Individual Responsibility for Crimes Set Out in Counts One, Two, Three and Four").[19]

These basic features of the charge of war crimes in the IMT indictment deserve attention in our present analysis of the IMTFE indictment, because the prosecution at the Tokyo Trial almost completely *disregarded* the essential features of the IMT model and instead came up with a distinct one of its own. What accounts for this departure?

The first of the three counts on war crimes in the IMTFE indictment is a conspiracy count (Count 53). The IMT indictment also alleged an overarching conspiracy to commit war crimes, but the construction of this count in the IMTFE indictment is quite complicated, as it frames an extremely broad conspiracy and enumerates a number of ways in which the accused could be charged with participation as co-conspirators. Following the IMT indictment, the Tokyo prosecution alleged that the accused participated in the conspiracy as either "leaders, organizers, instigators, or accomplices in the formulation or execution of a common plan."[20] In defining the substance of the charges, however, the Tokyo indictment charged that twenty-six of the twenty-eight accused participated in a common plan or conspiracy whose object was[21]:

*to order, authorise and permit* the commanders-in-chief of the several Japanese naval and military forces ... and the officials of the Japanese War Ministry, and the persons in charge of each of the camps and labour units for prisoners of war and civilian internees in territories of or occupied by Japan and the military and civil police of Japan, and their respective subordinates *frequently and habitually to commit the breaches of the Laws and Customs of War*, as contained in and proved by the Conventions, assurances and practices referred to in Appendix D [of the indictment], against the armed forces of the countries hereinafter named and against many thousands of prisoners of war and civilians then in the power of Japan ... *and that the Government of Japan should abstain from taking adequate steps in accordance with the said Conventions and assurances and Laws and Customs of War*, in order to secure observance and prevent breaches thereof.[22] (emphasis added)

---

[19] Eighteen of the accused at Nuremberg were charged with having "authorized, directed, and participated in War Crimes," and one other was charged with using his official positions "to advocate, encourage and incite the commission of the War Crimes." The remaining six accused were not charged with war crimes, but they faced the charges of crimes against peace and crimes against humanity.
[20] *Documents*, 32.
[21] The ones not charged of conventional war crimes are Ōkawa and Shiratori.
[22] *Documents*, 32.

In the above statement of offense, the accused was charged with having been party to a conspiracy, whose goal was both (1) *to order, authorize and permit* various military units, army-ministry officials, prisoner-of-war camp authorities, and their subordinates to commit war crimes, *frequently and habitually*, and (2) for the Japanese government *to abstain from taking adequate steps* as set out in the international conventions, assurances, and the laws and customs of war.

While one might readily ascertain the meaning of "ordering" and "authorization" as that of the affirmative acts of commissioning war crimes what should "permitting" mean? This particular word had been used in the murder counts under Group Two as well, but what was the exact nature of offense? Was the prosecution alleging that the accused issued *express permission* for the commission of criminal offenses? Or, was it that the accused did not issue any express permission, but rather *condoned* their commission? If "permission" was being used in the latter sense, what mental element (mens rea) was presupposed? Were the accused charged with condoning the commission of criminal offenses *purposely*, *knowingly*, *recklessly*, or *negligently*? The conjunctive use of "permitting," together with "ordering" and "authorizing" obscures the issue.

Furthermore, Count 53 alleged that the accused permitted, authorized, and ordered the specified officials to commit war crimes "frequently and habitually." What, exactly, was the function of this phrase? What constituted the "frequent and habitual" commission of war crimes, and how did the prosecution plan to prove it? What conduct of an accused would consist in ordering someone to habitually commit a crime? Further, what did the prosecution mean by alleging that the accused ordered, authorized or permitted "the Government of Japan" to "abstain from taking adequate steps" to prevent breached of the relevant international norms? How, for example, could an accused have permitted, or ordered the Government of Japan as an abstract entity to refrain from following international legal norms?

Count 53 provides no satisfactory answers to any of these questions. However, the two ensuing counts on war crimes may offer some clues. While Count 53 alleges a conspiracy to commit war crimes, Counts 54 and 55 charge the accused with individual responsibility for these crimes. Count 54 focuses on the actual commission of the crimes while Count 55 charges a culpable failure to prevent their commission. Count 54 thus charges that the accused (save two) "ordered, authorized, and permitted the same persons as mentioned in Count 53 to commit the offences" specified as war crimes in that previous count.[23]

It again can be assumed that the words, "ordered" and "authorised," denoted the affirmative acts of commissioning war crimes, but the meaning of the word

---

[23] Ibid.

"permitted" remains unexplained and ambiguous as a mode of liability. It is here, however, that the influence of the Yamashita Case makes itself felt.

The prosecution at the Yamashita Trial developed a single count of war crimes, the main part of which read as follows:

[Yamashita,] while a commander of armed forces of Japan ... unlawfully disregarded and failed to discharge his duty as commander to control the operations of the members of his command, *permitting* them to commit brutal atrocities and other high crimes.[24] (emphasis added)

This word, "permitting," was repeated also in the bills of particulars of offense that accompanied the charge above at the Yamashita Trial. A total of 123 concrete episodes of war crimes were listed in them, enumerating specific dates, locations, types of offense, and victims involved. Since Yamashita could not be directly linked to ordering or even knowing of even one of the crimes charged, the prosecution at the US military commission resorted to the tactic of alleging that in some undefined manner he "permitted" them.

A further exploration of the record of the Yamashita Trial reveals that the use of the word "permitting" was highly controversial because – as defense counsel representing Yamashita objected – the substance of the offense was obscure. The US military commission rejected the defense objection, however, and found the accused guilty, by drawing upon the prosecution's evidence that "the crimes were so extensive and widespread, both as to time and area, that they must either have been *willfully permitted* by the accused, *or secretly ordered* by the accused"[25] (emphasis added).

It is worth noting that, when convicting Yamashita, the US military commission did not attempt to clarify the meaning of "permitted," let alone the even more obscure formulation of "willfully permitted." Although the language of the commission's decision *suggested* that the conviction was supported by the proof of Yamashita's orders or knowledge of atrocity, the actual record of the trial did not support any findings of criminal orders or knowledge. The formulation of "secretly ordered" apparently rises from the brute fact that the prosecution could not find a single order linked to the commission of a war crime and therefore postulated that because they could not be found they must have been secretly promulgated. Apart from the absurdity of such a formulation, one may recall that the burden of proof was on the prosecution to show beyond a reasonable doubt that Yamashita issued such orders. They clearly did not meet this burden.

---

[24] "Case No. 21. Trial of General Tomoyuki Yamashita," in United Nations War Crimes Commission, *Law Reports of the Trials of War Criminals*, vol. IV, 3–4.
[25] Ibid., 34.

The basis of Yamashita's conviction appears to have been the sheer fact that he had held the position of commander. In other words, it was a "strict liability" standard by which the commission convicted Yamashita, and not the evidence of orders, knowledge, or even negligence. The finding of "willful permission and secret ordering" conveniently obscured this controversial decision.[26] Given the authoritative role of MacArthur as commander-in-chief of the US Army Forces, Pacific theater, and as SCAP in the management of both the Yamashita and Tokyo trials, one may perhaps infer that the incorporation of the word "permitting" in the IMTFE indictment arose at the very least from awareness on the part of the prosecution of the advantages of the prosecutorial strategy employed in Yamashita. As we will see in Chapter 9, the majority judgment explicitly adopts the "secretly ordered or willfully permitted standard" in its treatment of the war crimes charges.

Count 55, as noted earlier, alleged a different theory or responsibility for war crimes. The formulation of the charge in Count 55 also departed from the theory alleged in Count 53, which stated that the accused had ordered, authorized, or permitted that "the Government of Japan should *abstain from taking adequate steps* to secure observance and prevent breaches" of international law. Count 55 instead references the official positions of the accused by which they had a duty to ensure respect for international legal norms, a duty which they "deliberately and recklessly" disregarded.[27]

Yamashita had also been charged with having "unlawfully disregarded and failed to discharge his duty." The formulation in the IMTFE indictment, however, differs in important respects. The contemporary doctrine of command responsibility is based upon a failure to prevent the commission of war crimes where the accused either knows, or has sufficient actual information to be on inquiry notice, that crimes are being committed by their subordinates. Indeed, the doctrine of command responsibility is predicated upon the "superior-subordinate" relationship of authority. Even under the strict liability standard employed in the conviction of Yamashita, the basis of the conviction was that crimes were committed by military units under his command. As the charges against Yamashita specified, Yamashita, "while a commander of armed forces

---

[26] For discussion of the strict liability standard at the Yamashita Trial, see Cohen, "Beyond Nuremberg."

[27] "The Defendants ... being by virtue of their respective offices responsible for securing the observance of the said Conventions and assurances and the Laws and Customs of War in respect of the armed forces in the countries hereinafter named and in respect of many thousands of prisoners of war and civilians then in the power of Japan ... deliberately and recklessly disregarded their legal duty to take adequate steps to secure the observance and prevent breaches thereof, and thereby violated the laws of war." *Documents*, 32–3. The name of Hirota does not appear in Count 54 of the indictment reproduced in the Boister & Cryer edition, but it is included in the original copy. See the digital copy reproduced on the Harry S. Truman Library & Museum Web site.

## 5.1 Counts on Conventional War Crimes

of Japan ... unlawfully disregarded and failed to discharge his duty as commander to control the operations *of the members of his command,* permitting them to commit brutal atrocities and other high crimes"[28] (emphasis added).

The indictment at Tokyo, however, refers rather vaguely only to "respective offices" held by the accused, not predicating that they held a position of authority tantamount to that of a military commander over the forces who committed war crimes. This broad formulation opened the door for conviction of civilian officials who may not have had any authority over, or capacity to control, military personnel engaging in war crimes. It was left to the judges to determine how to define a theory of liability that might encompass the disregard of duty by those who had no de facto authority to discharge that duty in an effective manner. As we will see, the majority judgment did so through an ill-defined theory of cabinet responsibility.

Another key feature of Count 55, however, appears far more restrictive in defining the scope of liability. It requires that the prosecution prove beyond reasonable doubt that the accused "deliberately and recklessly disregarded their duty" to ensure compliance with international law. The conjunctive formulation here is again striking. The term "deliberately" implies purposive behavior, that is, that it was the aim or objective of the accused not to fulfill their legal duties. The term "recklessly," however, involves a far lower mens rea, or mental element. Recklessness involves the conscious disregard of a risk. In other words, the prosecution would only have to show that the accused were aware that there was a possibility that crimes were being committed and ignored this information in failing to follow up to prevent the crimes as their duty required. Again, it was left to the judges to determine what standard should be applied to the conduct of the individual accused and we will see in ensuing chapters how they met this challenge.

What bears underscoring in anticipation of ensuing chapters is that Counts 54 and 55 focus on the accused as individuals and require the prosecution to prove beyond a reasonable doubt for each of them that they were responsible for war crimes in the manner specified respectively in these counts. Count 53, on the other hand, treats the accused as a collectivity, a conspiracy, and requires only a demonstration that they participated in the conspiracy to commit the crimes as alleged in that count. The latter point became moot, however, because the Tokyo judges, like their counterparts at Nuremberg, rejected these charges by maintaining that the Charter did not authorize conviction for conspiracy to commit war crimes. Both tribunals interpreted their Charters to authorize only prosecution for conspiracy to wage aggressive war.

---

[28] "Case No. 21, Trial of General Tomoyuki Yamashita," United Nations War Crimes Commission, *Law Reports of the Trials of War Criminals*, vol. IV, 3–4.

## 5.2 Implications of Appendices D and E in the Indictment

As noted earlier, the reference to the official position of the accused in Count 55 scarcely clarified how it should be applied to the diverse group of accused who had held a variety of governmental, military, diplomatic, or consultative positions. In order to shed some light on the prosecution's theory of liability, one must refer to the appendices to the indictment treated in Chapter 2.

Appendix E of the indictment articulates an astonishingly broad scope of liability:

It is charged against each of the Defendants ... was one of those responsible for all the acts and omissions of the various Government of which he was member, and *of the various civil, military or naval organizations in which he held a position of authority.* (emphasis added)

This charge appears to impose a form of vicarious liability in the sense that the accused are to be held accountable for "all the acts and omissions" of the government or any organization in which a particular accused "held a position of authority." The charge does not require a connection of specific accused to those acts, rather just that he occupied a position of authority and was thereby responsible for "all" criminal acts which were committed under the administrative or policy purview of the "Government" as a collectivity or the respective governmental agency or entity. In other words, mere membership or official position would be enough to convict. In this sense the charge is reminiscent of the standard under which Yamashita was convicted, simply by virtue of his position of command. But even in the case of Yamashita, the indictment required that the crimes be committed by troops under his command. In the formulation of Appendix E there is no such requirement.

Appendix D of the indictment casts additional light on the prosecution's theory of responsibility, indicating that the responsibility of individual members of a government flows from the general responsibility of the "government" as a collective abstraction. In this sense, we might refer to this theory as "government responsibility," though Appendix E also extended it to accused who were members of the military or other organizations. Whether the convictions rendered in the majority judgment were based upon such a theory, or that of "cabinet responsibility," or some other theory will be discussed in ensuing chapters.

Appendix D, referenced in Count 53 earlier, contains a list of "the Conventions, assurances, and practices" relating to the laws and customs of war. Three of these conventions – the Hague Conventions No. 4 Concerning the Laws and Customs of War of 1907 ("Hague Convention No. 4"), the International Convention for the Amelioration of the Condition of the Wounded and Sick

5.2  Implications of Appendices D and E in the Indictment

in Armies in the Field of 1929 ("Red-Cross Convention"), and the International Convention Relative to the Treatment of Prisoners of War of 1929 ("Prisoner-of-War Convention" or "Geneva Convention") – contained stipulations that identified the "hostile Government" as the one primarily responsible for the observance of the laws and customs of war, and secondarily, commanders of the armed forces. The Hague Convention No. 4, for example, specifies that "Prisoners of War are *in the power of the hostile Government*, but not of the individuals or corps who capture them"[29] (emphasis added).

It is, of course, the states that sign, ratify, and become parties to international treaties and conventions. This was the case with the Japanese government and the 1929 Prisoner-of-War Convention, when the Japanese government agreed to assume the obligations of the convention even though Japan have not ratified it.[30] The prosecution appears to have derived from the responsibility of states to abide by the obligations of such conventions the principle that members of the governments of those states have the duty *as individuals* to ensure that the state does so. In other words, in light of the principle of individual responsibility as set out in Appendix E, the prosecution theorized that *all* members of a government bear that duty, regardless of the nature of the position they hold. This principle is sweeping in its scope, because it does not require the official to have authority in regard to the area of governmental or military activity within which crimes were committed.

Another aspect of Appendix D bears scrutiny because it indicates another prong of the prosecution's theory of the case. Appendix D contains the prosecution's allegations of "Particulars of Breaches" relative to the counts of war crimes. Just short of four pages in the forty-six-page Bill of Indictment, the list of particulars indicates fifteen categories of war crimes that allegedly were commonplace occurrences in the Japanese conduct of war and military occupation during the period covered by the indictment.[31] The brevity and

---

[29] *Documents*, 57.
[30] Ibid., 57–8.
[31] The fifteen categories of war crimes as listed in Appendix D are as follows:

1. Inhuman treatment ... prisoners of war and civilian internees were murdered, beaten, tortured and otherwise ill-treated, and female prisoners were raped by members of the Japanese forces.
2. Illegal employment of prisoners of war labor.
3. Refusal and failure to maintain prisoners of war.
4. Excessive and illegal punishment of prisoners of war.
5. Mistreatment of the sick and wounded, medical personnel and female nurses.
6. Humiliation of prisoners of war, and especially officers.
7. Refusal or failure to collect and transmit information regarding prisoners of war, and replies to enquiries on the subject.
8. Obstructions of the rights of the Protecting Powers, of Red Cross Societies, or prisoners of war and of their representatives.
9. Employing poison [with a notation that this allegation is confined to the wars of Japan against the Republic of China].

generalized nature of the list stands in stark contrast with its counterpart in the IMT indictment, which, as mentioned earlier, enumerated *concrete instances of atrocity* exhaustively and in great detail, some 7,900 words in length. The prosecution at the Tokyo Trial may well have prepared the list of particulars the way it did as a prosecutorial strategy designed to deal with certain shortcomings in the evidence, and more specifically, evidence directly linking individual accused to specific crimes. We will see in Chapter 6 that the prosecution indeed focused on documenting the *widespread and recurrent character of the categories of war crimes* as illustrated in Appendix D during the trial, and used such evidence to argue for an inference of a policy that might connect the accused to this criminal conduct.[32] Subsequent chapters will explore to what extent the judges found this method of linking the accused to crimes to which they had no apparent connection sufficient to meet the required burden of proof. We turn first, however, to the prosecution's presentation of evidence to support such a theory.

  10. Killing enemies who, having laid down their arms or no longer having means of defence, had surrendered at discretion.
  11. Destruction of Enemy Property.
  12. Failure to respect family honour and rights, individual life, private property and religious convictions and worship in occupied territories, and deportation and enslavement of the inhabitants thereof.
  13. Killing survivors of ships sunk by naval actions and crews of captured ships.
  14. Failure to respect military hospital ships.
  15. Attacks, and especially attacks without due warning, upon neutral ships.

*Documents*, 59–62.

[32] No evidence in support of Item 9 in Appendix D (the use of poison gas in China) was presented during the trial. The reason for this particular omission cannot be established conclusively. One can only speculate that the Chinese prosecution team either suffered from a lack of investigative resources, or received conflicting instructions from its own government about prosecutorial priorities, or had both problems. It is also worth noting that, according to the internal records of the Prosecution, the Chinese and Soviet prosecution teams on different occasions proposed the inclusion of the Japanese development and use of bacteriological weapons in the prosecutorial effort. But it never materialized, due apparently to US obstructionism. For internal discussion of the International Prosecution Section regarding evidence of the Japanese use of bacteriological weapons, see the following documents: Matters to be Included in Indictment According to Views of Chinese, French, Dutch and Philippine Associate Prosecutors, April 14, 1946, p. 2. M1668, roll 1; Memorandum from Eugene D. Williams to Frank S. Tavenner, Jr., December 4, 1946, MSS 78-3, Box no. 3; and, Memorandum for Major-General A. N. Vasilyev, December 13, 1946, MSS 78-3, Box no. 3. University of Virginia Law Library Special Collection. There are many Japanese-language publications on the Japanese development, experiment, and deployment of bacteriological weapons, and the US cover-up efforts. The path-breaking piece is Morimura's *Akuma no hōshoku*. For a list of book-length studies on Unit 731 in Japanese, see Nichigai Associates, ed., *Taiheiyō sensō tosho mokuroku 45/94*, 634–6. For the English-language publications, see Powell, *Japan's Germ Warfare*; Powell, "A Hidden Chapter in History"; and Harris, *Factories of Death*.

# 6  Accountability for War Crimes

In this final chapter in Part I, we delve into the remainder of the record of the Tokyo Trial to illuminate how the counts on war crimes were substantiated during the actual court proceedings. As will become apparent in Part II, such an inquiry is important because the majority afforded the war crimes evidence only summary attention, thus providing insufficient insight into the massive scope of the evidence that the prosecution brought before the court. The majority judgment also gives little sense of how the defense confronted that evidence. In other words, it is important to have an overview of the evidentiary basis of the war crimes charges in order to assess the way in which the majority judgment and separate opinions arrived at their respective legal conclusions. This is particularly important in regard to the linkage evidence that could connect individual accused to the far-flung atrocities perpetrated across the Japanese Empire.

The pages that follow are divided into five sections. The first section discusses the methods of proof that the prosecution adopted for documenting war crimes and linking them with the individual accused. The second section then turns to an array of evidentiary materials that the prosecution presented during its three phases on war crimes.[1] The third and fourth sections do the same with respect to the defense cases on China and the Pacific region.[2] The last section touches briefly on the prosecution's summation concerning its theory of government responsibility. This chapter brings to light the full range of evidentiary materials and theoretical arguments made by the prosecution and the defense to persuade the judges of the validity of their respective arguments on guilt and innocence.

---

[1] The three phases on war crimes appear in the transcripts of court proceedings under the following headings: "Phase V: Atrocities Connected with Japanese Military Aggression in China and in the Traffic in Opium & Narcotics," "Phase XIII: Class C Offenses," and "Phase XIV: Class B Offenses." The second phase was titled as "Class C Offenses," but its substance was conventional war crimes, and not crimes against humanity. Evidence relating to China can be found at T2527–692, 3269–542, 3886–944, and 4451–663, and the Pacific, 5351–846, 11403–628, and 12348–15533.

[2] The two defense phases on war crimes were delivered under the following headings: "Sub-Division 4 of Division III (China) – the Japanese occupation of Nanking and Japanese Peace Initiative," and "Sub-Division 5 of Division V – The Pacific War." (T21431–804, 27117–390).

## 6.1 Challenges and Methods of Proof

"Mr. Justice Mansfield, we are all very much concerned with the length of the evidence dealing with conventional war crimes, that is, alleged atrocities." This was the remark with which Justice Webb, president of the tribunal, began the court proceeding for the day of December 4, 1946. Seven months had already passed since the arraignment, and much of the prosecution's presentation concerning crimes against peace was complete. Evidence on atrocities relating to China had been admitted, too, in late July, August, and early September. Three former Allied prisoners of war took the witness stand as well, in September and November, to provide detailed testimony regarding mistreatment of prisoners of war in general and in connection especially with the Burma-Siam Death Railway (or "Death Railway" hereafter). At the start of December 1946, however, a full presentation on war crimes relating to the Pacific War was yet to begin. The International Prosecution Section, by then, had amassed a tremendous amount of oral and documentary evidence under the able leadership of the Australian associate prosecutor, Alan J. Mansfield. However, the tribunal seemed apprehensive about its volume and its relevance to individual accused. Elaborating the tribunal's concern, Webb remarked,

> It is not very clear yet to what extent the accused can be associated with that particular class of crime. I know that you will contend that the Burma-Thailand Railway was a military project and that the prisoners of war were unlawfully employed thereon. There is also evidence that that particular project was authorized by the Japanese cabinet, and there was a report to the accused TOJO covering the operations on the line and the treatment of prisoners. The accused SHIGEMITSU is also mentioned in that regard. *But there are other conventional war crimes with which the association of the accused had not been made so clear up to date.* It would, of course, be regrettable should we hear a vast amount of evidence extending over many weeks, only to discover that the accused could not be associated with the matters dealt with.[3] (emphasis added)

The above statement reveals that the judges were unsure at this stage as to how the prosecution was going to link the mass of evidence on war crimes with individual accused. From a modern perspective such concern was not misplaced, as it is generally the case when dealing with political and military leaders at the national level that they may have no direct connection to the actual commission of many of the crimes. The burden is then upon the prosecution to provide the vital linkage evidence and a theory of the case that proves the culpable role of the accused beyond a reasonable doubt. This is what Webb, in the passage quoted above, asked the prosecution to clarify.

[3] T11759–60.

## 6.1 Challenges and Methods of Proof

Mansfield's response to the president of the tribunal was brief but reassuring. He stated that the prosecution's case rested upon "several factors." They included admissions made by the accused themselves during the pretrial Allied investigations of Japanese war crimes suspects.[4] Moreover, there were "certain direct acts of some of the accused with regard to orders, and the formulation of" war crimes. For instance, Mansfield explained, the prosecution had documentary evidence of "the Prisoner of War Punishment Act and the act under which the American aviators who were shot down in Japan were executed without trial." Furthermore, evidence specifically against the accused Tōjō would show that "he directly announced on one occasion that Japan would not follow the Geneva Convention," and also that he "gave instructions to camp commanders, at meetings of camp commanders, which were contrary to the rules of international warfare."[5] In short, the prosecution's case would contain a variety of "linkage evidence," i.e. the evidence that would show the direct connection of the accused with the commission of war crimes.

The actual case that the prosecution presented did not betray Mansfield's words. However, the linkage evidence introduced was limited in both quantity and quality and did not always show conclusively the culpability of individual accused in terms of ordering, authorization, or knowledge of war crimes. The bulk of the prosecution's case, as a matter of fact, was "crime-base evidence," whose function was to document the occurrence of various episodes of war crimes while not necessarily linking them to the accused. How did the prosecution propose to deal with this particular problem?[6]

Mansfield had a ready answer to this question, too, when he took the podium again about two weeks later to deliver the opening statement for the main phase on war crimes relative to the Pacific region. He first acknowledged that an inordinate amount of evidentiary materials was at hand for the war crimes phase and that it would be "impossible in any reasonable length of time to put before the tribunal detailed evidence of all the offenses committed by the Japanese against the recognized laws and customs of war." For this reason, and as had already been approved by the tribunal in preceding months, "a method has been devised which will be relatively short and which will not omit any important matter."[7] The method being referred to involved using synopses for organizing and presenting the mass of evidentiary materials for the sake of saving time and resources. (See Chapter 1 under 1.4.) Mansfield went on to explain that in this manner the episodes of war

---

[4] Some of those who investigated the accused in the pretrial phase served also as members of the International Prosecution Section.
[5] T11760.
[6] See Chapter 10 for the discussion of "crime-base evidence" and "linkage evidence" in present-day international and hybrid criminal proceedings.
[7] T12859.

crimes would be "classified by areas, and in each area it will be shown that the mistreatment of prisoners of war, civilian internees and native inhabitants was *similar*"[8] (emphasis added). In other words, the evidence would be presented to establish a pattern in the ways in which members of the Japanese armed forces treated prisoners of war, civilian internees, and non-interned civilians across regions. Elaborating further, he stated:

*This similarity of treatment* throughout the territories occupied by the Japanese forces will, it is submitted, lead to the conclusion that such mistreatment was the result not of the independent acts of the individual Japanese Commanders and soldiers, but of the general policy of the Japanese forces and the Japanese government.[9] (emphasis added)

Mansfield's strategy thus aimed at inferring governmental policies from a widespread pattern of conduct. While this method of using circumstantial evidence to connect high-level officials to specific criminal conduct is legitimate, it also requires the prosecution to provide specific criteria for the analysis of crimes committed under varied circumstances by different military units in a variety of settings.[10]

The prosecution at Tokyo thus aimed not only to document the broad geographical distribution and recurrence of war crimes, but also to show similar patterns in the ways in which the Japanese committed war crimes at different places and times. The proof of patterns of culpable activities would, the prosecution argued, establish an inference that the commission of war crimes was an integral part of the Japanese war policy. What did the word "similarly" mean, though? How did the prosecution plan to document such patterns? As it turns out, members of the prosecution had different answers to these questions.

The Chinese associate prosecutor, Xiang Zhejun, for example, invoked the concept of "similarity" to argue that the Nanjing Massacre (also known as the "Rape of Nanjing") was not an isolated instance of atrocity, but that the types of crimes witnessed at Nanjing – murder, massacre, torture, rape, robbery, looting, and wanton destruction of property, as Xiang named them – "*took place in*

---

[8] T12859–61. The prosecution identified twenty-one general "areas" at which war crimes were committed. They were namely: (1) Singapore and Malaya; (2) Burma and Thailand; (3) Hong Kong; (4) Taiwan; (5) Hainan Island; (6) Andaman and Nicobar Islands; (7) Java; (8) Borneo; (9) Sumatra and Banka Island; (10) Celebes; (11) Ambon; (12) Timor; (12) New Guinea; (14) New Britain; (15) Solomons, Gilberts, Nauru and Ocean Islands; (16) other Pacific Islands; (17) French Indochina; (18) China other than Hong Kong; (19) sea transportation; (20) Japan; and (21) atrocities at sea.

[9] T12861.

[10] Some of the factors used in contemporary tribunals to demonstrate patterns of systematic conduct include the "organized nature of the acts of violence and the improbability of their random occurrence." Patterns of crimes can be established by demonstrating "the non-accidental repetition of similar criminal conduct on a regular basis." *Prosecutor v. Blaskic* Case IY-95-14-A, Appeals Chamber Judgment of July 29, 2004, p. 36.

## 6.1 Challenges and Methods of Proof

*every province* in occupied China *and covered the entire period* from 1937 to 1945"[11] (emphasis added).

The Philippine associate prosecutor, Pedro Lopez, meanwhile, attempted to use the concept of "similarity" of offense in the sense of *"the technique and method used* in the wholesale murder, torture, and rape, and the wanton destruction of property"[12] (emphasis added). The techniques and methods he documented, however, were not particularly unique or peculiar to the Japanese conduct of war. For instance, massacring civilians and prisoners of war by assembling them in close confinement, carrying out scorched-earth policy to destroy suspected guerrilla bases, and using torture during interrogations of enemy nationals to extract confessions, have often been employed in waging war. Without further evidence of common patterns by which these crimes were committed, these might not be sufficient to establish that they were perpetrated according to national policies to which the accused could be connected.[13]

The Dutch prosecutor, Sinninghe Damste, on the other hand, attempted to use the notion of "similarity" to show the widespread and recurring nature of the same *categories* of war crimes. He singled out as recurring categories of offense the following acts: murder, summary execution, torture by the military police force (hereafter "Kenpeitai"), general mistreatment of prisoners of war and civilians at internment camps, forced labor on civilians (known as "*rōmusha*"), and "forced prostitution."[14]

Mansfield himself and other American and British Commonwealth prosecutors gave the word "similarity" no particular meaning but enumerated various *categories of offense as listed in* Appendix D, which they alleged were commonplace occurrences for the duration of the war in the Pacific theater. Chapter 9 will examine how the Majority Judgment responded to these various prosecution approaches to demonstrating a common pattern sufficient to link the accused to the war crimes charged in a manner satisfying the burden of proof beyond a reasonable doubt.

The indefinite manner in which the prosecution deployed the concept of similarity presented the defense with an opportunity to attack the prosecution case on war crimes at its core. During its summation, the defense pointed out that the notion of similarly patterned war crimes was "far too vague to be made the foundation of a highly criminal charge," and that the prosecution "does not

---

[11] T3886–7.
[12] T12351.
[13] Some methods of torture used by the Japanese military force ("Kenpeitai") may well be considered as unique, such as "water cure" (which simulated drowning, somewhat like waterboarding). The prosecution argued during the summation that the "uniformity" of Kenpeitai cruelty "must have been the result of a common training," and that, "if such a common training had been given it must have been a matter of Government policy." (T40101).
[14] For the Dutch presentation of war crimes, see T13476–14051.

208    Accountability for War Crimes

even say that the 'pattern' was uniformly found everywhere. In some cases admittedly it was not."¹⁵ Tacitly admitting that the crimes occurred, the defense offered an alternative explanation for the similarities in the Japanese conduct of war and military occupation:

> Even if the alleged atrocities or other contraventions assume a similar singular pattern of acts it cannot justify such an assumption [of orders by higher authorities]. Such a pattern may have been a sheer reflection of national or racial traits. Crimes no less than masterpieces of art may express certain characteristics reflected the mores of a race. Similarities in the geographic, economic, or strategic state of affairs may in part account for the "similar pattern" assumed.¹⁶ (emphasis in the original)

If the defense's explanation as above were to stand, it might as well serve to support the prosecution's contention that the Japanese "frequently and habitually" committed war crimes as alleged in the indictment. This part of the defense's argument appeared to escape the attention of the judges, however, who focused on assessing the validity of the prosecution's contention of "similarly patterned" atrocities. As will be seen in Part II, the majority found that evidence supported this contention and, based on the finding, concluded that the atrocities were "either secretly ordered or willfully permitted by the Japanese Government or individual members thereof and by the leaders of the armed forces."¹⁷

## 6.2    The Prosecution's Case

### 6.2.1    China: The Nanjing Massacre

The prosecution's strategy in presenting the evidence of war crimes relative to China was to organize it around the documentation of the Nanjing Massacre. The Central China Area Army, under command of defendant General Matsui Iwane, captured the city of Nanjing on December 13, 1937. Contemporaneous reporting by the Japanese and Western witnesses revealed that mass executions, mass looting, large-scale destruction of property, mass rape, and other acts of violence were committed by the Japanese servicemen at an alarming rate in the initial days, and lasting for several weeks.

The Chinese associate prosecutor, Xiang Zhejun, contended that the Nanjing Massacre was "no isolated instance" but, as cited above, an "outstanding example" of the Japanese conduct of war in China.¹⁸ He further held that the

---

[15] T42261.
[16] T42203.
[17] Justice Webb did not make the same findings in his draft judgment. See Chapter 10 for full analysis of the matter.
[18] T3887.

Japanese armed forces continued to commit these types of offenses throughout the theater of war in China, regardless of the "frequent notification and protest" by which the Japanese high-command organs and central government authorities were repeatedly put on notice. "This was the Japanese pattern for warfare," Xiang maintained.[19] We should note here that there are two possible interpretations of how these widespread crimes might establish the culpability of individual accused. On the one hand, the duration, repetition, scale, and geographical spread of these crimes could give rise to an inference of a policy. A theory of liability such as "cabinet responsibility," or "government responsibility," or actual participation by individual accused in the formulation, approval, or implementation of such policies, could then connect individuals to that policy. On the other hand, the widespread and systematic nature of the crimes, if proved, could give rise to an imputation of knowledge of the crimes to the accused. In such a case, it would be their failure to prevent such crimes, as charged in Count 55 of the indictment, that would ground their culpability.

The prosecution began its case by detailing the circumstances of the Nanjing Massacre. It called to the stand 13 American, Chinese, and Japanese witnesses. (This was the only single episode of war crimes for which the prosecution introduced multiple witnesses in excess of 5.) The witnesses included the former members of the International Committee for the Nanjing Safety Zone, which the foreign residents in Nanjing established shortly before the Japanese invasion for the purpose of protecting the civilian population in the city. Twenty-seven court exhibits containing corroborative evidentiary documents were also presented. They comprised affidavits and statements taken from victims and witnesses of atrocity; excerpts from a book of documents compiled and published by Kelly & Walsh in 1939 by the International Committee for the Nanjing Safety Zone[20]; charts tallying burials conducted at the time of atrocity; a summary report on the investigations of Japanese war crimes in Nanjing, prepared by the procurator of the Nanjing District Court; and diplomatic dispatches and correspondence. The prosecution also introduced records of the pretrial Allied interrogation of two accused, Matsui and Lieutenant General Mutō Akira, the latter having served as vice chief of staff of the Central China Area Army at the time.[21]

This substantial body of evidence aimed to support two of the core contentions of the Chinese associate prosecutor: (1) that murder, massacre, torture, rape, robbery, looting, and wanton destruction of property were the types

---

[19] The presentation of evidence on war crime in China was made by a joint team of Chinese and American prosecutors.
[20] PX323, T4508–36. For a brief account of the publication, see Testimony by Miner Bates, T2626–7.
[21] Evidence relating to the Nanjing Massacre can be found at T2527–692, 3369–89, 3435–9, 3453–65, 3505–13, 3886–44, and 4451–604.

of offense commonly committed by the Japanese servicemen during the initial weeks of the Japanese military occupation of Nanjing; and (2) that the Japanese military and government authorities were put on notice about the mass atrocity from early on. The prosecution alleged that Matsui, Mutō and Foreign Minister Hirota received various reports from the Japanese diplomatic corps represented in Nanjing and from other sources. This latter contention, if proved, would establish knowledge on the part of Japanese officials, on which basis they might be convicted for failing to prevent these crimes.

The prosecution's key evidence against Matsui was his pretrial Allied interrogation record, dated March 8, 1946, in which he readily admitted that he acquired knowledge of his troops' acts of violence shortly after the fall of Nanjing. Matsui had commanded the military operations of the Central China Area Army from his headquarters in Shanghai, but he made a one-week visit of Nanjing starting on December 17, whereupon he received reports on atrocity as well as observing the condition of the city himself.[22] On this particular matter, the following dialog between the Allied interrogator and Matsui was recorded during the pretrial interrogation:

> Q. [Allied interrogator]. When did you first hear, if you did hear, that Europe and America got the idea that your troops committed many outrages in Nanking?
> A. [Matsui]. Almost as soon as I entered Nanking.
> Q. You heard about it?
> A. Yes.
> Q. From what source did you hear about it?
> A. From Japanese diplomats.
> Q. Who was the Japanese diplomat?
> A. It was a very small diplomatic official and I do not remember his name, the Consul at Nanking.[23]

Matsui went on to state that while he believed the behavior of the Japanese soldiers to be excellent insofar as obeying orders was concerned, the troop conduct was bad when it came to their "behavior towards the Chinese population and their acts generally." He also acknowledged that "there were some lawless elements in the army." When asked about his general orders regarding

---

[22] According to Matsui's former vice chief of staff, Mutō Akira, the headquarters of the Central China Area Force was initially set up in the suburbs of Shanghai city, and moved to the forward base at Suzhou on December 5, 1937. After the visit of Nanjing, Matsui returned to Shanghai. Several defense witnesses, including Matsui and Mutō, subsequently testified (during the defense phase) that their stay in Nanjing actually lasted "for four or five days" only. DX3454, T33087–91.

[23] PX257, T3453–4.

## 6.2 The Prosecution's Case

the maintenance of military discipline prior to the invasion, Matsui stressed that he was personally committed to "strict discipline and the punishment of all evil doers," and that he "advocated the thorough investigation of the Nanking Incident."[24] That said, he could only recollect one case of court martial involving an officer and three more involving enlisted men, and he had no further information concerning these court-martial cases. What was more, he himself was subjected to no disciplinary action. He was recalled to Tokyo in February 1938 but that he was not required to report on the conduct of his forces in Nanjing.[25]

A pretrial Allied interrogation record of Mutō, dated April 16, 1946, provided more details as to how Matsui and Mutō received reports on atrocities and what steps they took to address the problem. Mutō recounted that Matsui was suffering from tuberculosis in those days, but that he travelled to Nanjing shortly after the city fell in order to participate in the takeover ceremonies. Mutō accompanied him and purportedly stayed in Nanjing for ten days. According to his account, both men learned upon arrival in Nanjing that the Japanese servicemen committed acts of violence, the source of information being Major General Tsukada Osamu, chief of staff of the Central China Area Army.[26] The gist of information was that "there were incidents of stealing, killing, assault and rape." The nature of information was sufficiently upsetting that Matsui became "mad and bawled out," so Mutō stated, and Matsui was said to have issued orders that all units except security troops leave the city.

Mutō's account revealed that only a selection of "fine troops" had been allowed entry to begin with, out of concern that those men who had been "under pressure for such a long time" might cause trouble.[27] In other words, Matsui and his subordinate officers had been aware of the low morale of the troops due to the prolonged tour of duty, and they could foresee the probable adverse consequence of letting these men participate in the invasion of Nanjing. Matsui's prior order to limit the troops' entry appears to have been ignored, however, as the chief of staff's reporting on "stealing, killing, assault and rape" suggests. This caused Matsui to issue another order during his one-week visit that excess troops be moved out of the city. But this order does not appear to have been followed either, given the overwhelming evidence that the Japanese servicemen continued to commit acts of violence at an alarming rate in the ensuing weeks.

As regards evidence against Hirota, two witnesses and several documents showed that the Japanese Ministry of Foreign Affairs received various reports

---

[24] Ibid., T3458–9.
[25] Ibid., T3464.
[26] PX255, T3552–9.
[27] Ibid., T3553–4.

and protests emanating from China, and that Foreign Minister Hirota was personally put on notice of the incoming information. One of the witnesses, Itō Nobufumi, was formerly minister-at-large in China and posted at Shanghai between September 1937 and February 1938. He testified that he "received reports from members of the [Japanese] diplomatic corps and from press men that the Japanese Army at Nanking had committed various atrocities at the time," and that he transmitted all of his reports "to the Foreign Office – in form they were all addressed to the Foreign Minister."[28] Itō appeared reluctant to single out Hirota as the recipient of the reports, however, as he insisted that he did not know to whom these reports ultimately should be directed.

Another prosecution witness attested to his personal knowledge that the reports and protests forwarded to the Japanese government came to the personal attention of Foreign Minister Hirota. The witness in question was Miner S. Bates, a founding member of the International Committee for the Nanjing Safety Zone and one of those foreign nationals who repeatedly visited the Japanese embassy in Nanjing in those days to file complaints. In Bates's case, he attested to having frequented the embassy "almost daily for the first three weeks," to submit a typed report or protest. "These men were honestly trying to do what little they could in a very bad situation," so Bates remarked on the Japanese embassy officials, "but they themselves were terrified by the military and they could do nothing except forward these communications through Shanghai to Tokyo."[29] When cross-examined about the final destination of the filed reports and complaints, Bates testified that "I have seen telegrams sent by Mr. [Joseph] Grew, the Ambassador in Tokyo, to the American Embassy in Nanking, which referred to these reports in great detail and referred to conversations in which they had been discussed between Mr. Grew and officials of the Gaimusho [the Japanese Ministry of Foreign Affairs], including Mr. HIROTA."[30]

The prosecution provided little information regarding the actions taken on the part of Hirota upon receipt of incoming reports and protests about the Japanese military violence. However, one document brought to light that Hirota was concerned about reports of the vandalizing of US property in Nanjing and that he personally took initiatives to have his government take a prompt remedial step. The document in question was a dispatch from C. E. Gauss, the American consul general at Tokyo, Japan, to the US embassies in Shanghai, Nanjing, Beiping, and Hankou, dated January 20, 1938. Gauss stated that, just recently, "the Minister for Foreign Affairs laid before the Cabinet the note mentioned [regarding the Japanese illegal entry into American property in Nanjing],

[28] T3505–6.
[29] T2638.
[30] T2661.

and that a drastic measure to assure compliance by forces in the field with instructions from Tokyo is being considered." The Japanese government was expected to provide Gauss with further information the following day about the exact measure the Japanese government was to take.[31] This sequence of events shows that Hirota was willing and able to take such issues to the Cabinet. The ability to take such initiatives became a contested issue during the defense phase (see Section 6.3 below) and also played an important role in the majority judgment.

### 6.2.2    China: The Post-Nanjing Period

After completing the documentation of the Nanjing Massacre, the prosecution introduced further evidentiary materials concerning other episodes of war crimes in the post-Nanjing period. The emphasis of this part of the presentation was not to substantiate every single known episode of atrocity. Rather, the prosecution limited its task to presenting a minimal amount of evidentiary materials, which would be just enough to sketch out the geographical distribution and recurrence of Japanese military violence.[32] To this end, the prosecution presented 49 statements that were taken from the victims and witnesses of atrocity at different combat zones and occupied territories in China. Most of them were formulaically written, single-page statements of offense that contained bare minimum information about dates, locations, types of offense, and victims involved. In a word, there was not much substance in them. This shortcoming elicited criticism from Justice Webb, who remarked, "There is hardly evidence. There are no details. What court could act on evidence like that?"[33] He expressed his dissatisfaction by further stating, "What they are doing is using, I have no doubt, affidavits which were used before the United Nations War Crimes Commission to establish a mere prima facie case and which contained a minimum amount of facts, just enough for very limited purposes."[34]

These remarks point to the tribunal's skeptical views about the adequacy of the evidence being introduced regarding war crimes in China in the post-Nanjing period. As we will see, this became a point of contention in the judgment and separate opinions. A total of three prosecution witnesses for this phase did not help improve the quality of the presentation either, as they testified only briefly, and on discrete episodes of atrocity.[35] The prosecution also

---

[31] PX328, T4558.
[32] Some of the documented instances of atrocity relating to China are itemized as murder counts (Counts 44–50).
[33] T4609.
[34] T4610.
[35] Testimony by Albert Dorrance, T3390–414; Testimony by Liu Yao-Hwa, T4614–18; and Testimony by Ti Shu-tang, T4618–29. These three witnesses gave testimony on war crimes in connection with the fall of Hankou in October 1938, and the Japanese invasion and military occupation in Hebei Province in 1941–4.

presented no evidence that contained affirmative proof of orders, authorization, or knowledge of war crimes by any individual accused.

That said, the evidence thus presented did bring out that a number of episodes of atrocity occurred in the post-Nanjing period, which included murder, massacre, torture, arson, plunder, mass deportation and mass forced labor, rape and abduction of women, and forced prostitution. What is more, the prosecution presented the postwar interrogation records of two accused, General Hata Shunroku and Mutō, to bring out that the Government of Japan in 1938 adopted a formal policy not to recognize the applicability of the laws and customs of war in China.

The pretrial interrogation record of Mutō, dated April 16, 1946, showed that, as former director of the Military Affairs Bureau of the Ministry of the Army (1939–42), Mutō had been responsible for the construction of prisoner-of-war camps. He also acknowledged that, in addition, he was in charge of formulating policies governing the treatment of prisoners of war until the start of the Pacific War, when the Prisoner-of-War Information Bureau took over this task. (The Japanese government established the Prisoner-of-War Information Bureau on December 27, 1941 in compliance with the Hague Convention No. 4.[36]) Having made these admissions, however, Mutō denied that the Military Affairs Bureau formulated any prisoner-of-war policies during the armed conflict with China, because his government did not recognize the existence of a state of war between the two countries. He briefly explained the wartime government's stance as follows:

The question of whether Chinese captives would be declared prisoners of war or not was quite a problem and it was finally decided in 1938 that because the Chinese conflict was officially known as an "incident" that Chinese captives would not be regarded as prisoners of war.[37]

The policy to reject prisoner-of-war status for Chinese soldiers in Japanese custody appears to have remained in force for the duration of the war. In a separate pretrial interrogation, Hata was asked about his own opinion on the nature of the Sino-Japanese armed conflict. Hata had previously served

---

[36] For the imperial ordinance on the Prisoner-of-Information Bureau, see PX92, introduced at T505.
[37] PX255, T3436–7. Nakayama Yasuto, a defense witness and formerly a staff officer of the Central China Area Army, explained during the defense phase that "what Colonel MUTO has stated concerns merely the aspects of the problem as it relates to international law, and the actual situation was that in Central China prisoners were accorded fair treatment as prisoners of war. Not only that, but those among the prisoners who grasped a true understanding of the Sino-Japanese conflict were later recruited for the regular troops of the Chinese Army, that is to say, the army which was under the Wang Ching-wei Regime." (T21939).

as commander-in-chief of the Central China Expeditionary Army[38] (February–December 1938), and subsequently as commander-in-chief of the China Expeditionary Force (1941–4) to oversee the entire military operations of the Imperial Japanese Army in the China theater. His response was that, "Although it actually was a war all they ever considered it as was a China Incident. Actually it was a war."[39]

The prosecution faced an enormous challenge in proving its China case. While it was relatively easy to produce evidence on Nanjing, how much and what kind of evidence would have been necessary to prove beyond a reasonable doubt common patterns in the way certain categories of crime were committed across a huge country over a period of eight years? To make matters more difficult, the prosecution was also under time pressure from the judges. Because crimes against peace were the priority, the China case beyond Nanjing was presented in summary fashion.

### 6.2.3 The Pacific Region

#### 6.2.3.1 The Prosecution Strategy

While the prosecution's case of war crimes relating to China was centered on a single episode of mass atrocity, the two remaining war crime phases relating to the Pacific region presented even greater challenges. The size of evidentiary materials for the Pacific phases was far greater than the one prepared for the Chinese phase. A total of 614 court exhibits were admitted, which served to document the broad geographical distribution and recurrence of war crimes.[40] The exhibits comprised affidavits, statements, and depositions that had been taken from victims, witnesses, and perpetrators of war crimes; captured Japanese military records, such as battlefield reports, military orders, instructions, and private diaries; reports of war crimes investigations by the Allied authorities as well as by the Government of Japan, produced at the war's end[41]; and excerpts from the records of contemporary Allied war crimes trials, such as

---

[38] After Matsui's recall to Tokyo, the Central China Area Army was reorganized to form the Central China Expeditionary Army.

[39] PX256, T3451.

[40] The prosecution's court exhibits included synopses, to which the Tokyo Tribunal assigned exhibit numbers. When the prosecution presented in evidence a document *and* one or more excerpts from the same document, the tribunal usually assigned a numerical number to the former (such as PX1984, Allied Postwar Interrogation of Tōjō Hideki), and then assigned to the latter the same numerical number plus an alphabet (such as PX1984-A and PX1984-B). For the purpose of this book, we regard them as constituting one court exhibit, i.e. not counting those exhibits that contain the excerpts of the admitted evidence.

[41] The Japanese government voluntarily set up a "Central Committee for Investigations Concerning Prisoners of War" at the war's end, and carried out its own war crimes investigations. The final reports were turned over to the Allied authorities. These reports, in turn, were put to use at the Tokyo Trial, by both the prosecution and the defense. See PX475-6, PX1921-4, and

the Yamashita Trial and the Honma Trial by the US Army at Manila (1945–6), trials held by the US Navy at Guam and Kwajalein (1945–7), and the British war crimes trials held at Singapore (1946–8).

In addition to documentary and affidavit evidence, twenty-four witnesses – mostly former Allied prisoners of war – took the witness stand to offer oral evidence concerning the general mistreatment of prisoners of war, civilian internees, and the non-interned civilian population in Japanese-occupied territories. Their testimony detailed the episodes of war crimes that the witnesses had personally experienced, such as, the Burma-Siam Death Railway, the Bataan Death Marches, the Sandakan Death Marches, the "Hell Ships" (prisoner-of-war transport by sea in overcrowded, inhumane conditions), and the massacre of Australian nurses at Banka Island, among other infamous cases.

The foregoing evidence aside, the prosecution's phases on war crimes relating to the Pacific region contained both an additional 172 court exhibits and 6 more witnesses to provide vital linkage evidence. What evidence, for example, could be adduced to link the accused in Tokyo to an incident of murder of a group of Australian nurses on a remote island in the Pacific? The strategy of the prosecution was to present the court with evidence designed not so much for documenting the link between specific war crimes and the individual accused in any affirmative manner, but rather for illuminating *the institutional and organizational dimensions* of the Japanese breach of the laws and customs of war.

More specifically, the bulk of the linkage evidence comprised (1) basic laws, rules, regulations, orders, notifications, instructions, and statements issued by the Ministry of the Army for the establishment of the prisoner-of-war administration; (2) requests, approvals, and reports regarding the use of prisoner-of-war labor, made to and from the Ministry of the Army on the one hand and, on the other, the army units at theaters of war, business leaders, and other non-military local authorities; (3) army-ministry's reports concerning the conditions of prisoner-of-war transfer, internment, labor, court-martials and punishments, and health; and (4) diplomatic records between the Japanese government and the protecting powers representing the Allied governments regarding the Japanese mistreatment of Allied prisoners of war and internees.

The six witnesses similarly gave testimony mainly on the institutional and organizational dimensions of war crimes, and especially with respect to the Ministry of the Army. One of the witnesses, Colonel Yamazaki Shigeru, who was a former official of the Prisoner-of-War Information Bureau, testified that the decision-making authority relating to prisoner-of-war affairs practically rested with the director of the Military Affairs Bureau. This position was

DX3128 (T5513–681, 14204–21, and 27894–900). For more information about the genesis of the government-led war crimes inquiries and reports, see Nagai, ed., *Sensō hanzai chōsa shiryō*.

## 6.2 The Prosecution's Case

"a kind of Chief of Staff to the War Minister,"[42] Yamazaki maintained, and "in so far as actual work [of the Prisoner-of-War Information Bureau] was concerned, nothing could be done without going through the Director of the Military Affairs Bureau."[43] Oral evidence such as this could be used against Mutō and Major General Satō Kenryō, who served as director of the Bureau successively (1939–42, and 1942–4, respectively).

There was just one instance during the witness testimony relating to the Pacific region where an accused was expressly named as a culpable individual. Captain James Chisholm from Australia, a former prisoner of war, attested not only to widespread prisoner-of-war mistreatment at the Naoetsu Camp in Niigata Prefecture (where he had been interned), but also to his personal knowledge of a tour of inspection carried out by defendant General Dohihara Kenji, then serving as commander of the Eastern District Army in central Japan. When asked by Justice Webb if he could identify the accused, this witness pointed at Dohihara in the dock and said, "That is him there."[44]

The prosecution thus introduced a very substantial body of evidence to support two of the core contentions of its case on war crimes in the Pacific region: (1) that the general categories of offense identified in Appendix D of the indictment were committed by the members of the Japanese armed forces throughout the theater of war and recurred for the duration of the war; and (2) that the members of the Japanese government and the military authorities were repeatedly put on inquiry notice about the Japanese mistreatment of prisoners of war and civilians in their custody, by way of protests from foreign governments, and also by internal reporting within the Ministry of the Army. It was, of course, the task of the judges to weigh this evidence, consider it in light of the arguments and evidence tendered by the defense, and reach factual findings on what the prosecution had succeeded in proving beyond a reasonable doubt. In principle, these factual findings would have to include a conclusion beyond a reasonable doubt that specific massacres or other crimes had occurred, because if the prosecution could not prove that the specific incidents had occurred there would be no basis for linkage to the accused. These factual findings, in turn, would provide the basis for assessing the culpability of individual accused according to criteria advanced by the judges as the appropriate legal standards. We will see in Part II to what extent the majority judgment and separate opinions actually proceeded in this manner in assessing the prosecution's war crimes case.

---

[42] T14846.
[43] T14847. Another former army-ministry official, Tanaka Ryūkichi, also testified on the relative superiority of the director of the Military Affairs Bureau vis-à-vis other army-ministry bureau chiefs. T14285–7.
[44] T14278.

Apart from evidence establishing institutional or organizational linkages to the crimes charged, the prosecution also introduced evidence against specific individual accused. For example, some of the army-ministry documents showed that at least two accused – Tōjō (army minister, 1940–4) and General Kimura Heitarō (vice army minister, 1941–3) – took affirmative steps to either formulate or issue certain prisoner-of-war policies, whose substance was in violation of the laws and customs of war.[45] In point of fact, Tōjō admitted during pretrial interrogations his responsibility for various instances of war crimes, and the records of the interrogations were admitted in evidence.

The army-ministry documents in evidence also contained correspondence in 1942 between Vice Army Minister Kimura and Itagaki, commander-in-chief of the Korea Army (1941–5), regarding transfer of prisoners of war from Singapore to Korea for labor and propaganda purposes.[46] The names of two former foreign ministers, Tōgō Shigenori and Shigemitsu Mamoru (1941–2 and 1945; and 1943–5, respectively), repeatedly appeared in evidentiary documents as well, as they were the ones to represent their government in their official capacity, and to respond to numerous incoming Allied queries and protests regarding the Japanese mistreatment of prisoners of war and civilian internees. This kind of evidence, of course, would have had far greater probative value than circumstantial inferences linking accused to a general policy or blanket failure to prevent crimes.

Furthermore, there was inculpatory evidence against certain accused relating to submarine atrocities. In his pretrial interrogation, Lieutenant General Ōshima Hiroshi (ambassador in Germany, 1940–5) admitted that he passed onto the Japanese naval attaché in March 1943 a German recommendation to kill the crews of enemy merchant vessels. This record was admitted in evidence.[47] A captured Japanese naval operation order, dated March 20, 1943, and also admitted in evidence, partly corroborated Ōshima's account. It showed that the First Submarine Force of the Sixth Fleet (headquartered at Truk in Japanese-controlled Caroline Islands in the Central Pacific; present-day Chuuk) ordered the carrying out of submarine atrocities.[48] Above all, a number of Allied protests (also admitted in evidence) showed that the Japanese government was

---

[45] For the relevant court exhibits, see PX1960–78, T14422–549.
[46] See PX1973–6, T14512–39.
[47] PX2106, T15187–9. For additional evidence by the prosecution concerning submarine atrocities, see PX3813A and PX3817 (T37907–12 and 37926–34).
[48] The relevant segment in the submarine operations order read, "Do not stop with the sinking of enemy ships and cargoes; at the same time that you carry out the complete destruction of the crews of the enemy's ships, if possible, seize part of the crew and endeavor to secure information about the enemy." PX2015, T15185. This document, notated as "Copy 24 of 70," was captured by the Allied forces during the Battle of Kwajalein in February 1944, and it subsequently was brought to the attention of the British government. A British protest, dated May 19, 1945, made direct reference to this captured naval operation order. See PX2103, T15180.

repeatedly put on inquiry notice in 1944–5 about the occurrence of individual episodes of submarine atrocity.[49] While not expressly named, these evidentiary materials could be held against two navy accused, Admiral Shimada Shigetarō (navy minister, 1941–4, and navy chief, 1944), and Vice Admiral Oka Takazumi (director of the Naval Affairs Bureau of the Ministry of the Navy, 1940–4).[50] To explore the prosecution's strategy in greater detail toward proving its case against specific accused, we may examine further some of these key evidentiary materials.

### 6.2.3.2. The Case against Tōjō

The prosecution appears to have had the least difficulty in making the case against Tōjō, partly because of his wartime positions that put him at the pinnacle of the Japanese government. He served as prime minister and concurrently army minister (1941–4) as well as army chief (February–July 1944), among other high positions held. Tōjō himself was prepared to admit that he had indeed held positions of authority, and that he accordingly bore individual responsibility. Building a strong case against Tōjō could assist in connecting other members of key bodies to policies and decisions attributed to his leadership role.

There was significant documentary evidence against Tōjō with regard to his authorizing the use of prisoner-of-war labor for work related to the operation of the war in direct contravention of the Hague Convention No. 4 and the Geneva Convention. Specifically, he was shown to have issued instructions to prisoner-of-war camp commanders, in mid-1942, that they must place prisoners of war under strict discipline and allow no one "to lie idle doing nothing but eating freely," so that the prisoners' labor and technical skills would be used for the waging of the "Greater East Asiatic War."[51] The army-ministry records revealed several instances when Tōjō and the vice army minister, Kimura, signed off on requests and queries from various quarters in the early months of the Pacific War, approving the transfer of prisoners of war to the inner territory of the Empire of Japan to address labor shortages.[52] What is more, a report generated by the postwar Government of Japan on the Death Railway singled out Tōjō as having a share of responsibility in the decision to use prisoner-of-war labor for the railway project.[53] This report had been voluntarily prepared and

---

[49] For the Allied protests regarding submarine atrocities, see PX2076–86, T15088–106.
[50] There was a third navy accused – Admiral Nagano Osami (navy chief, 1941–4) – but he died shortly after the start of the court proceedings at the Tokyo Trial.
[51] PX1960, T14422–4; PX1961, T14425; PX1962, T14427; and PX1963, T14429.
[52] For relevant court exhibits, see PX1967–78, T14484–549; and PX2002–2015, T14708–28.
[53] PX475, introduced at T5513. This report is reproduced as "Japanese Government Report on Employment of War Prisoners in Siam-Burma Railway Construction," in Kratoska, ed., *The Thailand-Burma Railway, 1942–1946*, vol. 1, 342–403. For reference to responsibility of Tōjō, Sugiyama, and Terauchi, see p. 391.

submitted to the Allied authorities by the Japanese government as early as January 1946. It was put to use at British war crimes proceedings and at the Tokyo Trial.[54] A former staff officer of the Army General Staff, Lieutenant General Wakamatsu Tadakazu, verified the substance of the postwar government report. When taking the stand as a prosecution witness, he testified that Sugiyama, Tōjō, and Kimura were chiefly responsible for sanctioning the use of prisoner-of-war labor for the railway construction. But he added that Kimura assisted only "through his official position, though not basically responsible." Kimura became party to the decision-making on the use of prisoner-of-war labor merely because of his "official position" as vice minister, and therefore, he was "not basically responsible."[55]

Further, Tōjō incriminated himself by his admission that he personally ordered the trial and punishment of eight captured "Doolittle Flyers," three of whose death sentences he confirmed. These American airmen, under the command of Lieutenant Colonel James Doolittle, had carried out on April 18, 1942 the first Allied air attacks against the Japanese homeland, launched from the aircraft carrier *Hornet*.[56] The prosecution's case also implicated two other accused for the trial and punishment of Allied airmen as well.[57]

Quite apart from proof of the issuance of these various military orders and instructions, the prosecution's case also contained evidence of Tōjō's awareness about the widespread mistreatment of prisoners of war and civilian internees as well as specific instances of atrocity involving civilian victims in occupied territories. He was the one to establish the Prisoner-of-War Information Bureau to begin with, which provided his government with a formal institutional mechanism for gathering, maintaining, and transmitting information about the enemy nationals in Japanese custody.[58] Proving the existence and functions of this institution was of vital importance for the prosecution's case both against Tōjō and other accused that could be connected to decisions or policies regarding prisoners of war.

Tōjō readily admitted that, since the early months of the Pacific War, the Ministry of the Army routinely received inquiries and protests from foreign

---

[54] For discussion regarding the use of this report at the British war crimes trials in Singapore, see Totani, *Justice in Asia and the Pacific Region, 1945–1952*, chapter 3.

[55] PX1989, T14634.

[56] Tōjō stated during the pretrial Allied interrogation that he came under great pressure from Army Chief Sugiyama to mete out stern punishment to Doolittle Flyers, but that he confirmed the execution of three only out of consideration for Emperor Hirohito's will. PX1984-A, T14600–3. Hirohito remarked approvingly on Tōjō's handling of the Doolittle Flyers after the war. See Terasaki, ed., *Shōwa tennō dokuhakuroku*, 89.

[57] See PX1991–3, T14662–73. For summations relating to the Japanese mistreatment of Doolittle Flyers, and especially those concerning the responsibility of Hata, see T40762–75 and T43399–431.

[58] According to the record of Tōjō's pretrial interrogation, "there was no organization set up to deal with Chinese prisoners" in connection with the so-called China Incident. PX1980-B, T14559.

governments regarding the treatment of Allied nationals under Japanese control. The inquiries and protests were usually forwarded from the Ministry of Foreign Affairs by way of the Prisoner-of-War Information Bureau, and they were then "taken up at bi-weekly meetings," which were held within the Ministry of the Army.[59] To elaborate the nature of information sharing within the army establishment, Tōjō offered the following additional explanation:

These matters were usually brought up at the meetings of the bureau chiefs of the War Department [the Ministry of the Army]. These meetings were held twice a week. Either the Chief of the Prisoner of War Information Bureau or the Military Affairs Bureau would bring them up. They were referred by the bureau chief meetings to the commander in the field who had the authority to act. If there was inhumane treatment, he would take measures accordingly, and the report would probably come back to me as War Minister.[60]

The above statement shows that the Ministry of the Army, as well as the Ministry of Foreign Affairs, were put on inquiry notice on a regular basis, and that they had the incoming inquiries and protests forwarded to the army units concerned for the latter's further actions and reporting.

When questioned during the pretrial interrogation about steps taken regarding the incoming inquiries and protests, Tōjō replied that there were "many instances" of follow-up investigations. "There was a case of mistreatment of prisoners of war during the building of the Burma-Thai Railway," he stated, "and I ordered a court martial in this connection."[61] It appears that Tōjō rarely carried out tours of inspection to ascertain the prisoner-of-war conditions himself, but he admittedly visited at least once the Ōmori Prisoner-of-War Camp in Tokyo, Japan.[62] Moreover, he received "rumors" of prisoner-of-war mistreatment in the wake of the Battle of Bataan and the Battle of Corregidor (April–May 1942). He inquired into the matter one year later, in May 1943, when he visited the Philippines to discuss the preparations for independence of the Philippines. Tōjō's inquiry about the Death Marches amounted to a passing reference only, however, and he accepted the explanation by the then chief of staff of the 14th Army, Lieutenant General Wachi Takeji, that "due to lack of transport facilities, the prisoners of war had to march long distances in the heat and that there was some suffering, and deaths resulted."[63]

---

[59] PX1980-D, T14565.
[60] PX1983-B, T14599.
[61] PX1980-E, T14565–6.
[62] PX1982-A, T14588. The prisoner-of-war camp at Ōmori served as the headquarters of the Tokyo Area Prisoner-of-War Camps. They comprised prisoner-of-war camps in Kawasaki, Mizushima, Naoetsu, Tokyo, and Yokohama.
[63] PX1980-E, T14572.

During the pretrial interrogation, Tōjō expressed regrets about the allegations of widespread atrocity. He nonetheless maintained that the army and navy authorities in those years "did not even suspect that such things happened."[64] The record shows that this particular remark elicited further questioning from the Allied interrogator. The following dialog ensued:

> Q. [The Allied interrogator]. You mentioned today that you did not even suspect the occurrence of these atrocities and the inhuman treatment of prisoners. How can you say this when the United States and Great Britain, through the Swiss and other governments, made numerous written and detailed complains to your Foreign Office about these very matters?
> 
> A. [Tōjō]. The matter of responsibility for humane considerations and the following of treaty provisions were *the responsibility of the various army commanders*. I believed that they were following them. This is my answer.
> 
> Q. So that, although these numerous complaints were made on these matters, you still trusted the commanders in the field and did not believe the complaints. Is that true?
> 
> A. As I said before, when a protest would come in, I would forward it to *the responsible army commander involved* for action which I thought was taken. I could not tell whether the protest was appropriate or not, and I presumed that investigations were made, followed by courts martial or other suitable action.[65] (emphasis added)

In the dialog above, Tōjō maintained that his duty as army minister was to have the incoming inquiries and protests forwarded to the army units concerned, and not necessarily to act on the inquiries and protests himself. He conceded, "Of course, since I was the supervisor of military administration, I am completely responsible."[66] Even so, he repeated that he was justified to entrust every military commander to dispose of the incoming inquiries and protests properly, "because it was *his* responsibility" to take appropriate actions[67] (emphasis added). This particular line of argument is important because – as we will see in our analysis of the defense case under Section 6.4 – it clashed with the arguments made by those other individual accused who had served as "various military commanders" in theaters of war.

---

[64] PX1981-A, T14575–6.
[65] PX1981-B, T14580.
[66] PX1981-A, T14576.
[67] PX1981-B, T14581.

## 6.2 The Prosecution's Case

### 6.2.3.3 Circulation of Information on Atrocities

While Tōjō's pretrial interrogation records shed light on how the Ministry of the Army dealt with the Allied inquiries and protests, the testimony by a prosecution's witness, Suzuki Tadakatsu, revealed not only that the Ministry of the Army was put on inquiry notice repeatedly, but that *other* government ministries, too, were alerted just the same. Suzuki was a career diplomat and served as chief of the "Bureau in Charge of Japanese Nationals in Enemy Nations," an office established within the Ministry of Foreign Affairs in mid-November 1942 to take charge of processing the incoming inquiries and protests on Japanese violations of laws and customs of war, and preparing replies on behalf of the government.[68] The successive foreign ministers were the immediate superior of this bureau's chief.

Suzuki's testimony confirmed that there was an established channel of communication between the Ministry of Foreign Affairs and the Ministry of the Army, as already explained in Tōjō's pretrial interrogation. But Suzuki had more details to offer:

The notes were received either in French or English and were translated into Japanese. A copy of the note with its Japanese translation was sometimes addressed to the Minister of War, the Vice Minister of War, the Military Affairs Bureau, or the Prisoner-of-War Information Bureau, depending on the importance and also the contents of the note ... In sending those notes, together with their translation, we accompanied them with a covering note which was either a simple note in itself, or accompanied by our own comments or recommendations.[69]

He added that, "in order to speed up the routine business, it was requested from the War Office that the documents be sent to the chiefs of the bureaus and sections and not to higher levels than that." Accordingly, the Ministry of Foreign Affairs usually forwarded the incoming inquiries and protests to the director of the Prisoner of War Information Bureau and the director of the Military Affairs Bureau of the Ministry of the Army, "except in the case of very important documents." The ones considered very important purportedly were forwarded directly to the army minister or the vice army minister, or both.[70]

Upon further examination, Suzuki testified that incoming inquiries and protests were also forwarded to multiple government agencies "simultaneously and independently and separately."[71] A small sample of documents from the foreign-ministry archives (which the prosecution presented in evidence) showed that the recipients of incoming inquiries and protests indeed were not

---

[68] For further evidence regarding the functions of this Bureau see DX3895, T38780–3.
[69] PX1489, T12833–4.
[70] T12841–2.
[71] T15523.

limited to the army minister, vice army minister, the director of the Military Affairs Bureau of the Ministry of the Army, or the chief of the Prisoner-of-War Information Bureau. There were other addressees, which included the minister and vice minister of the Ministry of the Navy, the Ministry of Home Affairs, the Ministry of Legal Affairs, the Ministry of Colonial Affairs, and the Ministry of Greater East Asia. One of the admitted documents also identified the director of the Naval Affairs Bureau of the Ministry of the Navy as yet another addressee.[72] On this basis, the prosecution supported the imputation of knowledge to a number of ministries and, by further inference, to the Cabinet. This provided a foundation from which to link specific accused to a failure to prevent such crimes under Count 55, as long as the prosecution could also establish that in the case of each accused such a duty existed.

Regarding the broad dissemination of information on mistreatment, Suzuki testified that the Ministry of Foreign Affairs commonly forwarded the incoming inquiries and protests to multiple government agencies, because "the text of the protest itself is rather large and bulky and containing many and various items; and the investigations into the subjects inquired into in the protest are carried on by various agencies concerned with the matter."[73] From this particular remark, one can learn that the Ministry of Foreign Affairs did not consider the Prisoner-of-War Information Bureau as the sole clearing house of prisoner-of-war information. The Ministry, at least, doubted the comprehensiveness of the bureau's information-gathering capacity, and it thus cast its net wide, requesting other ministries and agencies to also review the forwarded inquires and protests and to take necessary actions in order to help ascertain the facts.[74]

"The Foreign Office's part in this matter," Suzuki continued to explain, "is to assemble the reports and information obtained as a result of investigation and to coordinate them and, on the basis of the results drawn up by the Foreign Office, to consult with the government departments concerned – government departments and other agencies concerned."[75] The Japanese replies (which were signed off by the successive foreign ministers, including Tōgō and Shigemitsu) usually were of the nature that denied various allegations of atrocity, or that refused to cooperate with the protecting powers in facilitating the prisoner-of-war camp inspection. Many inquiries and protests were simply unanswered.

---

[72] See PX2170–74, T15507–15.
[73] T15522.
[74] For further evidence by the defense concerning the involvement of various government offices, including the Government of Manchukuo, in the management of the Allied prisoners of war and civilian internees, see the testimony by Matsumoto Shun'ichi, T27139–40; and the testimony by Odajima Tadashi, T27871–2.
[75] T15522.

The foregoing discussion and analysis summarize the case by the prosecution on war crimes. Before discussing the defense case it is worth remembering that, apart from individual accused such as Tōjō, the vast majority of the prosecution's evidence was "crime-base evidence," in which the names of individual accused rarely appeared, if at all. What is more, those evidentiary materials whose ostensive purpose was to offer "linkage evidence" carried information mainly about *the institutional and organizational dimensions* of war crimes, and not always proof of criminal orders, authorization, or knowledge, by the individual accused. This state of affairs in the prosecution's case needs not be construed as a shortcoming, but rather as the expression of a distinct method of proof and a theory of responsibility. The approach was two-pronged.

On the one hand, the prosecution aimed at establishing the guilt of the accused not only by presenting affirmative evidence of criminal orders or authorization, but also by documenting the broad geographical distribution and recurrence of similarly patterned war crimes, *so that the inference of policy could be made in the Japanese commission of war crimes*. At the same time, the prosecution built its case on the theory of government responsibility as articulated in the indictment (Appendix E), by which the prosecution treated the accused as "one of those responsible for all the acts and omissions of the various governments *of which he was member*, and of the various civil, military, or naval organizations *in which he held a position of authority*." It follows that, under the prosecution's scheme of things, the required proof (1) would be one of the widespread and recurring characters of war crimes, and (2) the accused's having held the positions of authority in the government must be proven.

The second focus of the prosecution's theory centered on alleged omissions, that is, a failure to take action to prevent the occurrence of war crimes. This theory built upon the evidence discussed earlier showing that specific ministries, agencies, and individuals had received (constructively or otherwise) sufficient information on the basis of which they either knew, or were put on inquiry notice, that crimes had occurred. If the prosecution could also prove that these individuals holding positions of authority in those ministries and agencies had a duty to take effective action to prevent the crimes but failed to do so, they would have gone a long way toward proving their case.

With these features of the prosecution's method of proof and theory of responsibility in mind, let us now turn to the defense case.

## 6.3   The Defense Case on China

### 6.3.1   *The Nanjing Massacre*

The defense case relating to war crimes was delivered in two parts, one focusing on China and the other the Pacific region. Additional evidence on behalf of each accused was introduced during the individual phases and the sur-rebuttal phase. In this and the next sections, we will analyze first the defense evidence relating to war crimes in China, including the evidence concerning those individual accused whom the prosecution had expressly or tacitly implicated during the China phase, then the evidence relating to war crimes in the Pacific region, including the evidence concerning a dozen or so individual accused whom the prosecution had expressly or tacitly implicated during the Pacific phases.

Following the organization of the prosecution's case, the defense presented their evidence first relating to the Nanjing Massacre and then to war crimes in China in the post-Nanjing period. One outstanding feature of the defense case on China was that the defense left the prosecution's evidence on the Nanjing Massacre virtually uncontested, a fact too often overlooked in debates about that event and in historical research on the Tokyo Trial. On the other hand, the defense attacked the validity of war crimes charges relating to the post-Nanjing period with great vigor. The defense's uneven approach to the two facets of the China phase is apparent in the divergence in the volume of evidentiary materials. The defense introduced only three witnesses and one exhibit in relation to the Nanjing Massacre, as opposed to twenty-six witnesses and seven exhibits in relation to war crimes in the post-Nanjing period.[76] The sheer quantity of evidentiary materials, of course, does not tell us much about their *quality*, to which we now turn.

The single exhibit admitted in evidence relating to Nanjing need not detain us, since it merely contained biographical information about accused Matsui. The three witnesses for the Nanjing case, meanwhile, deserve attention: Lieutenant General Nakayama Yasuto, formerly a staff officer of the Central China Area Army; Hidaka Shunrokurō, a former councilor at the Japanese embassy in Shanghai; and Tsukamoto Kōji, a legal officer who successively held the positions of the chief of the Judicial Department of the 10th Army, judge and prosecutor of the Shanghai Expeditionary Army, and prosecutor, preliminary judge, and judge of the Central China Area Army, in the period between August 1937 and January 1939.[77] The 10th Army and the Shanghai Expeditionary Army both came under the command of the Central China Area Army at the time of the invasion of Nanjing.

---

[76] These numbers do not take into account additional witnesses and documents that the defense presented during the individual phases.
[77] Tsukada's military rank is not indicated in the transcripts of court proceedings. These three witnesses aside, eight additional witnesses gave evidence either orally or by way of affidavits during the individual case for Matsui. See T32587–616, 32619–88. The defense also produced two additional evidentiary documents during Matsui's individual phase. See DX3397, Instructions on Military Discipline issued to his Forces by General Matsui Iwane, Commander-in-Chief, Central China Area Army (December 18, 1937), T32616–8; and DX3402, Photograph of a Bulletin posted on a wall at the Chinshan Temple in Chinkiang, T32688–9.

## 6.3 The Defense Case on China

Rather than casting doubt on the prosecution's account of the events at Nanjing, the testimony of the three witnesses generally confirmed what had been shown in the prosecution's case. Moreover, their testimony provided important details concerning the Japanese servicemen's acts of violence and steps taken by the members of the Japanese civilian and military authorities during the occurrence of mass atrocity.

The factual matters arising from the testimony of these witnesses can be summarized under the following six points: (1) that Matsui issued orders before the invasion of Nanjing regarding the maintenance of military discipline and orderly conduct; (2) that, upon his entry into Nanjing on December 17, 1937, he received reports from the military police, commanders of subordinate armies and divisions, and Japanese diplomatic corps, regarding his troops' "looting, rape, burglary, and so forth," in direct contravention of his prior orders[78]; (3) that Matsui issued fresh orders for the removal of excess troops and the enforcement of strict military discipline; (4) that, after his return to Shanghai in about five days, Matsui continued to hear rumors about his troops' unlawful conduct in Nanjing; (5) that the Japanese diplomatic representatives in China contemporaneously transmitted to the Japanese Ministry of Foreign Affairs various reports on the Japanese troops' violence; and (6) that the Judicial Department of the Central China Area Army handled about ten criminal cases involving an unspecified number of Japanese criminal offenders between December 1937 and January 1938.[79]

These factual matters aside, one of the witnesses, Nakayama, brought to the tribunal's attention some organizational details about the Central China Area Army that suggested certain limitations in Matsui's command authority. According to his testimony, this army was established to bring two other armies already deployed in central China "under unified control" in preparation for the invasion of Nanjing.[80] As such, the headquarters of the Central China Area Army was equipped with a minimal staff department of seven officers alone, which was just enough to engage "solely in commanding operations." The headquarters of the two subordinate armies, by contrast, were complete with the ordnance, finance, medical, and judicial departments.[81] Nakayama testified that the Central China Area Army did not at the relevant time have its own Judicial Department or court-martial.

When Matsui took the witness stand on his own behalf during the individual defense phase some six months later, on November 24, 1947, he gave further evidence concerning the organizational limitations of the Central China

---

[78] Testimony by Tsukamoto Kōji, T21568.
[79] Ibid., T21564, 21579.
[80] DX2577, T21891.
[81] Ibid., T21889–90, 21892.

Area Army. He testified that the mission of the Central China Area Army was "to unify the command of these two units," and that "since it had only seven staff officers, its duty was limited to giving operational instructions to the two headquarters." He went on to underscore his limited command authority, stating that his "relation with officers and men in the field in regard to the command and supervision was entirely indirect."[82] When cross-examined by the prosecution regarding his authority on matters of discipline and morale of the troops, Matsui pointed not to himself but to the divisional commanders as being chiefly responsible:

> Ordinarily discipline and morals within an army was the responsibility of the Division Commander. The Commander of the Army above the Division Commander supervised these Division Commanders and maintained the court martial under his jurisdiction. I was above them. I was the Commander above them and my Area Army Headquarters had no legal organ nor any military police or gendarmerie under its direct control, and therefore reports were not made to my headquarters or to me directly.[83]

In this self-serving explanation, Matsui maintained that the responsibility on matters of military discipline and morale stopped at the level of commanders of the Shanghai Expeditionary Army and the 10th Army since they alone were equipped with judicial officers. When cross-examined further regarding his share of responsibility, Matsui insisted on his lack of authority on matters of military discipline: "I have no legal right to issue such an order [of a court-martial]. I had no authority except to express my *desires* as over-all Commander-in-Chief to the commander of the army under my command and the divisional commanders there under"[84] (emphasis added). Matsui's argument of limited authority ultimately failed to convince the judges and several other accused who advanced the same defense were also unsuccessful in most part.[85] While Matsui argued that he had no authority to court martial soldiers for crimes already committed, what remained uncontested was his power and duty to use his command authority to prevent further crimes from being committed.[86]

---

[82] DX3498, T33819–20.
[83] T33871.
[84] T33875.
[85] Similar arguments of limited command authority were made at other contemporaneous Allied war crimes trials as well, and some proved successful, such as the Toyoda Trial (1948–9). See Totani, *Justice in Asia and the Pacific Region, 1945–1952*, chapter 6.
[86] The High Command Case had also considered the situation where crimes were committed but the commander had no court-martial authority: "while commanding generals might not be able under the provisions of the Barbarossa Jurisdiction Order to establish courts martial to try them ... such commanders were nevertheless responsible, within the areas of their commands, for the summary execution of persons who were merely suspects" p. 525.

6.3 The Defense Case on China            229

With regard to the evidence relating to accused Hirota, one of the three defense witnesses, Hidaka, offered critical details as to the witness's personal knowledge of how the information of atrocities in Nanjing was handled by the Ministry of Foreign Affairs. Hidaka worked as a councilor for the Japanese embassy in Shanghai between August 1937 and March 1938, and had the opportunity to visit Nanjing in his official capacity on four separate occasions.[87] He testified that many reports on wrongful acts of the Japanese soldiers were submitted from foreign residents to the consulate general, and that he forwarded all of the reports he received to the Ministry of Foreign Affairs. Moreover, he testified that he received reports on atrocity in person when visiting the consulate general in Nanjing, that he saw the existing conditions himself, and that he talked also with foreign residents. After conducting these surveys, he is said to have taken the following steps:

I submitted a written report of those items to the Foreign Ministry, and made the same report orally to Foreign Minister HIROTA and other Foreign Ministry Staff members when I returned home for instructions at the end of January 1938. Then I heard that whenever reports were submitted from the officials on the spot the authorities in Tokyo called the attention of the Army to them.[88]

Hidaka further testified that the armed forces in Nanjing received some directives "about this [affair]" from the army high command in Tokyo, thanks to having been alerted by the foreign ministry. Eventually, Lieutenant General Honma Masaharu, then in the rank of a major general, was dispatched by the Army General Staff to Nanjing, in early February 1938, purportedly on a mission concerning "problems of foreign relations" and "other matters concerning the Chinese people."[89] Matsui's recall to Tokyo took place shortly after this.

During Hirota's individual phase, the defense had another foreign-ministry official, Ishii Itarō, take the stand to offer additional evidence regarding the foreign ministry's handling of the incoming information on atrocity. (Hirota elected not to testify on his own behalf.) Ishii served as director of the Bureau of East Asiatic Affairs of the Ministry of Foreign Affairs between May 1937 and November 1938, and was directly subordinate to Hirota. The testimony by this witness revealed that the Ministry of Foreign Affairs indeed gave warnings to the Ministry of the Army repeatedly and emphatically about the incoming reports on atrocity, demanding that proper actions be taken immediately to stop the violence. That said, Ishii's testimony also indicated that the one to apply pressure on the army authorities was Ishii himself rather than Foreign Minister Hirota. The witness revealed that, even before being asked by Hirota,

[87] DX2537, T21445.
[88] Ibid., T21453.
[89] Ibid., T21454.

Ishii transmitted the first incoming telegraphic report on atrocity to his army counterpart, the director of the Military Affairs Bureau in the Ministry of the Army. Ishii also brought up on his own initiative the incoming reports on atrocity repeatedly at the "liaison meetings" regularly convened among the bureau chiefs and the section chiefs of the Ministry of the Army, the Ministry of the Navy, and the Ministry of Foreign Affairs. At these meetings, Ishii demanded that the army authorities "take strict measures to stop them immediately."[90]

As regards actions taken by Hirota, Ishii readily confirmed that "the Foreign Minister, being alarmed and worried about the matter, urged me that some steps or other should be taken quickly to suppress such disgraceful deeds." Moreover, Hirota is said to have told Ishii that he met in person with Army Minister Sugiyama with a request "to take strict measures promptly with regard to the case of Nanking atrocities."[91] When questioned further, Ishii conceded that Hirota spoke to the army minister "once or twice" as far as his own knowledge went. He did not know if Hirota took any other actions.[92] This reply elicited additional questioning by the prosecution, and the following dialog ensued:

Q. [Prosecution]. Did HIROTA ever discuss with you any further steps that should be taken to get these atrocities stopped?
A. [Ishii]. I think we had several discussions.
Q. What did he suggest doing?
A. He told me quite frequently to lodge serious warning to the authorities concerned in the War Ministry.
Q. But we know that he had produced no effect. *Didn't you suggest to him that he should bring it up in the cabinet?*
A. We have never talked about bringing this question up before the cabinet. My reason for saying so is that I did not regard that the cabinet was a body to discuss such a question.
Q. Why not?
A. I think it so because the cabinet, as a cabinet, was not in any position to deal with questions which concerned the military in the field.
Q. *Was it not necessary, in your position, for you to know something about international law?*

---

[90] DX3287, T29972. By "liaison meetings," Ishii meant the meetings that were held among the second-tier officials of the Ministries of the Army, Navy, and Foreign Affairs, and *not* the meetings of the Liaison Conference at which members of the cabinet and the Imperial Headquarters met. However, this part of Ishii's testimony was misrepresented as meaning the "Liaison Conference" in the prosecution's summation (T40028), and the same error was repeated in the Judgment of the Tokyo Tribunal (*Documents*, 538).
[91] DX3287, T29970–1, 29973.
[92] T29990.

A. Yes, of course.

Q. *And did you not know that the responsibility was on the government and not on the commanders in the field for the treatment of prisoners?*

A. I can't quite comprehend the point in the question.[93] (emphasis added)

In the exchange above, the prosecution appears to cross-examine the witness along the lines of the theory of government responsibility as had been set out in the indictment (Appendices D and E). The prosecution thus asked, "Didn't you suggest to him that he should bring it up in the cabinet?"; and, "Did you not know that the responsibility was on the government and not on the commanders in the field for the treatment of prisoners?" Interestingly enough, these lines of questioning only elicited puzzlement on the part of the witness. Ishii's notion of the foreign minister's duty apparently was at odds with that of the prosecution's, and, as we shall see, with that of most of the judges.[94]

### 6.3.2 The Post-Nanjing Period

If the defense's response on the prosecution's case on Nanjing was somewhat limited in scope, the defense seemed better prepared to grapple with war crimes charges relating to the remainder of the Sino-Japanese armed conflict. The defense, at least, was able to assemble a comparatively larger quantity of evidentiary materials: twenty-five witnesses, three affidavits, one map, two photos, one operations order, and two other pieces of army records. From this perspective, given the relative paucity of prosecution evidence regarding war crimes alleged to have been committed across all of China over a period of several years, subsequent chapters in Part II will examine to what extent the judges consistently recalled that the burden of proof was on the prosecution and the standard of proof was beyond reasonable doubt. The defense, of course, did not have to prove that no war crimes were committed. They only had to introduce sufficient evidence to raise reasonable doubt as to the prosecution's allegations of both specific crimes alleged as well as the further inference of a broad temporal

---

[93] T29992–3.
[94] The defense evidence on the Nanjing Massacre touched on the knowledge of other cabinet members as well. Accused Kido was education minister at the time of the Nanjing Massacre, and he was not charged in connection with war crimes in China either. However, the prosecution presented a piece of evidence against him during the rebuttal phase. See PX3342-A, Excerpt from *Japan Times and Mail*, T31515–18; and PX3737, Extract from the Minutes of Meeting of the Budget Committee of the House of Peers, February 16, 1938, T37285–9. In a 1964 interview, Kido remarked that, "During the court proceedings, I, too, was accused vehemently of responsibility for the Nanking Incident in my capacity as education minister, but the verdict was 'not guilty' on grounds of insufficient evidence." This outcome struck Kido as strange, as he believed that, "from the viewpoint of the same minister of state, I do not fully comprehend how much difference there was between Hirota's and my responsibility." Kido, *Kido nikki, Tōkyō saibanki*, 449.

and geographical pattern of such crimes to which individual accused could be connected.

The defense witnesses were mostly former members of the Central China Expeditionary Army or the China Expeditionary Force, i.e. army officers who had served under command of accused Hata during the war against China. It did not take long for the judges to find out that these witnesses were wont to give lengthy testimony on extraneous matters while invariably attesting to Hata's strictness with military discipline, the exemplary conduct of the troops, and no personal knowledge whatsoever of any instance of atrocity. The judges were unimpressed. Webb notified the defense that the tribunal disapproved of these kinds of defense evidence. "From my colleagues this morning and yesterday afternoon," he interjected, "I have heard many adverse comments on the length of these affidavits." By "these affidavits," Webb was referring to the affidavit evidence that the defense introduced in place of taking direct oral examination from the Japanese-speaking witnesses (as was required by the applicable rules of procedure; see Chapter 1 under 1.4). "They certainly are unduly prolix," Webb concurred, and the defense evidence relating to war crimes in the post-Nanjing period was "really repetitive." He went on to remark that "another member of the tribunal observes that the affidavits are directed to disprove matters not alleged."[95] When the defense continued to introduce the same kinds of affidavit evidence regardless, Webb interjected again and said, "this affidavit, like many others, is nearly all husk and contains very little kernel."[96]

There were, nonetheless, important factual revelations that appeared in the defense witness testimony. While witnesses testified to the strictness of military discipline in the post-Nanjing period, their testimony could also reveal underlying attitudes and problems that might support the prosecution's case. The testimony by Yoshibashi Kaizō is a case in point. This witness was formerly an army captain and attached to the staff of the 2nd Army that participated in the invasion of Hankou in October 1938 under the command of the Central China Expeditionary Army, commanded by Hata. Like other witnesses, Yoshibashi attested to the strictness of military discipline and the exemplary conduct of the troops at the time of the Hankou invasion. But he then offered additional personal observations regarding military discipline and troop morale that, though intended to assist the defense, in fact revealed both the potential lack of discipline as well as criminal conduct:

Our army commander had issued very strict order concerning military discipline. On the other hand, our army authorities made every effort to establish recreation centers in

[95] T21646.
[96] T21745.

order to prevent, positively, the occurrence of vicious crimes, and *you can imagine how surprised I was at the sight of the Japanese female recreation corps which came up the Yangtze River to Hankow as early as November 1* [1938].[97] (emphasis added)

What Yoshibashi effectively told the tribunal was that the army authorities were extremely sensitive about lax military discipline and low troop morale of their men, *so that* they regarded the immediate dispatch of Japanese "comfort women" as a top priority, to prevent the occurrence of "vicious crimes" in the newly occupied city. (The phrase, "Japanese female recreation corps," in Yoshibashi's original testimony appears as "the Japanese female comfort unit [*Nihonjin onna no ian-tai*].") In other words, Japanese high-level field commanders were well aware of the propensity of their troops to commit such crimes, and particularly the kind of mass rape that had occurred in Nanjing, and in order to attempt to forestall such behavior they provided military brothels. This leaves open the question of what would happen when such "comfort stations" were not available and also reveals the underlying problem of discipline.[98]

Another defense witnesses who offered more substantive evidence concerning the problem of poor military discipline of the Japanese servicemen in the post-Nanjing period was Lieutenant General Ōyama Ayao, who served as chief of the Army Judicial Affairs Bureau in the Ministry of the Army between December 1933 and March 1945. His testimony revealed that, despite the effort to enforce military discipline, rape remained prevalent in the Japanese conduct of war and military occupation in China.

This situation was regarded as serious enough that his Army Judicial Affairs Bureau revised the army criminal code in the hope of tackling the problem more effectively. Ōyama explained that "The Japanese Army Penal Law had formerly contained no provision relating to rape and it was treated in conformity with the general Penal Law, as constituting a crime in case its victim should bring forward a complaint." He continued that "such treatment of this offense was insufficient for enforcing military morality, and therefore, with the enactment of Law, No. 3 on February 20, 1942, the Army Penal Law was revised, making rape a non-complaint-based crime and its punishment was also

---

[97] DX2551, T21594. For the Japanese original, see *Kyokutō kokusai gunji saiban sokkiroki*, vol. 5, 293.
[98] A path-breaking study on comfort women is Yoshimi, *Jūgun ianfu*, available also in English translation as *Comfort Women*. For a guide to archival materials on comfort women, see Yoshimi, Sensō no kioku, sensō no kiroku.

increased."[99] At the very least, this testimony reveals the awareness in Tokyo of the failure to limit the occurrences of rape by troops in the field. It also reveals that this problem was regarded as serious enough to require a revision of the army penal code.

During cross-examination, Ōyama was asked if the cause of this revision had to do with many rape cases being brought to the attention of the Army Judicial Affairs Bureau. Ōyama replied to this question affirmatively, saying, "Yes, it was known to us by reports from the field that there were many offenses, that is, offenses and numerous cases of rape in the field."[100] This reply elicited further questioning from the prosecution as to whether or not the rape cases occurred mainly in Nanjing. Ōyama replied to the question negatively this time. The following dialog is recorded in the transcripts of court proceedings:

Q. [Prosecution]. And were not those numerous cases mostly in China and particularly in Nanking?
A. [Ōyama]. Not necessarily.
Q. Where were they then?
A. In China. Not only in Nanking but in other areas of China there have been cases of offenders being punished for such offenses.[101]

The dialog above is significant, since it acknowledged that the Japanese armed forces committed war crimes, including rape, *repeatedly and across the region*, as had been alleged in Counts 53–55 and Appendix D of the indictment.[102] On this basis, knowledge could potentially be imputed to high-ranking accused, laying the foundation for liability on the basis of failure to prevent such crimes under Count 55 or command responsibility for their actual commission.

The poor discipline of Japanese servicemen in China received further documentation when General Yamawaki Masataka took the stand as a defense witness during the individual case for the accused Itagaki. Yamawaki served as vice army minister when Itagaki held the position of army minister (1938–9). When cross-examining this witness, the prosecution introduced a top-secret army-ministry order on censorship, dated February 1939 and titled, "Concerning the Instruction and Control of the Speeches and Actions of the Army Units and Units and Army Men Returned from the China Incident Area." Yamawaki

---

[99] DX2560, T21660.
[100] T21683–4.
[101] T21684.
[102] Item 1 of Appendix D in the IMTFE indictment set out the following offense as commonplace occurrence: "Inhuman treatment ... prisoners of war and civilian internees were murdered, beaten, tortured and otherwise ill-treated, and *female prisoners were raped by members of the Japanese forces*" (emphasis added).

6.3 The Defense Case on China 235

himself had issued this order in his capacity as vice army minister, and had it transmitted to the army forces in Japan proper, Korea, Manchuria, and Taiwan. The instruction stated that the speeches and actions of returning soldiers had not been controlled satisfactorily despite repeated warnings, and that the army authorities were gravely concerned about unchecked talk by the returning officers and enlisted men impacting negatively the popular confidence in the army as well as the war effort itself. "The damage is extremely large," the censorship order read, and "I repeat the order again to make the control of the directing even more strict and consequently glorify the meritorious deeds, raise the Japanese army's military reputation and insure that nothing will impair the accomplishment of the object of the Holy War." The full text of the instruction reveals clearly both the widespread commission of rape, murder, and plunder throughout the China campaign as well as the tolerance, if not encouragement, of field commanders toward such crimes. The examples of prohibited speech in the instruction are horrific in their detailing of rape, torture, and murder of civilian women.[103]

---

[103] PX3304: Extracts from *Army Records of the China Incident*, 1939, vol. 7, introduced at T30126. This army-ministry instruction contained a long list of the types of statement that were subject to strict censorship. This list is representative:

> The thing I like best during the battle is plundering. In the front lines the superiors turn a blind eye to plundering and there were some who plundered to their heart's content.
> At XX we captured a family of four. We played with the daughter just as we would with a harlot. But as the parents insisted that the daughter be returned to them we killed them. We played with the daughter as before until the unit's departure and then killed her.
> Our company commander unofficially gave instructions for raping as follows: 'In order that we won't have problems, either pay them money or kill them in some obscure place after you have finished.'
> If the army men who participated in the war were investigated individually they will probably be all guilty of murder, robbery or rape.
> In the battlefield we think nothing of rape. There are even some men who resisted with firearms when discovered by the military police in the act.
> In the half a year of battle about the only things I learned are rape and burglary.
> In the unit they were issuing three-yen tickets to officers, two-yen tickets to non-commissioned officers, [and] one-yen tickets to the men for prostitutes and thus provided recreation for the soldiers.
> Some Japanese soldiers are quite hard. They examined the corpses of their comrades individually to extract even the gold teeth.
> The plundering by our army in the battle area is beyond imagination. Pacification is being practiced in only a small part of the occupied area.
> The prisoners of the Chinese Army were sometimes lined up in one line and killed to test the efficiency of the machine gun.

The prosecution read into the record some of these example sentences in the list, but not all of them. See T30127–30.

**6.4  The Defense Case on the Pacific Region**

In regard to war crimes in the Pacific region, the defense delivered its evidence in three separate sub-divisions: (1) Japan's obligation under international treaties and agreements regarding the treatment of prisoners of war; (2) treatment of prisoners of war and civilian internees by the army; and (3) treatment of prisoners of war and civilian internees by the navy. The first sub-division was designed for the defense to present evidence concerning the Japanese government's own interpretation about the applicability of the Prisoner-of-War Convention of 1929. The second and third sub-divisions focused on addressing the prosecution's evidence of war crimes relating to the army and navy personnel, respectively. There was no independent sub-division to address the prosecution's case relating to non-military branches of the government, but additional evidence about them was introduced during the individual phases and the sur-rebuttal phase. In the pages to follow, then, we will discuss the defense evidence by clustering it in terms of the "army" cases, the "navy" cases, and the "non-military government" cases.

*6.4.1  The Army Cases*

The defense's strategy in tackling the army cases was to leave much of the crime-base evidence uncontested, and to focus instead on disputing the alleged policy dimension of army war crimes and the evidence against specific individual accused.[104] For the former purpose, the defense called to the stand four former army officers and one civilian. These witnesses admitted in varying terms to the army authorities' awareness about unsatisfactory prisoner-of-war conditions, but they also emphasized the authorities' good-faith efforts to treat prisoners of war fairly and lawfully.[105] A selection of army-ministry records in evidence partly corroborated the witness testimony, as they indicated not only that the top army-ministry officials knew about poor health and poor treatment being meted out to prisoners of war, but also that they repeatedly issued instructions for improved treatment.[106] The testimony about awareness actually supported the prosecution's case and it was therefore vital for the defense to

---

[104] For the defense phase on army war crimes in general, see T27190–244, 27390–963, and 28085–8.

[105] For the testimony of five defense witnesses to testify for the army phase, see T27190–6, 27201–37, 27391–5, and T27803–78.

[106] See the following army-ministry documents: "Transportation of Prisoners of War" (Army Ministry-Asia-Confidential Report No. 1504, December 10, 1942) in PX1965, introduced at T14439 (p. 32 of the exhibit); "Re Improvement of PW Administration" (Army-Asia-Secret No. 696, March 3, 1944) in DX3051, introduced at T27806 (p. 2 of the exhibit); and DX3111, Report Published on February 23 [of 1943] by the Army Medical College, T27810–12. For testimony by a defense witness regarding the circumstances of the issuance of the first of these three army-ministry documents, see DX3109, T27806–7.

## 6.4 The Defense Case on the Pacific Region

show that the accused had actually effectively mitigated the ill-treatment and done everything in their power to meet Japan's obligations regarding proper treatment of prisoners of war.

The defense introduced a war crimes report produced by the postwar Government of Japan that similarly conceded that "some unauthorized punishments" were indeed inflicted by the Japanese servicemen, but not that such acts were ever intended or authorized as a matter of policy. "Upon inquiries among the prisoners' camps in Japan proper, it was revealed that, with few exceptions, atrocious and inhuman acts of violence were never done deliberately upon the prisoners of war," so the report read.[107]

Aside from evidence pointing to the army ministry's efforts to ameliorate the prisoner-of-war conditions, the defense also presented several affidavits, letters, and reports in which former prisoners of war, civilian internees, and representatives of the International Committee for Red Cross provided positive assessments of internment conditions or, alternatively, conveyed personal gratitude for generous treatment. This type of evidentiary materials did not impress the tribunal, however, as Justice Webb interjected:

Do you think you are going to meet the sweeping charges made against you by reading the individual experiences of a few people? We know that there are tens of thousands of kind-hearted Japanese. We would assume in the army itself, in the navy, in the air force, many Japanese behaved very well *but that is not an answer to these charges. Meet the charges made against you and do not try to prove that in other cases where no charges were made no faults could be found.* That is what you are doing.[108] (emphasis added)

The above remark is important, as Webb made it clear to the defense that the tribunal was weighing evidence regarding those instances of war crimes *which had been documented in the prosecution's case*, and not some general allegations of war crimes. In other words, the requirement for an effective defense was to cast doubt upon the specific crimes alleged by the prosecution, and the tribunal, for this reason, had little patience for the foregoing type of evidentiary materials.

The defense's case on individual accused did address substantive issues in a manner that could undermine the prosecutorial strategy that sought convictions on proof of the widespread and recurrent character of war crimes. The defense, in particular, raised two new questions that had not been explored in the prosecution's case, but that could be material to determining the individual responsibility of the accused. One of the two concerned *the context of war* in which war crimes had occurred, and the other was *the legal authority or duty*

[107] DX3128, T27895.
[108] T27474.

of individual accused during their service as army-ministry officials at Tokyo or as military commanders at theaters of war.

### 6.4.1.1 The Context of War

On the first point, the defense generally held that the context of war was largely overlooked in the prosecution's case, even though the deteriorating war conditions – especially in the last year when Japan fought losing battles practically everywhere except in China – had greatly impacted the ability of army commanders to exercise control over their own troops and provide for prisoners of war. This type of argument was advanced, for example, on behalf of accused Kimura, Mutō, Dohihara, and Itagaki in regard to war crimes committed in Burma, the Philippines, and British Borneo, Java, Malaya, and Singapore.

A number of witnesses took the stand on behalf of these accused. The testimony by witnesses for Kimura and Mutō brought out the desperate situations in maintaining the lines of communication amid a series of Japanese military defeats and retreats in Burma and the Philippines, respectively. Mutō himself took the stand for three days in mid-November 1947, during which he gave testimony on the utter disorganization of the 14th Area Army resulting partly from the poor operational plans that the Southern Army had ordered for implementation, and partly from the extraordinary fire power of the invading American assault forces. Mutō's testimony, one may note, was substantially the same as the one he had given when taking the witness stand at the Yamashita Trial back in Fall 1945. In both instances, Mutō emphatically argued that General Yamashita – with whom he stayed at all times in the last battles in the Philippines – was in no position to know the commission of war crimes or to establish control over the troops, given the extreme circumstances of the war resulting in a complete breakdown of his communications network.[109]

A key witness for Dohihara and Itagaki, navy captain Watanabe Yasuji testified on the grave situation of the Japanese supply lines in maritime Southeast Asia. He revealed that incessant Allied aerial and naval attacks caused huge shipping losses, which, in turn, adversely impacted the Japanese military operations as well as the livelihood of the people in the Japanese homeland.[110] The trial record shows that Watanabe's testimony drew keen attention of Justice Webb, who remarked that "the percentage of decrease of supplies to the Japanese forces overseas may be very material to the question of the treatment

---

[109] For Mutō's testimony regarding the battles in the Philippines, see DX3454, T33134–50. For the defense evidence concerning the Burma Area Army, see T27595–619, 31722–48.
[110] DX3103, T27789–93.

## 6.4 The Defense Case on the Pacific Region

of prisoners of war in Malaya and elsewhere."[111] Upon further questioning by the defense, the witness offered additional data regarding the volume of shipments, including the following:

In 1944, shipments were made in response to demands from all theaters, but only 56 per cent of the demands could be met. The supplies to French Indo-China, Sumatra, Java, and Borneo was only 35 per cent that year, supplies to Burma 41 per cent, to the Philippines 47 per cent. These are destinations to which supplies were under average or below level.[112]

The above statement is significant, since the dramatic drop in shipment likely cut into the ability of the 7th Area Army to provide both its own forces and the Allied nationals in its custody with essential items such as food and medicine.[113] This line of defense, as indicated by Webb's remark, raised the issue for the judges of determining the standard of liability for commanders under exigent battlefield conditions such as those described by these witnesses.

### 6.4.1.2 *The Legal Duty or Authority of Individual Accused*

The second point the defense raised against the prosecution's case had to do with the blanket presumption that the army accused derived from their respective wartime positions the legal authority or duty to ensure proper treatment of prisoners of war and civilian internees. The defense was ready to concede that such was indeed the case with Army Minister Tōjō, but not with respect to other army-ministry accused such as Kimura, Mutō, and Satō. Moreover, the defense faulted the prosecution for alleging the same with those accused who had served as high-ranking army officers in theaters of war, namely, Kimura (commander-in-chief, Burma Area Army); Dohihara and Itagaki (commander-in-chief, 7th Area Army); and Mutō (commander of the Imperial Guards Division [later reorganized as the Second Imperial Guards Division[114]], Sumatra, 1942–4; and chief of staff of the 14th Area Army, 1944–5). A number of witnesses took the stand to give testimony on the nature of the legal authority or duty vested in various positions held by these accused. Some of their testimony relating to army-ministry officials was partly supported by regulations of the army ministry which the defense presented in evidence.[115]

---

[111] T27794.
[112] T27795.
[113] The defense provided additional accounts on the adverse circumstances of shipping later on. See the testimony by Hazeyama Tetsuo, T30195–213.
[114] DX3450, Affidavit by Ōhira Hideo, T33062.
[115] For army-ministry regulations that the defense presented regarding vice army minister, see DX3349, Excerpt from Army Ministry General Regulation regarding the treatment of the business of the Ministry, comprising Appendix 1, "Matters entrusted to the Vice Minister of War,"

With respect to those three accused who had served as area-army commanders (i.e. Kimura, Dohihara, and Itagaki), the defense contended that the position of an area-army commander did not entail any legal authority or duty to take control of prisoner-of-war affairs in the first place. It was thus mistaken, so the defense asserted, to hold them accountable for prisoner-of-war mistreatment, even if the alleged offenses had, in fact, occurred in territorial jurisdiction of the respective area armies. This contention turned out to be difficult to maintain, however, since key defense witnesses offered mutually contradictory oral evidence.[116]

Major Ikejiri Satoshi, a defense witness and formerly adjutant of the commander-in-chief of the Burma Area Army (1944–5), testified that the area-army commander lacked the power to control the prisoner-of-war camps in Burma.[117] However, Captain Tazumi Genzō, a former prisoner-of-war camp commandant at Rangoon, stated during the postwar Allied interrogation (whose record the defense submitted into evidence) that his camp, in fact, came within the military chain of command of the Burma Area Army and hence was controlled by it.[118] Testimony by Colonel Fuwa Hiroshi – formerly a staff officer of the Burma Area Army (1943) and subsequently of the 7th Area Army (1944) – aligned with the one by Ikejiri, as he testified that an area-army commander did not have command authority vis-à-vis prisoner-of-war camps.[119] But then, Major Hazeyama Tetsuo, formerly a staff officer of the 7th Area Army, disputed the validity of Fuwa's testimony, as he testified that the area-army commander was vested with the authority to decide the details of prisoner-of-war policies. Hazeyama further revealed that the area-army commander, Itagaki, "conducted an inspection tour of POW camps, and finding out in detail about the conditions of supply in those camps, he ordered that the rations be increased."[120] Major General Saitō Seiei, formerly chief of

---

T31663–8; and DX3462, Regulations governing the Duties of Officers of the Wartime Superior Headquarters, introduced at T33283. For army-ministry regulations concerning the director of the Military Affairs Bureau that the defense referred to, see PX1965, *Laws, Rules and Regulations Pertaining to Prisoners of War*, T27694–702 (introduced initially at T14439); and PX74, Imperial Ordinances and Charges on the Organization of the Ministry of the Army, T27714–17 (introduced initially at T504).

[116] In a far more nuanced, detailed, and acute analysis of the law and the evidence than that of the Tokyo majority judgment, the High Command Case held that field commanders and commanders of occupied territories did have such duties in regard to prisoners of war. See, for instance, High Command Case, 534–49, as well as the extensive analysis of the evidence as to each accused.
[117] T27538, 27543–53.
[118] DX3087, T27566.
[119] T28723–30. This witness's testimony elicited the prosecution's remark that "this is a most unusual setup that the witness is describing. It is quite opposite the ordinary set up." Justice Webb appeared to agree, and let the prosecution leave it at that by saying, "That is sufficient." (T28730).
[120] T30206 and 30210.

### 6.4 The Defense Case on the Pacific Region 241

the Malay Prisoner-of-War Camp at Singapore (1944–5), partly corroborated Hazeyama's accounts. "The Commander-in-Chief of the Area Army was in direct command of P.W. Camps and the military detention camps," so Saitō testified, although he added that "orders covering the overall management of prisoners were issued by Commander-in-Chief of the Southern Army Marshal TERAUCHI and received through the Area Army."[121] Lieutenant General Ayabe Kijutsu, formerly chief of staff of the 7th Area Army, tended to support that the area-army commander was indeed in charge. He recounted that there was "marked improvement" in prisoner-of-war conditions since Itagaki's assumption of command of the army.[122]

Regardless of these contradictions, what the defense testimony failed to address is the duty of high-ranking commanders to take effective action when they became aware of mistreatment of prisoners of war in their command area. Could they rely on a type of bureaucratic defense and say that formal command authority over the camps was vested in another administrative division and hence they, despite their general command authority, were entitled to do nothing in the face of such conditions? Or did they have a duty to take whatever measures that were in their power to try to ensure that the mistreatment ended or was ameliorated? Like the authoritative High Command Case at Nuremberg, the Tokyo Tribunal held that they did.[123]

In contrast to contradictions regarding other accused, the defense argument for Mutō's case was generally consistent. During his testimony, Mutō explained that his duty as commander of the Imperial Guards Division had been "to take charge of the defence of Northern Sumatra in accordance with the order from the 25th Army Commander." He was, in other words, an operational commander without the responsibility of dealing with the administration of prisoners of war or civilian internees in occupied territory. He emphasized that "a clear line was drawn" between operational and administrative duties among various military authorities on the ground, and also contended that "I never employed war prisoners for labor."[124] His former chief of staff, Major General Ōhira Hideo, provided corroborative evidence. He testified that the commander of the Imperial Guards Division "had nothing to do with military administration established in the garrison-area," but that Commander Mutō rather took charge of the defense of the garrisoned area from enemy attacks.[125] According to Ōhira, the divisional commander had no part in the administration of civilian internment either. The one responsible for the affairs of civilian internees was "the governor of the province, an official of the military

[121] DX3313, T30230.
[122] DX3312, T30218.
[123] See note 116 supra.
[124] T33131–2.
[125] DX3450, T33063.

government organization," so he testified.¹²⁶ In other words, the defense argued that bureaucratic fragmentation of authority shielded Mutō for responsibility for certain administrative functions within his command area.

As regards Mutō's legal authority or duty as chief of staff of the 14th Area Army, the defense presented "Regulations Governing the Duties of Officers of the Wartime Superior Headquarters" to bring out that Mutō was vested with no power to command in the first place. The relevant articles in this document defined the duty of an army chief of staff as to "assist the Army Commander," so that a chief of staff "shall direct and supervise the work of the Staff officers and, in accordance with the intent of the Army Commander, shall exercise a general control over all business of the Headquarters."¹²⁷ Colonel Kumegawa Yoshiharu, formerly a staff officer of the 14th Area Army, confirmed that a chief of staff "was not invested with the authority of deciding principal matters." With respect specifically to Mutō, Kumegawa testified that Mutō made no pretence of assuming command authority and issued "no order to any unit."¹²⁸ (The defense had also used the same document to show Mutō's lack of command authority during his service as vice chief of staff of the Central China Area Army back in 1937–8.¹²⁹) The issue of the responsibility of staff officers was analyzed extensively in the Nuremberg High Command Case but, as subsequent chapters will indicate, the Tokyo judges failed to subject this issue to systematic analysis.¹³⁰

### 6.4.2 The Navy Cases

In regard to the allegations of mistreatment and atrocities in the navy cases the defense adopted a different strategy.¹³¹ The trial record shows that the main defense strategy on navy war crimes was quite straightforward: they attacked the prosecution's case by denying the existence of any order, authorization, or knowledge on the part of the individual navy accused concerning the

---

¹²⁶ Ibid., T33064.
¹²⁷ DX3462, introduced at T33283. See pp. 2–3 of the exhibit.
¹²⁸ DX3451, T33076.
¹²⁹ The duty of a vice chief of staff was defined in the regulations as to "assist the Army Chief of Staff and endeavor to replete the fighting strength of the Army," and "for this purpose he shall maintain a close contact with other Departments in the Headquarters (as well as with the Army Supply Department) and make arrangements on necessary matters so as to ensure a smooth executing of all business." DX3462, p. 3.
¹³⁰ See High Command Case, 512–15.
¹³¹ For the defense's phase on navy war crimes in general, see T27245–390. The defense case on the army war crimes comprised twenty-two witnesses and fifty-one court exhibits, while the one on the navy war crimes was limited to seven witnesses and ten court exhibits. In addition to these, further witnesses and evidentiary documents were presented during the individual phases of the accused.

6.4 The Defense Case on the Pacific Region        243

documented instances of naval atrocities.¹³² To this end, the defense called to the stand seven witnesses during its general phase on navy war crimes. Two of the witnesses were Rear Admiral Tomioka Sadatoshi and Rear Admiral Yamamoto Chikao, who had alternately served as chief of the First Section of the Navy General Staff (1940–5). The gist of their testimony was that the Navy General Staff had nothing to do with the alleged instances of naval war crimes, since it never issued orders of their commission, or acquired knowledge about them. With regard specifically to submarine atrocities, these witnesses pointed out that the Navy General Staff actually issued two directives – in November 1941 and March 1942 – which expressly prohibited the killing of survivors of torpedoed enemy ships.¹³³

Further evidence concerning orders and authorizations from the Ministry of the Navy was provided during the testimony of Rear Admiral Takata Toshitane and Rear Admiral Yamamoto Yoshio, successive chiefs of the First Section of the Naval Affairs Bureau of the Ministry of the Navy (1940–5). These two witnesses testified mainly on the navy share of legal authority or duty in managing the affairs of prisoners of war. According to Takata, the Ministry of the Navy had its own system of prisoner-of-war administration, which operated independently of and separately from the one run by the Ministry of the Army.¹³⁴ (This aspect of Japanese prisoner-of-war administration had not been brought out during the prosecution's case.) Yamamoto corroborated Takata's account and also testified that the Ministry of the Navy received copies of some incoming inquiries and protests regarding, at least some of the alleged instances of submarine atrocity. His section accordingly had investigations carried out, and made no finding that could authenticate the wrongdoing as alleged in the inquiries and protests.¹³⁵ Rebuttal testimony led by the prosecution, however, indicated otherwise.¹³⁶

---

[132] The episodes of naval atrocity for which the prosecution sought to hold the navy accused accountable generally came down to the following three kinds: (1) submarine atrocities in the Indian Ocean, December 1943–October 1944; (2) summary execution of American prisoners of war and civilians at Kwajalein, October 1942, and Wake Island, October 1943; and (3) widespread prisoner-of-war mistreatment at the navy-run prisoner-of-war camp at Ōfuna, Japan. For the prosecution's evidence on naval war crimes, see T14233–5, 14911–5281.

[133] The testimony by Yamamoto Chikao, T27245–68; and the testimony by Tomioka Sadatoshi, T27282–309. The defense also presented in evidence various navy-staff directives that the witnesses referred to in their testimony, namely, DX3058-A, Excerpt from *Collected Volume of the Imperial General Staff Headquarters' Instructions, Naval Section*, comprising Navy General Staff Directive No. 15, November 30, 1941, T27301–3; and DX3054-C, Excerpt from *Collected Volume of the Imperial General Staff Headquarters' Instructions, Naval Section*, comprising Navy General Staff Directive No. 61, March 1, 1942, T27387–90. See also the testimony by Mito Hisashi, T34635–45.

[134] DX3065, T27358–62.

[135] DX3066, T27382–3.

[136] Jirō Nakahara, formerly a civilian *Nisei* interpreter attached to the commander of submarine *I-8*, testified that, "Soon after I reported back at the Naval General Staff I was told by the Chief

When the two navy accused – Oka and Shimada – took the stand, they testified that they had been completely left in the dark about the alleged navy war crimes, if these crimes had occurred at all. In the case of Oka, he confirmed that the Ministry of the Navy had an established system of prisoner-of-war administration, but he downplayed the legal duty of the Naval Affairs Bureau (of which he served as director between 1940 and 1944). He portrayed the work of the Naval Affairs Bureau relating to prisoners of war as comprising "routine" tasks only, which his subordinate officials disposed of as a matter of course and without involving personal attention of the bureau chief. Oka stated that, "during my tenure in office as Director of the Naval Affairs Bureau, I have never heard, seen, or recall any note of protest."[137]

Shimada similarly testified that he was utterly ignorant of the alleged instances of naval war crimes. He expressed personal regrets at the revelation of naval atrocities, but pleaded that he was not informed of any of those occurrences until the opening of the criminal proceedings at the Tokyo Trial. "As I sat in this court room [sic] and heard *for the first time* the recounting of many instances where Japanese naval personnel mistreated prisoners of war, I was both shocked and ashamed," so he remarked[138] (emphasis added). Shimada conceded that the protests from foreign governments might have been forwarded to his ministry but insisted on his ignorance, stating, "but certainly they were never routed to my personal desk."[139] When cross-examined about his knowledge of submarine atrocities in his capacity not only as navy minister but also as navy chief (February–July 1944), Shimada simply reiterated his position. "No, I learned nothing. I knew nothing."[140] It was thus left for the prosecution to prove that information about atrocities was in fact circulating in the relevant Navy circles.

### 6.4.3   *The Non-Military Government Cases*

The defense strategy relating to "non-military government" cases, in some ways, was comparable to the strategy for the navy cases, pleading general ignorance of war crimes. These included Kaya Okinori (finance minister, 1937–8,

---

of the Third Section not to relate my experience overseas." (T38144). In support of Nakahara's testimony, the prosecution presented in evidence a top-secret navy communication, dated August 14, 1944, and transmitted from the Eighth Submarine Squadron to the Ministry of the Navy. This document contained a report on military operations of subordinate submarines. PX3841, T38130–1.

[137] DX3473, T33420.
[138] DX3565, T34670.
[139] Ibid., T34671.
[140] T34774.

and 1941–4); General Koiso Kuniaki (prime minister, 1944–5); and Lieutenant General Suzuki Teiichi (president of the Planning Board, 1941–3). Kaya, for example, testified:

> As to the treatment of prisoners of war, I was not informed nor consulted about it either in the Cabinet meetings or elsewhere, nor was I informed about the protests from foreign countries ... Concerning the treatment of prisoners of war during the Pacific War, I was not in a position to even dream that ill-treatment was being accorded the prisoners of war. I did not even hear of rumors that prisoners of war were being ill-treated. The press and radio made no mention of it.[141]

During his testimony, Koiso, too, denied that he was ever put on notice of any incoming inquiries and protests from foreign governments. Moreover, he insisted on his ignorance on grounds that the prime minister was in no position to participate in "matters concerning the Command," including matters relating to the treatment of prisoners of war and internees.[142] The veracity of Koiso's testimony was put to test during the sur-rebuttal phase, however, when a defense witness testifying on behalf of Shigemitsu gave oral evidence to the contrary (as discussed later).

Accused Suzuki's denial of knowledge of war crimes followed a different line as his defense was compelled to discredit evidence that the prosecution had presented against him. The evidence in question comprised excerpts from a monthly publication of the Ministry of Home Affairs, dated September 1942. It contained a brief report on the conference held between the Planning Board and the Prisoner-of-War Administration Section of the Ministry of the Army on August 15, 1942, whereby it was agreed to use prisoners of war to make up for domestic labor shortage. The gist of the agreement, as shown in the publication, was that the initial transfer of some 3,500 prisoners of war would be made to various locations in Japan for "mining, stevedoring and engineering and construction work for national defense," and that, under the direction of the Ministry of Welfare and in consultation with the army authorities concerned, prefectural governments would take the necessary steps to accommodate the prisoners of war.[143]

During his testimony, Suzuki conceded that the Planning Board had authority over matters of supply and demand of labor in Japan, but asserted that the Board "had not the slightest authority concerning the treatment of prisoners of war." This is another version of the kind of "bureaucratic defense" referred to above where an accused seeks to shift responsibility to another administrative

[141] DX3337, T30658–9.
[142] DX3375, T32246.
[143] PX1791-A, T14506–7.

unit that allegedly was the only one concerned with the relevant criminal conduct. Suzuki claimed to have no personal knowledge of the said conference, stating it to be "unimaginable that the planning board should, even without my knowledge, have had a conference under its auspices or to have participated in any way in the formation of policies therein [regarding the transfer and use of prisoner-of-war labor]."[144]

While Kaya, Koiso, and Suzuki could readily advance a claim of ignorance of mistreatment of prisoners of war, leaving it to the prosecution to produce evidence to the contrary, the defense for Tōgō and Shigemitsu confronted a very different challenge. This was understandable. The names of these two accused appeared repeatedly in voluminous wartime diplomatic correspondence between the Japanese government, the Allied governments, and the protecting powers concerning the mistreatment of Allied nationals in Japanese custody. These accused were the ones officially to represent the Government of Japan in their capacity as foreign minister, and to handle numerous inquiries and protests from overseas. In short, Tōgō and Shigemitsu were hardly in the position to claim ignorance. Tōgō might assert that there were limited opportunities for him to acquire knowledge or to take actions, given his comparatively brief terms as foreign minister (October 1941–September 1942, and April–August 1945).[145] The same could not be said of Shigemitsu, however, whose service as foreign minister was far longer and continuous, covering the last third of the Tōjō Cabinet (April 1943–July 1944) and the entirety of the Koiso Cabinet (July 1944–April 1945). Under those circumstances, the defense made no attempt to deny Shigemitsu's awareness about various incoming inquiries and protests, but focused rather on illuminating what Shigemitsu *did* do to address the problem.

The key – and only – testimony that the defense presented for accused Shigemitsu regarding war crimes charges was Suzuki Tadakatsu, an individual who had already taken the stand as a prosecution witness. During the sur-rebuttal phase, the defense presented a fresh affidavit taken from this witness and then called him to testify. Suzuki was formerly a direct subordinate of Shigemitsu and was responsible for processing the incoming inquiries and protests regarding Japanese war crimes, as well as for preparing the official responses of the Japanese government. As it turned out, this witness, whom the prosecution had presented to the tribunal as credible, had quite a lot to say about Shigemitsu's personal efforts to force his government to change its

---

[144] T35247.
[145] Tōgō's main argument was that, despite the difficult circumstances of the war in 1945, he fully discharged his duty as foreign minister, which was, "the transmitting of the protests or inquiries received from the Allied countries to the Japanese authorities concerned, and the sending to the former of the replies received." DX3647, T35773.

attitude on prisoner-of-war affairs and to take practical steps to address the incoming inquiries and protests.

Suzuki stated in his affidavit that the Ministry of Foreign Affairs had "no means to make direct inspections, or directly to collect information concerning them," but that it had the authority merely to make such "requests to competent authorities and await their action."[146] The witness went on to explain that, while serving as foreign minister, Shigemitsu made a series of attempts to work within the given institutional constraints, and to mount pressure on his government. For example, Shigemitsu directed Suzuki to maintain close contact with the army and navy authorities, not only by forwarding copies of incoming inquiries and protests but also by Suzuki conveying concern in person to his army and navy counterparts during twice-a-month liaison meetings of bureau chiefs and section chiefs of the Ministry of Foreign Affairs, the Ministry of the Army, and the Ministry of the Navy. Shigemitsu also spoke personally to the army minister, urging that the army authorities take ameliorative steps to rectify the situation. Concurrently, Shigemitsu directed his subordinates within the Ministry of Foreign Affairs to collect information about the Japanese conduct of war and military occupation overseas by using foreign news sources, so that the foreign ministry would be able to ascertain facts independently of the military authorities.[147]

Above all, Shigemitsu took two innovative steps in his effort to draw the *collective attention* of the members of the Cabinet and of the military high-command organs to various problems associated with the Japanese mistreatment of Allied nationals. One was that he developed a plan in April or May 1944 to establish an "international laws and customs committee" as a new cabinet organization. The purpose of the committee, according to Suzuki, was to help raise awareness among the cabinet members about the gravity of the Allied protests. Suzuki conceded, however, that the plan failed to materialize, the reason being that "the administration of matters relating to prisoners of war was under the jurisdiction of the army."[148] Another step Shigemitsu took was to bring up for discussion the Allied protests at a meeting of the Conference for the Supreme Direction of the War, held in October 1944. The gist of Shigemitsu's statement during this meeting was reported as follows:

At this meeting Foreign Minister SHIGEMITSU pointed out to the members who were present that, according to recent information from enemy sources, it was reported that the Japanese treatment of prisoners of war left much to be desired. He further stated that the humanitarian treatment of prisoners of war had been from old times a virtue of our country, and that this was a matter of importance from the point of view of our

---

[146] DX3898, T38789.
[147] Ibid., T38789–91.
[148] Ibid., T38793.

international reputation and future relations. As it was a matter for profound regret if by any possible chance we should have committed the slightest possible fault in this matter, *he desired that direction should be issued to responsible persons among the competent authorities*, so that the matters might be fully discussed.[149] (emphasis added)

Suzuki testified that the prime minister, the foreign minister, the army minister, the navy minister, the army chief, and the navy chief comprised the conference members (which, in turn, implicated one of the accused, Koiso, then serving as prime minister). Suzuki added that the discussion at the conference caused the Prisoner-of-War Information Bureau to take a follow-up action, to dispatch its men to prisoner-of-war camps at theaters of war, and to have them pass onto the military officers concerned the instruction "to be considerate in the treatment of prisoners of war."[150]

What should one make of the foregoing accounts by this witness? Given the nature of Shigemitsu's wartime initiatives as outlined earlier, the judges faced the question of whether his conduct was sufficient to exculpate him from responsibility. The answer to this question would depend on what standard of liability the judges would impose. For example, if the standard was that a concerned official was required to do everything within his scope of authority to address the issue then, if credible, Suzuki's testimony might have considerable weight in favor of the accused. If, on the other hand, the judges imposed a standard that required the accused to take *effective* measures to end the mistreatment, or required him to resign if such measures were not effective, then Suzuki's testimony might well not be sufficient. All three of these standards were imposed by various war crimes tribunals. In the High Command Case, for example, the answer depended upon the nature of the crimes and the nature of the position and authority of the accused. What is significant for other defendants about this account of Shigemitsu's initiatives is that it indicates how, at least at this stage of the war, more high-level officials were made aware of the apparent mistreatment of POW.

The trial record indicates that by this time the prosecution had come to develop an interpretive position on *the theory of government responsibility that a foreign minister, who acquired information of war crimes, had the duty to bring it up with the Cabinet*. (In the case of the Tokyo Tribunal, subsequent chapters in Part II will indicate that the majority judges applied little analytical capacity to addressing this issue and largely followed the standard advanced by the prosecution.) The prosecution advanced this particular position when cross-examining Suzuki, as it asked, "Now, did Mr. SHIGEMITSU ever take any of these matters up with the cabinet as regards the treatment of prisoners of

---

[149] Ibid.
[150] Ibid., T38794.

war?" Suzuki replied to this question in the negative, as he said, "I do not think Foreign Minister SHIGEMITSU himself submitted anything of the kind to the Cabinet meetings."[151] Suzuki then offered the following explanation:

If I am permitted I should like to say, with regard to the question of whether or not this matter was brought up at the cabinet meeting, that according to Japanese practice and custom one cannot conceive of the question of the prisoners of war – anything relating to prisoners of war being taken up by the cabinet unless that matter were submitted by the War Minister.[152]

It is worth recalling that the prosecution had previously posed the same question and received a similar reply during cross-examination of Ishii Itarō, a key defense witness for Hirota. These two instances of cross-examination indicate that the prosecution had come to argue that proof of the accused's action vis-à-vis the cabinet should be the key to determining whether or not the foreign minister discharged his legal duty. How the majority judges applied such a standard will be taken up in Chapters 7 and 9.[153]

The conviction of Shigemitsu proved to be one of the most controversial results of the Tokyo Trial. From the standpoint of assessing the defense strategy, it is worth noting that the defense rejected the prosecution's position on the foreign minister's duty as not having any valid theoretical or factual grounds. During the summation of Shigemitsu's case on April 1, 1948, the defense faulted the prosecution for failing to prove the alleged legal duty of the foreign minister to take action vis-à-vis the Cabinet.[154] Furthermore, the defense criticized the prosecution's insistence on treating *the Cabinet* as the highest executive body of the Japanese government when, *in reality*, the one to function as the highest government organ as of 1944 was the Conference for the Supreme Direction of the War. Indeed, the defense maintained "that this body was a more effective instrument for dealing in such matters than the Cabinet and that, its decisions governed the decisions of the Cabinet, has been admitted by the prosecution."[155] If one was to apply the theory of government responsibility as set out in the Bill of Indictment,

---

[151] T38911.
[152] T38913.
[153] Shigemitsu declined to take the witness stand in his own behalf, but he kept in his prison diary a personal record of the daily developments in the courtroom. In one diary entry, he expressed regret over Suzuki's testimony because, "If the truth be told, I actually brought up the matter [of incoming inquiries and protests] with the cabinet and discussed it more than once." What is more, Shigemitsu confided in the diary that he also brought up the matter with Emperor Hirohito and, as a result, "His Majesty frequently issued various orders to the military authorities [*heika yori tabitabi gunbu tōkyoku ni shushu gokamei ga atta*]." Shigemitsu, *Sugamo nikki*, 39, 343.
[154] T46390.
[155] T46392–3.

and if one was to accept the complex structure and workings of the Japanese government as documented by the prosecution and the defense throughout the court proceedings (as explored in Chapter 3), the defense made a strong argument that Shigemitsu did discharge his legal duty. As we will see, however, this argument appears to have made little impression on most judges. The majority failed utterly to systematically consider the defense case and weigh it according to the burden of proof against the prosecution's evidence in regard to each of the charges against each of the accused.

## 6.5 The Prosecution's Summation on Government Responsibility

This chapter completes the exploration of the strategy and evidentiary materials that the prosecution and the defense presented concerning the counts of war crimes. What remains to be discussed are the standards of responsibility for war crimes that the prosecution proposed during the summation, representing what we might call a "four-tier conception of government." The prosecution had separately proffered another conception of the structure of the Japanese government concerning mainly crimes against peace (as explored in Chapter 3). In regard to war crimes, the prosecution advanced the four-tier conception of government, discussed below, as a simple legal tool whose purpose seemingly was to enable the judges to weigh evidence on war crimes and determine the responsibility of the accused in an expeditious manner. The fact that the prosecution offered these legal tools is significant, since the prosecution effectively urged the tribunal not to get too caught up in the extreme complexity of theories and facts arising from voluminous evidentiary materials, but rather to use a set of simple standards of proof to determine the verdicts. It appears from their judgment that the majority accepted a shortcut, which would enable them to avoid careful analysis of the dynamics of authority and decision-making as it evolved over the seventeen years under consideration by the tribunal. The president of the tribunal, Justice Webb, as we will see, was far less ready to forgo the kind of careful analysis and weighing of the evidence that forms the basis of a reasoned judicial decision.

The four-tier conception of government had a simple formula. It posited first that "it is the Government as a whole which is primarily responsible for the prevention of breaches of the Laws of War," and then classified the constituent elements of the "Government" in question into four general categories of individuals. The four were namely: (1) members of the Cabinet; (2) "every official" who acquired knowledge of war crimes, and who also possessed such power to rectify the matter; (3) military officers in charge of armed forces as well as staff members; and (4) bureau chiefs in the Ministry of the Army and the Ministry of

## 6.5 The Prosecution's Summation on Government Responsibility 251

the Navy. The prosecution did not elaborate any further the standards of proof for each of these categories *except* the first one, i.e. members of the Cabinet. To set out the standards of proof for one category alone appears not very helpful, given the fact that the Cabinet was hardly the only government body in which the accused had served or that played a significant role in policy formation. In any event, it is worth quoting in full the standards of proof relating to the cabinet members, as the prosecution set out in its summation:

> As regards a Cabinet Minister it is clearly his duty, *upon learning of the commission of these crimes, to bring the facts to the notice of his colleagues in the cabinet, and to resign unless effective steps are taken to prevent their commission.*
>
> Singularly little evidence has been given by the defense, who alone are in a position to know the facts, as to the steps, if any, taken by any of them for this purpose. There is no evidence that any of them ever raised the question of war crimes in the cabinet. Their failure to do so makes their guilt the greater. If they did raise the question and acquiesced in no effective steps being taken they must still bear the responsibility.[156] (emphasis added)

In the above statement, the prosecution offered three tests of guilt that the judges might apply when dealing with the cases involving former cabinet members. They were namely: (a) whether or not the accused acquired knowledge of the commission of war crimes; (b) whether or not the accused brought up to the Cabinet his knowledge of war crimes; and (c) if the accused insisted on the Cabinet taking effective steps to address the problem, or resigned in protest.

These standards appear concise and practical enough. But the question is, what is their legal foundation, and how should they be defined and applied? In the broad strokes painted by the prosecution, *every* member of the cabinet, including the education minister, the finance minister, and so on, could be held liable for not resigning without any showing either that they had participated in the formation of such policies, or had approved them, or that it was within their de facto authority to influence the implementation of the policies let alone to cancel them. In other words, this standard represented a form of collective cabinet responsibility solely based on upon formal membership in that body. At Nuremberg, for example, formal position was not decisive but rather substantive participation in the policy circle or in the actual formulation of implementation of criminal policies or orders.

The alternative for the Tokyo judges, of course, was to create a standard that focused liability on ministers with *specific* de facto power, duty, and knowledge relating to discharging the responsibility of the government to prevent

---

[156] T40112.

breaches of the laws and customs of war. The prosecution offered no additional explanations or legal analysis to help address these questions. Consequently, the theory of the responsibility of cabinet members – and the theory of government responsibility more generally – remained under-developed and under-defined at the closure of the court proceedings. It was, then, left to the judges to sort out unresolved theoretical questions and determine whether and how the theory of government responsibility should apply, if at all, to individual cases. In Part II we now turn to how the various judges dealt with this task.

*Part II*

The Law and Jurisprudence of
the Judgments and Separate Opinions

# 7 The Majority Judgment: Crimes against Peace

## 7.1 Introduction

As noted earlier in the Introduction, criticisms and assessments of the IMTFE typically focus more on political, cultural, and procedural aspects of the trial as a whole rather than on the law and jurisprudence of the tribunal as reflected in the judgment, separate opinions, and prosecution and defense theories of the case. For a variety of reasons, not the least of which is the bulk of the trial record and of the judgment and five other dissenting and concurring opinions, close analysis of the application of legal doctrine to the evidence before the court has not been a priority for many historians and commentators.[1] Previous chapters have analyzed the way in which the legal strategies of the prosecution and the defense developed. Such analysis is a necessary step toward an assessment of the jurisprudence of the judgment and opinions because the Tokyo judges depended on the evidence introduced by the parties. The majority largely accepted the case as it had been framed by the prosecution, and by the defense in the case of the dissenting opinions.

Differences of opinion over the structure of political authority in the Japanese government, the interrelations of the military, political bodies, and the imperial institution, as well as the nature of command responsibility and the chain of command itself, were central to disputes over who should be held legally liable for crimes against peace and war crimes in 1931–45. Even more fundamental for determination of the individual criminal liability of the accused, however, was the dispute over whether the charge under the indictment of various crimes against peace had been previously established in international law during the period under indictment. This issue divided the tribunal and provided the most important basis for the dissenting opinions that will be considered in subsequent chapters. Moreover, even if one assumes that crimes against peace was

---

[1] There is one major exception to this generalization. Boister and Cryer's *The Tokyo International Military Tribunal* stands apart from and above the existing Japanese and English language secondary literature as a serious and invaluable commentary on the legal issues raised at and by the Tokyo Tribunal. Rather than make multiple references to this important work throughout the ensuing chapters on the majority and separate opinions we suggest readers to give this seminal work the careful attention which it deserves.

a legitimate category of crime in prevailing international law rather than an ex post facto imposition of a new legal norm, the question remains as to whether each of those individuals charged with crimes against peace could be proved guilty beyond a reasonable doubt. This question also divided the tribunal, as reflected in the judgment and separate opinions. This chapter will focus on consideration of the treatment of these issues in the majority judgment.

Before considering the jurisprudence of the majority judgment on crimes against peace, two preliminary comments may be appropriate. The first is that at the time when the IMTFE judges deliberated on their legal findings in regard to crimes against peace, as indicated in Chapter 2, precisely the same issues have already been considered at Nuremberg before the IMT. Not only had the Nuremberg judgment found that charges of crimes against peace were valid under established international law, but their decision had already given rise to a significant body of legal commentary, including by many of the leading international law scholars of the day.

Many assessments of the Tokyo Tribunal, however, tend to neglect systematic comparison with Nuremberg, tacitly or explicitly according greater legitimacy to the proceedings and conclusions of that tribunal. It has too often been overlooked that the Nuremberg judgment was subjected to many of the same objections as have preoccupied scholars of the IMTFE for decades. There is also little doubt that most of the accused at Tokyo could also have been found guilty under the standards applied by the judges of the IMT.[2] Yet postwar German scholars, like critics of the IMTFE, vehemently attacked the legitimacy of the Nuremberg Tribunal as a whole on the basis of the alleged ex post facto nature of crimes against peace, often failing to mention the well-established basis for the conventional war crimes of which most of the accused were found to be guilty. These criticisms have been muted by the passage of time, however, as the Nuremberg judgment is now widely accepted, both in Germany and beyond, as the foundation of modern international criminal law, including the "crime of aggression" which is now enshrined in the Rome Statute of the International Criminal Court. Indeed, the Nuremberg Tribunal Museum and Academy have recently been established to carry forth the legacy of Nuremberg. Why is this not the case with the IMTFE, we might ask?

In regard to the IMTFE the same objections to crimes against peace and to the tribunal as a whole appear to remain as vivid today as they were seventy years ago, attesting to the different political and ideological dynamic that

---

[2] Fritzsche, Schacht, and Von Papen, acquitted at Nuremberg, had no real counterparts among the accused at Tokyo with the exception of Hashimoto Kingorō in terms of their remoteness from policy circles planning aggressive war, or from direct or indirect linkage to waging aggressive war or committing war crimes. There were far more accused at Tokyo who were members of the military or who held the highest cabinet level positions (foreign minister or prime minister in particular) than was the case at Nuremberg where the selection of defendants was more diverse.

## 7.1 Introduction

impinges upon discussion of the IMTFE and distracts from sober consideration of the law and jurisprudence of the tribunal as reflected in the work of the judges who produced the majority judgment and separate opinions. This provides all the more reason why close analysis of all the judgments and opinions is required to assess the performance of the IMTFE as a court. As noted earlier, while the politics of the formation of the IMTFE and the creation of its mandate are important subjects for historical research, it is also important to assess the work of the tribunal in terms of the quality of its judicial craftsmanship. In doing so one of the most important criteria must be the required standard of proof beyond a reasonable doubt. While historians have the luxury of determining their own individual standards as to the plausibility of an interpretation, judges do not. The judges and the prosecution at Tokyo were bound to the presumption of innocence and the burden of proof rested with the prosecution to prove the guilt of each accused beyond reasonable doubt in regard to each of the crimes charged. The defense, on the other hand, was only required to raise reasonable doubt in regard to each of the charged crimes, not to prove its own version of events. Our task, then, is to consider the extent to which the judgment and separate opinions engaged in the type of systematic legal analysis required to correctly apply that standard of proof. This is what the chapters in Part II aim to do in the case of the majority judgment and the separate opinions.

While it is clear that politics played a role in the formation of the court and in its proceedings and deliberations, this was no less true in regard to Nuremberg. At Tokyo, it is often overlooked by critics that, as we will see, external politics and ideologies played an even greater role in regard to the dissenting opinions than in the case of the majority judgment or the separate concurring opinion of Webb. It should also be recognized, however, that in reality all international criminal tribunals are political creations whose work is to a greater or lesser degree impacted by the larger political context which produced them.[3] That said, while political dynamics may shape the way in which a court is created or its jurisdiction defined in its statute, such considerations should play no role in the judges' application of the law to the evidence before them.

While others may focus on the political and historical context of the Tokyo Tribunal, what is specifically important here is a careful analysis of the way in which the law was actually defined and applied by the tribunal, because such analysis is a necessary preliminary to a determination of whether non-legal factors may have played a role and influenced the course or outcome of the proceedings. In other words, an assessment of the jurisprudence and application of the law by the various judges of the IMTFE must be framed within the

---

[3] International criminal courts are created by and overseen by states, whether through the mechanism of the UN Security Council or the Assembly of State Parties of the ICC, and they critically depend upon state cooperation to function effectively.

most fundamental obligation of judicial institutions under international law: the requirements of competence, independence, impartiality, and fairness in the application of the law to the evidence before the court. The ensuing chapters use the final written decisions of the judges as the benchmark for assessing their performance.

The claim that Nuremberg and Tokyo represented "victor's justice" because only German and Japanese war criminals were on trial is not a criticism of the trial proceedings themselves unless it can be shown that the accused were denied fundamental fair trial rights or that the judges acted in a manner that reflected incompetence, prejudice or a lack of independence and impartiality. In other words, the claim of "victor's justice" because of the one-sidedness of the proceedings is a criticism of the way in which the tribunal was created and operated as an institution, not a valid criticism of the fairness and soundness of the verdicts against individual accused.

For example, the fact that the International Criminal Tribunal for Rwanda (ICTR) has for political reasons never investigated or indicted members of the Rwandan Patriotic Front (RPF), the force that ousted the genocidal regime and formed the current government of Rwanda, does not establish that the proceedings against, and convictions of, individual accused were unfair or illegitimate. The fact that the RPF is widely regarded as having been responsible for some tens of thousands of revenge killings does not indicate that there were flaws in the trials that convicted members of the Hutu Power regime, responsible for the murder of 800,000 to 1 million Rwandans in 100 days. We may criticize the United Nations, members of the Security Council, and the Office of the Prosecutor for not having prioritized such prosecutions of the victorious side of the conflict, but such criticisms do not bear upon the fairness and validity of the trial proceedings. An assessment of the proceedings and verdicts requires an analysis of the conduct of the trials and the quality of the judgments according to prevailing international fair trial standards and criteria for assessing final written decisions.

Likewise, with respect to the IMTFE the salient question in regard to the validity of the verdicts against individual accused is the legal and factual justification of the verdicts as embodied in the majority judgment. The goal of legal analysis of the majority judgment and the separate opinions should not be to substitute our opinions on the guilt or innocence of individual accused for that of the judges, let alone to allow our views or prejudices about the politics of WWII in the Asia-Pacific to obscure our analysis of the trial and the final judgment and opinions. Our task is rather to dissect the factual analysis and legal reasoning on which the individual verdicts are based and determine whether the judgment and separate opinions meet the standards of a well-reasoned final decision based upon applicable law and the evidence before the court. Only in this manner can analysis of the judgment and separate opinions as *legal*

## 7.1 Introduction

*decisions* transcend the interminable political and ideological disputes that have much more to do with presuppositions about the Japanese and Allied war efforts as a whole than they do with the trial and judgment of twenty-five individuals accused of international crimes.

From this analytical perspective, it will be seen in the ensuing consideration of the jurisprudence of the judgments and opinions that the independence, competence, and impartiality of both majority and dissenting judges must be called into question. While the lack of full judicial independence may appear to be most obvious in the attempts by the majority, following the lead of both the prosecution and the defense, to minimize the role and responsibility of the Emperor, it is also the case that the dissenting opinions, and particularly those of Pal and Roeling, reflect to an equal or greater degree a lack of independence and impartiality.

The second preliminary comment is that the dissenting opinion of Justice Pal has in many quarters skewed or even short-circuited substantive consideration of the jurisprudence of the majority judgment and some of the other separate opinions. The veneration accorded Pal's dissenting opinion by some Japanese and American commentators has served perhaps to discourage taking that judgment seriously as a judicial reasoned opinion that meets required standards of impartial consideration of the evidence and the applicable law. As will be seen below, however, it is Pal's opinion itself that should not be taken seriously as jurisprudence, as opposed to a political tract that bends and twists both international law and the evidence before the court to reach a conclusion determined by presupposition and ideology rather than by a competent and impartial examination of the evidence and the charges in regard to each accused. Indeed, it is precisely its ideological stance rather than its juristic qualities that have won it admiration in Japan and among some western commentators. Even the group of Japanese researchers who promoted the dissemination of Pal's dissent in the 1960s privately conceded the negligible import of his opinion for international law.[4] Nonetheless, Pal's Opinion continues to overshadow objective consideration of the majority judgment by its facile dismissal of *all* the charges and convictions against *all* of the accused at Tokyo.

The widespread celebration of this conclusion of Pal's dissent points up another fundamental shortcoming of many of the treatments of the judgment of the IMTFE: The outcome of the Tokyo Trial cannot be assessed in a collective framework. While historians may look at the Japanese and Allied governments as collectivities, the obligation of the prosecution is to prove the guilt of *each* of the accused beyond a reasonable doubt. The obligation of the judges, on

---

[4] See Nakazato, *Neonationalist Mythology in Postwar Japan*, 169. See note 2 in Chapter 12 for related information.

the other hand, is to make individual determinations of the liability of *each of the accused* for *each* of the charges that have been brought against them. This, after all, remains the most fundamental contribution of Nuremberg and Tokyo, the principle that liability for international crimes attaches to individuals, not to states or collectivities.

In order to convict the accused persons the judges must therefore impartially, fairly, and competently weigh the evidence against each of them on each of the charges against them. The ultimate outcome by which this trial is to be measured is accordingly the legal and factual justification for each of the individual verdicts. In the final analysis, the fairness of the proceedings must be judged on this basis as well as the extent to which the defense was given an adequate opportunity to make its case. The obligation of a final written decision in international criminal proceedings is to provide a reasoned account of the weighing of the evidence and arguments adduced by both prosecution and defense, to make factual findings that logically follow from careful consideration of all the relevant evidence, to clearly articulate the applicable legal standards and apply those standards to the factual findings, and to reach individual verdicts based on these conclusions.

As we will see, both the Majority Judgment and Pal's dissent fail miserably in regard to these most basic criteria. In the case of the majority it is their reliance on the charge of conspiracy and a narrative of the collective activity of the Japanese government and military that serve to obscure the analysis of the liability of each individual accused. In the case of Pal, it is rather his willful blindness to the evidence and to the actual conduct of individual accused in order to condemn the proceedings as a whole that leads to his failure in this most fundamental responsibility of the judge as opposed to the external critic or academic commentator.

The soundness of our criticisms of the majority and dissents is reflected in the documents themselves. In the Majority Judgment the verdicts that justify the findings of guilt against twenty-five individuals comprise only 29 out of 558 pages devoted to analysis of the evidence, or 5 percent of the whole. The narrative verdicts, as we will see, hardly represent a careful assessment of the evidence against each of the accused, even more so in regard to war crimes than in regard to crimes against peace. In the Webb draft judgment, on the other hand, the individual verdicts comprise some 395 pages of the 638-page typescript, or 60 percent. This draft judgement, which the majority refused to accept as the judgment of the tribunal, thus provides the detailed examination of the relevant evidence against each of the accused that is missing in the majority judgment.

In Pal's dissenting opinion, some 616 printed pages in length, which also purports, as will be seen later, to be a complete final judgment of the case as a whole, there is *no* systematic treatment of the individual accused. What we find instead is a collective judgment that none of them were guilty of any of the crimes of which they were accused. In regard to some of the war crimes charges Pal takes the government as a collectivity and concludes that none of its members bear any responsibility for these war crimes.[5] When he does briefly take up the responsibility of nine military defendants, in five pages he concludes that not one of them is responsible for any of the many war crimes with which they have been charged. Needless to say, the treatment of nine defendants in five pages does not include an analysis of the prosecution case and evidence against each of them or a systematic application of the law to factual findings based on the evidence.

Roeling, on the other hand, in a briefer, but still quite substantial dissent of 128 printed pages, devotes some 32 pages, or 25 percent of the whole, to the individual verdicts involving just five of the accused where his opinion differed from that of the majority.[6] In other words, even upon a brute quantitative assessment it appears clear that neither the majority nor Pal engaged in a substantive analysis of the liability of each accused based upon a careful examination of the evidence bearing upon each of the charges against them. Webb and Roeling, on the other hand, by this same measure appear to have taken much more seriously their fundamental judicial task of rendering a reasoned judgment and verdict against each individual. The legal and evidentiary basis on which the various judges based their verdicts will be taken up in this and subsequent chapters.

## 7.2 Chapter II of the Majority Judgment and the Law of Crimes against Peace

In one sense it is quite easy to review the law applied in the majority judgment, in another sense quite difficult. The relative ease derives from the brevity of the section of the judgment entitled "The Law," for it consists of a mere 7 pages out of 628 of the complete judgment. The difficulty arises because the inadequacy of the brief section on "The Law" necessitates uncovering the legal standards that are actually applied by the tribunal. This is no simple task for two principal reasons. The first is that the judgment not only often does not make clear what definition or standard is being applied but is also at times inconsistent and unclear. The second reason has to do with its length and its organization. In comparison with the relatively short and incisive document produced by the IMT, the Tokyo judgment seems almost interminably long.

---

[5] Pal Opinion, 1363.
[6] Roeling also sent Webb a 100-page memorandum setting out in detail what he considered to be the case on conventional war crimes. January 23, 1948 M1417 25, National Archives of Australia (hereafter NAA).

## 262    The Majority Judgment: Crimes against Peace

As we will see, the narrative account of the conspiracy to engage in aggressive war takes up many hundreds of pages with detail on internal Japanese political developments and Japanese relations to China 1931–41 that would benumb all but the most dedicated reader. In the sections that follow we will first consider what the Majority Judgment explicitly articulates as the law of crimes against peace. The discussion will then turn to inferring what standards were actually applied by the majority in reaching their legal conclusions and individual verdicts. Whatever one's view of the proceedings at Tokyo, the judgment itself, like the separate opinions, must be analyzed as a legal document according to the expectations and standards that should be brought to bear upon a final written decision in an international criminal trial adjudicating charges of the most serious international crimes.

As noted earlier, the section of the judgment devoted to articulating the legal standards is remarkably abbreviated. In fairness, it should be noted that the Nuremberg judgment also engaged in relatively little explicit discussion of the definitions of crimes, modes of responsibility, or other doctrinal issues. The IMT's discussion of the standing of crimes against peace is considerably lengthier than that of the IMTFE, but that is due to the fact that the Tokyo majority, as will be seen, felt that the same issues had already been authoritatively dealt with at Nuremberg and contented themselves with adopting the findings of that tribunal. It should also be pointed out that while the Nuremberg judgment dealt at some length with the issue of the development of the law criminalizing aggressive war, it also never clearly defined the elements constitutive of that offense. Since the requirement of explicit definition of elements to be proved, as is required practice today, was not yet established in the jurisprudence of the 1940s, this is not surprising. The failure of the Tokyo Majority Judgment to define the elements of initiating, planning, preparing or waging of aggressive war is thus reflective of the general practice of criminal law at the time. Indeed, among the thousands of postwar national war crimes trials conducted across Europe and Asia it is rare indeed to find an attempt to define the elements of the crimes charged.

The seven-page section of the judgment (Part A – Chapter II) entitled "The Law," consists of three sections (a–c),[7] one of which deals with crimes against prisoners of war (or "POW" hereafter), and is thus irrelevant for crimes against peace.[8] The two relevant sections for crimes against peace are Chapter II(a) "Jurisdiction" and Chapter II(c) "The Indictment."[9]

---

[7] MJ 79–86.
[8] MJ Part A – Chapter II(b) "Responsibility for Crimes against Prisoners" 82–4.
[9] Since crimes against POWs are included in the indictment section, it is not clear why this topic received a separate section and why it came before "The Indictment" section.

## 7.2 Chapter II of Majority Judgment

### *7.2.1 Jurisdiction*

The jurisdiction of the IMTFE to try the accused for crimes against peace is established by the Charter that created the tribunal. The defense advanced seven challenges to the jurisdiction of the tribunal and it is these challenges that provide the focus for this initial section of the judgment. The strategy adopted by the majority was to follow the precedent set by Nuremberg, where the jurisdiction of the IMT had been challenged on similar grounds. The argument advanced by the Majority Judgment in affirming its jurisdiction follows, and in many cases quotes or closely paraphrases, the unanimous rejection of those challenges by the Nuremberg judges.[10] The majority's basic argument, as reflected in the first sentence of the section on jurisdiction, precisely follows Nuremberg in holding that, "the law of the Charter is decisive and binding on the Tribunal."[11] In words further echoing the Nuremberg judgment the majority affirms that the Allied Powers in constituting the tribunal under its Charter do not "have the right under international law ... to enact or promulgate laws ... in conflict with recognized international law."[12] They continue to note that as the law of the Charter is binding upon the tribunal the four principal challenges to jurisdiction must be rejected. Exactly like the Nuremberg judgment, however, they note that "given the great importance of the questions of law involved" the judgment will nonetheless address the questions raised by the defense.[13]

What is striking about the way in which the majority chose to address these questions is that they do not do so in their own voice. What follows instead is simply a long quotation from the Nuremberg judgment containing in abbreviated form the central argument on which the IMT upheld its jurisdiction. Unlike the IMT, the majority did not feel compelled to actually review the development of international law in the first forty-five years of the twentieth century in order to demonstrate that individual criminal responsibility had already been established in international law prior to the period under indictment. The reason why the majority judges did not feel compelled to provide such a legal analysis appears in the paragraph immediately following the quotation from the IMT:

With the foregoing opinions of the Nuremberg Tribunal and the reasoning by which they are reached this Tribunal is in complete accord. They embody complete answers

---

[10] That there were internal divisions within the tribunal on jurisdiction is indicated in Judge Cramer's memorandum to Webb of January 29, 1947 urging postponement of announcing a decision on jurisdiction because "the members are so divided in their opinion, two of whom do not believe that they are bound by the Charter nor that aggressive warfare is criminal" (AWM 3DRL 2481/5 p. 1). Justice Jaranilla also expresses his concern at the depth of the divisions on the issue of jurisdiction and deplores the fact that three judges did not take part in the deliberations. January 22, 1947 AWM 3DRL 2481/5 pp. 1–2.
[11] MJ 79.
[12] Ibid.
[13] MJ 80.

to the first four of the grounds urged by the defence ... In view of the fact that in all material respects the Charters of this Tribunal and the Nuremberg Tribunal are identical, this Tribunal prefers to express its unqualified adherence to the relevant opinions of the Nuremberg Tribunal rather than by reasoning the matters anew in somewhat different language to open the door to controversy by way of conflicting interpretations of the two statements of opinions.[14]

As will be seen, the dissents of Roeling and Pal disagree with the majority, and also with Nuremberg, on the issue of jurisdiction in regard to crimes against peace. From well before the creation of the IMTFE and until today, international law scholars have differed in opinion over the status of crimes against peace as an emerging doctrine in international law in the years following WWI. Those differences of opinion are reflected in the divergence between the majority judgment and the dissenting opinions. While Pal, as will be discussed in Chapter 12, engaged in a voluminous and rambling debate with the major international legal scholars who took the same position as that adopted by the Nuremberg Tribunal, the majority refrained from doing so. They chose instead to rely upon the conclusions and reasoning of Nuremberg, which they regarded as both correct and authoritative.

From the standpoint of evaluating the Majority Judgment as a final written decision providing justification for its findings and conclusions, our task is not to decide whether from the standpoint of international legal scholarship the conclusions reached by Nuremberg and the Tokyo majority are correct or incorrect. The status of crimes against peace in the pre-WWII period is a matter on which some of the leading international legal experts of the day were divided. The obligation of the majority was to provide a reasoned account of their decision on jurisdiction and they did so, in time honored juristic fashion, by following the reasoning and conclusions of a tribunal which they regarded as valid and authoritative. If one is to reject the ruling of the IMTFE on the status of crimes against peace, then one must necessarily also reject the identical ruling by the IMT and conclude that both of these tribunals were for this reason illegitimate and had no jurisdiction to try these international crimes. Few critics of the IMTFE have ventured such an opinion, singling out the Tokyo Tribunal as a kind of politically motivated aberration rather than seeing it for what it was: the Asian counterpart of Nuremberg, based upon the same legal foundation that defined its jurisdiction and the body of law it was to apply.

To digress for a moment with a contemporary example, we may consider the path breaking decision of the Appeals Chamber of the International Criminal Tribunal for the former Yugoslavia (ICTY) in the first case brought before that court: *Prosecutor v. Tadic*. In the Tadic Appeals Judgment the Appeals

[14] MJ 81.

Chamber essentially created a new mode of liability in international law, joint criminal enterprise (often referred to as JCE).[15] The chamber of course did not indicate that it was creating a new doctrine ex post facto, as had been argued by the defense. They relied instead on a series of decisions in rather obscure WWII British, American, and Italian cases conducted before military tribunals in which the Appeals Chamber found the nucleus of such a mode of liability, though it was nowhere referred to as joint criminal enterprise.

While scholars may disagree over the ICTY Appeals Chamber's interpretation of these WWII precedents, the chamber provided a reasoned justification for its interpretation of the law in holding that joint criminal enterprise was in fact an established doctrine prior to the commencement of the period under the jurisdiction of the ICTY. That doctrine of joint criminal enterprise, "found," as opposed to "created," by the ICTY Appeals Chamber in the Tadic Case is now an established doctrine widely used in international criminal prosecutions. Yet this holding was based on a far more tendentious reading of previous authorities than what one finds in the Nuremberg judgment on jurisdiction, nor was there a voluminous scholarly literature in support of such a doctrine at the time the Appeals Chamber rendered its decision. In assessing the decision of the Appeals Chamber one may criticize the acumen of the analysis while acknowledging that the judges met their obligation of providing a reasoned account to justify their holding.[16]

### 7.2.2 The Indictment

The "Indictment" section, (c), of Chapter II covers, in three pages, the legal foundations of the fifty-five counts of the indictment. Given the brevity of the treatment it follows that the discussion is hardly substantive. The first three paragraphs consider crimes against peace, encompassing five separate categories of crimes: "These are planning, preparation, initiation and waging aggressive war or a war in violation of international law, treaties, agreements or assurances; to these four is added the further crime of participation in a common plan or conspiracy for the accomplishment of any of the foregoing."[17] This formulation indicates that conspiracy is a "further crime" in itself, that is, a substantive offense rather than a mode of liability. This gave rise to a fundamental split of opinion between Webb and other judges, as will be seen in the next chapter, with Webb arguing in vain that "naked conspiracy" did not constitute an independent crime.

---

[15] *Prosecutor v. Dusan Tadic*, Case IT-94-1-A, Appeals Chamber Judgment pp. 80–107.
[16] The ICTY Appeals Chamber considered some of the essential criteria for a reasoned opinion in the context of its Judgment on a Rule 98 *bis* ruling in the Karadzic Case (Case IT-95-5/18 p. 17).
[17] MJ 84.

The judgment then defines conspiracy: "A conspiracy to wage aggressive or unlawful war arises when two or more persons enter into an agreement to commit that crime." It does not, however, treat the other four offenses as crimes which they will consider apart from the conspiracy:

Thereafter, in furtherance of the conspiracy, follows planning and preparing for such war. Those who participate at this stage may be either original conspirators or later adherents. If the latter adopt the purpose of the conspiracy and plan and prepare for its fulfillment they become conspirators. For this reason, as all the accused are charged with the conspiracies, we do not consider it necessary in respect of those we may find guilty of conspiracy to enter convictions also for planning and preparing. In other words, although we do not question the validity of the charges we do not think it necessary in respect of any defendants who may be found guilty of conspiracy to take into consideration nor to enter convictions upon Counts 6–17 inclusive.[18]

In other words, when the judgment states that when an accused adopted the purpose of the conspiracy and planned or prepared for "*its*" fulfillment, it follows that the accused is guilty of the crime of conspiracy to wage aggressive war. The judgment reasons that because all of the accused are charged with conspiracy as a crime in itself there is no need to consider the underlying crimes of planning aggressive war or preparation of aggressive war. Hence, the judges found it proper to ignore Counts 6–17 of the indictment which charge individual accused with the crimes of planning or preparing aggressive war. The judgment then applies the same reasoning to "initiating and waging aggressive war" and dismisses the necessity of making findings on Counts 18–26 as well. What may seem to be a mere technical matter at this early point in the judgment actually has far-reaching consequences.

This holding by the majority has the effect of relieving it, in their view, of the need to make concrete findings as to the conduct of each individual accused that might have met the requirements of proof for planning, preparing, initiating, or waging aggressive war.[19] Meeting such requirements of proof beyond a reasonable doubt would have necessitated a detailed examination of the conduct of each of the accused in regard to their participation in policy decisions, or the implementation of those decisions through their participation in concrete planning, preparation, or the conduct of the war. This was the kind of analysis which the Nuremberg judgment provides in regard to each of the accused. Instead, the Tokyo Tribunal felt that it satisfied the requirements of proving conspiracy by merely demonstrating agreement with or adherence

---

[18] Ibid.
[19] That this was the intention of the majority is indicated in Justice McDougal's memorandum to Webb of August 23, 1948 stating that the majority had decided that planning, preparation, and initiating would not be dealt with specifically because they were subsumed under conspiracy. AWM 3DRL 2481/16.

to the "purpose of the conspiracy" at any stage of its development from the period before the war to its end. Because of the notorious fluidity of the concept of conspiracy, which does not require an explicit agreement, the actual articulation of the criminal purpose, or that the alleged conspirators every met to formulate the conspiracy, it may be considerably easier to prove than the underlying conduct. And because new individuals can enter the alleged conspiracy at any time, their "agreement" with the conspiratorial purpose which is now in its stage of implementation may be inferred from their conduct that involves participation in that implementation.

Eliminating the requirement of establishing that the evidence was sufficient to prove Counts 6–26 of the indictment thus had the consequence of focusing the majority's complete attention on the conspiracy as opposed to the conduct of each individual accused that would have had to be established to convict or acquit for each one of the four other substantive offenses named in the indictment: planning, preparing, initiating, and waging aggressive war. As will be seen later, this central focus on the "conspiracy" operates to obscure the specific acts of each individual accused.

Because conspiracy is defined here as merely "an agreement" by two or more persons to wage aggressive war, the focus becomes that implied agreement, that unity of purpose that allegedly defines the group of "conspirators." With the corporate conduct of the "conspirators" as a collectivity in the forefront, the individual actions of each accused as a planner, initiator, preparer, or wager of aggressive war recede into the background. This approach operated to relieve the majority of deciding which, if any, of these four categories has been proved beyond a reasonable doubt in regard to each of the accused. The judgment's focus shifts instead to a narrative form describing the unfolding of a conspiracy from the 1920s onward that allegedly, and however implausibly given the deep divisions within the Japanese political and military elites, encompassed every one of the accused.[20]

Conspiracy, like its contemporary international law counterpart of joint criminal enterprise, is a tool beloved of prosecutors because it makes it so much easier to prove their case against a myriad of defendants all of whom played different roles in a complex set of decisions and events that took place over a number of years and in different institutional settings. At Tokyo it also relieved the majority judges of the necessity of analyzing the factual basis for twenty counts of the indictment against each of the twenty-five accused.

---

[20] For an example of this approach of the majority, see Justice Mei's memorandum to Justice Bernard (undated) that the conspiracy encompassed far more individuals than the twenty-five accused and included the army general staff and other "persons or organizations" who participated in the common plan. NAA M1417/1 28, pp. 3–4.

Focusing solely upon conspiracy to wage aggressive war seems to have also obviated the need, in the view of the majority, for defining "planning" or "preparation" or explaining the distinction between these two crimes. In regard to "initiating" and "waging" on the other hand, the judgment does make some attempt to define them:

> Although initiating aggressive war in some circumstances may have another meaning, in the Indictment before us it is given the meaning of commencing the hostilities. In this sense it involves the actual waging of the aggressive war. After such a war has been initiated or has been commenced by some offenders others may participate in such circumstances as to become guilty of waging the war.[21]

Although this passage is far from clear, it indicates a basic distinction between those who "commence hostilities" and those who participate in hostilities after they have commenced. It leaves undefined, however, the distinction between "planning," "preparing," and "commencing." Since these are all, according to the indictment, separate crimes, and according to the judgment, separate categories of conspiratorial conduct, it would seem important to explain how they relate to one another. Focusing solely upon the fifth category of crime, conspiracy, as subsuming all of the first four categories, allows the judgment to consider all of these categories of conduct simply as means of "fulfillment" of the conspiracy. Conspiracy, then, emerges as virtually the sole focus of the 75 percent of the total judgment which deals with the aggressive war counts.

In defining the scope of the liability of those defendants accused of the crime of conspiracy to wage aggressive war, the judgment refers to Article 5(c) of the Charter, which provides that "Leaders, organizers, instigators and accomplices participating in the formulation or execution of a common plan or conspiracy to commit any of the foregoing crimes are responsible for all acts performed by any person in execution of such plan."[22] The judgment interpreted this clause to apply only to crimes against peace, thus eliminating the possibility of conviction for conspiracy to commit murder, war crimes, or crimes against humanity. In this regard the Tokyo majority follows the lead of the Nuremberg judgment. In another, more important, respect, however, they did not.

At Nuremberg, as at Tokyo, the prosecution, and particularly the American prosecution team, relied heavily upon conspiracy as their overarching theory of the case. As the IMT judgment reveals, however, they were not successful in convincing the judges that the theory of a grand conspiracy could explain and encompass the complex and emerging patterns of planning, policy formulation, and conduct that led Germany from rearmament in the early 1930s

---

[21] MJ 84–5.
[22] MJ 85 and IMT judgment, 226. Note, however, that the judgment does not define precisely what constitutes instigating or organizing.

to catastrophic defeat in 1945. While the IMTFE majority relieved itself of making findings on the counts of the indictment relating to the planning, initiating, and so on of aggressive war, the judges at Nuremberg insisted that in regard to the accused "their guilt under each Count must be determined."[23] The IMT judgment goes further, however, in circumscribing and ultimately rendering almost useless the prosecution's theory of conspiracy under the indictment.

The Nuremberg judgment addresses the conspiracy theory by noting that the prosecution has essentially argued that "any significant participation" in the German government or Nazi Party provides "evidence of participation in a conspiracy." This amorphous concept of conspiracy, which is largely accepted by the Tokyo majority, is rejected by their Nuremberg brethren: "But in the opinion of the Tribunal the conspiracy must be clearly outlined in its criminal purpose ... The Tribunal must examine whether a concrete plan to wage war existed, and determine the participants in that plan."[24] One finds no counterpart in the IMTFE majority judgment to the IMT's careful dissection of the conspiracy theory advanced by the prosecution. The Nuremberg judgment maintains that although there is no doubt that war planning took place, the evidence does not establish "a single master conspiracy."[25] What the evidence does indicate is the "existence of many separate plans rather than a single conspiracy embracing them all."[26] The conclusion the Nuremberg judges drew from this more nuanced appreciation of the evidence essentially negated the prosecution's entire theory of the case as based upon a master conspiracy:

In the opinion of the Tribunal the evidence establishes the common planning to prepare and wage war by *certain* of the defendants. It is immaterial to consider whether a single conspiracy to the extent and over the time set out in the Indictment has been conclusively proved. Continued planning, with aggressive war as the objective, has been proved beyond doubt.[27] (emphasis added)

In other words, the IMT judgment rejects the theory of an overarching conspiracy and focuses instead on whether the involvement of each individual in planning or waging aggressive war has been proved by the evidence before the court. They conclude that the evidence adduced is sufficient to prove beyond a reasonable doubt that certain of the defendants engaged in the actual conduct of planning aggressive war and therefore there is no need to rely upon the conspiracy theory to connect all of them to the aggressive war charges.

---

[23] IMT judgment, 224.
[24] Ibid., 225.
[25] Ibid.
[26] Ibid.
[27] Ibid.

270     The Majority Judgment: Crimes against Peace

The majority judges at Tokyo, on the other hand, chose precisely the opposite path. They rejected the counts of the indictment requiring proof of individual conduct establishing which accused actually participated in a "concrete plan" to wage aggressive war and whether their participation met the requirements of proof for planning, preparing, initiating, or waging. They relied instead *solely* upon the conspiracy count to establish that all of the accused participated in a master conspiracy that embraced them all, from 1928 to 1945.

## 7.3 Chapter III of the Judgment and the Framework of International Treaty Law

In Chapter III of the judgment, the tribunal considers Japan's obligations under a variety of international treaties and instruments. For the most part these are enumerated rather than analyzed in regard to substantive legal doctrine. While Chapter II, *The Law of the Charter,* attempted to identify, however sketchily, the legal norms that the court would apply in considering the charges before it, Chapter III does not indicate the relation of the many provisions of the twenty-eight treaties, conventions, protocols, and other international legal instruments which it discusses to the law of the Charter.[28] While this may be understood to reflect the tribunal's statement that the law of the Charter is strictly binding upon it, the tribunal also specified in Chapter II(a) that this statement does not reflect an authority of the convening powers to *create* a legal framework in contravention of existing international law. As the judgment concludes, "In the exercise of their right to create tribunals for such a purpose and in conferring powers upon such tribunals belligerent powers may act only within the limits of international law."[29]

This section of the judgment thus provides an outline of the international legal framework that on the majority's view validates the law of the Charter and legitimizes prosecuting the accused for violations of international law (as *expressed* in the Charter). This enumeration of the relevant body of international law also serves for the majority to demonstrate, against the arguments of the defense and the dissents by Pal and Roeling, that Japan had assumed obligations under this framework and to a significant extent participated in its creation. This argument thus aims to support the majority's holding that Japan's aggression and conduct of hostilities violated the international normative framework by which it was bound. This rehearsal of Japan's international obligations is summarized in a very brief concluding section, tellingly entitled, "Japan Was a Member of the Family of Nations." Like the preceding parts of

---

[28] On this section see Boister and Cryer, *Documents*, lxxii–iv.
[29] MJ 79.

this chapter, this conclusion provides little in the way of reasoning or analysis. It states in its entirety:

> Thus for many years prior to the year 1930, Japan had claimed a place among the civilized communities of the world and had *voluntarily* incurred the obligations designed to further the cause of peace, to outlaw aggressive war, and to mitigate the horrors of war. It is against that background of the rights and obligations that the actions of the accused must be viewed and judged.[30] (emphasis added)

In regard to crimes against peace, then, the majority establishes, to its own satisfaction, a legal framework for holding individuals accountable for aggressive war. In limiting their focus to the conspiracy charges in the indictment they avoid the necessity of defining what specific conduct and mental element is required to prove that an individual planned, prepared, initiated, or waged aggressive war. How this legal framework was in practice applied to the evidence advanced by the prosecution against each of the accused must be distilled from the parts of the judgment that focus on the evidence regarding their conduct. This task is not an easy one, however, because of the way in which the judgment on crimes against peace is constructed. In particular, as will be seen, the focus on conspiracy as the "master offense" subsuming all four other categories of crimes related to aggressive war tends to obscure the legal standards that the court applies to individual defendants.

## 7.4 Chapters IV–VIII of the Judgment: The Master Conspiracy Narrative

### 7.4.1 Overview

Having briefly discussed the legal framework, the majority turn to the body of evidence to which that framework will be applied in regard to the aggressive war charges. They do not do so through a systematic referral to actual evidence in the form of testimony and exhibits but rather in the form of an historical narrative encompassing 75 percent of the judgment. That narrative not only rarely cites specific portions of the transcript or refers to documents in evidence but it also seldom refers to the prosecution or defense cases or their arguments on specific factual issues in dispute. The bulk of the majority judgment comprises what is essentially a chronological narration of Japanese internal politics and foreign policy formulation of the years 1928–45, informed by an overarching theme that from the beginning to the end the conspirators were united by a common purpose to wage aggressive war to secure Japanese domination of the Asia-Pacific region.

---

[30] MJ 110.

The remainder of the judgment after the majority's review of the legal framework, thus consists of three parts: In the first part, Chapters IV–VII provide an historical narrative of 420 pages, which the majority later refers to as "the recital of facts."[31] Chapter IV sets out a summary chronological narrative of some 194 pages of Japanese policy decisions and machinations that led to war, covering 1928–41 and including alleged planning to wage war against China and the USSR as well as preparations for the Pacific War. Chapters V–VII each provide a chronological narrative of roughly the same period, but they focus on China, the USSR, and the war against the Western Powers respectively, and together comprise 293 pages. The second part, Chapter VIII "Conventional War Crimes," consists of a mere sixty-two pages covering all the conduct of war and occupation from 1931 to 1945. The third part provides the tribunal's findings and verdicts. Chapter IX, "Findings on Counts of the Indictment," despite its seemingly crucial importance, is radically abbreviated, consisting only of four pages. Chapter X, "Verdicts," contains the reasoning behind the convictions of the accused and consists of only thirty pages (or approximately one page per defendant).

One might find surprising the way in which the vast bulk of the judgment is confined to a chronological narrative that resembles a historical treatise more than a legal analysis of evidence, arguments, and responsibility. The gross imbalance between the "recital of facts" in narrative form as opposed to the findings based upon that recital is particularly striking. The reason, however, seems clear. The theory of a single grand conspiracy from 1928 to 1945 dominates the approach of the majority as it did the summation of the prosecution.[32] For the majority, establishing what they take to be the unbroken, linear development of the conspiracy is in the foreground, overshadowing focused analysis on the conduct of each individual accused. The form of a chronological historical narrative is the perfect vehicle for revealing the unfolding of the conspiracy over seventeen years, but it necessarily obscures the role of individuals, especially because of the form the narrative takes. Because the narrative focuses on the chronological flow of events rather than carefully considering the role of individuals and institutions, and because the findings and individual verdicts are so abbreviated, there is no place in the judgment where the majority weighs and analyzes the actual evidence against each accused and considers the arguments of the defense and prosecution on that evidence. Because different accused play different roles at different times, and because some of them leave the alleged conspiracy at an early date and others come in late in the war, the narrative form is even more inadequate as a mechanism to focus upon them as individuals systematically

[31] MJ 598.
[32] See Chapter 4.

## 7.4 Chapters IV–VIII of Judgment

in relation to the available evidence. As we will see, the roles of individuals as reflected in the evidence and upon the inferences that can be drawn beyond a reasonable doubt from that evidence, remain largely unanalyzed. This is a fundamental shortcoming of the judgment and stands in stark contrast, as we will become apparent, with the approach of Webb in his draft judgment that the majority refused to accept.

Before proceeding further with the consideration of the majority judgment, one point deserves repeated emphasis. These criticisms of the majority judgment do not provide a basis for any conclusions as to the actual guilt or innocence of any of the accused. The fact that the majority do not carefully weigh the evidence as to each accused does not mean that the evidence was not there. Indeed, Webb's draft judgment shows clearly how evidence could be analyzed and marshalled to ground the liability of the accused. We must distinguish between, one the one hand, the majority's failure to provide an adequate justification of their verdicts through a carefully reasoned analysis of the evidence that was before them, and, on the other hand, the absence of such evidence in the prosecution case. The former is a fundamental shortcoming of the judgment in setting out a reasoned account of the verdicts, but only the latter would provide the basis for concluding that the verdicts themselves were factually incorrect because they were not supported by the evidence.

Webb's draft judgment shows that sufficient evidence had indeed been presented by the prosecution in order to provide a reasoned account justifying the verdicts. As always, we must remember that the relevant issue in a trial is whether on the basis of the evidence actually presented by both parties the judges could or could not reasonably conclude and justify that guilt had been established beyond a reasonable doubt. That is a different assessment than the judgement of a historian based upon a very different kind of analysis which might arrive at historical conclusions as to whether specific individuals should or should not have been convicted. It is a fundamental premise of this book that for our purposes the Tokyo Trial should be evaluated as a trial and the judgment and separate opinions assessed *on the basis of the quality of their reasoning and analysis as juridical products in light of the evidence before the court.*

In setting out to narrate over 420 printed pages the development and implementation of policies that resulted in aggression encompassing most of the Asia-Pacific region one might expect the majority to first establish the structure of authority for policy formation and for political and military decision-making in Japan and trace how it developed over the seventeen-year period under the jurisdiction of the tribunal. Since the primary obligation of a judgment is to provide factual and legal findings on each of the charges against each of the defendants, a clear delineation of their individual places within

274  The Majority Judgment: Crimes against Peace

the de facto structures and processes of war policy formation and implementation would seem to be essential to a determination of their liability for crimes against peace perpetrated by the Japanese government.[33] Chapter 3 has shown how the prosecution in fact labored to establish and clarify the complex interrelations and development of various institutions and bodies that each played a significant part in that process. Chapter 3 also indicated that the defense did not contest this central part of the prosecution's case by advancing an alternative account of the structure of authority in regard to war policy and strategy.

The path was thus open for the majority to construct the aggressive war part of the judgment around an analysis of the role and interplay of the different institutions, an account of how those roles developed in the course of the hostilities from 1931 to 1945, and a careful weighing of the evidence as to the place of each individual accused in those institutional developments that led to war. The judgment instead charts a different path.

The 420 pages of this part of the judgment are instead constructed around a chronological narrative of how the events unfolded, and particularly in the period from 1931 to 1941. Nowhere does the judgment systematically weigh the evidence adduced by the prosecution to support its theory of through what institutional structures decisions were made and implemented that involved the planning, preparation, initiation, and waging of the wars which Japan undertook. Especially in light of the fact that, as Chapter 3 has shown, the prosecution's account of the structures of authority shifted from its initial presentation of the evidence to its closing statement, one would think that the judges would be obliged to consider the evidence supporting these different perspectives and make clear findings as to the prosecution's account, the arguments of the defense, and as to its own view. They do not undertake any of these basic tasks. Indeed, Justice Northcroft, as one of the majority, argued in a memorandum that they should "state the facts as we find them" rather than setting out the evidence for and against.[34]

That Webb disagreed fundamentally with such an approach is made clear in his memorandum of February 21, 1947 which states that apart from a history of Japanese operations in China, Manchuria, and so on,

It will, of course, will be necessary to deal separately with the case of each of the individual accused in a full statement of all his activities gathered from *the evidence for both the prosecution and the defense*. Following this statement in respect of each

---

[33] The majority judgment (MJ 598) briefly set out this obligation at the beginning of the individual verdicts: "Article 17 of the Charter requires that the judgment shall give the reasons on which it is based. Those reasons are stated in the recital of facts and the statement of findings."
[34] January 5, 1948 NAA M1417/1 32.

accused there will be findings of fact and the application of the law in his case, thus leading to the verdict.[35] (emphasis added)

These two sentences set out the basic requirements for a reasoned final decision based upon the application of the law to findings based upon a weighing of the available evidence. One of the fundamental questions raised in assessing the majority judgment is why the majority did not follow what Webb, as president of the tribunal, had so clearly and accurately prescribed as their duty as judges.

Chapter IV of the judgment is entitled *The Military Domination of Japan and Preparations for War.* Its focus is on the domestic context of Japanese history from 1928 onward. This 190-page chapter presages the even more detailed narratives of the war in China and preparation for the Pacific War that make up Chapters V–VII. Chapter IV establishes, in the majority's view, the overarching conspiracy and thus already determines the conclusions of the narrative of the ensuing three chapters. For this reason our analysis focuses largely on Chapter IV. Considerations of length also preclude detailed analysis of Chapters V–VII, and, in any event, all of the key events considered in these latter chapters have already been dealt with in Chapter IV.

As the title of Chapter IV implies, the general theme is the domination of Japanese policymaking by a conspiratorial elite within the military, an elite that gains power and co-opts key civilian officials for its aggressive ends. The tribunal justifies its approach based on historical narrative by arguing that it is essential to understand this history in order to answer two questions raised by Japan's illegal actions in regard to its neighbors: "'Why did these things happen?' and 'Who were responsible for their occurrence?'"[36] The tribunal here understands that the historical analysis it provides must ultimately relate to the central question before it, which is the guilt or innocence of the twenty-five accused. As the judgment explicitly acknowledges, "The Tribunal must deal with the history of these attacks ... but its most important task is to assess the responsibility of individuals for these attacks." The judgment must, then, strike a balance between, on the one hand, the mode of historical narrative that it views as essential for making events comprehensible, and, on the other hand, the legal analysis of the responsibility of each individual accused under the legal standards articulated by the judgment.

That the tribunal does not succeed very well in this task may be due to a variety of factors that we will see at work in the analysis of the relevant parts of the judgment. These include: (1) the scope of the historical period deemed relevant, encompassing seventeen years (1928–45) of Japanese domestic and

---

[35] NAA M1417/1 32.
[36] MJ 110.

international politics; (2) the mass of evidence produced on these matters as bearing upon twenty-five individual accused, most of whom played a prominent role in this period; (3) the tendency of the judgment's focus on the crime of conspiracy to obscure the role of individual actors (whereas a focus on the four underlying offences on the basis of individual responsibility would necessarily have highlighted the conduct of individual defendants in regard to specific criminal acts).

The general conclusion of Chapter IV is articulated at the end of its introductory section. This conclusion is important, for while it sets out the central theme of the judgment as a whole, it also raises important questions about the theory of conspiracy on which the judgment so heavily relies. The tribunal reasons that,

The outstanding feature of the period under review is the gradual rise of the military and their supporters to such a predominance in the government of Japan that no other organ of government, neither the elected representatives of the people, nor the civilian ministers in the Cabinet, nor the civilian advisers of the Emperor in the Privy Council and in his entourage, latterly imposed any effective check on the ambitions of the military ... The varying fortunes of the protagonists in the political struggle which culminated in the supremacy of the military will be found to provide the explanation of many of the events abroad. Japanese warlike adventures and the preparations therefore ebbed and flowed with the varying fortunes of the political struggle in the Japanese homeland.[37]

Two questions are raised here that should guide any analysis of the tribunal's conclusions on crimes against peace. First, if there were fundamental divisions between various military and civilian ministers and other officials, how can there have been a single conspiracy between the defendants, who encompassed virtually all of the leading civilian and military leaders of wartime Japan? In other words, since the judgment defines conspiracy for purposes of the indictment as an "agreement between two or more persons" to wage aggressive war, how can there have been such an agreement between civilian and military leaders when according to the judgment the whole history of the period was defined by ever-shifting alliances and struggles between them? (This leaves aside the question of the deep divisions within the military itself, both between the Imperial Japanese Army and the Imperial Japanese Navy, and within each of those two services, as had been brought out in the admitted evidence. See Chapters 3 and 4.)

The second related question is how can civilian leaders be held accountable for actions of the Japanese government which they appear, on the tribunal's account of the predominance of the military, powerless to change? In other words, if, in the judgment's words, the eventual supremacy of the military

[37] MJ 110–11.

was so great and so complete that "no other organ of government ... imposed any effective check" on their aggressive ambitions, how can the civilian members of that government be held accountable for crimes committed as a result of these ambitions? The rest of the chapter will largely focus on the answer to these two questions and an elucidation of the way in which the judgment uses the conspiracy theory to link together all of the major defendants in a web of liability for aggressive war.

The narrative of the seventeen-year period is structured first around a general introductory narrative of the political developments within Japan from 1928 to 1940 that on the view of the majority prepared the path to war for the conspirators. The topics of the consolidation of the military's power in Japan and the war against China make up the bulk of the narrative (320 of 420 pages), most of which is concentrated on the period 1931–41. For the majority, it is this period in which the conspiracy to wage aggressive war is formed and implemented by the conspirators.

In the passage quoted earlier, the majority identified the overarching theme of the narrative as the political domination of Japan by the military to the point where no other organ of government could provide a counterweight to the policies they advocated. What must be considered in analyzing the historical narrative section of the judgment is how that "political struggle which culminated in the supremacy of the military"[38] relates to the participation of individual accused in a conspiracy that begins in 1928 and continues without interruption until defeat in 1945. The conspiracy has been defined by the majority as an agreement to wage aggressive war to achieve the political domination of East Asia and the Pacific by Japan. The ultimate question to be established by the judgment, then, is the existence of such a conspiracy and proof beyond a reasonable doubt that each of the accused was a member of that conspiracy and contributed to its implementation. As we will see, however, the role of each of the accused is not the focal point of the narrative and there is actually no place in the judgment that weighs the specific evidence advanced by the prosecution and the defense to establish that each individual was or was not a co-conspirator.

When the judgment finally turns to the verdicts, it refers to the narrative section as a "recital of facts."[39] This is indeed the way in which the entire narrative reads, that is, as a history, in "recital" rather than analytical form, of the period, chronicling one event and decision after another. The "facts" on which that chronicle are based are taken as established and just recited as if the judgment were a history textbook. But *how* were these facts established? On this the judgment is wholly silent, simply taking the facts as given and weaving

[38] MJ 111.
[39] MJ 598.

them into a historical account without detailed analysis of the evidence and arguments advanced by the parties to support or contest them. It is for this reason, we may assume, that the section on "Findings" is only 4 pages as opposed to the 420 pages of the narrative. The narrative section is in fact the findings, or conclusions of the majority as to the way in which, on their view, a single conspiracy to wage aggressive war inexorably unfolded over seventeen years. For this reason the "Findings" section consists rather of general overall conclusions summarizing the narrative section. What the judgment should have done, as Webb's draft judgment amply demonstrates, is to weigh and analyze the testimony, documents, and arguments advanced by the parties relevant to each of the key factual issues pertinent to the charges against the accused. The "Findings" should then have systematically expounded the findings that followed from that analysis.

The negative impact of this manner of proceeding is compounded further by another striking feature of the judgment. When the majority announces its factual findings, which will be examined in detail below, even then they do not include findings as to the role of the individual accused. The findings are largely devoted to a summary of the theory of an overarching conspiracy and the judgment states, "The question whether the defendants or any of them participated in that conspiracy will be considered when we deal with the individual cases."[40] The fact that after 424 pages of "recital of facts" and "findings" the majority has not yet established whether the accused were members of the conspiracy is striking enough. The greater problem is that the individual verdicts do not, in fact, address this task. Instead, there appears to be an inherent contradiction between the statement just quoted and what the judgment says in the introduction to the verdicts. Referring to the "recital of facts and that statement of findings," the opening of the "Verdicts" section maintains that,

Therein the Tribunal has examined minutely the activities of each of the accused concerned in relation to the matters in issue. Consequently, the Tribunal does not propose in the verdicts now to be read to repeat the many particular findings on which the verdicts are based. It will give its reasons in general terms for its findings in respect of each accused, such general reasons being based on the particular statements and findings in the recital already referred to.[41]

This statement explains why the factual conclusions as to the charges against each accused in the individual verdicts are so abbreviated, comprising only 29 pages in total for twenty-five accused, each charged with multiple counts of the indictment. As indicated earlier, neither the "Findings" section nor the individual verdicts contain either a systematic analysis of the evidence against each

[40] MJ 596.
[41] MJ 598.

accused or specific detailed findings. One would expect that since it is individuals who are on trial, a section entitled "Findings" would in fact make specific factual findings bearing upon on each of the accused. What it does instead is to make findings on the scope and development of the overarching conspiracy without referring to the individual alleged conspirators.

The judgment, in the passage just quoted, justifies this omission by averring that the narrative section of the judgment "has examined minutely the activities of each of the accused." It is, then, to this section we must turn to determine whether or not the judgment meets the obligation it acknowledges of examining in detail the conduct of each individual accused in relation to each of the crimes charged. As had already been suggested, the narrative form of the "recital of facts" chapters is hardly well-suited for this task.

*7.4.2 Narrative Form and Individual Accountability*

While the indicted individuals do appear in the historical narrative, they are neither the focal point nor the systematic object of analysis. Rather their names appear and reappear as the narrative develops its chronological account of the unfolding of events, but it is the narrative that is always in the forefront, not the individuals. There is thus no place in the narrative, or in any other part of the judgment, where the evidence and arguments against or on behalf of each individual are brought together with an analytical focus on the sufficiency of the evidence to prove the charges beyond a reasonable doubt. Nor is there a systematic or coherent consideration of the defense evidence and arguments on each of the accused. There are indeed connecting threads that run through the narrative, but they are focused not on individuals but on institutional developments and shifting political alliances, always with a view toward the inexorable progress of the conspiracy. There is indeed a "minute" account, but it does not center on the evidence that relates to the charges against individuals. Rather it describes the myriad events, disputes, setbacks, and political conflicts and upheavals that characterized the conspiratorial road to war.

In order to analyze the role of each individual accused one would have to extract from the narrative every reference to them and put them together in some kind of systematic fashion. This is what the judgment fails to do, leaving that task to the Webb draft judgment that the majority rejected. Even this would only be a first step, for what is essentially required is a weighing of the evidence behind those references and an analysis resulting in specific factual findings in regard the requirements of proof needed to establish each of the charges against each accused. This also the judgment fails to do. What we are left with is a bewilderingly detailed and ill-organized account of an

280    The Majority Judgment: Crimes against Peace

exceedingly complex flow of events in which individuals surface, disappear, and reappear as the chronology moves on. It is in fact the alleged overarching conspiracy as an abstract entity that organizes and drives the narrative, as the "Findings" section ultimately reveals. Before turning to that crucial section a few examples from the narrative may illustrate the points made here.

### 7.4.2.1  The Case of Hirota

As stated earlier, in the 420-page historical narrative the role of individuals is not systematically analyzed. Indeed, because it is the flow of events that is in the forefront, the judgment seldom relates its references to individuals to the charges against them. This of course undercuts the claim of the majority that their individual conduct has already been "examined minutely" so that there is no need for systematic analysis in the individual verdicts or findings. It is of course impossible to go through the 420-page narrative exhaustively, but a few representative examples may illustrate this point. As the conviction of Hirota Kōki has given rise to so much criticism we may take it as a suitable example.

When the judgment describes the creation of the Imperial Headquarters it is in relation to the general theme of the ascendancy of the "Army's influence over the cabinet."[42] They state that, "On 19 November 1937, the Cabinet, of which HIROTA, KAYA, and KIDO were then members gave consideration to the matter; and, on the following day, Imperial General Headquarters was established."[43]

While this may be an interesting fact for historians of prewar Japan, what is its legal significance in regard to the three named accused? The judgment gives no hint. Did they attend the November 19 cabinet meeting? Did they speak on the issue and if so did they oppose or support the establishment of the Imperial Headquarters? If they supported it, what is the legal significance of them supporting an institution whose stated purpose was merely to improve communication between the army and navy? Similar bodies were established in most of the major military powers of this era.

The judgment provides no information on any of these issues. Moreover, the ensuing discussion of the Headquarters indicates that it, on the account of the majority, had little relevance to the accused. They first note that the operation of the Imperial Headquarters, "was a sphere of secrecy ... In which the Cabinet was to have no part."[44] They go one to state that in any event, "There is little evidence to indicate the importance of the part played by Imperial General Headquarters in the events of subsequent years. It was a poorly coordinated body ... But by its very establishment, the armed forces

---

[42] MJ 168.
[43] Ibid.
[44] MJ 169.

## 7.4 Chapters IV–VIII of Judgment

were given the opportunity to make important decisions without the approval, or even the knowledge of the Cabinet of the day."[45]

Two points deserve emphasis here. The first is that the judgment does not even attempt to explain how this section bears upon the culpability of the named accused. Their names appear only in a tangential, cursory manner, indicating that at this time they were members of the cabinet. The very next paragraphs explain that the cabinet had no connection to the work of the IHQ. The second point is related and concerns the overarching conspiracy of which the three named accused, Hirota, Kaya, and Kido were allegedly a part. How does this factual account (which cites no evidence or arguments of the parties) show that these three men were co-conspirators, sharing a common purpose with the army, with whom they have at this point already allegedly been planning to wage aggressive war since at least 1931? Doesn't this narrative rather suggest that the army was operating independently of these civilian leaders, creating an institution for coordinating military strategy and operations from which they would be completely excluded? It certainly does not establish any relevant fact beyond a reasonable doubt. Indeed, the judgment is silent on how these developments illustrate an overarching conspiracy to wage aggressive war that encompasses the named accused.

In the judgment's lengthy treatment of the events of the crucial period of 1936–8 Hirota emerges as a central figure whose name appears again and again in the narrative. This is only natural in that in his roles as prime minister and foreign minister he was intimately involved in cabinet policy discussions. The judgment most closely identifies what they regard as Hirota's central role in the conspiracy with the "national policy decision, which proved to be the cornerstone in the whole edifice of Japanese preparations for war."[46] This "national policy decision" (discussed at length in Part I) plays an essential role in the majority's theory of an overarching conspiracy and is referred to again and again in the account of the period leading to the Pacific War in 1941.[47]

How, then, does this national policy decision establish Hirota as a member of the conspiracy to plan, prepare, initiate, and wage aggressive war? The judgment notes that the "national policy decision" did not originate in the cabinet itself but in the Ministry of the Army and the Ministry of the Navy.[48] The army and navy ministers then presented the proposed policy statement to Hirota and the finance and foreign ministers, Baba Eiichi and Arita Hachirō. The judgment states that in the discussion of the proposal Baba suggested that although Japan should aim at the ousting of the "military rule policy of the Powers"

---

[45] Ibid.
[46] MJ 129. The full text of the Basic Principle of National Policy is reproduced in Chapter 4.
[47] As seen in Chapter 4, Hirota's Basic Principle of National Policy was essential in the prosecution's case of the overarching conspiracy.
[48] MJ 129–30.

282    The Majority Judgment: Crimes against Peace

(i.e. the Western colonial countries) "it was essential for Japan herself not to practice military despotism."[49] Arita noted that it was also essential to retain the "goodwill of Great Britain and the United States." In this context Baba, Arita, and Hirota "had no fault to find with the proposal" and left it to the army and navy "to draw up a detailed plan."[50]

We must again ask how this narrative of the origin of the national policy decision that was a "cornerstone" of the conspiracy bears upon Hirota's liability. The facts taken to be established by the judgment indicate that Hirota supported a policy of Japanese expansion in the Asia-Pacific region at the expense of the colonial powers. Rivalry of colonial powers was not exactly new and this goal is by no means criminal or coterminous with a common purpose to wage aggressive war. The judgment provides no analysis on this point and the historical narrative simply moves on to other developments, where Hirota's name often appears but again without the essential reasoning to make the connection to the charges against him. That connection, however, is made in Webb's draft judgment.

The majority judgment, on the other hand, provides little analysis on the crucial points from which Hirota's participation in the conspiracy could be inferred beyond a reasonable doubt. For example, the section entitled "Naval Preparations" begins by stating that "While HIROTA was Prime Minister, the Navy was not less active than the Army in promoting the national mobilization for war."[51] There is no mention at all of how Hirota might have been connected to these preparations or how they indicate that he aimed at aggression, for this is the only reference to him. The central thrust of the narrative thus far has been to establish the absolute domination of the army and navy over the cabinet, so how does the fact that the navy was building up during Hirota's brief term as prime minister indicate his role in the conspiracy? It was also true, of course, that all the major powers were increasing their naval capacity in anticipation of possible war. The question for the tribunal was whether specific individuals involved in that buildup were planning to use that naval capability to wage aggressive war.

The fact that numerous cabinets were assembled and fell during this period, while the military preparations continued unabated throughout, might indicate that neither Hirota nor other prime ministers were responsible for such developments. In fact, as the judgment acknowledges, Hirota's Cabinet fell because

---

[49] MJ 130.
[50] Ibid. As the judgment summarizes, the "fundamental principle" of this policy was to strengthen Japan to become "the stabilizing power, nominal and virtual, in East Asia" and to "secure peace in the Orient and contribute to the peace and welfare of mankind throughout the world." The policy maintained that "diplomatic skill" and a strong national defense would be the means by which Japan would increase its power in the region (MJ 127).
[51] MJ 132.

## 7.4 Chapters IV–VIII of Judgment

of army dissatisfaction with his policies.[52] His successor, Konoe, the judgment states, acceded to the army's policies in order to avoid a similar fate.[53] Where in such narratives are we to find the criminal "agreement" and "common purpose" to wage aggressive war which defined the overarching conspiracy alleged by the prosecution and confirmed by the majority?

In regard to Hirota, the judgment relies heavily on his role as foreign minister subsequent to the fall of his cabinet to establish his culpability as a conspirator, but again they do not analyze the facts they narrate to demonstrate his connection to the crimes charged. The judgment maintains that it was in his dealing with the United States that Hirota's "policy as Foreign Minister is plainly revealed."[54] Their reference for this finding is again the national policy decision of August 1936. On this basis they conclude that as foreign minister Hirota adhered to that policy which aimed at achieving Japanese dominance in the Asia-Pacific on the basis of the "co-existence and co-prosperity principle" which would be pursued in a "smooth and amicable manner" while maintaining "most amicable relations with the Powers."[55]

While one might maintain, as the judgment suggests, that the veneer of amicability concealed an intention to wage aggressive war to achieve Japan's aims, this is something that must be proved beyond a reasonable doubt by weighing and analyzing the evidence for and against as it bears specifically upon Hirota. While Roeling and Webb both engage in such an analysis in regard to Hirota, reaching opposite conclusions, the majority judgment merely narrates the facts as given, inferring without demonstration that they reveal his participation in the conspiratorial common purpose of waging aggressive war. What the judgment should do, but does not, is to consider what other inferences could be drawn from the evidence and whether the inference it prefers has been proved beyond a reasonable doubt.

It must be underlined that this is not to suggest that Hirota was innocent of the charges against him. Webb's draft judgment shows that there is a great deal of evidence that the majority might have adduced to establish Hirota's guilt. Roeling, as we will see, stretches to interpret damning evidence in a light favorable to Hirota. Our point, however, is *not* to argue for Hirota's guilt or innocence, but rather to point out the shortcomings of the judgment *as a reasoned decision* with an obligation to justify its legal conclusions based upon weighing and analysis of the prosecution and defense evidence before it.[56] As discussed above, subsequent historical research about Hirota, like facts not in

---

[52] MJ 184–85.
[53] MJ 185.
[54] MJ 179.
[55] Ibid.
[56] Hirota's conviction in regard to war crimes committed during the Nanjing Massacre will be considered in Chapter 9.

### 7.4.3 Army Domination and the Conspiracy

evidence before the tribunal, is irrelevant from this perspective of the assessment of the judgment.

Central to the judgment's narrative is the domination of Japanese policymaking by the army. A rather strange feature of the judgment's portrayal of this process is the way in which its temporal development is portrayed. On the one hand its course is inexorable from 1928 onward, but on the other hand there are constant changes of direction, conflicts between alleged participants, setbacks, doubts, and reassessments. It was precisely such dynamics that led the Nuremberg judges of the IMT to reject the idea of a single overarching conspiracy.

For example, in the cabinet crisis of December 1931 the army succeeds in bringing down the government, with Prime Minister Wakatsuki resigning "after admitting his Cabinet's inability to control the Army."[57] The majority concludes that at this point in 1931, "The Army had achieved its goal of a war of conquest in Manchuria, and had shown itself to be more powerful than the Japanese Cabinet."[58] We should also note here that the personification of the army, like the consistent personification of the cabinet, obscures the role of individual accused in these events. While assigning agency to the "Army" as a collectivity may be sufficient for a historical narrative it is the conduct of individual accused that is relevant for purposes of assigning responsibility for crimes charged.

When the new cabinet under Prime Minister Inukai Tsuyoshi (succeeding Wakatsuki) is seen as not sufficiently compliant with the militarists' wishes, the judgment describes how he is assassinated. While it seemed that the judgment had already concluded that the military had achieved its goals in December 1931, and perhaps consolidated them with the assassination of Inukai and the fall of his government within months of the Wakatsuki resignation, the judgment then states that the new cabinet under Saitō Makoto (succeeding Inukai) worked to achieve a compromise with the army and "would control the military."[59]

It appears from the judgment's narrative, however, that on the one hand the Saitō Cabinet's policies largely followed the army's aggressive policies, making "Araki's principle of national defence the overriding consideration in its Manchukuoan policy."[60] The judgment infers that "national defence" "meant

---
[57] MJ 116.
[58] Ibid.
[59] MJ 118.
[60] MJ 121.

the conquest of other countries through force of arms" and notes that in the months after Army Minister Araki's speech the "policy gained both popular support and Cabinet recognition."[61] What the judgment fails to do is demonstrate how Araki's speech invoking the national spirit and the Imperial Way was an expression of the conspiracy to wage aggressive war. Likewise, unclear is how Araki's "emotional appeal to the patriotism of the Japanese people"[62] is translated into policy, yet that would seem to be crucial for establishing responsibility for the sentiments he expressed becoming national policy.

Apart from the attribution of agency to personified institutions like "Cabinet" or "Army," the judgment's frequent use of passive constructions also obscures which individuals are connected to or responsible for developments. For example, the judgment states that under Saitō, "In April 1934 a new policy in respect of East Asia was formulated." Not only does the judgment not indicate who formulated it, but it goes on to say that it was "quickly disclaimed by the Saito government." This would seem to undercut the previous conclusion that the army had succeeded in imposing its policy upon the cabinet. The judgment then maintains that this policy that was disclaimed "was much the same policy that War Minister ARAKI had enunciated ten months earlier."[63] What the import of this statement is for Araki's potential criminal liability is not explained. Nor does the judgment explain why his policy, that had been previously accepted by a cabinet that was allegedly prostrate before the army, is now easily disclaimed by a cabinet that had, we have been told just three paragraphs earlier, "made Araki's principle of national defense the overriding consideration" of its policy. The contradictions in the majority's attempt to construct a linear narrative are apparent.

Considering the activities of the ensuing Okada Cabinet (July 1934–March 1936) the judgment refers to Okada's testimony that during his term in office once more "the power of the Army was increasing."[64] The extent of what the judgment refers to as the "power and ruthlessness" of the army appears from the attempted coup and assassination of Okada by a group of army officers. Okada tenders the resignation of the cabinet after the February 26 Incident of 1936, "being unable to control the military."[65] While, as seen above, the judgment presents the Hirota Cabinet as being virtually under the control of the army, in January 1937 the army brings down his government as well because of lack of compliance by members of the cabinet with army wishes.[66] As also seen above, the judgment presents Hirota's policy as foreign minister as in complete

[61] MJ 120.
[62] Ibid.
[63] MJ 121.
[64] MJ 124
[65] MJ 125.
[66] MJ 144.

accordance with army wishes, indicating on their view, his participation in the conspiracy. Konoe, in February 1938, in order to avoid the downfall of his government, accedes to the army's "schemes" for nation-wide mobilization for war.[67] With this, the judgment concludes, "the Army had moved one step nearer to the achievement of complete political supremacy in Japan" and, "had made itself the master of Japan's destiny."[68] At this point in 1938, according to the judgment, the army is "one step closer" to what it had, according to the judgment, supposedly achieved already in 1931, 1934, and 1936. Thus, "at the Army's instigation the nation had embarked upon a programme of aggrandizement through expansion of military power."[69]

Who is "the Army" here and what is its relation to the alleged conspirators? The "Army" is not on trial but rather a group of individuals many of whom have no connection to that institution. Further, at every point where the judgment presents the army as having achieved political domination there appear to follow events that indicate the situation is rather more complex.

Thus, in May 1938, just a few months after the events where the judgment portrays the army as the master of Japan's destiny, another crisis ensues which leads to the army bringing down the Konoe Cabinet as well. This, the judgment indicates, aims at meeting "the threatened breakdown of the Army's plans."[70] In order to gain firmer control of the government Foreign Minister Hirota and Finance Minister Kaya leave the government and the cabinet "is strengthened by the addition of two military men."[71] If Kaya and Hirota were key members of the conspiracy who, on the judgment's portrayal, had worked tirelessly to advance the conspiracy to wage aggressive war, why did they have to be pushed aside, as the judgment implies they were? On the other hand, if the army was so firmly in control as the "master of Japan's destiny," why did it need to strengthen the cabinet by adding more of its own men? Moreover, the judgment maintains that under the new "strengthened Cabinet" the goal remained the same of "fulfilling the aims of the basic national policy" laid down in 1936.[72] Since the judgment has spelled out in detail how all cabinets since 1936, and especially those of Hirota and Konoe, had faithfully strived to implement that policy, how does the theory of conspiracy explain the constant need for cabinet reshuffling?

The point here is that the judgment's adherence to a theory of an overarching conspiracy pursued without interruption from 1928 to 1945 requires a reductive account of what was an incredibly turbulent period in Japanese politics. The

[67] MJ 185.
[68] MJ 185, 187.
[69] MJ 187.
[70] MJ 190.
[71] Ibid.
[72] MJ 191.

judgment presents the "Army" as a monolithic element (typically ignoring the navy) that seems to stand in for "the conspiracy" in the narrative account. Yet what the judgment's narrative actually reveals is that just as there was considerable dissension within the political circles and the cabinet, so there were also important differences in policy within the army and the navy. Thus, in light of the lack of progress in bringing about a quick resolution to the war in China in 1938, a strong faction in the cabinet argues that the goal of military conquest in China "should be abandoned." The judgment continues in the next sentence, "Nor was this disagreement confined to the Cabinet ... Among the members of the army general staff this was the prevailing opinion."[73] Indeed, as seen in Chapter 4, some high-ranking army officers wanted peace in China so as to pursue war against the Soviet Union. The struggle within the army was ultimately resolved in favor of those who wanted to pursue the war in China and this led to yet another cabinet reorganization. This passage reveals what the personification of the "Army" and the "Cabinet" have too often occluded: the path to war was not linear and the theory of a single overarching unbroken seventeen-year conspiracy with one consistent aim is not supported by the evidence adduced by the judgment, let alone by other evidence which informs Webb's draft judgment.

These divisions within the army and the cabinet resurface in the judgment as the narrative continues through the events of 1938–41.[74] Deep divisions arise not only between factions in the cabinet and the military over, for example, an Axis alliance, war with the Soviet Union, or relations with the US, but emerge within the Ministry of Foreign Affairs, and include the Emperor, imperial advisors, and others.[75] The judgment notes that, "The situation within the cabinet was one of unresolved conflict." Lest one think that situation was confined to the cabinet, the judgment reports that the Emperor had reprimanded Army Minister Itagaki, and the Lord Keeper commented, "The Army is confused and everything is lost." This was in July 1939, long after the judgment had concluded that the army was the master of Japan's destiny and in complete control of the government. While the judgment reports this turn of events it never analyzes its import for the conspiracy theory being advanced.

In regard to another one of the leading players in this drama, Prime Minister Hiranuma, one of the alleged leading conspirators, the judgment initially presents him as having "achieved a position of pre-eminence among the leaders

---

[73] MJ 204.
[74] See, for instance, MJ 236–51.
[75] See MJ 247–8 on the Emperor's role. Hirohito's role was of course a point of contention among the judges, and especially Bernard and Webb vis-à-vis the majority. See Webb's memorandum to Cramer of October 4, 1948 expressing regret of "the failure to refer to KIDO's Diary ... showing the part played by the Emperor in starting the war." AWM 3DRL 2481/8.

of the military faction" even before the campaign in Manchuria in 1931.[76] Hiranuma is accordingly portrayed as unremittingly supportive of the army's position in the crisis of 1939 over the Axis alliance, but then the judgment indicates that by August of that year "HIRANUMA had withdrawn somewhat from his position of complete acquiescence in the Army's plans."[77] Here he is portrayed as a follower, not as a leader, and his shift of position seems not to comport with the previous narrative. Despite his "pre-eminence" among the military activists, his cabinet also falls in August 1939. The new cabinet is instructed by the Emperor to adopt a policy of "cooperation with Great Britain and the United States."[78]

This cabinet soon fails as well, as described in the section "The Army brings about the downfall of the Yonai Cabinet."[79] The judgment describes this situation as "indicative of the commanding attitude which the Army had assumed."[80] Yet this statement refers to the situation in July 1940, years after we had previously been told that the army controlled the destiny of the nation, etc. In its efforts to describe a linear trajectory of dominance by the "Army" as a stand-in for the conspiracy, the judgment fails to provide the analysis required to support this theory and fails to consider the other inferences that could plausibly be derived from the facts it narrates.

The account of the army's quest for political domination reaches its culmination in the section entitled "The Liaison Conference and the manner in which the domination of the military was made complete."[81] While it has several times earlier appeared that the army was already dominant, this section describes the emergence of this new body which "was to ensure the unity of military and Cabinet policy." Although the judgment subsumes the importance of this body within its argument about military domination, the situation appears to require a more nuanced analysis. The judgment states that this new entity "for the first time enabled the leaders of the Army and Navy to take a direct part in the formulation of Cabinet policy, became itself a very important policy-making body ... During the year 1941 Liaison Conferences were held frequently and came more and more to usurp the functions of the Cabinet meeting."[82]

Several points deserve emphasis here. First, the navy suddenly appears as an important voice in policy formation, when heretofore the "Army" has been the primary and often sole agent. Differences of opinion between the army and navy have been obscured by general reference to "the Army" as representative

[76] MJ 225.
[77] MJ 248.
[78] MJ 250.
[79] MJ 284–5.
[80] MJ 284.
[81] MJ 289–90.
[82] MJ 289.

## 7.4 Chapters IV–VIII of Judgment

judgment presents the "Army" as a monolithic element (typically ignoring the navy) that seems to stand in for "the conspiracy" in the narrative account. Yet what the judgment's narrative actually reveals is that just as there was considerable dissension within the political circles and the cabinet, so there were also important differences in policy within the army and the navy. Thus, in light of the lack of progress in bringing about a quick resolution to the war in China in 1938, a strong faction in the cabinet argues that the goal of military conquest in China "should be abandoned." The judgment continues in the next sentence, "Nor was this disagreement confined to the Cabinet ... Among the members of the army general staff this was the prevailing opinion."[73] Indeed, as seen in Chapter 4, some high-ranking army officers wanted peace in China so as to pursue war against the Soviet Union. The struggle within the army was ultimately resolved in favor of those who wanted to pursue the war in China and this led to yet another cabinet reorganization. This passage reveals what the personification of the "Army" and the "Cabinet" have too often occluded: the path to war was not linear and the theory of a single overarching unbroken seventeen-year conspiracy with one consistent aim is not supported by the evidence adduced by the judgment, let alone by other evidence which informs Webb's draft judgment.

These divisions within the army and the cabinet resurface in the judgment as the narrative continues through the events of 1938–41.[74] Deep divisions arise not only between factions in the cabinet and the military over, for example, an Axis alliance, war with the Soviet Union, or relations with the US, but emerge within the Ministry of Foreign Affairs, and include the Emperor, imperial advisors, and others.[75] The judgment notes that, "The situation within the cabinet was one of unresolved conflict." Lest one think that situation was confined to the cabinet, the judgment reports that the Emperor had reprimanded Army Minister Itagaki, and the Lord Keeper commented, "The Army is confused and everything is lost." This was in July 1939, long after the judgment had concluded that the army was the master of Japan's destiny and in complete control of the government. While the judgment reports this turn of events it never analyzes its import for the conspiracy theory being advanced.

In regard to another one of the leading players in this drama, Prime Minister Hiranuma, one of the alleged leading conspirators, the judgment initially presents him as having "achieved a position of pre-eminence among the leaders

---

[73] MJ 204.
[74] See, for instance, MJ 236–51.
[75] See MJ 247–8 on the Emperor's role. Hirohito's role was of course a point of contention among the judges, and especially Bernard and Webb vis-à-vis the majority. See Webb's memorandum to Cramer of October 4, 1948 expressing regret of "the failure to refer to KIDO's Diary ... showing the part played by the Emperor in starting the war." AWM 3DRL 2481/8.

288    The Majority Judgment: Crimes against Peace

of the military faction" even before the campaign in Manchuria in 1931.[76] Hiranuma is accordingly portrayed as unremittingly supportive of the army's position in the crisis of 1939 over the Axis alliance, but then the judgment indicates that by August of that year "HIRANUMA had withdrawn somewhat from his position of complete acquiescence in the Army's plans."[77] Here he is portrayed as a follower, not as a leader, and his shift of position seems not to comport with the previous narrative. Despite his "pre-eminence" among the military activists, his cabinet also falls in August 1939. The new cabinet is instructed by the Emperor to adopt a policy of "cooperation with Great Britain and the United States."[78]

This cabinet soon fails as well, as described in the section "The Army brings about the downfall of the Yonai Cabinet."[79] The judgment describes this situation as "indicative of the commanding attitude which the Army had assumed."[80] Yet this statement refers to the situation in July 1940, years after we had previously been told that the army controlled the destiny of the nation, etc. In its efforts to describe a linear trajectory of dominance by the "Army" as a stand-in for the conspiracy, the judgment fails to provide the analysis required to support this theory and fails to consider the other inferences that could plausibly be derived from the facts it narrates.

The account of the army's quest for political domination reaches its culmination in the section entitled "The Liaison Conference and the manner in which the domination of the military was made complete."[81] While it has several times earlier appeared that the army was already dominant, this section describes the emergence of this new body which "was to ensure the unity of military and Cabinet policy." Although the judgment subsumes the importance of this body within its argument about military domination, the situation appears to require a more nuanced analysis. The judgment states that this new entity "for the first time enabled the leaders of the Army and Navy to take a direct part in the formulation of Cabinet policy, became itself a very important policy-making body ... During the year 1941 Liaison Conferences were held frequently and came more and more to usurp the functions of the Cabinet meeting."[82]

Several points deserve emphasis here. First, the navy suddenly appears as an important voice in policy formation, when heretofore the "Army" has been the primary and often sole agent. Differences of opinion between the army and navy have been obscured by general reference to "the Army" as representative

[76] MJ 225.
[77] MJ 248.
[78] MJ 250.
[79] MJ 284–5.
[80] MJ 284.
[81] MJ 289–90.
[82] MJ 289.

of the military establishment as a whole, or by references to "the military faction." Second, if the army has achieved such a position of dominance over the cabinet as the judgment describes, why was it this Liaison Conference that "for the first time" enabled army and navy leaders to take part in cabinet policy deliberations? This is especially questionable given the presence and tremendous influence of the army and navy ministers within the cabinet, who were nominated by their respective services. Third, how does the Liaison Conference and its increasing importance as a policy making body relate to the simplistic theory of a conspiracy that had already been firmly established many years before and had allegedly dominated Japanese war policies since 1931, and had been enshrined in the national policy decision formulated by the army in 1936, which the judgment says had been adhered to strictly by every cabinet since?[83]

Finally, although the title of the section indicates the ultimate achievement of military domination over the cabinet, the narrative reveals that the situation was not so simple after all. The judgment recounts that at the Liaison Conference of July 27, 1940, "the Army and Navy had signified their acceptance of the Cabinet's policy" to avoid "friction" with the United States and avoid causing a war with "a third power."[84] The judgment concludes that this position was in accordance with the national policy decision of 1936 in that it aimed at extending Japanese influence through diplomacy and a strong military "while attempting to avoid the needless aggravation of other nations." On the other hand, just a few pages after narrating these differences of opinion and the acceptance of the need to avoid war with the United States and Great Britain, the majority provides a summary of Chapter IV which concludes that by September 1940, "The conspirators now dominated Japan. They had fixed their policy and resolved to carry it out." That policy, they conclude, led directly to the attacks that launched the Pacific War.[85] How this confused and contradictory narrative reflects an unchanging conspiracy that aimed at aggressive war since 1928 is never explained or justified through a systematic evaluation of the available evidence.

It is striking that Chapter IV only refers explicitly to the conspiracy in the last two paragraphs. As seen earlier, the overarching theme of the chapter is, as announced on its first page, "the gradual rise of the military and their supporters to such a predominance in the government of Japan that no other organ of government, neither the elected representatives of the people, nor the civilian ministers in the cabinet, nor the civilian advisors of the emperor in the Privy

---

[83] Note the judgment's conclusion that the Konoe Cabinet of 1940 "placed renewed emphasis on the unchanging aims of the Army's planning which had been settled in the basic national policy decision of August 1, 1936" (MJ 293).
[84] MJ 294.
[85] MJ 304.

Council and in his entourage, latterly imposed any check on the ambitions of the military."[86] We have seen, however, that the majority's own description indicates serious dissension within and between all of these groups and organs of government over fundamental policies. Yet at the same time that complete dominance of the military had been achieved and the cabinet rendered impotent (recalling that it had been declared so on several previous occasions by the judgment), the judgment recounts that a new policymaking body emerges, the Liaison Conference, and plays a central role. Indeed, in the verdict against Suzuki Teiichi that body is referred to as the "virtual policy making body for Japan."[87] Rather than tacitly relying on the reductive closing arguments of the prosecution, the judges' own systematic accounts of the complex structures of authority in Japanese policymaking during the crucial years, and a clear specification of the roles of the key accused in those structures, would have been more productive in delineating individual responsibility for the ultimate decisions to wage war in Manchuria, China, the Soviet Union, Southeast Asia, and the Pacific.

What the judgment, preoccupied with maintaining the flow of a linear chronological historical narrative, never analytically confronts is the exact nature of the relationship between individual agents, institutions, and other consultative bodies on the one hand, and the conspiracy on the other. The substitute for specific references to the conspiracy throughout the main body of the narrative is, as we have seen, attribution of agency to vague collectivities like "the military," "the Army," "the military faction," "the Cabinet," and so on. While individual names appear, the majority seems to assume that the narrative speaks for itself and no analysis of evidence or even of the "recital of facts" is necessary to establish the connection of individuals to the particular event that is the subject of that part of the narrative.

Sometimes, to be sure, the narrative states that the individual in question proposed or supported a policy or made a specific statement. But just as often, as we have seen, there is simply a reference to an event that took place while the accused person served in the cabinet or the like. Moreover, when the judgment does refer to a specific act that could show support for a policy or action there is typically no weighing, or even reference, to the evidence that supports that conclusory assertion, the defense arguments, or a consideration of whether the inference drawn by the majority has been proved beyond a reasonable doubt. This, for example, is the case where the crucial inference is repeatedly drawn that when a politician advocates for the expansion of Japanese influence through the combination of "diplomatic skills" and building a strong "national

---

[86] MJ 110.
[87] MJ 621.

## 7.4 Chapters IV–VIII of Judgment

defense," what they actually mean is that they are advocating actual aggressive war to achieve Japanese military domination of Asia and the Pacific.

To be sure, they were advocates of expansion by force. But there were other voices who may have argued that Japan's goals of increasing political power could be achieved through other means, backed by the capacity to go to war if necessary. Such a policy was by no means criminal under international law and was the basic posture of all the great powers of the era: strong diplomacy backed by the capacity to defend national interests by military means. There is a crucial difference there, because the essence of the charge against all of the accused is, as the tribunal states in its definition of the crimes of conspiracy, "A conspiracy to wage war aggressive or unlawful war arises when two or more persons enter into an agreement to commit that crime. Thereafter, in furtherance of the conspiracy follows planning and preparing for such a war."[88] That is, the majority must show beyond a reasonable doubt that every one of the accused shared the same common purpose of waging aggressive war and participated in the planning or preparation.

Although the majority never states what the requisite mental element is for this offense, it is clear that the elements of "agreement" and "common purpose" require a showing of intent to wage aggressive war. Mere knowledge of the agreement of other persons does not establish that one shares their common purpose. Because the mental elements are not clearly specified, the judgment also does not distinguish between: (1) those individuals who knew of the conspiracy to wage aggressive war and participated in government, but did not share that purpose; (2) individuals who advocated military force and conquest as the preferred means for achieving Japanese pre-eminence in Asia; and (3) individuals who supported Japanese expansion, saw that it could lead to military confrontation, but advocated diplomacy and other nonviolent means, backed by the capacity to use force, as the means for achieving Japan's aims. Such differences are crucial for proving the charge of conspiracy to wage aggressive war, but the judgment typically both deviates from its definition of the crime and conflates the support of Japanese expansion with the intention to use aggressive war to achieve that expansion.

The majority judgment again and again draws the conclusion of intent to wage aggressive war, based upon the inference that various policy statements, expressed in different and nuanced ways, that refer to political and economic expansion and the buildup of national military capacity actually demonstrate that intent and hence the sharing of the criminal common purpose.[89] The

---

[88] MJ 84.
[89] See, for instance, the conclusion that "HIROTA had been true to the basic aim of 'securing a steady footing in the Eastern continent as well as developing the South Seas, under the joint efforts of diplomatic skill and national defense'" (MJ 179).

principle vehicle that drives the conflation of conspiracy to wage aggressive war with other means of achieving political aims is the acceptance without demonstration that the national policy decision of 1936 embodied the conspiracy and that all who indicated support for that policy statement were ipso facto advocating aggressive war. What the majority never does is to demonstrate, based upon weighing the evidence before it, the proof beyond a reasonable doubt of the legitimacy of those inferences and conclusions in regard to each individual accused in each of the myriad instances in the 487-page narrative where that inference is implicitly made. This, however, is what is required to provide a reasoned account of the participation in the conspiracy during the period under indictment. In the final section of this chapter we now consider whether the findings and verdicts provide such a reasoned justification.

## 7.5 Chapter IX: Findings

Chapter IX of the judgment is entitled "Findings on the Counts of the Indictment." Only Count 1, the charge of the master conspiracy, receives more than the most cursory treatment. One would expect the findings to fulfill a crucial role in the judgment. After such an extensive and convoluted historical narrative that does not focus systematically on any of the accused but rather on the development of events, the judgment should pull together all of the specific "recitals of facts" pertinent to each of the accused. This it never does, neither in the findings nor in the section on individual verdicts.

The findings section devotes just three pages to Count 1 of the indictment. All the other counts, 5–55, are treated in less than one page. What is particularly striking in regard to the three pages devoted to findings on Count 1, is that *not one* of the accused is even named in this section. Of those indicted, only Ōkawa Shūmei, a relatively minor figure is mentioned, and he was found incompetent to stand trial. Against whom, then, are the findings directed? The answer is actually quite simple: the "conspirators" and the "conspiracy."

What the findings conclude in this brief summary is that a conspiracy existed to wage aggressive war in order to achieve the domination of Asia and the Pacific. This conspiracy came into being when in the 1920s Ōkawa advocated that, "Japan should extend her territory on the continent of Asia by threat or, if necessary, by use of military force."[90] Ōkawa alone could of course not constitute a conspiracy, because as the judgment has established the agreement and common purpose of two or more persons is required. As to when the conspiracy actually came into being the judgment is vague and devotes only one sentence to this important fact. The judges assert that in the period from 1927 to 1929, "a party of military men, with Okawa and other civilian supporters"

[90] MJ 594.

advocated "that Japan should expand by the use of force. The conspiracy was now in being. It remained in being until Japan's defeat in 1945."[91]

There are several points that deserve mention here. First, it is striking that the judgment is vague as to the temporal dimension of the initiation of the conspiracy (1927–9) and as to the initial conspirators. They only say that some unnamed "military men" and "civilian supporters" shared Ōkawa's policy. Were none of the accused involved at this stage? Why are none of the accused mentioned here?

Second, we note that within one paragraph the judgment's description of what was the aim of the conspiracy has shifted in an important manner. In the first sentence, quoted immediately above the judgment, it is said that the conspirators conspired to extend Japanese domination in Asia "by threat or, if necessary, by use of military force." In the second formulation the use of threat has disappeared, along with the crucial qualifier "if necessary." This slippage between different formulations of the conspiracy occurs throughout the majority judgment and is of crucial significance. We may recall that the Nuremberg judgment concluded that there was no master conspiracy but rather many difference conspiracies or initiatives at different times and with different compositions. What the majority judgment's historical narrative has made clear, without intending to do so, is that this is also the case at the IMTFE.

There may well have been some military leaders in Japan who always advocated the use of force and conquest. It is clear from the judgment that there were, for example, members of the Army General Staff and the navy who did not share this view, though they were not opposed to Japanese expansion. There were both political and military leaders who advocated an aggressive policy of expansion that was backed by the implicit threat of force that a strong military establishment implies. There were also important figures like Shigemitsu, who played no significant role until the Pacific War was well underway, advocated against the use of military force, but then, found themselves in a government that was hopelessly embroiled in a losing war that as individuals they had no power to stop.

All of these views, and others, are encompassed within the group of accused, all of whom are identified by the indictment and the judgment as agreeing to a single common purpose that was crystallized in 1928 and did not change until 1945 when the war ended. The judges at Nuremberg had the good sense to recognize that the reductive quality of such a generalization was inadequate to comprehend the complexity of events and political rivalries, conflicts and dynamics leading to war. Although the judges at Tokyo confronted an even more complex situation because of the lack of a single "inner policy circle" dominated by one person (Hitler), the majority embraced the conspiracy theory

---

[91] Ibid.

advanced by the prosecution most likely as the simplest way of connecting all of the accused to the charges against them without having to provide a detailed analysis of all of the evidence bearing upon the actual conduct of each accused in regard to each of the charges.

The judgment notes that from the very beginning of the conspiracy there was strong disagreement in policy circles between those who advocated the use of force and those who urged expansion by peaceful means. The way in which the findings describe this conflict is both reductive and illustrative of the crucial slippage noted earlier. The judgment concludes that under the Tanaka Cabinet in the late 1920s, there began the "long struggle between conspirators, who advocated the attainment of their object by force, and those politicians ... who advocated Japan's expansion by peaceful measures *or at least by a more discreet choice of the occasions on which force should be employed*"[92] (emphasis added). Here the conspirators are narrowly defined as those who agree that Japan should use military force to expand. Those falling outside of the conspiracy are those who advocate that Japan should expand by peaceful measures and by a more "discreet" use of force.

On this view of the conspiracy, that the judgment avers existed unchanged from this point to 1945, how could the national policy decision of 1936 discussed earlier be a manifestation of the conspiracy? That policy, which the judgment repeatedly refers to as the guiding principle of Japanese policy from 1936 to 1941, advocated, according to the majority, for expansion by peaceful means backed by a strong national defense. This is an even weaker formulation than that stated by the judges as falling outside the conspiracy because it advocated "a more discreet" use of aggressive force. Yet the historical narrative repeatedly used the national policy decision of 1936 as evidence that every individual who advocated for, or even agreed with it, shared the aim of waging aggressive war to achieve Japan's domination over Asia and the Pacific.

The findings are also puzzling when, in the next paragraph, the judgment concludes that when they had "finally overcome all opposition the conspirators carried out in succession the attacks necessary to effect their ultimate object that Japan should dominate the Far East."[93] The examples they give are the attack on Manchuria in 1931, and aggression against China from 1934 to 1937. These attacks, on the judgment's own account, can hardly be the product of having overcome all internal opposition by the conspirators by 1937, let alone 1931. There is thus repeated ambiguity and slippage in the historical narrative as to when this occurs. In fact, the judgment repeatedly recounts that the military faction (never using the term "conspirators") was repeatedly on the verge of achieving, or had achieved, complete domination of the cabinet and

---

[92] MJ 595.
[93] Ibid.

## 7.5 Chapter IX: Findings

government when the ensuing part of the narrative shows that they had indeed not done so. The final conclusion in the narrative, as discussed earlier, was that such complete domination of policymaking was achieved only in Fall 1941, yet here the findings conclude that already in 1931 that process was complete. The preceding narrative itself has shown that this was by no means the case.

Astonishingly, the Findings section concludes without making a single finding against any one of the accused. The only findings are about the conspiracy, as indicated earlier. The findings on Count 1 of the indictment thus conclude by stating that, "These far reaching plans war waging wars of aggression ... were not the work of one man. They were the work of *many leaders* acting in pursuit of a common plan for the achievement of a common object. That common object that they should secure Japan's domination by preparing and waging wars of aggression, was a criminal object"[94] (emphasis added). We may note here that the formulation of the common purpose has again been defined as an agreement among unnamed persons that wars of aggression should be the means for Japan's expansion. We will see in the next section if the individual verdicts apply this definition.

Thus the findings conclude by stating that a conspiracy to wage aggressive war existed among a group of unnamed persons. The majority justify making findings only on the conspiracy as an abstraction rather than on the conduct of each of the accused by referring to the ensuing section on individual verdicts: "The question whether the defendants or any of them participated in that conspiracy will be considered when we deal with the individual cases."[95] As noted earlier, however, the treatment of these issues of individual responsibility is as cursory in the verdicts as it is in the findings.

The majority thus relieve themselves of systematically analyzing specific cases through the dual means of making findings only on "the conspiracy" as a collective abstraction and by deferring consideration of individual cases to a section of the judgment that also does not consider them in a systematic and reasoned manner. As we will see in the next chapter, Webb's draft judgment stands in stark contrast to that of the majority in both rejecting the overarching conspiracy charge of Count 1 and by its overwhelming attention to the evidence against each of the accused.[96]

---

[94] MJ 596.
[95] Ibid.
[96] In the concluding paragraph on Count 1 the judgment states that all of the accused who "were parties to the conspiracy or who at any time with guilty knowledge played a part in its execution" are guilty of the charge contained in Count 1. The judgment has never indicated what mental element, or mens rea, is necessary for conviction on the conspiracy charge, though it is presumably intent. The reference in the sentence quoted here to accused who knowingly "played a part" in the execution of the conspiracy, presumably refers to the accomplice liability included in Count 1. Here the judgment says nothing about what is necessary to prove that someone was an accomplice to the conspirators, beyond that they had "guilty knowledge." The

### 7.6 The Verdicts

As discussed earlier, the judgment introduces the verdicts by stating that they will not give "particular reasons" for the verdicts but rather "general reasons." This is justified by referring to the "many particular findings in which the verdicts are based." As has just been seen, however, the Findings section refers only to the conspirators and never to individual accused.[97] While the judgment maintains that the "recital of facts and the statement of findings" have already "examined minutely" each of the accused, we have seen that this is not the case.

In the historical narrative that makes up the so-called "recital of facts" the individual accused are not treated systematically but emerge as part of the narrative. The term "recital of facts" is also telling, for it is true that that the narrative reads like a recital of facts already established rather than an analysis to *justify* factual findings. In other words, the "recital of facts" is, as the term implies, conclusory rather than analytical and systematic in regard to the evidence on the specific conduct of each accused relevant to the charges against them. What we find in the verdicts, then, are the "general reasons" rather than an analysis of the evidence based on the definition of the offenses with which they are charged. While the Nuremberg judgment does not engage in very lengthy analysis in the verdicts, they do cite and discuss specific evidence that is directly relevant to the charges against each individual and base their conclusions on that evidence. It is particularly striking that the majority judgment not only does not cite specific evidence but does not even provide references to the portions of the judgment that in their view "minutely" examine the conduct of the accused. A few examples will suffice to demonstrate the consequences of this approach and the lack of systematic application of a common standard of liability to all of the accused charged under Count 1.

#### 7.6.1 *Dohihara*

Dohihara Kenji, who was colonel in 1931 and had advanced to general by 1941, is convicted of conspiracy under Count 1 because, "as the aggressive policy of the Japanese military party was pursued in other areas in China DOHIHARA took a prominent part in its development by political intrigue, by threat of force and by the use of force ... DOHIHARA acted in close association with other leaders of the military faction in the development, preparation, and execution

---

judgment defines neither exactly what they have to have knowledge of, nor the required nature of their contribution to the execution of the conspiracy or by what mental element that participation must be accompanied.

[97] MJ 598.

7.6  The Verdicts

of their plans to bring East and South East Asia under Japanese domination."[98] We must first note that Dohihara is described here as associating himself with the "military faction" and "military party." Does this refer to the conspirators as a whole or to the faction within the military that is often vaguely referenced in the historical narrative? If the "military faction" is not coterminous with "the conspirators" then why does this show Dohihara's common purpose with the conspiracy as opposed to this undefined "military faction"? Why is the conspiracy nowhere referred to in the discussion of Dohihara? The judgment is silent on all of these issues. Also, what is relevance of the reference to political intrigue and threat of force when the judgment has just defined the conspiracy as the agreement to wage aggressive war to achieve Japanese domination?[99] The general summary of conclusions with which the majority contents itself leaves open more questions than it answers.

### 7.6.2  Hashimoto

In regard to Hashimoto Kingorō, whom the judgment describes as primarily a propagandist, he is specifically convicted as "*a principal* to the formation of the conspiracy and contributed largely to its execution" (emphasis added). The judgment made no such specification as to Dohihara. The judgment finds that Hashimoto detested democracy and admired military dictatorship. He "was a principal" in the conspirators' efforts to suppress democracy in Japan and control the government. The relation of these political views to the charges arises from the finding this control was necessary to realize the goal of aggression. Here it appears that Hashimoto's adherence to a political faction that opposed democratic institutions is a key element in his conviction, but the judgment never explains how this meets their definition of conspiracy to wage aggressive war. They conclude that his publications aimed at the destruction of democracy and the creation of "a form of government more favorable to the use of war for achieving expansion of Japan."[100] Such an aim does not demonstrate membership in a conspiracy that aims to actually wage aggressive war against specific countries.

The only concrete action referred to, if vaguely, is that "He played some part in planning the occurrence of the Mukden Incident."[101] There is no

---

[98] MJ 599.
[99] Justice Mei refers to what he calls "the criminal psychology" of Dohihara in a memorandum (undated) to Justice Bernard. In this memorandum he also gives his view of what kind of weighing of the evidence the judgment should provide: "We are justified to make our own conclusions after a review of all the evidence, but we are not obliged to detail all the evidence that supports our conclusions." (NAA M1417/1 28 pp. 5–6).
[100] MJ 600.
[101] Ibid.

explanation of his specific role ("some part") and how that role proves beyond a reasonable doubt an inference that he was doing so as part of the conspiracy to wage aggressive war to achieve Japanese domination of Asia and the Pacific. The treatment of Count 1 concludes by saying that through his denunciation of treaties and his passionate support for increased armament he aimed to secure domination through "force or the threat of force."[102] We note here the slippage between increasing military capacity and the implicit threat of force by that increase and the advocacy of aggressive force itself to advance Japan's ambitions. The ambiguity is left unresolved as the next sentence states that he is convicted as a principal in the conspiracy.

### 7.6.3   Hata

In regard to Hata Shunroku, who served as army minister for eleven months in 1939–40, the judgment concludes that he "contributed substantially" to planning and executing aggressive war. The examples they give, however, do not indicate the nature of his connection. The judgment states that during his term in office, "the war in China was waged with renewed vigor; the wang ching wei [wang jingwei] government was established at Nanking; the plans for control of French Indo-China were developed."[103] All of these formulations are in the passive voice and simply state that these events occurred in a specific time period. The inference is that Hata was responsible for these developments but the judgment gives no indication of his relevant conduct or the evidence to support their conclusion. Given the dissension noted in the historical narrative about this period and the numerous players, both institutional and individual, who were involved in resolving the major conflicts over policy at this time, a specification of Hata's role, at least through citation of the relevant pages of the historical narrative would seem to be essential to provide a reasoned account of the grounds of the conviction.

The conclusion as to his overall participation in the conspiracy is even vaguer. In regard to the conspiratorial common purpose the judgment only states that he "favored domination of East Asia and the areas to the South."[104] This does not meet the definition of conspiracy they have established as they do not say that he advocated for or contributed to the common purpose of achieving domination through aggressive war. The conduct they cite as illustrating this conclusion is also not directly relevant because they only state that he "approved the abolition of political parties" and helped make the way for creation of a totalitarian state in Japan. Again the inferences from these statements

---

[102] MJ 601.
[103] Ibid.
[104] Ibid.

## 7.6 The Verdicts

to the requirement of proof under the definition of conspiracy is unstated. The ultimate verdict merely states that he is guilty under Count 1 and, unlike for Hashimoto, does not specify if he is found to be a principal or accomplice. This omission is important because the judgment finds primarily that he "contributed" to certain events or policies. Whether he did so with the intent to wage aggressive war as part of the common purpose, or whether he merely knew of the criminality of the common purpose and knowingly or intentionally contributed to it, should determine whether he is found to be a conspirator or an accomplice. The judgment, however, entirely refrains from such legal specifications in its verdict.

### 7.6.4 Hiranuma

Another illustration of the lack of attention to important legal issues is found in the treatment of Hiranuma Kiichirō, who held many important posts throughout the period under indictment. While, as Webb will show, there is in fact a great deal of evidence linking Hiranuma directly to aggression against China and other nations, the judgment only devotes sixteen lines to summarizing his role and convicting him. Two points merit attention here. First, one of the few specific instances referred to relates that Hiranuma, as one of the *jūshin* (senior statesmen; ex-premiers), was present at the November 29, 1941 meeting to advise the Emperor on war and peace. The inculpatory fact cited by the judgment is that Hiranuma "*accepted* the opinion that war was inevitable and advised the strengthening of public opinion against the possibility of a long war"[105] (emphasis added). It is difficult to see how accepting as "inevitable" an opinion advanced by others, just a few days before Pearl Harbor, proves either membership in a conspiracy to start the Pacific War or the required intent to wage aggressive war that defines the conspiracy.

The second point to be made here concerns the slippage in the definition of the parameters of the conspiracy. It will be recalled that in its findings the judgment distinguished between the conspirators on the one hand and those who advocated expansion by peaceful means but by resorting to force "discretely" as necessary. In the conclusion as to Hiranuma, however, the verdict seems to put him in that latter camp but nonetheless qualifies this as conspiracy, stating that throughout the period under consideration Hiranuma supported the policy of "domination by Japan in East Asia and the South Seas by force when necessary."[106] The verdict against Hirota reaches a similar conclusion, though again with a different nuance, finding that Hirota was in favor of a peaceful means of expansion, though "he consistently agreed to the use of force if diplomatic

---

[105] MJ 602.
[106] Ibid.

negotiations failed to obtain fulfillment of the Japanese demands."[107] Although the judgment reaches this conclusion it in fact neglects to state whether the majority found Hirota guilty under Count 1, with which he had been charged.

### 7.6.5   Kaya

The abbreviated consideration accorded the verdicts is perhaps nowhere more apparent than in the treatment of Kaya Okinori, who held primarily administrative and financial positions, culminating in serving as finance minister from 1941 to 1944. Apart from an eight-line recitation of the offices he held, the entirety of the treatment of Kaya consists of the following:

> In these positions he took part in the formulation of the aggressive policies of Japan and in the financial, economic and industrial preparations for the execution of those policies. Throughout this period, particularly as Finance Minister in the first Konoye and TOJO Cabinets as a President of the North China Development Company, he was actively engaged in the preparation and carrying out of aggressive wars in China and against the Western Powers. He was an active member of the conspiracy alleged in Count 1 and is adjudged guilty under that Count.

Again, what the judgment nowhere discusses is whether in taking part in financial and economic activities Kaya did so with the requisite intent to wage aggressive war, which alone would establish that he was a co-conspirator by virtue of sharing the common purpose. In his case they also make no specification as to whether he is adjudged to be a principle or accomplice.

### 7.6.6   Kimura

Defendant Kimura Heitarō never reached the cabinet level, rising from administrative positions in the Ministry of the Army until becoming vice minister in 1941, a post from which he was relieved in 1943. He is convicted as an accomplice in the conspiracy on the basis that because of his close contact with the army minister and others he "had full knowledge of the plans and preparations for the Pacific War and the hostilities in China."[108] The judgment further explains its verdict by stating that, "though not a leader, he took part in the formulation and development of policies which were either initiated by himself or proposed by the General Staff or other bodies and approved and supported by him."[109] Curiously, however, in the next paragraph they refer to

---

[107] MJ 603.
[108] MJ 609.
[109] Ibid.

Kimura not as an accomplice, but "as one of the conspirators."[110] The ultimate verdict does not resolve this ambiguity, simply stating that Kimura is "guilty under Count 1."[111]

### 7.6.7 Satō

The majority's lack of precision in following the legal standard it had established in regard to being a conspirator as opposed to an accomplice to the conspiracy is further evidenced by the treatment of Satō Kenryō. Like Kimura, Satō gradually rose in the military hierarchy in the 1930s, but never attained the rank of vice minister. In 1941 he became chief of the Military Affairs Section of the Military Affairs Bureau. At this point, according to the judgment, he was able "to influence policy," though no events or evidences are referenced to support that conclusion or to indicate which policies he actually influenced. The judgment, moreover, does not continue to find that he did in fact influence policy. Instead, it states that, "The crucial question is whether by that date he had become aware that Japan's designs were criminal and thereafter he furthered the development and execution of these designs."[112] This is a correct statement of the requirements of proof for accomplice liability under the majority's definition (apart from the fact that it fails to state the required mental element for his furtherance of the designs). That is not, surprisingly, the basis on which he is convicted. Instead, the verdict on Satō concludes that, Satō, having "*guilty knowledge*, was clearly a member of the conspiracy from 1941 onward"[113] (emphasis added). This, of course, contradicts the standard they have established which requires an agreement reflected in a common purpose to conspire to wage aggressive war, and the mental element required would be intention rather than awareness of knowledge. Their finding that he had "guilty knowledge" of the conspiracy and contributed to its fulfillment can only ground a conviction for complicity in the conspiracy, not as a principal.[114]

### 7.6.8 Shimada

Before October 1941 accused Shimada was a naval officer "who had no part in the conspiracy." He became navy minister in the Tōjō Cabinet and in only

---

[110] MJ 610.
[111] Ibid.
[112] MJ 616.
[113] MJ 617. The only basis cited for this conclusion is a speech Satō made in 1938 on Japan's policy toward China. The majority concludes that this speech establishes his awareness "beyond reasonable doubt" but it is not clear that their paraphrases from this speech do not admit of other plausible inferences. For evidence relating to Satō's speech, see PX270, T3612–39.
[114] Article 5(c) of the IMTFE Charter provides for the liability both of those who play a principal role in an alleged conspiracy as "Leaders, organizers, instigators" as well as for those who assist them as "accomplices."

ten lines the judgment finds that he at this time became a conspirator. The judgment devotes only one sentence to establishing his participation in the conspiracy: "From the formation of the TOJO Cabinet ... until 7th December 1941 he took part in all decisions made by the conspirators in planning and launching that attack."[115] Whether he took part because his office merely required him to attend those meetings and whether he did or said things at the meetings that indicate he shared the common purpose of the conspiracy is not addressed. What appears here is that his mere membership in the cabinet in a position that necessarily included him in policy meetings at the crucial time is enough to justify his conviction. Unlike the case of Satō, where a speech he made three year earlier is cited as indicating his common aim with the conspiracy, the judgment explicitly states that Shimada had previously "played nothing but the part of a naval officer carrying out his duties."[116] The judgment's justification for proof beyond a reasonable doubt of intentional participation in the common purpose of the conspiracy seems flimsy indeed.[117]

### 7.6.9 Shigemitsu

In contrast, the majority acquit Shigemitsu Mamoru on Count 1 because by the time he became foreign minister in 1943 "the policy of the conspirators to wage certain wars of aggression had been settled and was in the course of execution. Thereafter there was no further formulation of that policy."[118] The majority's historical narrative had in fact concluded that, as was seen above, the conspiracy to wage war had already been settled in Fall 1941. This same argument should, then, apply to Satō. In his case, however, the conviction on Count 1 turned on his guilty knowledge of the aims of conspirators and actions to further the conspiracy.

Why was the same standard not applied to Shigemitsu? Under the majority's logic applied to Satō this would seem to require a similar conviction of Shigemitsu under Count 1 because the judgment has concluded that, like Satō, Shigemitsu (1) was aware of the conspiracy and (2) waged aggressive war against the United States, Britain, and other nations, thus supporting the conspiracy. Further, the grounds for excusing him on Count 1 seem quite flimsy because although the aggression was underway in 1943, the judgment's findings concluded that "The conspiracy existed ... for many years. Not all the conspirators were parties to it at the beginning ... All of those who at any time were parties to the conspiracy or who at any time played a part in its execution are guilty

---

[115] MJ 619.
[116] Ibid.
[117] The treatment of Oka, formerly director of the Naval Affairs Bureau of the Ministry of the Navy from 1940 to 1944, is also abbreviated to say the least.
[118] MJ 617.

## 7.6 The Verdicts

of the charge contained in Count 1."[119] It is very difficult to see under this definition how, having convicted Shigemitsu under Counts 27, 29, and 31–33 of having "played a principal part in waging" aggressive war, the majority could find him not guilty under Count 1 as well.

### 7.6.10 Tōgō

The justification for the acquittal of Shigemitsu on Count 1 also seems inconsistent with the legal standard applied to another Japanese diplomat, Tōgō Shigenori. The basis of the charges against Tōgō centers only on his activities as foreign minister for the eleven months he served in that position. He took up his position in October 1941, by which time, as discussed above, the historical narrative concluded that the aggressive policy had been largely settled and the military was in total control of the government. The very abbreviated verdict against Tōgō finds that he "attended Cabinet meetings and conferences and concurred in all decisions adopted."[120] Apart from the fact that the majority have previously repeatedly found that the "military faction" totally controlled the cabinet at this point, passive concurrence in collective decisions would not necessarily indicate agreement with the criminal common purpose. The judgment sets out no evidence about what he said or did at these meetings to indicate that he shared the criminal purpose. Likewise, in what appears to be the crucial point, the judgment finds that he played a prominent role in the "duplicitous" negotiations with the US leading up to the war. (Of course there was less than a two-month interval between his assumption of office and the Pearl Harbor attack.) The judgment again does not indicate how his criminal intent can be inferred from his conduct in the negotiations.

The judgment also indicates that Tōgō's defense argued that he had received assurances that there was a genuine effort to bring the negotiations with the US to a "successful conclusion."[121] If there was a plausible inference from the evidence that Tōgō did participate in negotiations in such a belief, this would completely negate the majority's crucial finding that he intentionally engaged in negotiations which were duplicitous so as to bring about an aggressive war. The only reason they advance for rejecting this defense is that when the negotiations failed he stayed in the cabinet for ten more months. The fact that he did so does not support beyond reasonable doubt an inference that he shared with the conspirators the required intent to wage aggressive war, for he could have stayed in the cabinet for many other reasons. The burden is on the prosecution, and the required elements of conspiracy must be established beyond

[119] MJ 597.
[120] MJ 622.
[121] Ibid.

reasonable doubt. The reasoning of the judgment does not appear to meet this standard in finding Tōgō guilty of conspiracy under Count 1. The comparison with the acquittal of Shigemitsu on this count also appears inconsistent with this verdict. The judgment does not consider whether Tōgō might have been found guilty as an accomplice of the conspiracy based on his knowledge of the conspirators' aims and his actions as foreign minister that contributed to implementing them.[122] As will be seen in the next chapter, however, Webb's consideration of the evidence against Tōgō casts such questions not addressed by the majority in a very different light.

---

[122] MJ 619.

# 8 An Alternative Perspective on Accountability for Crimes against Peace: The Two Webb Judgments

## 8.1 Introduction

The concurring opinion of Sir William Webb, the President of the IMTFE, was promulgated with the judgment of the majority and is widely referred to by scholars. Less well known is a document that Webb entitled "The President's Judgment" but never published.[1] Webb completed and revised a draft of this judgment he had hoped would be adopted as the majority judgment of the tribunal.[2] The judgment was circulated as the "First Draft Judgment" and then as the "Second Draft Judgment."[3] When the majority refused to accept it Webb in the end decided to use the vastly shorter text that he provided to the IMTFE as his concurring opinion, discussed later in Chapter 14.[4]

"The President's Judgment" is a complex and comprehensive document, comprising some 658 pages in typescript. It is nothing less than a complete alternative account of the trial and the grounds of liability for the twenty-five defendants, which Webb had proposed as the majority judgment. While Webb

---

[1] To avoid confusion, the unpublished manuscript will be referred to by the title Webb gave it: "The President's Judgment," abbreviated in the notes as the TPJ. The published opinion of Webb will be referred to as Webb's Concurring Opinion.
[2] In a letter to MacArthur of August 13, 1947, which was apparently never sent, Webb referred to his activity in drafting as follows: "I am quite sure you intend that I should have all the help I need to write the Court's judgment, or, in any case, the leading judgment. This will be one of the most important and the longest in history. The law alone will be dealt with at considerable length." (NAA M1418/1 6). In a memorandum to all the judges on December 20, 1946 Webb invited their comments "on the first draft which I framed to meet what I thought might be the opinion of the majority." (NAA M1417 24 p. 1).
[3] See, for instance, Webb's memorandum of December 27, 1946 entitled "Second Draft Judgment" which sets out the general strategy for the second draft. (NAA M1417/25.)
[4] On 17 May 1948 Webb noted how long it was taking the majority to draft a judgment and suggested they use his own (AWM 3DRL 2481). Justice Northcroft of New Zealand had expressed his refusal to accept a judgment drafted by Webb as that of the tribunal and indicated similar sentiments on the part of Justice Mei of China (NAA M1417 24 p. 1). As of July 9, 1948 Webb was in the process of completing his own judgment, which at that point he still intended to be published (AWM 3DRL 2481/4). Later that month he appears to have been reconsidering, as a memorandum of 24 July from the Australian Mission reports that Webb was considering whether to concur in the majority judgment and "to scrap his own." (NAA A1838 1550/6 part 2 p. 2). This is, of course, what he in the end decided to do.

agreed with the majority that all of the defendants should be found guilty, he disagreed with them on almost everything else, particularly on the law, and the legal and factual basis for the guilty verdicts. Webb's "President's Judgment" commands our attention because it provides what the majority judgment sorely lacks: a coherent, well argued, reasoned account of the basis for its findings and conclusions, particularly in regard to the individual accused. In February of 1947 Webb prepared an outline, entitled "Form of Judgment," for his intended majority judgment. He included under the heading "Evidence" the following: "Full statement of evidence in relation to different phases and showing *in detail* the association of any accused" (emphasis added). In the next section, "Verdicts," Webb provides a: "Full statement of evidence against and for each accused, followed by finding of fact, application of relevant law, and finally the verdict in his case."[5] This is precisely what is lacking in the majority judgment. If Webb's "President's Judgment" had been adopted as the majority judgment of the tribunal, much of the criticism leveled at the court might have been deflected.

Webb, of course, was eminently qualified to produce such a reasoned opinion. As President of the IMTFE he took a leading role in the proceedings and was present at the trial sessions far more than some of his colleagues, especially the notoriously absent Justice Pal.[6] He was also a distinguished and experienced judge in Australia, having served as the chief justice of the Supreme Court of Queensland. Finally, he possessed far greater knowledge of the subject matter of the proceedings than any of the other judges by virtue of his having presided over three commissions appointed during the war by the Australian government to investigate and report on Japanese war crimes.[7] His judgment, unlike that of the majority or the dissenting opinion of Justice Pal, bases its ultimate conclusions as to liability upon systematic factual findings drawn from careful review of the trial transcript and the exhibits tendered as evidence. Also unlike these two accounts, it articulates the legal standards that

---

[5] NAA M1417/25 21, February 21, 1947, p. 2.

[6] Justice Webb presided over the court proceedings daily without fail, except in the period between November 10 and December 12, 1947, during which he was called back to Australia to fulfill his other duty as chief justice of the Supreme Court of Queensland. The number of days that other judges absented themselves from the proceedings varied, falling in the range of 10–40 court days or so. Justice Pal alone repeatedly took prolonged absences (October 28–December 2, 1946; September 3–26, 1947; and October 6–November 26, 1947). The total days of Pal's absence are 91 out of 466 court days, plus 9 additional days when he did not attend part of the day's proceedings (a total of 21 percent). For more information about Pal's absences, see Nakazato, *Neonationalist Mythology in Postwar Japan*, 15–16, 18–20.

[7] For an account of the three Australian war commissions that investigated Japanese war crimes and Webb's role, See Sissons, "Australian War Crimes Trials and Investigations." For guide to archival information on Webb Papers, visit the guide to the papers of Sir William Webb at the website of the Australian War Memorial. www.awm.gov.au/findingaids/private/webb/. Last accessed July 11, 2018.

## 8.1 Introduction

it will apply and, with few apparent exceptions, does carefully apply them to the factual findings for each individual defendant.

Whereas the bulk of the majority judgment is taken up by a narrative of the conspiracy to wage aggressive war that tends to obscure the role of individual actors in favor of generalizing about the conspiracy, Webb focuses on the role of each individual in the complex chain of events that led to Japanese attacks against China and subsequently against other countries. Webb also, unlike the majority, considers both the prosecution and defense contentions. The difference between Webb's approach and that of the majority, in regard to both crimes against peace and war crimes, is that Webb considered it essential to weigh the evidence in this way. He in fact suggested to the judges that they draft their judgment in this manner, "but as a majority of the members preferred to find facts without reference to the Defence summations, I made my first draft in accordance with their wishes." It is astonishing that the majority took the view that they did not need to refer to the defense case in their judgment as Webb notes that even in the first draft he decided to incorporate "the main Defence submissions." Significantly, he underscores that it is the duty of the judges to do so: "We must do that to be fair."[8] The final version of Webb's draft judgment reflects this principle. As Webb noted in a memorandum to all judges concerning his second draft judgment, the judgment of the tribunal must sum up the arguments by both defense and prosecution. Their task as judges, he asserts, is not *"to write any phase of history"* (emphasis added) but to ascertain the guilt of the accused based upon the evidence and by a statement of factual findings as to each of them.[9]

In the majority judgment the individual verdicts comprise some 66 pages out of a total of 1,211 in the original typescript promulgated by the court, or approximately 5 percent of the total. In The President's Judgment, on the other hand, the individual verdicts comprise 395 pages out of a total of 658. This means that some 60 percent of The President's Judgment is devoted to "Part VI Individual Verdicts" providing specific factual findings against each of the individual accused persons. When one reads the verdicts of the majority it is easy to conclude that they often do not provide a substantial evidentiary basis for the conclusion of guilt. Indeed, the preceding chapter has pointed out how the verdicts often do not refer even to the evidence adduced against that particular accused in the narrative part of the judgment. It is thus perhaps understandable that critics of the judgment, unfamiliar with the contents of the 48,412 pages of transcript, the 4,335 supporting exhibits, and 779 depositions and affidavits, have concluded that the verdicts are based upon "victor's justice" rather than

---

[8] Memorandum of Webb to all judges May 17, 1948, AWM 3DRL 2481.
[9] NAA M1417/1 32.

the conduct of the individual accused.[10] The majority judgment's neglect of systematic factual findings against each defendant is a glaring shortcoming that The President's Judgment addresses. It, rather than the majority judgment, thus provides a better basis for assessing whether the verdicts against individuals are in fact supported by the evidence or dictated by prejudice or politics. It also provides a far better focus for assessing whether the legal framework applied to these factual findings coherently supports the conclusions of individual culpability.

It will be the task of this chapter to provide such an assessment of the legal and factual analysis through which Webb arrived at his conclusion that all of the twenty-five defendants should be found guilty. Webb clearly had the Nuremberg judgment in mind as he drafted his own opinion and he was concerned about the appearance of the lack of acquittals at Tokyo in contrast to the acquittals of Schacht, von Pappen, and Fritzsche at Nuremberg. In the beginning of Part VI of The President's Judgment, "Individual Cases," he states, "Acquittals like that of Schacht and others at Nuremberg are not possible here. Hitler's foreign policy appeared vacillating, and judging from the Nuremberg findings, his purpose of aggressive war was known to only a few of the German accused until Poland was invaded in 1939."[11] Webb's concern, and the fact that he was not simply blindly following Nuremberg, appears as well from a memorandum where he states that, "The chapter on individual responsibility should be dealt with more fully than it was at Nuremberg."[12] Webb's proposal to the majority to deal fully with principles of individual responsibility unfortunately fell on deaf ears.

Whatever the merits of Webb's account of Nuremberg, the starting point for his analysis of the liability of individuals is the conclusion arrived at from his general factual findings in Part IV, "Japan's Recourse to War" and from his findings against each of the accused. As he put it, "I find it impossible to believe that in the offices these accused held they could fail to know all that this tribunal has ascertained about the attitude of Japan. There is no immunity for anyone, soldier or civilian, who takes part in what he knows, or should know, to be an illegal and criminal war."[13]

While Webb used the lack of clarity about Hitler's evolving intentions as a way of distinguishing the German context from that of Japan, The President's

---

[10] These are the numbers given in the majority judgment, p. 76.
[11] TPJ 268.
[12] NAA M1417/ 25.
[13] TPJ 267. In revising the judgment Webb added a qualifying note to the "There is no immunity" phrase: "There is no principle of law or justice which gives immunity." The following handwritten insertion appears immediately following the sentence quoted here: "It may be expedient not to make mere combatants responsible; but immunity cannot be granted by this Tribunal which has no power to alter the law but can only ascertain and apply it."

Judgment makes clear that the Japanese political and military leadership was wracked by sharp divisions of opinion and by competing policies in regard to war in China and beyond in 1931–45. How does Webb, then, account for holding all the accused liable in this context of apparent uncertainty about whether and when to go to war? This will be one important criterion for testing the consistency of Webb's approach, analyzing whether the individual verdicts bear out the general position he takes justifying the lack of acquittals.

What seems to be the underlying rationale is that at certain points in time every one of the accused became aware that Japan was either deciding to engage in war that could not plausibly be justified on legal grounds or was actually engaged in such a war, and that possessing this knowledge they nonetheless supported and participated in planning or implementation of this undertaking. Whether Webb's factual findings are based on sufficient evidence to support such conclusions in the case of individual defendants will be a focal point in the ensuing inquiry. Another key analytical question will be how the conclusions on guilt in regard to aggressive war compare with the findings and conclusions on conventional war crimes. Before addressing these questions, however, it is important to consider the preliminary and more basic issue of the legal basis for the verdicts. How did Webb, in The President's Judgment, define the body of law to be applied in reaching his verdicts? How does his account of the law of the tribunal compare with the majority judgment?

## 8.2 The Law of the Tribunal

### 8.2.1. The Charter and its Authority

Section II of The President's Judgment, "The Charter and the Law," takes, as it must, for its starting point the Charter of the IMTFE. Webb characterizes the Charter as binding not just because it is, in fact, the tribunal's Charter and thus the basis of its legal authority, but because, "it is International Law, the Natural Law, the Potsdam Declaration and the Instrument of Surrender put into operation – perfected – by the martial law of the Supreme Commander Allied Powers in occupation of Japan."[14] While some of the other judges appear to have suggested that they should follow the Charter even if aspects were not based on international law, Webb rejected such views.[15]

---

[14] TPJ 12. Webb took this issue very seriously as shown in a memorandum to the judges of June 12, 1946, stating that if the Charter goes beyond international law their duty would be "to disregard its terms pro tanto. We cannot bind ourselves to commit judicial murder if we think we will be involved."(NAA M1417 24 p. 1).

[15] See for instance, Judge Patrick's memorandum to Webb of December 23, 1946 and Webb's response of December 24. (NAA M1417 24 pp. 1–5).

The martial law Webb refers to, Webb explains, is the Supreme Commander's proclamation of the tribunal and the Charter enacted to "implement the term of surrender that stern justice be meted out to war criminals." Webb thus makes explicit that the highest Japanese authorities have assented to and accepted the jurisdiction of the IMTFE by signing the Instrument of Surrender which required carrying out in good faith the Potsdam Declaration. "This," Webb reasons, "imposed upon the Japanese Government the obligation, among others, of apprehending and surrendering persons named by the Supreme Commander as required for trial on charges of war crimes."[16]

### 8.2.2  The Charge of Crimes against Peace

While this reference to the Instrument of Surrender provides a basis for finding that the Japanese government has assented to the jurisdiction of the tribunal for charges of war crimes, it requires a further step to argue that this assent includes charges of crimes against peace, or aggressive war. This step, Webb argues, arises from the fact that "the Emperor and Government of Japan understood the term 'war criminals' to include those responsible for the war." Although he does not cite it again here, Webb had previously described the response of the Japanese government to the demands of the Potsdam Declaration. There he noted that the Japanese government, on August 9–10, 1945, had decided not to press for the condition that those responsible for the war should be dealt with through the Japanese government itself. Webb quotes, and underscores, that, "on the same day the Japanese Emperor told KIDO that he could not bear the sight of those responsible for the war being punished but that he thought it was then the time to bear the unbearable"[17] (emphasis in The President's Judgment).

Webb thus takes great pains to establish the sources of the legal authority of the tribunal beyond what the Nuremberg judgment termed the sovereign legislative authority of the victorious Allies. Indeed, this was a point of contention with other judges who were of the opinion that the sole source of authority of the tribunal was the Charter.[18] In addition to the Japanese assent to the Potsdam Declaration and the Instrument of Surrender, Webb also argues that under International Law, and Natural Law, belligerents, as occupying Powers, have the right to punish war criminals. He also notes that under international law a victorious power may require as a condition of armistice, that the defeated state hand over those suspected of war crimes. Citing the standard contemporary treatise, *International Law* by L. Oppenheim and H. Lauterpacht, he qualifies

---

[16] TPJ 12–13.
[17] TPJ 2, paraphrasing the August 10, 1945 entry in *The Kido Diary*, the Lord Keeper of the Privy Seal, as quoted at T31178 of the trial transcript. See PX 3340, and also note 40 in Chapter 2.
[18] See, for instance, the memorandum of Justice Northcroft to Webb of December 24, 1946 NAA M1417 24 p. 1.

## 8.2 The Law of the Tribunal

this by noting that punishment in such a case can only be upon determination of guilt, from which arises the provision to create a tribunal that is based upon the recognition of the accused war criminal's right to a fair trial. This he takes to be the foundational basis for the IMTFE.[19]

Despite having found that in accepting the terms of surrender the Japanese government also accepted submitting to trial for war crimes and for responsibility for war itself, Webb embarks, as does the Nuremberg judgment, on an examination of the legal status of crimes against peace. Webb clearly recognized that this was the most contentious part of the Charter and of the judgment of the tribunal. Indeed, as discussed in the preceding chapter, it is this part of the legacy of Nuremberg and Tokyo that remains controversial and most often gives rise to the charge of victor's justice whereby those who won the war label as aggressors and criminals those who lost.

The defense had raised objections to the status and legality of charging crimes against peace, as discussed in Chapter 2, and the majority judgment had chosen not to respond to those objections except through a single extended quotation from the Nuremberg judgment.[20] As noted in Chapter 7, this strategy allows the majority to avoid stating their understanding of this important issue and its application to the Japanese context. Webb, on the other hand, chooses to directly address this important question.

The declarations of the League of Nations in 1925 and 1927 designating aggression as an international crime provide the starting point for Webb. He then turns to the most important and most contentious source for regarding aggression as criminal, the Pact of Paris of 1928 that sixty-three nations, including Japan, had adopted. As the Nuremberg judgment had noted, the Pact of Paris does not explicitly refer to aggressive war as criminal. Like the Nuremberg judgment Webb nonetheless concludes that, "the conclusion is irresistible that the illegality of aggressive war and its criminality were perceived and acknowledged."[21] At this point, however, Webb departs from the line of reasoning adopted by Nuremberg and develops an argument specific to the case of Japan's view of its obligations under international law. Webb's argument has no counterpart in the majority judgment which chose to simply quote Nuremberg with no additional commentary or application to the case before the IMTFE.

Webb begins by noting that the negotiations surrounding the Pact of Paris make clear that the recourse to war in self-defense was widely discussed by the major powers, including Japan. This is highly relevant to the IMTFE context because defense counsel had argued, as many Japanese conservatives continue

---

[19] TPJ 13.
[20] See TPJ 20–2.
[21] TPJ 14.

to do today, that Japan was merely acting in self-defense and hence not as an aggressor. On May 26, 1928 the Japanese government responded to a note from the United States by indicating that while recognizing the principle of renouncing war as an instrument of national policy, they understood the proposed principle to contain "nothing that would refuse any independent state the right of self-defense."[22] The US government replied, according to Webb, by affirming that the American draft proposal did not restrict or impair the right of self-defense, which was "inherent in every sovereign state and implicit in every treaty."[23] The US note went on to state that it was unwise to define either aggression or self-defense in the treaty, "since it was far too easy for the unscrupulous to mould events to accord with an agreed definition."[24] The Japanese government, Webb notes, replied on July 20, 1928 by asserting that, "their understanding of the draft was substantially the same as that entertained by the United States."[25]

On this basis Webb establishes that the Japanese government, in its negotiations connected to the Pact of Paris, had acknowledged that it regarded self-defense as the only legal exception to the prohibition of war as an instrument of policy as expressed in the Pact. This understanding, Webb argues, extended to the inadvisability of providing a legal definition of self-defense that some nations would inevitably exploit through discovering loopholes to justify their aggressive intentions. This raises the fundamental question of how, in the absence of definitions in the instruments, a determination is to be made in concrete cases whether the resort to arms is in self-defense or constitutes an illegal act of aggression. Here Webb again relies on Oppenheim and Lauterpacht's authoritative treatise which maintains that under international law the state resorting to war purportedly in self-defense cannot hold "the right of ultimate determination ... of the legality of the action. No such right is conferred by any other international agreement."[26] What follows for Webb is the conclusion that Oppenheim and Lauterpacht draw from this reason: "The legality of recourse to force in self-defense is in each particular case a proper subject for impartial determination by judicial or other bodies."[27]

What Webb does here is to move beyond abstract discussions of the interpretation of the Pact or Paris to the position that the Japanese government itself took in negotiations clarifying its understanding of its obligations under the

---

[22] TJP 15.
[23] Ibid.
[24] Ibid.
[25] TJP 16. The US-Japan exchange regarding the interpretation of the Pact of Paris is reproduced in the prosecution's summation. T39019–20. For the defense's argument on the same matter, see T42155–69, and T42239–42.
[26] TPJ 16, citing Oppenheim, *International Law*, ed. Lauterpacht, 6th edn, vol. II, 154–5.
[27] Ibid.

## 8.2 The Law of the Tribunal

Pact. These negotiations reveal, on his view, that the Japanese government acknowledged that the only legal justification for recourse to war was legitimate self-defense. From this perspective, the claims by defense (and Justice Pal) that the tribunal was applying an ex post facto norm could be dismissed as without merit, for the Japanese government itself had accepted that recourse to war, unless in self-defense, violated international law.

For Webb, it inevitably followed that only a judicial body, in this case the IMTFE, could make the determination as to whether that resort to violence in a specific case constituted aggression or was in fact undertaken in self-defense. If the determination of aggression as opposed to self-defense is to be made by a judicial body rather than the belligerents themselves, on Webb's view it also followed that a legal standard was required to make this determination. Here again Webb differs from the majority. In the section of the majority judgment entitled, "The Law" (Chapter II), no discussion of this issue is to be found.[28] While finding that the attacks against the United States were "unprovoked," the majority concludes that, "Whatever may be the difficulty of stating a comprehensive definition of 'a war of aggression', attacks made with the above motive cannot but be characterized as wars of aggression."[29]

Webb's approach to defining aggressive war appears in the section immediately following his discussion of self-defense, a section entitled "Individual Responsibility." Webb opens this section by indicating what conduct constitutes a crime against peace: "The conduct perceived and acknowledged as illegal and criminal is recourse to war for the solution of international controversies: as an instrument of national policy."[30] The standard for determining liability for crimes against peace thus becomes whether the state in question has engaged in hostilities to further its national policies or in legitimate self-defense. If the engagement in hostilities does not arise from self-defense then, on Webb's understanding of the Japanese interpretation of the Pact of Paris, that engagement is necessarily a violation of the norm. This, as will be seen later, is the test that Webb applies in his factual findings and individual verdicts where he inquires whether warlike actions undertaken in China and elsewhere were implemented to advance Japanese policy objectives or were responses to military force directed at Japan. This follows, of course, from Webb's previous determination that claims of self-defense must be evaluated by an impartial judicial body on a case by case basis.

---

[28] MJ 990–1000.
[29] MJ 1000. Defining aggression has proved enormously contentious and elusive. The UN 1974 Definition of Aggression was immediately recognized as unsatisfactory and impossible to apply. Considerable negotiation and controversy has also attended the development of the definition of aggression for the Statute of the International Criminal Court.
[30] TPJ 16.

Whatever one may think of the substantive merits of Webb's definition, what is important here are three factors that distinguish it from the approach of the majority judgment:

1. He articulates a definition and adduces evidence to show that it was a definition acknowledged by the Japanese government and other nations.
2. He bases that definition upon generally accepted standards from contemporary international legal instruments and the leading jurisprudence.
3. He applies this standard to test the evidence in making his factual findings and ultimate determinations as to guilt.

These factors together distinguish The President's Judgment as a reasoned opinion in support of its conclusions in contrast to the more haphazard approach of the majority judgment. Webb, of course, had the advantage both of a more experienced and capable legal intellect than many of his colleagues, and of being a sole drafter rather than a member of a group piecing together a judgment like a patchwork quilt.

### 8.2.3  Individual Responsibility for Crimes against Peace

Having established the standard for making findings on the characterization of a state's participation in a conflict Webb then moves to address two related questions: (1) Do those individuals who implement state policies found to be criminal bear individual responsibility for their actions? (2) What individual roles or kinds of conduct in the implementation of criminal policies incur individual criminal responsibility? These questions are not addressed directly by the majority judgment, which, as already seen, merely substitutes a lengthy quotation from Nuremberg for its own reasoning.

The first question formed the substance of objections to the jurisdiction of the tribunal raised by the defense (and echoed by Justice Pal in his dissent).[31] For Webb, the answer to the first question follows from the position he has taken on the criminality of aggression under the Pact of Paris: "Every state that became a party to the Pact of Paris perceived and acknowledged the illegality and criminality of recourse to war ... as an instrument of national policy. If, nevertheless, any such state resorts to aggressive war, those individuals through whom it acts, *knowing as they do that their state is a party to the Pact*, are criminally responsible for this derelict of state"[32] (emphasis added). Webb thus follows Nuremberg in rejecting the defense contention that individuals cannot be held responsible for "acts of state." This was, of course, one of the most fundamental contributions, perhaps the most important contribution,

---

[31] See MJ 24.
[32] TPJ 17.

of the IMT's judgment to the development of international law. This holding by the Nuremberg judgment destroyed once and for all the legal fiction that states "act" rather than the individuals who possess the legal authority and power to determine, control, and implement the policies of those states. The demise at Nuremberg of the Act of State doctrine has provided the foundation for contemporary international criminal law, premised upon the principle that individuals who hold high office in a state may be held individually criminally responsible for the actions undertaken by the institutions of the state when elements establish the necessary degree of connection of those individuals to the criminal acts. As the Nuremberg judgment was promulgated before that of Nuremberg's corresponding tribunal in Tokyo, the IMTFE applied this groundbreaking precedent.[33]

Webb's reasoning on the issue of the accountability of individuals as opposed to states follows that of Nuremberg: states act through individuals, and those individuals, in acting for the state, bear responsibility for their conduct. But Webb also makes clear that in the specific case of charges of aggressive war individual responsibility also follows from (1) a state's adherence to the Pact of Paris; and (2) the individual's knowledge that the state for which he or she acts is a party to the Pact of Paris and, on his view, has both renounced war as an instrument of policy and accepted the illegality of violation of that norm.[34]

The question that follows from this determination is which individuals through whom the state acts may be held criminally accountable. Here Webb's answer is sweeping in its implications.

Initially, Webb states that, "Where the war takes place those responsible necessarily include those who decided on it and those who planned and prepared for it. Preparation embraces crimes against humanity committed to facilitate war."[35] This statement follows the IMTFE Charter, the IMT Charter, and the Nuremberg judgment. Of particular interest here is the way in which Webb includes crimes against humanity under the rubric of preparation. In other words, persecution or murder perpetrated to facilitate war before the outbreak of hostilities can also be prosecuted as, or in connection with, crimes against peace. This qualification is significant because the Tokyo Charter, like that of Nuremberg, limited crimes against humanity to acts of murder, extermination, enslavement, persecution, and other crimes, "in execution of or in

---

[33] Pal attempts to use the "act of state" doctrine to excuse Japanese war crimes. He says that punishment of escaped prisoners of war or killing prisoners of war when they were too numerous to be conveniently accommodated were "mere acts of state" and provided no grounds for individual liability (Pal Opinion, 1170/1393).

[34] The majority judgment does not address this issue, again, because of its reliance on a quotation from Nuremberg that simply asserts the illegality of aggression under the Pact of Paris (MJ 25).

[35] TPJ 16.

connection with any crime within the jurisdiction of the Tribunal."[36] In the case of Nuremberg this meant that crimes committed before the outbreak of hostilities on September 1, 1939 were not prosecuted. Webb, here, in linking crimes against humanity to preparation of aggression, opens the door to prosecution of crimes such as those committed by Japanese forces in China prior to the Sino-Japanese War commencing on July 7, 1937.

In reviewing his draft judgment Webb seems to have noticed that in enumerating those who decide upon, plan, or prepare for aggressive war he had omitted to mention those who actually wage it. He added two paragraphs in an addendum that is also sweeping in its implications:

> The view that aggressive war is illegal and criminal must be carried to its logical conclusion, e.g., a soldier or civilian who opposed war but after decided it should be carried on until a more favorable time for making peace was guilty of waging aggressive war.
>
> There are no special rules that limit the responsibility for aggressive war, no matter how high or low the rank or status of the person promoting or taking part in it, *provided he knows or should know it is aggressive.*[37] (emphasis added)

Neither the Nuremberg judgment nor the Tokyo majority judgment explicitly addresses the issues raised by Webb here.[38] The Nuremberg Tribunal appears to have resolved that in regard to crimes against peace participation in the inner policy circle, rather than official rank, title, or position, was determinative of liability. Webb, on the other hand, is prepared to encompass all those soldiers and civilians who participate in an aggressive war within the circle of liability, *if* they have, or should have had, knowledge of its illegality. How is the "should have known" standard to be applied and how wide should the net of accountability actually be cast in regard to bureaucratic functionaries and field officers and soldiers? Analysis of Webb's individual findings and verdicts may clarify his position, but the broad principle of individual responsibility for waging or promoting aggressive war goes far beyond that contemplated at Nuremberg.

### 8.2.4  The Law of Conspiracy

As was seen in Chapter 7, the majority judgment is largely built around a narrative of the development of a conspiracy to wage aggressive war. What is almost entirely lacking from that judgment is a discussion of the law of conspiracy. In The President's Judgment, Webb directly addresses the issue of the legal status

---

[36] IMTFE Charter Article 5(c).
[37] This addendum was added as page 17a. It is in typescript and a handwritten annotation indicates where it belongs in the manuscript: "Transfer to bottom of page 17."
[38] Technically speaking there is no section on the law of crimes against peace. As noted in Chapter 5, Chapter II, The Law, is divided into two sections: "(a) Jurisdiction of the Tribunal," and "(b) War Crimes against Prisoners."

of conspiracy and reaches conclusions that form the basis for a very different approach than that adopted by the majority. The difference in his interpretation of conspiracy is particularly significant in that it allows him to bring out the divisions within the Japanese leadership over war policy rather than tending to ignore or elide them as the majority does. Indeed, as seen earlier, the majority's reliance on a conspiracy narrative allowed them to refrain from making specific findings and conclusions as to the particular role of each accused in regard to waging, planning, preparing, or instigating aggressive war. Webb's approach, on the other hand, brings squarely into focus the specific conduct of each individual accused rather than subsuming them within generalizations about the conspiracy. As in regard to other issues, Webb's approach brings out the failure of the majority to address fundamental legal issues.

For Webb, the starting point is the insight that under international law conspiracy cannot be charged as a substantive offense, that is, as a crime in and of itself. This flies directly in the face of the majority judgment which had, as seen in Chapter 7, done precisely this. Whereas the majority had offered no explanation for the legal basis of the charge of conspiracy, Webb justifies his position by arguing that except in the Anglo-American world conspiracy is not normally charged when the crime has actually been committed. In such cases, he states, it is usual to charge the commission of the crime itself. What Webb terms "naked conspiracy" (i.e., conspiracy as an independent offense) is not known to international law either in the Pact of Paris or in the laws and customs of war: "It may well be that naked conspiracy to have recourse to war or to commit a conventional war crime or crime against humanity should be a crime, but this tribunal is not to determine what ought to be but what is the law ... [I]t has no authority to create a crime of naked conspiracy based on the Anglo-American concept; nor on what it perceives to be a common feature of the crime of conspiracy under the various national laws."[39]

Webb here rejects both a central thrust of the prosecution case, as well as of the majority judgment. He goes farther than the Nuremberg Tribunal, where conspiracy was central to the American prosecution team's case, in squarely refusing to read into international law a substantive offense of conspiracy. He instead interprets the Charter as providing for "participation in a common plan or conspiracy" as a mode of commission, as "a means of committing a crime against peace."[40]

Webb notes that Article 5 of the Charter provides that "leaders, organizers, instigators, and accomplices" who participate in the formulation or implementation of a conspiracy or common plan can be held accountable for all the acts

---

[39] TPJ 18. This comment by Webb also makes clear how alive he was to the impermissibility of establishing ex post facto norms and applying them in a criminal prosecution.
[40] TPJ 18.

committed by other persons who act to execute the plan. This, he observes, is simply the traditional form of criminal responsibility based upon complicity. That is, individuals whose only role is to plan, prepare for, or assist in waging aggressive war are held accountable for the acts of those who actually carry out the plan. Rather than holding these individuals liable for what, in Webb's view, would be a novel criminal offense under international law, he reads the Charter's provisions regarding conspiracy to be no more than an application of traditional criminal law doctrines regarding modes of liability.[41] In a context in which significant concerns had been raised regarding ex post facto application of the law, Webb's approach has considerable merit.

## 8.3 Individual Factual Findings and Verdicts on Crimes against Peace

Webb's draft judgment allocates a substantial section to general factual findings on crimes against peace. Unlike the majority judgment these resemble actual factual findings based on the evidence before the court rather than an historical narrative that states facts as given. Of greater relevance in underscoring the essential differences between the majority and Webb are the individual verdicts which, as noted earlier, take up substantially more than half of the judgment and comprise some 395 pages. In this section each of the verdicts consists of two sections: "Facts Found," taking up the bulk of the verdict, and "Conclusion." The conclusions summarize the factual findings and explain and justify the verdict of guilty. In most cases Webb's "Conclusion" for each of the accused is longer and more detailed than the total individual verdict of the same accused in the majority judgment. This section will consider Webb's findings against each of the accused that were examined in the preceding chapter on the majority's verdicts on crimes against peace. This will allow us to highlight the fundamental differences in form and substance between Webb's draft judgment and that of the majority.

### *8.3.1 Dohihara*

Unlike the general findings in the majority judgment that Dohihara associated himself with "the military faction" and took a prominent part in advocating the use of force in Japan's China policy, Webb details Dohihara's actual role and refers to some of the specific evidence against him on which his factual findings are based. For example, Webb notes that when Dohihara was called to Tokyo in September 1931 to report on the military's schemes in Manchuria, he "was quoted in the Tokyo press as an advocate of the solution of all pending

[41] TPJ 18a.

## 8.3 Individual Factual Findings and Verdicts on Crimes against Peace

issues in Manchuria by force, if necessary, and as soon as possible." He then notes that although Dohihara was not in Mukden on September 18, 1931 when the Mukden "Incident" occurred, his office "was the centre of invasion operations," serving as a communications link between the outposts and the headquarters of the Kwantung Army.[42]

In the aftermath of the Japanese takeover Webb details Dohihara's roles and actions in securing Japanese control and domination of Manchuria. To cite one example, Webb recounts how Dohihara had been instructed by the Japanese government through the Tianjin consul-general, Kuwashima Kazue, that creation of an independent state in Manchuria could violate the Nine-Power Treaty. Webb explains that despite this Dohihara insisted on carrying out the plan and devised a strategy for pretending that Japan had no hand in it. Further, Dohihara informed Kuwashima "that in the case of interference by the Government the Kwantung Army might separate from the Government and accidents graver than assassination might occur in Japan."[43]

After further detailing of Dohihara's key role, Webb quotes at length the telegram of Consul-General Kuwashima to the foreign minister. The telegram recounts in detail Dohohara's role in undermining Japanese policy: "For this matter he repelled all intervention and remonstrance; and at times, knowing that it was against the national policy, he would resort to all sorts of plots ... His desperate actions are beyond our imagination ... The riot [instigated by Dohihara] has turned into a clash between Japan and China."[44]

Webb goes on to detail how in his interrogation Dohihara admitted that he had deliberately violated orders and that he "knew that when the Kwantung Army was planning to set up an independent state, it was going to violate the Nine-Power Treaty."[45] These examples are just a few from the first five pages of the fifteen pages Webb devotes to factual findings on Dohihara. He continues beyond the Manchuria phase to make findings on Dohihara's role in North China in 1935–7. After the beginning of Japan's invasion of China in 1937 Dohihara assumes command of the 14th Division and "participated in the Peiping-Hankow drive."

Based on these findings Webb arrives at conclusions that are much more nuanced and more directly founded upon specific findings than the general conclusions of the majority opinion. He concludes that Dohihara "with others" was responsible for resorting to force in Manchuria and "knew that there was no justification for it."[46]

---

[42] TPJ 293.
[43] TPJ 295. The prosecution uses this and other similar quotations in their summation, seemingly unaware that this highlighting of Dohihara's individual role might call into question their theory of an overarching conspiracy. See Chapter 4.
[44] TPJ 296. This quote appears in PX300, T4395–7.
[45] TPJ 297. This admission appears in PX2190-A, T15729–30.
[46] TPJ 306.

On the other hand, Webb finds that Dohihara cannot be held accountable for initiating or planning the war in China or the Pacific War, though he is liable for waging war because of his direct participation, "knowing its illegality," as an "army Commander" in both cases.[47] Webb's conclusion on Dohihara's responsibility for the Pacific War is particularly important in contrast to the methodology of the majority.

Webb first notes that Dohihara cannot be held liable based upon an inference from the offices he held alone. While noting that Dohihara attended a crucial Supreme War Council meeting on June 30, 1941, Webb concludes that he "does not appear to have said or done anything" at this meeting to justify a finding of guilt on this count.[48] As seen earlier, the majority repeatedly infers culpable participation from mere attendance at meetings or from the fact that meetings took place while a particular accused was in the cabinet. When reaching a conclusion of liability, whether for crimes against peace or war crimes, Webb is also nearly always careful to note that the required mental element is met, of knowledge or information sufficient to put the accused on inquiry notice.[49] Note also that Webb does not find Dohihara guilty under Count 1, the grand conspiracy charge regarding domination of the entire Asia-Pacific region, relied on by the majority. His findings are specifically directed to the particular theaters of war where he finds Dohihara to have been either engaged in instigating, planning, or waging aggressive war.

### 8.3.2  Hashimoto

Webb's findings on Hashimoto are among the shortest in his draft judgment, comprising only some six pages (TPJ 308–14). This is likely due to the limited nature of his conclusions in regard to Hashimoto's liability. The limited nature of his findings starkly points up the difference between his approach and that of the majority. In the majority judgment, it will be recalled, Hashimoto was treated largely as a propagandist, rather than in relation to his activities in his military positions. For this role the majority held him to be a principal in the formation and execution of the grand conspiracy charged in Count 1 of the indictment. The shortcomings of the majority's treatment of Hashimoto were noted in Chapter 7 and are underscored by the contrast with Webb's analysis.

Webb recounts Hashimoto's admission that in 1930 and afterwards he was active in devising "schemes" to achieve greater global prominence for Japan, though he did not admit that these schemes were "the only cause" of the Manchurian and other "incidents."[50] Webb cites specific testimony in regard

---

[47] TPJ 306–7.
[48] TPJ 307.
[49] Ibid.
[50] TPJ 309.

8.3 Individual Factual Findings and Verdicts on Crimes against Peace    321

to Manchuria, both that of Hashimoto himself as well as others. For example, "Hashimoto admitted to TANAKA, Ryukichi, in 1934 that he had assisted the Kwantung Army to bring about the Manchurian Incident."[51] Webb also considers at some length Hashimoto's writings and speeches advocating attacking England and America and bringing virtually all of the Asia-Pacific region under Japanese control. Despite these writings and propagandistic activity, Webb declines to hold Hashimoto accountable for anything other than Manchuria and China because of the lack of evidence concerning the connection between his writings and other activities and the outbreak of war: "His writings including press articles and the secret report may or may not have contributed to war. That is as much can be said."[52]

In other words, in contrast to the majority that finds the evidence of his writings sufficient to regard him as a principal in the formation *and* execution of the Pacific War, Webb finds that the evidence is not unambiguous and hence does not meet the required burden of proof. That is, he actually weighs and analyzes the applicable evidence in relation to the standard of reasonable doubt. The majority never considers such questions about the sufficiency of the evidence where more than one inference is plausible. Webb only finds the evidence sufficient to hold Hashimoto responsible for bringing about and waging the war in Manchuria and China, "knowing that Japan was the aggressor."[53] For establishing the mental element he refers to ample evidence in support of his finding and conclusion. Webb's refusal to hold Hashimoto responsible under Count 1 points up the dangers of the majority's approach in narrating a single overarching conspiracy from 1928 to 1945 in which each of the accused played a part.

### 8.3.3  Hata

As discussed earlier, the majority's guilty verdict on Hata was quite general, finding that while he was army minister the war in China was waged "with renewed vigor" and that he was a member of the conspiracy to achieve domination of East Asia and the Pacific.[54] Webb, on the other hand, first considers Hata's role after he "assumes command in Central China" on February 14, 1938. Webb quotes Hata's admission about the nature of the conflict in China in his interrogation that, "Although it was actually a war, all they ever considered it as was a Chinese Incident!"[55] This admission is significant, of course,

---

[51] TPJ 311.
[52] TPJ 314.
[53] Ibid.
[54] Unlike the brief treatment accorded Hata by the majority, Webb devotes thirteen pages to his findings and conclusions: TPJ 315–328.
[55] TPJ 315. This quote appears in PX256, T3451. See also Chapter 6 under Section 6.2.2.

because it undercuts the defense position on China as well as indicating Hata's complete awareness of the true nature of the conflict and of the hollowness of the Japanese interpretation. Webb goes on to detail that while Hata was in command in Central China the stated policy of the Japanese government was that they would continue military operations until the "National Government was 'completely annihilated.'"[56]

Turning to Hata's role as army minister from 1939, Webb's discussion again points up the vagueness of the conclusions of the majority as to the grounds of Hata's liability. As we have already seen, Webb cites records of interrogations, quotes Hata's own words in his official capacity, refers to the testimony of witnesses, and provides exact dates of relevant evidence. For example, Webb provides a lengthy quotation from Hata's statement at a committee meeting of the Imperial Diet on March 22, 1940: because of the "anti-Japanese policy" of the Nationalist Government (i.e., that they refuse to surrender or be defeated on the battlefield) Japan is now fighting a "Holy War" to bring about peace in Asia. He goes on to argue that Japan should ignore the Nine-Power Treaty and should focus on overcoming any resistance to "the establishment of the new order in East Asia."[57]

Webb then refers to Hata's testimony that he had studied international law and knew that the war in China was a violation of the treaty. Hata stated, "There seemed to be no other way out but to resort to armed force when other means failed."[58] Such examples could be multiplied from Webb's treatment. The most striking contrast between Webb's approach and that of the majority is that Webb finds Hata guilty for aggressive war only in relation to his activities regarding China. Although Webb details Hata's key role in the downfall of the Yonai Cabinet in 1940 and in proposing Tōjō as prime minister, Webb, unlike the majority, relies on the overwhelming evidence regarding China, noting also that Hata resumed command in Central China from March 1941 to November 22, 1944. The majority on the other hand rely on generalities to find Hata responsible for conspiring to dominate all of the Asia-Pacific region.

### 8.3.4  Hiranuma

In contrast to the mere sixteen lines the majority devotes to Hiranuma and the important political roles he assumed, Webb spends fifteen pages analyzing his contribution to the Japanese war policies. Whereas one of the few specific instances

---

[56] TPJ 315, quoting Prime Minister Konoe's public statement, dated January 16, 1938. The relevant sentence in the speech read, "But, so far as the same Government adheres to the pro-communism and anti-Japanese policy, we will never lay aside our arms until they are *completely annihilated*" (emphasis added), in PX 268, T3564.

[57] TPJ 317. These quotes appear in PX3832, T38017–8, 38021–3.

[58] TPJ 317–18. This quote appears in PX 256, T3451.

## 8.3 Individual Factual Findings and Verdicts on Crimes against Peace 323

cited by the majority against Hiranuma merely found that he attended the November 29, 1941 meeting that advised the Emperor on going to war, Webb analyzes Hiranuma's particular roles from 1931 to the end of the war. Webb first details the role of the Privy Council in the Manchurian "Incident," during which time Hiranuma was vice president of that body (in 1936 he became president of the Privy Council until assuming the position of prime minister in 1939), referring specifically, for example, to his statements on September 13, 1932 regarding the creation of a puppet independent state. Webb does sometimes merely refer to decisions of the Privy Council without specifying what Hiranuma said and did, perhaps imputing these decisions to him by virtue of his leadership role as Vice President of the Council.[59] On the other hand, his treatment of Hiranuma's tenure as prime minister is replete with specific references to his words and deeds as related to the charges against him.

To cite but a few examples, Webb recounts how, in order to retain Itagaki as army minister in his cabinet, Hiranuma agreed to seven specific demands of the "Army Senior Chiefs" that aimed at victory in China and at putting Japan on a war footing.[60] In regard to his China policy, Webb cites evidence against Hiranuma that is, astonishingly, omitted by the majority in their verdict despite its obvious inculpatory relevance. Webb recounts that on January 21, 1939 Hiranuma tells the Diet that he intends to pursue the previous China policy at all costs. Webb continues, "There was no alternative, he concluded, but *to exterminate* those who persisted in opposition to Japan"[61] (emphasis added). Webb also quotes at length the "HIRANUMA Declaration of May 4, 1939 addressed to Hitler" which pledges Japanese political, economic, and military support to Germany in the event of war and references the cabinet decision of June 5, 1939 to implement this pledge to participate "in a German war against England and France."[62]

Webb details the many cabinet decisions in which Hiranuma participated, and the Liaison Conference meetings and other key meetings he attended. In some cases Webb only notes the decision that was reached while in other cases

---

[59] TPJ 331. PX241, T297–82. Part of the minutes is discussed in Chapter 4 under Section 4.1.
[60] TPJ 332–3. The fact that Army Minister Itagaki made seven demands on Hiranuma was publicized by the press at the time, as shown in PX3303, a newspaper article entitled, "Execution of Seven Items: Hiranuma Requested by the Army," published in the *Chūgai shōgyō shinpō*, January 6, 1939, T30120–2.
[61] TPJ 334. The relevant segment in the speech reads as follows: "I hope the above intention of Japan will be understood correctly by the Chinese so that they may cooperate with us without the slightest apprehension. Otherwise, the construction of the new order would be impossible. As for those who fail to understand to the end and persist even hereafter in their opposition against Japan, we have *no other alterantive than to exterminate them*" (emphasis added), in PX 2229-A, Excerpt from *Tokyo Gazzette*, March 1939, T15989–90.
[62] TPJ 337–9. The full text of the Hiranuma Declaration can be found in PX503, Telegram from Ambassador Ott in Tokyo, to State Secretary von Weizsaecker, May 4, 1939, T6104–6.

he states, for example, that "Hiranuma agreed."[63] Like the majority, in many of these cases he omits to state more specifically what Hiranuma actually said. In regard to the most important of these meetings, however, Webb does go into considerable detail. As stated earlier, the majority referenced Hiranuma's agreement with the conclusion of the November 29, 1941 meeting of the senior statesmen that war with the United States was "inevitable." Unlike this statement of dubious inculpatory weight, Webb details Hiranuma's actual contribution to the discussion. In response to Tōjō's assertion that war with the Western Powers could not be avoided, Hiranuma "remarked that he agreed that Japan was equal to a prolonged war with the United States in spiritual strength but doubted its ability in material power. He urged that adequate measures be taken to awaken patriotic sentiment."[64] Webb also takes up Hiranuma's opposition to peace negotiations in 1945. Among other actions of Hiranuma, Webb recounts how at a meeting held on April 5, 1945 Hiranuma said he was "strongly opposed to any advocacy for peace and cessation of hostilities and so there was no way out but to fight to the end."[65]

Webb thus provides evidence based on factual findings, unlike the majority's grossly abbreviated individual verdict on Hiranuma. Also unlike the majority, Webb provides a conclusion that links the factual findings to specific legal conclusions. For example, Webb not only cites but also analyzes words attributed to Hiranuma at the November 29 meeting of the senior statesmen to show that although he "doubted Japan's material strength" he nonetheless *counseled for and supported* the intended war.[66]

### 8.3.5  Hirota

The conviction of no other accused at Tokyo has aroused so much controversy as that of Hirota Kōki. Defended by the dissenting opinions of Pal and Roeling, Hirota has been portrayed as a martyr to "victor's justice." Apart from other reasons, this is in part due, no doubt, to the inadequacies of the majority judgment, discussed in Chapter 7, in failing to make individualized analyses

---

[63] TPJ 340, and see 339–341.
[64] TPJ 342. See also Chapter 4 under Section 4.4.
[65] TPJ 342–3. The minutes of proceedings of the senior statesmen's meeting, held on April 5, 1945, are incorporated in Kido's affidavit, DX3340. For Hiranuma's statements, see DX3340, T31124 and T31134.
[66] TPJ 344. The transcripts of the November 29 meeting are not in evidence. Instead, oral evidence was taken from some of those individuals who had attended the meeting, such as, Tōjō, Yonai, and Wakatsuki. An excerpt from *The Kido Diary* was also presented in evidence (PX1196, T10452–4), in which Kido recorded the gist of the meeting although he himself was not present. He offered additional explanatory remarks about the meeting in his affidavit evidence (DX3340, T31040–4).

8.3 Individual Factual Findings and Verdicts on Crimes against Peace 325

of the available evidence and reach reasoned conclusions applying the law of the tribunal to that evidence. At the same time, perhaps no other verdict makes clearer how one's perspective on the evidence might change as seen through the lens of the Webb's draft judgment. A reading of the findings and conclusion of Webb's draft judgment indicate that a reasoned case could have, and should have, been made by the majority to support their verdict against Hirota. The evidence relied upon in Webb draft judgment also casts important light upon the attempt by Roeling, as will be seen in Chapter 11, to explain away Hirota's role at the center of Japanese policymaking in the critical period of 1936–8. It must again be emphasized, however, that our purpose is *not* to arrive at a conclusion concerning the guilt or innocence of Hirota or any other of the defendants. What this treatment of the Webb draft judgment aims at is, on the one hand, to underscore the shortcomings of the majority judgment and, on the other hand, to show what kind of case Webb was able to make to support his verdicts, based upon the available evidence.

Webb's draft judgment devotes twenty pages to close analysis of Hirota's role as foreign minister and prime minister through the crucial period from 1933 to 1937 when Japan's policy toward China hardened and the foundational decisions that led to the Pacific War were taken. Webb, unlike the majority, takes Hirota's own words and deeds as the basis of the evidence that leads to the legal conclusions he reaches at the end of his treatment.

Webb begins by noting that already as ambassador to the USSR in 1930–2 Hirota had stated that Japan's policy should be to be ready for war and that the "purpose of such policies was not defense against communism, but rather the conquest of East Siberia."[67] Webb quotes *The Saionji-Harada Memoirs* and other sources to show Hirota's commitment to abrogate the Washington Naval Treaty, a position on which he stated, "We are taking an unconditional stand."[68] Such evidence provides only the introductory backdrop to the far more detailed account of Hirota's actions and intentions in regard to Japanese expansion in China.

Webb begins by noting that Hirota was a member of the cabinet that on December 22, 1933 reached a key decision on the independence of Manchukuo. To show that Hirota personally favored such a policy, Webb cites Hirota's speech of January 23, 1934 to the Imperial Diet in which "he acclaimed the establishment of Manchukuo as an independent country."[69] In regard to the army's preparations for and advance into China, Webb provides detailed evidence showing that Hirota, as foreign minister, had been apprised of these intentions and preparations. He also cites Hirota's statements, diplomatic

---

[67] TPJ 345–6. This quote originally appears in PX693, T7452.
[68] TPJ 346. See PX3777-B, T37669.
[69] TPJ 347. See DX3237, T29453–4.

communications and policy briefs to show that Hirota was actively engaged in promoting these plans for further Japanese expansion into China.[70]

After the Japanese initiated outbreak of hostilities in China (the Lukouchiao Incident, also known as the "Marco Polo Bridge Incident"), Hirota supported cabinet decisions for further military activity against China and, in a speech to the Imperial Diet on 27 July, "blamed China for the incident" and made further statements that were contradicted by the actual decisions already taken by the cabinet. Webb goes on to cite the August 7, 1937 draft terms of settlement with China that had been prepared by Foreign Minister Hirota, the premier, and navy and army ministers. This draft stated that, "we should be determined to exercise military power on a large scale and for a long time."[71]

To cite only some of the most inculpatory evidence considered by Webb, he notes that when Japan had commenced full scale military operations in China, Hirota and the army and navy ministers decided on August 7, 1937 "that the principal areas for using military force on land should be Hopei-Chahar and Shanghai."[72] Webb notes that apart from a similar speech to the Imperial Diet, on September 5, 1937 Hirota blamed the Chinese for the Japanese attack on Shanghai and gave his approval to increasing Japanese forces and the dispatch of warships there.[73]

Webb next provides a detailed account of the Japanese negotiations with the Nationalist government, showing how the cabinet, with Hirota in a key role, overrode the Army General Staff's desire to reach a settlement, by insisting on terms that he knew the Chinese would not agree to. Webb cites evidence showing that even the Germans understood Japan's policy to be in bad faith and communicated as much to Hirota. This policy culminated in a decision of the Cabinet Council on January 15, 1938, that Japan will replace the current government of China with one that "will be a worthy coalition with our Empire."[74] To demonstrate Hirota's position on these "epoch-making"[75] policy decisions Webb cites Hirota's speech of February 16, 1938 to the Imperial Diet, where Webb states that Hirota admitted that Japan "had never tried to compromise with Chiang Kai-shek ... and that Japan had pursued a policy of chastising China in order to change her attitude."[76] Webb again cites *The Saionji-Harada Memoirs* on Hirota's attitude, citing his statement that because

---

[70] TPJ 349.
[71] TPJ 351. See PX3735, T37223.
[72] TPJ 352. See PX3735, T37221.
[73] TPJ 352.
[74] TPJ 358. See also Chapter 4 under Section 4.2.
[75] TPJ 358, quoting Kido, originally appearing in PX2260, T16223.
[76] TPJ 358. See PX3737-A, T37295–6.

## 8.3 Individual Factual Findings and Verdicts on Crimes against Peace 327

the Chinese were bluffing "there was nothing to do but launch the alternative plan of long-term warfare."[77]

Although Webb continues to detail Hirota's activities up to the outbreak of the Pacific War, the discussion earlier should be sufficient to demonstrate that Webb, unlike the majority, relied upon specific evidence of what Hirota actually said and did in making his factual findings. He also appears to have done so in a balanced way, noting, for example, that in the November 29, 1941 meeting of senior statesmen Hirota advised that Japan should not rush into war, should postpone the attack and should seek a diplomatic solution after the initiation of hostilities.[78]

Having made factual findings on the evidence he deemed immediately relevant to Hirota's culpability, what conclusions did Webb reach on the basis of these findings? Webb argues that "no other civilian prime minster, except perhaps HIRANUMA, supported" the militarists with such consistency.[79] To support this conclusion Webb refers to some of the evidence on which he has made findings, from Hirota's advocacy of the conquest of East Siberia, to his position on Manchukuo and the further aims "to dismember China and bring it under Japan's control ... This was in reality taking part in the waging war against China."[80] Webb concludes from the disingenuous settlement negotiations with Chiang Kai-shek and Hirota's articulation of the necessity for a "long term" war that, "He was determined to wage war to destroy China and get complete control of China."[81]

On the other hand, unlike the majority, Webb again considers the sufficiency of the evidence against the burden of proof and concludes that although Hirota "did as much as any civilian to prepare" for the Pacific War, the fact that he at the critical moment suggested postponement "precludes a finding beyond a reasonable doubt that he initiated the Pacific War."[82] One would scour the majority opinion in vain to find a similar weighing of the evidence and an explicit expression of the application of the reasonable doubt standard. Webb goes on to note, however, that in regard to waging the Pacific War, when Koiso became prime minister in 1944 "Hirota advocated the prosecution of that illegal and criminal war."[83] Whatever one's personal conclusion as to Hirota's culpability, there is little doubt that Webb's verdict provides a reasoned decision based upon consideration of the evidence which Webb deemed relevant to the charges. This, along with other evidence Webb cites in his general treatment of

---

[77] TPJ 357. See PX3789-A, T37723.
[78] TPJ 363–4. See PX1196, T10453–4.
[79] TPJ 364–5.
[80] Ibid.
[81] Ibid.
[82] TPJ 366.
[83] Ibid.

the developments of these years, presents the case that needs to be answered by the dissenting opinions.

### 8.3.6 Kaya

Webb's treatment of Finance Minister Kaya is one of the briefest in his draft judgment, comprising only six pages. Yet, in comparison with the majority judgment, Webb engages in a serious analysis of the evidence on Kaya's role. Having enumerated the offices Kaya held, the majority judgment based its conviction of Kaya entirely upon the following seven lines:

In these positions he took part in the formulation of the aggressive policies of Japan and in the financial, economic and industrial preparations for the execution of those policies. Throughout this period, particularly as Finance Minister in the first Konoye and TOJO Cabinets as a President of the North China Development Company, he was actively engaged in the preparation and carrying out of aggressive wars in China and against the Western Powers. He was an active member of the conspiracy alleged in Count 1 and is adjudged guilty under that Count.

Webb begins his consideration of the evidence by explaining that after Kaya entered the cabinet in June 1937 not only were important decisions made as to the expansion of military efforts in North China but under him there was a huge increase in the national budget "70% of which was to be used by the Army and Navy."[84] To make Kaya's attitudes toward these developments in China clear, Webb quotes from a book of his speeches that Kaya stated "that the China Incident was actually a war between Japan and China" and that Japan should prepare accordingly.[85] Webb continues to quote other passages of the speeches, including on how "Economic war" is of decisive importance and that the demands of the Army and Navy must be met with adequate budgets to enable their successful prosecution of the war effort.[86]

Until his resignation from the cabinet on May 26, 1938, Kaya, according to the evidence cited by Webb, played an important role in financing the Japanese occupation of North China. While the defense claimed that after his resignation Kaya had no further connection with the government until 1941, Webb cites evidence that undercuts this claim. For example, Webb cites an appeal Kaya made on November 2, 1938 at the "Japanese-Manchukuo-China" roundtable conference where he called Japan's war in China "a holy war" and stressed the

---

[84] TPJ 394. This figure draws upon the prosecution's summation at T41030, which, in turns, is based on Testimony by John G. Liebert, SCAP Legal Advisor in the Economic & Scientific Section and Chief of the Cartel & Controls Section, T8541–2.
[85] TPJ 394. This quote appears in PX3338-A, T30667.
[86] TPJ 395. This word, "economic war," appears in PX3338-C, Excerpt from book entitled *War Time Economic Life*, T30677.

need to expand armaments and economic power for Japan to achieve its goals in East Asia.[87] During the period in which he denied having a governmental role, Kaya, according to the evidence cited by Webb, served as the president of the North China Development Company. Webb states that Kaya explained the role of this company as supplying "Japan with war materials to be used in the conduct of Sino-Japanese hostilities."[88]

Kaya again became finance minister in the Tōjō Cabinet on October 17, 1941. Webb cites Kaya's decision to approve the decision of the Liaison Conference of November 5, 1941 to continue with preparations to attack the United States and the Imperial Conference of December 1, 1941. At that conference, where the decision to go to war was made, Kaya gave a report on Japanese economic and financial strength. He had, Webb notes, "told the Prime Minister that he would not oppose war and at the conference he did not oppose war. He knew in advance that hostilities were to be opened against the United States."[89]

This is not a complete summary of the evidence considered by Webb concerning Kaya's role, but the comparison with the seven lines of the majority opinion is clear enough. As in his other individual verdicts, Webb cites dates, events, and specific words and actions of Kaya. On this basis Webb concludes that Kaya "knew the hostilities in China were war and he knew or should have known that it was not a war in self-defence of Japan. Yet he was a strong supporter of that war."[90] In regard to the Pacific War, Webb similarly reaches a conclusion that flows directly from the evidence he has cited: "As Tojo's Finance Minister he agreed to the war after mature deliberation. He knew it was launched to enable Japan to retain her grip on China and so like the China war was also illegal and criminal."[91]

### 8.3.7  Kimura

One gains a very different perspective on the role and responsibility of Kimura, both as an Army general and as vice army minister, from Webb's analysis as opposed to the brief treatment by the majority. Of particular note is the long and detailed treatment by Webb of Kimura's role in regard to war crimes, which will be discussed in a later chapter. In regard to aggressive war, the majority, as seen earlier, characterized Kimura as a mere accomplice to the conspiracy. Webb, on the other hand, adduces evidence to show that Kimura actually had

---

[87] TPJ 396. See PX3339, T30690.
[88] TPJ 397. Kaya gave this explanation when interviewed by a foreign correspondent, John Goette, T3872.
[89] TPJ 398. See Testimony by Kaya Okinori, T30704–5; and DX3665, Affidavit by Tōjō Hideki, T36374.
[90] TPJ 400.
[91] Ibid.

an active and important role in a number of contexts. While Webb's treatment of the aggressive war charges is shorter than his much more detailed analysis of Kimura's role pertaining to the treatment of POW, he nonetheless makes evidence-based findings to support his legal conclusions.

In regard to Kimura's role in the war in China, Webb notes that apart from his earlier role as a major-general in Tokyo, on March 9, 1939 he is promoted to lieutenant-general and receives a field command in China. In 1940 he is made chief of staff of the Kwantung Army as well as serving on key committees charged with the economic exploitation of Manchukuo.[92] Webb spends more time, however, detailing Kimura's conduct as vice army minister from April 10, 1941. He notes that Kimura's duties in this position included "the control and utilization of Manchurian resources; general mobilization in Korea, Formosa, and the Colonies" and other matters.[93]

With the outbreak of the Pacific War evidence considered by Webb shows Kimura involved in issuing orders and engaging in correspondence concerning deployments, finance, and logistics. For example, Webb notes that Kimura "countersigned the order issued immediately after the Imperial Conference on 1st December 1941" notifying field commanders that war "would commence on 8th December 1941."[94] It is also Kimura, Webb recounts, who notified the foreign ministry on January 23, 1942 that Japan would follow the Geneva Convention on POWs. While the voluminous evidence presented by Webb on Kimura's important role in regard to mistreatment of POW bears more directly upon the war crimes charges, that evidence also shows Kimura not as a mere accomplice but as an individual directly involved in policy formulation and implementation at the highest levels.

Webb also makes findings concerning the important role Kimura played when Tōjō was absent or involved in other matters because of his dual role as

---

[92] TPJ 414.
[93] Ibid. This finding draws upon the prosecution's summation at T41136, which, in turn, is built on PX3365, Tables 1–10 in Article 27 of the Army Ministry General Affairs Regulations, introduced at T31768. This exhibit, which was not read into the record, contains "Matters Entrusted to the Vice-Minister of War," a list of 69 matters that came within the responsibility of the vice army minister. See pp. 1–4 of the exhibit.
[94] TPJ 415. This finding is based on Testimony by Tanaka Shin'ichi, formerly chief of the First Bureau of the Army Department of the Imperial Headquarters. He testified that, following the December 1 Imperial Conference, he was directed by his superior and army chief, General Sugiyama, to draft an alert order to all commanding generals of troops in the South Seas Areas about X-day of the impending war against Great Britain, The Netherlands, and the United States. He further testified that "before the order could be wired to the various commanders in the South Pacific it also had to have the signature of approval of Generals TOJO, KIMURA and MUTO in their respective capacities as War Minister, Vice Minister of War and Chief of the Military Affairs Bureau. *It was the customary rule in our office to obtain the signatures of the War Minister, the Vice War Minister and the Chief of the Military Affairs* [Bureau] *on those important orders before they could be sent out*" (emphasis added), T16146–7. The date given by Webb may be a typographical error as the correct date is December 1.

army minister and prime minister. As Webb notes, "Before any important matters were formulated by the Bureau Chiefs, they had to receive the approval of the Minister and the Vice-Minister for War and the Bureau could not carry any decision into effect without the approval of the Minister and Vice-Minister."[95] Webb also cites as evidence of Kimura's policy level role the dispatch of German Ambassador Ott to Berlin in which he states that "as Vice-Minister of War he was one of the principal advocates of German-Japanese military cooperation."[96]

The conclusion that Webb draws from his consideration of the evidence is that Kimura "took an active part in the China war." Further, as vice army minister and commander-in-chief of the Burma Area Army "he took a prominent part in planning, preparing, initiating, and waging war in the Pacific." Webb also concludes that Kimura knew that these wars were not in self-defence, "particularly from his close association with TOJO."[97] Consideration of the available evidence leads Webb to give a reasoned justification for the conclusion about the importance of Kimura's role, a conclusion that differs from the less evidence-based assessment of the majority.

### 8.3.8 Satō

As seen in the preceding chapter, the majority was inconsistent as to whether Satō should be treated as an accomplice to the conspiracy or as a conspirator. The majority judgment adduced virtually no specific evidence to support either position, relying instead on generalizations about his roles. Webb, as we might expect, was much more specific in his consideration of what factual findings to make on the basis of the evidence.

Webb traces Satō's career from relatively modest beginnings to his increasingly important roles, ending his career as a lieutenant-general with field commands in Southeast Asia. Of most relevance concerning the charges against him was his appointment in April 1942 as director of the Military Affairs Bureau of the Ministry of the Army. This role involved "explaining" military policy to the Diet. For example, Webb states that on March 11, 1942 Satō addressed the Diet on the need for mobilization to facilitate the "Greater Asia War."[98] Webb also quotes his admission in his interrogation that he felt his

---

[95] TPJ 418–9. This finding draws upon the prosecution's summation at T41150, which, in turn, is built on DX3348, excerpt from Army Ministry General Regulations, T31658–62.
[96] TPJ 419. See PX1272, telegram from the German ambassadors in Tokyo, Major General Eugene Ott and Heinrich Stahmer, May 17, 1942, T11355.
[97] TPJ 423.
[98] TPJ 549. For Satō's own admission of serving as army spokesman (or the so-called "explainer," see PX2238-A, excerpts from Allied Postwar Interrogations of Satō Kenryō, T16090–94. For the test of his March 11, 1942 speech, see PX849, T8413–15.

explanation of policy to the Diet "was the most powerful."⁹⁹ Webb then relates that at an earlier period Satō had already proved himself as an able "Army Spokesman" on policy and strategy against China and the Soviet Union. Webb quotes such a speech at length and notes that Satō "criticized the Cabinet and the Foreign Office for offering China peace conditions which were too mild."¹⁰⁰

Satō became chief of the Military Affairs Section of the Military Affairs Bureau and in that capacity, Webb relates, he either prepared or oversaw the preparation of a document dated November 11, 1941 which set "out the reason for Japan's determination to fight the United States and Great Britain." The document was adopted by the "pre-Liaison Conference of the War and Navy Ministries and the General Staff."¹⁰¹ Webb also quotes the speech that Satō made at the Army Day celebration on March 10, 1942 where Satō not only praised Japan's attack on the Allies without a declaration of war but also "went on to say that Japan had been preparing for a war to break out in 1941 or 1942, that throughout the China Incident sixty percent of the Budget was used for the purpose of preparing for this war whilst the remainder was used for the fighting in China."¹⁰²

On the basis of such evidence and factual findings Webb reaches conclusions much more specific, clear, and better grounded than those of the majority. Satō, he concludes, was not a "mere soldier or civil servant: he engaged in important political activities." Satō, Webb adds, not only learned of Japan's preparations and intention to go to war but was aware that these preparations "*were not based on the needs of self-defense*" (emphasis added). "Knowing this," Webb continues, "he still took an active part in these preparations, in shaping Japan's course for war, and in the waging of war in China and the Pacific."¹⁰³ While the majority relied on vague and inconsistent generalizations to find Satō liable under the grand conspiracy charge in Count 1 of the indictment, Webb systematically eschewed findings on Count 1 in all of his conclusions. In the case of Satō he found him specifically guilty of conspiring to wage war, and actually participating in the planning, initiating, and waging of war in China and the Pacific under specific counts of the indictment.

### 8.3.9    Shigemitsu

Like the conviction of Hirota, the conviction of Shigemitsu Mamoru, diplomat and ultimately foreign minister, has aroused controversy and charges of victor's justice. As in the case of Hirota, the majority judgment might appear

---

⁹⁹ TPJ 549. PX2238-A, T16094. See also Satō, *Tōjō Hideki to Taiheiyō senso*, 91.
¹⁰⁰ TPJ 550.
¹⁰¹ TPJ 551–2. For the draft memorandum, see PX1175, T10362–5.
¹⁰² TPJ 553. See PX849, T8414.
¹⁰³ TPJ 555.

## 8.3 Individual Factual Findings and Verdicts on Crimes against Peace 333

not to offer an adequate evidence-based analysis and reasoned decision on his liability. Webb's account on the other hand provides factual findings based upon evidence that formed the basis for his legal conclusion of responsibility. Webb first details Shigemitsu's role as ambassador to China and then turns to his actions as ambassador to the Soviet Union in 1936. In this capacity he met with the People's Commisar for Foreign Affairs on several occasions and made demands for the withdrawal of Soviet troops from the west bank of Lake Khasan, etc. On one such occasion he stated that, "Japan has the rights and obligations to Manchukuo to use force and make the Soviet troops evacuate."[104]

Shigemitsu's next posting, as Webb recounts, was to London as ambassador to Great Britain. Webb quotes from a series of telegrams that Shigemitsu sent after the outbreak of war in Europe, advising Tokyo on how to take advantage of the German conquest of European colonial powers. The majority judgment considers none of this evidence, but Webb quotes at length as support for his findings. Shigemitsu's telegram of August 5, 1940 conveys the importance of such evidence in assessing Shigemitsu's liability:

In order to establish our position in Greater East Asia, it would be necessary to consider measures for gaining the maximum benefits at the minimum loss by carrying them out at the direct expense of small nations (for example France and Portugal) (although indirectly it may turn out to be at the expense of Britain and America) and by avoiding conflict with other countries so as not to make many enemies at once but to dispose of them one by one.[105]

Roeling, as will be seen, portrays Shigemitsu as steadfastly a man who sought peace. The majority, on the other hand, do not discuss the evidence such as that examined by Webb. His draft judgment shows the importance of systematically weighing the evidence in order to demonstrate support for legal conclusions and to construct a reasoned decision that supports them. To reiterate, the purpose here is not to arrive at a conclusion about Shigemitsu's guilt or innocence but to point up the blatant differences between the judgments of Pal, Roeling, and the majority on the one hand and the draft judgment of Webb on the other. Only Webb, as we see, lives up to the core obligation of a judge in an international tribunal to base the ultimate decision upon a careful and impartial weighing of the evidence so as to arrive at sound factual findings to which the relevant legal norms may be applied.

Though Shigemitsu claimed that when he became foreign minister in April 1943 he did so in order to work for peace, Webb quotes his statement of September 27, 1943 on the Tripartite Pact: "The Pact of alliance shines forth as brightly as ever to illumine our road to victory ... It is well for us to renew

[104] TPJ 558. See PX754, T7763.
[105] TPJ 561. This quote is contained in PX1023, T9713.

our firm determination to prosecute the common war ... the spirit of Japan who is fighting in East Asia is the spirit of Germany and her allies fighting in Europe."[106] In a similar vein, Webb quotes Shigemitsu's statement in an article of December 12, 1944: "on December 11, 1944, the three nations, concluding a new treaty, firmly pledged themselves to fight out the common war until final victory."[107] Webb also quotes at length a statement by Shigemitsu of December 12, 1944 in which he extols Hitler as a hero who will save Europe and pledges that Japan will fight "to the last together with our allied countries at any cost."[108]

In arriving at legal conclusions based upon these factual findings Webb again adopts a balanced approach requiring the evidence to prove the charges beyond a reasonable doubt. Thus he does not find Shigemitsu guilty in regard to the charges on China or the USSR because, he reasons, in these cases Shigemitsu did not go beyond the duties required of him as ambassador in his negotiations and actions in regard to those countries. On the other hand, Webb concludes that because of the policy advice he gives the Japanese government on how to exploit the German victories in Europe, Shigemitsu "exceeded" these duties. Webb calls particular attention to Shigemitsu's suggestion *"to attack and plunder the small nations ... who had never threatened Japan"* (emphasis added). As to his role as foreign minister, on the basis of the evidence cited, Webb concludes that, "when Japan resorted to war he was as Foreign Minister a strong advocate of its continuance until final victory. He was responsible for waging war." On this basis Webb finds him guilty.[109]

### 8.3.10 Shimada

As discussed earlier, the majority conclude that Shimada, as navy minister in the Tōjō Cabinet, was a participant in the overarching conspiracy and they convict him, among other things, on Count 1, devoting only one sentence to justify this conclusion: "From the formation of the Tojo Cabinet ... until December 7, 1941 he took part in all decisions made by the conspirators in planning and launching that attack."[110] Webb, on the other hand, spends eight pages discussing Shimada's role in regard to policy matters and the conduct of the war in China and the Pacific. While the majority contents itself with noting that Shimada attended meetings, with no reference whatsoever to what he said or did at those meetings, Webb refers to much more specific evidence. For example, Webb states that, "Shimada admitted that he ... on 30 November 1941 ... joined with

---

[106] TPJ 561. See PX773, introduced at T7876. See pages 1–3 of the exhibit for the quoted passages.
[107] TPJ 561. See 828-A, extract from the *Nippon Times* issue of December 12, 1944, T8066.
[108] TPJ 562. For the quoted passage, see PX829-A, T8068.
[109] TPJ 567.
[110] MJ 619.

Nagano ... in advising the Emperor that the Japanese Navy's preparations for war against the United States and Great Britain were adequate and satisfactory."[111] While the majority cite only attendance at key meetings, Webb states that Shimada "also admitted that he, as Minister of the Navy and Minister of State, at the Imperial Conference on 1st December 1941, joined in making the final decision to wage war against the United States and Great Britain and their allies."[112]

It is not necessary to detail Webb's further discussion as the statements just quoted indicate the nature of the evidence on which Webb relied. Webb's lengthy discussion of the Navy's involvement in war crimes will be discussed in Chapter 10. On the basis of his findings, Webb concludes that, "Shimada, as Admiral, played a leading part in the war against China ... and as navy minister he voted for war in the Pacific, knowing that these wars were not in self-defence of Japan."[113] While the majority convict Shimada, among other counts, on the grand conspiracy charged in Count 1, Webb is again more specific, finding him guilty of conspiracy only on Count 4, the Pacific War, as well as substantive charges of waging war under other counts.

### 8.3.11 Tōgō

Webb's treatment of the charges against senior diplomat and Foreign Minister Tōgō is among the lengthiest, comprising some 23 pages. Tōgō was one of the civilian officials whom Roeling, in his dissent, had concluded should be acquitted because they worked for peace. Webb goes into great detail in his careful examination of the evidence against Tōgō to reach a very different conclusion.

In regard to Manchuria, Webb states that Tōgō supported the policy in regard to Manchukuo and the Soviet Union through his advice to the Ministry of Foreign Affairs. Tōgō, Webb recounts, also admitted that "the Russian danger had no relation to Japanese aggression in Manchuria; the Soviet Union was afraid of Japan and not Japan of the Soviet Union."[114]

---

[111] TPJ 569. See DX3565, Affidavit by Shimada Shigetarō (direct), T34667; and Testimony by Shimada Shigetarō, T34696–704.
[112] TPJ 569. DX3565, T34666.
[113] TPJ 577.
[114] TPJ 607–8. DX3609, Affidavit by Arita Hachirō, regarding a memorandum entitled, "On the Foreign Policy of Japan vis-à-vis Europe and America Following Withdrawal from the League of Nations," April 1933, prepared for Arita, then vice minister for Foreign Affairs, by Tōgō Shigenori, director of European and American Affairs Bureau, T35349. Webb is referring to those segments that are not read but to which the prosecution alerted the tribunal's attention during the summation. See T41873. For the relevant passages, see DX3609-A, memorandum entitled "On the Foreign Policy of Japan vis-à-vis Europe and America Following Withdrawal from the League of Nations," April 1933, pp. 15–24.

After Tōgō is appointed ambassador to Germany in October 1937, Webb details his important role in Japanese policy toward Germany and German support of Japan's activities in China. Tōgō told the German foreign minister on January 10, 1938 that although Japan desired peace with China it "was determined to carry on the war to its bitter end" and had decided to bypass Chang Kai-shek in its dealings with China unless he capitulated to all Japanese demands. He also made clear that Japan's ambitions extended "to the whole of China."[115]

The bulk of Webb's analysis of Tōgō's role, however, focuses on his conduct as foreign minister in the Tōjō Cabinet from October 1941. Webb details how various individuals, including Japanese ambassador to the United States, Admiral Nomura Kichisaburō, asked Tōjō why he was agreeing to join a war cabinet under Tōjō. Nomura himself had asked to be relieved of his post in Washington "because he did not want to continue deceiving other people and himself and resignation was the only way open for a man of honor." Tōgō, according to Webb, had no such compunctions.[116] Indeed, Webb devotes eight full pages to considering Tōgō's role in the November-December negotiations, analyzing in detail, for example, his communications with Nomura in Washington and others.[117] While Nomura made clear that he considered the risks for Japan to be too great if America entered the war, Tōgō opined that "Japan had been engaged in hostilities for four years and was not prepared to give up the fruits of these hostilities." Webb underlined this phrase to indicate its importance in his factual findings.[118]

As foreign minister at this critical juncture in the preparation for war, Tōgō was tasked with analyzing and reporting on crucial questions concerning the broader international prospects for Japan "assuming Japan would initiate war in the southern regions in autumn 1941." In regard to his role in the decision-making process about when to go to war Webb cites significant admissions

---

[115] TPJ 608–9. PX486-D, Telegram from Ambassador Trautman, Hankou, to Berlin, January 11, 1938, T5991. The relevant part in the exhibit contained an office memorandum by Foreign Minister von Neurath, part of which read as follows: "Mr. TOGO has explained on his side, that Japan wishes to work for peace cooperate [cooperation] with China and wishes conclusion of the hostilities as soon as possible. But, on the other hand, the Japanese Government is determined to carry on the war to its bitter end ... the Japanese Government no longer considers today Chiang Kai-shek as representative of the Chinese Central Government. Japan is still willing to negotiate with him. However, if he would not accept the Japanese peace conditions, the Japanese would make peace with each provincial governors. *To believe the military victory of China is a fantasia*" (emphasis added). T5991.

[116] TPJ 610. See PX1161, Telegram from Ambassador Nomura Kichisaburō in Washington, DC, to Foreign Minister Tōgō Shigenori, October 22, 1941, T10312–3; and PX2917, Telegram from Foreign Minister Tōgō Shigenori to Admiral Nomura Kichisaburō, the Japanese ambassador in Washington, DC, October 21, 1941, T25920.

[117] TPJ 612–20.

[118] TPJ 613. Tōgō made this remark during his conversation with Joseph Grew, the US ambassador in Tokyo. See PX2918, T25936–7; and T25925–37.

## 8.3 Individual Factual Findings and Verdicts on Crimes against Peace

made by Tōgō. Tōgō, he recounts, not only assented to the decision of the Liaison Conference of November 1 and the Imperial Conference of November 5, 1941 but he also "admitted that by refusing to agree to the decision for war and refusing to resign he could have made agreement impossible, bringing about the fall of the Cabinet."[119] Although at the November 1 meeting he counseled waiting until the United States had entered the war in Europe before initiating hostilities in the Pacific, Tōgō said he reserved his decision and would report his conclusion the next day. The conclusion he reached, however, was not for delay, but rather that "he was in no position to prove that Japan's military strength was insufficient" and he thus gave his agreement to the decision for war "on the morning of 2nd November."[120] After the final decision to go to war had been reached at the end of November, Webb recounts how Tōgō admitted that rather than give up her gains in China, "the only way open to Japan was the way of self-defense."[121] If the United States would not give in to Japan's demands in regard to China Tōgō stated "he could only agree that Japan must wage war."[122]

What appears in Webb's account, unlike that of the majority or the Roeling and Pal dissents, is that Tōgō, like Hirota and some other figures, expressed misgivings as to the timing for Japan's initiation of the Pacific War in 1941 but did not oppose that policy in principle. Whether they inwardly opposed and used the issue of timing as an excuse is legally irrelevant because whatever their intentions they wound up supporting the decision for war at the highest policymaking level. Webb's treatment demonstrates the importance of careful analysis of the available evidence as to what the accused actually said and did at all the important junctures related to each of the charges against them.

The discussion above has highlighted only key parts of the evidence Webb considered in his lengthy discussion of the evidence against Tōgō. The conclusions he reached on the basis of these findings flow from the evidence itself rather than from the kind of generalizations relied on by the majority. Tōgō, Webb concludes, "was foremost in advancing, influencing, and realizing Japan's remaining in virtual control of Manchuria and extending her

---

[119] TPJ 611. The following exchange between the prosecution and Tōgō is recorded in the transcripts. "Q [Prosecution]. The plain fact of the matter is, is it not, that if you have refused to resign and had refused to have joined in the decision for war affirmatively, the Cabinet would have had to fall on bloc, would it not? A [Tōgō]. Yes." (T36110). For Tōgō's explanation as to why he decided not to resign, see DX3647, T35708–10.
[120] TPJ 611. See DX3647, T35695–6.
[121] TPJ 621. Webb underlines this statement to emphasize its importance. This quote is actually a paraphrase that the prosecution provided during the summation at T41923. The original statement by Tōgō reads, "Japan was now asked not only to abandon all the gains of her years of sacrifice, but to surrender her international position as a power in the Far East. That surrender, as we saw it, would have amounted to national suicide. *The only way to face this challenge and defend ourselves was war*" (emphasis added) in DX3547, T35706.
[122] TPJ 621.

domination to the rest of China." In regard to the decision to go to war in 1941 Webb concludes that Tōgō joined the Tōjō Cabinet "knowing that it supported war; yet he did nothing to change its attitude. To retain the 'fruits of hostilities' in China' TOGO was fully prepared to fight the Western Powers. He voted for war against them, with full knowledge and after mature deliberation."

On this basis Webb finds Tōgō guilty in regard to the specific charges related to these events, while the majority also found him guilty under Count 1 of participation in the overarching conspiracy. In regard to evidentiary foundation and careful weighing of the evidence Webb's findings and conclusions stand in stark contrast not only to those of the majority but also to those of the dissenting opinions that portrayed Tōgō as a diplomat who desired only peace.

# 9 The Majority Judgment on War Crimes

## 9.1 Introduction

As noted in the preceding chapters, the IMT at Nuremberg had already addressed the major questions about the jurisdiction and authority of the tribunal. The IMTFE judgment thus broke little new ground on jurisdiction or on crimes against peace. In this light it is apparent that a consideration of the jurisprudential contribution of the IMTFE judgment must focus primarily upon the treatment of conventional war crimes. This chapter addresses how the majority judgment articulates and applies the legal standards for war crimes. As in the two previous chapters we assess the majority judgment based upon its treatment of the legal issues, the quality of the analysis of the evidence, and the application of the law to factual findings in a reasoned decision.

The judgment contains five main sources relevant to analysis of war crimes:

- Chapter II of the judgment, Section (b) Responsibility for War Crimes against Prisoners
- Chapter VIII of the judgment, *Conventional War Crimes*
- Chapter X of the judgment, Verdicts
- Judgment, Annex 6, Appendix D, *Incorporated in Group 3* (dealing with relevant articles of applicable international conventions)
- Judgment, Annex 6, Appendix E, Statement of Individual Responsibility

As indicated above, the judgment applies no clear legal analytical framework that is systematically articulated. On the whole, the judgment fails to discuss definitions or elements of war crimes offenses. Chapter II does provide a treatment of theories of liability, but as we will see, the theories articulated there are not rigorously applied, and are often not referred to in the verdicts or the discussion of particular offenses. Chapter VIII deals with "Conventional War Crimes," but most of the exposition is factual rather than legal, and in any event it is rarely analytical. Finally, it is often difficult to link the justification of the individual verdicts either to the analysis of patterns of war crimes in Chapter VIII or to the theories of liability expounded in Chapter II. The remainder of this section will proceed by examining first the legal framework articulated in

Chapter II and in the two appendices to Annex 6. Then we will analyze how and to what extent this legal framework is applied in Chapter VIII. Finally, examining the basis of the individual verdicts will, together with the discussion of Chapter VIII, provide the basis for determining what legal standards were actually applied to the facts to justify the verdicts against the individual accused.

## 9.2 Standards of Responsibility in Chapter II of the Judgment

One of the greatest challenges facing the judges at the IMTFE, and at WWII tribunals more generally, was to articulate the standards that would determine legal responsibility for the international crimes with which the defendants were charged. This challenge arises most acutely in the trial of high-level individuals where tribunals consider the modes of liability that link the accused to war crimes to which in many circumstances they had no direct connection. At Nuremberg the recovery by investigators of massive documentary evidence provided a basis for the direct connection of the accused to criminal policies and actions through their participation in the formulation of those policies or through implementation of the policies through orders and institutional mechanisms.

At Tokyo, on the other hand, where there was ample documentation on policymaking in regard to aggressive war, the prosecution faced greater challenges in documenting the role of each individual accused in regard to war crimes. This challenge was most forcefully felt in regard to the role of civilian members of the cabinet for crimes committed by military units against civilians and POW in far-flung theaters of war. While Chapter 7 focused on the way in which the majority judgment relied on the doctrine of conspiracy as the dominant mode of liability for crimes against peace, this strategy was not available to them in regard to war crimes. What theories of liability did the prosecution and majority judgment resort to in order to prove the critical linkage beyond reasonable doubt?

Although Chapter II(b) is entitled "Responsibility for War Crimes against Prisoners," it actually articulates a more general theory of liability which the judgment can be seen to apply to other war crimes as well. The treatment is abbreviated and compressed, however, taking up only two full pages of the judgment.[1] The essence of this theory is that it is the responsibility of "the Government" to ensure that duties under international conventions, such as

---

[1] See MJ 82–4. The abbreviated and compressed nature of the theory of liability in the majority judgment mirrors the one that the prosecution set out during the summation. See Chapter 6 under Section 6.5.

## 9.2 Standards of Responsibility in Chapter II of the Judgment

the 1907 Hague Conventions, are effectively carried out.[2] Having followed Nuremberg in denying the legitimacy of the Act of State doctrine, the tribunal thus reasons that the duties that reside in the "Government" as a collective entity must be carried out by "persons."[3] Those persons, in turn, may be held individually and criminally accountable for the actions of their government that violate international law. Of the thousands of persons who constitute a government and its institutions, who should be the object of judicial scrutiny and what standards of responsibility should direct that scrutiny?

As the judgment states in a key passage, the individuals responsible for carrying out these international duties "are those persons who direct and control the functions of Government." Who, then, in the case of Imperial Japan, were the individuals who were vested with exercising such control and direction? The tribunal's response was that, "In this case and in the above regard we are concerned with the members of the Japanese Cabinet."[4]

As previous chapters indicated, the prosecution in the course of making its case had established a much more complex picture of what bodies and individuals directed and controlled "the functions of Government." The statement that the cabinet is the sole focal point of authority grossly oversimplifies the dynamics of policy formation. Indeed, Part I has demonstrated the difficulties faced by the prosecution in analyzing the shifting dynamics of de iure and de facto authority as they evolved from 1928 to 1945. Apart from its other shortcomings the judgment's standard fails to mention the ultimate source of political authority in Japan, Emperor Hirohito, as Webb's draft judgment indicates. As emphasized in Chapter 7, it is a striking failure of the majority judgment not to provide an accurate and detailed analysis of the structures of authority in Japan in the period of 1931–45 and locate each individual accused within those structures.

Leaving that matter aside for the moment, the tribunal here is applying the theory of individual responsibility, first articulated at Nuremberg, which holds that "States" as abstractions are not responsible under international law but rather the individuals who exercise control in those states. As the Tokyo judgment eloquently puts it: "The duty to prisoners is not a meaningless obligation cast upon a political abstraction. It is a specific duty to be performed in the first case by those who constitute the Government."[5] Having stated that the cabinet is the relevant organ that possesses such authority, the judgment qualifies that statement by expanding the scope of potential responsibility of echelons far below the cabinet level. Rather than considering the role of other

---

[2] MJ 82.
[3] Ibid.
[4] Ibid.
[5] Ibid.

policy-level bodies, or the roles of the Army and Navy General Staffs, the Privy Council, and so on, the judgment focuses responsibility downward rather than upward in regard to the treatment of POW. The judgment thus further defines those who "constitute the Government" by identifying four categories of individuals bearing responsibility for prisoners by virtue of their positions:

1. Members of the Government
2. Military or Naval Officers in command of formations having prisoners In their possession
3. Officials in those departments which were concerned with the wellbeing of prisoners.
4. Officials, whether civilian, military, or naval, having direct and Immediate control of prisoners.[6]

It seems apparent that the principal criterion that distinguishes the cabinet from the other three groups is that all three have a direct connection to the treatment of POW. The cabinet, on the face of it, might have no such connection because it is a largely civilian body that might have had no role in determining policies or making decisions as to treatment of POW. The connection of the cabinet to POW mistreatment must be established beyond reasonable doubt by the prosecution and the judges must articulate the standard that in the absence of explicit policy formulation or decision making can link the cabinet to the mistreatment sufficiently to satisfy the requirements for criminal liability.

What standard then does the majority judgment articulate and how do they in fact apply it? Having defined these four groups of responsible individuals, the judgment delineates the basis on which they may be held liable for failing to fulfill their duty to "secure proper treatment of prisoners" and to prevent their ill-treatment by "establishing and securing the continuous and efficient working of a system appropriate for these purposes."[7] The conditions for liability, or, to put it in a more contemporary terminology, the elements of the offense with which such individuals might be charged, appear to include:

- A duty, by virtue of holding an office in the four categories defined above, to secure proper treatment of POWs.
- Failure to establish a proper and effective system to prevent ill-treatment of POWs.
- Or, having established such a system, failure to secure its continued and "efficient working."
- Knowledge that ill-treatment was occurring and failing "to take such steps as were within their power to prevent the commission of such crimes in the

---

[6] MJ 82–3.
[7] MJ 83.

## 9.2 Standards of Responsibility in Chapter II of the Judgment 343

future."[8] The subsequent paragraph makes clear that such knowledge may be imputed.
- In the absence of such knowledge, "fault in having failed to acquire" it. The following sentence makes clear that "fault" should be understood, in a legal sense, as negligence.[9]

It is apparent here that criminal liability is primarily based upon omissions rather than upon criminal conduct. All of these standards involve a failure to act, a failure to prevent, or a culpable failure to acquire knowledge.

In other words, individuals, civilian or military, who hold certain military or governmental positions are primarily held liable for their failure to ensure protection of POW rather than for instigating, committing, ordering, or aiding and abetting criminal acts against them. This focus is presumably because of the lack of evidence that directly connected the accused to the commission of the crimes against POW through one of the conventional modes of liability just mentioned: instigating, committing, ordering, or aiding and abetting. The language of "failure to prevent" invokes the doctrine of what in WWII was termed "command responsibility" and today is often referred to as "superior responsibility." Despite the highly influential body of jurisprudence developed in the Nuremberg subsequent proceedings on command responsibility it is interesting that the majority judgment does not formulate the categories of conduct listed above under that conceptual rubric. If the judgment had done so it would have provided greater conceptual clarity as to the legal standard by which the accused were being held to account.

There are a number of issues raised by the five criteria listed above that require elaboration. The first is that the duty to protect POW appears to devolve upon *all* individuals who hold certain formal positions in the government regardless of their actual functions, authority, or activities. All individuals in the enumerated categories are liable for a failure to fulfill this duty if they (1) hold a certain position, (2) are aware of ill-treatment or are negligent in not acquiring such awareness, (3) do not take such steps *as were within their power* to prevent the ill-treatment. The italicized phrase "as were within their power" is crucial, for it is only this qualification which prevents liability from attaching when an individual was powerless to attempt to exert any influence over the ill-treatment.[10] While this provision appears at first glance to prevent an individual from being convicted for ill-treatment of prisoners when they had no role in that ill-treatment and no capacity to prevent it, the actual situation proved to be more complicated.

---

[8] Ibid.
[9] Ibid.
[10] This would be like the "strict liability" standard that was applied to General Yamashita at his trial in Manila in 1945. See Totani, *Justice in Asia and the Pacific Region, 1945–1952*, chapter 1.

Having set out these five criteria, the judgment makes a crucial qualification of the way that they should be applied to the four categories of officials. This qualification is significant, because it provides the basis upon which accused persons such as Hirota were convicted for war crimes in addition to crimes against peace. The judgment returns to the premise noted earlier that it is the Japanese cabinet that "direct(s) and control(s) the function of government."[11] Using this premise to consider the issue of liability for members of the cabinet for ill-treatment of prisoners, the judgment states,

> A member of a Cabinet, which *collectively,* as one of the principal organs of the Government, *is responsible* for the care of prisoners, is not absolved from responsibility if, having knowledge of the commission of the crimes in the sense already discussed, and omitting or failing to secure the taking of measures to prevent the commission of such crimes in the future, he elects to continue as a member of the Cabinet. This is the position, *even though the Department of which he has charge is not directly concerned with the care of prisoners*. A Cabinet member may resign. If he has knowledge of ill-treatment of prisoners, *is powerless to prevent* future ill-treatment, but elects to remain in the Cabinet thereby continuing to participate in *its collective responsibility* for protection of prisoners he willingly assumes responsibility for any ill-treatment in the future.[12] (emphasis added)

The responsibility of cabinet members is thus distinct from the other categories of actors. While the elements elaborated above only require individuals charged with a duty toward prisoners to take such steps as are in "their power," a cabinet member is required "to secure the taking of measures." In other words, if a cabinet member does everything within his power to prevent ill-treatment but the measures are ineffective, he must resign or will incur criminal liability. Thus, even where the cabinet member is factually "powerless to prevent future ill-treatment" of POW he incurs criminal liability by remaining in the cabinet.

The discussion of the prosecution's case on the structure of authority in the Japanese government in previous chapters made clear, however, that it is far from clear that the cabinet was the organ that possessed the authority to oversee the treatment of POW. The judgment does not provide an analysis of evidence that the cabinet in fact did have such authority, but rather simply states that they will treat the cabinet as "the Government" for the purposes of managing the POW system. Since in fact cabinet members did not have the power *in that specific capacity* to prevent crimes by ordering that they cease, the entire cabinet would have no option but to resign upon receiving credible information that crimes were being committed. This would hardly appear to be a realistic

---

[11] MJ 82.
[12] MJ 83–4. Note that this passage acknowledges other "principal organs of government" but fails to specify them or to indicate why they do not also bear responsibility for the treatment of POW.

standard for the conduct of a government and raises the issue of who in fact had ultimate authority to determine the treatment of POW.

In regard to the other three categories of military officers and civilian officials, they could only be held liable if they had the requisite knowledge and the power to prevent the crimes, or were negligent in not acquiring such knowledge. This presumably implies that they were in a position where such knowledge was available to them if they fulfilled their duty to protect POW. This distinctive standard of accountability for the civilian cabinet we may term, for the sake of convenience, "cabinet responsibility." We use this term because the majority judgment fails to predicate the responsibility of cabinet members on the most essential element of command responsibility: The prosecution must prove beyond a reasonable doubt that those committing the crimes are the *subordinates* of the accused.

The Japanese cabinet did not in fact have authority in the chain of command, which may explain why the judgment scrupulously avoids referencing the doctrine of "command responsibility" as applied by US military commissions in the Yamashita and Honma cases and in the Nuremberg subsequent proceedings. The distinct scope of liability the majority applies to the cabinet appears clearly from the contrast with their treatment of military commanders, where they explicitly invoke the doctrine of command responsibility. In regard to army and navy commanders the majority judgment holds that, "If ... it be shown that within the units under his command conventional war crimes have been committed ... a commander who takes no steps to prevent the occurrences of such crimes in the future will be responsible for such future crimes."[13]

The IMT Nuremberg judgment does not explicitly address the issue of whether a government official must resign to avoid liability where he or she does not have the power to change or reverse a policy. This issue did not arise because the IMT predicated liability primarily upon de facto participation in policy formulation and decision making, the issuance of criminal orders, and the implementation of criminal policies and orders. This issue did arise, however, in the Nuremberg subsequent proceedings in regard to officials below the cabinet level.

In one of the subsequent proceedings, the treatment of Ernst von Weizsaecker in the Ministries Case, is instructive because it points up a fundamental failing in the majority judgment in justifying the standard it applies in regard to the cabinet.[14] Von Weiszaecker was *Staatssekretaer (Secretary of State)* in the foreign ministry directly under von Ribbentrop, the foreign minister who was sentenced to death by the IMT. As to the mass shootings of the Einsatzgruppen

---

[13] MJ 84.
[14] *US v. Ernst von Weiszaecker et al.* (The Ministries Case).

in the East, although von Weizsaecker had initialed reports which showed that he knew of these mass shootings, the Foreign Office was not in any way connected to their implementation. Here, the tribunal found, von Weizsaecker had to be acquitted, because although there was knowledge, there was no participation. As to the deportation of Jews and others to the killing centers in Poland, the matter was different. Von Weizsaecker argued that the Foreign Office had neither initiated nor executed these policies, nor could they have prevented their implementation. The court found, however, that where von Weizsaecker both knew of the policy and made a substantial contribution to its implementation, he was responsible for crimes against humanity and war crimes because he did not resign. Where his contribution was slight, he was not to be held accountable.[15]

Beyond the duty to resign even where there is no authority to prevent crimes from being committed, what is particularly troubling about the holding of the IMTFE judgment, however, is its explicit statement that the liability of the cabinet is "collective." That is, all members of the cabinet are responsible for all acts of mistreatment of prisoners of which they aware, and for the failure to ensure a properly functioning system of protection, regardless of the nature of their function or portfolio in the cabinet. The cabinet is treated as a collective entity of government, with all members responsible for any ill-treatment of which they become aware regardless of whether their de iure position or de facto authority enables them to have any influence over those who are responsible for, or might prevent, that mistreatment.[16] This is a far different standard than that applied in Nuremberg both at the IMT and the subsequent proceedings.

Having set out the distinctive and collective liability for the cabinet, the judgment then considers the other enumerated groups of persons with responsibility for prisoners. In regard to army and navy commanders, the judges do not appear to consider the situation where a commander might be powerless to prevent the occurrence of ill-treatment. The judgment simply states that army or navy commanders can, "by order, secure proper treatment and prevent ill-treatment of prisoners. So can army and navy ministers. If crimes are committed against prisoners *under their control* ... they are responsible for those crimes"[17] (emphasis added). It is not clear here whether army and navy ministers are being held to a stricter standard than other cabinet members. Does the phrase "under their control" refer to de iure control or de facto? It is also not

---

[15] Ministries Case, 497–8.
[16] As Chapter 7 on the judgment's treatment of crimes against peace indicates, that section of the judgment itself makes clear that civilian cabinet members were in no position to substantially influence the policies of the military let alone prevent them from carrying out courses of action in which they had decided.
[17] MJ 84.

## 9.2 Standards of Responsibility in Chapter II of the Judgment 347

clear whether the "duty to resign" standard applies only to ministers or to other army and navy commanders as well. As mentioned earlier, for the doctrine of command responsibility articulated in the High Command Case and in contemporary tribunals the relevant issue is whether the individuals committing the crimes were under the effective (i.e. actual de facto as opposed to de iure) control of the accused commander. For the IMTFE the question is whether the POW were under the hierarchical control of the accused without any inquiry as to whether they were actually in a position to prevent the crimes.[18]

The final paragraph of Section (b) considers other government officials ("Departmental Officials") below the cabinet level. Here the tribunal holds that such officials are not responsible through a failure to resign. They immediately qualify this statement, however, in a manner which leaves some confusion as to what the judgment intends: "[B]ut if their functions included the administration of the system of protection of prisoners, and if they had or should have had knowledge of crimes and did nothing effective, to the extent of their powers, to prevent their occurrence in the future then they are responsible for such crimes."[19] This standard applies to such officials whether they actually had knowledge (imputed or otherwise) or were reckless or negligent ("should have had knowledge" is ambiguous in this regard) in not acquiring such knowledge. It also requires that the action required of such officials be "effective" in preventing such crimes from being committed in the future, but adds that this effectiveness is qualified by "The extent of their powers." This seems to imply that if they had knowledge of the crimes and no authority to prevent them they would not have to do anything "effective" to do so. What, then, were they required to do?

Two things are not entirely clear here. First, since all of the four enumerated groups were defined as those who bear "responsibility for prisoners," and since group (3) was defined as "Officials in those departments which were concerned with the wellbeing of prisoners," what group is subject to the exemption from the duty to resign? Does the judgment mean officials in departments that do not have responsibility for prisoners as defined by the four groups? Or does it mean officials within those departments responsible for prisoners, whose

---

[18] The High Command Case also considered in a far more nuanced analysis the case of the liability of the commander of an army or army group who knows that mass murder is being committed *by security forces not under his command.* They held, inter alia, that only the commander of occupied territory incurs such liability because he possesses a special duty under international law to protect the civilian population under the occupation over which he has authority. See High Command Case, 544–9.

[19] MJ 84. Note that the explicit qualification of "to the extent of their powers" suggest that in regard to military commanders the majority simply assumes they have such authority by virtue of their position. Under chaotic conditions prevailing in the last phases of the war, for example, this assumption might be of questionable validity. See, e.g. of Lieutenant General Baba (NAA A471 81631 Parts A and B) discussed in Cohen, "Military Justice from WWII to Guantanamo."

individual functions do not relate to prisoners? Further, does the duty to resign extend to those officials defined by the clause beginning, "But if their functions included administration of the system"? The judgment only says that they are responsible, but does not state that they can escape this responsibility only by resigning. It also does not make clear what actions are required of them to escape liability where they do not have clear authority to prevent the reoccurrence of such crimes.

To sum up this discussion of the applicable legal standards in Chapter II, a few points deserve emphasis. First, liability for war crimes involving prisoners is defined through breach of an affirmative duty arising from the relevant provisions of the Hague (1907) and Geneva (1929) Conventions.[20] The crime of which the defendants at Tokyo are accused is breach of that duty to ensure the proper treatment of prisoners and the failure to prevent ill-treatment.

Second, the standard to which the accused are held extends to both knowledge and negligence. That is, in a situation in which they had no knowledge of the crimes, or knowledge of conduct sufficient to put them on inquiry notice, they are nonetheless liable if they can be found negligent in not acquiring that information.[21] Third, the judgment places great emphasis upon the position which the person held rather than the scope and nature of their actual functions and authority. That is, unlike the contemporary jurisprudence on this issue, the emphasis is on their *de iure* rather than their *de facto* position.[22] This is particularly true in regard to the cabinet, where responsibility is held to be collective rather than individual.

It may be here that the tribunal was influenced by the document setting out the prosecution's position on individual responsibility (Appendix E of the indictment and Annex 6 to the judgment).[23] On the one hand, that document begins by stating that the defendants are charged "with using the power and prestige" of their positions and their "personal influence" to promote and carry out the crimes with which they are charged. On the other hand, in the specifications to the grounds of individual responsibility of each of the accused, in most instances there is simply an enumeration of the offices or positions they held.

---

[20] Appendix 6 to Annex D of the judgment specifies all of the relevant sections and the duties that arise under them.

[21] As the judgment puts it, "If, such a person had, or should, but for negligence or supineness, have had such knowledge he is not excused for inaction" (MJ 83).

[22] The cases at the ICTY and ICTR dealing with the responsibility of military commanders and civilian superiors have consistently held that it is their de facto authority that is decisive. This is captured in the required element of this mode of liability (under Article 6(3) of the ICTR Statute and Article 7(3) of the ICTY Statute) that a commander or superior must actually have "*effective*" control" of the subordinates who commit the crime. See Celebici Appeals Judgment supra note 13.

[23] Annex E is discussed in Chapter 5.

## 9.3 Standards of Responsibility and Factual Findings in Chapter VIII

Having explored the way the IMTFE defines the body of law it intends to apply to conventional war crimes, one must next look to see how the judgment actually justifies its legal conclusions in Chapter VIII, "Conventional War Crimes," Chapter IX, "Findings on Counts of the Indictment," and Chapter X, "Verdicts." In particular, we will compare the discussion of categories of crimes in Chapter VIII with the verdicts on individuals in Chapter X.

Such comparison is necessary because, as the judgment itself explains, the narrative of the occurrences of conventional war crimes only refers to the roles or acts of the individuals accused *"where it may be convenient."*[24] Indeed, the judgment goes on to state that in some cases it may be "convenient" to consider the role of individuals, in other cases "and generally, as far as it is practicable, circumstances having relevance to the issue of responsibility will be dealt with later."[25] In fact, in regard to most of the accused, those issues are not "dealt with later." They are treated only in the most cursory manner, if at all. Again, one must question why issues of "practicability" limit the most important analysis required of the judgment, which is the analysis of the evidence indicating that the prosecution has proved its case beyond a reasonable doubt against each individual. This is particularly the case in regard to war crimes, where the tribunal is not applying a conspiracy theory that connects all of the accused, as was the case in regard to crimes against peace. The rather cavalier manner in which the majority disposes of this issue of fundamental importance is indicative of their willingness to see the accused in collective terms. It cannot be emphasized enough that "convenience" and "practicability" are not excuses for the failure to consider the requirements of proof for each individual before the court.

In fact, nowhere in the judgment is there a systematic analysis of the conduct of each accused or consideration of the defense case on war crimes.[26] As in the case of crimes against peace this is one of the most significant shortcomings of the judgment from the perspective of judicial best practices on providing a reasoned final decision. Although the IMT adopted a similar strategy they nonetheless provided a far more substantive treatment of each individual accused than did the IMTFE majority. The extent and importance of these shortcomings is amply demonstrated by the treatment of war crimes in Webb's draft judgment, considered in the next chapter.

---

[24] MJ 531.
[25] Ibid.
[26] Justice Northcroft, for example, was assigned by the majority to deal with the Pacific War. In a memorandum of January 20, 1948, he strikingly notes that in preparing that case he relied "upon the case tendered by the prosecution without consideration of the defence" (AWM 3DRL 2481).

In the first sentence of Chapter VIII the judgment notes that because of the mass of evidence heard on conventional war crimes it is "not practicable" to provide a complete statement of the atrocities on which the tribunal heard evidence.[27] Given that they had already devoted more than 400 pages to a similarly massive body of evidence on crimes against peace one may question this justification for the brevity of their treatment. What strategy, then, does the IMTFE adopt in order to make factual findings on war crimes that may ground the verdicts against the accused? In the second paragraph of Chapter VIII the judgment states that,

> During a period of several months, the tribunal heard evidence, orally or by affidavit, from witnesses who testified in detail to atrocities committed in all theaters of war on a scale so vast, yet following so common a pattern in all theaters, that *only one conclusion is possible – the atrocities were either secretly ordered or willfully permitted* by the Japanese Government or individual members thereof and by the leaders of the armed forces.[28] (emphasis added)

This statement is of fundamental importance in the judgment. It provides the actual basis on which the accused persons are linked to the vast number of crimes on which the tribunal heard evidence. Such a theory of liability is crucially important because much, if not most, of the evidence referenced in the judgment on specific atrocities never mentions names of high-level accused. A person testifying to mass rape in the Philippines, mistreatment of prisoners or civilian detainees on the Death Railway or Sandakan Death Marches would likely have never seen or perhaps heard of most of the accused and would not be able to provide evidence that linked them to the particular criminal acts to which they were testifying. In the absence of orders, minutes of policy decisions, reports of field commanders, or other documentary evidence, the linkage of high-level officials to such crimes would have to be inferred by other means.[29]

Several points deserve emphasis here. First, the statement that the criminal acts were ordered or permitted by "the Japanese Government or individual members thereof" seems to follow from the framework laid out in Chapter II. That is, the "Government" is treated as a collectivity and all of the high-level accused were "individual members thereof." Chapter VII does not specify exactly what is meant by the "Government." Although Chapter II of the judgment identifies the cabinet as the embodiment of "the Government," the

---

[27] MJ 531.
[28] Ibid.
[29] Roeling argued that a pattern cannot be inferred from crimes that are permitted rather than ordered, but his reasoning on this point is far from clear. Memorandum of August 23, 1948 NAA M1417/1 28 p. 1.

individual verdicts as well as some of the language of Chapter VII itself, reveal that liability of members of the government extends beyond the cabinet.

As seen in previous chapters, the prosecution had presented a much more complex view of the decision-making structures that collectively constituted the "Government." Further, unlike the four groups enumerated in Chapter II, the judgment here mentions three groups: the "Government" as a collectivity, individual members of the "government," and "leaders" of the army and navy. The description here differs significantly from the treatment in Chapter II. This incoherence about the nature of the Japanese policymaking structures is troubling because it is an issue of central importance in determining the responsibility of the individual accused who participated in the key institutions. Treating them as a collectivity of course also obscures individual roles and makes it easier to justify conviction.

There is also an apparent difference in the treatment of the "Government" here. Chapter II of the judgment grounded the liability of members of the government upon their duty under the Hague and Geneva Conventions to establish and maintain a system that would prevent mistreatment of prisoners. The basis of liability was therefore a breach of that duty, whether knowing, reckless, or negligent. In Chapter VIII, on the other hand, the judgment states that the members of the government may be held liable because they either "secretly ordered or *willfully* permitted" the atrocities which the judgment then proceeds to enumerate[30] (emphasis added). The phrase "willfully permitted" implies that they both had knowledge of the crimes or of the likelihood of their occurrence and intended (not just "permitted" but "*willfully* permitted") in some manner that such crimes would be committed. Such knowledge is not required under the breach of duty standard. Exactly what is meant either by "permitted" or "willfully permitted" is never specified.

There is thus an apparent contradiction here between Chapters II and VIII in regard to conventional war crimes. On the one hand, Chapter VIII infers from the vast scale and common pattern of the crimes that the "Government" must have either ordered the crimes or known that they were occurring and deliberately allowed them to continue. The term "secretly" reveals that there is no actual *evidence* that the crimes were actually ordered, but rather that the widespread nature of the crimes indicates that they *might have been*. In other words, it is the *pattern and scale* that the judgment invokes to link the crimes

---

[30] MJ 531. The way that the judgment sometimes treats the "Government" as a collectivity and might thereby obscure the individual roles of the various accused is shown, for example, in the discussion of the Death Railway, where the tribunal refers to the evidence establishing, "that the Government had knowledge of the casualties and failed to remedy these conditions" (MJ 556). Roeling, on the other hand, suggested to the majority that they add much more specific detail on war crimes, for example on the Death Railway, including rebutting defense argument. See, e.g. his memorandum to the judges of August 23, 1948 NAA M1417/1 28 pp. 13–16.

to the individual accused under the vague rubric of the "Government."[31] In Chapter II, on the other hand, because the accused in the four enumerated categories had an affirmative duty to prevent mistreatment of prisoners, they are liable for such mistreatment when they knew or merely should have known that it was occurring (i.e. they could be held liable when they were not, in fact, aware but should have been). "Deliberately ordering" and a common pattern would be irrelevant to a determination under these latter criteria. Lest one think that the distinction lies in the fact that the relevant parts of Chapter II deal with prisoners, Chapter VIII for the most part indiscriminately describes atrocities perpetrated against prisoners, civilian internees, and civilian nationals of occupied countries. There is no explanation in the judgment about how these two chapters should be read together or why these two quite different theories of liability have been developed for treating conventional war crimes.

Another feature of the standard set out at the beginning of Chapter VIII is even more curious. The judgment's phrase "a scale so vast, yet following so common a pattern that only one conclusion is possible – the atrocities were either secretly ordered or willfully permitted" follows a similar finding made by the US military commission in Manila in its judgment against General Yamashita (as discussed in Chapter 5). In the words of the military commission, "the prosecution presented evidence to show that the crimes were so extensive and widespread, both as to time and area, that they must either have been *willfully permitted* by the accused, *or secretly ordered* by" him[32] (emphasis added).

As in the Yamashita Case, such a standard is puzzling in a number of respects. First, to infer that crimes were *"secretly ordered"* because of their extent and commonality is clearly not, in terms of logic or common sense, the *"only one conclusion ... possible"*[33] (emphasis added). The fact that the judgment must *presume* that the accused might have *"secretly* ordered" the criminal conduct is because no such orders, or evidence of the existence of such orders, had been found, despite intensive investigation by the prosecution. From the very fact that no such orders were found the inference is drawn that they therefore

---

[31] In memoranda of December 3 and 4, 1946 (AWM 3DRL 2481) Justice Northcroft suggests this strategy if the prosecution cannot provide "the necessary evidence to link the defendants with the atrocity allegations." The next day Northcroft writes again and notes that the prosecution may rely on evidence of widespread crimes, which could provide the basis of an inference for breach of a duty by the "Commanders-in-Chief and by the Government of Japan."

[32] Decision of the Military Commission in *US* v. *Yamashita*. As the dissenting opinions in the Supreme Court review of Yamashita's *habeas corpus* petition, noted, the charge itself was vague and incoherent, and the basis of liability in the mere fact of the widespread nature of the crimes did not make clear what, if any, was the connection of the conduct of the accused to the crimes committed by Japanese troops. See, e.g. Rutledge dissenting, In Re Yamashita, 327 US 1, 52–3 and fn. 17.

[33] MJ 531.

9.3 Standards of Responsibility and Factual Findings in Chapter VIII   353

existed but must have been secret.[34] On the other hand, the reason that no such orders can be shown to link the accused to the thousands of atrocities charged could arise from other factors, such as common programs of training, military culture, or indiscipline in certain contexts. Indeed, the whole notion of a "pattern" is inadequately analyzed by the judgment.

Judges such as Mei Ruao, Delfin Jaranilla, and B. V. A. Roeling provided the majority with a detailed analysis of specific evidence. Roeling wrote extensive and detailed memoranda with explicit references to exhibits and statements, for example, from which an explicit policy of authorizing the killing of POW could be inferred.[35] Although these judges urged the incorporation of this evidence, the majority judgment, puzzlingly, did not incorporate these suggested additions on war crimes.

For example, the judgment lists more than a hundred massacres simply by the enumeration of the geographical location and the approximate date. The conclusion drawn as to the common pattern in these massacres relies on the following reasoning: "There is a similarity of method to be found in most of the massacres. The victims were first bound and then shot, bayoneted, or decapitated by swords." Since rifles and bayonets were the standard weapons in the possession of Japanese infantry, and swords in the case of officers, this "similarity" is hardly surprising and is hardly sufficient to give rise to an inference that such events must have been "secretly ordered" by the accused. Indeed, the very fact that there is such variation in the manner of execution also permits an inference that there was no unifying order or policy from the central authorities as to such executions.[36]

The judgment tacitly admits that there was no uniformity in the perpetration of massacres, for following the passage just quoted it continues by noting that, "In some places, "even more dreadful methods were employed." A number of examples of such methods are given, such as killing groups of victims by burning, explosives, machine guns, or drowning.[37] Again, this hardly supports the conclusion of a pattern of criminal conduct so similar in the details of its

---

[34] The judgment refers to a few instances where policy orders regarding prisoners were issued and stamped "Secret." The treatment of orders in wartime as "secret" is routine in most armed forces and this sense of "secret" is quite different that that referred to by the judgment in the passage discussed above. In the former sense, "secret" orders are routinely filed and would be discoverable as part of a war crimes investigation. In the passage referring to the accused having "secretly ordered" the crimes, on the other hand, the meaning is rather orders to which no reference or evidence has been found so one must infer that that they secretly existed.

[35] See in general his lengthy memoranda of January 23 (NAA M1417 25), February 5 (NAA M1417 28), and August 23 (NAA M1417 28) 1948, and on the point of the policy on POW, memorandum of February 5 pp. 9–12 and memorandum of January 23 pp. 69–100. See also the following footnote 44 below on Jaranilla.

[36] The defense disputed the validity of the charge of "similarly patterned" war crimes, as discussed in Chapter 6 under Section 6.1.

[37] MJ 545–9.

execution in disparate times and places so as to justify an inference that it must have been "secretly ordered" by the accused. We must also recall that the inference must be established beyond a reasonable doubt, a standard of proof rarely referenced in the judgment. In regard to such inferences, as discussed earlier, reasonable doubt should be understood to mean that there is only one plausible inference to be drawn which is hardly the case in regard to the patterns of atrocities considered by the judgment.[38]

Perhaps the somewhat more plausible case where such inferences from a common pattern might be justified is found in the judgment's treatment of torture by the Kenpeitai (military police force). The judgment finds that, "Methods of torture were employed in all areas so uniformly as to indicate policy both in training and in execution."[39] The judgment relies principally upon showing that certain kinds of torture (water torture, suspension, electric shock, etc.) were used in many places where the Kenpeitai operated. The judgment reasons that, "The Kempeitai were administered by the War Ministry. A Kempeitai training school was maintained and ordered by the War Ministry in Japan. It is a reasonable inference that the conduct of the Kempeitai and the camp guards reflected the policy of the War Ministry."[40] This is a far better reasoned account of a common pattern than that provided in regard to the methods by which massacres were perpetrated. Even here, however, it is not clear that the inference of common training in interrogation methods for Kenpeitai recruits can be imputed without documentation or reasoned argument to an actual policy at the level of the Ministry of the Army let alone the cabinet or the "Government."[41]

Apart from "secretly ordering," the other theory of liability articulated by the judgment is that the crimes were so widespread that they must have been "willfully permitted" by the accused. "Willfully permitting" is not an established theory of liability in the criminal law. One of the dissenting opinions in

---

[38] The institution of forced prostitution euphemistically referred to as the "comfort women" system would have seemed to have furnished an excellent example of a systematic practice and pattern indicating official policy and acquiescence. This was not brought forward by the majority despite evidence in the Dutch and Chinese prosecution cases on war crimes. See, for instance, Justice Mei's memorandum of August 24, 1948, recounting that during the occupation of Guiilin the Japanese forces engaged not only in rape but, "They recruited woman labour on the pretext of establishing factories. They forced the women thus recruited into prostitution with Japanese troops." (NAA M1417/1 28 p. 2). The evidence that Justice Mei referred to is PX353, Statement by nine Guilin citizens, T4654–5. This exhibit describes how the Japanese occupation authorities in Guilin in the last year of the war falsely advertised the establishment of factories and recruited woman labor. The statement read that the women thus assembled were forced into "prostitution for the Japanese troops."

[39] MJ 557–60.

[40] MJ 557. The prosecution argued during the summation that the similarity of Kenpeitai torture must have resulted from the type of training they receive. See note 13 in Chapter 6.

[41] See the memorandum of Justice Bernard to Webb and the other judges of August 31, 1948 where Bernard makes the point that the evidence does not show that the training encompassed the treatment of POW. M1417/1 28 p. 3.

the US Supreme Court review of Yamashita's *habeas corpus* petition focused on the vagueness of the term "permitting":

> At the most, "permitting" could charge knowledge only by inference or implication. And, reasonably, the word could be taken in the context of the charge to mean "allowing" or "not preventing" – a meaning consistent with absence of knowledge and mere failure to discover. In capital cases, such ambiguity is wholly out of place.[42]

Willfully allowing or not preventing implies knowledge that the acts were occurring, or also points to the conscious and deliberate (in legal terms "reckless") disregard of the risk that they might occur. As we have seen, however, the judgment does not restrict the scope of liability to knowledge or recklessness, but also includes, at least in the case of crimes against prisoners, the failure to acquire such knowledge in the absence of any awareness of a risk. This is a negligence standard based upon an affirmative duty to acquire such knowledge by ensuring a system for the enforcement of the protections of the laws of war. From the unsystematic references to the accused in the course of the review of war crimes in Chapter VIII, it is impossible to tell which standard the tribunal actually used, or whether it applied one standard uniformly. Accordingly, we must turn to the verdicts against the individual accused in an attempt identify the basis of liability and to determine to what extent it follows the standard articulated in Chapter II.[43] As will be seen, the tribunalin consistently applies the standards set out in Chapter II and fails to connect the factual findings of Chapter VIII to the individual verdicts.[44]

## 9.4 Standards of Responsibility in the Individual Verdicts

It may be useful to consider first several military commanders convicted by the IMTFE of war crimes and then compare their treatment to the civilian accused. This manner of proceeding is relevant for consideration of the jurisprudential

---

[42] In Re Yamashita, 327 US 1, Rutledge dissenting opinion fn. 17.
[43] One might expect that Chapter IX, "Findings on Counts of the Indictment" would provide relevant information, but it does not. The entire findings on war crimes, however, consist of the following passage: "Count 54 charges ordering, authorizing, and permitting the commission of Conventional War Crimes. Count 55 charges failure to take adequate steps to secure the observance and prevent breaches of conventions and laws of war in respect of prisoners and civilian internees. We find that there have been cases in which crimes under both these counts have been proved" (MJ 597). Note that there is no identification of the theory of liability under which "these counts have been proved."
[44] It is curious that neither Justice Mei of China nor Justice Jaranilla of the Philippines appear to have participated in the drafting of the sections of the majority judgment dealing with war crimes committed in their countries. This is reflected in their memoranda that suggest changes to sections of the judgment dealing with these issues and provide greater and more accurate detail. See Jaranilla's memorandum to Cramer as chair of the drafting committee, August 23, 1948 NAA M1417 28 and Mei, August 24, 1948 NAA M1417 28.

356    The Majority Judgment on War Crimes

legacy of the Tokyo Trial, for in contemporary tribunals a careful distinction is made between civilian and military superiors. It should preliminarily be noted that the discussion in the IMTFE's individual verdicts of liability for war crimes is even more abbreviated and cursory than the treatment of the charges of aggressive war. This follows the general pattern of the judgment whereby the treatment of aggressive war is much longer and more detailed than is the case with war crimes. Consideration of the individual verdicts on war crimes in Webb's draft judgment will highlight this point.

### 9.4.1   The Responsibility of Military Commanders: Dohihara, Hata, Itagaki, Kimura

For accused Dohihara, the verdict on war crimes focuses only upon his activities as commander of the 7th Area Army from April 1944 to April 1945, covering Malaya, Sumatra, Java, and for part of this time, Borneo. The tribunal found that there were conflicts in the evidence as to "the extent of his responsibility for protecting prisoners of war within the area of his command."[45] In light of these evidentiary problems the tribunal concluded that his responsibility was only clear in regard to the provision of food and medicine, though the prosecution had argued that the 7th Area Army had general administrative authority over prisoner of war camps under its jurisdiction. The judgment further concludes that deaths from malnutrition and disease were rampant among the prisoners. On what theory of liability, then, do they connect Dohihara to these deaths? The tribunal finds that because food and medicine were available that could have been used care for the prisoners, "these supplies were withheld upon a *policy* for which Dohihara was responsible" (emphasis added). On this basis Dohihara is convicted under Count 54 (presumably for "authorizing") and acquitted under Count 55.

This result is puzzling in two regards. First, the judgment does not refer to the mental element required for conviction. That is, they make no finding as to whether Dohihara knew that terrible conditions prevailed among the prisoners scattered across the vast area of his command, late in the war when communications were difficult at best, let alone whether he "willfully" or intentionally withheld supplies. They also make no finding as to whether he knew that food and medicine were being withheld. This, of course, fails to meet the standard articulated in Chapter II, where, as noted earlier, the tribunal stated that liability must be grounded either upon *knowledge* that such crimes were being

---

[45] This in itself is odd in that in Chapter VIII the judgment makes an explicit finding that Dohihara was one of the accused who "administered detention camps as military commanders during the Pacific War." The entire treatment of Dohihara on all counts takes up just one page of text (MJ 599–600).

## 9.4 Standards of Responsibility in the Individual Verdicts

committed and a concomitant failure to prevent their further occurrence, or upon a *negligent failure to acquire such knowledge*. One might argue that knowledge is implicit in the finding that Dohihara was responsible for the policy, but the tribunal nowhere states what the policy was, how its existence was proved beyond reasonable doubt, or whether knowledge of the mistreatment could be inferred from it.

The second surprising aspect of the conviction of Dohihara is the lack of conviction under Count 55. Dohihara appears to provide a perfect example of a commander who, according to the tribunal's criteria in Chapter II, should be convicted under Count 55 for a failure to carry out his duty under international law to prevent mistreatment of prisoners. Finally, while the criteria for military commanders in Chapter II focuses upon prisoners held by units under their command, the verdict against Dohihara finds that prisoners "within the area of his command" were mistreated. They make no finding that the mistreatment was perpetrated by soldiers under his command. This issue should have been made clear because, as the High Command Case held, a field commander in a combat area is not normally held responsible for crimes committed by security or other formations not under his command, while a commander of occupied territory may be held liable because of the special duty he has to protect the civilian population of the territory.[46] It is precisely such nuanced and careful analysis that is almost entirely lacking in the individual verdicts of the IMTFE in regard to war crimes.

Comparing the conviction of Dohihara with that of Hata, one may indeed wonder at the difference in the treatment of the two cases, for which the judgment provides no explanation.[47] Hata was convicted of war crimes in relation to his command of expeditionary forces in China in 1938 and 1941–4.[48] In the extremely short part of the verdict devoted to his liability for war crimes the judgment states that while he was in command in China,

> atrocities were committed on a large scale by the troops under his command and were spread over a long period of time. Either Hata knew of these things and took no steps to prevent their occurrence, or he was indifferent and made no provision for learning whether orders for the humane treatment of prisoners of war and civilians were obeyed. In either case, he was in breach of his duty as charged under Count 55.[49]

Here the tribunal appears to follow the standard set out in Chapter II, holding that the perpetrators of the crimes were units under Hata's command and that

---

[46] High Command Case, 544–9.
[47] In a memorandum to all judges of November 1, 1948 Webb points out such glaring inconsistencies in the majority judgment's treatment of individual cases. They were obviously not corrected (AWM 3DRL 2481).
[48] On the evidence against Hata see Chapter 6.
[49] MJ 602.

he knew or should have known (i.e. was negligent in not acquiring knowledge) of their crimes and thereby breached his duty to prevent such conduct. This case, therefore, could be construed as a command responsibility case, though as we have seen, Chapter II does not frame the theory of liability in that manner. What is puzzling is the lack of consistency in the assessment of the liability of Hata and Dohihara under the standards articulated in previous parts of the judgment. Equally puzzling is the conviction under Count 54 for Dohihara and Count 55 for Hata, despite their being similarly situated. Also troubling is the failure of the tribunal to weigh and analyze the evidence against Hata on which its verdict is based.

The tribunal treats the defendant Itagaki in a manner similar to Dohihara. Itagaki, the judgment finds, from April 1945 to the surrender, commanded an area including Java, Sumatra, Malaya, Borneo, and the Andaman and Nicobar Islands.[50] They also find that during this period the camps in these areas were not under his command, but he, like Dohihara, was responsible for food and medical supplies. The tribunal briefly considers Itagaki's defense that supplies were short and that he did the best that he could under the circumstances. The judgment rejects this defense because they find that after the surrender supplies were made available to the camps and that Itagaki should have done so earlier and made adequate arrangements for better treatment of the prisoners. Whether or not this finding was an appropriate conclusion under the difficult and chaotic circumstances in April–August 1945, the judgment makes the same inference as in the case of Dohihara, namely that Itagaki was responsible for the *policy* that "was responsible for the deaths and sufferings of thousands of people whose adequate maintenance was his duty."[51] In neither case is there a reasoned argument based upon analysis of the available evidence as to the justification for such an inference, let alone beyond a reasonable doubt.

It is also very puzzling that the judgment fails to mention factual findings in Chapter VIII that apparently linked Itagaki to other war crimes apart from his activities in 1945 (which formed the sole basis in the verdict of his liability for crimes of war). For example, in Chapter VIII the judgment found that Itagaki, as army minister in 1939, received a policy advisory from the Central China Expeditionary Army that explicitly advocated a policy of terror against the civilian population so as to weaken their resistance.[52] As army minister this

---

[50] On the evidence against Itagaki on war crimes charges, see Chapter 6. Note how the verdict against Itagaki does not refer to his activities in Korea which Chapter VIII found to violate the rules regarding proper treatment of prisoners. (MJ 573–4) This is likewise the case with Kimura. See note 46 in Chapter 6 for the prosecution's evidence on prisoner-of-war transfer from the outlying areas to Korea, arranged by Itagaki (then serving as commander of the Korea Army) and Kimura (vice army minister).

[51] MJ 606–7.

[52] MJ 532. See PX272, Central China Expeditionary Army Situation Estimate, July 20, 1939, issued by the Headquarters of the Central China Expeditionary Army, and distributed to Vice

## 9.4 Standards of Responsibility in the Individual Verdicts 359

report (as well as many others) at the least put Itagaki on notice that crimes might be committed against enemy civilians and prisoners. Here the existence of a policy need not be inferred from circumstantial evidence. Since this policy was in fact carried out, Itagaki would also seem to bear responsibility for its consequences. Yet these facts are not considered in the verdict. The verdict also fails to consider the finding in Chapter VIII that in 1939 "the War Ministry under Itagaki" became so concerned about the extent to which Japanese soldiers returning from China were telling stories of the atrocities they had perpetrated or witnessed, that his ministry issued special orders to deal with this situation.[53] Yet the verdict makes no mention whatsoever of his activities prior to April 1945 in regard to war crimes.

The salient difference between the judgment's treatment of Itagaki and Dohihara on the one hand and Hata on the other appears to be that the Chinese victims were mistreated by troops under Hata's command, whereas Dohihara and Itagaki only had responsibility for providing food and medical supplies for the prisoners and detainees. In the latter two cases, they infer a policy from this conduct and convict, presumably, for "authorizing under Count 54." In neither case do they state which of the several grounds of liability in Count 54 (ordering, authorizing, or permitting) they rely on. In the case of Dohihara they entirely ignore the mental element, while in the case of Itagaki they conclude that he either knew or was indifferent. This latter finding is strange, for although either ground might justify a conviction one would expect the judgment to specify on which of these grounds the prosecution had succeeded in meeting their burden of proof beyond a reasonable doubt. Further, whether Itagaki was guilty of knowingly inflicting such mistreatment or was only negligent in doing so would, one presumes, make a difference in sentencing.

Apart from the issues raised above, one may wonder why, since the judgment explicitly found that both Itagaki and Dohihara had an affirmative duty to prevent mistreatment of prisoners and civilians, they would not have been convicted under Count 55 for breach of that duty under the standards laid out in Chapter II. In the tribunal's mind the difference might have resided in the distinction between crimes committed in an *area* under one's command as opposed to by *units* under one's command, but there is no analysis of the issue and no explanation as to whether that is the case.[54] Since the tribunal also

---

Chief of the Army General Staff, Vice Minister of the Army, Commander of the 11th Army, Commander of the North China Expeditionary Army, and Commander of the "Nami" Air Group, T3657 and T3666.

[53] MJ 541. The special orders (PX3304) were presented during cross-examination of vice army minister Yamawaki, who took the witness stand on behalf of accused Itagaki. For more information on PX3304, see note 103 in Chapter 6.

[54] Neither the prosecution nor the defense had focused on this issue until cross-examining some defense witnesses during the individual phases. When this issue did emerge the prosecution and defense differed little on the 7th Area Army's territorial jurisdiction. In its summation for

explicitly found that Dohihara and Itagaki had a responsibility for the food and medicine and an affirmative duty to ensure proper treatment of the prisoners but failed to do so, this would seem like the kind of conduct that would fall directly under a culpable breach of duty as outlined in Chapter II and as charged in Count 55 of the indictment. In many ways the drafting of the individual verdicts appears to have been an afterthought.

The treatment of defendant Kimura may cast some further light on the tribunal's thinking. Kimura was charged with war crimes for his conduct while serving as vice army minister from April 1941 to March 1943, and commanding the Burma Area Army from August 1944 to the Surrender.[55] Unlike Hata, Itagaki, or Dohihara, the Tribunal convicted him under both Counts 54 and 55. The rationale for the conviction under Count 54 was that Kimura "in a positive way was a party to breaches of the Rules of War." In other words, the tribunal reasons that when he approved or transmitted orders for the labor of prisoners of war, such as in the Death Railway, he was actually *committing* a criminal act rather than merely failing in his duty to prevent mistreatment. This falls under "ordering" in Count 54, though again the judgment is not absolutely explicit on this point. In regard to Count 55 on the other hand, the tribunal finds that he had knowledge of mistreatment of prisoners in all theaters of war, and that when he took over command of the Burma Area Army he took no effective disciplinary measures to stop such crimes. He was thus "negligent in his duty to enforce the rules of war."[56]

In the first instance, from a legal doctrinal standpoint Kimura could not be "negligent" in the breach of his duty if he had *knowledge* of the atrocities as the tribunal found he did. The judgment should have held that he knowingly or deliberately violated his duty. The final sentence of the verdict uses the word "deliberately," but this is of course inconsistent with their explicit finding of "negligence" at the beginning of the same paragraph.[57]

In this case, however, why did they not conclude, as they did in the case of Dohihara and Itagaki, that such mistreatment was the result of a *policy* of the accused, which on their reasoning would have again justified a conviction under Count 54 rather than Count 55? It seems that if Kimura was convicted under both 54 and 55, the same should have been true of Itagaki and Dohihara. Conversely, if Dohihara was convicted only under Count 54, despite his negligent breach of duty, the same should have been true for Kimura. The judgment also makes no explicit finding as to whether the mistreatment of prisoners of

---

Dohihara the defense admitted that "we do not deny that there were prisoners of war camps located within the territorial jurisdiction of the 7th Area Army, but we do state that such camps were never under the control of the 7th Area Army." (T43845).

[55] On the prosecution's case against Kimura, see Chapter 6.
[56] MJ 610.
[57] Ibid.

9.4 Standards of Responsibility in the Individual Verdicts        361

war in the Burma theater was perpetrated by troops under his command or merely within his command area, the difference that appeared to have distinguished the treatment of Hata.

### 9.4.2 The Convictions of Mutō, Oka, and Satō

As one of two final examples of the treatment of military commanders we may turn to the puzzling case of defendant Mutō.[58] Mutō was also convicted under both Counts 54 and 55. The first ground for conviction arises out of his activities as commander of the Second Imperial Guards Division in Northern Sumatra from April 1942 to October 1944. The entirety of the judgment's discussion of his conviction in this regard consists of the following two sentences:

> During this period, *in the area occupied by his troops*, widespread atrocities were committed, for which MUTO shares responsibility. Prisoners of war and civilian internees were starved, neglected, tortured and murdered, and civilians were massacred.[59] (emphasis added)

Here the judgment makes no finding that the perpetrators of the atrocities were troops under his command. They also make no finding as to the required mental element. One may infer that they intended their use of the word "widespread" to imply an inference of knowledge, but there is no statement to that effect, let alone analysis of Mutō's particular situation or what information he possessed.[60] The judgment here appears to follow not the standards laid out in Chapter II, but rather the logic of Chapter VIII, that when crimes are committed on "a scale so vast, yet following so common a pattern in all theaters, ... only one conclusion is possible – the atrocities were either secretly ordered or willfully permitted." The judgment, however, makes no explicit reference to this standard and no finding as to whether the accused is being held liable because he "willfully permitted" the crimes, secretly ordered them, or failed to prevent them. They also do not even state whether this conviction falls under Count 54 or under Count 55. In other words, the judgment fails completely to offer a reasoned justification for his conviction based upon specific analysis of the available evidence and the applicable legal standards in accordance with the burden of proof.

The second basis of conviction for Mutō arises from his activities as General Yamashita's chief of staff in the Philippines from October 1944. The verdict had previously acquitted him on charges that as a member of General Matsui's staff in Nanjing he was liable for the massacres and mass rapes committed

---
[58] See the account of the prosecution's case against Mutō in Chapter 6.
[59] MJ 614.
[60] For the defense evidence on this matter, see Chapter 6 under Section 6.4.1.

there.⁶¹ The rationale was that although Mutō knew of these atrocities, as a subordinate he was in no position to stop them. In regard to the Philippines, on the other hand, they find that he was in a position to "influence policy" but failed to do so while "a campaign of massacre, torture, and other atrocities was waged by Japanese troops on the civilian population."⁶²

The verdict in regard to Mutō's role in the Philippines also seems inadequate in several respects. First, it is not clear how or if the "ability to influence policy" on the part of a military subordinate fits into the criteria for liability established in either Chapter II or Chapter VIII. Next, the judgment does not make clear whether the ability to influence policy provides the basis of a conviction on the basis of *complicity* in the perpetration of the crimes under Count 54 or for a breach of duty by failing to prevent them under Count 55. One would assume that analysis, or at least an explicit finding would be required here. There is also no evidence or analysis as to his actual ability to influence policy on these matters. The judgment appears to merely infer this ability from Mutō's title.

Mutō's defense, following the defense employed by General Yamashita, was that he had no knowledge of these crimes.⁶³ The judgment dismisses this, in language that recalls the decision of the military commission that convicted General Yamashita, solely by stating that they find his defense "wholly incredible."⁶⁴ The burden of proof, however, is on the prosecution to prove beyond a reasonable doubt all of the elements of the offense, including the requisite mental element. The only evidence referenced by the judgment is the widespread nature or the crimes with no analysis as to whether and how Mutō was in a position to acquire the knowledge imputed to him, let alone whether he or his commander had the ability, under the prevailing circumstances, to prevent them. The judgment, again, does not provide a reasoned account of what evidence introduced by the prosecution established beyond a reasonable doubt that Mutō had actual knowledge of these crimes.

Further, the judgment makes no explicit finding as to the standard on which they convict Mutō. One may assume that they imply he *knew* of the crimes from their scale, but one might also infer that they are holding him liable because he *should have known*.⁶⁵ In terms of the jurisprudential legacy of the

---

⁶¹ Webb, on the other hand, convicted him for the crimes in Nanjing, as will be seen in the next chapter. Justice Mei provided a great deal of detail and argument on Nanjing to add to the case against Matsui, Mutō's superior, but in vain. See Mei's memorandum to the judges of November 1, 1948 NAA M1417 30.

⁶² MJ 613–14. One may note that the judgment fails to even mention that Mutō also served in the important position as director of the Military Affairs Bureau of the Ministry of the Army, a position which was the basis of the prosecution of Satō, and, in the naval counterpart, Oka.

⁶³ For the defense evidence see Chapter 6 under Section 6.4.1.

⁶⁴ MJ 613–14.

⁶⁵ As Justice Murphy's dissenting opinion in the Supreme Court review of Yamashita's *habeas corpus* petition notes in language that could equally be applied to Mutō, "Many terrible

## 9.4 Standards of Responsibility in the Individual Verdicts 363

IMTFE judgment, the holding that a chief of staff shares responsibility with a commander simply by virtue of his position could have established an important principle if it had been clearly stated and supported by a reasoned opinion. It was not. Further, the tribunal appears to be relying solely on the *de iure* positions that Mutō held in China and the Philippines, for they make no reference in either case to whether he was *in fact* able to influence policy. The Nuremberg judgment, on the other hand, like the contemporary international criminal tribunals, held that it is only the actual ability to influence policy rather than mere position that must provide the basis for individual criminal responsibility. The contrast between the treatment of Mutō's liability as chief of staff and the very careful and detailed analysis of the roles and responsibilities of staff officers in the High Command Case underscores the shortcomings of the majority judgment in this regard.[66]

As a final example of the verdicts on high ranking military defendants one may take the puzzling acquittal of Vice Admiral Oka on war crimes charges.[67] Oka was not a field commander, but rather held the important position of director of the Naval Affairs Bureau of the Ministry of the Navy from October 1940 to July 1944. The judgment, in a previous section, had explained the importance of this navy office and of its army counterpart. The judgment explicitly finds that Oka participated influentially in "the Liaison Conference at which the policy of Japan was largely decided." He was thus no mere functionary. Moreover, in its detailed examination of the system set up to manage prisoners of war held by the armed forces, the Naval Affairs Bureau, like its army counterpart, had chief responsibility for administration of the system designed to deal with prisoners.

Oka, then, as the director of this key bureau for four years, would seem to fit perfectly within the categories established in Chapter II for those bearing the affirmative duty to ensure the proper treatment of prisoners: "(3) Officials in those departments which were concerned with the well-being of prisoners; (4) Officials, whether civilian, military, or naval, having direct and immediate control of prisoners."[68]

In its elaboration of what it calls "The System" to deal with prisoners, the judgment concentrates on the army, which held most of the prisoners, but goes on to explicitly hold that the navy's system of POW administration resulted in gross mistreatment in all areas in which Japanese naval forces operated. The

---

atrocities were committed by your disorganized troops. Because these atrocities were so widespread, we will not bother to charge or prove that you committed, ordered, or condoned any of them. We will assume that they must have resulted from your inefficiency and negligence as a commander." Murphy Dissent, In Re Yamashita, 327 US 1, 35–6.

[66] See High Command Case, 512–15.
[67] Chapter 6 has discussed the prosecution's evidence against Oka.
[68] MJ 83.

judgment explicitly states, "the enforcement of the laws of war in those areas became the responsibility of the Navy under SHIMADA and OKA."[69]

In light of the important role of the Naval Affairs Bureau in policymaking, orders, and regulations regarding prisoners, and in light of Oka's key position in that office, how does one explain the judgment's acquittal of Oka in regard to the war crimes charges under Counts 54 and 55? The entire treatment of Oka on the charges of war crimes consists of the following: "There is some evidence tending that Oka knew or ought to have known that war crimes were being committed by naval personnel against prisoners of war *with whose welfare his department was concerned*, but it falls short of the standard of proof which justifies a conviction in criminal cases"[70] (emphasis added). The acquittal of Satō on similar charges for his role in the Military Affairs Bureau of the Ministry of the Army is consistent on the one hand, but seemingly directly contrary to the standards established by the majority in Chapter II.

This verdict thus seems difficult to reconcile either with the cases examined above or with the various standards of liability employed by the tribunal. As was noted earlier, as one of the Japanese government's chief officials charged with the welfare of prisoners held by navy, Oka would seem to fall within the purview of the theory of liability for breach of an affirmative duty articulated in Chapter II. While the judgment holds that the prosecution did not prove beyond a reasonable doubt that Oka "knew or ought to have known," this alone is not the standard set out in Chapter II for those who bear responsibility for the prevention of crimes against prisoners. Webb's draft judgment, as the next chapter will show, provides a clear account of how Oka's liability should be assessed.

The treatment of Oka thus does not fit the criteria which the judgment had so clearly articulated in Chapter II for a determination of liability for those charged with the care of POW. It is equally puzzling that both Mutō and Satō served as the director of the Military Affairs Bureau of the Ministry of the Army, but that neither was convicted in connection with this role. The verdict for Satō reads, "There is no doubt that SATO knew of the many protests against the behavior of Japan's troops, for these protests came to his Bureau and they were discussed at the bi-weekly meetings of Bureau Chiefs in the War Ministry. TOJO presided at these meetings and he it was who decided that action or inaction should be taken in regard to the protests. SATO, his subordinate, could not initiate preventive action against the decision of his chief."[71] This is not, however, the standard articulated in Chapter II. Oka, Satō, and Mutō clearly fall under the third of the four categories enumerated by the judgment: "Officials in those departments which were concerned with the well-being of prisoners." Further,

---

[69] MJ 583.
[70] MJ 615.
[71] MJ 617.

the fact that decision was ultimately taken by Tōjō is irrelevant in terms of the specific standards of culpability set out in Chapter II, which provided that persons in this category would be held accountable if they possessed knowledge that ill-treatment was occurring and failed "to take such steps as were within their power to prevent the commission of such crimes in the future."

Examining the treatment of these military officers by the tribunal one must conclude that there is little systematic analysis in the judgment providing a justification for the respective verdicts. The failure to articulate the theories of liability, to specify the grounds of conviction in regard to specific counts, to systematically weigh the evidence and provide a reasoned account for findings in regard to the mental or other elements, and the inconsistencies between the various verdicts and between the verdicts as a whole and the criteria for liability articulated in Chapters II and VIII reflect poorly on the majority in regard to the quality of the judgment. Clearly, the judgment does not follow the basic principle of justice of treating similarly situated accused in a similar manner. As we will see, the treatment of civilian officials presents similar difficulties.

### 9.4.3 The Responsibility of Civilian Officials: Hirota, Koiso, Shigemitsu, and Hiranuma

Hiranuma was charged for various counts relating to waging aggressive war through his participation in policymaking at the highest levels of the Japanese government as, at various times, prime minister, president of the Privy Council, home minister, and minister without portfolio. No mere figurehead, the tribunal, in four brief paragraphs, found Hiranuma to be "not only a supporter ... but ... one of the leaders of the conspiracy and an active participant in furthering its policy."[72] Hiranuma was also charged with war crimes under Counts 54 and 55 of the indictment. The judgment's entire treatment of Hiranuma's responsibility for war crimes consists of the following two sentences: "There is no evidence *directly* connecting him with the crimes charged in Counts 33, 35, 54, and 55. We, therefore, find him not guilty on these counts"[73] (emphasis added). This verdict, completely ungrounded in a reasoned application of the articulated standards of responsibility to the evidence, appears almost incomprehensible in light of those standards given the exalted level at which Hiranuma operated in governmental and policy circles. The discussion of Hiranuma in Chapter 7 has already indicated what evidence was actually available to, but ignored by, the tribunal, as also made clear by Webb's treatment, taken up in Chapter 10.

---

[72] MJ 602.
[73] Ibid.

As seen earlier, Chapter II finds that the cabinet, as the embodiment of the Government of Japan, is collectively responsible for the mistreatment of prisoners of war and civilian internees. They hold that a cabinet member aware of such mistreatment must resign to avoid criminal liability. Nowhere in Chapter II does the tribunal suggest that there must be a "direct" connection between a cabinet member and the criminal activity. Hiranuma was not only a cabinet member but also served as prime minister, wielded considerable de facto influence, and as the judgment found, was an active and important member of the group involved in the policy of waging war in China and elsewhere. Under the standard articulated in Chapter II all that would be necessary to convict would be a finding that he knew or should have known of the mistreatment and failed to resign. Yet the judgment does not make any mention at all of the state of Hiranuma's awareness, or what information was conveyed at the cabinet and other meetings he obviously regularly attended that should have at the least put him on inquiry notice. After all, the judgment explicitly finds that he was one of the government members with what the Chapter II calls *"the principal and continuing responsibility" for the treatment of prisoners.*[74] It is odd, to say the least, that they engage in no such analysis to determine whether, under the standard clearly articulated in Chapter II for cabinet members, Hiranuma was negligent or reckless in failing to fulfill his legal duty to ensure the proper treatment of prisoners of war and civilian internees.

Apart from the standards of Chapter II, it would also appear that the tribunal should have considered Hiranuma's liability under the "secretly ordered or willfully permitted by the Japanese Government" standard articulated in Chapter VIII.[75]

Hiranuma's acquittal on war crimes charges seems even more puzzling in light of some of the evidence which the judgment had referenced in its examination of war crimes in Chapter VIII but did not mention in its verdict. For example, in discussing war crimes perpetrated by Japanese forces in China, the judgment refers to a speech given by Hiranuma on behalf of the cabinet to the Imperial Diet in January 1939. In that speech, the judgment continues, he expressed the hope that the Chinese people would "understand" Japan's "immutable policy" in China. In regard to those Chinese who did not wish to cooperate, Hiranuma's policy was chilling in its clarity: "As for those who fail to understand, we have *no other alternative than to exterminate them*"[76] (emphasis added). This statement as one of Japan's highest level policymakers, combined with what the tribunal found to be his unrelenting efforts advocating for the war effort in China, would surely seem to be sufficient to connect him

---

[74] MJ 82.
[75] MJ 531.
[76] MJ 532. See note 61 in Chapter 8 for the exhibit in which this statement is documented.

9.4  Standards of Responsibility in the Individual Verdicts      367

to war crimes in China under Count 54 as either "authorizing" or "permitting" or under a theory of complicity. Hiranuma's acquittal on these charges calls into question the coherence of the judgment's theory not only of cabinet or "Government" responsibility, but individual responsibility as well.

Hiranuma's acquittal seems even more puzzling in light of the conviction under Count 55 of Koiso, who served as prime minister from July 1944 to April 1945. The Tribunal found that when Koiso became prime minister Japanese war crimes were so notorious that it was "improbable" that he would not have known of them. At a meeting in October 1944 the foreign minister reported that according to information from enemy sources, Japan's treatment of prisoners of war "left much to be desired." The judgment concludes that because Koiso remained prime minister for six months after that meeting and there was no improvement in the treatment of prisoners, he was guilty of "a deliberate disregard of his duty."[77]

The crimes committed by the Japanese forces in China, and particularly in Nanjing, were also "notorious" and subject to voluminous and continuing international protests to the Ministry of Foreign Affairs. Was it not equally "improbable" that Hiranuma, especially given multiple positions at the highest level and his advocacy of the use of exterminatory violence against the civilian population in China, would not have been aware of them and of the execution of Chinese prisoners of war? One would have hoped for a reasoned account of these seemingly discrepant findings that would explain the criteria the tribunal applied in each case to reach its conclusions.

The treatment of Kido is also puzzling in this light. Kido, like Hiranuma, was acquitted under Counts 54 and 55. The tribunal finds that though Kido was a member of the cabinet during the Nanjing massacre, "The evidence is not sufficient to attach him with responsibility for failure to prevent."[78] Since the judgment argues that the protests about Nanjing were discussed at the meetings of the Liaison Conference and brought forward by Foreign Minister Hirota, why would this awareness and a failure to prevent or resign not have triggered liability for Kido under the standards for cabinet members articulated in Chapter II?[79] The judgment offers no explanation and does not even mention the state of Kido's knowledge in regard to the events in Nanjing. Perhaps out

---

[77] MJ 611. The majority judgment appears to refer to testimony taken from Suzuki Tadakatsu during the sur-rebuttal phase. As already shown in Chapter 6, Suzuki testified that Shigemitsu brought up the Allied protests on prisoner-of-war mistreatment at a meeting of the Conference for the Supreme Direction of the War, in October 1944.

[78] MJ 609.

[79] MJ 538. Although the majority judgment found that "the protests about Nanjing were discussed at the meetings of the Liaison Conference," this finding is based on an erroneous understanding of evidence. A prosecution's witness and a former foreign-ministry official, Ishii Itarō, testified that the incoming protests were discussed repeatedly at the liaison meetings of *bureau chiefs* of the Ministry of Foreign Affairs, the army, and the navy, which were separate from the meetings

of a desire to make their acquittal plausible they deliberately neglect to go into any detail on these matters.[80]

The conviction of Hirota has remained one of the most controversial decisions of the Tokyo Tribunal. It was criticized in the dissenting opinion of Justice Roeling, in the Japanese press, and in subsequent literature on the trial. In the late 1930s Hirota served as prime minister and as foreign minister during the Nanjing Massacre. The Tribunal found that this was the only event that linked him to conventional war crimes under Count 55.

The judgment finds that because he received reports from foreign sources about the atrocities in Nanjing he should not have been content to rely upon assurances from the Ministry of the Army that the crimes would not continue. His failure to follow up and insist before the cabinet that action must be taken "amounted to criminal negligence."[81] If the court had applied the standards of Chapter II consistently, one would have expected them to state that Hirota had a duty to resign if he could not prevent the crimes in Nanking. Since foreign protests continued, he must have been on notice that it was likely that the army had not, in fact, put an end to the atrocities. The only factor which appears to distinguish the fate of Hirota from that of Kido and Hiranuma is that he was the direct recipient of information about the massacre in Nanjing. If this is the basis of the distinction, however, the tribunal does not make this explicit, and it certainly does not appear to follow from the standards articulated in Chapter II.

The fact that according to the majority's account of the influence and authority of civilian cabinet members, Hirota and the cabinet would have been powerless to change the conduct of army operations is not mentioned by the verdict, which simply states that he should have "insisted" before the cabinet. The evidence against Hirota was clear in regard to his knowledge of the events in Nanjing. What the verdict should have done, but utterly failed to do, was to frame its analysis of Hirota's culpability within the framework set out in Chapter II of the judgment. Under this framework the case for Hirota's guilt beyond a reasonable doubt would have been clear. Why the verdict failed to apply the judgment's own articulated standard of liability for cabinet members to Hirota remains unclear. In Chapter 10 we shall consider the way in which Webb's draft judgment treats these issues.

As a final example, the case of Shigemitsu is illustrative of the judgment's inconsistency. The tribunal found that Shigemitsu, as foreign minister, received continuous information from foreign governments from 1943 to 1945 about the mistreatment of prisoners and civilian internees. In the case of Shigemitsu

---

of the Liaison Conference of the cabinet members and IHQ members. See note 90 in Chapter 6 for more information as to how this misinformation made it to the majority judgment.

[80] See note 94 in Chapter 6 for the prosecution's evidence against Kido concerning the Nanjing Massacre, and Kido's post-trial comment on the conviction of Hirota.

[81] MJ 604.

## 9.4 Standards of Responsibility in the Individual Verdicts 369

the judgment seems to apply the standard set out in Chapter II. They find that Shigemitsu,

> took no adequate steps to have the matter investigated, although *he, as a member of the government, bore overall responsibility* for the welfare of the prisoners. He should have pressed the matter, *if necessary to the point of resigning*, in order to quit himself of a responsibility which he suspected was not being discharged.[82] (emphasis added)

So in regard to Shigemitsu, the judgment bases his conviction under Count 55 of the indictment squarely on the theory of liability set out in Chapter II. The cabinet as the embodiment of the government bears collective responsibility for the welfare of prisoners. Shigemitsu, as "a member of the government" shared that collective responsibility. In addition, the judgment finds that he possessed sufficient information to put him on notice that further investigation was required. His duty required him to pursue this matter to the point of resigning his office if he was unable to assure himself that mistreatment was not occurring. This treatment of Shigemitsu, although not expounded in tremendous detail, is exceptional in the clarity of the legal basis of its findings when compared to the previous examples. The reasoning for this discrepancy is not apparent.

This examination of the verdicts against individual civilian and military accused shows that apart from the inconsistencies within and between the standards of liability articulated in Chapters II and VIII those standards are not systematically applied to the accused. It further shows that there is no consistency in the way in which similarly situated accused are treated. The judgment's assessment of the liability of the individuals discussed earlier displays an incoherence that is baffling. The brevity of the analysis, which is often not analysis but merely two or three sentences of conclusion, is also troubling. Why the judgment does provide a somewhat more detailed analysis in regard to some individuals but not to others is also never explained.

What one may surmise from the individual verdicts in regard to war crimes confirms that in the view of the majority, war crimes occupied a secondary place in regard to crimes against peace. The judgment as a whole devotes vastly more space to crimes against peace and engages in a far lengthier exposition of the evidence. The verdicts in regard to crimes against peace are also more lengthy and detailed, though still abbreviated. The IMTFE, not unlike the IMT, gave priority to the convictions on aggressive war. Unlike the IMT, however, the IMTFE judgment seems to consider the war crimes charges as an appendage to the main case, to be disposed of quickly and apparently with little application of juristic acumen.

---

[82] MJ 618.

## 10  An Alternative Tokyo Judgment

*The Draft Webb Judgment on War Crimes*

### 10.1  Issues and Context

This chapter provides an assessment of the legal and factual analysis through which Webb arrived at his conclusion that all of the twenty-five defendants should be found guilty of war crimes. A comprehensive treatment of Webb's extensive analysis of the individual culpability of all twenty-five accused in regard to war crimes charges would be too lengthy given the bulk of his treatment of the individual accused, which comprises some 60 percent of his 658-page judgment. This chapter will instead focus on some of the military and civilian defendants and discuss the legal and factual basis of Webb's verdict. For the purposes of highlighting the contrast with the majority judgment, whose shortcomings have been detailed in the previous chapter, we will focus on the same individual accused as discussed there.

As noted in Chapter 8, Webb clearly had the Nuremberg judgment in mind as he drafted his own opinion. He was concerned about the appearance of the lack of acquittals at Tokyo in contrast to the three acquittals at Nuremberg. In the beginning of Part VI of the President's Judgment, "Individual Cases," he states, "Acquittals like that of Schacht and others at Nuremberg are not possible here."[1] Whereas the IMT at Nuremburg based their convictions on the criteria of participation in Hitler's inner policy circle or on direct connection to the crimes against peace of war crimes through contributing to the formulation, dissemination, or implementation of criminal orders or policies, Webb's starting point for crimes against peace was his finding that, "I find it impossible to believe that in the offices these accused held they could fail to know all that this Tribunal has ascertained about the attitude of Japan. There is no immunity for anyone, soldier or civilian, who takes part in what he knows, or should know, to be an illegal and criminal war."[2] While this is the general position Webb takes

---

[1] TPJ 268.

[2] TPJ 267. As mentioned in note 13 of Chapter 8, in revising the Judgment Webb added a qualifying note to the "There is no immunity" phrase: "There is no principle of law or justice which gives immunity." The following handwritten insertion appears immediately following the sentence quoted here: "It may be expedient not to make mere combatants responsible; but immunity cannot be granted by this Tribunal which has no power to alter the law but can only ascertain and apply it."

## 10.1 Issues and Context

in regard to crimes against peace, what of his treatment of war crimes where the evidentiary situation was far different because of the lack of the kind of detailed documentation of policy formulation that was available in analyzing the decision to go to war?

In answering this question we must bear two factors in mind. The first is that in regard to crimes against peace Webb could draw on extensive evidence that directly bore upon the roles of many of the individual accused. There was extensive evidence about what individuals said or reported in regard to cabinet meetings, the Imperial Conference, speeches before the Imperial Diet, and a variety of other settings in which they expressed their views. This evidence was directly relevant to the attitudes, communications, and participation of particular individuals in policy formation and implementation in regard to the war in China and later in the Asia-Pacific theater. Such evidence, for example, shows how individuals who for purposes of diplomacy characterized Japan's war in China as an "incident" in fact acknowledged that it was a war, or in today's vocabulary, an international armed conflict.

While a massive amount of such evidence was available to shed light on individual roles at the policy level in regard to war planning, the situation was rather different in regard to the Japanese armed forces' treatment of civilian populations and POW in occupied territories. The first reason for this is that such matters were not as important at the highest policy levels so as to produce the kind of extensive and ongoing policy-level debates and discussions as did overall war strategy and decisions about such vital issues as whom, how, and when to attack.

While international protests about Japanese treatment of civilian populations and POW were known by at least some members of the cabinet, we have relatively little *direct* evidence about the extent of knowledge or the expressed views of many of the accused on specific issues relating to specific war crimes, let alone the extent to which they reflect actual policies. The second reason has to do with the destruction of the records that would undoubtedly shed more light on these matters. Webb, of course, was well aware of this issue and addressed it directly in The President's Judgment. In regard to the orders that went out from the army headquarters to destroy all documents and conceal guilt, Webb reasoned that this demonstrated awareness at the governmental level of large scale atrocities.[3] For example, he references the order sent out by the POW Information Bureau providing that, "Personnel who ill-treated

---

[3] Lieutenant General Kawabe of the Army General Staff testified that general orders of document destruction were issued by the Army General Staff. The prosecution also presented two army-ministry documents showing instances of the orders of document destruction and permission for war criminals to flee. See also Chapter 1 under Section 1.5.

prisoners of war and internees ... are permitted to take care of it by ... fleeing without a trace."[4]

The second reason for the differences in the evidentiary basis for war crimes charges as opposed to crimes against peace has to do with the nature of such crimes. As Justice Pal points out, in the case of Nuremberg the prosecution was in possession of some orders that directly linked specific individuals at the policy level to criminal conduct against civilians and POW. The notorious Kommisarbefehl is one such example, the *"Nacht und Nebel"* decree is another.[5] But it should also be remembered that such orders, and even high-level discussions about such matters, never spoke directly of murder or mistreatment. Even at the Wannsee Conference in January 1942, where Reinhard Heydrich and a group of ministerial officials in less than two hours constructed the institutional architecture of the systematic extermination of millions of persons in killing centers to be specifically constructed for that purpose, there is no explicit mention of the true nature of the undertaking. Heydrich explained that an "evacuation" of Jews to "the East" was now a "solution possibility" (*"Loesungsmoglichkeit"*) and in the implementation of that evacuation many would "fall away through natural decline." Those who did not "naturally" decline would be "treated accordingly."[6] Despite the opaque language, everyone present understood exactly what was meant and exactly what was required of them in their various ministerial occupations. Yet in carrying out this program of mass murder they too only spoke in the bureaucratic euphemisms of "migration," "resettlement," and "wandering off."[7]

Whether in WWII contexts or in the Bosnian war of 1992–5, we should thus not expect to find direct expressions of criminal policies. They are the

---

[4] TPJ 260. See PX2011, T14718–9. Also discussed in Chapter 1.

[5] Pal overstates the case, however. The prosecution had, for example, no written orders from Hitler and the policy level establishing the extermination centers in Poland. The orders that were the basis of the *Sondermassnahmen* through which millions of Poles and Soviet citizens (both Jewish and non-Jewish) were systematically shot in mass executions do not directly authorize such killings but use euphemism and other circumlocutions to create a sphere of action in which those carrying out the orders understood what was to be done without explicit written authorization. As Adolf Eichmann later testified, the order for the *Endloesung*, the "final solution to the Jewish question in Europe" (itself a vague euphemism) was, according to Himmler, given to him orally by Hitler and then orally transmitted to Heydrich, who in turn orally disseminated it to officials at the Wannsee Conference. On this, see Hilberg, *The Destruction of the European Jews*, 163–8. The only written authorization that Heydrich received (signed by Goering, not Hitler) for the implementation of what would later be known as The Holocaust is extraordinarily general: "Complementing the task already assigned to you in the directive of 24 January 1939, to undertake, by emigration or evacuation, a solution of the Jewish question as advantageous as possible under the conditions of the time, I hereby charge you with making all necessary organizational, functional, and material preparations for a complete solution of the Jewish question in the German sphere of influence in Europe" (quoted by Hilberg, *The Destruction of the European Jews*, 163).

[6] Hilberg, *The Destruction of the European Jews*, 166.

[7] Ibid., 167.

10.1 Issues and Context 371

in regard to crimes against peace, what of his treatment of war crimes where the evidentiary situation was far different because of the lack of the kind of detailed documentation of policy formulation that was available in analyzing the decision to go to war?

In answering this question we must bear two factors in mind. The first is that in regard to crimes against peace Webb could draw on extensive evidence that directly bore upon the roles of many of the individual accused. There was extensive evidence about what individuals said or reported in regard to cabinet meetings, the Imperial Conference, speeches before the Imperial Diet, and a variety of other settings in which they expressed their views. This evidence was directly relevant to the attitudes, communications, and participation of particular individuals in policy formation and implementation in regard to the war in China and later in the Asia-Pacific theater. Such evidence, for example, shows how individuals who for purposes of diplomacy characterized Japan's war in China as an "incident" in fact acknowledged that it was a war, or in today's vocabulary, an international armed conflict.

While a massive amount of such evidence was available to shed light on individual roles at the policy level in regard to war planning, the situation was rather different in regard to the Japanese armed forces' treatment of civilian populations and POW in occupied territories. The first reason for this is that such matters were not as important at the highest policy levels so as to produce the kind of extensive and ongoing policy-level debates and discussions as did overall war strategy and decisions about such vital issues as whom, how, and when to attack.

While international protests about Japanese treatment of civilian populations and POW were known by at least some members of the cabinet, we have relatively little *direct* evidence about the extent of knowledge or the expressed views of many of the accused on specific issues relating to specific war crimes, let alone the extent to which they reflect actual policies. The second reason has to do with the destruction of the records that would undoubtedly shed more light on these matters. Webb, of course, was well aware of this issue and addressed it directly in The President's Judgment. In regard to the orders that went out from the army headquarters to destroy all documents and conceal guilt, Webb reasoned that this demonstrated awareness at the governmental level of large scale atrocities.[3] For example, he references the order sent out by the POW Information Bureau providing that, "Personnel who ill-treated

---

[3] Lieutenant General Kawabe of the Army General Staff testified that general orders of document destruction were issued by the Army General Staff. The prosecution also presented two army-ministry documents showing instances of the orders of document destruction and permission for war criminals to flee. See also Chapter 1 under Section 1.5.

prisoners of war and internees ... are permitted to take care of it by ... fleeing without a trace."[4]

The second reason for the differences in the evidentiary basis for war crimes charges as opposed to crimes against peace has to do with the nature of such crimes. As Justice Pal points out, in the case of Nuremberg the prosecution was in possession of some orders that directly linked specific individuals at the policy level to criminal conduct against civilians and POW. The notorious Kommisarbefehl is one such example, the *"Nacht und Nebel"* decree is another.[5] But it should also be remembered that such orders, and even high-level discussions about such matters, never spoke directly of murder or mistreatment. Even at the Wannsee Conference in January 1942, where Reinhard Heydrich and a group of ministerial officials in less than two hours constructed the institutional architecture of the systematic extermination of millions of persons in killing centers to be specifically constructed for that purpose, there is no explicit mention of the true nature of the undertaking. Heydrich explained that an "evacuation" of Jews to "the East" was now a "solution possibility" (*"Loesungsmoglichkeit"*) and in the implementation of that evacuation many would "fall away through natural decline." Those who did not "naturally" decline would be "treated accordingly."[6] Despite the opaque language, everyone present understood exactly what was meant and exactly what was required of them in their various ministerial occupations. Yet in carrying out this program of mass murder they too only spoke in the bureaucratic euphemisms of "migration," "resettlement," and "wandering off."[7]

Whether in WWII contexts or in the Bosnian war of 1992–5, we should thus not expect to find direct expressions of criminal policies. They are the

---

[4] TPJ 260. See PX2011, T14718–9. Also discussed in Chapter 1.
[5] Pal overstates the case, however. The prosecution had, for example, no written orders from Hitler and the policy level establishing the extermination centers in Poland. The orders that were the basis of the *Sondermassnahmen* through which millions of Poles and Soviet citizens (both Jewish and non-Jewish) were systematically shot in mass executions do not directly authorize such killings but use euphemism and other circumlocutions to create a sphere of action in which those carrying out the orders understood what was to be done without explicit written authorization. As Adolf Eichmann later testified, the order for the *Endloesung*, the "final solution to the Jewish question in Europe" (itself a vague euphemism) was, according to Himmler, given to him orally by Hitler and then orally transmitted to Heydrich, who in turn orally disseminated it to officials at the Wannsee Conference. On this, see Hilberg, *The Destruction of the European Jews*, 163–8. The only written authorization that Heydrich received (signed by Goering, not Hitler) for the implementation of what would later be known as The Holocaust is extraordinarily general: "Complementing the task already assigned to you in the directive of 24 January 1939, to undertake, by emigration or evacuation, a solution of the Jewish question as advantageous as possible under the conditions of the time, I hereby charge you with making all necessary organizational, functional, and material preparations for a complete solution of the Jewish question in the German sphere of influence in Europe" (quoted by Hilberg, *The Destruction of the European Jews*, 163).
[6] Hilberg, *The Destruction of the European Jews*, 166.
[7] Ibid., 167.

## 10.1 Issues and Context

exception rather than the rule. As Zygmunt Bauman and Raul Hilberg have demonstrated, bureaucracies engaged in criminal activity operate through a language of euphemism that masks a collective understanding of the nature and goals of the governmental policies they implement. This is one of the main ways in which bureaucrats and government officials distance themselves from moral responsibility for the outcomes of their policies. It is also the basis on which they seek to deny such responsibility when they are called to account, whether at Nuremberg, at Tokyo, or at a national tribunal. In this regard, we should no more take at face value denials of knowledge and responsibility at Tokyo than we do similar claims and excuses offered by the accused at Nuremberg. But, we must also always remember that regardless of what we may think of such denials, in the setting of the trial of these individuals the burden is always upon the prosecution to establish that such protestations of innocence are false and to prove guilt beyond a reasonable doubt on each of the specific charges in the indictment. The duty of the judges in such trials, on the other hand, is to analyze all the evidence which the defense and prosecution have offered and provide a reasoned account of whether or not the prosecution has met their burden in regard to each accused for each of the crimes with which they are specifically charged.

In the Japanese context, from the order to burn documents and for personnel to "vanish without a trace," and from the evidence of the actual systematic destruction of documents, we know that there was evidence that Japanese officials considered would be incriminating. If such evidence had survived, as much did in Nazi Germany, documenting the implementation of criminal policies in the field, the prosecutors at Tokyo might have found themselves in a different position. But it cannot be emphasized enough that in general, war crimes trials against high-level officials are typically based upon inference from a variety of kinds of circumstantial evidence rather than the "smoking gun" that every war crimes investigator dreams of. Convictions are based upon "linkage" evidence that provides the connection between high-level officials and crimes committed far away from the quiet of their ministerial or executive offices. In this regard, as pertaining to war crimes, the Tokyo trial was typical rather than exceptional. Let us briefly consider the nature of such evidence as a prelude to looking at how Webb arrived at his conclusions.

In mass atrocity cases from WWII to Rwanda, Bosnia, Cambodia, or Kosovo, there is ample evidence that crimes have been committed on a large scale against civilians and other protected persons. Those who point to Justice Pal as substantiating the innocence of Japanese policymakers should perhaps read his dissenting opinion more clearly, for Pal repeatedly states that what he calls "devilish and fiendish" crimes were committed by Japanese forces on such a widespread scale that they undeniably occurred.[8] His conclusion, however, is that while those in the field of operations were justifiably punished for such crimes by national tribunals, the high-level accused at Tokyo had nothing to do with such "overzealous" behavior by their subordinates and hence cannot be held accountable.[9] In considering Pal's dissent in Chapter 13 we will see to what extent this conclusion was justified by the evidence or motivated by other agendas.

It is, however, precisely the challenge that faces prosecutors in trials of high-level accused persons to link them to the crimes that typically take place in distant locales they have never seen and are perpetrated by persons they have never met. In the contemporary international and hybrid criminal tribunals, prosecutors distinguish between "crime-base evidence" and "linkage evidence." Crime-base witnesses testify to the murders, rapes, deportations, or torture that they personally experienced or witnessed. These witnesses typically know nothing of the role of the high-level defendants on trial or of the deliberations, policies, orders, or decisions that may have led to the crimes. In the case of widespread crimes and atrocities, establishing the crime base is usually quite straightforward, as is documenting the liability of those who were directly connected to the commission of such crimes. Linkage of high-level accused to those crimes, and delineation of their exact roles and responsibilities, however, can be quite difficult and is often based upon inferences from evidence about the scope, nature, and manner in which the crimes were perpetrated. Disagreements between the judges over the solidity of such inferences has very recently produced extremely controversial acquittals at the ICTY of high-level military and security commanders in the Yugoslav conflict.[10]

Seen in this perspective, the two key issues in assessing the Webb and majority judgments at the IMTFE are: (1) On the basis of what evidence and inferences from that evidence do the judgments link each accused person to the crimes of which he was convicted? (2) On what theory of liability does the judgment rely in the case of each accused person to ground their culpability?

Chapter 9 has already demonstrated the failing of the majority judgment to provide a reasoned analysis of linkage evidence or a clear articulation and application of established theories of liability. How, then, did Webb address

---

[8] See, for instance, Pal's conclusion on Nanjing: "even making allowance for everything that can be said against the evidence, there is no doubt that the conduct of Japanese soldiers at Nanking was atrocious and that such atrocities were intense for nearly three weeks and continued to be serious to a total of six weeks" (Pal Opinion, 1099/1359).

[9] On "overzealousness" by local Japanese commanders as Pal's explanation for what he admits were tens of thousands of deaths of "coolies" and POW on the Death Railway, see Pal Opinion, 1183–90, where the phrase is used by him repeatedly.

[10] We refer to the acquittals in the Gotovina, Perisic, and Stanisic cases at the ICTY.

these questions? In regard to civilian officials holding the highest offices Webb sometimes devotes relatively little space to analysis of the specific evidence against some of them. Shigemitsu's liability is treated in some detail, whereas the cases of Hiranuma and Koiso are treated with great brevity. In regard to military officials, on the other hand, Webb tends to provide a much more detailed analysis. In the concluding part of this chapter we will consider why this might be the case.

## 10.2 Individual Cases

In order to evaluate Webb's analysis of the liability of individuals accused for war crimes we have to look at two distinct parts of The President's Judgment and read them together. The first of these is Part V of the judgment, "Convention War Crimes and Crimes against Humanity." The second is Part VI, "Individual Cases." Part V is relatively abbreviated, comprising only twenty-five pages. This relatively brief treatment may have had two grounds. The first is that in light of the mass of evidence, of which Webb, as head of three commissions in Australia that investigated war crimes by the Japanese military forces, was more than well aware, he may have considered the evidentiary issue as to the "crime base" straightforward and unproblematic. Then Part V essentially sets the stage for Part VI. It provides an overall account of the range and scope of crimes of which the defendants stand accused and it sets out the theory of liability that Part VI will apply.

The concluding section of Part V "Common Plan of Atrocities Conclusion"[11] summarizes this foundation for the verdicts in Part VI: "The war crimes committed by the Japanese armed forces ... were so many and so terrible and raised such a storm of protest throughout the Allied world that they *must have been known* to all Japanese leaders, and more particularly to the accused. Yet nothing effective was done to prevent them"[12] (emphasis added). This is the core of Webb's theory of liability, captured in the "must have known" standard. The requirements for this theory are very close to some of the elements of the contemporary doctrine of superior responsibility.[13] On Webb's view Japanese leaders are responsible when they had knowledge that war crimes had been or were going to be committed but they did not take effective action to prevent these crimes or punish those responsible for them.[14]

---

[11] The original title of this section was merely "Conclusion – Common Plan." Webb crossed that out by hand and wrote in the title given above.
[12] TJP 261.
[13] For example, as defined in Article 7(3) of the Statute of the ICTY and Article 6(3) of the Statute of the ICTR.
[14] As articulated in the Celebici Appeals Judgment of the ICTY (*Prosecutor v. Delalic et al.*).

The crucial difference with the modern doctrine, as discussed in Chapter 9, is that today a required element is the proof of a superior-subordinate relationship between the perpetrators and the accused. This relationship is defined as de facto effective control, that is, the power to prevent the crimes or punish those responsible for committing them. Webb seems to be articulating a version of such a theory that maintains that those in a position of national leadership have the duty, by virtue of holding key ministerial positions and being members of the cabinet, to take such effective preventative action when they have knowledge that such crimes may have been or will be committed ("cabinet Responsibility").[15]

For Webb, however, the formal position alone was not enough to ground liability and knowledge was also required. In his memoranda he also makes clear that in addition to knowledge under Count 54 participation was a required element: "a cabinet minister was not responsible unless it was shown that he was a party to the act constituting the crime." Under Count 55 which defined a crime of omission in failure to prevent, a cabinet minister would be held accountable "if he remained passive despite his knowledge and his power – and duty – to act."[16] Because of the difficulty in finding direct evidence of knowledge of specific incidents, as opposed to general categories of crimes, that would link each accused to those crimes, Webb drew inferences from the available evidence to impute knowledge to the accused.[17] The clarity with which he sets this out distinguishes his draft judgment from that of the majority, who avoid this issue completely. What Webb does in Part V of his President's Judgment is to demonstrate that given the scale of the crimes, the volume of international protests, and the circulation of information within policy circles, the high-level defendants "must have known" of the kinds of crimes being committed by Japanese forces in occupied territories. Webb then relies on this inference of knowledge to link particularly the high-level civilian accused to the war crimes charged in the indictment.

A central part of Part V is thus devoted to establishing this required element of knowledge in regard to the higher levels of the government as a whole. Webb proceeds systematically, beginning with a section entitled "The Japanese Government's Knowledge of War Crimes: The Rape of Nanking."[18] He establishes there that because of the vast scale and duration of the atrocities and

---

[15] Justice Roeling also articulated a clear standard along these lines, providing that knowledge, a duty to prevent, and the power to prevent were required elements. (See Roeling's memorandum to Webb of January 23, 1947 NAA M1417/ 1 25 p. 49.) Unfortunately the majority failed to follow either Roeling or Webb in providing such a definition and applying it. Whether Roeling actually consistently applied such a standard will be discussed in Chapter 11.
[16] Memorandum of November 1, 1948 NAA M1417 30.
[17] See also the section, "Imputing Knowledge to the Accused." (TPJ 266–7).
[18] TPJ 239.

## 10.2 Individual Cases

the circulation of information in government circles an inference of knowledge is justified. Although he does not go into great detail, perhaps because he regarded the case of the Nanjing Massacre as so clear, he does provide specific evidence, noting that protests received by the foreign ministry were discussed with War Ministry officials at the Liaison Conferences, that "more than 70 cases of rape were sent to Foreign Minister HIROTA," and that "newspaper reports of the atrocities were referred to in the Budget Committee of the House of Peers on 16th February 1938."[19]

Webb next briefly considers "Knowledge After Nanking and Before Pacific War." After noting atrocities committed in Hankou he states that, "On 15th February 1939 the Vice-War Minister issued an order that men returning from the Chinese Incident Army should be properly controlled so that they should not talk about atrocities."[20] Webb then provides a much lengthier account of what information was available to and brought to the attention of governmental circles after the commencement of the Pacific War. He begins this section, "Knowledge During the Pacific War," with an account of how, after foreign protests were received, copies of the protests were passed not only to the Ministry of the Army but also to those of the Navy, Home Affairs, and Legal Affairs. They were discussed at bi-weekly conferences of the army ministry, and then forwarded to the relevant Army Commander and head of the POW camps. They then supplied information to the Military Affairs Section of the Military Affairs Bureau of the Army Ministry, which in turn sent them to the Ministry of Foreign Affairs.[21]

On this basis Webb concludes, "This system ensured that information of atrocities should be well circulated throughout the Government offices."[22] In addition, Webb describes how transcripts of Allied broadcasts with details of atrocities and warnings to the Japanese government and military that they would be held accountable "were circulated throughout the Foreign Office, the Board of Information and the War and Navy Ministries."[23] Having set out the system for the distribution of information Webb then devotes individual sections

---

[19] TPJ 239. By "Liaison Conferences," Webb appears to limit its meaning to "liaison meetings" between the officials of the Foreign Ministry and the Army Ministry. For the evidence regarding newspaper reports on atrocities being referred to the Budget Committee of the House of Peers, see PX3342-A, T13514–18; and PX3737, T37272–96. See also note 93 in Chapter 6.

[20] TPJ 239. See PX3304, T30126–30. Full listing of types of speeches subject to censorship is reproduced in note 103 in Chapter 6. As already indicated above, Webb also adduced other orders to suppress such information. See TPJ 260.

[21] Webb relied mainly on testimony of Tōjō Hideki and Suzuki Tadakatsu as well as other Japanese witnesses. See also Chapter 6 under Section 6.2.3

[22] TPJ 240.

[23] TPJ 246. This finding is based on the information provided by the Japanese government, in two certificates attached to PX1488, certified transcripts of Allied radio broadcast concerning Japanese atrocities and official Allied protests regarding Japanese mistreatment of prisoners of war, as monitored by the Japanese Ministry of Foreign Affairs between January 24 and December 19, 1944, T12821.

to a number of particular protests ranging from the Burma-Siam Railway to atrocities in Rangoon, China, the Philippines, and so on.[24] Throughout this account Webb notes the role of specific accused, such as Shigemitsu, Kimura, and Itagaki, in the specific protests or events.

Apart from his consideration of the circulation of protests, Webb also considers Japanese documents and reports in evidence that indicate awareness of war crimes being committed. For example, he notes the "Japanese Censorship Instructions" of December 20, 1943 which "prohibited any reports which might give the impression of cruel treatment of POW."[25] He likewise cites the report of a conversation on January 3, 1942 between Ōshima and Hitler where they both indicate that their navies have issued orders to kill all seamen who survive the sinking of their ships so as to heighten the shortage of US ships crews. In support of this evidence he also cites the operational order of the First Submarine Force of March 20, 1943 instructing submarine commanders to kill ships' crews after they have been interrogated for intelligence information.

One would search the majority judgment's section on individual verdicts in vain for such references to specific evidence on these matters. As noted above, the majority relies on the "secretly ordered or willfully permitted" standard, where the inference of the orders or purposive acquiescence is almost exclusively established through a simple recitation of atrocities by place and date. Webb on the other hand devotes most of this important section of the judgment to provide examples of the evidence that demonstrated the basis for his inferences and the conclusion that the highest-level government officials "must have known" of the atrocities.[26]

It is important to note here a fundamental difference in approach to the majority judgment. As noted above, while Chapter II of the majority judgment does set out a framework for a failure to prevent, that standard is not systematically applied in the individual verdicts. In Chapter VIII the theory of liability was that the war crimes of the Japanese armed forces were so widespread and followed such a similar pattern in such diverse geographical areas that they must have either been "secretly ordered or willfully permitted" by the accused.[27] Webb, unlike the majority, weighs the evidence against the applicable standard of proof beyond a reasonable doubt. Thus, though he explicitly accepts that the available evidence can "*suggest* a common plan" (emphasis added), he rejects the sufficiency of the evidence for establishing guilt unequivocally.[28] Fulfilling

---

[24] TPJ 246–50.
[25] TPJ 250. See PX1977, Memorandum concerning Revision and Adjustment of Precautions on Censorship, from Colonel Matsumura Shūitsu, Chief of Information Bureau, the Ministry of the Army, December 20, 1943, T14540.
[26] TPJ 262.
[27] The majority takes this language from the decision of the US Military Commission in Manila in the Yamashita Case, as noted in Chapter 8.
[28] TPJ 262.

his obligation to analyze and weigh the evidence he notes that other inferences could account for apparent patterns of atrocities, for example the training and disciplinary methods of the army and Kenpeitai.[29]

In the concluding passage of the War Crimes section of his draft judgment, Webb is responding to what he regards as the erroneous views of both the majority judgment and the dissenting opinion of Pal. He states that, "Of course, the accused are not excused because the Army and police were the actual perpetrators." This sentence appears to directly respond to the repeated assertion by Pal that those responsible for atrocities had already been punished by national tribunals, that this was sufficient retribution, and that there was hence no need to punish the accused at Tokyo who in any event, on Pal's view, had no connection whatsoever to those crimes.[30] Webb's point, in contrast, is that, "Even the civilians among the accused, like TOGO and HIROTA, were in a position to protest *or to appeal to the Emperor*, and, if necessary, to bring about a crisis in the Japanese government in order to prevent atrocities" (emphasis added). This, he goes on to say, is the burden of holding high office: great responsibilities on his view bring with them great duties, and the failure to carry out those duties is the ultimate basis for their liability when they know or have reason to know that crimes are being committed and they do not do all within their power to prevent them.[31] Whereas the majority judgment requires cabinet level officials to resign if they cannot prevent crimes of which they are aware Webb focuses on what such officials can do, which is to force the matter up to the highest political and military authority in Japan, Emperor Hirohito.

From this perspective another crucial difference with the majority judgment emerges, a difference which will be further emphasized by Webb in the individual verdicts. Whereas the majority judgment also concludes that the accused who held key cabinet positions should have brought such matters before the full cabinet, they studiously avoid the mention of the Emperor in such contexts. This comports with the British and American strategy, to which the Australians vehemently objected, to deflect responsibility away from the Emperor. As we will see, Webb on the other hand always states that they had the duty to bring the matter to the cabinet and failing effective action there to take it to the Emperor himself.[32] Rather than requiring resignation because of

---

[29] TPJ 262. Pal, on the other hand, denies that there is a pattern and hence rejects the notion that the crimes reflect a policy. See Pal Opinion, 1165/1391 and 1171/1394.

[30] See, for instance, Pal Opinion, 1145/1381, to cite just one such example of many from his opinion.

[31] TPJ 262. Webb's language in regard to the mental element is very similar to modern doctrine. He indicates, for example, on p. 267 that those in high positions "knew or must have known" and adds that if they did not have actual knowledge of the specific findings and evidence they were "at least put in inquiry" sufficiently that knowledge may be imputed to them.

[32] Though Webb is well aware that the Emperor cannot be brought before the IMTFE because of decisions of political expediency by the Allies (see TPJ274, i.e. the United States and the United Kingdom), he uses the section "Immunity of the Emperor" to underscore that the

the futility of resorting to the cabinet, which as we have seen was scarcely the nexus of political and military power, Webb requires high-level officials to first take the issue to Hirohito, whose word did have the authority to rein in the military and determine policy.[33]

The part of the introduction of Chapter VI, "Individual Verdicts," devoted to the authority and responsibility of Hirohito, flew in the face of British and American policy and was likely one of the main reasons why the majority refused to accept Webb's proposed judgment as the judgment of the tribunal. Webb had warned the majority, however, that ignoring the role of the Emperor could backfire and damage the credibility of the tribunal, which it did. As Webb noted in a memorandum to Justice Cramer of the United States on the majority's draft, "I notice the complete absence of any reference to the part played by the Emperor in starting and ending the war. I think that if the judgment plays down his part to this extent it will lead to devastating criticism." [34]

In his own draft judgment, Webb justified his inquiry by arguing that Hirohito's ultimate authority should be taken into account in sentencing members of the government who did not have decision-making power. This device gave Webb the excuse he clearly sought to go on record in a way that indicated why the Emperor should have also been in the defendants' dock. He devotes a section to this issue, "Immunity of the Emperor," which begins by stating that "The great authority of the Emperor was proved beyond question when he ended the war. The outstanding part played by him in starting as well as ending it was the subject of unimpeachable evidence led by the Prosecution."[35] That he also concluded this section with a brief section entitled "Emperor's Prosecution not Suggested" indicates that he knew perfectly well that was just what he was suggesting. Indeed, the previous section, "The Emperor was the Leader," began with the statement, "The Emperor's authority was required for war ... He was the only man in Japan who could decide on peace or war." Webb goes on to reject all of the excuses made for protecting Hirohito. For example, he argues that, "The suggestion that the Emperor was bound to act on advice is contrary to the evidence. He was not a limited Monarch. If he acted on advice it was because he saw fit to do so. That did not limit his responsibility. But in any event a limited Monarch would not be excused for committing a crime at International Law on the advice of his Ministers."[36]

---

Emperor was the ultimate source of authority: "He was the only man in Japan who could decide on peace and war ... The suggestion that the Emperor was bound to act on advice is contrary to the evidence." (TPJ 272).

[33] See the discussion in Chapters 3–4 of Hirohito's key role in critical decisions on war policy.
[34] Webb memorandum entitled "Your Draft of the Pacific War" to Cramer and marked "Personal," indicating the sensitivity of the issue. (NAA M1417/1 25), September 15, 1948.
[35] TPJ 272.
[36] TPJ 273–4.

## 10.2 Individual Cases 381

### 10.2.1 The Responsibility of Civilian Officials for War Crimes

Turning to Webb's treatment of the individual accused, we may begin with Hiranuma, who served as vice president and later president of the Privy Council and also as prime minister. Webb spends fifteen pages detailing what he documents as Hiranuma's key role in formulating an aggressive Japanese policy toward China in the 1930s. He cites, for example, Hiranuma's speech to the Imperial Diet in which he says that there is no alternative but to "exterminate those who persist in opposition to Japan."[37] Such statements clearly reflect not only Hiranuma's views on the necessity of pursuing conquest in China but also reveal his acceptance of a policy of systematic war crimes in China. What may appear puzzling, however, is that after such detailed analysis of the inculpatory evidence on crimes against peace, his treatment of Hiranuma's liability for war crimes is perfunctory, taking up only one paragraph. In the course of his analysis of the aggressive war charges Webb has also occasionally referenced Hiranuma's position on war crimes, but there has been no substantive analysis of the evidence.

As noted earlier, Webb's treatment of military commanders is much more detailed, raising the question of why Hiranuma's liability is established with such brevity. Webb appears here to rely on his extensive treatment of the circulation of knowledge to show that high-level officials "must have known" of the war crimes charged against them. In regard to China, Webb has already established in earlier parts of his judgment that war crimes in China were known in high-level policy circles because of the protests of foreign governments and because of the order issued by the Ministry of the Army to stop Japanese soldiers returning home from China from speaking of what they did and saw. Webb thus concludes that Hiranuma by virtue of his position and the information that must have been available to him "must have known" of atrocities. In this situation, "As Prime Minister he had the clear right and the duty to bring the matter to the notice of the Emperor or Cabinet who could have ended them [i.e. the crimes], He must be held responsible for the consequences of his failure."[38] Webb thus convicts Hiranuma only for failure to prevent under Count 55 of the indictment and not for Count 54 which would have required a more substantive account. The majority, as seen earlier, acquitted Hiranuma on war crimes charges with no apparent justification; an inconsistent result in relation to their conviction on Count 55 of others, like Koiso, who held similar positions.

In regard to other civilian officials, however, Webb focuses in greater depth on their conduct, the information available to them, and the evidence of what

---
[37] TPJ 334.
[38] TPJ 344.

382    An Alternative Tokyo Judgment

they must have known. This appears to be his strategy when dealing with officials who were directly involved, for example in responding to foreign protests. In such cases he examines the evidence that shows not just that they had knowledge but also participated in some affirmative way. For example, in regard to Shigemitsu's service as foreign minister (1943–5) Webb examines his statements and actions extensively, devoting six of twelve pages to the war crimes charges. Shigemitsu as foreign minister received repeated protests about the treatment of POW. Webb documents how Shigemitsu thus had knowledge (or at the very least sufficient information to put him on inquiry notice) but he responded to Allied queries and protests with false information and refused to allow visits to relevant camps. Webb provides multiple examples of such conduct and adduces Japanese government documents that clearly demonstrate the falsehood of Shigemitsu's replies. Webb contrasts Shigemitsu's duties in his lower position as ambassador to those he assumes when he rises to the cabinet level. At that level he had the responsibility to take effective action to protect POW and civilians in occupied territory. Webb finds he disregarded this duty when he made "no proper inquiries and would not allow the Swiss or the International Red Cross representative to do so." He also never took up the issue with the cabinet or the Emperor, "let alone to resign or force a crisis." Shigemitsu's knowing provision of false information about the treatment of POW and internees goes beyond omission and failure to prevent and provides an inference of his acquiescence in the criminal activities.[39]

If that standard seems strict, one might refer again to the Ministries Case and Ernst von Weiszaecker who had a significantly lower position than Shigemitsu, as State Secretary in the foreign ministry. As we have seen, he was held accountable for mass murder and atrocities perpetrated in the Soviet Union and Poland because he did not resign when he became aware of them. Being below the cabinet level he could not directly influence policy or provoke a crisis, as could Shigemitsu. The tribunal convicted him on this basis even though they explicitly found that he had remained in office to continue his work in the resistance against Hitler. Despite the protestations of Pal and Roeling there was nothing exceptional in the WWII context about the conviction of a foreign minister on such a basis.

Webb's treatment of Koiso is strikingly abbreviated. Almost all of the eleven pages he devotes to Koiso's career concerns his role in regard to aggressive war. His conviction on Counts 54 and 55 is explained, in its entirety, by the following two sentences: "In all the offices he held he had a duty to see that

---

[39] TPJ 563–6, 568. Webb reaches a similar conclusion in regard to Kimura, who in January 1942 advises the foreign ministry that Japan will observe the 1929 Geneva Convention on POW. He receives protests about mistreatment of POW and does not reply except when giving false information.

the Laws and Customs of War were observed by the Japanese. He had ample warnings that they were not being observed [illegible addition of three words here in the manuscript] in the protests of the American and British governments and he did nothing effective to prevent them."[40] While this brief conclusion is in line with the treatment of Hiranuma, there is no explanation of why Koiso is also convicted under Count 54 as well as Count 55. The conviction for failure to prevent follows from Webb's position that as premier and the holder of other high offices he had knowledge of the crimes being committed by the Japanese military. The conviction of Count 54 is not explained or justified, though presumably it had to do with Koiso's direct role in operations in China as chief of staff of the Kwantung Army and for his role in regard the opium traffic, to which Webb devotes a paragraph.[41] The treatment of Koiso's liability for war crimes is thus far from satisfactory.

The differences in the treatment of Koiso and Hiranuma on the one hand and Shigemitsu on the other are striking, especially in light of the detail of his consideration of the evidence on crimes against peace. Shigemitsu is not the only civilian official whose role in regard to war crimes receives greater attention. In his 24-page discussion of the liability of Foreign Minister Tōgō, for example, Webb devotes two pages to an analysis of his role in regard to POW and cites specific evidence on which he grounds his legal conclusion that Tōgō could have brought about an improvement in the conditions of the POW if he had "forced a Cabinet crisis or appealed to the Emperor."[42] Shigemitsu and Tōgō were both foreign ministers while Hiranuma and Koiso both reached the level of premier. This again appears to arise from his direct involvement. Likewise, Webb devotes seven full pages to a careful and detailed account of the evidence regarding Tōjō's connection to war crimes.

### 10.2.2 The Responsibility of Military Offices for War Crimes

In the case of the defendants who occupied military roles Webb typically goes into far more detail about the factual context in which they operated. This is required in some cases because they operated below the national policy level of the cabinet and their liability is predicated upon a direct connection, if proved, to specific atrocities or to the implementation of policies with criminal consequences. In other cases Webb provides another explanation. For example, in regard to Ōshima, the Japanese military attaché to Berlin, Webb provides one of the lengthiest discussions from the twenty-five accused because,

---

[40] TPJ 435. Koiso served as chief of staff of the Kwantung Army from August 1932 to March 1934. For evidence concerning Koiso's involvement in opium traffic in Manchukuo, see the summation by the prosecution, T41189–90.
[41] TPJ 429.
[42] TPJ 630.

"No other part of the evidence shows so clearly the extent of German-Japanese cooperation for and in war as that involving Oshima's activities; so I have set it out at some length."[43]

The bulk of Webb's 16-page treatment of General Dohihara focuses on the charges of crimes against peace, as was discussed in the previous chapter. Webb also convicts Dohihara of failing to prevent war crimes under Count 55, but only in relation to POW. Webb discusses that when Dohihara was commander of the Eastern District Army in September–October 1943 he "had jurisdiction over POW camps located around Tokyo." Webb recounts that Dohihara inspected the Naoetsu Camp, where sixty prisoners died from starvation and ill-treatment during the period it was under Dohihara's command. Webb finds that there was no improvement in conditions at the camp after Dohihara's inspection.[44] He likewise finds that when Dohihara was Commander of the 7th Area Army in Singapore there was also widespread "ill treatment of prisoners and civilian internees." Webb cites an affidavit of Lieutenant General Ayabe Kijutsu that when Itagaki took over the Singapore command "there was marked improvement in the camps." Webb cites this evidence to indicate that Dohihara should have been aware of the conditions and had the capacity to improve them. Webb concludes that Dohihara's "inspection of Naoetsu Camp indicates his responsibility." He further states that the "world-wide protests" against Japanese ill-treatment of POW should have at least put Japanese commanders on inquiry notice. Webb's previous discussion of the circulation of information about protests has also indicated the way in which the system of handling protests provided specific information to local commanders.[45]

In contrast to the cursory explanation of the conviction of Hata in the majority judgment, Webb's 14-page treatment of Hata focuses in some detail on his connection to war crimes. Again, unlike the majority, Webb discusses specific evidence linking Hata to the crimes charged. He explains, for example, how troops under Hata's command, waging what Hata himself called a "Holy War" in China,[46] committed widespread atrocities in 1938 and the Japanese foreign office received protests concerning these.[47] Taking up Hata's next command in China from March 1941 to November 1944, Webb's discussion of war crimes committed under Hata's command during that period take up five pages. He deals in some depth with Hata's orders concerning the trial and punishment of the Doolittle Flyers, noting that Hata received reports on the trial

---

[43] TPJ 546.
[44] Key testimony against Dohihara as commander of the Eastern District Army was provided by James S. Chisholm, T14270–80. See also Chapter 6 under Section 6.2.3.
[45] TPJ 305, 307. See affidavit DX3312, excerpted at T30217–27. See also Chapter 6 under Section 6.4.1.
[46] TPJ 317.
[47] TPJ 316.

10.2 Individual Cases
385

and "requested the Prosecutor to ask for the death penalty."[48] Webb explains that at the time of the trial there was no Japanese legal provision for such a proceeding because regulations only provided for POW.[49] Later in the war, in July 1945, Hata also approved the death penalty for American flyers. In his conclusion on the war crimes charges, Webb, following the standard he previously articulated, imputes knowledge to Hata because of the "vast scale," geographical scope, and temporal duration of the crimes in China in the area under his command. These are all factors that would be relied upon today in contemporary international criminal tribunals, though they would need to be found to be established beyond a reasonable doubt, which the majority fails to do in regard to Hata. Taking these criteria into account together with the "repeated protests at the highest levels," Webb's judgment states that it is reasonable to conclude that although Hata had "the authority and the power to prevent" these crimes he knew to be occurring, he failed to do so.[50]

Webb reaches similar conclusions about Army Minister Itagaki. Webb found that he knew of war crimes perpetrated in China and that his vice minister issued an order for soldiers coming back from China not to discuss or reveal the atrocities that were taking place there.[51] Webb finds that Itagaki was also responsible for mistreatment of POW in Korea. Though as army minister he could have taken effective action in regard to war crimes by going to the cabinet or the Emperor he did nothing and hence breached his duty.[52] The treatment of Itagaki's involvement in war crimes is much less detailed than Webb's treatment of the evidence regarding aggressive war, but Webb makes clear, as follows from his previous discussion of the imputation of knowledge to officials at Itagaki's level, that as army minister he must have had knowledge yet failed to take any action to prevent such crimes from occurring.

Webb's treatment of Kimura's connection to war crimes while serving as vice minister of the army, taking up 9 pages of his judgment. He thus goes into much greater detail than in regard to Itagaki, perhaps because Itagaki as army minister could be, as Webb had previously argued, presumed to have knowledge as a member of the government. For Kimura, on the other hand, Webb cites specific evidence that links him directly to a wide range of war crimes.

---

[48] TPJ 325. For the comprehensive review of evidence against Hata regarding the trial and execution of Doolittle Flyers, see the prosecution's summation at T40762–75 and the defense summation at T43339–431.
[49] TPJ 324. Webb recounts how the flyers were not informed of the charges against them or even that they were facing a court martial, were not asked to plead nor provided with interpretation so that they could understand the proceedings, and so on. "The entire proceedings lasted 20 minutes to half an hour" (TPJ 325).
[50] TPJ 327.
[51] TPJ 387, 393.
[52] TPJ 393.

Webb begins by stating that while he was vice minister important protests of war crimes were referred directly to him.[53] Of the many protests received regarding Burma, China, and the Philippines, Webb notes that the Ministry of the Army responded only once and that was with false information. POW camps were under the supervision and authority of his ministry and the Imperial Ordinance provided that as vice minister he had shared responsibility for oversight of the relevant bureaus and divisions.[54] As an illustration of Kimura's direct involvement in POW affairs, Webb recounts how Kimura sent British and American POW to Korea in March 1942 and "complained that the accommodation which it was proposed to provide for them was too good."[55] Webb further specifies how Kimura took an active part in policy level discussions regarding the treatment and employment of POW in the Death Railway and elsewhere, and was aware of the mortality rates resulting from such employment.[56]

Taking up the period when Kimura assumed a field command as commander-in-chief of the Burma Area Army in September 1944, Webb goes into even greater detail analyzing the evidence on the basis of which he infers Kimura's knowledge of the widespread atrocities committed there in that period. As with Hata, Webb examines the nature of the atrocities, which included large scale massacres under orders of the field commanders. He refers to the geographical scope and proximity to Kimura's headquarters, the protests received by Kimura's command, the chain of command structure, and testimony by a camp commander that he was "ordered and directed" by Kimura.[57] Webb, like the majority, convicts Kimura under both Counts 54 and 55, but unlike the majority he provides specific evidence and a reasoned account to support his conclusion that Kimura not only failed to prevent crimes he knew were occurring but that he also was a party to the commission of those crimes.

Webb's treatment of Mutō, whom he regards as a key figure in Japanese war policy and planning, is puzzling in some respects. Because of Mutō's role Webb devotes twenty-three full pages to examining the evidence against him. In these, however, only two deal with war crimes charges. This imbalance in the verdicts as a whole has already been noted and reflects tribunal priorities apparently shared by all the judges, including the dissenters. What is puzzling about Webb's treatment of war crimes allegations against Mutō is that in regard to some of

---

[53] TPJ 416.
[54] TPJ 416–17. For the relevant army-ministry regulations, see note 115 in Chapter 6.
[55] TPJ 417. For reference to relevant court exhibits, see note 46 in Chapter 6.
[56] TPJ 417–18. No records of policy-level discussions *per se* regarding the use of prisoner-of-war labor for the Death Railway were presented at the Tokyo Trial. However, admissions were made by Japanese witnesses that some accused, including Kimura, had a share of responsibility for the policy decision. See Chapter 6 under Section 6.2.3.
[57] TPJ 422–3. The defense evidence concerning area-army commanders' responsibility for prisoner-of-war administration, see Chapter 6 under Section 6.4.1.

## 10.2 Individual Cases

the charges Webb is, as is usually the case, quite specific in linking Mutō to the criminal conduct. For example, he begins the section entitled "Atrocities" by demonstrating Muto's role in policy formulation regarding POW when he was the director of the Military Affairs Bureau of the Ministry of the Army: "MUTO admitted that the policy pertaining to prisoners of war emanated from the Prisoner of War Information Bureau ... and that Prisoners of War camps were built under his Bureau." Webb also cites testimony by one of the officers from the "Prisoner of War Control Bureau" of the Ministry of the Army (or also known as the Prisoner-of-War Administration Section) affirmed Mutō's role in issuing orders and implementing policy.[58]

The other main charge against Mutō that Webb considers at length concerns Mutō's role in the Nanjing Massacre, where he was vice chief of staff for General Matsui. Webb relies on Mutō's admission that he was in Nanjing for ten days at the relevant time and his acknowledgment that rape and plunder occurred, though he denied the extent of those crimes. Webb also cites Mutō's admission that a book subsequently published on the Nanjing Massacre was read with shame by Japanese officers and that the misconduct was "a demonstration of weakness on the part of Japanese military education" which he was powerless to influence.[59]

The aspect of Webb's treatment of Mutō that is problematic concerns his findings that Mutō was responsible for atrocities in the Philippines while chief of staff for General Yamashita. In contrast to his treatment of Mutō's role at Nanjing, Webb cites no evidence beyond the fact that Mutō held this position "at the time of Manila atrocities."[60] On this basis alone Webb concludes that, "As Matsui's vice chief of staff at Nanking and Yamashita's chief of staff in the Philippines MUTO *must have known* of the dreadful conduct of the Japanese troops but he did nothing to correct or to discipline the troops"[61] (emphasis

---

[58] TPJ 493. Mutō's admission regarding the role of the Military Affairs Bureau in prisoner-of-war policy can be found in PX255, T3436. See also Chapter 6 under Section 6.2.2. The officer from ther Prisoner-of-War Administration Section that Webb refers to is probably Colonel Yamazaki Shigeru, who took the stand as a prosecution's witness and later as a defense witness. His testimony included the following: "The Prisoner of War Information Bureau and the Prisoner of War Control Bureau [the Prisoner-of-War Administration Section] acted according to the orders of the Military Affairs Bureau," (T14840); and, "The chief of the Prisoner of War Information Bureau, and concurrently the chief of the Prisoner of War Management Bureau [the Prisoner-of-War Administration Section], was given the power of decision only to a very limited extent and on important matters he had to receive his orders from the Military Affairs Bureau," 14841–2.

[59] TPJ 494. Webb's finding is probably based on PX255, Allied Postwar Interrogation of Mutō Akira. It records the following admission made by Mutō: "When I went to North China, I did hear that such a book was published in America concerning the rape of Nanking, but due to the fact that I could not read English, I was unable to read the book." (T3557). The book being referred to was probably the one admitted in evidence as PX323, which is referenced in Chapter 6.

[60] TPJ 495.

[61] TPJ 496.

added). While in the case of Nanjing, Webb has provided a reasoned account of how he reached this conclusion based one the application of his "must have known" standard. In regard to the Manila atrocities, however, Webb provides no information as to where Mutō was located at the time, what information he had, etc. While his conclusion as to Nanjing differs from that of the majority, who acquitted Mutō on the problematic grounds that despite his knowledge as vice chief-of staff he could not influence policy, Webb consistently applies his legal standard and finds him guilty of those charges. In regard to Manila, however, Webb takes the same position as the majority but unlike them he does not even mention Mutō's defense that he had no knowledge of the crimes. Because the burden of proof is on the prosecution, Webb's failure to cite evidence to support the conclusion that Mutō "must have known" of the atrocities is as flawed as that of the majority. Given his careful exposition of Mutō's accountability for the other war crimes charges, as well as his exhaustive discussion of the aggressive war charges, this shortcoming remains unexplained.

In contrast to this omission in regard to Mutō, Webb pays considerable attention to the evidence against Vice Admiral Oka Takazumi, director of the Naval Affairs Bureau of the Ministry of the Navy after 1940. As with Mutō, Webb details Oka's role and influence at policy levels in regard to war planning and preparations. As to the war crimes charges, largely concerning mistreatment of POW, Webb spends four of twenty one pages considering the context and evidence. He reviews key parts of Oka's testimony, including his admission that his bureau had responsibility for regulations and reporting on POW and for furnishing information to the Ministry of Foreign Affairs for replies to protests about mistreatment.[62] Webb also details how the Naval Affairs Bureau undertook investigations and issued instructions about the treatment and transportation of POW in navy custody. On this basis he convicts Oka under Count 55 for his failure to prevent mistreatment. On the other hand, in regard to charges concerning Oka's accountability for murder of POW ordered by camp commanders and other officers, Webb, after considering the evidence in detail, concludes that Oka "cannot on the evidence be found to have been a party to those orders."[63] As seen in the previous chapter, the majority, without careful consideration of the evidence, acquitted Oka on all war crimes charges. Webb's judgment provides a contrasting reasoned account that is based on the evidence and nuanced in its application.

Another example may further underscore the difference in the way Webb treats some cabinet-level accused from those with bureaucratic positions. Satō served as government commissioner for army matters in the Imperial Diet and director of the Military Affairs Bureau of the Ministry of the Army (from 1942). In his capacity as director of the Military Affairs Bureau, he had

[62] TPJ 513.
[63] TPJ 517.

responsibility for construction of POW camps and for replies to protests of mistreatment there. He attended bi-weekly meetings and those where Tōjō's policy that all POW must work was announced. Reviewing all the evidence Webb concludes that, "SATO was not satisfied to remain a mere soldier or civil servant: he engaged in important political activities."[64] As director of the Military Affairs Bureau responsible for the proper care of POW, he did nothing to prevent their exploitation through labor on war-related projects or to ensure that they were not otherwise mistreated. In other words, Satō's liability, like that of Oka or Matsui and Mutō, is rooted in his specific spheres of activity and the way in which he managed their specific duties and responsibilities.

In regard to cabinet-level officials, Webb argued that a system for the circulation of information was in place that permitted an imputation of knowledge because it ensured that all such individuals "must have known" of reports of criminal conduct in the field. At this higher level, in exalted positions of power and authority, the possession of information concerning atrocities was enough to require cabinet members to take all steps within their power to alter the policy of their government, even to the point of taking the matter to the Emperor and provoking a governmental crisis if their protests were not effective. On Webb's analysis, there were no accused in cabinet positions who took such action and therefore individuals such as Hirota, Kaya, Shigemitsu, and Hiranuma had to bear the "consequences" of their actions. Webb did not, however, apply this standard blindly. In regard to Araki, for example, Webb makes the specific finding that his position as cabinet councilor alone was not enough to establish his liability for Nanjing or other crimes against humanity and war crimes. Webb also finds that there was no evidence that in his role as education minister he received enough information about war crimes in China to put him on inquiry notice. For this reason Webb acquits him on the charges related to war crimes.

## 10.3 Conclusion

Webb's analysis of the liability of the individual accused on war crimes charges is, on the whole, balanced, careful, and consistent in its application of a clear standard of responsibility. He first articulates the standard he will apply and then elaborates on it by describing a system that justifies the imputation of knowledge to certain levels of the government. In the individual verdicts he usually cites specific evidence that prove knowledge or that provide sufficient grounds for inferences imputing knowledge beyond a reasonable doubt. The majority, on the other hand, do not sufficiently link their treatment of the individual accused in regard to war crimes charges to the section of the judgment on the general context of war crimes. Because the majority judgment focuses

---

[64] TPJ 555.

the substance of its individual verdicts almost exclusively on the charges of planning and waging aggressive war, it too often provides only sketchy, if any, references to the evidence on that basis of which it convicts for war crimes charges. In contradistinction to Webb, the majority judgment almost never actually quotes or cites specific evidence on war crimes let alone weighing that evidence to justify its conclusions. This is not to say that the evidence does not exist, but rather that the majority, unlike Webb, typically fails to analyze it in any depth. If Webb's draft judgment had been adopted by the majority we would have been provided with a very different perspective from which to view the verdicts of guilt against the accused.

In the end, Webb's draft judgment places its overwhelming emphasis on the responsibility of each individual accused. The majority's overemphasis on the theory of a conspiracy to wage aggressive war, which occupies such a large portion of its judgment, tends to efface the role of specific individuals in favor of a sweeping narrative that places an abstract collectivity, "the conspirators," in the foreground. For many of the accused, though not all, the majority's consideration of their role in regard to the war crimes charges seems almost to be an afterthought.

Pal's dissenting opinion in a sense goes a step further. He too often appears to ignore that a trial is about individual guilt, not national guilt or innocence. His desire to exculpate the Japanese government or state as a collectivity overshadows the fact that the IMTFE is a trial of individual accused persons for each of whom the prosecution has to prove guilt beyond a reasonable doubt and *for each of whom* the judges have the responsibility to provide a reasoned account of the findings and evidence that grounds their conclusions of guilt or of innocence. Webb, in his draft judgment, most fully fulfills the role of judge who weighs the evidence against each accused in turn on each of the charges against them and provides a reasoned decision in each individual case. He spared the majority the embarrassment his draft judgment would have caused if it had been published as his concurring opinion. Unfortunately, however, his decision not to adopt it as his concurring opinion has provided posterity with a very incomplete sense of the evidence before the court that on Webb's view justified the convictions of the accused.

# 11 The Dissenting Opinions of Justices Bernard and Roeling

## 11.1 Bernard's Dissent

As noted earlier, the majority judgment has seldom been analyzed systematically in regard to its qualities as a final written decision providing a reasoned justification of its findings and conclusions. Likewise, the legal content of the separate opinions has been significantly neglected.[1] This chapter examines the separate opinions of Justices Bernard and Roeling. While of all the separate dissenting opinions Bernard's has received relatively little attention, at the same time it can shed light on internal differences among the judges as to some of the most fundamental jurisprudential issues before the court.[2] It also reveals the way in which the legal culture of these eleven judges from such disparate backgrounds shaped the way they viewed such issues. While Bernard's separate opinion may not have had the political impact as those of Pal and Roeling, that it did not, for the thrust of Bernard's objection to the proceedings at the IMTFE is that the Japanese emperor was not also on trial. This uncomfortable fact for many Japanese critics of the trial may explain why Bernard has received so much less attention than Roeling and Pal. The grounds of this neglect are also interesting because Bernard's opinion is in some ways similar to those of Pal and Roeling in offering an alternative account of the basis of international law and the conceptual and philosophical foundations of the very idea of international justice.[3] For this reason alone it should compel our attention.[4]

---

[1] Sellars, "The Legacy of the Tokyo Dissents on 'Crimes against Peace,'" points up the juristic importance of the dissenting opinions on crimes against peace.
[2] Bernard participated in the drafting of the majority judgment and his memoranda indicate some of these differences of opinion. See, for instance, his memorandum of April 28, 1948 to the members of the tribunal as well as his memorandum "Remarks Concerning the Draft of Judgment of the Majority," which deals in considerable detail with the Japanese operations in Manchuria in 1931–2. NAA M1417/25.
[3] On Bernard, see Esmein, "Le juge Henri Bernard au procès de Tôkyô."
[4] Bernard's memorandum to Webb of January 31, 1947 indicates that he was prepared to write a dissent if the majority did not accept his "opinion on the non-criminality in itself of violations of treaties." (NAA M1417/ 25).

At the outset of his opinion Bernard rejects the defense and Pal's arguments on the legitimacy of the tribunal.[5] He states that the Allied nations were, by virtue of the criminal nature of the war waged by Japan, "perfectly qualified to create the International Military Tribunal for the Far East." He also finds that the charge of "victor's justice" is without merit because (1) the Allies created a tribunal and turned the accused over to it; (2) there was no alternative mechanism because of the lack of an international authority; (3) the Allies provided the procedural basis for a fair trial. He concludes his discussion of the issue of the legitimacy of the IMTFE by saying that failure to create such a court "would have deprived the world of a verdict, the necessity of which is universally felt."[6] It is small wonder that critics of the tribunal prefer to focus on Pal and generally ignore the salient points made by Bernard. This is also the case because, as will appear, the central thrust of Bernard's objections to the outcome of the tribunal's proceedings is that Emperor Hirohito was not the principal defendant.

Bernard, like Webb in his unpublished draft judgment, criticizes the position taken by the majority on conspiracy.[7] He finds that the majority erred in dismissing the counts of the indictment on planning and preparation of aggressive war on the grounds that findings of guilt on conspiracy subsume the other modes of liability. On Bernard's view, "planning and preparation are more serious matters than the mere conspiracy; consequently they must be taken into consideration by the tribunal and should be taken as the basis for conviction if found established."[8] Bernard's view proceeds from the position that sole reliance on the vague notion of conspiracy obscures the nature of the accused's *individual participation* in the crimes of which they have been found guilty.

His argument, though not articulated in detail, seems to be that subsuming all accused in a grand conspiracy, and at the same time refraining from making specific findings on counts of the indictment that charge specific modes of conduct by which crimes were perpetrated, makes it difficult to fairly assess the culpability of individual accused. Bernard is indeed correct that taking part

---

[5] Bernard prepared a lengthy memorandum (January 4, 1947) on the rationale for the rejection of the defense motions challenging the jurisdiction of the IMTFE. This memorandum follows on his previous draft presented to Webb on October 10, 1946 (NAA M1417/25). In the January memorandum Bernard indicates that he had hoped that the Nuremberg judgment would provide answers to all such objections but notes that because it did not he provides his own substantive treatment expressing his views. NAA M1417/24. We might also note Justice Mei's memorandum of December 8, 1946 on the same issue, entitled "Rambling Remarks on the Draft Judgment." (NAA M1417/25).

[6] Bernard Opinion, 665.

[7] Bernard provided the tribunal with memoranda setting out in detail his arguments on conspiracy, which on the contentious issue of "naked conspiracy" echoed those of Webb. See, for instance, his memoranda of October 13, 1948 AWM 3DRL 2481/5 and October 7, 1948 AWM 3DRL 2481/4.

[8] Bernard Opinion, 666.

## 11.1 Bernard's Dissent

in the actual planning and preparation of an aggressive war is more serious than merely being part of a group that has agreed that Japan should wage such a war. Such differential roles should be reflected in sentencing and should be based upon factual findings that support the conclusions about the culpability of each accused. In this regard, as argued above, the majority judgment is sorely deficient.

A major thrust of Bernard's opinion, and one of its most interesting aspects, bears not upon the findings of guilt or innocence, but upon the majority's position on the foundation of the law of the tribunal. According to Bernard, the majority position is that objections made by the defense to the jurisdiction of the tribunal (and echoed by Pal) must be rejected because "the law of the charter is decisive and binding."[9] These objections include that aggressive war is not illegal, that there is no individual responsibility for war, and that the Charter is ex post facto legislation and thus itself illegal.

The majority judgment addresses objections to the legitimacy and jurisdiction of the tribunal through a lengthy citation of the Nuremberg judgment which locates the binding nature of the Charter in the "sovereign legislative power" of the victorious Allies to whom Germany unconditionally surrendered. Although Bernard recognizes the right of the Allies to convene such a tribunal he nonetheless believes that there is a foundation for what he calls the "substantive law" of the tribunal that transcends such "legislative" authority.[10] Bernard, in articulating this view, goes beyond the Nuremberg judgment's discussion of the evolution of international law in the first half of the twentieth century as the basis for the criminalization of aggressive war. Implicitly rejecting this justification rooted in legal positivism he invokes another, and on his view higher, source of law.

The Nuremberg judgment went beyond the statement of the binding nature of the Charter and elaborated at some length upon the justification for establishing aggressive war as a crime. It explained this manner of proceeding by indicating that even though the Charter was legitimate and binding the issues raised by the defense objections were important for international law. The majority judgment does not engage in such an extended jurisprudential discussion, though Webb does so in his unpublished draft judgment. It is the majority's bald reliance on the Charter alone that is the focus of Bernard's objection.[11]

How, then, does Bernard justify his position that aggressive war is indeed an international crime and a crime for which there is individual criminal

---

[9] Ibid., 668.
[10] Ibid.
[11] Bernard acknowledges that the majority at times indicates its awareness of other grounds but he argues that the positivistic reliance on the Charter is the real basis of its position (Bernard Opinion, 669).

responsibility? In contradistinction to the approach of the majority and of Webb, he turns to the European tradition of natural law jurisprudence. He rejects the majority's view that in accepting appointment as a judge at the IMTFE they accept the validity of all of the substantive law articulated by the Charter. On Bernard's view such legitimacy must be measured against a higher source of law and not, for example, on interpretation of the Pact of Paris, etc. He states this position quite clearly:

There is no doubt in my mind that such war is and always has been a crime in the eyes of reason and universal conscience – expressions of natural law upon which an international tribunal can *and must* base itself to judge the conduct of the accused tendered to it.[12] (emphasis added)

Bernard goes even further, however, and maintains that it is natural law, and not the Charter, which also establishes the responsibility of individuals for state-organized criminality:

There is no doubt either that the individual cannot shelter behind the responsibility of the community the responsibility which he incurred by his own acts. Assuming there exists collective responsibility, obviously the latter can only be added to the individual responsibility and cannot eliminate the same. It is because they are inscribed in natural law and not in the constitutive acts of the Tribunal by the writers of the Charter, *whose honor it is, however, to have recalled them*, that those principles impose themselves upon the respect of the Tribunal. (emphasis added)

In regard to the substantive issue of the legitimacy of charging aggressive war as an international crime for which there is individual responsibility, Bernard is in complete agreement with the majority and with Webb. It is in regard to how this position is justified that he dissents. He invokes natural law in maintaining that the judges of the IMTFE are only "recalling" principles already grounded in an eternal natural order. He does not elaborate upon the philosophical basis of such claims but it is clear that he is both standing in a certain European tradition and also that his position must be seen in the context of jurisprudential debates that raged in the postwar years over the status of the positive law as against higher principles of justice. In attacking the legitimacy of, for example, the laws of the Nazi regime, scholars such as Radbruch and others turned to the natural law tradition to argue that an unjust and iniquitous law is not a law at all and may be set aside. Bernard stands in this tradition in claiming that the legitimacy of the IMTFE and of the law it applies can only be found in the "higher" sphere of natural law and universal reason.[13]

---

[12] Ibid., 670.
[13] On Radbruch see, for instance, Radbruch, "Fuenf Minuten Rechtsphilosophie," and in the Anglo-American context the famous Hart-Fuller debate. For an overview of the literature and issues in regard to the legal legacy of the Nazi era see, Joerges and Singh Ghaleigh, eds., *Darker Legacies of Law in Europe*.

## 11.1 Bernard's Dissent

One of the most substantial sections of Bernard's Opinion concerns conventional war crimes. The first sentence of this section makes clear his differences with Pal and why his judgment is generally not examined by those who take a revisionist view:

> There can be no doubt that *on all steps of its hierarchy* the members of the Japanese Army and Police made themselves guilty of the most abominable crimes in respect to the prisoners of war, internees, and civilians of occupied territories.[14] (emphasis added)

Bernard then goes on to focus on crimes against prisoners of war and, while approving holding the accused liable for such mistreatment, criticizes the legal grounds on which the majority relies. He agrees with the majority that the four groups specified in the majority judgment can be held liable for such crimes:

> (1) Members of the Government; (2) Military or Naval officers in command of formations having prisoners in their possession; (3) … ; (4) officials, *whether civilian, military, or naval*, having direct and immediate control of prisoners.[15] (emphasis added)

He disagrees, however, that Article IV of the Hague Convention No. 4 of 1907, provides the correct legal basis for their liability and he further disagrees with the majority's reasoning as to what conditions are required to hold members of the specified groups accountable.[16] Although his interpretation of Article IV is implausible and unconvincing, his critique of the majority's reasoning is far more well-founded.[17] As will appear, the real reason for rejecting the majority's citation of Article IV appears to be that Bernard prefers to rely on natural law rather than international statutory law as the basis for assessing liability.

Bernard's analysis of the defects of the majority's reasoning follows a similar line as to his objections to the exclusive focus on conspiracy in regard to proving crimes against peace: the lack of individuation in regard to the specific conduct and specific culpability of each accused person before the tribunal. His disagreement with the majority is well founded. He objects to the majority's generalization of liability based upon institutional position rather than individual conduct and argues that culpability, and hence appropriate sentencing, must differ from individual to individual. One sees here again how much better

---

[14] Bernard Opinion, 671.
[15] Ibid.
[16] Ibid., 671–3. The section of the majority judgment Bernard refers to has been analyzed in detail in Chapter 6.
[17] Bernard, without providing any reasoning to back up his assertion, interprets the provision that prisoners of war "are in the power of the hostile government but not of the individuals or corps who capture them" to mean that those individuals or corps who capture the prisoners have absolutely no responsibility for any war crimes which they perpetrate against them (Bernard Opinion, 671).

served the tribunal would have been in adopting the Webb draft judgment as it to a significant degree addresses precisely Bernard's concerns.

The essence of Bernard's analysis is that "no-one can be held responsible for other than the necessary consequences of his own acts or omissions." In regard to omissions, for example, the crucial category for failure to prevent mistreatment of prisoners of war, Bernard correctly argues that an attribution of responsibility must rely upon "proving that the author of the omission could by an action of some kind prevent the commission and its direct harmful consequences."[18] That an individual cannot be punished for the acts of others of which he had no knowledge or was powerless to prevent is well established not only in the contemporary jurisprudence of the international criminal tribunals but also in fundamental principles of criminal law. Bernard points to the failure of the majority to provide factual findings on these issues for each of the accused convicted of such war crimes charges. Bernard specifically and justifiably rejects the imputation of knowledge to all of these accused on the general grounds that the crimes were widespread, etc. He correctly holds that, "No general rule can be made upon this point and proof that omission is the cause of harm done must be furnished in each case by the prosecution."[19] In other words, he rejects the general categorization of *classes* of individuals who can be held liable by virtue of their positions and recalls the legal burden of the prosecution of making the case against each of them.

Unlike the majority or Pal, Bernard articulates a clear standard of liability based upon what he takes to be established principles of criminal jurisprudence and natural law, to which he again reverts.[20] He maintains that there are two bases on which guilt may be established for the failure to prevent mistreatment. Although the first basis could be far more clearly formulated, in essence it provides that when a person is accused of a failure to prevent a war crime it must be proved that (1) he or she was able to prevent the commission of the crime; (2) no legal presumption suffices to establish such proof; (3) the crimes must be the direct result of their omission or negligence.

The second basis of liability is more clearly formulated and provides that an individual may be held liable for a failure of duty to protect prisoners of war when their imprudence, negligence, or disregard of regulations or orders "created a state of fact suited to the multiplication of violations of the laws of war."[21] In concluding the discussion of this section on conventional war crimes we should note that Bernard focused only on prisoners of war and did not

---

[18] Ibid., 673.
[19] Ibid.
[20] He concludes this section on conventional war crimes by criticizing the view that the treaties, conventions, and customary law encompass the whole of the legal sphere that applies to the regulation of conflict (ibid., 674).
[21] Ibid., 674.

## 11.1 Bernard's Dissent

consider crimes against the other two groups he mentioned at the beginning of the section. Given that he there indicated his conviction that Japanese forces were also responsible for the most serious crimes against these groups we are left in the dark as to whether he also had disagreements with the approach of the majority on convictions for such crimes.

The most striking feature of Bernard's standard of liability, however, is that he provides no basis for it either in international practice and custom or in the considerable body of conventional law represented by the Hague and Geneva Conventions. Considering that Japan had declared that it would respect the 1929 Geneva Convention one would have thought it appropriate that Bernard would at least refer to its provisions. He does not. What he does instead is to refer again to natural law as what he takes to be the proper basis for adjudicating war criminality. He does not cite any authority either for the general applicability of natural law or for the specific standards of liability that he articulates. Indeed, his position is baffling in its scope: "Several times in expressing my opinion I preferred the expression of natural or universal law to that of international law."[22]

Bernard here appears to venture into metaphysical terrain with his apparent disdain for the body of international legal doctrine. For his twin propositions that the natural law is higher and "above nations" and that concrete norms to define offenses and theories of responsibility can somehow be derived from it, he provides no argument, citation, or foundation. He contents himself with the sole remark that although there are differences of opinion as to the nature of natural law, "its existence is not seriously contested *or contestable* and the *declaration* of its existence is sufficient for our purpose"[23] (emphasis added).

Bernard's assertion that the mere "declaration" of natural law suffices and cannot be contested indicates that he leans on the natural law tradition that is grounded in faith and belief in a metaphysical higher authority. It is beyond the scope of this analysis to assess the biographical origins of Bernard's approach.[24] More salient for present purposes is Bernard's apparent conviction that he can simply sweep away any discussion of international law jurisprudence with a vague reference to metaphysics. When he states that natural law as the basis for substantive law is not "seriously contested or contestable" he also ignores major traditions of legal philosophy that do precisely that. Indeed, in Bernard's era, theories of legal positivism, associated with major figures like Hans Kelsen, but going back much further in the European tradition, were in the ascendancy and it is perhaps for this reason that he wanted to take a stand against such theories for reasons briefly alluded to above. In any event, it is

---

[22] Ibid.
[23] Ibid.
[24] For Bernard's biography, see Ōoka, *Tōkyō saiban*.

clear that Bernard stands apart from all of his fellow judges in his belief that the tribunal does have the authority to punish individuals for crimes against peace and for war crimes but that this authority, and the doctrines through which it is implemented, derive not from Charters, declarations, conventions, or custom, but rather from the metaphysical realm of natural and universal law.

Thus far, Bernard's dissent has supported the legitimacy of the tribunal and of the charges against the accused. He has provided alternative rationales for the proceedings but has not challenged the results. The final two sections of his dissenting opinion, however, do just that. In the penultimate section, "Opinion relative to the Proceedings of the Tribunal," Bernard articulates three grounds on which the fairness of the trial might be contested. What is perhaps most peculiar about these grounds is that they are not based upon any reference to the "natural and universal law" which he has previously emphasized as the ultimate and authoritative source of applicable norms.

The first objection made by Bernard is striking in its narrowly chauvinistic view of justice and fair trial rights. Bernard argues that principles of justice have been violated because the tribunal did not employ an investigating judge to collect and analyze the evidence for both prosecution and defense. Bernard's apparent belief that only the French civil law procedural provisions can provide a fair trial is baffling in its insularity and implication that all trials conducted under the common law and other civil law systems which do not follow the French civil law model are inherently and inescapably unfair. It is also striking that Bernard relies here not upon a reference to his "preferred" standard of natural law but rather upon the positivistic national institutional arrangements of particular countries (unless, of course he believes that the French system derives from divine law, but he does not say so). The inherent contradiction is clear.

The second objection made by Bernard has a valid political foundation but Bernard cites neither legal authority nor natural law as its basis. Bernard argues that the prosecution of the accused was "unequal" because Emperor Hirohito was not among those indicted. While one might agree on the substance of his claim that Hirohito should have been among the accused, Bernard makes no plausible or reasoned argument as to why it was unjust to convict those who were in fact demonstrated to be guilty of what he himself calls "the most abominable crimes."[25] Here he appears to confuse the political and moral objections that might be made to the exclusion of Hirohito with legal standards of fair trial rights. Where, one might ask, is there a recognized norm in international or domestic criminal law that if one individual potentially implicated in a crime is not indicted then no one else can be brought to trial for the same or related crimes? Further, at the time of the IMTFE judgment there was no legal bar to

---

[25] Bernard Opinion, 671.

## 11.1 Bernard's Dissent

subsequent prosecutions against other Class A war criminals, including the Emperor.[26]

Bernard's third and final ground is also puzzling. The essence of his objection on the grounds of fair trial rights was that, "the eleven judges which compose the Tribunal were never called to meet" to orally discuss the judgment.[27] Bernard explains that a committee of seven prepared a draft "majority" judgment and that the opinions of the other judges were distributed amongst all the judges for comment. In fact, the archival records of the tribunal provide us with a substantial body of such memoranda that commented upon, proposed revisions for, and debated many parts of this draft judgment. Those participating in that exercise included Bernard. He acknowledges this and also notes that the majority in fact modified parts of their judgment in response to such suggestions. He also noted that drafts of two dissenting opinions were also circulated.[28] He provides no legal basis whatsoever for the assertion that the lack of an oral deliberation of all the judges violated fundamental principles of fair trial rights to such a degree so as to invalidate the proceedings as a whole.

In sum, none of the three procedural grounds which Bernard views as such serious violations of fair trial rights have a firm legal basis. One is rooted in a blind belief in the unique superiority of the French system, seemingly unaware of the serious objections that had been raised inside and outside France of its fairness to the rights of the accused. The second is a political critique of the decision to try Japan's political and military leaders without Hirohito and offers no legal basis for claiming this as a violation of fair trial rights and due process. The third has no basis whatsoever either in the Charter of the tribunal or in international law. One is left to wonder whether perhaps Bernard simply felt slighted or left out when the majority did not accept his eccentric view of the foundation of the trial in "natural law."[29] He concludes this section of his opinion with the even more puzzling remark that although he in fact signed the judgment of the IMTFE his signature does not indicate an "acknowledgement thereof."[30] One again must wonder why a lawyer and judge would sign a judgment which he does not "acknowledge."

The trajectory of Bernard's opinion is a strange one. While the earlier sections make cogent legal arguments about the defects of the majority's approach to liability for war crimes or its sole reliance upon a conspiracy narrative, the

---

[26] See under Section 1.2. of Chapter 1, and also Totani, *The Tokyo War Crimes Trial*, chapters 2 and 3, on the ongoing discussions of the status of the Emperor and on the subsequent Class A proceedings against Admiral Toyoda Soemu and Lieutenant General Tamura Hiroshi, also held in Tokyo in the period of 1948–9. A detailed analysis of the trials of Toyoda and Tamura can be found in Totani, *Justice in Asia and the Pacific Region, 1945–1952*, chapters 2 and 6.
[27] Bernard Opinion, 675.
[28] Ibid., 675.
[29] On Bernard's motivation, see Ōoka, *Tōkyō saiban*, 22.
[30] Bernard Opinion, 676.

opinion increasingly wanders into questionable territory. The culmination of this tendency is perhaps most plainly seen in the two final sections, the second of which turns to the "Verdict and Sentences."

While Bernard has, correctly on our view, criticized the majority judgment for its failure to individualize the culpability of the accused with specific findings on their individual conduct, he appears to be guilty of the same error. His entire critique of the verdicts and sentences occupies less than two pages and does not refer to any of the individual accused but treats them as a group. Bernard articulates three grounds for his objection to the verdicts.

In regard to the charges related to aggressive war he argues that the meaning of the terms "conspiring," "planning," "preparing," "waging," and "initiating" were too vague for the accused to have known what conduct in relation to the war in which they participated was illegal. He states that only "the formal proof" that the accused had "succeeded" in understanding the meaning of these terms could ground their responsibility.

This is a strange argument to make considering that Bernard, as seen above, had accepted the illegality of aggressive war as founded in natural and universal law. If this was the natural and universal law which superseded the law of the Charter and all relevant international treaties, how could the accused have been unaware of it? It is perhaps for this reason that Bernard tries to rely on his assertion of the "vagueness" of what it means to plan, prepare, initiate, or wage war. But it surely stretches the imagination to contend that the Japanese high command was unaware of what it meant to "wage war" or to prepare or plan it. What Bernard appears to aim at here is to establish the crime of aggressive war as rooted in immutable natural law, and hence not ex post facto, but at the same time to find a way to exculpate the accused. The true reason for this strategy appears in his second and most interesting objection to the verdicts.

The second objection of Bernard addresses the conspiracy charge but quickly turns again to the role of Emperor Hirohito and it is here that Bernard's difficulty with the tribunal appears to reside. Bernard states that he regards the "declaration of the Pacific war" as "the most serious of acts committed against peace."[31] Why the fourteen years of the Japanese war and occupation in China were less "serious" he does not indicate. What he does state, however, is that of this "most serious act" there was "a principal author who escaped all prosecution and of whom in any case the present defendants could only be considered as accomplices."[32] That "principal author," he makes clear in the subsequent paragraph, was Emperor Hirohito.

Bernard's revulsion against the decision by the American and British governments to exclude the Emperor from the proceedings so they could continue to

---

[31] Ibid., 677.
[32] Ibid.

## 11.1 Bernard's Dissent

use him for their own purposes is understandable. The Australian government vehemently objected to this manner of proceeding. It must have indeed been galling for a judge convinced of the ultimate responsibility of the Emperor to have sat through a trial that only accused those who regarded him as their superior authority. Whatever his objections, however, Bernard's responsibility as a judge was to make findings against each of the accused on the basis of the evidence against them. He did not need to rely on the evidence adduced by the majority alone, for he had access to the complete record of the trial and could have, as Webb did in his draft judgment, analyzed this evidence and arrived at his own conclusions as to guilt and innocence. Indeed, since he criticized the majority for not meeting this standard he was surely bound to do so himself. What he did instead was to imply, though not state explicitly, that none were guilty of aggressive war because the Emperor did not join them in the defendant's dock. He rather refuses to make an explicit statement and instead of analyzing the evidence himself he contents himself with stating that the "defects of the procedure followed by the prosecution did not permit me to formulate a definite opinion concerning the questions raised by the accusations of crimes against peace."[33]

In this regard Bernard fails in his fundamental duty as a judge by refraining from clearly stating his findings on the guilt and innocence of the accused based on the facts brought into evidence. His apparent disgust at the exclusion of Hirohito does not justify either invalidating the whole proceedings without a legal justification for this position, or in refusing to make findings against the other accused. If they were "accomplices," as he himself states, that characterization needs to be documented for each of them, as he required of the majority. And if the evidence in fact supports the attribution of accomplice liability then the guilty verdicts would be justified. The fact that he disapproves of the treatment of Hirohito does not relieve him of his responsibility as a judge and if he found it morally distasteful to participate in such proceedings he should have resigned and in any event should not have signed the majority judgment.

Bernard's treatment of the verdicts in regard to war crimes and crimes against humanity is even more questionable on the same grounds. He disposes of these charges in seven obscurely formulated lines, though not by indicating that the accused bear no responsibility for them. This final paragraph speaks for itself in testifying to Bernard's abdication of his judicial responsibilities. He has rejected the majority's approach and articulated his own standards for assessing the liability of the accused for war crimes, yet he fails to apply these same standards to indicate where he may differ from the majority on their individual verdicts. He finds, as he has already indicated, that Japanese forces perpetrated the most serious international crimes. He also proposes standards

---

[33] Ibid.

for analyzing the individual responsibility of the accused for these crimes, yet he concludes his opinion as follows (quoted in full):

> The most abominable crimes were committed on the largest scale by the members of the Japanese police and navy I esteemed I could say nevertheless, and I will add there is no doubt in my mind that certain Defendants bear a large part of the responsibility for them, that others rendered themselves guilty of serious failings in the duties towards the prisoners of war and towards humanity. I could not venture further in the formulation of verdicts, the exactitude of which would be subject to caution or to sentences, the equity of which would be far too contestable.[34]

## 11.2 Roeling's Dissent

### 11.2.1 Introduction

Although Roeling did not attain the same heroic status granted to Pal by the Japanese arch-conservatives and many American scholars, because of his dissenting opinion he is nonetheless often accorded a second place in the ranks of those who had the courage to reject the Tokyo Trial's judgment. Like Pal, he is also often regarded as a great jurist who had a broader understanding of international justice than his brethren on the International Military Tribunal for the Far East. What is, however, typically not dealt with is that fact that although Roeling argued that five of the accused, and most notably former prime minister and Foreign Minister Hirota and Foreign Minister Shigemitsu, should not have been convicted, he concurred with the conviction of *all* of the other twenty defendants. What is even less often referenced, however, is the reasoning by which he justified his opinion on these two groups of defendants. In fact, while Roeling is frequently praised as a great jurist, his actual jurisprudence has received relatively little analytical attention.[35] This discussion of Roeling will seek to provide that critical assessment.[36]

Apart from the importance of actually dealing with the legal and political arguments which Roeling develops, his opinion is important in several other ways. First it points up how many assessments of the Tokyo Trial judgment are informed more by political stances about the individual verdicts than by objective analyses of the evidence, legal doctrine, and reasoning on which those verdicts are based. Second, it involves important issues of judicial independence and codes of conduct raised by the fact that Roeling, as is not widely

---

[34] Ibid.
[35] For the best English language treatment of Roeling's jurisprudence see Cryer, "Roeling in Tokyo. On Roeling's heroic stature see, e.g. Van der Wilt, "A Valiant Champion of Equity and Humaneness."
[36] The comprehensive treatment of Roeling's overall participation in the IMTFE and its broader Dutch context, see Van Poelgeest, *Nederland en het Tribunaal van Tokio*.

## 11.2 Roeling's Dissent

known, engaged in intensive discussions about his dissenting opinion with officials of the Dutch government and significantly altered his draft opinion in response to their concerns. Finally, consideration of the reception of Roeling's rejection of the guilty verdicts in regard to Hirota and Shigemitsu points up the double standard that is implicitly applied to the Tokyo Trial in comparison with Nuremberg. There is little doubt that both Hirota and Shigemitsu would have been convicted under the Nuremberg standard, as was their German counterpart, Foreign Minister von Joachim von Ribbentrop or State Secretary Ernst von Weiszaecker.[37] Yet the Tokyo judgment is often treated as a unique aberration in its conviction of such civilian officials. Little or no consideration has been given by critics of the Tokyo judgment as to how the defendants would have fared if the Nuremberg standards of responsibility had been applied to them.

Roeling's dissenting opinion is both complex and interesting, requiring careful analysis to arrive at an understanding of some of its central features. It is also curious in a number of regards.[38] The first, and most important from the standpoint of international law, section of the Opinion is largely based upon a memorandum that Roeling sent to Webb on January 23, 1947.[39] That memorandum, entitled "Interpretation of the Charter," contains all of the research on the status of aggressive war under international law that he later directly incorporated into the Opinion. The memorandum is attached to a letter of the same date in which Roeling apologizes for having taken so long to determine his stance on "the law of the case."[40] He also informs Webb that, "The enclosed writing is not to be regarded as a judgment. As you know it is not the custom in my judicial practice that the minority opinion is publicly expressed. I would prefer that this practice be followed in our Tribunal."[41] Indeed, Webb and Roeling had previously agreed that there should be one judgment for the tribunal to demonstrate the international cooperation on which it was based.[42]

---

[37] Von Weiszaecker was not a defendant at the IMT but was tried in the Nuremberg Subsequent Proceedings (NMT) in the Ministries Case. His conviction provides a stark contrast to Roeling's desire to acquit Hirota. See Ministries Case, pp. 496–98.

[38] There is first the question of why Roeling wrote a dissenting opinion at all (note that unlike that of Bernard and Pal it is not entitled as such but rather merely as the "Opinion of the Member of the Netherlands"). There is extensive correspondence on this issue, both internal to the court in his exchange of memoranda with Webb, but also in his communications with the Dutch government. Both of these aspects will be dealt with below.

[39] Roeling's letter to Webb of January 23, 1947 (NAA M1417 Item 24) contains the memorandum entitled "Interpretation of the Charter" (cited hereafter as Memorandum, "Interpretation of the Charter").

[40] Ibid., p. 1 (not numbered; the letter comprises 2 pages).

[41] Ibid. See also Webb's letter of August 24, 1948 to Roeling on this issue which indicates that at this late date the two of them were still discussing the "one judgment" question. AWM 417/1/7 Record 3DRL 2481/20.

[42] AWM 3DRL 2481/20.

Roeling did, however, publicly dissent, and his letter to Webb justifies this with an apparent reference to Pal, who had informed the other judges before the trial began that he intended to dissent. Referring to what he has called his preferred practice of not having dissenting opinions, Roeling states, "In the event that this would be impossible for the reason that one of the members of the Court would insist in giving a dissenting vote, I am prepared to write my own judgment."[43] He immediately qualifies this statement by adding that in this case his judgment "will be a short one without the quotations I needed in my memorandum to strengthen my argument."[44] In the end, however, Roeling's opinion was neither short nor without citations. Indeed, all of the rather tedious quotations of sources in the memorandum are incorporated fully into the opinion.

We suggest below that his decision to change the format of his opinion is in fact related to the change he made in its substantive conclusion. The memorandum argues at length that aggressive war is not a crime within the jurisdiction of the tribunal because it is not recognized, and, further, *should not be recognized*, in existing international law.[45] The opinion, however, while setting out all of the same evidence and arguments to support this position, in fact reaches the opposite conclusion: international law *does* permit the accused to be tried for the crime of aggressive war. This is the central paradox of Roeling's opinion, which we illuminate in the ensuing discussion. The explanation for this paradox casts a new light on Roeling as a judge and jurist, for it reveals that he fundamentally modified his opinion at the request of the Dutch government.

The structure of the Opinion is also rather odd in that it seems to consist of three independent parts that were merely stitched together, rather than a coherent whole. The first part gives no indication of the organization of the opinion and begins with a section entitled "Introduction," followed by a section entitled "Jurisdiction," and concludes with a short section titled "Responsibility for Omission." The introduction only comprises two short paragraphs and reads as a preface to the whole opinion. This first part of the opinion deals with some of the general legal issues facing the tribunal, though it is nowhere stated that this is the first of three sections or that it will focus on the law of the case.

The second part of the opinion (also not labeled as such) appears to begin anew. It starts, unlike the first section, with a title: "Some Observations on the

---

[43] Ibid. See also Roeling's letter to Tenkink of December 16, 1946. PIG/AR. The archival material on Roeling's consultations with Dutch jurists and his correspondence with the Dutch government concerning his dissenting opinion are the basis of the detailed analysis provided by Van Poelgeest, *Nederland en het Tribunaal*, 65–71, 82–96. For the research and analysis detailing the archival sources of Roeling's correspondence with Dutch jurists and government officials we are grateful to Nicole Brauchli-Jageneau.

[44] AWM 3DRL 2481/20. In fact Roeling's opinion comprises 127 pages in print.

[45] See memorandum, "Interpretation of the Charter" pp. 23–5, which will be more fully discussed below.

Facts," followed by a table of contents, and, again, an introduction. This section provides a lengthy and detailed account of the events leading to war in China and later in the Pacific, as well as defense arguments concerning the Greater East Asia Co-Prosperity Sphere and other matters. This section is followed by nineteen appendices, as if these marked the end of the opinion; but they do not. Instead, the opinion goes on to conclude with, "The Verdicts in the Individual Cases." This section, despite the title, focuses only on the five of the accused whom Roeling feels should have been acquitted. Although he notes his dissent on the findings and sentencing in regard to many others, he gives no analysis, argument, or evidence for his position. He merely includes a brief statement as to his disagreement in regard to the sentences, though not the findings of guilt, for the other accused.

The opinion as a whole reads as if the three parts were written independently and designed to stand alone.[46] Although there is some thematic consistency, the result is a rather disjointed text that is best assessed part by part rather than as a cohesive whole. While this assessment can cast some light on what might have been Roeling's motivations in dealing with certain issues the way he did, of greater significance are the internal memoranda he exchanged with other members of the tribunal and particularly with Webb. These memoranda, as well as his correspondence with the Dutch foreign ministry, provide the basis for a reassessment of Roeling's dissenting opinion and of his role as a judge at the IMTFE.

### 11.2.1.1 The Puzzle of the Charter

The first section of Roeling's opinion primarily consists of the section entitled "Jurisdiction." The argument here can be seen as addressing three issues: (1) Is the Charter of the IMTFE binding upon the judges in regard to the international law to be applied by the tribunal? (2) If it is not binding, is the crime of waging aggressive war as encompassed in the Charter in conformity with existing international law such that it is just to apply that standard of criminal liability to the accused? (3) If the crime of waging aggressive war was not known to international law at the time of the acts for which the defendants are charged is there nonetheless a legal foundation that legitimates holding the defendants liable for such a crime?[47]

---

[46] This is confirmed by the memorandum, "Interpretation of the Charter," which was written independently of the other parts of Roeling's Opinion. The cover letter to Webb of January 23, 1947 (cited above) indicates that at that time he intended a shortened version of the memorandum to be his dissenting "judgment."

[47] It should be noted that some of the judges argued vehemently that the tribunal had no authority to declare "the actions of the Allied Powers null and void" by rejecting parts of the law of the Charter. Justice Patrick, for example, argued that just as these same judges lacked such authority in their own countries so too they lacked it in Tokyo and it was a "radical error" for them to

We will deal with each of these in turn in order to come to a clearer understanding of what Roeling is aiming at in this section of his opinion. Such analysis must address the central puzzling feature of this section of the opinion: On the one hand Roeling appears to set aside the law of the Charter so that he can reach the conclusion that the accused cannot be charged with a crime of aggressive war. Indeed, reading through the first 2/3 of this first part of the opinion the central thesis is clear: aggressive war is not a crime that was recognized in international law before WWII. This is *not*, however, the result Roeling reaches, for in the end he concludes that this crime is cognizable under the Charter of the IMTFE. This apparent contradiction lies at the heart of Roeling's opinion and clouds whatever contribution to international law that it hopes to make.

*11.2.1.1.1 Is the Charter Binding Upon the Tribunal?* Roeling criticizes the majority judgment for taking the position "that the Tribunal is bound by its Charter."[48] Roeling notes that the Nuremberg judgment states that the Charter is binding upon the International Military Tribunal, but he then argues that this cannot be what the judgment really means: " ... it would be surprising if the Charter, laid down on behalf of the Allied Nations, should be intended to be binding upon the Tribunal even if it disregarded existing international law."[49] He then uses this as the basis for rejecting the position of the Tokyo majority that they are strictly bound by the Charter and a judge who disagrees with the law of the Charter can only either resign or refuse to accept the office. He claims that, "This standpoint seems to be not only dangerous for the future but incorrect at this moment."

We will explore in a moment Roeling's grounds for stating that the majority's conclusion is incorrect but it is first worth noting that Roeling does not pay sufficient attention to the actual language of the Nuremberg judgment in arguing that it cannot mean that the law of the Charter is strictly binding. Indeed, his argument seems to so deliberately misrepresent the Nuremberg judgment that it calls into question his objectivity and judicial impartiality in addressing these fundamental legal issues.

Roeling asserts that the Nuremberg judgment, like the majority judgment in Tokyo, in fact considers "whether or not the crimes mentioned in the charters were crimes according to international law."[50] This assertion is both disingenuous and misleading. In fact, the Nuremberg judgment is quite clear that: "These provisions are binding upon the Tribunal as the law to be applied

---

maintain otherwise (memorandum of Patrick to Webb of July 1, 1946 NAA M1417 25 pp. 2–3). See also Patrick's memorandum to Webb of October 11, 1946 NAA M1417 25 pp. 5–6.

[48] Roeling Opinion, 680.
[49] Ibid., 680–1.
[50] Ibid., 681.

## 11.2 Roeling's Dissent

to the case."[51] This is but one of a number of passages where the judgment affirms the status of the Charter as providing *the sole legal basis* for the tribunal's jurisdiction. Roeling asserts that the "sovereign legislative power" of the victorious Allies to which the Nuremberg judgment refers cannot be the basis for creating the law of the tribunal as opposed to the judges of the tribunal as a judicial body.[52] On his view it is the tribunal which must decide whether the crimes enumerated in the Charter are recognized under international law.[53] On precisely this point, however, the Nuremberg judgment is explicit as the paragraph which precedes the reference to the sovereign legislative power of the Allies makes clear:

The jurisdiction of the Tribunal is defined in the Agreement and Charter, and the crimes coming within the jurisdiction of the Tribunal, for which there shall be individual responsibility, are set out in Article 6. The law of the Charter is decisive, and binding upon the Tribunal.[54]

Although the Nuremberg judgment does discuss the status of aggressive war under existing international law it does not do so in the sense in which Roeling indicates when he says that it considers "whether or not the crimes mentioned in the Charter were crimes according to international law." In fact, the relevant passage in the Nuremberg judgment makes absolutely clear what the status of the Charter is in relation to the crimes it enumerates:

*The Charter makes the planning or waging of a war of aggression or a war in violation of international treaties a crime*, and it is therefore not strictly necessary to consider whether and to what extent aggressive war was a crime before the execution of the London Agreement. But in view of the great importance of the questions of law involved, the Tribunal has heard full argument from the Prosecution and the Defense, and will express its view on the matter.[55] (emphasis added)

The strained nature of Roeling's treatment of Nuremberg sets the tone for the entire section on Jurisdiction. Roeling appears desperate to reduce the Charter's status to merely creating a factual framework of inquiry to which the tribunal must add the law to be applied.[56] Arguing that it is the tribunal and not the

---

[51] IMT judgment.
[52] Roeling Opinion, 682. Roeling attempts to argue that the reference to the sovereign legislative power of the Allies only applies to the domestic law of the occupied country and not to the international law of the Charter. This is quite clearly not what the Nuremberg judgment states.
[53] Ibid.
[54] IMT judgment, 218.
[55] Ibid., 219.
[56] While in the Opinion Roeling indicates that the judges are applying existing international law to the Charter's framework in his internal memoranda he sees a broader role for the tribunal. While he denies the authority of the Allies and the Charter to make international law, ironically

Charter which must determine what is the applicable international law, Roeling states that, "it would be surprising indeed if such a tribunal had been convened almost exclusively for the purpose of finding facts."[57] An obvious retort, of course, would be that the task of the tribunal is to apply the law of the Charter to the facts it finds, but Roeling is determined to reduce the Charter to a jurisdictional framework with no legal content. He concludes his argument by stating that, "The Charter determines which facts may be subjected to a legal hearing. The Tribunal, having been invested by the Charter to 'try and punish' (Art. 5) will determine which of those facts are crimes according to international law. This follows from the general principles of international law."[58] What those general principles are or how they determine such a conclusion Roeling never states.[59]

It is today common practice in the international criminal tribunals to determine what was the *definition* of the crimes or theories of responsibility encompassed in their Statute Charter at the time the alleged crimes in question were committed. They cannot, however, deviate from the enumeration of those crimes in the Statute because the Statute defines exclusively what crimes fall under the jurisdiction of the tribunal.[60] At the time of the Tokyo Tribunal, the only precedent was Nuremberg and, as indicated earlier, the International Military Tribunal took a stand clearly in opposition to Roeling's interpretation of international law. This is also the position taken by the Dutch government in its objection to Roeling's position on the Charter.[61]

While Roeling attacks the position taken by Nuremberg and by the majority as wholly illegitimate and applying Charter provisions that are themselves "a violation of international law,"[62] on the other hand, he articulated a more moderate view in private. In a letter to Webb on March 20, 1947 Roeling in fact acknowledged that the majority's view on the status of the crime of aggression had, "a tenable basis – the binding force of the Charter together with a

---

he unproblematically casts the judges in a role equivalent to that of legislators: "The Tribunal creates here the law, and has, *as every legislator*, to realize what will be the results of *its law*" (emphasis added). Roeling, Memo to The President on Conventional War Crimes of February 5, 1948 p. 115, AWM File 417/1/7 Record 3DRL 2481/20.

[57] Roeling Opinion, 681. See Cryer, "Roeling in Tokyo," p. 1114 on this point.
[58] Roeling Opinion, 682. See also the passage on the same page where, "It is the Tribunal which is called upon to decide whether those acts or 'omissions' are crimes under international law" (ibid., 682).
[59] Roeling also attempts to argue that the "history of the Charter" supports his conclusion. Roeling claims that when the Potsdam Declaration refers to the punishment of "war criminals" it provides the basis only for the prosecution of "war crimes" under the Charter and not aggressive war (ibid., 682–3).
[60] See the AFRC Appeals Judgment at the Special Court for Sierra Leone, *Prosecutor v. Brima et al.*, Case. No. SCSL-2004-16-A pp. 52–6 for expanding the scope of the definition of Other Inhumane Acts as a category of crimes against humanity under the Statute of the Special Court.
[61] See letter of the Minister of Justice to Roeling of June 6, 1947, PIG/AR.
[62] Roeling Opinion, 680.

11.2 Roeling's Dissent

certain interpretation thereof."⁶³ The striking discrepancy between the letter's acknowledgment that the majority (and the Nuremberg judgment's) position is in fact a tenable interpretation of the Charter's status as opposed to Roeling's strident denial in his dissent that there is any possible rational basis for this position underscores the polemical nature of Roeling's Opinion.⁶⁴ One might then ask what is motivating the strident and complete disparagement of the majority's position? To answer this question we must turn to Roeling's ensuing discussion of the legal status of the crime of aggressive war.

*11.2.1.1.2 Is Aggressive War a Crime Under Existing International Law?* In order to argue that aggressive war was not a recognized crime under existing international law Roeling had first to eliminate the Charter as the source of law which the tribunal was bound to apply. Having accomplished that task to his satisfaction he then begins a new section of this first part of the opinion, entitled "Crimes against Peace."⁶⁵

Roeling takes as his starting point the position that until the "era of the League of Nations and the Pact of Paris, the waging of war was a sovereign right of states."⁶⁶ This statement is in a sense programmatic, because what underlies this entire section of the judgment is a commitment to an apparently *absolute principle of national sovereignty*. What seems to ground Roeling's apparent hostility to the notion of aggressive war as a crime is what we today would call a "realist" interpretation of international politics and a concomitant acceptance of strict legal positivism that dismisses legal limitations on sovereignty as wishful thinking in the absence of an overarching and statutorily enshrined international and universal governmental authority with the coercive powers of a national state.

This theme becomes explicit in the later parts of this section of his opinion and is the driving force behind the often tendentious and one-sided analysis of the various international legal instruments from the early twentieth century that he examines. One may get a sense of the vehemence of his interpretation by the position he takes on the 1928 Pact of Paris (also known as the Kellogg-Briand Pact), which his memorandum to Webb argues is not "of any real significance" and is in fact "merely an expression *of a pacific mood*"⁶⁷ (emphasis added).

---

⁶³ NAA M1417 Item 24. Letter of Roeling addressed to Sir William Webb.
⁶⁴ Roeling and Webb exchanged extensive memoranda over their differences of opinion on such issues. See AWM 3DRL2481/20, March 17, 1946.
⁶⁵ Roeling Opinion, 684–704.
⁶⁶ Ibid., 684.
⁶⁷ Roeling, memorandum, "Interpretation of the Charter," pp. 17–18. In his subsequent correspondence with Webb over the position he takes in the memorandum Roeling concedes that the Pact or Paris had in fact at least established the illegality of aggressive war: "I don't doubt that a war in violation of the Pact of Paris is an illegal one. It is probable that our Tribunal will find the Pacific war was a war in violation of the Pact of Paris. The evidence of the Prosecution was

The fact that a judge of an international criminal tribunal can dismiss an international treaty signed by sixty-three nations, including Japan and the Netherlands, as of no significance and only reflecting a "mood" says quite a lot about Roeling's position. It is especially telling given that he has stated that it is their role as judges, and not the role of the nations drafting the Charter, to determine what is international law. Roeling's view of the substantive content of international law appears limited indeed by his general dispositions on positive law and the primacy of national sovereignty.[68]

In his review of the international legal context in the prewar period, Roeling first takes up the various instruments, conferences, and declarations that from the League of Nations onward preceded the Pact of Paris and he dismisses them one by one as of no legal significance whatsoever.[69] He then frames the central question of this section of the Opinion as, "Did the Pact of Paris make aggressive war an international crime for which individuals can be held responsible?" As should by now be apparent, his answer to this question is that it did not. But how did Roeling reach and justify this conclusion?

Examining the preparatory work to the Pact and proceedings of the US Senate Committee on Foreign Relations, he argues that it was never the intention of the Pact of Paris to create an enforceable norm.[70] He concedes that the opinion of international legal experts is divided as to whether the Pact did more than "condemn" aggressive war as opposed to recognizing it as "a new international crime."[71] He concludes that it did not, relying *not* on legal principles but rather upon what he takes to be the reality of international relations: "As long as the relations between states are still such that any state, *in accordance with its sovereign right*, will decide its position in vital conflicts, there will be no place for outlawing war"[72] (emphasis added).

The phrase "in accordance with its sovereign right" not only reveals Roeling's realist bias but also begs the question. The whole point is whether the Pact of Paris limited such a sovereign right to wage war. Roeling in this

---

rather strong on this point and I don't think the Defense shall succeed in refuting that." This quotation is from Roeling's reply to Webb's comments on Roeling's memorandum of January 23, 1947. Roeling Memorandum to Webb of March 20, 1947 NAA M1417 Item 24, p. 1. See also the comment on p. 7, "But in view of the produced evidence it is probable that we accept the aggressive character of this war."

[68] The implications of his position for Dutch interests in the East Indies (Indonesia) were brought out in correspondence to Roeling from various Dutch officials including the Dutch prosecutor at Tokyo. See the sources cited in Van Poelgeest, *Nederland en het Tribunaal*, pp. 10–21, 71–96. See especially the letter of Boon to Roeling of August 18, 1948, Archief Ministerie van Buitenlandse Zaken, Den Haag (ABZ hereafter) 314.2.

[69] See, e.g. his statement that there is no basis for concluding that there was any change in the status of war before the Pact of Paris because, "Neither abortive treaties, nor misleading resolutions could effect this change" (Roeling Opinion, 691).

[70] Ibid., 692–4.

[71] Ibid., 694.

[72] Ibid., 695.

## 11.2 Roeling's Dissent

passage justifies his position that it did not, based on his view of the nature of the "relations between states." This, however, is an interpretation of international relations rather than international law.

As argued earlier, this position also rests upon a strong positivist interpretation of legal institutions which maintains that there is no law in the absence of a sanction backed by the coercive power of a government. This is clearly indicated by Roeling's reliance on the most prominent and extreme positivist theorist of this era, Hans Kelsen: "Kelsen rightly observed, 'The complete failure of the Briand-Kellogg Pact [i.e. the Pact of Paris] clearly shows that it is useless to outlaw war without eliminating the possibility of legally unsettled and untenable conflicts'"[73] (clarification in brackets added).

When Roeling dismisses the Pact of Paris as politically untenable, of "no real significance" and the product of a "pacific mood," he fully realizes the consequences of such a position on sovereignty and the limits of international law. He does so in a manner which makes clear just how strong his view of national sovereignty is in an era that has just seen the end of fourteen years of international conflict:

> The *price of unlimited national sovereignty is an occasional war*. If aggressive war is recognized as criminal, partial surrender of national sovereignty is indicated, and a community of nations must have developed which no longer tolerates violence between its members, and in which war in a sense acquires the character of civil war. Without this development, a declaration of on the outlawry of war as such is a fairly empty phrase.[74] (emphasis added)

Having concluded that neither the "lofty phrases" nor the ambiguous terms of the Pact of Paris outlawed war so as to make it criminal, Roeling takes up the question of law which, as yet unarticulated, has been hanging over his detailed discussion of the international legal developments of the interwar years. This question, of course, is whether the string of developments Roeling has traced between the League of Nations and the Pact of Paris were sufficient to constitute a norm under international customary law. Roeling cites Glueck as taking such a position.[75]

Roeling, quite predictably given the previous discussion, flatly rejects this position as based upon a "misunderstanding" of custom as a source of international law.[76] His conclusion is based upon the argument that it was "only towards the end of the war" that criminal responsibility for the "authors of aggressive

---

[73] Ibid.
[74] Ibid., 691.
[75] The leading treatise of the period, Oppenheim/Lauterpacht, elaborates the position that an international customary law norm matured in the Pact of Paris, but this discussion is not referenced by Roeling.
[76] Roeling Opinion, 695.

war" came under discussion.⁷⁷ The opinion cites various proclamations from 1941 to the Moscow Declaration of 1943 but concludes that they only refer to punishment for war crimes and not for the war itself. Such a conclusion seems like a narrow, if not deliberately misleading, interpretation of such documents. When, in a document cited by Roeling, the Soviet Government condemned the "inhuman and rapacious" conduct of German troops under the "criminal Hitlerite Government of Germany," one might well gather that they were referring to the invasion of the Soviet Union and its consequences together rather than neatly separating war crimes from aggressive war, as Roeling claims.⁷⁸ In regard to more explicit pronouncements of Axis aggression he also takes a similar tack. He cites, for example, the Cairo Declaration of December 1943 which explicitly states that the Allies are "fighting this war to restrain and punish *the aggression* of Japan"⁷⁹ (emphasis added). Here again summarily he dismisses the import of this declaration to punish aggression, rather implausibly given ongoing planning of war crimes tribunals at that period, because, "Only the punishment of Japan as a nation is here brought up."⁸⁰

The conclusion Roeling reaches on the basis of his dismissal of all policy discussions and pronouncements of the Allied governments in the first years of the war is that crimes against peace were not regarded as "true crimes" before the London Agreement of August 8, 1945.⁸¹ On this basis he is able to rephrase the salient question as whether or not the London Agreement could create such a category of international crimes.⁸²

*11.2.1.1.3 If There is No Basis in Existing International Law for Crimes against Peace, is There Another Foundation for Such a Category of International Crime?* Having dismissed the treaty and customary law bases for crimes against peace by concluding that it was only in August 1945 that this category was recognized as criminal in the strict sense, where can the opinion go from here? It is at this point where, rather than concluding the discussion with a finding that aggressive war was not a crime cognizable by the tribunal, Roeling's Opinion suddenly begins a startling reversal of course.

His entire argument to this point has been based upon the following chain of reasoning as analyzed above: (1) The Charter of the IMTFE cannot create

---

[77] Ibid., 696.
[78] Ibid. This is just one example of many that he cites, proffering the same interpretation.
[79] Ibid., 698.
[80] Ibid., 698–9.
[81] On March 2, 1947 Webb had already responded to Roeling's view that Allied declarations only applied to prosecution for conventional war crimes: "I cannot see the justification for your view that President Roosevelt, Mr. Churchill, and Generalissimo Stalin did not contemplate the prosecution of anything but atrocities. The Potsdam Declaration extends to 'all war criminals'." (NAA M1417 Item 24). Memorandum of Webb to Roeling.
[82] Roeling Opinion, 700.

## 11.2 Roeling's Dissent

crimes. (2) Only the judges of the IMTFE have the authority to determine if the categories of criminal acts enumerated in the Charter are recognized as crimes under existing international law. (3) If they are not so recognized then it would be a violation of international law to try and punish individuals for such crimes. (4) Existing international law did not recognize aggressive war as a crime until August 1945.

This chain of reasoning which Roeling has advanced over the first twenty pages of the opinion would seem to lead to the ineluctable conclusion that all of the accused persons must be acquitted of all charges under the Charter rubric of crimes against peace. This is not, however, the conclusion which Roeling reaches. Instead, he reaches *precisely the opposite conclusion:* that it is in fact in conformity with international law to punish individual defendants for their respective roles in what he characterizes as Japanese aggression. Any reader having made their way through these densely argued first twenty pages might well ask how is this complete *volte face* possible?

Roeling, apparently bowing to the influence of the Dutch government, abruptly reverses course.[83] At the juncture where he has claimed to establish that crimes against peace were not recognized as true crimes until August 1945 he launches into a new line of reasoning. This reasoning is based upon a conception of international law in some respects radically at odds with that which he has just expounded at length. The fact that he did not modify the argument of the first twenty pages of the opinion but left it in juxtaposition with what follows was perhaps his way of setting out what he really thought as opposed to the legal conclusions that he now felt compelled to reach. This interpretation is borne out both by his correspondence with the Dutch government and also by comparison with his memorandum to Webb of January 23, 1947. In that memorandum, as discussed earlier, the analysis of the legal basis of the Charter and crimes against peace is the same, but the ultimate conclusion of the memorandum is diametrically opposed to that of the opinion. Yielding to the foreign ministry's argument that he was not appointed as an independent judge but rather as a representative of the Netherlands, he abandons the position taken in his memorandum and upholds the law of the Charter.[84]

---

[83] Roeling's interaction with the Dutch government was initiated by his request of January 28, 1947 to the foreign ministry for advice as to a dissenting opinion on points of international law. He had previously also requested advice from Dutch jurists. There follows more than a year of correspondence in which more and more Dutch officials are drawn in to the attempt to influence Roeling. To his credit, Roeling did not follow their request not to publicly dissent (Letter of Roeling November 24, 1948). He did, however, present the Dutch government with different options that he might follow, and ultimately modified his position to accept the law of the Charter, as reflected in his letter to the foreign ministry of April 10, 1948, ABZ 314.2 and June 3, 1948, ABZ 314.2. For the detailed account of this web of correspondence see Van Poelgeest, *Nederland en het Tribunaal*, pp. 71–96.

[84] Ibid., and Roeling's reply of June 3, 1948.

At the end of the discussion of crimes against peace in the January 23 memorandum to Webb, he concludes in the final paragraph of that section that the outlawry of war presumed by the Pact of Paris would only be possible if there were a surrender of "sovereign rights" which in fact has not taken place. He states that interpreting the Pact of Paris as if such a surrender of sovereignty (and hence the sovereign right to wage war) had taken place would be deceptive. In the following final two sentences Roeling sets out for Webb what seems to be his real rationale for rejecting the law of the Charter:

> It would be better if mankind realized the true state of international relations rather than be misled by a false sense of security. Nothing is so detrimental to the healthy development of any legal institution as to live beyond one's means both morally and legally; i.e. to accept in law and in jurisdiction conceptions which are not true and not living. For the sake of the future development of international law, I should prefer to concede the poverty of our achievement at this moment rather than to indulge in presumptions.[85]

By what legal alchemy, then, does Roeling justify reaching the conclusion that crimes against peace *are* in fact legitimate grounds for convicting individuals accused of waging, planning, or initiating aggressive war? The first step is to minimize the significance of the principle of legality prohibiting ex post facto laws. He states that if the principle of *nullem crimen sine lege* were a principle of justice then the tribunal would be compelled to dismiss all charges violating the principle. He argues, however, that this principle is not a principle of justice, but only a "rule of policy" and "an expression of political wisdom."[86] Once this barrier of principle is dismissed he can move to an interpretation of the Charter that directly contradicts that which he proposed in the first section of the opinion. What he mysteriously characterizes as "positive international law" leads to a "special way" to interpret the Charter, namely to interpret it in such a way "that it is in accordance with international law."[87]

On this basis he proceeds to argue that since the Allies waged a just war[88] and are responsible for peace and order in its aftermath, they are entitled to take measures to prevent the reoccurrence of "gravely offensive conduct."[89] From this it follows that when the victorious Allies chose a "judicial way" rather than "political action" (i.e. summary execution) to protect the peace by prosecuting the authors of Japanese aggression, this "novelty ... cannot be regarded as a violation of international law."[90]

---

[85] Memorandum, "Interpretation of the Charter," p. 25.
[86] Roeling Opinion, 700.
[87] Ibid.
[88] Note here his fundamental disagreement with Pal who maintained that the Japanese acted only in self-defense and were thus the victims of Chinese and Allied aggression.
[89] Roeling Opinion, 701.
[90] Ibid.

Roeling thus shifts the basis of the legitimacy of the Charter, which he now implicitly acknowledges as a source for the creation of law, from the sphere of justice to the sphere of the political. He analogizes the prosecution of crimes against peace to, "political crimes in domestic law, where the decisive element is the danger rather than the guilt, where the criminal is considered as an enemy ... and where the punishment emphasizes *the political measure rather than the judicial retribution*"[91] (emphasis added). On this basis he concludes that the Charter's formulation of crimes against peace "is in accordance with international law."

Roeling's line of reasoning is quite astonishing. We may recall that at the beginning of his opinion Roeling dismissed the majority's arguments about the status of the Charter on the basis of his view of *the absolute primacy of principles of justice over the political authority of the Allied powers*. In the closing part of his treatment of crimes against peace, however, he justifies his reversal of course on a purely political characterization of the law. Following the passage quoted immediately above about punishment as a "political measure," Roeling unequivocally expresses the shift in his stance on the relation of crimes against peace to politics rather than justice: "As long as the dominant principle in the crime against peace is the dangerous character of the individual who committed this crime, the *punishment should only be determined by considerations of security*"[92] (emphasis added).

The implications of such a position would give most international lawyers considerable pause since it seems to exclude considerations of procedural fairness and reasoned proof of individual culpability in favor of basing guilt on political expediency. As we will see, this is also the basis for his argument of acquittal of certain accused.

In these passages Roeling thus now argues that the foundation of international law in regard to the category of crimes against peace is political expediency which requires the "punishment" of dangerous individuals who might threaten the peace won by force of arms. The very *creation* of international law is thus determined not by considerations of justice (as he had earlier argued) but rather by considerations of political security. Having clearly stated that crimes against peace were not recognized as criminal until August 8, 1945, the process that justifies overriding the *policy* against ex post facto punishment is the necessity to create a legal category that permits rendering harmless individuals who pose a security risk. Through this reasoning, the category of legal punishment – which Roeling's own principles of justice required to be based upon individual culpability – has been transformed into a mere political tool. By the same process of reasoning, the creation of international legal norms,

---

[91] Ibid., 702.
[92] Ibid.

which he earlier stated was beyond the political authority of the Allies, has now been legitimated as a justifiable political measure by those same Allies in order to deal with dangerous individuals.

Fully aware of the potential consequences in making punishment into a security measure, Roeling quickly tries to limit the damage. Immediately following his statement on "considerations of security" as the grounds for punishment he states, "In this case, this means that no capital punishment should be given to anyone guilty of the crime against peace only."[93] This conclusion follows, it would seem, from the security considerations that only necessitate removing the dangerous individuals from positions where they might do harm. Roeling makes this clear when he argues that there is no need to inquire into the "impulses" of individuals that led them to participate in the planning and initiation of what he terms Japan's "wars of conquest": "Insight into the genesis of the crime has but limited importance, as it is *not so much retribution for the offense by punishment* which is here being sought, as a *measure for protection by the elimination of dangerous persons*"[94] (emphasis added). While Roeling suggests that a sentence of life imprisonment will accomplish this purpose, why could it not be argued that no method removes potential enemies and dangerous individuals more effectively than execution? Moreover, why have a trial at all if the role of the court is simply to remove dangerous individuals from the public and political sphere?

*11.2.1.2 Roeling's "Observations on the Facts"*

As indicated earlier, this second part of Roeling's Opinion seems to stand alone and have been conceived independently from the first section discussed above. Indeed, its Introduction explains that Roeling felt it necessary to dissent on some of the findings of the majority on "the factual history of Japan, and with the part which the accused played in this history."[95] The legal theory of responsibility which informs this second part of the opinion, however, has already been set out at the end of the preceding section. It is this theory of responsibility which reveals the main aim of Roeling's "Observations on the Facts." That purpose is primarily to justify the exculpation of a group of five civilian officials whose individual verdicts Roeling will address in the third and concluding part of his opinion.

Having ultimately legitimized the crime of aggressive war, as noted earlier, Roeling, in the final pages of the section on crimes against peace, turns to the issue of defining that crime. He states that it is not necessary to clearly distinguish between planning, preparing, initiating, and waging aggressive war.

---

[93] Ibid.
[94] Ibid., 702–3.
[95] Ibid., 709.

## 11.2 Roeling's Dissent

There is, however, a question which he considers to be "more important" than such issues. And it is indeed one of the most significant issues of responsibility posed by trials such as Nuremberg and Tokyo where essentially a government is put on trial. This passage is worth quoting at length because it also provides the justification for the main argument of the remaining two parts of the opinion:

> More important in this case is the question of whether every single member of the government, who votes for war after having entered the government with the purpose of maintaining peace, can be considered to have initiated the war. A similar problem arises in case of someone having entered the government during the war, similarly with the intention to achieve peace as soon as possible. Decision on this point is of great moment for the future. The Judgment must by all means avoid establishing such norms as would tend to create the consequence that individuals supporting peace would be forbidden to hold high office in a government which is inclined to aggressive war, or is in the process of waging an aggressive war.[96]

This passage raises the important question left ambiguous in the majority's treatment of the responsibility of the civilian cabinet. As seen above, on the one hand the majority seems to be operating with a notion of "cabinet responsibility" where all members of the government at the ministerial level may be held liable for the actions authorized or tacitly permitted by that government. On the other hand, the majority does not apply that standard consistently.[97]

Roeling here suggests that even cabinet members and other civilian officials in key positions who actively engage in the planning or waging of aggressive war should not be held liable if they took up their positions with the intention of working for peace. That he means precisely this is made clear in the ensuing paragraph where he states, "The mere fact of having been a member of the government which decided for war, or which was in the process of waging war, is not sufficient. *The intention with which one enters such a government is decisive*" (emphasis added). At Nuremberg, of course, the standard of responsibility was not official position but whether one participated in the inner policy circle where decisions as to war were made. The true inner intention with which one allegedly exercised such a role in key political decision-making was understandably completely irrelevant to the Nuremberg judges in determination of guilt.

We may criticize Roeling's position as naïve in that even if we could truly know the inner motivations of such high-ranking individuals (which is dubious in itself) what is really decisive is the issue of what is meant by "peace" and on

---

[96] Ibid., 703.
[97] Ibid. See also p. 707, where Roeling applies a similar principle to the issue of responsibility for war crimes.

what terms. Both the German and Japanese governments initiated peace feelers at various stages of the war, conditional on being able to retain part of the territories they had conquered or on maintaining the same government in power. It was for this reason, among others, that the Allies decided to press for unconditional surrender. Such discussions between Japan, China, and other powers had been going on throughout the late 1930s. In the case of the Japanese government in the period 1937–41, however, the price of such "peace" was maintaining their occupation of China and their de facto colony of Manchukuo. We might recall here that the Imperial Government of Japan repeatedly justified its decision to wage war in China, and then in the Asia-Pacific region, on the grounds that the war's objective was to achieve "peace" in a Japanese-dominated Greater East Asia.

Roeling, in the "Some Observations on the Facts" part of his opinion, consistently avoids discussing the brute fact of the war being waged against China in this period (discussed later). Perhaps he was somewhat sympathetic to the Japanese attempts to justify their invasion and occupation of China, or perhaps their "right" to do so flowed from his commitment to an absolutist version of national sovereignty and of Dutch interests in the East Indies. Would he have been similarly disposed to exculpate Nazi leaders as seeking "peace" if the price they demanded was continued occupation of the Netherlands and its incorporation into the Reich?

Roeling nowhere specifies how such a determination of an individual's true motivation is to be made or according to what legal criteria it is to be assessed as sufficient. He does, however, use this principle of "intending peace" as the grounds for arguing for the acquittal of Hirota, Kido, Shigemitsu, and Tōgō. Whether or not Roeling genuinely believed that Hirota, for example, desired peace even at the cost of abandoning China we will never know. The majority, and to a far greater extent Webb in his draft judgment, produced enough evidence to compel a conclusion that Hirota preferred peace but was readily prepared to resort to force to maintain the Japanese occupation of China and to retain his influence with the militarists. Roeling's own comments in an internal memorandum to the judges of August 23, 1948 suggest that he knew perfectly well of Hirota's true role and that Hirota had in fact advocated armed force to achieve Japan's aims of domination in China. Indeed, Roeling suggests to the judges that in the part of the draft judgment treating Hirota they add two quotations from one of Hirota's speeches in 1938 which states that the Japanese leaders ("we") decided to "chastise" the Chinese through armed force as a matter of policy.[98] It is hard to see how the position Roeling takes in this memorandum is compatible with the view he later takes in his dissenting opinion.

---

[98] August 23, 1948 NAA M1471/1 28 pp. 1–2. Hirota's speech was delivered to the Budget Committee of the House of Peers on February 16, 1938 (PX3737-A). Roeling quotes Hirota

## 11.2 Roeling's Dissent

What is clear is that Roeling's primary motivations were considerations of policy and not of individual guilt. For this reason he was prepared to overlook inculpatory evidence to advance the policy he advocated. This is already implied in the passage quoted earlier in which he says they must not interpret the Charter in a manner in which would dissuade individuals from entering the government in order to work for peace. He reiterates this position at some length in regard to these specific officials. After having argued that Shigemitsu should not be convicted for his role in the war as foreign minister in 1943–5, Roeling restates his principle: "But he who assumes public office in order to oppose that war, who accepts his appointment in order to promote peace, cannot and should not be accused of waging an aggressive war."[99] The primacy of such considerations in Roeling's mind is clearly expressed in his correspondence with Webb on this issue.[100]

Beginning with the important point that the tribunal must determine the limits of liability for civilian officials who are indirectly implicated in the perpetration of crimes by the military, he employs a logic that follows his reasoning on making intention the primary factor in regard to crimes against peace. He has just been dealing with the responsibility of Hirota and Kido for war crimes committed in China such as the Nanjing Massacre and he states that his general observations will equally apply to the cases of Tōgō and Shigemitsu.[101]

Indicating that in regard to this issue the tribunal "creates the law," he goes on to say that it must take great care in regard to "the results of its law":

Now, if we establish a responsibility of the civil government for the behavior of the army, the results will be that at the ending of a war there will be nobody in the government inclined to make peace, because the whole government can expect to be tried and sentenced ... The exclusion of civilian authorities from responsibility for war crimes committed by the armed forces will leave a power in the nation able and prepared to finish that war.[102]

Roeling here indicates that general policy considerations should determine the verdicts against Hirota, Kido, Tōgō, and Shigemitsu rather than their

---

as saying: "Japan has been endeavoring to make the Chinese Nationalist Government make reflections, if possible, while chastising their mistaken ideas by armed force" (citing T37296). Roeling also quotes another passage from the same speech: "Since they were facing Japan with very strong anti-Japanese feeling, we decided on a policy whereby we had to necessarily chastise them" (citing T37293). The same evidence is referred to in Webb's draft judgment. See note 76 in Chapter 8.

[99] Roeling Opinion, 800.
[100] See also Roeling's argument that policy considerations should take precedence in determining convictions in his memorandum of February 3, 1948 NAA M1417 28 pp. 113–15.
[101] Roeling Memo to The President of February 5, 1948 p. 114, AWM File 417/1/7 record 3DRL 2481/20.
[102] Ibid., 115.

individual legal culpability. That such policy-oriented considerations rather than assessments of individual culpability are foremost in Roeling's mind is also indicated by his somewhat astonishing statement to Webb that, *"In this trial the fate of the accused is relatively of no importance. What matters is the decision about international law"*[103] (emphasis added). While Roeling had, as was seen above, articulated such policy considerations in regard to defining and applying the category of crimes against peace, here he extends this approach to the liability of civilian officials for war crimes committed by the national military. Such a manner of proceeding goes against the very notion of a fair trial where the verdict should be based solely upon whether the evidence presented establishes the guilt of each individual for the specific crimes with which they have been charged.

Allowing policy to determine outcome means that some individuals may be convicted of crimes against peace because they are "dangerous," to use Roeling's term, while others may be acquitted of war crimes because they are needed to perform a useful function in ending the war. This is the essence of *a political trial* rather than proceedings in conformity with principles of legality and the rule of law, and Webb is quick to point exactly this out in his terse rejoinder to Roeling:

But to me it seems the only question for us as regards Hirota and other civilians is whether there is evidence we believe that they were in fact responsible for the crimes of the soldiers. *The consequences of convicting them is beyond our province.*[104] (emphasis added)

Apart from responding directly to Roeling in the memo quoted immediately above, Webb also addressed this issue, in implicit reference to Roeling and Pal, in his draft judgment. In the introductory section to the individual verdicts discussed below in Chapters 8 and 10, Webb cuts through the rationalizations of the defense and dissenting opinions to note that,

The accused concerned in the Pacific wars also knew, or should be assumed to have known, that Japan preferred war with America to withdrawal from China, and could have secured peace with China, and successfully negotiated with America, if she had agreed to withdraw within a reasonable time. I find it impossible to believe that with the offices these accused held they could fail to know all that this Tribunal has ascertained about this attitude of Japan.[105]

---

[103] Roeling, letter to Webb of January 23, 1947 (cover letter for the Roeling Memorandum of that date), p. 1 NAA M1417 Item 24.
[104] Webb, Memo to The Hon. Justice Roeling, Conventional War Crimes, of February 6, 1948 p. 1 of 1, AWM File 417/1/7 Record 3DRL 2481/20.
[105] TPJ 267.

## 11.2 Roeling's Dissent

Building upon this conclusion it follows for Webb that, "There is no immunity for anyone, soldier or civilian, who takes part in what he knows, or should know, to be an illegal and criminal war."[106] In reviewing the draft, Webb at this point inserted a handwritten addition which deals directly with Roeling's argument that for reasons of political expediency civilian officials should not be punished so that they can work for peace. Webb articulates the principle, which follows from Nuremberg and is today a bedrock of international justice, that, "There is no principle of law or justice which gives immunity." Further, he notes, the tribunal has "no power to alter the law but can only ascertain and apply it."[107] He then compares the situation of the Tokyo accused to those at Nuremberg, where he argues that it was possible that accused like Schacht, who were not in Hitler's inner policy circle, did not know of his intentions. For Webb, however, the circumstances of the accused at Tokyo are different because of the widespread understanding of Japan's policy to China and its impact on the decision to launch the Pacific War. Hence, he concludes, "Acquittals like that of Schacht and others at Nuremberg are not possible here."[108]

Having illuminated this policy-oriented approach which guides Roeling through this and the final part of his opinion we may now turn to a brief analysis of the way in which it shapes the examination of the "events which led up to the Pacific War" and Roeling's verdicts in regard to specific individuals. It is the narrative of the pre-1941 era, informed by the policy considerations articulated above, that provides the foundation for the verdicts in the final part of the opinion.

The key assumption informing Roeling's analysis of the relevant historical events in the section entitled "Some Observations on the Facts" is that there existed a fundamental division in the Japanese government between "a group which in a peaceful way, was striving for a prosperous Japan, a Japan which would virtually dominate East Asia ... [and] a group which aimed at the expansion of Japan by means of force."[109] That these two groups can be neatly divided is the foundation, however dubious, for all that follows in his dissent on individual verdicts, building upon his previously established principle that intending peace forgives all sins.[110] As he clearly states, "The decisive question in this trial is to determine how the relationship of the two different concepts, of expansion by means short of war, and of expansion by force of arms, developed."[111] As one might predict, it is primarily the military that

---

[106] Ibid.
[107] Ibid.
[108] TPJ 268.
[109] Roeling Opinion, 709.
[110] As Chapters 3–4 have indicated the evidence before the tribunal did not supports such a reductive and binary concept of wartime Japanese leadership.
[111] Roeling Opinion, 709.

falls into the latter camp and the diplomats and statesmen who fall into the other. The statesmen, as he will argue, may have made fatal errors, but those errors are not culpable even though they led to war. What this clean bifurcation seems to ignore, however, is the view developed by the majority, and at length by Webb in his draft judgment, that no such clean division is possible because individuals like Hirota may have preferred peaceful expansion at some point but were also prepared to use force, particularly in China, to achieve Japanese aims.

In the section "Bearing of Japan's Internal Situation on the Question of Guilt," Roeling argues that in order to guide them "away from dictatorship and war" Japanese statesmen had no choice but to cooperate with the militarists.[112] Needleless to say, this approach did not exactly meet with success. Roeling, however, appears to regard this cooperation with the militarists as merely a well-intentioned failure:

In considering the parts played by the Japanese statesmen, this very conflicting situation should be kept in mind. That the policy of appeasing the aggressive groups was a mistaken policy, and, judging from its results, a fatal policy, does not necessarily indicate that, as a policy, it was criminal. There should be room here for a non-criminal error in judgment.[113]

The real point here is not whether "as a policy" this appeasement was criminal but rather whether each individual accused engaged in conduct that established their culpability for aggressive war.

One of the strangest features of this section of Roeling's Opinion is the way in which it seems to studiously ignore the fact that from at least 1937 forward Japan was in fact fighting a major war in China. For example, when speaking of the role of Hirota, Kido, and Konoe in working for the establishment of the New Order in a Japanese-dominated Asia, Roeling indicates that their endorsement of the policy of expansion made it easier for the militarists to argue for war in the face of Western opposition to Japan's aims. In the face of such Western opposition the militarists "had no difficulty in convincing the government that, in view of embargoes and freezing orders, no way other than was left to achieve this end [i.e. Japanese domination]."[114] What is missing from his account is that fact that at this point war on a massive scale, despite the euphemism of the "China Incident," had already been underway for four years and it is this Japanese aggressive war in China that is producing Western opposition. What the majority and Webb judgments make clear is that the "statesmen" like

---

[112] Ibid., 712.
[113] Ibid.
[114] Ibid., 718.

Hirota were no more prepared to give up Japanese occupation of China and Manchuria than were the proponents of war within the military.

This apparent blindness or indifference to the reality of the situation in China manifests itself in numerous passages of this part of Roeling's Opinion. When discussing the development of the policy of the New Order in Asia in 1938 Roeling states that Hirota articulated this policy to the Diet, explaining that ending all dealings with Chiang Kai-shek was the only way of securing the New Order and the "'stability of East Asia under Sino-Japanese cooperation."[115] What "cooperation" was Roeling thinking Hirota meant when he advocated severing all relations with the legitimate government of China and advancing Japanese "cooperation" through the puppet that had been set up by conquest and massacre?

To take another example, Roeling argues that the decisive turn toward war in Japanese policy occurred in September 1940 in the context of discussions with the Axis Powers. But, again, Japan had already been occupying Manchuria (where "Manchukuo" was established) for nine years and had already been at full-blown war with China since 1937. Roeling sees no apparent connection between the events of 1940–1 and those of the preceding decade of war and conquest in China. Similarly, he concludes that at the time of the Tripartite Alliance in September 1940, "Japan essentially intended to establish the 'New Order' *by means short of war*"[116] (emphasis added). This would have been news indeed to the millions of Chinese suffering under Japanese occupation.

Lest there be any doubt as to Roeling's intent to encompass China within this notion of peaceful expansion as allegedly proposed by the statesmen, one need only consider his conclusion in the section "Difference between the policies of 1936 and of 1940." There he states that whereas war was envisaged from September 1940, "The crucial decision of August 11, 1936 aiming at the domination of East Asia (by the New Order) by expelling Western Powers, envisaged achieving that goal *by means short of war*"[117] (emphasis added). Given that, even leaving aside the occupation of Manchukuo, Japan invaded China a year later as part of that very policy of "domination of East Asia," one can only wonder at Roeling's ellipsis of China. This, in turn, grounds his conclusion that, "It has been shown that the critical moment when the policy turned to the use of armed force as a means of achieving the domination of *East Asia,* occurred in the later days of 1940, specifically on

---

[115] Ibid., 726.
[116] Ibid., 732.
[117] The Hirota Cabinet adopted multiple resolutions in August 1936 on policy on armament and foreign relations. Most important was the "Basic Principle of National Policy" (see Chapter 4). Roeling on this occasion is referring to another policy document that the Five Minister Conference adopted, on August 11, 1936, titled, "The Fundamental Principle of Our National Policy." This policy document can be found as PX979, T9549–53.

September 19, 1940"[118] (emphasis added). How can the decision to dominate East Asia by force have been taken only in 1940 when the outright invasion to conquer China occurred in 1937? It would perhaps be a different matter if Roeling said this applied to Southeast Asia, but he is specific in his reference to "East Asia," which surely must be taken to include China. Postulating a version of the history of this period in which statesmen like Hirota worked for peace through the New Order policy until they were overcome by the force of events in 1940 when war becomes inevitable obscures the violence the Japanese had already inflicted on China and sets the stage for his argument in the final section of the opinion that none of these statesmen should be convicted. It is to that section that we now turn.

*11.2.1.3 The Verdicts in the Individual Cases*
Following on the principle he had elaborated in the previous section that those "dangerous" individuals guilty of crimes against peace should not suffer capital punishment but only be rendered harmless, Roeling's first sentence in his section on the verdicts states, "From the law as it now stands, it follows that no one should be sentenced to death for having committed a crime against peace. Internment for life is, at this state, the appropriate punishment for this crime."[119] On this basis he argues that Araki, Hashimoto, Hiranuma, Hoshino, Minami, Kaya, Ōshima, Shiratori, Suzuki, Koiso, and Umezu should receive this penalty. To dispel any doubt that Roeling accepted the death penalty as legitimate, the following paragraph articulates Roeling's disagreement with the life sentences that the majority applied to Oka, Satō, and Shimada. These individuals, he states, should have been sentenced to death. He also states his agreement with the majority that Dohihara, Itagaki, Kimura, Matsui, Mutō, and Tōjō should likewise be executed.

In the end, then, Roeling's dissenting opinion accepts that all but five of the accused should have been found guilty and argues that nine of the accused should receive the death penalty, the rest life imprisonment. While he disagrees with the majority's rationale on the status of crimes against peace he nonetheless agrees that it can form the basis for convicting both civilian and military officials. He also accepts the legitimacy of convictions based on conventional war crimes and argues that individuals so convicted should be sentenced to death. Thus, while much has been made of Roeling's critique of the IMTFE, in fact his only disagreement with the majority as to guilty verdicts focuses on the convictions of Hata, Hirota, Kido, Shigemitsu, and Tōgō. As his policy rationale for not convicting statesmen who intend to bring about a peaceful settlement has been dealt with above, we may briefly examine a few salient

---

[118] Roeling Opinion, 781 and see also 738.
[119] Ibid., 775.

features of his reasoning as to the acquittal of these five individuals. He refrains completely from discussing or analyzing his position in regard to the verdicts he suggests for the remaining accused.

*11.2.1.3.1 Hata*   Hata is the only military officer among these five individuals. Roeling states the appropriate standard in determining his liability: "No soldier should ever be found guilty of the crime of waging an aggressive war simply for the reason that he performed a strictly military function. Aggression is a political concept, and the crime of aggression should be limited to those who take part in the relevant political decisions."[120] As we have seen, in the previous section of his opinion Roeling argued that it is primarily the military who should bear responsibility for resorting to war and that the civilian leaders merely made the non-culpable error of appeasing them. In dealing with the case of Hata he reiterates that, "In this case, the danger of a situation where military men influence the policy of a country has been made clear for all time."[121] Hata, he claims, merely carried out the aggressive policy but was not responsible for it. On this basis he should be acquitted of crimes against peace. Here Roeling discounts, for example, Hata's statement to the Imperial Diet about "thoroughly crushing the Chiang Kai-shek government's pro-Communist and anti-Japanese policies." He reasons that "words spoken on official occasions often do not reveal the true story."[122] Contemporary tribunals, in contrast, have relied precisely upon such kinds of public or policy utterances to infer intent.

Roeling's position on Hata seems to more fundamentally be based on two factors. The first is that he accepts defense evidence that Hata as army minister attempted to bring about peace with Chang Kai-shek (he does not indicate on what terms Hata discussed peace). The second, and more puzzling reason is that Roeling maintains that "the relations between Japan and China ... have not been sufficiently clarified in the trial to prove Hata guilty of the crime of waging a war of aggression."[123] Exactly what he means by this is not made clear because Roeling limits himself to this statement, but judging by the discussion of the developments of 1936–45 reviewed in the previous section of his opinion the implication is that he hedges doubt as to whether the Japanese were really guilty of aggression in China and, if so, who was responsible. It may also be that Roeling felt that if he was to exonerate the statesmen for aggression in China he needed to also find grounds for exculpating the army minister who advanced the same New Order policy as they did.[124]

---

[120] Ibid., 779.
[121] Ibid., 776.
[122] Ibid., 778. As seen in Chapter 8, Webb treated the evidence against Hata quite differently.
[123] Ibid.
[124] His apparent conviction that Hata had nothing to answer for in China is also borne out by his argument that Hata should be acquitted for war crimes committed in Nanjing, Guangzhou, and

426    The Dissenting Opinions of Justices Bernard and Roeling

Roeling's treatment of the four statesmen, Hirota, Kido, Tōgō, and Shigemitsu, must be read against the policy that he has already articulated in the previous section, namely that civilian officials who intend peace should not be convicted of crimes against peace despite having played key roles in the government that decided upon or waged aggressive war. Roeling's treatment of Hirota may serve as an example of the sometimes tortured reasoning by which he argued for acquittal on legal grounds while the underlying justification was the general policy.

*11.2.1.3.2 Hirota*   Hirota, Roeling notes, is charged with conspiring to wage war in order to establish the New Order, and waging war in China. Roeling will thus have to directly deal with the issue regarding China that he has thus far managed to avoid. His starting point is that in the secret decision of 1936, "it is apparent that Japan did not plan the domination of East Asia by aggressive war ... The policy makers of 1936 and later had in mind other roads to the domination of Asia." He reiterates that "policy turned to the use of armed force as a means of achieving the domination of East Asia" occurred in September 1940.[125] Given that armed force had already been used by Japan in 1931 in Manchuria and that the outright invasion of China occurred a year after the 1936 policy decision, how does Roeling extricate Hirota, whose policy it was, from responsibility? Indeed, Roeling's own memoranda had made clear that Hirota had personally advocated and justified the use of armed force to achieve domination in China.[126] Roeling's memorandum, for example, suggests the judges add the following quotation from one of Hirota's policy speeches to indicate his views and role: "Since they [the Chinese] were facing Japan with very strong anti-Japanese feeling, *we decided on a policy whereby* we had to necessarily chastise them"[127] (emphasis added).

The first step is to continue to argue as if the policy for the domination of East Asia somehow, for reasons never specified, did not include China. Hirota's failing on this view was to understand that once that policy had been set war became inevitable, though "other Japanese" would lead in that direction,

---

Hankou, because it had not been proved that he knew of these crimes or could have prevented them. He applies the same logic to Hata's role as supreme commander of the Japanese army forces in China 1941–4, arguing that the crimes committed in China "were not of such magnitude that reports could not have failed to reach Hata" and that the prosecution had failed to prove that Hata "could and should have known of the events in time to put an immediate stop to them" (ibid., 777, 780).

[125] Ibid., 781.
[126] August 23, 1948 NAA M1471/1 28 pp. 1–2. Roeling quotes Hirota as saying: "Japan has been endeavoring to make the Chinese Nationalist Government make reflections, if possible, while chastising their mistaken ideas by armed force" (citing PX3737-A, T37295–6).
[127] Ibid, citing PX3737-A, T37293.

## 11.2 Roeling's Dissent

presumably first in 1940.[128] Hirota, on Roeling's view, thus did not foresee that he would not be able to maintain Japan on the peaceful path to domination. Consistent with the policy of exculpating statesmen who commit fatal errors but intend peace Roeling concludes that Hirota is not responsible for the consequences of his policy:

> His was a miscalculation of his own power. Hirota did not realize before the event that he would not be able to retain command of the evil spirits he was evoking by his policy ... However fateful for Japan this policy of 1936 may have been, it does not come under the concept of the crimes against peace as mentioned in the Charter.[129]

Roeling then turns to the issue of Hirota's responsibility for waging war in China. Here he argues that the major policy decision of 1936 for domination of East Asia *has no relation to waging war in China* and, hence, Hirota also bears no responsibility for that war.[130] He indicates that the majority judgment erroneously relies on such a connection on the basis that when Hirota and others saw that they could not achieve their ends in China through peaceful means they accepted that Japan would have to resort to war.

The reasoning Roeling uses to reject this conclusion is quite astonishing. He reasons backward from the policy decision of September 1940, arguing that since it was only then that Japan decided to resort to war, the majority view is in error. He is aware, of course, that the all-out war in China did in fact begin with the Japanese invasion of 1937, so he must explain away Hirota's role as foreign minister at that time. His argument relies on the same strategy he employed in the previous section of the opinion, the fatal, but non-culpable, error of appeasement: "Hirota was the outstanding advocate of the policy of appeasing the military by cooperating with them."[131] He argues that while Hirota advocated the New Order and a powerful military to achieve Japanese domination of East Asia he did not want to use armed force to achieve this end. Therefore, he concludes,

> The steps Hirota took, however fateful they may have been for the future of Japan and of the world, did not come under the scope of the *concrete* planning of aggressive wars. In retrospect, those steps may appear to have been conditions sine qua non for the latter developments towards aggression. He did, however, not take those latter steps.[132] (emphasis added)

The awkward fact for Roeling is that whatever Hirota's inner intentions might have been, once war with China was underway he took an increasingly hard line. While Roeling squirms to explain this away he must acknowledge that,

---
[128] Ibid., 781.
[129] Ibid.
[130] Ibid.
[131] Ibid., 782.
[132] Ibid.

It has been proved that he [Hirota] participated in the government's decision not to deal any longer with Chang Kai-shek. Even in case this should lead to the conclusion that he, as a member of the Japanese government, waged a war of aggression against China, the history of his role shows that, he did not belong to *those arch-aggressors* who are judged by this Tribunal to deserve he death penalty.[133] (emphasis added)

Whether Roeling is correct about Hirota's commitment to peace is a factual matter that can never be definitively resolved. It is clear, however, that from a legal standpoint in determining guilt for waging aggressive war there is no distinction between "aggressors" and "arch-aggressors." Roeling's argument here is specious and irrelevant. What is also clear from Roeling's Opinion, however, is that he agrees that Hirota's policy encompassed domination of East Asia and appeasement of the militarists. He seeks to exculpate Hirota from the consequences of that policy by arguing, however implausibly, that it bore no relation whatsoever to the decision to invade, conquer, and subjugate China a year later, despite Hirota's speeches, cited above, justifying just such a policy. His conclusion that the decision to use force only occurred in 1940, when Hirota was no longer prime minister or foreign minister, is thus entirely implausible.

Given that the policy explicitly aimed at the Japanese domination of East Asia, and that China was the major East Asian nation that had already been in Japan's sights since the takeover of Manchuria by military means in 1931, it seems inexplicable how Roeling could plausibly reject the majority and Webb's conclusion as to the connection between that policy and the decision to invade China. But Roeling had to reject that conclusion if he was to acquit Hirota.

The difficulty did not end there, however, because Roeling had to accept that as foreign minister Hirota took an increasingly tough line, supporting the military's position of breaking off peace talks with Chiang Kai-shek (apart from other evidence indicating Hirota's support of pursuing the military campaign in China). His conclusion is that because Hirota always wanted peaceful domination and because he was not one of the "arch-aggressors," he should be acquitted. The brute fact that Roeling, despite his best efforts, cannot efface, is that the majority and Webb, assisted by Roeling's own memoranda, have established that however much Hirota may have preferred peaceful domination of China he was prepared to advocate for armed force if he thought it was the only way to achieve Japan's aims. Roeling's attempt to cleanly sever the policy of domination from the resort to force is simply not supported by his arguments, which, as shown above, struggle to deny the obvious connections supported by the evidence adduced in the majority and Webb draft judgments.

In regard to Hirota's responsibility for war crimes in China, Roeling's internal memoranda to Webb make clear that he was under no illusion as to Hirota's

---

[133] Ibid., 785.

## 11.2 Roeling's Dissent

role. In a memorandum of August 23, 1948 when the judges were drafting their judgment, Roeling suggests that they add many more references showing the awareness of foreign governments of the huge scale and nature of the atrocities being committed in Nanjing as communicated in their protests over many weeks to Japanese diplomats during the time when Hirota was foreign minister. Roeling adds that they should also emphasize the duration of the hostilities, which is a key issue in regard to taking steps to stop and prevent them. Roeling unequivocally accepts that Hirota was fully aware of the atrocities and states that he personally spoke to Army Minister Sugiyama about them but then decided not to bring the matter to the cabinet because "it was not in a position to deal with questions regarding the military in the field." Given that Roeling explicitly acknowledges that in regard to the atrocities, "The time element is very important in relation to the responsibility," it seems clear that in this memorandum he is aware that Hirota was in a key position, had full knowledge, and after consulting with the army minister decided not to challenge what the army was doing in Nanjing.[134]

In conclusion, the explanation for Roeling's positions on the key issues in his opinion do not reflect well on his stature as a judge or as a jurist.

First, Roeling, while refusing to bow to the Dutch demand not to publicly dissent, sacrificed his independence as a judge by engaging in protracted discussion and negotiation with Dutch officials over the content of his dissenting opinion and was ultimately persuaded to completely reverse his opinion on the absolutely central issue of the law of the Charter on crimes against peace.

Second, he justified this reversal by resorting to arguments of political expediency to justify convicting individuals for acts he apparently considered not to be criminal. He also masked what he himself had referred to as principles of expediency in the clothing of the law in upholding crimes against peace as international law when he considered this not to be the case. As we have seen, he justified the conviction for crimes against peace on the analogy of domestic laws which punish political crimes for the purpose, he maintains, of eliminating dangerous persons. He had rejected precisely this expedient in his January 23, 1947 memorandum to Webb. Dismissing the notion that the victors can define who is a war criminal Roeling states, "I don't think war crimes trials can be used for this purpose. A victor has other means to achieve that." These means, he states, include the right of a victor to preserve the peace that has been won by taking dangerous persons into custody. This is also what he says in his opinion, but in the memorandum the conclusion is different. He argues that such preventative measure has "nothing to do with criminality." The conclusion he draws from this undercuts the very basis of his justification of the

---

[134] NAA M1417/1 28 pp. 2–7. Roeling also notes (p. 7) the importance of citing the evidence of reports that rapes were being committed in the presence of the Japanese commanders.

convictions for crimes against peace he approves of in his opinion: "*Using war crimes trials for the purpose of eliminating undesirable elements would mean the mixing up of justice and expediency, and would frustrate both*"[135] (emphasis added). His opinion itself thus appears to be an exercise in hypocrisy or political expediency.

Finally, his general policy on the desirability of enabling statesmen who desire peace to participate in government organized criminality appears to determine his verdicts on the individual accused such as Hirota, Shigemitsu, and others. While the policy of encouraging those who desire peace to work for that end within criminal governments may (or may not) be a wise principle of policy, it is not a legal standard for determining the culpability of individuals for alleged participation in criminal conduct. Indeed, Webb points this out quite forcefully to Roeling in the memorandum quoted above. A judge in criminal proceedings should not need to be reminded that his or her primary responsibility is to reach conclusions on the culpability of individual accused for the crimes charged on the basis of the evidence before them. To do otherwise would, in Roeling's phrase, mean the "mixing up of justice and expediency" and result in a political show trial.

---

[135] Roeling, Memorandum of January 23, 1947, p. 23.

# 12 Pal's "Judgment," or Dissenting Opinion, on Crimes against Peace

## 12.1 Introduction

There are several reasons to challenge to analyze what is commonly referred to as the dissenting opinion of Judge Pal but which he entitled "Judgment." The implication of that title will be considered below. In this chapter, however, Pal's "judgment" will simply be referred to as his "opinion" or "dissenting opinion" to avoid confusion with the judgment of the Tribunal.[1] We have placed this consideration of Pal's dissent after the treatment of Bernard and Roeling to provide a comparative perspective that reveals just how greatly Pal's treatment departs from their more juristic and sober assessments of the shortcomings of the majority judgment.

The first challenge in analyzing the jurisprudence of Pal's Opinion is its length. As we have seen, the majority judgment, taking up some 558 pages in print, is ill-organized and poorly written in comparison with its relatively terse Nuremberg counterpart of some 170 pages. Pal's Opinion – at 616 printed pages – is not only longer, but the first 530 pages are almost overwhelming in their tedium, their needlessly overly lengthy and often irrelevant quotations, their repetitive pseudo-scholarly disquisitions on points of international law, and their general lack of concision and clear organization. It would be surprising indeed if many of those commentators who lionize Pal as the great hero of the IMTFE had actually read through the entirety of his opinion and carefully considered the grounds on which he exculpates all of the accused at Tokyo.[2]

---

[1] The title page of the official version of Pal's opinion only contains the word "Judgment" as a title. In Pal's memorandum to Webb of November 5, 1948, delivering this opinion to the President, he refers to it as "my dissentient judgment" and as a "dissenting judgment." The other separate opinions refer to themselves as "Opinions." (NAA M1417/1 28).

[2] Some of Pal's commentators in Japan have also noted the needless length of the many quotations and their apparent lack of relevance. Members of a "Tokyo Trial Research group" (*Tōkyō saiban kenkyūkai*), which published a complete translation of Pal's dissenting opinion in 1966 (*Kyōdō kenkyū*), publicly celebrated it as a "'Book of Truth' that will be remembered forever in the history of mankind," and compared Pal with the towering seventeenth-century jurist of international law, Hugo Grotius (*Kyōdō kenkyū*, vol. 1, p. 3). Privately, however, they noted that the dissenting opinion was poorly organized, as the same issues were repeatedly raised and many bulk quotes were thrown in without any clear indication as to their relevance. Doubts were also expressed

If they had, Pal would be unlikely, as we will see, to have gained his reputation as a proponent of peace and international understanding.[3] The second difficulty arises from the fact that although his opinion is replete with massive numbers of quotations from legal sources it actually bears little resemblance to a dissenting opinion. Indeed, it fails even to consider the majority judgment from which it purports to dissent. The reasons for that will be made clear below.

As we will argue, Pal's opinion operates somewhere in the space between a legal treatise and a political tract, tending much more toward the latter rather than the former. It includes what can only be regarded as political commentary that not only points to the lack of impartiality on Pal's part but also reveals that his true purpose appears to have had little to do with the appropriate function of a judge writing a dissenting opinion on the case before him. Pal's opinion has found great resonance in Japan precisely for this reason. On the often flimsiest legal and factual grounds, it not only concludes that "each and every one of the accused must be found not guilty of each and every one of the charges in the indictment ... " but it also frequently suggests that the real criminals are the Allies and that they should have been put on trial *instead of* (not in addition to) the entirely innocent Japanese leaders. As we will see, Pal explicitly likens the Allied conduct of the war to that of Nazi Germany, suggesting that as the Nazi leaders were put on trial at Nuremberg, so the Allied leaders should have been tried at Tokyo rather than *any* Japanese government officials or military commanders. Needless to say, these conclusions and his obvious hatred of Western colonialism and imperialism were extraneous to the legal issues before him, but they were central to his true agenda, which was political rather than legal.

It is thus a central contention of the present chapter that Pal fails utterly to carry out his responsibilities as a judge at Tokyo. Indeed, his memorandum of July 5, 1946 indicates that he had already decided to dissent on key issues to be argued before the tribunal and was "preparing a detailed judgment of [his] own."[4] Pal assigns himself another function, that of judging the trial which in his view *should have occurred* instead of the one that did. In that imagined trial, the accused would have included the Allies, and he titled the "dissenting opinion" he wrote as "judgment" because he aimed to provide the justice that in his view neither the Nuremberg nor the Tokyo trials delivered.[5]

Webb had clearly and accurately set out the fundamental criteria by which the judges' impartiality and the legitimacy of their decisions were to be

---

about the contribution of Pal's dissenting opinion in the field of international law. See Nakazato, *Neonationalist Mythology in Postwar Japan*, 169. See also Nakajima, "The Tokyo Tribunal, Justice Pal and Historical Revisionism in Postwar Japan."

[3] See Kopelman, "Ideology and International Law."
[4] Pal memorandum to Webb NAA M1417 25 p. 3.
[5] Ushimura, "Pal's 'Dissentient Judgment' Reconsidered," notes that in Japan Pal's dissent was widely apprehended as an alternative "judgment" p. 215.

## 12.1 Introduction

measured: "[T]hat the members of the tribunal should not be prejudiced and should not be personally hostile to the accused and that they should thoroughly and objectively analyze the evidence to determine guilt or innocence."[6] As we will see, Pal utterly fails to live up to these obligations for his personal biases become manifest in shaping his conclusions and he makes no attempt to analyze the evidence "thoroughly and objectively." His "judgment," as we will see, was designed to give the appearance of rigor and logic but is shot through with contradictions, inconsistencies, obfuscations, superficial reasoning, and deliberate avoidance of the evidence before the court that did not fit with his predetermined aims.

Assessing Pal's opinion indicates he should be seen much more as a defense advocate rather than an impartial jurist. His opinion, as we will see below, and particularly in the two case studies on his treatment of war crimes, is blatantly partial to the defense case. Again and again Pal eschews balanced and impartial analysis and weighing of the prosecution and defense cases in arriving at his findings and conclusions. Indeed, in regard to his treatment of the war crimes charges against the accused it would be more accurate to characterize those eighty pages as defense advocacy devoid of any real legal analysis of the evidence before the tribunal. Such analysis fell outside the scope of his aims. He knew that no matter what he said all of the accused had been convicted in what he regarded as an illegitimate and unjust trial that never should have taken place and merely cloaked raw power with juristic garb.

Pal in reality used the opportunity to "dissent" as an opportunity to write his own, as he termed it, "judgment." A dissenting opinion by its very nature dissents *from* the majority judgment, whose arguments it should carefully consider. It is striking that Pal chose not to participate substantively in the deliberations of the majority on the points from which he dissented. *It is even more striking that had he not even seen the Majority judgment when his own "dissent" was already complete.*[7]

In the large corpus of internal memoranda between the judges debating points of law and evidence or reviewing drafts sections of the various versions of judgments being circulated, Pal is hardly present. Pal was quite obviously not interested in making his viewpoints heard within the court but rather in promulgating them to a global audience.[8] In this sense it is hard to encompass

---

[6] Webb "Draft No. 2" of November 1947 p. 21. (NAA M1417/1 32)

[7] Pal had made his intention to dissent and its purport publicly known before the promulgation of the judgment, as noted in a speech to the American Bar Association on September 7, 1948 by Ōshima's defense counsel, Owen Cunningham, who stated that although the judgment of the tribunal was not expected for many months, "One of the judges, the Indian, has already completed his dissentient judgment, recommending dismissal of all counts and acquittal of all defendants." (NAA M1417/1 25).

[8] One cannot excuse this on the grounds that they would have rejected his views, because Roeling and Bernard, not to mention Webb and Zaryanov, each participated extensively and effectively in the internal debates in regard to their strong objections to various points of law and evidence.

his opinion as a dissent from the judgment of the tribunal, as opposed to his own creation independent of the tribunal. This is in fact the way in which Pal worked from the beginning. He seized this opportunity to say all that he believed needed to be said about what he took as the centuries of Western domination of Asia that had only been reinforced by the Allied victory as well as what he regarded as the criminality of the Allied use of the atom bomb to end the war.[9]

For Pal the inhumanity of the Allied conduct of the war, and the use of this weapon in particular, so far outweighed anything the Japanese had done in their conduct of the war from 1931 to 1945 that it demanded a clear statement as to who were the real war criminals.[10] Pal underscores his point by demanding the acquittal of "each and every one of the accused on each and every one of the crimes" with which they had been charged. The implausibility of this conclusion as a *legal* conclusion in regard to the war crimes charges in particular is manifest in the face of the massive evidence of Japanese war crimes before the tribunal. Pal makes a show of examining some of that evidence but, as this and the next chapter will show, his conclusions are not based upon that evidence but upon other extrinsic factors that he deemed as essential to a "true" judgment of Japan's wars. Consideration of these factors leads Pal to conclude that not only are all the Japanese accused innocent, but their innocence arises from the injustice of the international system of Western domination that both made war inevitable and created victors' tribunals at Nuremberg and Tokyo. Such an approach might well befit a political critique of the system of western colonialism still in place at the start of WWII. It does not, however, fit within the ethical and professional obligations of a judge.[11]

However much some commentators may sympathize with the politics of Pal's judgment, or however much they may condemn the Allied bombing campaign in Germany or in Japan, they should acknowledge that it is those politics that have driven Pal's enterprise and not the impartial exercise of the judicial function. They may praise Pal as an anti-colonial and anti-imperialist political advocate and theorist, but they should also recognize that he deliberately chose that role over the proper role of a judge. Pal's disregard for the most basic judicial ethic of impartiality and reasoned analysis rather than prejudice and personal political convictions has, of course, been noticed. There is, for

---

[9] Pal's intentions also appear from his apparent frustration that his request to read out his entire Judgment in court was not approved by the majority. Memorandum of November 5, 1948 to Webb NAA M1417/ 1 28.

[10] In addition to the analysis of his treatment of war crimes below, see also the concluding paragraphs of his Opinion, in the final section entitled "Recommendations."

[11] Even from the standpoint of political critique, Pal seems oblivious to the reality of Japan's primary war aim which was to replace western colonial domination with its own, as it had already done in Korea, Taiwan, and Manchukuo.

example, his often-noted indication to Roeling before the beginning of the trial that he would likely dissent.[12] His behavior at the close of the defense case frames the nature of his role when he is reported to have rushed to congratulate defense counsel on the emotional power and content of their speech.[13] Needless to say, such action not only indicates a lack of impartiality but also constitutes a fundamental contempt for basic judicial ethics. A third point that reveals his disposition toward the trial is that he was absent at almost 1/4 of the trial sessions, scarcely appropriate for any judge, let alone for a judge who plans to reject the entire prosecution case and every aspect of the majority's and Webb's legal conclusions.[14]

From this perspective it is not surprising that unlike Roeling and Bernard, Pal does not even acknowledge the majority judgment, to which he only refers once, in the first sentence of his opinion. Roeling and Bernard wrote dissenting opinions that appropriately focused on their disagreements with the majority.

Pal sets out instead to answer the prosecution case in an opinion that serves at once as the case for the defense and an indictment of the tribunal on which he agreed to serve as a judge.[15] Apart from having absented himself from much of the trial, he also did not deign to actively participate in the internal debates around the drafting of the judgment.[16] The other dissenting Judges, Roeling and Bernard, on the other hand, were among the most active participants in these discussions. Pal thus appears to have operated in a vacuum where he followed his own predetermined agenda, divorced from deliberations of the other judges as well as from nearly a quarter of the trial proceedings. He would have presumably justified this because he regarded the entire trial as illegitimate and the other judges as instruments of Allied vengeance and power. Accordingly, he felt no need to even consider the majority judgment when drafting his own. Since his intention was clear from the beginning and since he seems to have seen his opinion as a political statement that would set the record straight on the pernicious nature of the Western Powers, there was no need for him to participate more fully in the judicial process. To the extent that his aim was

---

[12] Recounted by Roeling to Arnold Brackman and reflected in the memorandum cited immediately above in footnotes 4 and 5. See Brackman, *The Other Nuremberg*, 71.

[13] See Chapter 2 under Section 2.1.

[14] He seems to overlook his fully documented absences from nearly a quarter of the trial when he states that "I have heard the entire case" (Pal Opinion, 932).

[15] Pal sent a brief note to Webb stating that he wants it noted on the record that he had intended to read out in court his entire "dissentient judgment."(NAA M1417/1 28) Apart from the massive egotism in wanting to read in its entirety a dissent that took up 1235 pages in Pal's original version, this request also indicates how Pal viewed his work as an alternative "judgment," that is an account of the entire trial, coequal to the majority judgment and, on his view, superseding it. This is not, of course, the normal role of dissenting *opinions*.

[16] See e.g. Justice Jaranilla's apparent reference to Pal as one of the judges who did not participate in deliberations on the contentious issue of jurisdiction and expressing his hope such judges "may still be open-minded on the said question." January 22, 1947 AWM 3DRL 2481/5.

political, he succeeded in winning the admiration of a defeated nation as their spokesperson for the rejection of the IMTFE. His failure resided in another domain, that of jurisprudence and the proper exercise of the role of a judge.

This chapter consists of a general discussion of some of the main features of Pal's opinion on the nature of international law, the status of the crime of aggression, and his account of Japan's alleged conspiracy to initiate and wage aggressive war. The next chapter addresses how Pal dealt with the prosecution case on atrocities and provides two detailed case studies of the sections of his opinion devoted to charges of war crimes. Such a detailed examination Pal's judgment, as opposed to a more unsystematic and hence inevitably much shorter approach, is necessary for two reasons.

First, there is the massive length of the opinion – already mentioned – which precludes detailed analysis of the entire text but which nonetheless demands a systematic approach that does justice to his full methods and argument rather than an anecdotal one that might be regarded by defenders of Pal as unrepresentative. In other words, we need to make the full case for the shortcomings of his opinion. Second, because of the way Pal has been made into an enshrined national hero in Japan and also elevated to the rank of a great jurist, it is necessary to show in detail just how much he fails to live up to the basic requirements of a judge and jurist in regard to the impartiality of his judgment and the quality of his analysis and reasoning in support of his conclusions.[17] In calling into question the orthodoxies that have prevailed about Pal it is necessary to provide a rigorous analysis of what he actually wrote; an analysis largely absent from the literature lionizing him.

Because there is room for legitimate difference of opinion on the state of international law on the crime of aggression during the period under the jurisdiction of the IMTFE, we focus in Chapter 13 on two case studies on areas about which there can be no doubt as to an existing body of international law on war crimes, including international customary law, as well as the 1929 Geneva Convention on Prisoners of War and the 1907 Hague Convention No. 4, to both of which Japan was a signatory.[18]

---

[17] See, on Pal, Nakazato, *Neonationalist Mythology in Postwar Japan*, which in part III offers a definitive account of myths surrounding Pal in postwar Japan. See also Futamura, *War Crimes Tribunals and Transitional Justice*, 110. A monument dedicated to Pal can be found in the precinct of the Yasukuni Shrine in central Tokyo, where fourteen of the Class A war criminals tried by the Tokyo Tribunal are enshrined. The fourteen comprise the seven who were sentenced to death, and seven others who died while in prison.

[18] As the High Command Case said of international customary law, "The law of war is to be found not only in treaties, but in the customs and practices of states which gradually obtained universal recognition, and from the general principles of justice applied by jurists and practiced by military courts. This law is not static, but by continual adaptation follows the needs of a changing world. Indeed, in many cases treaties do no more than express and define for more accurate reference the principles of law already existing." High Command Case, 472–3.

## 12.2 Preliminary Overview

As noted earlier, one of the difficulties in providing an analysis of Pal's opinion is its length. The sections dealing with the charges of crimes against peace alone comprise some 510 pages of the Boister and Cryer text.[19] The entire majority judgment, from which Pal purports to dissent, consists of 558 pages, including all of the sections on war crimes, individual verdicts, etc. What explains the voluminous nature of Pal's dissenting opinion? The most obvious reason is Pal's aims not to identify, as the other dissenting judges did, the points on which he disagrees with the majority, but rather to provide his own full account of the actual trial and of the trial that should have been held in its stead. Thus, after stating in his first sentence that he regrets he cannot concur "in the judgment and decision of my learned brethren," he never mentions the majority judgment again.[20] The section of Pal's opinion on crimes against peace seeks to establish that Japan was in fact a victim of Western imperialist aggression.

The part devoted to crimes against peace takes up 83 percent of Pal's opinion for two reasons. Undermining the legitimacy of the Allied war aims and exonerating the Japanese from the charge that they were responsible for the war was one of his principal purposes. Second, Pal wanted a platform from which to attack the whole enterprise of international law as part of Western imperialism and domination of Asia. Because of his own manifest hatred of British imperialism, and in his desire to see India and the rest of Asia free from colonial rule, he sympathized with the notion of Japan's expansion at the expense of the Western Powers and wanted to delegitimize any doctrines of international law that would have condemned it.[21] These are his goals and it is of course for just these views that Pal has been lauded as a visionary and a great political thinker.[22] We will see more concretely how these views shaped the kind of "judgment" he produced and why he did so.

Pal's views on colonialism, imperialism, Western racism, and the international political system of the prewar era run through his treatment of the charges of crimes against peace. A substantive assessment of Pal's political views and ideology is outside the scope of this book because these views are

---

[19] In Pal's typescript version issues of conspiracy and the crime of aggression take up 946 pages out of 1235, or 1014 pages if one includes the section on procedure and evidence which is actually a continuation of the argument on aggressive war.

[20] Memoranda of some of the other judges indicate their criticisms of Pal's views on key legal issues. See, e.g. in the Webb papers Justice Mei's memorandum of March 1, 1948 to Webb (AWM 3DRL 2481/3 p. 2) and Webb's comments (AWM 3DRL 2481/61).

[21] In regard to the British, Pal's Bengali nationalism made them a chief target of his attack. Even though in 1948 when his Opinion was completed Britain's economic and political importance had been vastly diminished in relation to the prewar period, Pal still tellingly referred to the "Britanocentric economic world order" that had long since evaporated (Pal Opinion, 1299).

[22] For a biographical perspective on Pal's intellectual and ideological formation, as well as his reception in India, see Nandy, "The Other Within."

extraneous to the legal issues before the court. That they were not considered extraneous by Pal, but rather, as he admits, central to his whole purpose in writing this massive "judgment," is itself an indictment of his conduct as a judge. He would no doubt have readily accepted this "indictment" because his obvious purpose was to use the opportunity to "dissent" in order to express his views and especially his contempt for the tribunal as an institution and his condemnation of the Allied Powers.[23]

For these reasons the crimes against peace sections comprise the vast bulk of the opinion. The legal issues concerning crimes against peace, however, although open to serious debate, were not terribly complex. Roeling dissented about crimes against peace on the same legal grounds as Pal. Yet his analysis of the relevant legal issues, while in fundamental agreement with Pal's conclusions, take up only twenty succinct pages of legal argument. His discussion, like that of Pal, focuses on the three crucial issues before the court on the crimes against peace charges: (1) Is the law of the Charter binding upon the Tribunal? (2) Were crimes against peace, or the waging of aggressive war, recognized as criminal under international law during the time period for which the accused are charged? (3) If aggressive war was criminal did international law at the relevant time provide for individual criminal responsibility for this crime?

Pal agrees that these are the salient issues and reaches the same conclusions as Roeling does. The relevant corpus of legal documents required for addressing these issues is relatively small. Ultimately, as noted above, there were grounds for legitimate differences of opinion on points (2) and (3) in particular. The crux of the matter, after all, hinged primarily upon the meaning of a very few phrases in the Kellogg-Briand Pact of 1928 and the manner in which the Pact was received by the international community at the time prior to the commencement of hostilities. The Nuremberg Tribunal, Webb, Roeling, Bernard, and various other judicial bodies such as the Nuremberg subsequent proceedings all managed to deal competently and concisely with these legal issues in tens of pages, defending their various interpretations of the Pact. Pal took 510 pages to discuss these issues because they were the platform to develop his agenda that extended far beyond the issues of international law actually before the tribunal and far beyond the role of a judge.

What is particularly telling is that Pal's own conclusions obviate the need for such elaborate discussion of crimes against peace and conspiracy to commit such crimes. On the one hand, Pal toward the end of his opinion announces that he does not in general consider conspiracy to be a crime or an accepted mode of liability in international law. This comes after 340 pages of discussion

---

[23] See below pp. 449–51, 457–8 on Pal's justification of his expansive role.

of the conspiracy charges. Why, then, does he devote 351 pages of his opinion to a crime which he does not consider to exist? The Nuremberg judgment rejected the prosecution's conspiracy theory in two pages and Webb did much the same. Even more surprisingly, Pal also announces very late in the judgment, and after he has completed his voluminous treatment of crimes against peace, *that he made no findings and reached no conclusions on whether any of the wars in which Japan engaged were aggressive.* If this is the case, then why does he spend the bulk of his judgment considering the charges of aggressive war? The ensuing discussion will provide answers to these questions.

## 12.3 The Crime of Aggressive War

### 12.3.1 The "Material Questions of Law"[24]

Pal, as noted earlier, appears to write in a vacuum, completely isolated from the deliberations and conclusions of his fellow judges. His interlocutors on the crime of aggressive war, whom he engages at tremendous and unnecessary length, are not his fellow judges or the majority judgment, but some of the leading international scholars of the day. Although Bernard and Roeling had expressed similar views on the same issues of aggressive war that Pal dealt with, he also never refers to their dissenting opinions. On the basis of the substance of his opinion, Pal seems to have conceived of himself as an academic jurist whose real counterparts were the great Western legal scholars such as Lord Wright, Sheldon Glueck, Hans Kelsen, H. Lauterpacht, and L. Oppenheim, whose errors he would reveal. His aspiration seems to have been to write his own treatise that would both articulate his vision of international law, politics, and inter-state relations, and then use that vision to attack the work of the tribunal and the Allied Powers who created it, to justify Japan's war aims, and finally to enunciate the principles of what he considered to be a just postwar world order.

Pal devotes 119 pages to a discussion of the three core legal questions enumerated above. These pages are replete with numerous lengthy quotations and paraphrases from what he calls "the learned authors" mentioned above. He engages them in excruciating detail, critiquing, praising, debunking, and so on. Even marginal texts are exhaustively examined, like one article by the Russian lawyer A. N. Trainin which receives nine full pages of treatment by Pal.[25] These dense and virtually unreadable pages of quotation, paraphrase, and lengthy outlines of articles and treatises are reminiscent of an academic literature review as a preliminary prospectus for a dissertation. It is an academic

---

[24] Pal Opinion, 815.
[25] Ibid., 893–902.

exercise that is wholly unnecessary because these jurists, who in any event significantly disagree with one another on various points, are not authoritative for the tribunal. There is thus no need for Pal to treat them at any greater length than did Roeling, who refers to their views in a little more than one page. The IMT Nuremberg judgment does not mention the work of international law scholars at all in its treatment of aggressive war and conspiracy because those authors are not the authoritative reference point. The Nuremberg judgment focuses instead on the international legal instruments that it is the proper role of the tribunal to interpret.

The role of the judge is not that of the scholar who needs to engage the academic literature and locate themself within current debates. The role of the judge is to determine the law applicable in the case at hand based upon the authoritative sources of international law, which in this case are the various international legal instruments and international customary law. What Roeling appropriately does is to focus attention on his interpretation of the core legal instruments that are dispositive for reaching decision on the criminality of aggression.[26] It is the role of the judges to use their legal acumen to decide on the import of the provisions of these international legal instruments not to engage in an academic debate whose outcome has in any event been clear since the first page of Pal's opinion. If Pal wanted to engage in dialogue and debate about applicable international instruments then the appropriate counterparts would have been the majority and other separate opinions from the judges of the IMTFE, as well as the judgments from the IMT and subsequent proceedings at Nuremberg. It is remarkable that Pal's efforts to elevate himself into the highest ranks of (Western) jurisprudence have been taken seriously.[27] What is impressive about this part of Pal's opinion is the *Fleissarbeit* – "grindstone work" – that went into those interminable outlines of various scholars' positions rather than the results of his very partial and one-sided analysis rejecting them in what is clearly an ideologically – rather than juristically – pre-determined conclusion.

What a close examination of the 119-page discussion of the crime of aggression indicates is that Pal's real focus was not the issue of aggression itself but rather the general enterprise of international law, which he saw as enshrining, justifying, and maintaining Western domination and colonialism while denying the same "privileges" to Japan. This is the subtext that runs through the entirety of his treatment of aggression and that also explains why he treated it

---

[26] Roeling Opinion, 694–5.
[27] Nandy, "The Stranger Within," suggests that though Pal was deeply steeped in Indian law at the time of the Tokyo Tribunal he lacked knowledge of international law. He goes on to say it was because of his role at Tokyo that he learned enough about international law to later function as a commentator, pp. 58–9.

## 12.3 The Crime of Aggressive War

at such length rather than in the concise manner of the other opinions and the Nuremberg judgments.

In considering the charges against the accused in regard to aggressive war Pal begins by rejecting the principle of individual responsibility which was the foundation of the Nuremberg judgment at the IMT. He does so, however, without referring to or engaging with the pathbreaking findings of that court which have defined the course of international criminal law until today. The basis of Pal's position is the Act of State doctrine, which was explicitly rejected by Nuremberg and all other WWII tribunals. As Pal explains in regard to the aggressive war charges against the accused, "the acts alleged are, in my opinion, all acts of State and whatever these accused are alleged to have done, they did that in working the machinery of the government."[28] Pal thus accepts the notion that the "State" as a legal abstraction shields the individuals who govern that state from *any* accountability for crimes committed in the name of the state they serve.[29]

Defense counsel at Nuremberg had also argued that acts of state precluded individual accountability. The tribunal responded that, "It was submitted that international law is concerned with the action of sovereign States, and provides no punishment for individuals; and further, that where the act in question is an act of state, those who carry it out are not personally responsible, but are protected by the doctrine of the sovereignty of the State."[30] In response to this defense argument the Nuremberg judgment held:

That international law imposes duties and liabilities upon individuals as well as upon States has long been recognized ... Crimes against international law are committed by men, not by abstract entities, and only by punishing individuals who commit such crimes can the provisions of international law be enforced.[31]

Pal does not even consider the Nuremberg judgment on this issue or explain why he considers its rationale to be invalid. Moreover, Pal soon involves himself in contradictory explanations about the Act of State doctrine he has invoked.

The Act of State rationale articulated by Pal would provide an absolute defense for any crimes committed by high-level state officials acting in their official capacity. This was indeed the intention behind the doctrine. Moving

---

[28] Pal Opinion, 815.
[29] In regard to the legal fiction of "acts of state" as invoked by the Nazi leaders as a defense, Robert Jackson in his Opening Statement at Nuremberg aptly remarked, "Of course, the idea that a state, any more than a corporation, commits crimes, is a fiction. Crimes always are committed only by persons." For Jackson's Opening Statement, see Volume 2 of *Trial of the Major War Criminals before the International Military Tribunal*. The quoted passage appears at page 150.
[30] IMT judgment, 222.
[31] Ibid.

442    Pal's "Judgment," or Dissenting Opinion, on Crimes against Peace

from charges of aggressive war to conventional war crimes, Pal states that war crimes committed by individuals in their individual capacity do not qualify for this defense because, "These are not acts of State."[32] At the bottom of the same page Pal reiterates that criminal responsibility for war crimes applies "only within the limitation that the act in question is not an act of the enemy state."[33] He does not, however, explain the criteria by which in specific cases this determination is to be made. When, for example, would a high-level government or military official be acting "in an individual capacity" yet commit war crimes cognizable at a tribunal such as the IMTFE? In other words, Pal's qualification would appear to apply to low-level soldiers who might, for example, in a drunken rampage, exceed their orders and commit war crimes such as rape, plunder, or murder. This is hardly relevant, however, to the kinds of accused before the IMTFE, and Pal offers no explanation of how the doctrine should be defined and applied in concrete cases to the high-level figures it was intended to protect.

To make matters even more confusing, Pal immediately appears to acknowledge that the Act of State doctrine no longer provides an absolute bar to individual criminal liability of high-level state actors: "In my judgment, it is now well-settled that mere high position of the parties ... would not exonerate them from criminal responsibility in this respect if, of course, guilt can otherwise be brought home to them. Their position in the state does not make every act of theirs an act of state within the meaning of international law." It is not clear what precedents Pal refers to when he says that it is "now well-settled" because he offers no citation. The obvious reference would be to Nuremberg but if that is the case, what Nuremberg regarded as "well-settled" was that the Act of State doctrine has been entirely invalidated.

It is typical of the inconsistencies in his opinion that Pal, just three pages earlier, had taken the position that the Act of State doctrine provided an absolute defense to all the conspiracy charges against the accused, but he then qualifies this position in a manner that leaves the whole matter unclear. When later in his opinion he in fact applies this doctrine to exonerate the accused from responsibility for certain war crimes against POW he offers no explanation of why in those cases, as opposed to all the other cases he discusses, the acts constituted acts of state.[34]

There is apparent confusion as to even more fundamental legal matters in this section of the opinion. On page 815 Pal states that there are three "material questions of law" that the tribunal must decide. On page 820, however, Pal again says he will "take up the material questions of law involved in the

---

[32] Pal Opinion, 818.
[33] Ibid.
[34] See Chapter 13, pp. 489–90.

## 12.3 The Crime of Aggressive War

case as specified above ... The questions are: 1. Whether a war of the alleged character is crime [sic] in international law. 2. Whether individual members of a State commit a crime in international law by preparing, etc. for such a war." The confusing point here is that Pal has not only switched from three issues to two but has also changed the issues, despite the fact that he says he is referring to the same issues "as specified above." The points he has omitted were not trivial for they include, among others, "Whether military, naval, political, and economic domination of one nation by another is crime in international life." He also omits from the second list the salient issue of whether there have been ex post facto laws that "affect the legal character of the acts alleged in the indictment."[35]

Despite having set out these two dispositive material issues on page 820, he turns immediately instead to related but separate issues that he has *not* enumerated: the status of the Charter, the legislative authority of the Allies, and the key question of whether the Charter is binding upon the court.[36] Having spent twenty pages mostly by discussing quotations from various jurists on the issues related to the status of the Charter, Pal has apparently forgotten the two issues he previously set out on page 820 as dispositive, and, for the third time in twenty-five pages, he states, "Two principal questions therefore arise here for our decision, namely: "(1) Whether the wars of the alleged character became criminal in international law. (2) Assuming the wars of the alleged character to be criminal, whether the individuals functioning as alleged here would incur any criminal responsibility in international law."[37] We should note here that the second point has been significantly reformulated yet again, and without any explanation.[38] We give these examples because they illustrate that although Pal's superficially meticulous organization of numbered points and lengthy outlines give the impression of rigor, the argument is in fact inconsistent and poorly constructed even in its basic structure.

After having for the third time without acknowledgment reformulated the material issues for the tribunal to decide, Pal does turn to the first issue he has defined. He then engages in thirty-seven pages of dialogue, replete with lengthy quotations, with major authors of international law treatises and articles. The point of such elaborate consideration of these pre-eminent scholars is not clear because he reaches a conclusion contrary to almost all of them. As he states, "After giving my anxious and careful consideration to the reasons given by the

---

[35] Pal Opinion, 815 and 820.
[36] His answer to these latter questions is basically the same as that of Roeling and Bernard to whom he does not refer, nor does he refer to the positions taken on these issues by the majority and Webb.
[37] Pal Opinion, 840.
[38] These examples of needless repetition and confusing organization could be multiplied.

prosecutor as also to the opinions of the various authorities[39] I have arrived at the conclusion: (1) That no category of war became criminal or illegal in international life; (2) That the individuals comprising the government ... incur no criminal liability in international law for the acts alleged."[40]

One might well think that this conclusion would mark the end of Pal's Opinion because he has answered the two material questions of law he proposed for decision on page 840 in the negative, compelling the conclusion that the accused must be acquitted. He has concluded that all of the charges regarding aggressive war must be disregarded and that per se, under international law the accused cannot be held accountable for any of the crimes with which they have been charged. Logically speaking there is no need to go into the factual disputes as to evidence because Pal has concluded that there is no legal basis for trying or convicting the accused.

Despite this finding Pal nonetheless writes another 523 pages and turns to a major legal issue which he has *not* set out as one of the material issues he must take up: "We must determine what is meant by aggressive war."[41] In the section that follows, however, Pal does not provide a definition of aggressive war and says that first it must be ascertained "which of the views as to a certain category of war having become criminal is accepted by us."[42] This turn is puzzling, to say the least, because the previous section has just concluded an exhaustive discussion with the determination that the wars alleged in the indictment are NOT criminal under international law. Why then would he say it is now necessary to consider views on when war is criminal when he has already found that its most extreme form, aggression, is not prohibited? What Pal actually has in mind appears a few pages later, when he states that, "I believe I have said enough to indicate that in deciding whether or not any particular action of Japan was aggressive we shall have to take into account the antecedent behavior of the other nation concerned including its activity in adverse propaganda and the so-called economic sanction and the like."[43]

As Pal states much later, his opinion does not make findings as to whether particular military actions of Japan constituted aggressive war, because he denies that aggressive war is a crime under international law.[44] What then is the purpose of this apparently conclusionless inquiry into the definition of aggression and the determining of whether Japan's actions constituted aggression? The purpose is to open the door to the real agenda of the rest of the opinion, an

---

[39] Note that Pal refers to the case of the Prosecutor and does not mention the majority opinion from which he purports to be dissenting.
[40] Pal Opinion, 903.
[41] Ibid., 904.
[42] Ibid., 913.
[43] Ibid., 924.
[44] Ibid., 1422.

## 12.3 The Crime of Aggressive War

agenda enabled by Pal's statement that inquiry into "antecedent behavior" of other nations is necessary. We will now examine how Pal frames that "antecedent behavior" in terms of themes that inform and shape the rest of his opinion.[45]

### 12.3.2 "Antecedent Behavior"[46]

In considering the claim that international law had evolved since WWI and through the actions of the League of Nations in the direction of limiting the sovereign right of nations to wage war, Pal rejects the idea that such a development has taken place. While this conclusion addresses the legal issue before the tribunal it is only the starting point for expressing Pal's political views that are extraneous to the work of the IMTFE. Pal now begins a discourse on what he considers to be the true nature of *international relations* (as opposed to applicable international law) by noting that prior to WWII "the powerful nations" gave no indication of accepting a "widening sense of humanity."[47] What he means by this is made abundantly clear in the ensuing sentences when he invokes Lord Robert Cecil's negative reaction when Baron Makino Nobuaki of Japan "moved a resolution for the declaration of the equality of nations." Lord Cecil of Great Britain, Pal continues, "opposed the resolution on the grounds that it "raised extremely serious problems within the British Empire."[48]

Pal here explicitly invokes a theme that has been implicit in much of his narrative to this point but which henceforth in the opinion becomes a leitmotif that runs through every section and informs Pal's position on every issue. The theme is the way in which the pre-WWII international system, and the structure of international law that undergirded it, justify and perpetuate the predominance of the Western imperial and colonizing powers. Pal, as a Bengali

---

[45] The Nazi defendants at Nuremberg invoked the same justification for their actions as Pal attributes to the Japanese. They argued that the economic and political system of the post-WWI era, the hostility of Britain, France, Russia, and the United States, and Germany's limited natural resources and geographical space left them no choice but to expand or die. Although Pal frequently refers to Robert Jackson's Opening Statement for the prosecution at Nuremberg, including in his discussion of "antecedent conditions," he does not refer to Jackson's apt rebuttal of this defense: "It is important to the duration and scope of this Trial that we bear in mind the difference between our charge that this war was one of aggression and a position that Germany had no grievances. We are not inquiring into the conditions which contributed to causing this war. They are for history to unravel. It is no part of our task to vindicate the European status quo as of 1933, or as of any other date ... The remote causations avowed are too insincere and inconsistent, too complicated and doctrinaire to be the subject of profitable inquiry in this trial. A familiar example is to be found in the 'Lebensraum' slogan, which summarized the contention that Germany needed more living space as a justification for expansion ... We do not need to investigate the verity of doctrines which led to constantly expanding circles of aggression. It is the plot and the act of aggression which we charge to be crimes." Jackson, Opening Statement, 149.
[46] Pal Opinion, 924.
[47] Ibid., 867.
[48] Ibid.

nationalist sitting in Tokyo at the tribunal during the period in which India successfully struggled for independence, was naturally predisposed to view international relations in this way, and it is no coincidence that his first example of Western intransigence in the face of Asian aspirations for equality is of Great Britain.[49]

Moving beyond the League of Nations Pal voices his accusation even more directly. He points first to the fact that "there is still continued domination of one nation by another" and that what he terms "that servitude" is accepted by the international community. Here he clearly refers to the colonial system that WWII had shaken but not yet eradicated. He states that Robert Jackson at Nuremberg said that "a preparation by a nation to dominate another nation is the worst of crimes." Applying this principle, he then reasons that either every powerful nation was guilty of this crime or there was no such crime prior to WWII: "Instead of saying that all the powerful nations were living a criminal life I would prefer to hold that international society did not develop before the Second World War so as to make this taint a crime."[50] In other words, on Pal's view there is no international norm that prohibits one nation from resorting to war to impose its dominion over another.

Pal does not, however, as is his usual practice, put quotation marks on his citation of Jackson. These words do not, in fact, appear in Jackson's Opening Statement.[51] What Jackson actually does say on this point directly contradicts Pal's assertion:

Our position is that whatever grievances a nation may have, *however objectionable it finds the status quo*, aggressive warfare is an illegal means for settling those grievances or for altering those conditions. It may be that the Germany of the 1920s and 1930s faced desperate problems, problems that would have warranted the boldest measures short of war. All other methods – persuasion, propaganda, economic competition, diplomacy – were open to an aggrieved country, but aggressive warfare was outlawed. These defendants did make aggressive war, a war in violation of treaties. They did attack and invade their neighbors in order to effectuate a foreign policy which they knew could not be accomplished by measures short of war. And that is as far as we accuse or propose to inquire.[52] (emphasis added)

The juxtaposition of Jackson's position with that of Pal neatly frames the issue. For Pal, as for the Nazi defendants at Nuremberg, it was the political,

---

[49] For more information on Pal's intellectual biography in the context of Bengali nationalism, see Nakazato, *Neonationalist Mythology in Postwar Japan*, part II.
[50] Pal Opinion, 867. There is also a certain irony in Pal tactfully not mentioning here that Japan eagerly joined the ranks of colonizing powers.
[51] The closest remark in Robert Jackson's Opening Statement to these words is in fact quite different: "to start or wage an aggressive war has the moral qualities of the worst of crimes." Jackson, Opening Statement, 155.
[52] Ibid., 149.

## 12.3 The Crime of Aggressive War

economic, and historical "status quo" of the prewar decades that justified and explained the resort to war to acquire an empire, which in Japan's case stretched from Korea, Mongolia, and the borders of India to New Guinea. For Pal, Japan was merely doing what other nations had previously done; but those nations had now put in place an international legal regime that was designed to maintain the status quo to their advantage while preventing newer powers, like Japan, Germany, and Italy from expansion. Pal ignores, of course, the fact that Japan had long before WWII already participated in that regime of colonial domination through its colonization first of Taiwan and then Korea.

Jackson, on the other hand, reminds the Nuremberg Tribunal that their role is to apply the law and not to delve into matters that were extraneous to the charges against the defendants, however important they might be for an historical understanding of the complex politics of the prewar period. Jackson's point is that under international law Germany's economic grievances and feelings of humiliation after the Treaty of Versailles could not justify invading its neighbors to secure the advantages, the natural resources, and the *Lebensraum* it desperately wanted. Pal on the other hand, as we shall see, appears to at the very least condone – and at times approve of – Japan's resort to war to overthrow Western dominance of the international political system. It is ironic in this context that Pal is often considered to be a visionary of peace, for while he regularly invokes the ideal of peace, his position on international law clearly justifies the resort of nations to war to secure greater political and economic power. Like Roeling, he may deplore this state of affairs, but he consistently maintains that even in 1948, at the time of writing his opinion, international law had not developed a norm that prohibited aggressive war as a tool of domination. Neither Japan nor Nazi Germany, it follows, could thus be condemned for waging aggressive war.

That Pal aims not just to excuse or justify Japan's war aims but also to identify the true guilty parties in WWII is made plain in the paragraphs that follow his reference to Jackson. He immediately invokes, as he does many times, the use of the atom bomb to end the war, rejecting the view that the atomic age will awaken "the sense of the unity of mankind."[53] Referring again to the use of atomic weapons, he states, "I, for myself, do not perceive any such feeling of broad humanity in the justifying words of those who were responsible for their use." He continues by arguing, as he will repeat in later sections, that he sees no difference "between what the German Emperor is alleged to have announced during the First World War in justification of the atrocious methods directed by him in the conduct of the war and what is being proclaimed after the Second

---

[53] Pal Opinion, 867.

World War in justification of these inhuman blasts."[54] In other words, as the Germans were the criminals in the conduct of WWI, and so were the Allies in WWII.

If one detects that Pal has here moved far beyond both the charges against the accused and the prewar "antecedents" that he felt necessary in order to justify Japan's conduct, the ensuing passages affirm that this is the case. Pal next moves to speculate further on the "new problems" that are facing the world in the atomic age. He opines:

> There is no doubt that the international society, if any, has been taken ill. Perhaps the situation is that nations of the international group are living in an age of transition to a planned society. But that is the matter for the future and perhaps it is only a dream ... The dream of all students of world politics is to reduce the complex interplay of forces to a few elementary constraints and variables by the use of which all the past is made plain and even the future stands revealed in lucid simplicity.[55]

In other words, the complexity of political events cannot be captured in the "elementary" principles of international law so as to constrain state behavior. Pal's skepticism as to whether or not international law can ever be effective, or whether a true "international society" can exist, may be of no relevance to the proceedings of the tribunal, but they are an integral part of the historical and political treatise he is writing in the guise of a dissenting opinion. In the pages that follow Pal continues his speculation as to whether there is an "inchoate [international] society in a stage of its formation" or whether the reality is that a new precedent of individual responsibility for aggression will in reality "only be a precedent for the future victor against the future vanquished." The "misapplication" of such a doctrine, he speculates further, "will shake the foundation of any future international society."[56] In other words, the doctrine of individual responsibility that Nuremberg and Tokyo are applying is in reality a mask for the revenge of the victor. This principle, Pal warns, is not to be seen as progress in international law as it has been widely hailed, but rather a threat for the future. The Tokyo Trial, however, like any criminal trial, is necessarily focused on the past. That is the nature of criminal justice. Pal's speculations as to the future of international society are legally entirely irrelevant to the trial of Japan's leaders but essential to his real thesis: The Allied victory and use of the atom bomb have merely served to further solidify the oppression of Western

---

[54] Ibid., 867–8. Later he will also liken the American use of the atom bomb not only to Germany in WWI but also in WWII, and to proclaim the Japanese government innocent of any conduct resembling either that of Nazi Germany or the Allies in their conduct of the war. See Chapter 13, pp. 469–70.
[55] Pal Opinion, 868.
[56] Ibid., 869.

12.3 The Crime of Aggressive War 449

domination that it was Japan's justifiable aim to destroy in initiating wars in Asia and the Pacific.

Having expounded at length upon the abstract nature of law and the injustices of the current system of international relations, Pal finally acknowledges that he has stepped beyond his institutional role as a judge at the tribunal: "I know that as a judge, it is not for me to *preach* the need for wider social consequences or to propound practical solutions for the problems ... of the modern world. Yet the international relation has reached a stage where even a judge cannot remain silent"[57] (emphasis added). Pal's characterization of his Opinion as "preaching" is apt, for Pal appears to see himself as a prophet of the future and, like the Biblical prophets, a denouncer of the injustices of his age. He recognizes that this is not the accepted role of a judge according to judicial ethics but feels that the dangers of the postwar era compel him to speak. The opportunity to publish a "dissenting opinion" provides the means to do so.

Continuing his diatribe against the tribunal and the international law it applies, Pal goes on to say that while he agrees with Professor Lauterpacht that international law should recognize individual responsibility to develop as "an instrument of peace and progress," this cannot be done through trials such as that at Nuremberg or Tokyo. He formulates as his position that, *"This certainly is to be done by a method very different from that of trial of war criminals from amongst the vanquished nations"*[58] (emphasis by Pal). The reason is that there still persists an international system that legitimizes the actions of "dominating foreign powers."[59]

In other words, Pal has rejected the legal foundation of the tribunal in which he is participating as well as the other Allied war crimes tribunals such as Nuremberg as a foundation for future international law. Indeed, he continues, "There is already a greater fear – namely, the power, the right of the victor."[60] For Pal it is thus the Allied victory that poses the true threat to the future. He argues that if there were a true international law, it is in fact the Allies who would be sitting in the defendant's dock and not the Japanese. Referring to his statement that if there really was individual responsibility for violations of international law, he concludes, "I refuse to believe that had that been the law, none of the victors in any way violated the same and that the world is so depraved that no one even thinks of bringing such persons to book for their acts."[61]

What are we to make of this? It is obvious and hardly needs stating that Pal has shed the robe of the judge to take up the pen of the outraged critic of not

[57] Ibid., 870.
[58] Ibid., 870–1.
[59] Ibid., 871.
[60] Ibid.
[61] Ibid.

only the tribunal, but of the entire international legal and political system under which it has been convened, and the Allied Powers who have acted to constitute it. He rejects the tribunal and dismisses the present possibility of what he calls the "dream" of an international society that can fairly sit in judgment. Instead, he points the finger of accusation at the victors, whom he believes threaten the future of the world.

His rejection of the legitimacy of the tribunal, and his contempt for the prevailing system of international relations that he believes it represents, raise the question of why Pal would consent to participate in such an institution that he regards as fundamentally illegal and unjust. The argument of his "judgment" provides the answer to that question, for it is only by sitting through this trial, that he obviously regarded as a sham from the beginning, that he will have the opportunity to write the "judgment" that the true international tribunal he invokes would have passed on the victors had there existed a just international system to create it. That true "judgment," as will be made even more explicit in the later sections of his opinion that we discuss later, will exonerate Japan and make manifest the guilt of the Allies.

Examples such as those given above could be multiplied, due to the length and repetitiveness of Pal's opinion. One further example of Pal's conception of his role as a judge as extending beyond the application of the law to the facts of the case deserves mention. Having concluded yet again that under current international law, "no category of war became criminal or illegal in international life,"[62] Pal reiterates the need for his inquiry to go *beyond the scope of the charges before the Tribunal*. Questions of law, he states, "are not decided in an intellectual quarantine area in which legal doctrine and the local history of the dispute are retained while all else is forcibly excluded. We cannot afford to be ignorant of the world in which disputes arise."[63] While one might object that it is precisely the nature of a fair trial to exclude political considerations from impinging on judgments of guilt or innocence, what issues does Pal maintain has been "forcibly excluded"?

Pal's takes the position that sufficient attention to the "antecedent behavior" of the parties to the conflict has been illegitimately removed from consideration. Pal's inquiry into what he sees as the broader antecedent historical and political context will become the driving force behind his ensuing 350-page treatment of Japan's alleged conspiracy. Those antecedents, Pal will argue, make clear which nations are really responsible for the war. In this section of his judgement that purports to deal with the issues of legal doctrine before the Tribunal he points the way to the themes that he will develop in these ensuing sections on conspiracy.

[62] Ibid., 903.
[63] Ibid., 904.

## 12.3 The Crime of Aggressive War

Pal immediately elaborates on one of the key extraneous factors of which judges "cannot afford to be ignorant."[64] He returns to his theme that "no one will seriously contend that domination of one nation by another became a crime in international life." While Pal appears here to overlook that the charges against the accused are not domination but rather the use of aggressive war to achieve domination, it is precisely Pal's point that it is hypocritical to condemn aggressive war while domination is in fact the accepted international norm.

Pal states that if one were to accept that domination is illegal, then "the entire international community would be a community of criminal races." Of course it is not the entire international community who is in a position of domination, so Pal qualifies his statement: "At least many of the powerful nations are living this sort of life."[65] It is not just that the "powerful nations" practice domination, but on Pal's view such domination was legitimized and protected by the international legal order that has also created the IMTFE. That is, in the name of preserving the peace by banning aggressive war, international law maintains the status quo of domination: "Certainly dominated nations of the present day status quo cannot be made to submit to eternal domination only in the name of peace." That status quo, he continues, "has been organized and hitherto maintained only by force, by pure opportunist 'Have and Holders'."[66]

This is the crux of Pal's complaint against international law that he will develop in its specific application to Japan in ensuing sections of his Opinion. Japan, he will argue, came late to the game of colonial acquisition. The Western dominating powers now want to hold what they have and after WWI they invented a new legal regime that would allow them to do so by banning other nations from using the very force by which the Western nations acquired their colonial dominions. Pal has acknowledged that this perspective is outside the scope of the tribunal's inquiry and it is for that very reason that he rejects the tribunal's legitimacy. Lest there be any doubt that this is his aim, his continuing discussion makes it clear that his real target is what he terms "the actual plague of imperialism."[67]

---

[64] Another such factor that Pal deals with at length is the "notorious fact that that world's nightmare was Communism" (Pal Opinion, 917). Pal returns to this theme again and again, taking it as a given and as a justification for Japan's invasion of China – in order to eliminate the threat communism poses. His treatment in this passage in no way resembles that of the judge but could well serve as part of a brief for the defense. Pal reveals himself again and again not as impartial but as a de facto defense advocate. After expounding at length on the communist threat (ibid., 917–19) Pal cites Nehru to point out that "there was no lack of violence in the capitalist world" (ibid., 918). The relevance of his remarks to the case at hand is far from apparent but fits into his general condemnation of the international system.

[65] Ibid., 904.
[66] Ibid., 910.
[67] Ibid.

The international legal order invoked by Robert Jackson at Nuremberg, Pal concludes, is a mere "ideological cloak" and a "device to perpetuate a casual status quo without providing any machinery for peaceful change."[68] The further step of this argument is not hard to imagine and will in fact become clear in Pal's later examination of the causes of WWII. Where the current international legal regime protects the status quo of domination and provides no means for "peaceful" alteration of that situation, resort to the violence of war is the only path open to nations such as Japan. Japanese conquest of China, Southeast Asia, and the Pacific is therefore justified because it was the only way to change the status quo and remove the overarching evil of Western imperialism.

## 12.4  The Conspiracy Charges

We have seen that Pal has repeatedly concluded that aggression is not a crime in international law, that individuals cannot be held responsible for aggressive war, and that there is in fact no valid international law on the use war as an instrument of domination. One might again think that this would mark the end of his consideration of the charges concerning aggressive war. It does not. As Pal himself concedes, "The view of the law I have taken makes it *somewhat unnecessary* for me to enter into the evidence in the case in respect of the counts other than these relation [sic] to war crimes strict sensu. But as I have heard the entire case and have formed my own opinion of the facts ... I would prefer briefly to indicate my conclusions in respect of them"[69] (emphasis added). Far from being "brief," this part of the opinion takes up fully 351 pages after which Pal then proceeds to the two sections devoted to conventional war crimes. It is far from clear why this section of the opinion was necessary or relevant, let alone what justified its bulk. What then is the purpose that motivates the exhaustive factual account Pal provides on the conspiracy charges that he has already deemed unfounded?

In taking up the issue of conspiracy Pal states that, "I have not considered whether or not any of the wars against any of the nations covered by the Indictment was aggressive. *The view that I take as to the criminality or otherwise of any war makes it unnecessary for me to enter into this question*"[70] (emphasis added). If, on Pal's view, there were and could be no wars of aggression then how could there be a conspiracy to plan, initiate, or wage such wars? In other words, because the convictions from which Pal is dissenting are convictions for conspiring to wage, plan, or initiate aggressive war, it follows ipso facto from his conclusion that there are no such conspiracies as charged in the indictment. In other words, it contradicts Pal's own position to consider the charges of conspiracy to wage aggressive war and then make specific findings on each charge. Pal nonetheless devotes these 351 pages to a non-existent

---

[68] Ibid., 911.
[69] Ibid., 932.
[70] Ibid., 1422.

## 12.4 The Conspiracy Charges

crime because it serves his greater purpose to do so. It is the conspiracy charge which provides the main vehicle for the historical narrative of the events of 1931–45 with which he aims to redress unjust accusations against Japan and point to the parties who are actually responsible.

To uncover this alternative historical and political narrative which serves Pal's ultimate goal in writing his own "judgment" we must examine his account of the conspiracy charges. We may begin by recalling the provisions of Article 5(a) of the Charter that defines "Crimes against Peace" as the "planning, preparation, initiation, or waging of a declared or undeclared war of aggression ... *or participation in a common plan or conspiracy for the accomplishment of any of the foregoing*" (emphasis added). As the Charter indicates, an accused person may be held accountable for planning, initiating, or waging a war of aggression OR for conspiracy to do the same. In other words, liability may be predicated either upon one's individual conduct or upon one's participation in a group that conspired to the commit the prohibited acts.

While Pal spends 351 pages – or 58 percent – of his entire opinion, on the issue of conspiracy he entirely omits consideration of the substantive crimes provided for in the first part of Article 5(a) and covered in Counts 6–36 of the indictment. That is, he fails to address whether any of the accused were guilty of having participated in the actual planning, initiating, or waging of aggressive war. Given that he concluded that conspiracy was not a crime recognized in international law, he should have then passed immediately to these substantive offenses defined in Article 5. It is clear that in a sense there was no need to do so because he had already held aggression not to be a crime. But if this is the reason for omitting consideration of the substantive offenses related to waging aggressive war, then it should have applied to the conspiracy to wage aggressive war as well.

Pal's exhaustive treatment of the conspiracy is even longer than that of the majority, whose very different account of the same persons and events he never mentions or rebuts. The thrust of Pal's treatment of the conspiracy charge is that the Japanese leaders had independent and justifiable motivations for taking the actions that led them to resort to war. This, Pal contends, undermines the prosecution's case because there is a reasonable doubt as to whether the actions of the accused were in fact guided by an overarching conspiracy.

Pal's critique of the prosecution theory of an overarching conspiracy embracing all of the accused and extending for some seventeen years is in principle well-founded, as Webb pointed out as well in his draft judgment. Pal also need not have looked far afield for such criticism because the similar conspiracy provisions of the Nuremberg Charter were in fact rejected by the IMT in its judgment, as discussed in Chapter 7.

As discussed in our treatment of the majority judgment above, it is unfortunate that the prosecution team at Tokyo followed the same erroneous path as their counterparts at Nuremberg and focused on a single all-embracing conspiracy.

The IMT convicted individuals for their individual conduct in participating in the policy planning and decision-making that led to war as well as their participation in policy circles that shaped the way the war was waged. By rejecting the notion of a single conspiracy and focusing instead on the individual roles of the accused in planning Germany's invasions of its neighbors, the IMT was able to show how the individual conduct of the accused fit into the larger collective activity of the German policy circles that set in motion the events that led to aggression. The IMT judgment invokes the words of a member of the German Foreign Office that could as well have described the course followed by Japan without employing the notion of conspiracy theory:

> The general objectives of the Nazi leadership were apparent from the start, namely the domination of the European Continent to be achieved first by the incorporation of all German speaking groups in the Reich, and secondly, by territorial expansion under the slogan "Lebensraum." The execution of these basic objectives, however, seemed to be characterised by improvisation. Each succeeding step was apparently carried out as each new situation arose, but all consistent with the ultimate objectives mentioned above.[71]

The Nuremberg judgment disposed of the theory of an overarching conspiracy in approximately two pages while Pal unnecessarily devoted 351 pages to this subject. On the other hand, the Nuremberg judgment focused instead on the role of the accused in planning and waging of aggressive war. Pal, however, fully ignores this main part of Article 5(a) of the Charter for a reason. While it was not difficult to show that the prosecution had not proved beyond reasonable doubt that there was no single master conspiracy to wage aggressive war, it would have been a different matter for Pal to demonstrate that not one of the accused was ever engaged in the planning, initiating, or waging of aggressive war. Indeed, the evidence, as Webb makes clear, was overwhelming that many of them did so. In Pal's treatment of the conspiracy he often implies that they were not so involved, yet reiterates over and over again that he is merely demonstrating that other motivations can explain their actions rather than the theory of conspiracy. As he concludes,

> I would again emphasize here that it is immaterial for our present purpose to see whether any policy adopted at any particular time, or any action taken by Japan pursuant to that policy was justifiable in law; *perhaps it was not*. All that we are concerned with here is to see if the circumstances can explain the adoption of the policy or action without the existence of the alleged conspiracy. The statesmen diplomats and politicians of Japan were perhaps wrong, and perhaps they misled themselves. But they were not conspirators. They did not conspire.[72] (emphasis added)

---

[71] Ibid. Note also Pal's apparent approval of Japan's version of the need for Lebensraum: "The never-ceasing problem of Japan rendered it inevitable, at least to the then statesmen of Japan, that the Japanese Government and people must set themselves to provide for Japan's rankly growing population" (Pal Opinion, 1163 and see also 1299).
[72] Pal Opinion, 1299.

## 12.4 The Conspiracy Charges

After 340 pages of discussing the allegation of conspiracy Pal concludes, "I have given above my reading of the evidence relating to the charge of conspiracy. *I am, however, of opinion that conspiracy by itself is not a crime at all in international life*"[73] (emphasis added). It is bizarre that only at this point, at the *end* of his voluminous treatment of conspiracy, rather than at the beginning, that he states his position that conspiracy is not an international crime.[74] Only then does he discuss the elements required to prove "the requirements of the offense."[75] Why, however, enumerate the requirements of an offense that he has determined not to exist in international law? Indeed, the whole exercise would seem superfluous in that Pal's treatment of conspiracy rejects the general notion of international law providing for any criminal liability at all: "Keeping all this in view it may be safely asserted that the nations have not yet considered the rule of international life ripe enough for the transposition of principles of criminality into rules of law in international life."[76] This conclusion would also seem to apply to the well-established body of law on war crimes.

One can only wonder why Pal didn't start out by stating his position that conspiracy is not an independent offense and then explain why he was nonetheless devoting more than half of his opinion to this topic. Setting out the requirements of proof should, of course, have been done at the beginning of the conspiracy section so as to provide the appropriate framework for his conclusions that the requirements of proof had not been met. Apart from sheer disorganization, the only reason one can imagine is that Pal wanted to create a 350-page narrative that would provide an alternative historical and political account of the events of 1931–45; an account that would justify Japan's conduct and war aims. Consideration of the conspiracy provided the vehicle for doing so. Pal appears to tacitly acknowledge this interpretation when he tries to justify why his discussion has roamed so far afield from the legal issues he was called upon to decide:

To appreciate what happened, it is only just to see the events by putting them in their proper perspective. We should not avoid examining the whole of the circumstances, political and economic, that led up to these events. This is why I refer to matters like the *Britanocentric economic world order,* the diplomatic maneuvers of Washington, the *development of communism* and the world opinion of the Soviet policy, the *internal condition of China,* the China policy and practice of other nations and the *internal condition of Japan* from time to time.[77] (emphasis added)

---

[73] Ibid., 1303.
[74] Webb takes the same position on "naked conspiracy" but Pal refrains from discussing any of the other opinions.
[75] Pal Opinion, 1304.
[76] Ibid., 1309. If Pal were consistent this would also mean that there could be no criminal liability for war crimes. That he recognizes that international law does provide for criminal liability for war crimes calls into question the sweeping statement he makes here and points to the internal contradictions in his exposition.
[77] Pal Opinion, 1299.

It scarcely requires elaboration that factors such as the "world opinion of Soviet policy," Britain's international *economic* importance, or China's or Japan's internal political difficulties fall outside of the legal issues legitimately before the tribunal. This, however, is precisely Pal's reason for rejecting tribunals like Nuremberg and Tokyo *in toto*. Pal's premise is that international law is a sham and politics and power are everything, hence neither Germany nor Japan should be held to account.

The concluding pages of Pal's opinion clearly reflect this larger aim that transcends the trial itself and the fate of the accused. Here, in the final three pages, he ultimately reveals clearly the thinking and purpose that has guided the judgment since the beginning. He rejects the tribunal as an institution, stating that, "the setting up of the tribunal was only for the attainment of an objective which was essentially political though cloaked by a juridical appearance."[78]

Building upon his premise that the tribunal itself is merely a political tool of the Allies, he indicates that consideration of the real "political issues" would have produced proceedings which "would have assumed a different appearance altogether, and the scope of our inquiry would have been much wider than what we allowed it to assume."[79] This fits in, of course, with his previous remarks as to the issues that were "forcibly excluded" and must be considered for justice to be done.

From this broader perspective, he continues, the conduct of the accused "would have simply furnished some evidentiary facts."[80] What then would have been the object of this imaginary trial of broader political scope in which what Pal considers the real issues would have been brought before the court? Pal's answer is stunning in its simplicity: "The real ultimate probandum would have been the future threat to the 'public order and safety' of the world."[81] What, in Pal's view, constitutes the threat to the safety of the world that should have been put on trial at Tokyo?

The source of this threat is the theme on which he expounds in the final paragraphs of his Opinion, rejecting the "vindictive retaliation" of the tribunal which will contribute to "pointing to false causes as the fountains of all ills."[82] The "world's attention," he claims, "has not yet been directed in the right direction."[83] The real cause of the world's ills, and the genuine threat to world peace, he argues, was not posed by those on trial at Tokyo, whom he has found to be wholly innocent of all wrongdoing. Instead he points to the atom bomb and states that, "The trials should not be allowed to use up the precious little

---

[78] Ibid., 1424.
[79] Ibid., 1424–5.
[80] Ibid., 1425.
[81] Ibid.
[82] Ibid.
[83] Ibid.

## 12.4 The Conspiracy Charges

thought that a peace-bound public may feel inclined to spare in order to find the way to 'conquer the doubts and fears, the ignorance and greed, which made this horror possible.'"[84] He concludes by stating that it was not the "defeated leaders" who alone bear responsibility for the war. He ends his "judgment" by clearly implying that history will judge that the real responsibility lay with the Allied Powers whom his narrative of the conspiracy has attempted to show were responsible both for pushing a peace-loving Japanese government to a war they wished to avoid and then using the atom bomb to end it. This is the lesson Pal wishes the world to draw from his treatise on the history and politics of 1928–45.

Without passing judgment on the merits of his historical account one can nevertheless conclude that it was not only extraneous to his role as judge but also again reveals his true aim in creating this massive text which he appears to have considered his opus magnum on the state of the world. It is for this reason that he ends his opinion not with reasoned verdicts in regard to the individual accused, but with a sweeping vision of a postwar world order that requires new ways of thinking, ways of thinking that Pal has charted out as a prophet for the future. What is implicit in these final pages is that Pal believes that since the tribunal did not take up the global political questions it should have, it is he who must fulfill that function. This, of course, would no longer have been a judicial proceeding. Pal's "trial" would have considered not only the Western political and economic domination that in his view ultimately produced the war but also the threat to the future of the world that the Allied victory represents. For Pal, a Japanese victory in the war, despite its human cost, would have overturned the oppressive colonial and imperialist order that in his view had enslaved much of the world. The defeat of Japan has instead solidified the Western domination that has now, moreover, been strengthened through the use of the atom bomb. The trial, in his view, was merely a political act designed to legitimate the legal order that enshrines that domination "cloaked by a judicial appearance."[85]

As a Bengali nationalist, Pal presumably felt this oppression quite directly and his bitterness at the outcome of the war and the "triumph" of the Western Power can be felt on almost every page of his opinion. Pal's self-proclaimed judgment aimed to express that sense of oppression and frustration at the defeat of Japan. Impotent to change the course of the actual trial, he created his own alternative trial, a trial at which he alone would pass judgment on the accused and would produce the definitive account of the world order that would not only address the injustices of the past but also provide the way forward so that the world could "win the race between civilization and disaster."[86]

---

[84] Ibid., 1426.
[85] Ibid., 1424.
[86] Ibid., 1425.

This interpretation of Pal's opinion also answers the pressing question of why he chose to participate *as a judge* in a tribunal whose legitimacy he totally rejected, whose aims he considered dangerous and political, and whose scope was limited to exclude consideration of the true causes of war and the real guilty parties.[87] By participating, Pal acquired the pulpit to promulgate his treatise on the world political and legal order that he hoped would free the minds of the "peace-bound public" from the "delusion" created by the nefarious forces that were "whispering into the popular ear the means of revenge while giving it the outward shape of the only solution demanded by the nature of the evils."[88] It is ironic that in espousing the cause of peace Pal justifies war as the only means for ending a political order he viewed as unacceptable. Our conclusion that in setting out on this path Pal violated his most basic duties as a judge in favor of the role of self-anointed political prophet would quite possibly not have disturbed him in the least. Pal had likely made his peace with that accusation when before the trial began he informed Roeling that he would dissent.

[87] Ibid., 1424–6.
[88] Ibid., 1425.

# 13 Pal's Treatment of War Crimes Charges

## 13.1 Introduction

While Pal's political and ideological beliefs explain why he concludes that no Japanese military or political leader could be held accountable for crimes against peace, with what means does he justify holding all of the accused not guilty in regard to war crimes? After all, the aim of overturning Western domination does not necessitate committing massive crimes against civilian populations that Japan was "liberating" from the colonial yoke. The consideration of Pal's treatment of war crimes charges thus can serve as a counterpoint to the bulk of his opinion that deals with the political dynamics of the international order. To what extent are his conclusions on conventional war crimes charges based upon a lack of impartiality and issues irrelevant to consideration of guilt or innocence?[1]

Before considering in detail the two main sections of Pal's treatment of Counts 54 and 55 of the indictment charging the accused with war crimes, a preliminary comment as to some themes that inform his discussion in both sections is appropriate. At many points throughout the ninety-seven pages dealing with war crimes, Pal states or implies that the military in the field were the real perpetrators, operating far away from the government in Tokyo. Unlike his strategy on aggressive war he does not deny that war crimes were perpetrated. Instead, he repeatedly avers that because national war crimes tribunals had already convicted the immediate perpetrators of Japanese war crimes, justice had already been served: "It should be remembered that in the majority of cases 'stern justice' has already been meted out by the several victor nations to the persons charged with having perpetrated these atrocious acts along with their immediate superiors."[2] Therefore, Pal argues, it follows that there is no need to charge Japanese leaders with these crimes.

---

[1] For a consideration of the role of ideology and, specifically, Indian anti-colonial sentiment on Pal's treatment of war crimes charges for the Nanjing Massacre, see Brook, "The Tokyo Judgment and the Rape of Nanking."
[2] Pal Opinion, 1344. Pal repeats this numerous times.

In a concluding passage of the war crimes section of his draft judgment discussed in Chapter 10, Webb appears to respond to what he regards as the erroneous views of both the majority judgment and the dissenting opinion of Pal. He states that, "Of course, the accused are not excused because the Army and police were the actual perpetrators."[3] This sentence appears to directly respond to the repeated assertions by Pal that those responsible for atrocities had already been punished by national tribunals, that this was sufficient retribution, and that there was hence no need to punish the accused at Tokyo who in any event, on Pal's view, had no connection whatsoever to those crimes.[4] Webb's point, in contrast, is that, "Even the civilians among the accused, like TOGO and HIROTA, were in a position to protest or to appeal to the Emperor, and, if necessary, to bring about a crisis in the Japanese government in order to prevent atrocities." This, he goes on to say, is the burden of holding high office: great responsibilities, in his view, bring with them great duties, and the failure to carry out those duties is the ultimate basis for leaders' liability when they know or have reason to know that crimes are being committed and they do not do all within their power to prevent them.[5]

This conclusion by Webb is, of course, also the position adopted by the IMT at Nuremberg as well as in subsequent proceedings cases, such as the High Command Case, the Hostage Case, and the Ministries Case, which are the leading WWII-era cases on the responsibility of high-level military and civilian leaders. It is striking that Pal, as we will see, clearly misrepresents the treatment of war crimes charges at Nuremberg. He also studiously avoids crucial issues of international law such as the special obligations of occupying powers in regard to the civilian population of occupied territories, a topic treated at length by the IMT and Nuremberg subsequent proceedings.

The position taken by Pal is revealing in that it indicates the lengths to which he was prepared to go to find excuses for not convicting those whose policies, decisions, and culpable inaction authorized, encouraged, and turned a blind eye to crimes committed by the Imperial Japanese Army, the Kenpeitai, and the Imperial Japanese Navy. What Pal does is to invert the logic of responsibility. The basic principle of responsibility in military organizations, as well as governmental hierarchies, is that responsibility is directed upwards. In other words, the greater the position of authority the greater the responsibility that high rank brings with it. In the words of the High Command Case, the Generals of the Oberkommando der Wehrmacht (High Command of the Army)

---

[3] TPJ 262.

[4] See, for instance, Pal Opinion, 1381 to cite just one such example of many from his opinion.

[5] TPJ 262. Webb's language in regard to the mental element is very similar to modern doctrine. He indicates – for example on p. 267 – that those in high positions "knew or must have known" and adds that if they did not have actual knowledge of the specific findings and evidence they were "at least put in inquiry" sufficiently that knowledge may be imputed to them.

13.1 Introduction 461

did not "hold their high ranks and positions and did not bask in the bright sunlight of official favor of the Third and Thousand Year Reich" without having commensurate responsibility for the policies and actions that shaped German conduct of the war.[6] As the Ministries Case also held, even below the cabinet level, high-level ministerial officials may also be held accountable when they know of war crimes being systematically committed and continue to remain in their office.[7]

That accountability applies to those who operate at the top levels of governmental, military, and corporate hierarchies is a basic principle of bureaucratic organization. Pal, on the other hand, suggests that if those at the lowest levels of the hierarchy have been punished for criminal conduct in which they engaged, then justice has been sufficiently done and the demands for accountability have been satisfied. In his view, those who developed policies and commanded or oversaw the institutions in which the subordinates operated are relieved of responsibility because those beneath them have been called to account. In his view, only if there is direct perpetration of the crimes can they be held accountable.

The glaring illogic of this argument is twofold: (1) It acknowledges that criminal conduct took place on a widespread scale across the Japanese Empire and was legitimately prosecuted and punished. This of course validates the very legal framework of accountability for war crimes that Pal wants to reject. (2) It relies on the assumption that criminal responsibility is limited by the prosecution of those most directly responsible for a crime and that others, who had authority over those convicted, are per se immune from prosecution for those same acts. No criminal law system in the world operates according to such a principle. The burden is, of course, on the prosecution to prove the connection of each individual accused to the specific crimes with which they are charged. If the prosecution fails to meet this burden then guilt has not been established. There is, however, nowhere in international jurisprudence an accepted principle that provides blanket exculpation for other perpetrators because some (and particularly those in lower positions of authority) have been called to account.

The argument discussed immediately above also indicates another general feature of Pal's dissenting opinion. He too often appears to ignore the basic fact that a criminal trial is about individual guilt, not national guilt or innocence. As Roeling clearly recognized in his dissenting opinion, the ultimate responsibility of a judge in criminal proceedings is to render judgment on the culpability of each accused person on each of the acts with which they are charged. Pal's obvious desire to exculpate *Japan as a nation and the Japanese government or state as a collectivity* overshadows the fact that the IMTFE is

---

[6] High Command Case, 515.
[7] See, e.g. Ministries Case, 494–8.

a trial of individual accused persons for each of whom the prosecution has to prove guilt beyond a reasonable doubt and *for each of whom* the judges have the responsibility to provide a reasoned account for their conclusions of guilt or of innocence. Pal, as will be seen, instead finds that "each and every one" of the accused is innocent of all charges, treating them as a collectivity and not making individual findings justifying his dissent as to their innocence.

Pal's treatment of the charges of war crimes against the accused also indicates that he seems to confuse the role of judge with that of defense counsel for the accused. His treatment of war crimes in the two sections that will now be discussed would have fit much better in a brief for the defense than in a reasoned final decision that carefully weighs the evidence and in a balanced manner considers the allegations of the defense and prosecution.

## 13.2 War Crimes against Civilian Populations

Pal's disposition as advocate rather than judge is indicated by the way in which he deals with the international law framework governing war crimes, the conduct of war, and the treatment of POW. His argument, as will be seen, is replete with contradictions, inconsistencies, and omissions. Despite the praise that has been heaped upon him in some circles as a jurist, it is also apparent that both his understanding of the sources of international law, the case law, and of legal doctrine were quite incomplete (or that he chose to disregard what he knew when convenient).

For example, at the beginning of his discussion of war crimes in relation to civilian populations in occupied territories he attempts to distinguish Nuremberg as a precedent for holding the accused at Tokyo accountable for failure to prevent war crimes when they had a duty to do so. He states, "The Tribunal at Nuremberg, therefore, had no occasion to consider any charge like the one contained in Count 55 of the Indictment before us. Those of the defendants, who were found guilty of war crimes, were found guilty of having themselves participated in the atrocious doings."[8] This conclusion is part of Pal's strategy to discredit Count 55 and, as indicated above, to limit liability to direct perpetrators.

Pal's statement about the Nuremberg judgment is, however, incorrect, as a simple reading of the individual verdicts would have indicated. It is not clear whether he did not read or understand the judgment or whether he was deliberately misrepresenting it. In any event, the Nuremberg judgment provides examples of just the kind of liability for which the accused at Tokyo were charged under Count 55. For example, Wilhelm Frick, Minister of the Interior, "had knowledge that insane, sick and aged people, 'useless eaters,' were being

---

[8] Pal Opinion, 1335.

13.2 War Crimes against Civilian Populations 463

systematically put to death. Complaints of these murders reached him, but he did nothing to stop them."[9] He was convicted on these charges of war crimes. Likewise, Walter Funk, President of the Reichsbank and Minister of Economics argued that he did not know that the Reichsbank was a depository for the SS of valuables taken from the victims of concentration camps. The tribunal rejected this plea: "The Tribunal is of the opinion that Funk either knew what was being received or was deliberately closing his eyes to what was being done." Funk was found guilty of these charges and was also found guilty in regard to the use of slave labor because although he did not directly participate, he "was aware that the board of which he was a member was demanding the importation of slave labourers."[10] As a final example, Albert Speer was convicted for the use of slave labor in organizing armaments industries despite the fact that, "Speer's position was such that he was not directly concerned with the cruelty in the administration of the slave labour programme, although he was aware of its existence."[11]

To take another example, although Pal entitles this section of his Opinion "War Crimes Stricto Sensu in relation to the Civil population of the Territories Occupied by Japan," he neglects to state the legal standards that apply to commanders and occupying authorities of occupied territories. Under the 1907 Hague Convention No. 4, to which Japan was a signatory, special duties and rules apply in the case of occupying powers and commanders of occupied territory. Whereas at the beginning of the ensuing section on crimes committed against POW Pal argues as to why the Hague Convention is not applicable at the IMTFE, for reasons not apparent he does not mention the Convention in this section. This would appear to be a serious omission because on the one hand the 1907 Hague Convention No. 4 lays down the rules regarding civilian populations in general and the particular rules that apply in the case of occupied territory.[12] Those provisions and other applicable international law norms were applied in the Nuremberg subsequent proceedings in the High Command and Hostage Cases. Pal nowhere in this section defines the applicable legal standards and apparently simply accepts the general description of war crimes in Count 54 of the indictment. The inconsistency as to why he sets out an argument against the applicability of the Hague Conventions in the next section but not here remains unclear.

---

[9] Nuremberg verdict on Frick, IMT judgment, 301.
[10] Nuremberg verdict on Funk, ibid., 306.
[11] Nuremberg verdict on Speer, ibid., 332. As noted earlier, the Ministries and High Command Cases also held individuals accountable for failure to take action to prevent crimes when they acquired knowledge of their commission. See, for instance, Ministries Case on Ernst Von Weiszaecker, 696–8.
[12] See, for instance, the detailed treatment of the duties of occupying powers and commanders of occupied territories in NMT High Command Case, 542–8, and the careful way it is applied in regard to each of the accused who exercised such authority.

Pal's exposition acquitting all the accused of war crimes is surprisingly abbreviated. Given that he has devoted the preceding 524 pages of the judgment" to issues of the international law on crimes against peace, conspiracy, and so on, the thirty pages he devotes to his massive list of alleged war crimes seems short in comparison. Indeed, he takes up almost four pages just by enumerating the categories of war crimes with which the accused are charged. This switch from overly lengthy exhaustive elaboration to almost cursorily abbreviated treatment is surprising given that unlike in regard to crimes against peace there is no question as to the validity of the legal category of war crimes against civilians. As noted earlier, Pal offers no objection to the classification of categories of Japanese mistreatment of civilians as war crimes.

Before launching into his rather sketchy and incomplete consideration of the crimes themselves, Pal prefaces his treatment of the war crimes charges with a four-page discussion of how what he terms "propaganda" produces inaccurate testimony of criminal conduct. He gives two pages of what he alleges are examples of "exaggerated" accounts of rape at Nanjing, suggesting his "suspicion" that they did not occur.[13] Although "suspicion" is hardly a judicial standard for assessing evidence, Pal goes on to propose as a remedy to such inaccuracies the necessity "to weigh the evidence carefully."[14] As we will see, however, this is precisely what he fails to do in his abbreviated treatment that omits mention of the vast bulk of evidence on war crimes that was before the tribunal.

Somewhat confusingly, having spent four pages explaining how propaganda distorts accurate testimony and using rape at Nanjing as an example, he nonetheless states, "Keeping in view everything that can be said against the evidence adduced in this case in this respect, and making every possible allowance for propaganda and exaggeration, *the evidence is still overwhelming that atrocities were perpetrated* by the members of the Japanese armed forces against the civilian population of some of the territories occupied by the[m] as also against the prisoners of war"[15] (emphasis added).

---

[13] Pal Opinion, 1341–4. For example, Pal suggests that when Chinese victims and witnesses testify that someone was raped by a Japanese soldier they might be referring to what was actually consensual sex (ibid., 1343). In regard to such events he states that, "It seems these witnesses accepted every story told to them and viewed every case as a case of rape ... I am not sure if we are not getting accounts of events witnessed only by excited or prejudiced observers" (ibid., 1343). One of the examples he gives is indicative of his attitude where he says that it is implausible that two Japanese soldiers could have raped young girls in front of their families, suggesting that the family would have prevented the two soldiers from doing so. The fact that the soldiers were armed and the family was not does not seem to impinge on Pal's imagination, nor does the rampant rape, murder, and mayhem then underway in Nanjing (Ibid., 1343).

[14] Pal Opinion, 1343.

[15] Ibid., 1343–4.

Pal then provides a list of the various locations and incidents where war crimes were alleged to have occurred. The enumeration takes up ten pages even though it only extends to October 1944. Without any explanation he stops at that date, stating only that, "I need not give in detail the incidents taking place since November 1944. We are given several incidents taking place during this period and *certainly there were atrocious misdeeds*"[16] (emphasis added). Since these "incidents" were charged against the accused one would think that a "careful weighing of the evidence" would require taking them up, but Pal, without providing any reason, does not even list them, giving no reason why he has decided not to consider war crimes committed in the last year of the war. On this too, he is inconsistent because despite this statement he later does take up crimes committed in the Philippines in 1945.

### 13.2.1 War crimes in the Pacific Theater

Most tellingly, in the mere ten pages where he purports to both list locations and events and consider the evidence, he does not, as he has said is required, "weigh the evidence carefully." A few examples will suffice. For example, in regard to his category of war crimes in "Singapore and Malaya" his only statement is, in its entirety, "We are given six instances in the first period, none during the second and third, four cases in the fourth period and one during the fifth, sixth, and seventh period."[17] As this is his entire statement there is not even the kind of brief description of the nature of the war crimes that he provides for many of the other geographical areas.

This glaring omission requires explanation and the reason is actually quite obvious and revealing. Singapore was the headquarters for the British Southeast Asian war crimes investigations and they conducted 131 trials there.[18] The British attached priority to war crimes committed in Singapore and were able to assemble extensive documentation that was presented at the trials and available to the British prosecution team at Tokyo, who made good use of it. Singapore was thus the site of two of the most well-known trials involving large scale and systematic atrocities. Apart from the careful documentation in the "Double Tenth Trial" (March–April 1946) of systematic torture employed by the Kenpeitai against POW and Singaporean civilians,[19] there was also a trial for one of the worst and best known Japanese massacres of civilians in WWII. In February and March 1942, soon after the beginning of the occupation, the

---

[16] Ibid., 1354.
[17] Ibid., 1351.
[18] For an overview of the British war crimes trials in the Pacific region, see Hayashi, *Sabakareta sensō hanzai*.
[19] For the record of the Double Tenth Trial, see Sleeman and Silkin, eds., *Trial of Sumida Haruzo and Twenty Others (The "Double Tenth" Trial)*.

Japanese forces rounded up thousands of Singaporean Chinese considered to be potentially anti-Japanese. They were screened by the Kenpeitai and at least 5,000 were killed in mass executions with machine guns on Changi Beach and other locations. The trial for this massacre was not conclusive in identifying how orders had passed down the chain of command as key figures were either dead or had escaped.[20] But there was little doubt left as to the nature and extent of the massacre itself. These were the sorts of events whose documentation and systematic nature were established by the war crimes investigations and that not even Pal's ingenuity could explain away. So he simply chose to omit all reference to them, and to the other evidence of war crimes committed at Singapore, thereby contradicting his own requirement of a careful weighing of the evidence and revealing the biases, deeply flawed methodology, and lack of impartiality in his exposition.[21]

The example of Singapore is by no means exceptional, but rather representative of his attempt to underplay, mischaracterize, and ignore the scale and nature of Japanese war crimes that had been documented in many hundreds of Allied war crimes trials, trials in which the accused very often admitted that the crimes had occurred but argued that they had acted under superior orders.[22] Needless to say, Pal also ignores the implications of these admissions and the import of the claim of superior orders shifting of responsibility to higher command levels. If he had fully examined the evidence it would have demonstrated the implausibility of his complete rejection of the prosecution case on war crimes, which not only the majority and Webb had found to be valid but also the other two dissenting opinions by Roeling and Bernard. His conclusion that *not one* of these thousands of criminal acts covered by his description could in any way whatsoever be connected to the army or navy high command is not only implausible but is also contradicted by evidence before the tribunal, particularly in regard to crimes such as the Nanjing Massacre or mistreatment of POW where foreign protests to the Japanese government were numerous.

In regard to Pal's category of war crimes in "Burma and Siam," he states that the prosecution charged fourteen incidents from December 1941 to

---

[20] See Totani, *Justice in Asia and the Pacific Region, 1945–1952*, 132–3, 144–55. For the prosecution's evidence relating to the Double Tenth Case, see PX1519–1521 (affidavits taken from victims and witnesses of atrocity), T12934–45. For evidence relating to the Singapore Massacre, see PX476 (an investigative report produced by the Japanese government in November 1945), introduced at T5624; Testimony by Cyril H.D. Wild, T5365–72, 5627–81, 5717–9; and PX1498–1500 (affidavits taken from victims and witnesses), T12894–7.

[21] For an account of this event and the documentation and scholarship on the Singapore Massacre, see Hayashi, "The Battle of Singapore, the Massacre of Chinese and Understanding of the Issue in Postwar Japan"; and Hayashi, *Shingapōru kakyō shukusei*.

[22] Pal Opinion, 1351. See, for instance, Pal's one sentence characterization of Japanese war crimes in Java: "12. JAVA Fourteen instances are named occurring during the entire period from March 12, 1942 and ending in August 1945." This is his total account of these events.

13.2 War Crimes against Civilian Populations    467

August 1944. He dismisses all of these charges in one sentence: "At worst these are all stray instances of cruelty towards individuals over a period of 5 years." He adduces not one piece of evidence to support this conclusion. In regard to one of the most serious incidents alleged in the Andaman and Nicobar Islands, he refers to the testimony of a survivor that in August 1945 about 700 Indians were forcibly removed and taken out to sea where they were pushed overboard 400 yards from shore. All but 203 drowned. The remainder who made it to shore were "left in the island without food for 50 days when the Japanese returned."[23] Pal gives no reason for discounting the reality of this event except stating that only the testimony of the sole survivor was offered to support it. This notorious incident was the subject of British trials and members of the Japanese garrison also testified at the trial of Vice Admiral Hara Teizō at Singapore (April–May 1946), admitting what had happened but alleging that their actions were due to a "food crisis." Pal engages in no analysis and reaches no conclusion concerning this event, merely implying that the testimony of the survivor is insufficient. This also hardly amounts to a careful weighing of the evidence.[24]

In regard to Borneo he recounts several incidents of significant scale and duration in just a few lines. He treats the case made by the Dutch prosecution team as to systematic forced prostitution as follows: "The third one [incident] says that from early 1943 onwards throughout Western Borneo, Indian and Chinese women were arrested and forced into brothels."[25] This one sentence is his entire treatment of a whole case for forced prostitution presented by the prosecution covering numerous victims and areas over a two-year period of time. These examples are representative of the treatment in the 10-page list and could be multiplied at length.

The conclusion Pal draws from this ten-page enumeration of incidents is that, "These are the instances of atrocities perpetrated by the Japanese Army against the civilians at different theaters during the entire period of the war. The *devilish*

---

[23] Pal Opinion, 1348. For the evidence concerning the mass drowning of Andaman Islanders, see PX1614, Declaration by Mohamed Hussain, T14189.

[24] The record of the trial of Hara Teizō et al. is deposited at the National Archives, Kew, Richmond, Surrey, UK. Defendant Hara Teizo, Place of Trial Singapore, WO235/839.

[25] Pal Opinion, 1348. The evidence being referred to is PX1702, "Report on Enforced Prostitution Western Borneo, N.E.I. during Japanese Naval Occupation," prepared by Captain J. F. Heybroek, Royal Netherlands Indies Army, introduced at T13527. This evidence, which was admitted but not read in court, offers a detailed account of the Japanese naval garrison's operation of military brothels at Pontianak. Pal's sweeping treatment notwithstanding, this particular evidentiary material could have been treated as incriminatory for the accused at the Tokyo Trial, as it brought out a highly organized, large-scale operation of military brothels at Pontianak (or the "comfort stations [*ianjo*]" as the word is translated in the Japanese version of the same court exhibit) for an extended period of time. The report also reveals that the navy authorities deployed the naval special police force, *tokkeitai*, so that threats and the use of force could be applied to compel the local women into sexual servitude.

*and fiendish character* of the alleged atrocities cannot be denied"[26] (emphasis added). Pal apparently believes that his extremely brief comments have served as an examination of the evidence, for he follows immediately by saying, "I have indicated against each item the nature of the evidence adduced in support of the occurrence. However unsatisfactory this evidence may be, *it cannot be denied that many of these fiendish things* were perpetrated"[27] (emphasis added). As we have seen, however, he has not "indicated against each item the nature of the evidence," let alone weighed it carefully.

Further, as an examination of the trial record and exhibits would reveal, he has not listed nearly all of the relevant evidence before the court, and moreover he has not analyzed or weighed any of it. His conclusion that "many" of these events occurred is, from a juristic standpoint, entirely unsatisfactory. Which events does he find to have been proved beyond a reasonable doubt? It is his obligation to make this finding. Which does he consider not to have been proved and why? This is what a careful weighing of the evidence would require. In regard to the crimes that he finds to have been proven, what were the circumstances, who was responsible, and what was communicated to higher levels of command? Were there reports or other communications that would have put commanders on notice that crimes were, might be, or had been occurring?

These are absolutely essential findings that Pal needed to make under his own standard and especially if he was going to acquit the accused of responsibility for these crimes. Yet he provides no such findings. These are precisely the kinds of analyses that the High Command Case, the Hostage Case, and the Ministries Case conduct in exhaustive detail in order to determine whether higher levels of command or civilian authority may be held accountable for the crimes of subordinates. What Pal repeatedly does instead is simply to allege that the persons responsible have already been tried and that there is no connection of the accused to these events.[28] In one short paragraph of six lines he correctly states that "the prosecution has built its case on inferences from the alleged knowledge and inaction of the accused." He rejects this proposition without discussion, having nowhere explained what inferences the evidence supports or does not support about the knowledge of Japanese officials.

What is striking, and representative, of Pal's manner of proceeding here is that he creates the pretense of objective analysis by the ten-page enumeration of war crimes allegations that he says require careful weighing. That careful weighing, as we have seen, never occurs and there are in fact no specific findings at all on the enumerated war crimes. His conclusion is in fact the antithesis of proper juristic analysis of the kind that he himself has said is appropriate.

---

[26] Pal Opinion, 1354.
[27] Ibid.
[28] Ibid., 1354–5.

## 13.2 War Crimes against Civilian Populations 469

What Pal ultimately finds on the war crimes charges is instead a brief one-page conclusion consisting of two parts, neither of which addresses the requirements of making specific legal findings and applying them to specific accused. The first prong of the conclusion has been adumbrated above: Pal maintains that justice has already been meted out to those responsible for the "devilish and fiendish atrocities" and that none of the accused before the court has any connection to any of these events as alleged in Count 54 of the indictment.

Pal misleadingly states that there is no evidence of an *order* from any of the defendants to commit the enumerated crimes, but Count 54 charges the accused with having "ordered, authorised or *permitted*" military personnel to commit war crimes. His finding that there is no direct order to commit such crimes misses the point of the prosecution's case that the accused were aware of criminal conduct and, as in the case of Nanjing, "permitted" these crimes to continue or implicitly authorized policies of mistreatment of civilians and POW.

Even more striking is that Pal's conclusion as to orders is not what is charged under the more relevant Count 55, *which he neglects to even mention.* That Count provides liability for the failure to prevent war crimes. Justifying this glaring omission is only an oblique reference to his erroneous representation of convictions for war crimes at Nuremberg discussed above. There is no reasoned argument substantiated by evidence or detailed consideration of the prosecution case to support his sweeping conclusion that all of the accused "had no apparent hand in the perpetration of these atrocious deeds."[29] What is actually relevant, however, is not whether they were direct perpetrators but rather whether they gained knowledge of such criminal conduct and either permitted it to continue or did nothing to prevent it when it was within the field of their authority to do so. Pal's reasons for omitting reference to Count 55 are obvious given that there was unequivocal evidence establishing that some accused at the very least had information concerning the commission of mistreatment or atrocities and failed to prevent them.

The second prong of Pal's "conclusion" in regard to the 10-page enumeration of war crimes is even more telling. He first refers to the "reckless, ruthless way" in which Germany waged war in both WWI and WWII. He then says the only conduct in the Pacific War comparable to Germany's manner of waging war "is the decision coming from the Allied Powers to use the atomic bomb."[30] The implication is clear. Only the Germans and the Allies have waged war in a "reckless, ruthless way" that requires accountability. Lest one think this is merely a tangential aside rather than the conclusion of his discussion of the

[29] Ibid., 1354.
[30] Ibid., 1355.

ten pages of enumerated war crimes, he expounds upon this theme at some length, concluding again that, "in the Pacific war, this decision to use the atom bomb is the only near approach to the directives of the German Emperor during the first world war and of the Nazi leaders during the second world war. Nothing like this could be traced to the credit of the present accused."[31]

Here the real purpose of Pal's opinion appears in the same vein as in his treatment of crimes against peace. Pal's view is that the wrong persons are on trial. While the Japanese government is wholly innocent of any involvement in the "fiendish" and "atrocious" war crimes committed all over its empire by its subordinates, the Allies, akin the Nazis he likens them to, have waged war in an illegal manner. This is why Pal considers that no detailed findings or analysis of the long list of war crimes is required. It is the Allies and not the Japanese leadership whose crimes need to be documented and the responsible leaders punished, as those of the Nazis were at Nuremberg. This conclusion reveals not only Pal's lack of impartiality and ideological purpose but also his complete disregard for adequately fulfilling his role as a judge of the crimes charged in the case before him. This section of his opinion started out with an elaborate invocation of analytical rigor and juristic inquiry but that inquiry was never pursued through the careful weighing of evidence Pal said was required. This careful analysis instead turned out to be merely a stage where the Japanese leaders could be regarded as innocent in comparison with the Nazi regime and the Allies.

### 13.2.2 The Nanjing Massacre and Other Atrocities in China

Pal, however, seems to have been aware that an obvious retort to his sweeping statement that Japan never waged war in a manner comparable to Germany would be to point to the war in China 1931–45. Pal had referred to but not discussed alleged war crimes in China in his ten-page enumeration.[32] Having already reached his conclusion exculpating the entire Japanese government and military leadership for war crimes, he nonetheless begins again to consider first Nanjing, then China as a whole, and finally the "rape of Manila" in the Philippines. This lack of organization is strange, because Pal appeared to have concluded his discussion of the ten-page list but now he sets out again with a different methodology and engages in a fairly detailed discussion of Nanjing and a more abbreviated account of other events in China and the Philippines. There is no reason given to explain why these events have been considered separately from the previous discussion, but perhaps Pal himself felt that his conclusion as to the innocence of all the accused might require some actual

---

[31] Ibid.
[32] Pal Opinion, 1345–6.

## 13.2 War Crimes against Civilian Populations 471

factual analysis. Rather than building that into the previous part of the section prior to his conclusion, he tacks on further discussion that results in the same conclusion of complete innocence.

At the beginning of this new discussion he says he will "examine how far the evidence on record would go" to establish the prosecution's contention that the Japanese leadership was aware of war crimes such as those in Nanjing and made no real attempt to prevent them.[33] Taking up what he calls "the Nanking rape" Pal somewhat reluctantly acknowledges that "The above evidence no doubt shows that the reports of the Nanking atrocities reached the Tokyo Government."[34] Having conceded this key element of the prosecution case, how does he nonetheless exculpate that government from responsibility?

His first step is to call into question the accuracy of the reports of atrocities. Here Pal begins the process of denial about Nanjing that continues to this day in right-wing nationalist circles in Japan, but in fact he only calls into question the testimony of one witness, a witness the *defense had actually conceded to be credible*.[35] He then concludes, "even making allowances for everything that can be said against the evidence [he has only questioned the account of one witness by characterizing it as 'strange'], there is no doubt that the conduct of Japanese soldiers at Nanking was atrocious and that such atrocities were intense for nearly three weeks and continued to be serious for a total of six weeks."[36]

Since he has acknowledged that the Japanese government at the highest levels had knowledge of what was happening in Nanjing and that the atrocities occurred over six weeks, one would now expect a discussion of why that government failed to stop the atrocities and prevent further ones from happening elsewhere once they were on notice as to the capacity of their armed forces to go on such a prolonged rampage. Pal, however, engages in no analysis of the crucial finding he has just made and instead abruptly turns to other war crimes in China. If one expects that the required analysis in regard to Nanjing would come later, then one would be sorely disappointed; it does not.

Pal instead proceeds to review several other incidents by briefly summarizing the evidence and in each case dismissing the account. Rather than providing a reasoned analysis for doing so he contents himself with statements such as these about the prosecution evidence about war crimes in Guangdong Province: "I decline to attach any value to statements such as these in a case of such gravity. I cannot believe that had atrocities really been committed in that province, the Prosecution could not have adduced any better evidence of the

---

[33] Ibid., 1358.
[34] Ibid., 1357.
[35] See the Defense's cross-examination of John Magee, T3939–3.
[36] Pal Opinion, 1359.

same."³⁷ Pal does not explain why he finds the testimony not credible or accurate. The speculation that the atrocities did not occur because the prosecution did not introduce "better evidence" is entirely inappropriate as the salient issue is whether the evidence they did introduce is credible or was rebutted by the defense. Pal makes no reference to the defense here and offers no reason as to why the evidence is not credible.

Pal similarly dismisses *all* the other accounts of war crimes in China without adequately specifying the grounds for doing so. There is no mention here of the careful weighing of evidence he had said was required. For example, in regard to very specific allegations of a retaliatory massacre on June 17, 1944 by Japanese troops in Changsha, China, testimony was provided by one of the victims who managed to escape from the burning town. Pal's rejection of the testimony of this massacre consists of the following: "I *wonder* if this witness did really manage to escape before anything could happen to the city"³⁸ (emphasis added).

It is not the role of the judge to "wonder" in pure speculation but rather to point to inconsistencies or other features of the testimony that undermine its credibility. Pal, as usual, does nothing of the kind. His lack of impartiality and his failure to analyze the evidence before him is made manifest by his account of a *defense* witness, *who was not present at the scene* of the alleged crimes, but who was the commander of the 11th Army of which a small detachment was involved in the massacre. Pal merely states, "He testifies that there were no atrocities committed there."³⁹ This statement Pal is prepared to accept at face value without any discussion as to credibility or whether it is self-serving. In regard to the prosecution eye witness, on the other hand, he "wonders" whether his story of escape is true without citing any reason why it is not credible.

In regard to a body of testimony about ongoing instances of murder, rape, and plunder during the occupation of Guilin, Pal states that, "There might have

---

[37] Ibid., 1359.
[38] Pal Opinion, 1360–1. The evidence being referred to is PX342, statement by Hsieh Chin-hua, introduced at T4612. This statement, taken from a 40-year-old merchant in Changsha, recounts that: "After the Japanese forces had occupied Changsha, they freely indulged in murder, rape, incendiarism, and many other atrocities throughout the district. On June 17, 1944, more than 10 soldiers went to To-shi, Shi Shan [where the witness lived], to plunder. One of them was however shot to death by the Chinese Chen Ni troops, and this greatly enraged the Japanese soldiers who thus hit upon retaliation against civilians. On that evening, more than 100 Japanese soldiers, armed with machine guns, visited the place again. They machine-gunned and then set fire to all houses from both ends of the street. Over 100 business houses including stocks of goods were thus entirely reduced to ashes. I was one of the victims who managed to escape from the town. Deprived of all personal belongings by the fire, I became homeless and had to live on alms." (T4612–13).
[39] Pal Opinion, 1361. The defense witness being referred to is Lieutenant General Yokoyama Isamu, formerly Commander of the 11th Army. See Testimony by Yokoyama Isamu, T21794–804.

13.2 War Crimes against Civilian Populations 473

been stray cases."[40] The allegations of course were of systematic, sustained criminality, but Pal concludes that such "stray instances" might "provoke similar statement from the villagers."[41] He provides no reason to support his supposition that the villagers fabricated stories based on other instances. This is again mere exculpatory speculation on Pal's part. He then refers to two commanders called by the defense who denied that any misconduct occurred. Pal again accepts their testimony at face value with no discussion as to credibility. His entire analysis of this body of evidence consists of the following: "The Prosecution evidence does not convince me of the account given therein."[42] Why not? We may well ask. Again, no reason at all is given. Pal perhaps felt that he was being a bit cursory in his dismissal of the accounts of these atrocities, so he adds a one sentence paragraph following the statement just quoted above: "At any rate such stray cases prove absolutely nothing for our present purposes."[43] No reason is given as to why these are "stray cases" and not further manifestations of the widespread "devilish and fiendish atrocities" that he has himself acknowledged.

### 13.2.3 The Rape of Manila

Pal then takes up the "rape of Manila" because it is the other "instance of organized mass atrocity" which might, like Nanjing, reflect the attitudes of the government and military hierarchy to such events so large they cannot be dismissed as "stray cases." Without referring to any specific evidence or events he dismisses in one sentence all of the considerable body of evidence of atrocities throughout the Philippines prior to the American invasion in October 1944 that had been presented by the Philippine prosecution team. All Pal has to say is that, "There might have been some stray cases but such incidents are not at all unusual." He then offers an excuse which is completely irrelevant to the charges against the accused: "There is no army or navy in the world which has not committed crimes of this nature. Those who committed such acts have, I believe, already been punished."[44] He also never mentions what kinds of crimes these were, what is the relevance of them being "not unusual," or who was

---

[40] Pal Opinion, 1361.
[41] Ibid. The prosecution introduced detailed evidence concerning atrocities in Guilin, Guangxi Province: PX352, Group Statement by Guilin municipal officials, concerning atrocities in Guilin City in July 1945, introduced at T4651; and PX353, Statement by nine Guilin citizens, introduced at T4652.
[42] Pal Opinion, 1362. The two military commanders being referred to are probably the aforementioned commander of the 11th Army, Yokoyama, and his military superior, Major General Amano Masakazu, formerly commander of the 6th Area Army, August 1944–February 1945 (testifying at T21743–763).
[43] Pal Opinion, 1362.
[44] Ibid.

punished for what crimes and what evidence in those trials might have inculpated the accused before the IMTFE. His qualifier, "I believe," is also scarcely the basis for a proper judicial finding.

Pal acknowledges that the "real atrocities on a larger scale" were committed after the American invasion but he also dismisses the import of these crimes: "While considering the case of atrocities in the Philippines we cannot attach much importance to what happened there subsequent to October 9, 1944. That was a period when it became impossible for the Japanese commanders to control the troops effectively."[45] On this basis he excuses the commanders[46] and states that it would be "absurd" to hold that such large-scale atrocities "reflect on the policy of the government, which was operating far away from the field, having at the time even no satisfactory means of communication."[47]

The whole point of a juristic inquiry into the charges alleged in the indictment is whether such large-scale atrocities did in fact reflect an explicit or tacit policy or a pattern of acquiescence and approval from which a policy may be inferred. Pal's statement that it is "absurd" to draw such a conclusion hardly constitutes a reasoned analysis. The few words he devotes to explanation are inapposite. It is irrelevant that the Philippines is "far away" from Japan and equally irrelevant that communications were difficult if there was a policy or an attitude of permissiveness already in place. That communications were "difficult" is not a substitute for a finding that no reports of these events ever reached Tokyo. The prosecution's case here is in any event not that Tokyo ordered these crimes but that there was a pattern reflecting either a permissive disposition toward the commission of such crimes, a policy that permitted or encouraged them, or a failure to prevent such crimes from occurring. Pal offers no reason for why the massive violence against Philippine civilians from October 1944 does not provide evidence giving rise to an inference of such a policy or permissiveness.

Having completed his second survey of war crimes, in China and the Philippines, Pal again merely provides a conclusion without any analysis or reasoned argument: "On a review of the *entire evidence* on this point, I have come to the conclusion that the evidence would not entitle us to infer that the members of the government in any way ordered, authorized, or permitted

---

[45] Ibid.
[46] Pal excuses all of the commanders in the Philippines with this blanket statement. Pal provides similar excuses for the military commanders associated with the Nanjing Massacre. General Matsui, he suggests, was "allowed, even for such a short period, to wait and see whether the machinery was properly functioning" (Pal Opinion, 1367). As Pal himself acknowledges, the period was hardly short, for on his account the "intense" and "serious" atrocities continued for six weeks.
[47] Pal Opinion, 1363.

13.2 War Crimes against Civilian Populations 475

the commission of these offenses"[48] (emphasis added). The justification for this sweeping statement is omitted and as we have seen, Pal can scarcely claim to have reviewed "the entire evidence."

### 13.2.4 Pal's Conclusion on Individual Guilt

Listing all of the names of sixteen government officials (including Tōjō), Pal offers what is apparently his real reason for holding them all to be innocent of any connection to these crimes: "In my opinion, as members of the government, it was not their duty to control the troops on the field, not [sic] was it in their power to control them."[49] He further holds that the government was justified in relying on field commanders to control their troops. Apart from the fact that he offers no reason as to why it was not the duty of the Japanese government to prevent massive atrocities by troops their decisions had sent to invade and occupy foreign countries his conclusion here avoids the real issues. Likewise, he does not discuss the obligations of the government in wartime to ensure compliance with international law. Even if it were permissible for governments to rely upon their field commanders to respect international law, what is their duty when the highest levels of political and military authority learn that the commanders have failed in this duty? Pal has admitted, however reluctantly, that members of the cabinet and other bodies were well aware of the Nanjing Massacre. He later admits that they were also aware and discussed at length the mortality rates and atrocious conditions on the Death Railway and in other camps. The issue here he fails to discuss is what steps such a government is required to take when they realize they *cannot* rely upon field commanders.

The hollowness of his sweeping conclusion that no one in the Japanese government, including the army minister, could be held accountable either for the myriad "stray cases" or the "atrocities on a larger scale" was perhaps sensed by Pal, for he added two enigmatic final sentences to his conclusion. He states that, "These high-ranking members of the government were entitled to rely upon the proper functioning of the machinery. There is no evidence in this case that there was any willful distortion of this machinery."[50] What follows appears to be a non-sequitor that again reveals Pal's underlying bias that has shaped the juridically clothed conclusions he has reached. Immediately after the statement about the lack of "willful distortion" in the "machinery" he adds: "War is hell. Perhaps it has been truly said that if members of the government can be tried and punished for happenings like this, it would make peace also

---

[48] Ibid.
[49] Ibid.
[50] Ibid.

hell."⁵¹ We may well ponder the meaning of that sentence and its relevance for judging the accused at Tokyo.

## 13.3  Crimes against Prisoners of War

The 1907 Hague Conventions and the 1929 Geneva Convention on POW were the principal statutory foundations in place before and during WWII. As is the nature of international law, they were of course supplemented and qualified by the international customary law norms that had been established by the time of hostilities. In his efforts to relieve all the accused of any accountability for the war crimes committed across the Japanese Empire from 1937 to 1945 Pal found it necessary to eliminate these two foundational sources of law as binding upon the Japanese state. How he did so is again revealing both of the legal quality of his Opinion as well as of his political agenda.

### 13.3.1  Applicable Law

In a section of his Opinion dealing with "War Crimes Stricto Sensu," Pal concludes that neither the 1929 Geneva Convention on POW nor the 1907 Hague Conventions "shall apply to this case."⁵² In regard to the 1929 Geneva Convention Pal engages in long and tortuous reasoning to explain why the fact that Japan explicitly agreed to abide by the provisions of the Convention did not in fact produce any obligation to do so. His argument reads like that of defense counsel advocating a position rather than a judge objectively analyzing the legal framework.

Even more revealing in its brevity, perhaps, is his argument for relieving Japan of the obligation to follow the 1907 Hague Conventions which it had ratified. He bases his argument on the provision in Article II which establishes that, "The provisions contained in the regulations (Rules of Land Warfare) referred to in Article I, as well as in the present Convention, do not apply except between contracting powers, and then only if all the belligerents are parties to the Convention." His total justification for why the Convention does not apply to Japan comprises just one sentence: "Neither Italy nor Bulgaria had ratified the 1907 Hague Conventions."⁵³

The legal situation, as one might imagine, was a bit more complicated than implied by Pal's one-line dismissal of the foundational framework for the legal regulation of war, which Japan had signed and ratified. What basic

---

⁵¹ Ibid.
⁵² Ibid., 1379.
⁵³ Ibid. Both Italy and Bulgaria had in fact signed the 1907 Hague Convention No. 4 but had not ratified it.

## 13.3 Crimes against Prisoners of War

international jurisprudence would have required here was a reasoned analysis as to (1) whether Italy and Bulgaria should be considered to be belligerents *in the War in China and/or the Pacific War*; (2) whether that specific provision of the Hague Convention was still valid and applicable to the present conflict; and (3) whether the norms of the Hague Conventions had since 1907 become part of international customary law and thus binding on all parties to the conflict.[54] As we have argued, Pal, however, was not writing as a jurist and despite the hundreds of pages of references to international law treatises and doctrines in preceding pages of his opinion, there is *not one word* devoted to the legal basis for his conclusion as to the inapplicability of the Hague Conventions for war crimes. Naturally, as a de facto advocate for the defense case, Pal was anxious to exclude the body of law which could clearly establish the culpability of some of the accused for conventional war crimes. As a judge he was obliged to state his reasons in an impartial and balanced analysis.

What is also disingenuous about Pal's argument about how the Convention applies only if all parties to the conflict are contracting powers is that the same objection had been made by the defense at Nuremberg at the IMT and in the Nuremberg subsequent proceedings. Pal considers none of the relevant legal sources in announcing his conclusion. As the Nuremberg judgment states, "But it is argued that the Hague Convention does not apply in this case, because of the 'general participation' clause in Article II of the Hague Convention No. 4 of 1907 ... Several of the belligerents in the recent war were not parties to this Convention."[55] The Nuremberg judgment dismissed this objection on the following grounds:

The rules of land warfare expressed in the Convention undoubtedly represented an advance over existing international law at the time of their adoption. But the Convention expressly stated that it was an attempt "to revise the general laws and customs of war," which it thus recognised to be then existing, but by 1939 these rules laid down in the Convention were recognised by all civilised nations, and were regarded as being declaratory of the laws and customs of war which are referred to in Article 6(b) of the Charter.[56]

This issue was again raised by defense counsel in the subsequent proceedings where, as in the RuSHA Case,[57] it was again held that the norms of the

---

[54] Needless to say, it would have been difficult to show that Bulgaria and Italy were belligerents either in the war in China prior to the outbreak of the European war in 1939 or the Pacific War in 1941. Pal does determine that what Japan had euphemistically labeled as the "China Incident" was in reality a war.
[55] IMT judgment, 253–4.
[56] Ibid. Similarly, Czechoslovakia had not ratified the 1907 Hague Conventions, which was relevant for charges of war crimes committed in that country.
[57] RuSHA Case, 54.

convention had, by 1939, become part of international customary law and were hence binding on all belligerents. This was also the position taken by Oppenheim and Lauterpacht, in the authoritative international law treatise of the time, on the status of the Hague Conventions in WWII. They also point out that the 1929 Geneva Convention expressly rejected the "general participation" clause, thus also indicating the shift in international customary law.[58] None of this is considered by Pal.

In other words, it was held at Nuremberg and acknowledged by *opinio iuris* that the key provisions of the 1929 Geneva Convention had also become part of international customary law.[59] Whether Pal agreed with this conclusion or not, it was incumbent upon him in writing a reasoned opinion to deal with these issues. The fact that he studiously avoids discussing the position taken by the Nuremberg Tribunals or any other legal authorities on the status of the 1929 Geneva Convention and the 1907 Hague Conventions is illustrative of his lack of basic juristic standards and his self-assigned role of one-sided defense advocate as opposed to judge. Comparison of, for example, the detailed analysis of the applicability of specific provisions of the Convention to non-signatories in the IMT judgment and the High Command Case shows up the shallowness of Pal's treatment of this issue as well as his lack of competence as a jurist.[60]

### 13.3.2 Pal's Treatment of Factual Matters: "Two Very Pertinent Factors"

Having dismissed the legal framework applicable to Japanese war crimes against POW, Pal nonetheless proceeds with the discussion on the basis that his rejection of the Conventions "does not mean that the fate of the prisoners of war was absolutely at the mercy of the Japanese. All I find here is that those conventions, as conventions, would not apply to this case."[61] What then would, in Pal's view, potentially ground the liability of those responsible for the well-being of Allied POW? He in fact never articulates what those standards are or from what legal source they are derived.

Pal begins his discussion of the factual issues by noting "two very pertinent factors."[62] The first of these is that the large number of prisoners surrendering is, in his surprising analogy, an unexpected circumstance like the "atom bomb." However inapt the analogy, its use gives Pal the opportunity to again expound on the evil of the Allied use of this weapon, however extraneous that might be to the matter at hand. The use of the atom bomb, he states, has produced a need

---

[58] Oppenheim, *International Law*, vol., 2, 234–5.
[59] IMT judgment, 232, 235–6.
[60] See High Command Case, 532–42.
[61] Pal Opinion, 1379.
[62] Ibid.

13.3 Crimes against Prisoners of War    479

for inquiry into "the legitimate means for the pursuit of military objectives."[63] What he argues is that the large numbers of surrendering soldiers "have equally come to force a more fundamental searching of the victors' obligations to give quarters to the surrendering army ... with such technique of war involving possibilities of sudden surrenders like this, many of the provisions of the existing conventions may require fundamental modifications." He goes on at some length about the atomic bomb in supposed support of his conclusion that in conditions of surrender of unexpectedly large numbers of troops the traditional rules governing POW no longer apply.[64]

This lengthy disquisition on the atomic bomb and the need to modify the rules of war is not only flawed in its logic but is again indicative of the nature of Pal's opinion:

1. The analogy is a false one and is an obvious pretext for yet again declaiming on the Allied use of the atomic bomb. The surrender of large numbers of Allied troops was not produced by a sudden and transformative technological innovation but rather through the simple incompetence and ill-preparedness of the 100,000 British soldiers in Singapore/Malaysia to whom he refers.[65] Such circumstances have occurred many times in military history and were an even more common feature of warfare on the European Eastern Front where in the first six months of the German invasion of the Soviet Union more than *3 million* Soviet soldiers were taken prisoner. Their mortality rate in German hands was on the order of 70 percent but no one at Nuremberg would have been prepared to accept that because of the unanticipated numbers the rules governing POW no longer applied.

2. The example as given by Pal is entirely misleading. An unexpected surrender might be grounds for initial lack of preparation and organization in dealing with large numbers of POW. It can no longer, however, serve as an excuse for the prolonged conditions of detention and slave labor over a period of years, which was the case with the Allied POW. In other words, the "unexpected" nature of the surrender is actually irrelevant to the charges against the Japanese accused which pertain not to initial reception of POW but to the conditions of their confinement from 1942 to 1945. Moreover, the case of the American POW taken after the surrender in the Philippines undercuts Pal's argument. As appeared in his trial in Manila, Lieutenant General Honma repeatedly requested adequate supplies and medical personnel from Tokyo to deal with POW and his requests were

---

[63] Ibid.
[64] Pal Opinion, 1379–80.
[65] Pal clearly relishes recounting again and again the humiliating surrender of numerically superior British forces to Japan.

denied or ignored by army authorities in the central government. Honma even sent his chief of staff to Tokyo to press the case but to no avail. The prosecution failed to make use of these findings arising from the Honma Trial but, as already seen in Chapter 6, it did present as evidence Tōjō's admission that he was put on inquiry notice about the Bataan Death March. The problem thus lay in the policies and decisions of the Japanese high command, whose responsibility Pal entirely denied.[66] All of Pal's disclaimers are also irrelevant to the systematic mistreatment of Chinese POW whom Pal neglects to mention here.

3. It is a well-established principle of international law, of which Pal was presumably well aware, that adventitious developments in the combat situation do not relieve belligerents of their obligations. Indeed, Pal's special pleading here in the form of these "very pertinent factors" acknowledges the Japanese violation of their basic obligations. What a change in practice, if universal, can do is to change the customary law norm. The surrender of British forces in Singapore or US forces in Bataan clearly did not constitute a universal shift in practice sufficient to change the normative structure pertaining to POW in the way in which Pal suggests that the atom bomb did in regard to the means of war. Indeed, the relatively scrupulous care with which the Germans in Western Europe followed the Geneva Convention in regard to British, American, Canadian, and Australian forces, and the reciprocity which those countries extended to German and Italian POW indicates the shallowness of Pal's attempt to excuse Japanese conduct.

Pal's second "pertinent factor" attempts to provide the basis for "explaining" in regard to crimes against POW, what Pal explicitly acknowledges as the "*more general prevalence of such misdeeds in every theatre of war*"[67] (emphasis added). The overwhelming prosecution evidence of the universal Japanese practice of mistreatment of POW everywhere the Japanese army and navy forces operated constitutes a serious challenge to Pal's determination to acquit all the accused of all charges.[68] The prosecution's case, and the majority judgment, is built upon two pillars: (1) the practices occurred in every theater of war by all Japanese forces and (2) because of international protests, internal reports, and other factors, the cabinet must have been aware of these practices.

In this light Pal had to find a way to explain the universality of the pattern of practice as arising from a factor independent of the top echelons of the military,

---

[66] On Honma's efforts to get the attention of the central government about the dire conditions of prisoners of war, see Totani, *Justice in Asia and the Pacific Region, 1945–1952*, 40–4.

[67] Pal Opinion, 1380.

[68] On the system for prisoner of war administration see Totani, *Justice in Asia and the Pacific Region, 1945–1952*, chapter 2. It shows how closely involved the Tokyo administration were in issues regarding POW, and the inaccuracy of Pal's sweeping conclusion that the higher levels of command in Tokyo were in no way involved.

the administrators of the POW system, and the government. His strategy is to explain that on the one hand the Japanese contempt for those who surrender led all Japanese soldiers to be disposed to ill-treat POW. Because the Allied soldiers had not died rather than surrendered they deserved to be treated with brutality and callous indifference. On the other hand, the Japanese soldiers were themselves used to being ill-treated by their own armed forces, so it was only natural they would treat POW the same way. In support of this argument Pal cites an American anthropologist who concludes, "According to our standards a [sic] Japanese were guilty of atrocities to their own men as well as to their prisoners."[69] Pal considers that such attitudes and the practices that followed from them were thus "not a policy of the conspiratorial group; it is a policy *coeval with the Japanese national life*"[70] (emphasis added). In other words, he concludes, what he characterizes as this "inhuman behavior" toward POW is explained by unique Japanese cultural factors rather than government permissiveness or policy.[71]

This reasoning begs a question. Indeed, the government and military officials whom Pal seeks to exonerate would logically have shared these cultural dispositions that amount to a "policy coeval with national life" and these dispositions would have informed their decisions, policies, attitudes, and actions. In other words, if government and military officials shared this contempt for Allied POW then they too are responsible for the treatment these attitudes produced because they were responsible for overseeing the institutions through which these policies were expressed. Thus, in their case these cultural dispositions would have been reflected in their policies and the way they administered the POW system.[72] Further, if such practices were embedded in Japanese cultural life then government and military officials would have been aware of such dispositions and hence on inquiry notice as to their obligations to POW. Japanese accused at Tokyo generally acknowledged their awareness of their legal obligations under the Geneva 1929 Prisoners Convention and their knowledge that Japan had agreed to fulfill those obligations. In this light, failure to prevent such mistreatment would have been culpable under Count 55. Pal fails to consider if the evidence was adequate to support such a conclusion.

Pal also ignores that it was the government and military who created the conditions that, on Pal's view, produced an almost total indifference to the welfare of their own soldiers, and especially the sick, wounded, ill-equipped, and starving detachments found in ever increasing numbers across the Empire

---

[69] Pal Opinion, 1381.
[70] Ibid., 1380.
[71] Ibid., 1381.
[72] We may recall here the defense argument on national culture already referenced in Chapter 6: "Even if the alleged atrocities or other contraventions assume a similar singular pattern ... Such a pattern may have been a sheer reflection of national or racial traits" (T42203).

as the tide of war turned in 1942. It was also the high-level officials and government who created and administered the system for dealing with POW and it requires no great leap to infer that the same callousness for the lives and well-being of their own soldiers carried over into the system for management and exploitation of Allied POW and their labor.

Pal, as usual, argues in a one-sided manner as an advocate, not considering the two sides of the argument in a juristic and balanced manner. The ultimate contradiction of Pal's position that such conduct was not the product of decisions, policies, and institutional administration that created and reinforced indifference is provided by the Tokyo accused themselves. If in fact the imperative to die rather than surrender was a cultural disposition "coeval with the Japanese national life" then the Tokyo courtroom would have been empty. But in fact, those generals and military top brass who encouraged what Pal himself several times explicitly calls a "policy" of fighting to the death rather than surrendering[73] survived to stand trial in Tokyo and many other venues. Like the Emperor, they preferred to suffer the ignominy of defeat rather than apply to themselves the same "policy" imperative they inculcated in the Imperial Japanese Army and the Imperial Japanese Navy, and that Pal considered "coeval" with their national life, resulting in so many wasted and unnecessary deaths of ordinary Japanese soldiers, fliers, and sailors.

Pal's repeated use of the word "policy" to refer to what he tries to portray as an innate part of Japanese national character in fact betrays the very purpose he advocates. Policies, unlike cultural dispositions, are made and administered by persons. If this "policy" of indifference to human suffering and life was "coeval with the Japanese national identity" in the war period it was because the men in the dock at Tokyo were among those who played a leading role in making it so through the thoroughness of militarization and indoctrination they carried out from the late 1920s. To attempt to shift the responsibility from the top of the military hierarchy to the lowly Japanese soldiers who paid the ultimate price for the imperative of death over surrender is shameless in its deliberate obfuscation of where responsibility for so much death and suffering of the Japanese people ultimately resided.

The two preliminary steps in Pal's argument described above frame his ensuing treatment of the culpability of the government and the armed forces leadership for crimes against POW. He has now established to his satisfaction that (1) the framework of international law conventions does not apply; (2) the sudden surrenders of allied personnel have negated the prevailing standards (it is not clear which ones in light of his rejection of the conventions) for treatment of POW; and (3) independent cultural factors account for the universality of the

---

[73] For instance, Pal Opinion, 1380: "when the policy of one party is fighting to the death" or even in the phrase, "it is a policy coeval with the Japanese national life."

mistreatment of POW. While this might seem to have been enough to conclude the matter, Pal proceeds to discuss accountability without ever specifying what the legal foundation of such accountability might be. He focuses the discussion on whether any of the accused can be connected to the mistreatment of POW and whether the mistreatment should be ascribed to an "act of state" rather than to an individual.[74]

### 13.3.3 Evidence on Widespread Prisoner-of-War Mistreatment

Faced with a massive amount of evidence from what he acknowledges is mistreatment of POW in every theater of war where the Japanese armed forces were engaged, Pal develops a multipronged argument to deflect the inculpatory import of this evidence away from the accused. The tone and structure of his presentation is again akin to that of a defense brief of advocacy rather than a dispassionate judicial consideration of the evidence. As such it is tendentious in taking all Japanese testimony at face value and doubting the reliability, for example, of all of the international protests received by the Japanese government about the treatment of POW.[75] For example, he uses the testimony of Lieutenant General Tanaka Ryūkichi, formerly director of the Military Service Bureau of the Ministry of the Army, as his main source of evidence, taking all he says as credible without any analysis or consideration of the self-serving quality of the testimony or countervailing evidence or interpretations. At the end of his summary of Tanaka's testimony he enumerates twelve other bodies of relevant evidence introduced by the prosecution against the view expressed by Tanaka, but summarily dismisses them without discussion: "I need not examine this evidence in detail. For my present purposes the evidence of TANAKA Ryukichi gives a fairly accurate account of the workings of the state machinery."[76]

As but one small example of Pal's failure to analyze and weigh the testimony of witnesses like Tanaka that he takes to support his case for the defense, we may consider Pal's treatment of the decision to employ POW in labor forces. Pal recounts, one of the high-level conferences that took place in Tokyo to consider the situation of POW. Without considering the implications that this and other such conferences posed for his denial of responsibility of the Tokyo level of command, Pal merely concludes that "in light of the prevailing situation in Japan at that time ... and in light of the slogan ... 'No work, no food' ... at this meeting it was decided "to make all the prisoners of war engage in *forced labor*" (emphasis added).

[74] Ibid.
[75] See, for instance, Pal Opinion, 1384–6.
[76] Pal Opinion, 1386–7. For Tanaka Ryūkichi's testimony that centers on the prisoner-of-war administration of the Ministry of the Army, see T14282–94, 14308–422, 15852–951.

Pal thus acknowledges that a policy level deliberation of treatment of POW occurred. He also acknowledges that a decision was made to engage POW in what he himself terms "forced labor," including that of officers, which was prohibited by the Geneva Convention. Indeed, he explicitly notes that at that meeting, Lieutenant General Uemura Mikio, director of the Prisoner-of-War Information Bureau, objected to the decision on the grounds that to use officers "in *forced labor* would be in violation of the Geneva Convention"[77] (emphasis added). Pal continues his summary of Tanaka's testimony by noting that, "But in spite of the view thus expressed by Uyemuia [Uemura], War Minister TOJO gave the decision of utilizing these officers for labor purposes in light of the fact that Japan had not ratified the Geneva Convention, although it was the government's position to respect the spirit of that Convention."[78]

It is stunning that Pal provides no detailed discussion of what this high-level policy decision by Tōjō implied, particularly for Tōjō's own liability. He also neglects to consider the fact that a conference was convened to consider the appropriate policy to adopt in regard to treatment of POW, and that at that conference one of the key officials in the POW administration system objected to a policy of mistreatment and invoked the 1929 Geneva Convention on POW as applicable. He also does not comment that Tōjō accepted its applicability but considered that the circumstances at the time warranted ignoring Japan's obligations. Pal's analysis also should have focused on what was envisaged under the term "forced labor," which he repeatedly employs. While certain forms of POW labor of non-officers were permitted under the Geneva Convention, those forms were limited, and slave labor and forced labor were certainly prohibited by international customary law, as applied at Nuremberg and elsewhere.[79]

Pal himself denied that the Geneva Convention applied to Japan, but his own account of the Tokyo conference above has shown that high-level Japanese officials involved with POW administration accepted its applicability. Surely a judge assessing the prosecution case should have considered this issue. The fact that Uemura explicitly objects to what he regards as mistreatment of POW under the Geneva Convention also undermines the very premises of Pal's

---

[77] Pal Opinion, 1385. Pal is making this finding based on testimony by Tanaka Ryūkichi, T14290.
[78] Pal Opinion, 1385.
[79] Pal never considers whether any form of what he terms "forced labor" is permitted outside of the rules of the Convention, and if labor of POW is permitted in what sense may it be "forced." Again, Pal is silent because the object of the exercise is not to weigh the evidence against the law. It is worth noting that the meaning of the term "forced labor" came under further scrutiny during Tanaka's cross-examination. Tanaka confirmed that, by that term, he meant compulsory labor and testified that, "With respect to obligations not specifically stipulated in a treaty, there is no way of having that carried out except by compulsion. That is, you cannot compel labor without an order." (T14382).

13.3 Crimes against Prisoners of War    485

conclusion that Tokyo was unaware of mistreatment and not involved in such decisions. Surely these issues should have figured in Pal's discussion of the evidence, but he chooses to be silent on these points as on all else that might weigh against the accused.

Finally, what are the applicable standards for treatment of POW? Pal readily acknowledges that mistreatment and crimes occurred on a massive scale, which necessarily means that there were applicable legal standards. Since Pal has dismissed the Geneva Convention on POW he is naturally obliged as a judge to define the law applicable to the case. He does not do this and ignores that on his own account Japanese officials acknowledge their government's decision to respect the Convention. The blatant inconsistencies and gaps in Pal's argument reveal that his purpose was to reach a pre-determined conclusion regardless of the law and the evidence. How he, in light of the evidence he himself has cited, justifies acquitting Tōjō on the charges for mistreating POW also remains unexplained.

### 13.3.4  A Nine-Point Summary of Pal's Argumentative Strategy

As the preceding discussion indicates, to fully analyze even this one section of Pal's opinion would require a separate and very lengthy chapter. The examples given above are fairly representative of the general quality and tenor of Pal's treatment, so we may usefully just summarize the main steps of his argument:

1. The deliberate failure of officials in the position of highest responsibility to prevent war crimes perpetrated by those under their authority and of which they are aware is not culpable. This position of course directly contradicts the jurisprudence and doctrinal findings not only of the IMT and the Nuremberg subsequent proceedings but also the decisions of the British, American, Australian, and Philippine war crimes tribunals, among others.[80] In other words, it goes against the virtually universal practice and interpretation of relevant international law on war crimes.
2. Although Pal has announced that the 1907 Hague Convention No. 4 does not apply to the case, he contradicts himself again when he subsequently acknowledges the applicability of Article IV of the 1907 Hague Convention No. 4. He states that he disagrees with the prosecution's reference to the plain language of Article IV, which provides that "Prisoners of War are in the power of the hostile government, but not of the individuals or corps who capture them. They must be humanely treated."[81] He also acknowledges that Article II of the 1929 Geneva Convention has an almost

---

[80] See, Totani, *Justice in Asia and the Pacific Region, 1945–1952*.
[81] 1907 Hague Convention No. 4, Article IV as quoted by Pal Opinion, 1388.

identical provision (which Convention he has also previously decided was not applicable but is nonetheless acknowledging here as the applicable legal standard). The purport of Article IV could not be clearer. It places the responsibility for humane treatment of POW clearly upon the "*government*" rather than on the military units that hold them. Pal, on the other hand, without any reference to the case law or voluminous literature and Travaux on the Conventions decides that this interpretation is not correct and that only the "particular member" of the government assigned to this specific function is responsible for its implementation.

His reasoning in support of this interpretation is hardly that of a jurist. Rather than citing the relevant authorities and interpretations he states that the standard that the highest levels of the government bear the ultimate authority for the implementation of international obligations "may be an ideal one for the golden age of an international community ... At present no government in the world functions in that way."[82] In a non-sequitor he concludes this paragraph supporting his interpretation of the Conventions by observing that one must take into account that wartime conditions prevailed and that "We must not ignore the part which propaganda is made to play ... specially in war-time."[83] What relevance these extraneous observations about propaganda have to the interpretation of Articles II and IV of the Conventions and their applicability to the Japanese cabinet and military hierarchy remains unstated. Pal's speculations about "golden age" ideals are also irrelevant, for he has himself acknowledged the applicability and obligatory force of Article IV. Japan assumed this obligation when it signed and ratified the Hague Convention and thus the observation that only in a "golden age" would governments function in such a responsible manner is not only extraneous but reveals the desperate argumentative lengths to which Pal was prepared to go in order to find all the accused not guilty of all charges.

3. The third point in Pal's "defense brief" is to conclude that the Japanese government was justified in ignoring the protests of Allied governments about the commission of war crimes against POW and others.[84] The reason he gives helps to explain why he has previously introduced the theme of propaganda. In WWI, he argues, there had been a "vile competition" in the form of British and American propaganda to incite hatred against Germany. So too, he suggests, the reports and protests conveyed to Japanese authorities may also have been mere propaganda and "bizarre fairy tales" and hence could be ignored.[85] He concludes that for this reason the Japanese

---

[82] Pal Opinion, 1389.
[83] Ibid.
[84] Ibid., 1389-2.
[85] Ibid., 1390-1.

13.3  Crimes against Prisoners of War    487

authorities were entitled to rely completely on reports from their own personnel and to disregard Allied protests and other such external reports as mere propaganda.

This argument is either extraordinarily naïve or extraordinarily disingenuous. There are first of all obvious reasons, apparent to any government official, as to why subordinates in the field may color reports in a favorable way. More importantly, if there was in fact a policy that enabled such criminal practices (as the decision of Tōjō referred to above suggests there was) or a practice of silently acquiescing in them, there would have been no reason to report such "crimes" to military authorities in the central government and very good reason not to. Pal acknowledges the prosecution has introduced documentary evidence linking the Tokyo levels of command and administration to knowledge and acquiescence of crimes committed in POW camps but dismisses them in a few sentences without considering any of the actual evidence in detail.[86]

Second, the analogy to WWI propaganda is entirely false. Propaganda is directed at a mass audience with an ideological purpose. The factually based reports and protests with accompanying documentation conveyed to the Japanese government by neutral parties obviously belong to a different category of communication with a different purpose. They are also confidential rather than public. The most glaring flaw in Pal's attempts to negate the force of the years of Allied protests, protests that had been supported by detailed factual allegations, is that Pal made no attempt to examine whether these reports that he cursorily dismisses as propaganda were in fact true. Given that the evidence of many – if not most – of the incidents and practices that had been protested were before the court, Pal could have easily taken a sample of cases to demonstrate, as he suggests, that they were unreliable and, hence, the Japanese authorities were justified in dismissing them.

What Pal does instead, however, is instructive. In the face of the many weeks of testimony and documentary evidence that had been presented by the prosecution on war crimes, he rejects their veracity in four sentences, quoted here in their entirety:

I do not see anything of special reliability in the nature of the prompts or in the so-called supporting evidence that accompanied them. The protests came through neutral powers; but these neutral powers were only transmitting what they got from the protesting belligerents. *No evidence of any customary behavior of the Japanese forces is before us.* I have already examined how the stories of atrocities in China stood at the time and stand now.[87] (emphasis added)

---

[86] Ibid., 1390.
[87] Pal Opinion, 1391.

Here Pal, without any examination or analysis of their accuracy, dismisses the protests and their accompanying documentation as unreliable, and also dismisses all of the evidence presented by the prosecution that that there was a pattern of behavior throughout the POW camp system. Not only does the evidence clearly indicate otherwise, as all of the other opinions and judgments acknowledge, but here Pal again contradicts himself. As noted earlier, Pal had previously explained what he himself calls the "inhuman" behavior of Japanese personnel toward Allied POW and the "general prevalence of such misdeeds in every theatre of war" by reference to dispositions "coeval with Japanese national life."[88] In this later passage, however, in his attempt to at all costs discredit and dismiss the years of factually based Allied protests he says that there is *no evidence* of *any* customary practices.

4. The fourth step in Pal's argument follows from the third: Because, in his view, there is no similarity or pattern of misconduct in the operation of the POW camps there was thus no policy or directive that would connect the accused to whatever misdeeds might have occurred. As he concludes, again in contradiction as to the reliability of the protests, "There might have been many atrocities. Yet it must be said in fairness to the accused that one thing that has not been established in this case is that the accused designed to conduct this war in any ruthless manner."[89] Apart from statements to the Imperial Diet like that of Hiranuma saying that the Chinese should be exterminated,[90] Pal's excuse here is legally beside the point. The present section of his opinion deals with the charge that the accused *failed to prevent* crimes of which they were aware, NOT that they ordered or deliberately "designed" such criminal conduct. The fact that the Japanese government received large numbers of documented protests over a period of years clearly put them on notice that crimes may been occurring in a widespread manner. Their failure to follow up and fully investigate these reports and take the necessary measures to prevent any further criminal conduct provides the basis of their liability under Count 54 for "permitting" the conduct to occur and continue and under Count 55 for their failure to prevent. Pal, as he has done before, mischaracterizes the charges so as to make it easier for him to acquit those responsible.

5. In regard to charges such as punishment or execution of POW who attempted to escape, as they were entitled to do under the Conventions, Pal again reiterates that the Geneva and Hague Conventions do not apply to Japan. He ignores the fact that, as noted above, he has been regularly citing these conventions as applicable where convenient to his own discussion. In regard to these executions he adds that such misconduct was influenced

---

[88] Pal Opinion, 1380.
[89] Ibid., 1391.
[90] See above Chapter 8, pp. 322–4 and also similar statements by Hirota and others.

## 13.3 Crimes against Prisoners of War

by "the overwhelming number of surrenders" and for this reason he concludes that criminal conduct in regard to such POW "would be mere *acts of state*. I would not find any of the accused criminally liable for them ... The punishment of escaped prisoners, according to these regulations again would be mere *act of state*."[91] (emphasis added)

Here again there are glaring flaws in the argument: (1) There is no reference to what would be the international customary law norm if the Conventions do not apply. Moreover, the Tokyo Conference discussed above about the treatment of POW indicated that the Japanese authorities themselves, including Tōjō, recognized the applicability of the 1929 Convention. (2) Whatever would have been the immediate impact of the number of surrenders, the POW system developed over years and was designed to accommodate these numbers and to exploit their labor. The Japanese government had the resources to relocate some 50,000 Allied POW to remote areas of Burma and Thailand for the construction of the Death Railway, so how can Pal, without citing any evidence whatsoever, conclude that mistreatment over the course of three years continued to be due to the unexpected number of surrenders and justified summary executions?[92] (3) He provides no reasoned account of why these specific actions in regard to POW should be considered "acts of state." Why are these measures alone, of all that he has discussed, "acts of state"? (4) *The most damaging flaw in Pal's argument is that designating these crimes as "acts of state" undercuts his entire argument that there was no policy or pattern. An act of state that is applied across the POW system over a period of time is by definition a policy or decision by the Government – that is, the "state."*

The Act of State doctrine, discussed above in regard to the aggressive war charges, and unequivocally rejected by Nuremberg, was designed precisely for the reason that prompts Pal to invoke it. That doctrine operated to shield the highest level of government officials from liability for criminal conduct through the legal fiction that the "state" and not the individuals comprising the government has acted. As the High Command Case stated,

The state being but an inanimate corporate entity or concept, it cannot as such make plans, determine policies, exercise judgment, experience fear, or be restrained or deterred from action except through its animate agents and representatives. It would be an utter disregard of reality and but legal shadow-boxing to say that only the state, the inanimate entity, can have guilt, and that no guilt can be attributed to its animate agents who devise and execute its policies.[93]

---

[91] Pal Opinion, 1393.
[92] This number appears in the record of the Tokyo Trial from a postwar Japanese government report, PX475, introduced at T5513.
[93] High Command Case, 508. As noted, the IMT Nuremberg judgment has also unequivocally rejected this doctrine.

In light of the manifest illegality of the clear policy in regard to the referenced conduct, Pal apparently felt he had no other means to exculpate the accused than by resorting to this discredited doctrine for which he gives no reasoned argument.

6. In regard to some atrocities, such as those committed on the Hell Ships transporting POW under horrific conditions, Pal has to admit that general practices were criminal.[94] How does he then deal with such instances? In regard to the Hell Ships he again refers to the "overwhelming number of surrenders" (again wholly irrelevant to the Hell Ship transports in 1943–5). Implicitly acknowledging, however, the shallowness of such an appeal he continues, "I do not accept the evidence on this point at its face value; but even making every possible allowance for exaggeration and distortion, it cannot be denied that there was overcrowding, underfeeding, and inadequacy in sanitation and ventilation."[95] He also acknowledges that there were "instances of mistreatment of the prisoners during transit" but then immediately concludes: "but I cannot accept it as indicative of any government policy or indifference."[96]

Pal provides no evidence or reasoning whatsoever to support this conclusion. Even though he does not analyze the body of evidence introduced about the Hell Ships, and without indicating how he has made "every possible allowance for exaggeration and distortion," he concludes that there was no "indifference" on the part of the government.[97]

What would have been required here was to assess the evidence that government officials were aware of the appalling conditions Pal refers to. Since many of the ships were transporting the POW to Japan for labor these were not events occurring only "far away" in remote locations. Pal's concluding remark on the Hell Ship issue, given here in its entirety, is telling: "The Prosecution contention that the Cabinet ministers should have resigned on this issue really contemplates an ideal state of affairs, but I do not think we can measure for our present purposes the conduct of the prisoners with such an ideal standard."[98] Here Pal acknowledges that cabinet ministers were aware of the horrific conditions on the Hell Ships but excuses them on the basis of some "ideal state of affairs" in the same way that he previously invoked a "golden age" as an excuse. The role of the judge, however, is to determine liability under the applicable legal standards, not to speculate that only under some unspecified ideal the accused would have acted to prevent these crimes of which they were aware.

---

[94] Pal Opinion, 1393–4. On the Hell Ship cases see Cheah, "Post-World War II British 'Hell-Ship' Trials in Singapore."
[95] Pal Opinion, 1394.
[96] Ibid.
[97] For the affidavit evidence on the Hell Ships, see, for instance, PX1633–PX1653, T13227–311.
[98] Pal Opinion, 1394.

## 13.3 Crimes against Prisoners of War

7. Pal is likewise compelled to admit the criminality of events he cannot deny, for example, the "Bataan Death March," which he states was "really an atrocious brutality." This event, however, he classifies as an "isolated instance of cruelty."[99] Likewise, he dismisses the years of abuse and atrocities associated with the Death Railway by saying that it was "the overzealousness of the local officers that was mostly responsible for the disaster that happened." He repeats the term "overzealous" several times and also blames the "roguish character" of Major General Arimura Tsunemichi, commander of the Prisoner-of-War Administration in Singapore.[100] Because the documentation of the mortality rates and conditions of slave labor on the Death Railway is so comprehensive, Pal makes no attempt to dismiss it but instead relies on characterizing what he acknowledges as systematic abuse committed through this multi-year operation involving tens out thousands of laborers as another isolated incident due solely to the "overzealousness" of the local commanders and engineers. He ignores the fact that orders as to the construction of the Death Railway and the acceleration of the construction schedule at all costs originated – which the prosecution had shown – in the Imperial Headquarters.[101] Such arguments as he makes might be advanced by defense counsel, but is it really worthy of a judge bound by the standard of impartiality?

Even documents that Pal himself references indicate the incoherence in his argument. For example, he quotes several reports from the chief of staff of the Southern Army fully admitting the human consequences of the strategic decisions made about the pace of railway construction. To give two such examples of reports quoted by Pal: "Moreover, for strategic reasons, it was necessary to complete the railway by August and the work was pushed forward at a terrific rate, *with the result that many prisoners became ill and many died*" (emphasis added). Or, in the words of another report from the Southern Army to the director of the Prisoner-of-War Information Bureau, "Since the proposed site of this railway line was a virgin jungle shelter, food, provisions, and medical supplies were far from adequate and much different from normal conditions for prisoners of war."[102] Pal also notes that the decision to construct the railway

---

[99] Pal Opinion, 1394–5.
[100] Major General Arimura Tsunemichi was responsible for transferring to the Death Railway in April 1943 a reinforcement prisoner-of-war work party, known as "F Force," which comprised 7,000 Australian and British prisoners of war. See testimony by Cyril H. D. Wild, T5445–58. For the British war crime trials, see the Totani, *Justice in Asia and the Pacific Region, 1945–1952*, chapter 3.
[101] For the prosecution's evidence concerning the circumstances of the construction work, including its acceleration in the first half of 1943, see PX475, introduced at T5513; and testimony by Wakamatsu Tadakazu, T14629–55. The full text of PX475 is reproduced in Kratoska, *The Thailand-Burma Railway, 1942–1946*, vol. 1, 342–403.
[102] Both reports quoted by Pal Opinion, 1397. The evidence being referred to is PX473, introduced at T5491, and the quoted passage at T5506–7 and 5511.

492    Pal's Treatment of War Crimes Charges

was made by Imperial Headquarters and that it was this body that also made the decision to speed up the construction of the railway.[103]

Here Pal himself presents evidence that links individual accused to orders, policies, and decisions. He also provides the evidence that the government was aware of the disastrous human cost of these policies and later received reports on how and why this occurred. Yet Pal does not at all examine this evidence or inquire as to when information about conditions was transmitted and to whom, or when cabinet members were made aware of the situation. These internal Japanese reports would also have confirmed the reliability of the many Allied protests that Pal so cursorily dismissed. Instead, he attributes all responsibility to what he terms the "overzealousness" of local officers and engineers and acquits all the accused of the charges without any of the required analysis of the relevant evidence. Even if the local officers were "overzealous," how does this relieve the higher-level officials in Tokyo if they were aware of the conditions of the railway and did not address the issue? Pal omits any mention of this, the crucial issue.

8. In regard to the seventeen pages of evidence Pal cites concerning illegal torture and execution of Allied aircrew, he makes every possible attempt to dismiss as much of the evidence as possible, characterizing the prosecution evidence such as the Report of the Judge Advocate General as "mostly worthless" without any explanation, analysis, or justification.[104] The bulk of the evidence, however, makes it impossible to dismiss in their entirety, so Pal simply concludes as follows: "The cases of execution without trial are really all stray cases at different theaters of war far away from Japan. In Japan proper there are several cases, all occurring in 1945 when everything was in a chaotic condition here ... In any case, in view of the conditions in Japan at the time, I would not hold them criminally responsible for failing to prevent these unfortunate executions. Every failure does not imply fault."[105]

This is the final sentence of the war crimes section of Pal's opinion and he does not explain why this particular failure "does not imply fault." He does not discuss whether the executions that took place "far away from Japan" were reported to Tokyo, nor does he analyze why the "chaotic condition" of 1945 specifically negates responsibility for illegal executions carried out in Tokyo and elsewhere in Japan. The underlying theme of the previous seventeen pages of discussion of illegal executions of Allied air crew is that it was the bombing

---

[103] Pal Opinion, 1397.
[104] Pal is probably referring to two court-martial reports on the trial and execution of Allied airmen in Japan in the last weeks of war. The prosecution obtained the reports from Ōyama Ayao, chief of the Legal Research of the First Demobilization Bureau. The reports appear in the record of the trial as PX1994 and 1995, T14674–80.
[105] Pal Opinion, 1420.

13.3  Crimes against Prisoners of War    493

of Japan that was really to blame and no one should be held accountable for the "unfortunate executions" that ensued. Indeed he suggest that "history" will decide whether the "outburst of popular sentiment" against bombing, and particularly the atom bomb, has "become legitimate" by virtue of the decision to "win the victory by breaking the will of the whole nation to continue to fight."[106] It is an understatement to say that such discussions and speculation go beyond the permissible scope of judicial activity and are irrelevant to the charges of failing to prevent illegal execution of Allied air crew who were in any event executed before the atomic bombings. What Pal suggests instead is that the illegal executions of Allied flight crew were justified because of the public outrage at Allied bombing policy. Apart from its questionable morality it is definitely not a legal basis for relieving those responsible of liability.

9. The final strategy employed by Pal in the face of the massive evidence on mistreatment of Allied POW is to argue that the problem of accountability had already been resolved in the national trials and there was no need to hold the accused accountable. As noted above, in his discussion of war crimes against civilians in occupied territories Pal had already stated that, "It should be remembered that in the majority of cases 'stern justice' has already been meted out to the persons charged with having actually perpetrated these atrocious acts along with their immediate superiors." He then states that he will "dispassionately ... see if the guilt would reach the accused before us."[107] As we have seen, his treatment is anything but dispassionate and impartial.

At the outset of his discussion of the treatment of POW Pal states that, "The evidence is overwhelming to establish the maltreatment of the prisoners of war in various ways. It will serve no purpose to discuss this evidence in detail. The actual perpetrators of these brutalities are not before us. Those of them who could be got hold of alive have been adequately dealt with by the allied powers."[108] He further invokes this point in his discussion of specific crimes. For example, in discussion of the Death Railway he references the 400 cases that had been brought to trial before American, Australian, and Dutch courts (neglecting to mention the many British trials on the Death Railway in particular).[109] He concludes that this shows that "there is no scope for any apprehension of any mistaken clemency" for these "foul acts." He then states, "We are here concerned with a different set of persons. Certainly nothing has been

---

[106] Ibid., 1355.
[107] Ibid., 1344 and see also 1354 where Pal repeats this passage.
[108] Ibid., 1371.
[109] Pal here is referring to testimony by Colonel Wild, a leading British war crimes investigator, although Pal got the information wrong. See T5684–5.

placed before us which would entitle us to say that they should have foreseen such brutalities or overzealousness on the part of these persons."[110]

The salient legal point is not whether the accused could have "foreseen" these acts but rather what they did or did not do to prevent them when they became aware of them. Pal systematically dodges this point in regard to the Death Railway cases. Likewise, in regard to the Bataan Death March he notes that the responsible person has been tried and punished (Lieutenant General Honma and some of his subordinates), and that General Yamashita was tried and punished for the Rape of Manila.[111] The fact that they were punished is irrelevant to whether the accused before the IMTFE should be held accountable.

### 13.3.5  Pal's Imaginary Tribunal

These nine aspects of Pal's argument are transparent in their partiality to the defense and manifestly inadequate as a careful weighing of the evidence which Pal himself sets out as the obligation of a judge. Pal's argument twists and turns as it confronts each set of accusations, involving him in contradictions and inconsistencies as he steers his treatment of crimes against POW to fit in with his overall conclusion that "each and every one of the accused" should be found entirely innocent of "each and every" charge contained in the indictment. As the war crimes charges are the final sections of the substantive parts of his Opinion, Pal views this ultimate conclusion as necessary for establishing what a true tribunal would have accomplished. That imaginary tribunal, whose "judgment" Pal has just written, would have considered, as Pal does, the broader context of the international system in the prewar era, the ways in which that system instantiated and justified the domination of the Western colonial and imperialist powers, and the way those powers had now used an international law they constructed in order to prevent Japan from acquiring an empire and then punishing Japan's leaders through a sham tribunal for having done so.

Above all, that imaginary tribunal Pal invokes would have held, as Pal repeatedly suggests, that the Allied use of the atom bomb was comparable as a means of war only to the Nazi devastation of Europe. Pal's ideal tribunal would have thus examined fully the evidence that was "forcibly" excluded from the IMTFE and would have found, as Pal did, that in light of this broader context no guilt could be assigned to any of Japan's military or political leaders for any of the crimes with which they were charged. The "judgment" of that ideal tribunal, which Pal believes he has now written for the world and for history, would also have found that it was the Western Allies who should have been

---

[110] Pal Opinion, 1400–1.
[111] Ibid., 1394–5; 1368.

13.3  Crimes against Prisoners of War    495

found guilty and punished both for their responsibility for driving a peaceful Japan into war and for the use of the atom bomb to end that war.

This interpretation of Pal's Opinion explains why it bears no relation to a dissenting opinion, such as that of Roeling or Bernard. It also explains why Pal never references, or even mentions, the majority judgment he purported to be dissenting from. Finally, it also explains why Pal repeatedly, as we have seen, expresses his contempt for the trial that did take place before the IMTFE and the need to broaden the frame of reference beyond the scope of the actual trial in order to achieve justice.[112]

Pal's vision of the role of a true judge required him to exculpate all the actual accused at Tokyo and provide a judgment on the issues that should, in his view, have been the focus of the trial. As he explicitly says, had the tribunal "been openly called upon to decide such political issues" that Pal deemed decisive, it would have been an entirely different trial, a trial in which the Japanese accused would have only played a minor part.[113] That trial would have focused on what Pal regarded as the true "future threat" to world peace, the continuing dominance of the victorious Allies. Pal's conclusion, like his likening the Allies to the Nazi leaders, leaves no doubt as to what the ultimate outcome of that ideal trial would have been. He leaves us with no doubt because his Opinion should actually be read as the judgment for that "trial." In this "judgment" Pal appoints himself as judge for the trial that did not take place. That trial, unconstrained by the sham norms of international law and the irrelevant legal arguments of the other Tokyo judges, would have considered all of those broader political and historical concerns and placed the true criminals rather than innocent Japanese leaders in the dock as accused. Pal could thus justify ignoring the opinions of the other judges because as the only true judge at Tokyo his historic mission was to deliver the truth for posterity. That in his self-righteous mission for the future well-being of the world he abandoned every basic professional and ethical standard of a judge would likely not have troubled him in the least.

---

[112] See Pal Opinion, 1424, where Pal says that the "one thing the victor cannot give to the vanquished is justice." At least, if a tribunal be rooted in politics as opposed to law, no matter what its form and pretenses, the apprehension thus expressed would be real, unless "justice is really nothing else than the interest of the stronger." He immediately follows this sentence with the account discussed above of what a real tribunal would have considered.
[113] Pal Opinion, 1424–5.

# 14 The Concurring Opinions of Justices Webb and Jaranilla

## 14.1 Jaranilla's Concurring Opinion

Justice Delfin Jaranilla of the Philippines wrote a concise voncurring opinion that aims to address a few discrete points on which he differs from the majority.[1] These include his more narrowly legal disagreements with the majority on issues such as the scope of the conspiracy charge and the counts of the indictment that the majority judgment dismissed, as well as more fundamental principles of jurisprudence on questions concerning the legitimacy of the tribunal.[2] It is these that are the most interesting aspects of his opinion and they shall be the primary focus in our treatment of his concurring opinion.

### 14.1.1 Victor's Justice?

After dealing with the more technical issues concerning the conspiracy and murder charges in the indictment, Jaranilla turns to fundamental issues on which the legitimacy of the Charter and the tribunal had been called into question. Here he addresses issues raised by the defense as well as by some of the dissents. He first turns to a section he entitles "Objection to the Tribunal." Here he considers the victor's justice charge. Pal, as we have seen, rejected the IMTFE on such grounds, arguing that the trial was merely politics "cloaked by a judicial appearance" because the larger framework of international politics and imperialist domination had not been included in the trial and the victors were not the accused. Pal also implied that as instruments of Western imperialism his fellow judges were not impartial and the trial was thus a sham. As we have argued in the previous chapter devoted to Pal's own "judgment," his view that the other judges were not impartial provides a classic example of the "pot calling the kettle black."

---

[1] Jaranilla's Opinion consists of 17 pages of text (*Documents*, 643–59).
[2] In regard to conspiracy, Jaranilla's primary point is that a plain reading of the Charter indicates that the conspiracy charge extended to war crimes and crimes against humanity and was not limited to crimes against peace. Jaramilla also argues that the tribunal should not have dismissed Counts 6–26 of the indictment as subsumed under the more general charges of Counts 1–5 (Jaranilla Opinion, 643–8).

14.1 Jaranilla's Concurring Opinion 497

It is against this framework of allegations of "victor's justice" that we must consider Jaranilla's treatment of this issue. Jaranilla understands the objection to be that "the members of this Tribunal, being representatives of the victorious nations which defeated Japan, cannot administer justice and that the accused are denied a fair and impartial trial."[3] Jaranilla begins his refutation by noting that the tribunal was established under the authorization of the Instrument of Surrender which was signed by Japan. He states that SCAP could have created a military commission or a national court, but instead the Allies decided, as they had at Nuremberg, to establish a tribunal composed of representatives of eleven nations, "carefully chosen as to their qualifications, fairness, and impartiality."[4] He adds that having executed the instrument of surrender which provides for such trials Japan had no standing to "repudiate what she has solemnly entered into."[5]

Jaranilla's argument is accurate up to a point. While it is certainly true that the Allies had the authority under the unconditional surrender, as reflected in that Instrument, to convene such a tribunal it does not follow that the proceedings of that tribunal are necessarily "fair and impartial." While Japan, as he states, cannot object to the convening of such a tribunal this does not mean that the accused individuals have no right to object if the trial does not meet prevailing basic international fair trial standards. Jaranilla answers this objection by arguing that the Charter "has assured the application of democratic practices and guarantees as enjoyed by the foremost nations of the world."[6]

Given the state of due process in national criminal courts in most countries in that era, Jaranilla's assessment is a fair one and it is hard to contend that the proceedings of both the IMT and the IMTFE did not meet the basic fair trial standards of the time. Many of the due process rights which we consider today to be essential to a fair trial, and which have been enshrined in documents such as the International Covenant on Civil and Political Rights (ICCPR) or the European Convention on Human Rights, had not been recognized as basic fundamental rights at that time.[7] The trials before the Nuremberg and Tokyo Tribunals must be judged according to the fair trial standards and best practices of that epoch. While it is indisputable that some of the national military commissions or military courts that tried German or Japanese war criminals after 1945 did not meet those standards, it is also quite clear that Nuremberg and Tokyo did. Indeed, it was to meet possible objections about the competence of the judges and the fairness of the proceedings that led the Allies to establish international tribunals as opposed to mere military courts in the first place.

---

[3] Jaranilla Opinion, 648–9.
[4] Ibid., 649.
[5] Ibid.
[6] Ibid., 650.
[7] These documents are available online at the websites of the United Nations Human Rights Office of the High Commissioner and European Court of Human Rights.

It should also be noted that the IMT trial at Nuremberg, of an approximately equal number of accused and covering a similarly large and complex geographical area and timeframe, was completed in about 1/3 the time as the Tokyo Trial. Most German critics who argued that there was victor's justice at Nuremberg did not dispute the fundamental fairness of the proceedings measured by the standards of the day. Indeed, in comparison with the standards practiced by Germany and Japan during the war period, both the IMT and the IMTFE vastly exceeded them and were commensurate with prevailing conceptions of due process. In this light, Jaranilla's argument that the proceedings were fair in regard to the standards by which they were conducted appears well taken.

A further objection might be that even if the proceedings were fair the verdicts were determined by the biases of the judges or the politics of the convening powers. Jaranilla answers such a critique by pointing out that the "Tribunal has absolved the defendants of various charges and have [sic] differed on certain issues."[8] Indeed, one may point out that over the objections of judges such as Jaranilla, the majority of the charges of the indictment were dismissed by the majority and various accused were acquitted of specific charges. While some of the judges objected to sentences of some of the accused as too harsh, others objected that some sentences were too lenient. It should also be remembered that Roeling, despite his dissent about the status of international law on crimes against peace, while opposing the conviction of five of the accused diplomats agreed that all of the other accused had been proven beyond reasonable doubt to be guilty. The fact that a judge like Roeling, who viewed the tribunal with such a critical eye and dissented in regard to some accused, nonetheless agreed with the guilty verdicts against twenty of the twenty-five defendants, points up that ability of the evidence justifying convictions to sustain scrutiny. In other words, Jaranilla is well-grounded in pointing out that this was no "kangaroo court," such as the wartime Japanese military tribunal in Shanghai, where all of the accused had been subjected to coercion and denied defense counsel, and where all of the judges had been instructed what to say and what to decide. All the Japanese judges in those proceedings complied with the directives they had received and obediently handed down convictions and the predetermined sentences.[9]

Jaranilla also raises the objections to the trial brought forward by Pal. He notes that even Pal has made no allegations against the judges themselves and has "found no fault with their moral integrity, independence of character and rectitude of judgment in the discharge of their functions."[10] As critics of

---

[8] Jaranilla Opinion, 650.

[9] For the IMTFE record concerning the wartime Japanese military proceedings at Shanghai, see PX3834, excerpts presented at T38026–30.

[10] See also Webb's "Draft No. 2" of the Judgment of November 1947 pp. 20–1 (M1417/1 32) where he considers the accusation that the tribunal represents the "Victor Nations." He points out that, "A military tribunal is generally, if not invariably, composed of nationals of the victors."

## 14.1 Jaranilla's Concurring Opinion

the IMTFE again often overlook, Jaranilla tellingly points out that Pal *"therefore voted to overrule the defense challenge to the fairness and impartiality of the Tribunal"*[11] (emphasis added). As we have seen, Pal's objections to the fairness of the proceedings have to do in their essence with the objection that it is the Allies who should be on trial for their use of the atom bomb and for their imperialist domination of Asia, which on Pal's view was the true cause of the war.[12]

### 14.1.2 Retroactive Laws?

Jaranilla next considers the objection that the IMTFE has applied retroactive standards in convicting individuals for crimes that had not yet been defined at the relevant time period. His arguments on this point, however, leave much to be desired. It is also not clear why Jaranilla considered it necessary to treat this point at all since it had been dealt with sufficiently by the majority.

Jaranilla first argues that the principle of nullum crimen sine lege does not apply to international law. This is a surprising position to take and Jaranilla's analysis appears to be confused. While on the one hand he avers that the bar on ex post facto laws applies only to national judicial contexts, on the other hand he also states that the Allied Powers "may legally try and punish individuals who have violated the laws and customs of war ... The offenders of international law are citizens of the world and as such are subject to international law whether or not that law has been made the law of the land."[13]

Jaranilla appears here to conflate a number of issues. First, is there individual responsibility for either the commission of war crimes or crimes against peace? In regard to the former it is clear that the punishment of the perpetrators of such crimes is well established in both international conventional and customary law, or, to use the usual phrase as invoked by Jaranilla, "the laws and customs of war." The point in this regard is not whether such crimes have been "made the law of the land" but whether the war crimes charged are cognizable under applicable international conventions and/or international customary law, the dual sources of international law. Since Japan, Germany, the United States, and Great Britain were signatories of the Hague Convention No. 4, and since it

---

He goes on to say that the authority of the court is not based upon "the right of the conqueror" but on the justice and impartiality of the judges. The criteria by which these are to be measured are, for Webb, "that the members of the tribunal should not be prejudiced and should not be personally hostile to the accused and that they should *thoroughly and objectively analyze the evidence to determine guilt or innocence*" (emphasis added).

[11] Jaranilla Opinion, 650.
[12] Pal also makes objection to the rules of evidence employed by the IMTFE, which were essentially the same as those at Nuremberg. Judging by prevailing international practices, especially in many civil law systems, it is hard to agree with Pal's criticisms on this point.
[13] Jaranilla Opinion, 651.

was universally acknowledged that that the main provisions of that convention had passed into international customary law, their applicability seems non-controversial and it is difficult to understand Jaranilla's concerns in regard to the "laws and customs of war." It should also be noted, in addition, that such war crimes were widely if not universally recognized in the national military law of the belligerents in WWII. Indeed, the Japanese government had itself put Allied flight crew on trial for war crimes, alleging they had attacked civilian targets.

To the extent that Jaranilla was also referring to the status of the crime of aggression in international law his response to the ex post facto objection is also not persuasive. Rather than embarking on a discussion of the status of the Kellogg-Briand Pact and other instruments, which in any event had been dealt with in the majority and other opinions, Jaranilla argues that the leaders of Japan had been repeatedly warned by the Allies "and were perfectly conscious that they were embarking on a war of conquest and hate, in defiant violation of her commitments and of international law."[14] This argument is again not entirely to the point, for the real issue is not whether the Japanese leaders were aware that they were initiating wars of conquest, which they clearly were.[15] The issue in contention is whether wars of conquest were illegal at the time period covered in the indictment. The majority and Webb and Roeling said they were, Pal said that they were not and that all nations were permitted under the then-prevailing principle of absolute national sovereignty to engage in war to further national policies. Jaranilla's discussion of the issue of retroactive application of the law thus contributes little, if anything, to the discussion in other opinions. The next section of his Opinion, "On Individual Responsibility," is more interesting.

### 14.1.3 *Individual Responsibility or "Acts of State"?*

From the next section, "On Individual Responsibility," Jaranilla increasingly turns to issues raised by Pal. It must have been galling for the judges when Pal, who had missed nearly 1/4 of the trial sessions and not actively participated in the circulation of memoranda concerning legal issues and the preparation of the tribunal's judgment, presented a massive "Judgment" of his own that aimed to completely discredit the two years of work that his "learned brethren" had devoted to this trial. It must have been even more appalling to Jaranilla in particular, who had experienced the worst of Japanese war crimes at Bataan and Manila first hand, that Pal so lightly dismissed the massive numbers of

---

[14] Ibid., 652.
[15] See, for instance, the remarks by Foreign Minister Matsuoka in note 96 of Chapter 4. Even Roeling, as we have seen, despite his critical position in regard to the legal status of aggression in international law, admitted that the Greater East Asia Co-Prosperity Sphere was a sham façade for Japanese conquest and armed domination of her neighbors.

atrocities committed in the Philippines, as we have seen, as "stray cases" or the unavoidable result of chaotic conditions.[16]

One of the major purposes of Jaranilla's Opinion is clearly to respond to and refute some of Pal's central legal arguments. In the section on individual responsibility Jaranilla deals with the Act of State doctrine, in the next section the Allied use of the atom bomb, and he then directly devotes a section to Pal's dissenting opinion.

Jaranilla begins by stating that the theory that only states are liable for crimes committed in their name, rather than the individuals who constitute the government of a state, is contrary to the Charter of the Tribunal. More substantively, he then accurately notes that the doctrine that an abstraction – the "state" – commits crimes is a legal fiction designed to shield state leaders for crimes they have perpetrated. Consequently, "The accused cannot shield themselves ... in the fact that their acts were acts of state ... Frankly speaking, crimes are always committed by persons, whether the act be that of the state."[17] This latter point goes to the essence of the position taken by the IMT at Nuremberg and by all of the Nuremberg subsequent proceedings tribunals.[18]

### 14.1.4 Was Nuremberg a Precedent?

Jaranilla thus considers the objection that in regard to acts of state the judgment of the Nuremberg IMT "should not be considered as a precedent."[19] Jaranilla points out that on December 13, 1946 the General Assembly of the United Nations unanimously adopted a resolution affirming the "principles of international law by the Charter of the Nuremberg Tribunal and the judgment of the Tribunal."[20] Apart from this obvious indication of the authoritative nature of that judgment, Jaranilla points out that by virtue of it being the first international criminal tribunal to consider this issue, its decision has precedential weight. This position also reflects the deliberations of the majority and Webb, as expressed in their internal memoranda prepared during the drafting phase

---

[16] It is surprising that Jaranilla did not address these shortcomings in Pal's Opinion by pointing to the evidence on Philippine atrocities that was before the tribunal. Indeed, Jaranilla had written internal memoranda indicating his awareness that the majority had not fully analyzed and incorporated into the judgment all of the Philippine evidence that had been presented. He suggests a number of specific atrocities that should be described in detail (NAA M1417 28 pp. 1–2). What Jaranilla and the majority did not anticipate was that apologists for Japanese atrocities would not be aware of the mass of documentation that was introduced into evidence as exhibits but not discussed in the judgment (and often not read into the transcript for considerations of time; see Chapter 6 under Section 6.1).
[17] Jaranilla Opinion, 652.
[18] IMT judgment, 233.
[19] Jaranilla Opinion, 653.
[20] Quotation from GA 95 (1) December 13, 1946. Jaranilla quotes a secondary source on the resolution.

of their judgment. They explicitly express what they regard as the authoritative status of the Nuremberg judgment *not because of formal precedent but because of its reasoning* and because it embodies "complete answers" to the major objections made by the defense at Tokyo.[21]

In other words, the memoranda of the judges during the drafting phase reveal the inaccuracy of the criticism about precedent. The majority was not blindly following Nuremberg because it was formally a precedent but because they approved of the reasoning of the tribunal and the substance of its legal conclusions.[22] While it is true that international law does not follow a formal system of precedent whereby decisions of previous tribunals are binding and obligatory in the strict sense, it is nonetheless the case that the decisions of the major international judicial bodies carry considerable authority and that their authority is proportional to the quality and the importance of the decision. It is also the case that one of the basic principles of legality, that of certainty and consistency of the law, mandates that due attention be paid to previous decisions of similarly placed tribunals. This is one of the principles cited by the drafters of the majority judgment so as to avoid "suggestions that it in any way differed from the law as stated in the Nuremberg Judgment."[23]

The Nuremberg judgment, with its decisive rejection of the Act of State doctrine and its articulation of the principle of individual responsibility for international crimes, has been recognized as the foundation for the subsequent seven decades of development of international criminal law. This provides a validation of the unique place in international jurisprudence accorded Nuremberg by the UN General Assembly's 1945 resolution. It is difficult to call into question the wisdom of Webb and the majority at Tokyo in following the jurisprudence of Nuremberg and its interpretation of the law of the Charter.[24]

### 14.1.5 Extraneous Issues: The Atom Bomb

Thus far in his Opinion Jaranilla has addressed legal issues that had been raised by the defense and supported by Pal. He apparently felt compelled, however, to also address an issue that, while outside the jurisdiction of the Tribunal and not a matter before the judges for decision, nonetheless weighed on the minds

---

[21] As the Canadian and British judges conveyed to Webb, "With the foregoing conclusions of the Nuremberg Tribunal and the reasoning by which they are reached this Tribunal is in complete accord ... In view of the fact that in all material respects the Charters of this Tribunal and the Nuremberg tribunal are identical, this Tribunal prefers to express its unqualified adherence to the relevant decisions in the Nuremberg Judgment." Memorandum of Patrick and McDougal to Webb of February 18, 1948 p. 3 (NAA M1417/1 32).

[22] See Webb's memorandum of November 6, 1947 to all of the judges (NAA M1417/1 32).

[23] Memorandum of Patrick and McDougal to Webb of February 18, 1948 p. 3 (NAA M1417/1 32).

[24] As we have seen above, Roeling could not deny the authoritative position of the Nuremberg judgment but sought to reinterpret it to suit his ends.

of many, as manifested by its rather random appearance in the opinions of the judges. This issue is the Allied use of the atomic bomb.

From a juristic point of view, it is unfortunate that Jaranilla devoted a section of his Opinion to an issue that was legally extraneous. The issue of Allied methods of waging war was not within the jurisdiction of the court and no evidence was introduced on the subject of the use of the atom bomb or on Allied bombing policy in general. Without jurisdiction, without the introduction of evidence, and without consideration and argument by defense and prosecution, this matter, whatever its historic and political significance and interest, was beyond the legitimate purview of the tribunal.[25] For this reason it was just as inappropriate for Jaranilla to raise this issue as it was for Pal.

The use of atomic weapons was an issue of political significance for the postwar era but while it may be entirely appropriate for historians to debate the various rationales for the use of these weapons, these matters do not concern the judges whose sworn duty is solely to weigh the evidence placed before the court as it pertains to the guilt or innocence of the accused persons. Nuremberg and Tokyo were trials, and the greater the extent to which they strayed into territory beyond the scope of their legal mandate the more they would have threatened to become the kinds of show trials that are actual instantiations of victors' justice.

The limitation of a criminal trial to the legally circumscribed jurisdiction of the court and to the charges presented in the indictment is one of the most basic principles of procedural justice. From the standpoint of judicial ethics it is a fundamental duty of the judge to keep the trial within these limits. If, on the other hand, judges in their personal capacity consider a court illegitimate and illegal because its jurisdiction did not include certain matters, then they should refuse to accept judicial appointment. Wearing the robes of a judge is not an excuse to pontificate on matters of international politics or to take up the mantle of the historian, the advocate for political change, or the legal scholar. The job of the judge in a criminal proceeding is solely to ensure that the trial meets legally defined standards of fairness and justice and that the ultimate verdict is based upon the law and upon an impartial weighing of the evidence

---

[25] At the start of the trial, the defense challenged the Tribunal's jurisdiction on the grounds partly that no American leaders were being criminally prosecuted for the atomic bombing of Japan, and argued that the Japanese accused, too, should be spared criminal prosecution (T212–13). The Japanese media outlet subsequently sensationalized this episode when it became known that the court interpreter failed to provide a complete Japanese translation of the defense challenges (*Kyokutō kokusai gunji saiban sokkiroku*, vol. 1, 22–3). Critics of the Tokyo Trial allege that the tribunal deliberately cut off the flow of court interpretation to prevent the Japanese public from hearing the defense argument. The transcripts of court proceedings show otherwise. It is rather that the sheer translation difficulty caused the court interpreter to stumble. The language arbiter brought the matter to the tribunal's attention following the defense challenges, and a prolonged discussion of this problem ensued between the president of the tribunal, the language arbiter, and the Language Section chief. See T215–20.

and a reasoned justification of the decision.[26] It is upon this basis that we have assessed the work of the judges as manifested in the majority judgment and separate opinions.

Like Pal, Jaranilla tries to explain his discussion of the atomic bombings in a strained and unconvincing manner. Jaranilla contends that the argument of the "inhuman" use of atomic weapons was introduced so as "to minimize the responsibility of the defendants in this case for the atrocities and inhuman acts committed during the war."[27] If he had ended the discussion at this point by saying that there is no legal basis for such a contention, this would have been sufficient. Instead, Jaranilla launches into a discussion of whether the use of these weapons was in fact justified on strategic grounds as a way of ending the war more quickly. This point is entirely irrelevant to the trial and beyond the scope of the issues and evidence before the court. That he quotes at length from the US Secretary of War Henry Stimson explaining the US rationale is indicative of how far Jaranilla has strayed.

Jaranilla's proper role, as is the case with Pal, is not to judge the logic of the strategies of how one side or another proposed to win the war but to judge the case before him. Jaranilla makes the point that each side strove to develop new weapons and used them – in the case of the Germans he mentions the V-1 and V-2 rockets, and in the case of Japan he points to the secret weapons program and how it "manufactured its own flying balloons with which it attempted to bomb the United States."[28] However effective or pathetic these various technological innovations may have been is not germane to the proceedings of the IMTFE. It is a historical fact that Germany, Britain, the Soviet Union, Japan, and the United States were all engaged in various kinds of research about atomic weapons and, in the case of Japan, the development and actual use of bacteriological weapons, but Jaranilla's speculation that Japan would have used them if they had possessed them is likewise inappropriate.[29]

It is likely that Jaranilla raised this issue because it had been, as we have seen, so central to Pal's argument that it was the Allies and not the Japanese leaders who should have been tried and convicted at Tokyo. While he may have

---

[26] See, for instance, for an example of the framework of basic international fair trial rights, in the *OSCE Legal Digest of International Fair Trial Rights* (OSCE Office for Democratic Institutions and Human Rights 2012). The International Covenant on Civil and Political Rights (ICCPR) Article 14 is the fundamental international human rights convention on this topic. This document can be accessed at the Web site of the Organization for Security and Co-operation in Europe.

[27] Jaranilla Opinion, 654.

[28] Ibid. By "flying balloons," Jaranilla is referring to balloon bombs that the Imperial Japanese Army developed in the last phase of the war using a large amount of *konnyaku* potato and Japanese *washi* paper (with which to make the balloons). The original idea was to release bacteriological weapons against the US mainland by launching those balloons, but the weapons attached to the 9,300 balloons actually deployed were incendiary bombs. For more information, see Yamada, *Rikugun Noborito kenkyūjo*, 57–76.

[29] Jaranilla Opinion, 654–5.

been incensed at Pal's own politically motivated judgment this did not require him to rebut the substance of Pal's arguments by justifying the American use of the atom bomb. Confirmation of Jaranilla's motivation in raising this issue to counter Pal is perhaps reinforced by the fact that he moves immediately to direct consideration of the "Dissenting Opinion of the Member from India."

### 14.1.6 Criticism of Pal

Jaranilla tackles directly the legitimacy of Pal's rejection of the validity of the Charter as the law of the tribunal. It is commonly accepted today by the various criminal international tribunals that they are bound by the definitions of the crimes provided by their Charters or statutes. For example, the Statute of the International Criminal Tribunal for Rwanda defines crimes against humanity in a manner that differs from the Statute of the International Criminal Tribunal for the former Yugoslavia, the Statute of the International Criminal Court, and from the international customary law definition of that category of international crime. The Statute of the International Criminal Court (ICC) also provides definitions that differ in important respects from other international criminal tribunals. Despite the fact that the ICTY and the ICTR share an Appeals Chamber, each tribunal is bound by the definition provided in its respective Statute, as is the ICC.[30] In other words, it is the Charter or Statute that determines which crimes are within the jurisdiction and competence of the court to try. This was also the position taken by the Nuremberg Tribunals at the IMT and the subsequent proceedings as to the law of the Charter as binding upon the tribunal.

What is commonly accepted practice today is for the judges to determine how the crime or mode of liability encompassed within their Statute was in fact defined in international customary law at the time that the alleged crimes were committed.[31] The IMT at Nuremberg stated that they were bound to apply the law as defined in the Charter but they also took up the question of whether the crime of aggressive war was established at the outbreak of WWII in Europe, finding that it was. What Jaranilla objects to in Pal's opinion is that Pal rejects the validity of the Charter and says that it does not have the authority "to define any crime."[32] Pal thus believes that it is for the judges to determine what – if any – crimes are within their competence to try and that they alone have the

---

[30] Such examples could be multiplied, for example with reference to the statute of the Extraordinary Chambers in the Courts of Cambodia. Roeling likewise rejects the authority of the Charter to define the legal framework of the court. See Chapter 12.

[31] For example, the jurisdiction of the Extraordinary Chambers in the Courts of Cambodia is limited to the period of the crimes of the Khmer Rouge (1975–9) and the judges look to the state of international law at that time on relevant points.

[32] Jaranilla quoting Pal at Jaranilla Opinion, 656.

authority to determine if those crimes exist in international law and to define them. It goes without saying that in most domestic systems it is not judges who decide whether murder is a crime under their jurisdiction but rather the criminal codes of their national jurisdiction.

What Jaranilla argues is that Pal himself does not have the authority to reject the validity of the Charter because his appointment as a judge rests upon that very Charter. As Jaranilla points out, under Article 2 of the Charter all the judges are "appointed by the Supreme Commander for the Allied Powers."[33] He goes on to say that that the Special Proclamation of the Supreme Commander for the Allied Powers that established the tribunal provided that "the constitution, jurisdiction and functions of this Tribunal are those set forth in the Charter."[34]

The next step in Jaranilla's argument is to point out that Pal took the oath of office under that Special Proclamation prior to assuming his role as judge and that by this oath of office he accepted the validity of the Charter and the duties it imposed upon him as a judge. Jaranilla on this basis concludes that Pal, "is thereby bound ... to give effect to the provisions of the Charter which alone gave him jurisdiction and define his functions."[35] It follows for Jaranilla that for Pal to hold that the Charter is invalid "is to hold that his appointment as such member is invalid ab initio, because he derives his appointment from the authority of the Charter."[36]

As was seen above, the legal grounds for Roeling's rejection of the Charter as providing the legal basis for the trial conducted by the IMTFE are equally implausible. Jaranilla points up the contradiction inherent in Pal's extreme position on the Charter and also offers sound legal arguments against the conclusions Pal draws. It follows from the position that Pal adopts that only the judges can define the crimes which the tribunal may consider. On this view, the judges could opine that not only the Charter that defines the crimes within their jurisdiction has no authority whatsoever but that all of the crimes charged in the indictment are in fact not crimes and there should be no trial at all because there is no legal basis for the judges to apply. Jaranilla points out that Pal views the position of the judges as identical to judges of a national Supreme Court empowered by the Constitution under which it operates to determine whether laws enacted by the legislature are constitutional.

The error in Pal's argument, Jaranilla points out, is because the authority of such a Supreme Court (or Constitutional Court as the case may be) derives from the Constitution "the Supreme law of the land," which assigns it that authority.[37] In other words, the authority of a judicial body to question the

---

[33] Ibid. The Special Proclamation is reproduced in *Documents*, 5–6.
[34] Jaranilla Opinion, 657.
[35] Ibid.
[36] Ibid.
[37] Ibid.

constitutionality of a law is premised upon the language of the Constitution and the nature of the authority it grants. In Jaranilla's view, only the national courts which have that constitutionally determined authority may rule on the constitutionality of a law. The flaw in Pal's reasoning, Jaranilla continues, is that in the case of international courts there is no such "international supreme court that is *above* the Allied Powers and the Supreme Command to which we owe our appointment." In the case of the IMTFE, he concludes, "Its constitution is its Charter, the only source of its creation, jurisdiction, powers, and functions."[38] Since the Charter explicitly sets out the law of the tribunal, he reasons, and since the Charter does not grant the judges the authority to overrule the law of the Charter, they are bound by its provisions. He has, of course, already pointed out that each of the judges swore an oath to uphold the Charter.

What follows from this for Jaranilla is that while the tribunal may acquit a defendant of crimes as defined in the Charter it may not determine that those crimes do not exist in international law. As noted above, contemporary practice, like the Nuremberg judgment, would accept the binding nature of the crimes provided by a tribunal's statute as defining its jurisdiction and competence. Contemporary practice does, however, authorize the judges to determine the *status* of those crimes during the period of the temporal jurisdiction of the tribunal as obligatorily defined by its statute or Charter. This is precisely what the judges at Nuremberg did by inquiring into the status of aggressive war during the relevant time period and holding that the crime of aggression had been established in international customary law. The IMTFE judges at Tokyo, as Jaranilla indicates, followed the same path.

### 14.1.7 Sentencing the Accused

Jaranilla concludes his Opinion with a section that has given rise, especially among Japanese critics, to accusations that he was biased against the accused and vindictive. The basis of these charges is that he finds that "a few only of the penalties" of the tribunal are too lenient because they do not reflect the gravity of the crimes or provide enough of a deterrent effect.[39] Strangely, however, he does not specify which defendants have in his view been treated too leniently, nor does he state what, in his view, the proper penalty should have been.

This is a serious defect because if Jaranilla were going to reject some of the sentences he should have specified which ones and also laid out the grounds on which, in consideration of both aggravating and mitigating circumstances, a different penalty should have been assigned to that specific person. This is, as noted above, a shortcoming common to Roeling, Bernard, and to Pal in that they reach general conclusions, verdicts, and sentences about groups

---

[38] Ibid.
[39] Ibid., 659.

of defendants without providing a reasoned account, based upon a weighing of the evidence, as to each individual accused in regard to whom their opinion differs.

The accusation of vindictiveness against Jaranilla arises from both his statement that some of the sentences were not harsh enough, and from his personal background. Jaranilla survived both the Bataan Death March and the Rape of Manila. He experienced first-hand some of the very war crimes that were before the tribunal. Jaranilla had been put forward by his government for appointment as the Philippine judge at Tokyo.[40] It would have been difficult to find any Philippine or Chinese jurist who had been in the country during the war who had not experienced the hardships that the Japanese occupation brought with it. Given the participation of the Indian National Army on the side of the Japanese, the perpetration of systematic atrocities against Indian POW in Japanese hands, as well as the failed Japanese attempt to invade India in 1944 and the massive loss of life that occurred as a result to Indian soldiers in the British Army, one might as well have raised this question concerning Pal.[41] Indeed, as we have seen, Pal, sitting in judgment at Tokyo during the culmination of the Indian struggle for independence, repeatedly railed against Western colonial and imperial domination of Asia.

The real point, however, is that any judge at Tokyo should have recused himself if he felt he could not carry out his function with the impartiality and other qualities that Webb rightly defined as incumbent upon all judges and as necessary conditions for justice to be done. From this perspective, Jaranilla's performance – including his impartiality – as a judge should be assessed on the basis of the way he conducted himself at the trial and on the basis of his Opinion. The fact that he stated that he differed in regard to only "a few" of the penalties determined by the tribunal is hardly enough to establish personal bias. Webb and Roeling both differed with their brethren as to certain penalties and, like Jaranilla, gave general reasons for doing so. In the previous chapter we have considered to what extent Pal, who, without specifying individual grounds, argued that every one of the accused should be acquitted "for each and every one" of the charges against them, meets the standard of judicial impartiality. As in the case of Jaranilla, Roeling, and all the other judges, such an assessment must be based upon analysis of their performance of their duties and not upon supposition based upon their personal background.

---

[40] For more information about Jaranilla's biography and wartime experiences, see Nagai, "Wasurerareta Tōkyō saiban Firipin hanji."

[41] The Imperial Japanese Army created the Indian National Army during the invasion of British Malaya, using surrendered Indian soldiers as the nucleus of this puppet all-India army. For a path-breaking study on the Indian National Army, see Lebra, *Jungle Alliance*. For a study of Japanese atrocities against those surrendered Indian soldiers who refused to join the Indian National Army, see Totani, *Justice in Asia and the Pacific Region, 1945–1952*, chapter 4.

In the end, Jaranilla's Opinion contributes relatively little to the jurisprudence of the IMTFE. Most of the topics he deals with had been addressed in the majority judgment. What it does reflect, however, are the concerns of the majority judges as to the public perceptions of their work because of the issues raised by Pal and to a lesser extent Roeling. This explains, for example, why Jaranilla, who indicated to the majority that he was concerned about the lack of sufficiently detailed examination of the evidence on war crimes in the Philippines, did not address that concern in his opinion by discussing that evidence himself. What this seems to indicate is that rather than thinking about the way in which their judgment would be read by posterity as to the scope and nature of Japanese war crimes, they were focused more on the challenges to their legacy posed by the attacks on the legitimacy of the tribunal as a judicial institution. These are the primary issues that Jaranilla chose to address.

## 14.2 Webb's Separate Opinion

The draft judgment which Webb wrote in the hope that it would be the basis of the majority judgment has been analyzed at some length in preceding chapters. Instead of using that judgment as a concurring opinion, Webb chose to withdraw it and substituted a very brief separate opinion comprising only some 8 pages in print. As Webb's view of the trial and the liability of the accused has already been discussed, two questions arising from his published concurring opinion require our attention. The first is why Webb withdrew an opinion on which he lavished so much time and effort. The second concerns what he intended to accomplish in the opinion that he did publish.

In regard to the first question, Webb provided an answer in the foreword of his separate opinion. The foreword states that Webb decided to withdraw his judgment, "to the extent to which I found myself in substantial agreement" with the majority. He added that, "in most matters the majority judgement is to the same effect as mine."[42] On this basis, he continues, he withdrew his judgment except for the few pages he chose to publish.

Webb's explanation is hardly satisfactory. Chapters 7 and 9 have demonstrated the glaring gap between the approach of the majority and that of Webb in regard to methodology, standards of liability, attention to the factual basis of the case against each accused as an individual, etc. Why, then, does Webb appear to have decided to paper over these discrepancies? The foreword offers two clues that may assist in answering this question.

First, Webb does not say that the two judgments in fact turned out to be in "substantial agreement." What he says instead is that the majority judgment was "to the same effect" as his. In terms of "effect," both judgments reached

---

[42] Webb Separate Opinion, 631.

the same conclusion that all of the accused should be found guilty. What Webb does not directly indicate is how greatly the two judgments differed in the way in which they justified these guilty verdicts. Webb does, however, allude to this discrepancy indirectly when he states that, "As to particular accused, I have devoted over 380 pages of my judgement to the individual accused." These 380 pages, of course, are in the draft judgment he did not publish, not in the eight pages he put forward as his separate opinion. Webb here clearly points out one of the most important aspects in which he parted ways with the majority. Whereas he devoted extended systematic analysis to the evidence against each of the accused and weighed its sufficiency against the required standard of proof beyond a reasonable doubt, the majority, as we have seen, failed miserably in meeting this fundamental obligation of a reasoned opinion.

There was no apparent reason for Webb to refer to 380 pages of a document that he did not publish or otherwise bring into the public realm. Why then did he reference this specific aspect of his judgment? It seems clear that Webb was, to say the least, disappointed that the majority refused to accept the product of his labors. Moreover, given how he constructed his judgment he must have found that of the majority clearly insufficient in its analysis of the case against each of the accused as opposed to its narrative of an overarching conspiracy that Webb had rejected. What seems to be the case is that on the one hand Webb, as President of the IMTFE, did not want to discredit the work of the court by publishing a judgment that would have constituted a plain rebuke of the insufficiency of the legal and factual analysis of the majority. Since, as he noted in the foreword, he and the majority reached the same conclusions as to the ultimate verdicts, he would not want to have cast doubt upon how those verdicts were justified by the majority when they were "to the same effect" as his own. On the other hand, Webb does appear to have felt compelled to point out what the majority failed to do, which was to provide an equivalent of the 380 pages Webb thought it necessary to devote to weighing the evidence against each of the accused. Rather than formulating this directly as an insufficiency of the majority judgment he instead indicated that he had provided such an analysis in the opinion the majority refused to accept. An acute reader of the two judgments would have understood Webb's point.

In regard to the differences with the majority judgment that prompted Webb to include the eight pages that he did publish, his separate opinion hardly makes them clear. Webb first takes up the "The Law" and summarizes his views on the law of the Charter and its relation to international law. While his condensed one-page treatment is perhaps much clearer than that of the majority it does not differ greatly in substance. Whereas the majority relied upon a lengthy quotation from the Nuremberg judgment to resolve this issue, Webb sets out his views in his own words. The second section of his judgment focuses upon "Crimes against Peace" and again he merely provides a condensed, one-page version of the argument he had developed at length in his draft. There are no major differences in substance from the majority on the legal issues and the same is largely true for the subsequent short section on "Individual Responsibility."[43]

Where Webb's separate opinion does differ from the majority in important respects appears in three of the issues he goes on to treat. The first of these involves the use of the conspiracy doctrine. The internal memoranda of the judges indicate that Webb was at odds with the majority as to whether conspiracy was itself a crime, as charged in the indictment, or merely a mode of liability, that is, a way of committing a substantive crime, akin to aiding and abetting, ordering, or inciting. While the majority maintained that what Webb referred to as "naked conspiracy" was indeed a crime under the Charter, Webb rejected such a view. He chose to set out his case briefly in the published separate opinion, arguing that whatever might be the case in English domestic law conspiracy was not itself a crime under international law: "It may well be that naked conspiracy to have recourse to war ... should be a crime, but this Tribunal is not to determine what ought to be but what is the law."[44] He goes on to explain that under the Charter, Article 5, conspiracy is only "a means of committing a crime against peace."

The second point on which Webb set out a different approach from that of the majority appears in the section entitled "Punishment."[45] Here, unlike the majority, Webb sets out criteria for the sentences of death as opposed to life imprisonment. Also unlike the majority, he approaches this task by analyzing the sentencing standards of the Nuremberg Tribunal. On this basis he concludes that, "Unless the Japanese accused are to be treated with less consideration than the German accused no Japanese should be sentenced to death for conspiring to wage aggressive war." Webb's point is that at Nuremberg, of the twelve accused found guilty of crimes against peace, all seven sentenced to death had also been found guilty of war crimes or crimes against humanity. Such a consideration of criteria for the death sentence or of consistency with Nuremberg are lacking in the majority judgment.

The most important regard in which Webb departed from the majority involves his treatment of the Japanese Emperor. In a section somewhat curiously entitled "Immunity of the Emperor," Webb addresses an issue that was clearly taboo for the majority.[46] Webb's views on the Emperor's responsibility appeared clearly in his draft judgment, as indicated in Chapters 8 and 10, and this was doubtless a ground upon which the majority felt compelled to reject his draft. While Webb in this section pays lip service to the political decision

[43] Ibid., 632–4.
[44] Ibid., 635.
[45] Ibid., 637–3.
[46] Ibid., 638–9.

made in Washington and London not to indict the Emperor, he also makes clear that Hirohito in fact bore the ultimate responsibility for the war. This, we argue, is the real impetus behind Webb's otherwise relatively bland separate opinion.

Webb does not flinch from making his case clear from the very first sentence: "The authority of the Emperor was proved beyond question when he ended the war."[47] His choice of words, referring to the legal burden of proof, is not coincidental, as the next sentence indicates: "The outstanding part played by him in starting as well as ending the war was the subject of evidence led by the Prosecution." Not content to leave matters at that, Webb goes on to counter every argument made on behalf of the Emperor to deflect his liability. He argues that, "The Emperor's authority was required for war. If he did not want war he should have withheld his authority."[48] He then rejects the arguments that the Emperor was justified because he might have risked his life in preventing war and that he "was bound to act on advice" as "contrary to the evidence."[49]

The answer to the question of why Webb chose to publish such a short separate opinion now appears clear. On the one hand, having withdrawn his massive alternate judgment in order not to discredit the majority and their ultimate verdicts with which he concurred, he obliquely pointed out the superiority of his draft judgment and the central inadequacy of the majority's approach by indicating, with no apparent need to do so, that he had provided 380 pages of analysis to justify his legal conclusions as to the liability of each accused. On the other hand, in regard to the responsibility of the Emperor, he felt compelled to be much more direct. His account of what has been "proved beyond question" in regard to the Emperor's ultimate responsibility is an indictment of both the prosecution and the Allied governments who ordered the prosecution to exclude him from the indictment. Read in conjunction with the previous paragraphs on the Emperor's actual role, Webb's statement that this decision was "*no doubt* ... in the best interests of the Allied Powers" must be read as condemnation rather than assent[50] (emphasis added). This condemnation also, of course, reflects the position advocated most forcefully by the Australian government, as discussed in Chapter 1.[51]

---

[47] Ibid., 638.
[48] Ibid.
[49] Ibid., 639.
[50] Ibid.
[51] See especially note 19 in Chapter 1.

# Conclusion

Foregoing chapters have carried out a systematic inquiry into the prosecution and defense cases as they developed over the course of two and a half years of the Tokyo Trial, the majority decision and five separate dissenting and concurring opinions, and Webb's draft judgment. By producing a new basis for the understanding of the Tokyo Trial by such an inquiry, we aimed at calling into question some existing orthodoxies about the trial's historical, legal, and jurisprudential legacies. Furthermore, we discussed Webb's draft judgment as an important and neglected resource, whose adoption as the IMTFE judgment would have greatly bolstered the jurisprudential contributions of the Tokyo Trial in the field of international law, and whose adoption might have provided a powerful counterpoint to some of the "victor's justice" criticisms still prevalent.

Rather than tediously summarize the conclusions of each of the previous 14 chapters we close our discussion of the IMTFE by noting that its jurisprudential legacy and significance has been brought out by the way in which it has been referenced and discussed in contemporary international and hybrid criminal tribunals. While it might be of future interest to examine the way in which the Tokyo judgment has been interpreted and used in the various tribunals, from the Extraordinary Chambers in the Courts of Cambodia to the International Criminal Tribunal for the former Yugoslavia (ICTY), we confine ourselves to examining one of the most salient points raised at the IMTFE. Previous chapters have noted the difficulty faced by the prosecution and the majority in detailing the role of specific organs, such as the cabinet, or of individual accused, in the structures of decision-making authority and policy formation as they evolved from 1928 to 1945. More specifically, our account has focused on the shortcomings of the majority in establishing the crucial linkages between high-level civilian and military officials and war crimes carried out in distant areas under Japanese occupation. It is this issue of command or superior responsibility that has provoked some of the most interesting discussions of the majority judgment in contemporary international criminal trials. The following provides a brief illustration of the way in which the legacy of the IMTFE continues to inform doctrinal discussions in international criminal law. It also points to the way in which tribunals still grapple with issues of responsibility for those – in particular civilian leaders – in a position of authority.

The reception of the jurisprudence of the Tokyo Trial was particularly influential when the ICTY and the ICTR (International Criminal Tribunal for Rwanda) were reaching the judgment stage of their early cases involving persons in a position of authority. These courts naturally turned to the most authoritative WWII precedents for guidance. These were in the first instance Nuremberg and Tokyo, and then the best-known command responsibility cases, primarily the Yamashita Case, the High Command Case, and the Hostage Case. Nuremberg was of little help in this regard, for the IMT on the whole held individuals liable for their participation in the formulation and implementation of policies, decisions, and orders that led to criminal activity. The Nuremberg judgment did not use the failure to prevent war crimes as a primary ground of liability and was thus of relatively little interest to the new international criminal tribunals. One important reason for this has to do with a significant difference that had arisen in the approach to command responsibility.

In the most authoritative and thorough explication of the contours of command responsibility as a theory of liability, the High Command Case, and others in the European theater, had considered the formulation, issuance, and transmission of orders as grounds for command responsibility. When the ICTY and ICTR Statutes were drafted, however, "ordering" was interpreted as a form of individual perpetration under Article 7(1) of the ICTY Statute and Article 6(1) of the ICTR Statute, both under the heading "Individual Responsibility." In both Statutes "Superior Responsibility" was defined under a separate heading: Article 7(3) in the case of the ICTR, Article 6(3) in the case of the ICTR. In substantially identical wording superior responsibility was limited to a failure to prevent or punish crimes of subordinates when the superior *knew or had reason to know* that crimes had been or were about to be committed.[1]

Having defined superior responsibility in this manner it was only natural that the Tokyo judgment would become an important reference point, as this appeared to be the major theory of liability that the IMTFE had used to convict Japanese military and civilian superiors for war crimes. As elaborated above, however, it is far from clear that the IMTFE understood itself to be applying this doctrine in regard to most of the accused, a doctrine to which it nowhere explicitly referred despite the fact that this terminology had become common by this time due to its application in many national war crimes trials in the

---

[1] Note the crucial difference between the "knew or had reason to know" definition of the mental element under the ICTR and ICTY Statutes and the "knew or should have known/negligently failed to acquire knowledge" standard articulated by the IMTFE judgment.

Conclusion                                                              515

European and Asia-Pacific regions. The IMTFE majority did not endeavor to clearly identify the relation of its theories of responsibility to those employed in other proceedings. Nor did the majority explain if there was a difference between the standard of responsibility used in the case of individuals who were in direct positions of command authority over military or security formations that had engaged in criminal activity as opposed to the standard to be used in regard to individuals who had some connection to or responsibility for prisoners of war, civilian populations, or civilian internees, but had no relation of authority to those who perpetrated crimes against these groups.

The fact that Count 55 of the IMTFE indictment was cast in terms of a failure to prevent crimes easily enabled researchers from later tribunals, knowing little of the context of the WWII trials and having little time to study them fully, to conclude that this was a charge under a theory of command responsibility. Whatever the prosecution may have intended, however, as was seen above, the IMTFE judgment understood the basis of liability to be an affirmative duty of governments to ensure the well-being of prisoners of war and civilian internees, and to prevent their mistreatment. This duty, the judgment held, was incumbent upon all members of a collectivity they identified as "the Government of Japan," embodied primarily in the cabinet and in other lower-level groups of civilian officials. This duty, they held, was also binding upon military officers and civilian officials who had a connection to the management and well-being of prisoners of war and civilian internees. In articulating the contours of this duty and the criteria for liability for its breach, they explicitly stated in numerous ways that the duty was not limited to those who had command authority over military units in possession of prisoners. Thus, in this section of the IMTFE judgment that is nowhere cited by ICTR and ICTY judgments, the tribunal appears to make clear that their primary theory of responsibility for war crimes is not command responsibility but rather the knowing, reckless, or negligent breach of a more general duty to protect prisoners regardless of whether a superior-subordinate relationship existed.

The potential for confusion over the grounds of conviction at the IMTFE was heightened, as we saw, by the articulation of the "secretly ordered or willfully permitted" language in Chapter VIII of the judgment and by the unsystematic treatment of the individual verdicts in Chapter X. The fact that the judgment typically dealt with the grounds for conviction for war crimes in such an abbreviated fashion, and so loosely and vaguely defined the criteria and findings it was using to convict or acquit, added to the possibility of misinterpretation, especially when it appears that ICTY and ICTR judgments for the most part only cite the passages from Chapter X. The result of all of this was that while the Tokyo judgment was an important reference point for certain issues in early cases, its application was in many instances based upon misinterpretations of the relevant parts of the judgment. Despite the misunderstanding as to the basis for the conviction of accused such as Hirota, there were nonetheless points on which the Tokyo judgment made a positive contribution to the jurisprudence of the ICTY and the ICTR, for example in regard to its holding that a commander cannot rely upon the mere issuance of orders to respect the civilian population or prisoners but must instead ensure that the orders are effective.[2] Examination of a few key ICTY and ICTR cases on command responsibility will enable us to understand the evolution of the reception of the jurisprudence of the IMTFE by the contemporary tribunals.

The first case to invoke the Tokyo judgment was the first trial at the ICTR, the Akayesu Case.[3] Akayesu was the chief municipal official (*bourgmestre*, roughly equivalent to a mayor) of a Rwandan community that was engulfed by the genocide. The Trial Chamber carefully considered the nature of Akayesu's de iure and de facto authority. While they indicated that they would have been willing to make a finding of command responsibility, they refrained from doing so because that theory of liability had not been properly pled by the prosecution. Akayesu, of course, was a civilian official, so in its judgment of September 2, 1998 the Trial Chamber referred to the conviction of Hirota on what it understood to be a theory of civilian superior responsibility:

As to whether the form of individual criminal responsibility referred to Article 6 (3) [i.e. "superior" or command responsibility] of the Statute applies to persons in positions of both military and civilian authority, it should be noted that during the Tokyo trials, certain civilian authorities were convicted of war crimes under this principle. Hirota, former Foreign Minister of Japan, was convicted of atrocities – including mass rape – committed in the "rape of Nanking," under a count which charged that he had "recklessly disregarded their legal duty by virtue of their offices to take adequate steps to secure the observance and prevent breaches of the law and customs of war."[4]

The Akayesu Trial Chamber cautioned, however, that Judge Roeling strongly dissented from the conviction of Hirota:

"Generally speaking, a Tribunal should be very careful in holding civil government officials responsible for the behavior of the army in the field. Moreover, the Tribunal is here to apply the general principles of law as they exist with relation to

---

[2] See, for instance, the Strugar Trial Judgment (*Prosecutor v. Pavle Strugar*, ICTY IT-01-42-T) citing the IMTFE judgment for the principle that a superior's duty to prevent cannot be discharged "by the mere issuance of routine orders and that more active measures may be required" (paragraph 374). See also Strugar footnotes 1093–1095, citing convictions of Hirota and Kimura, and footnotes 1099–1101, regarding Tōjō and Shigemitsu, on the necessity of undertaking an effective rather than a token or merely routine investigation. The Strugar Appeals Judgment also cites the IMTFE judgment on issues of command responsibility in footnotes 706 and 707 (ICTY IT-01-42-A).

[3] *Prosecutor v. Jean-Paul Akayesu*, ICTR-96-4-T.

[4] Akayesu Trial Judgment paragraph 490.

the responsibility for omissions. Considerations of both law and policy, of both justice and expediency, indicate that this responsibility should only be recognized in a very restricted sense."[5]

On this basis the Trial Chamber declined to regard the IMTFE conviction of Hirota as reflecting settled law and held that the principle of superior responsibility as applied to civilians "remains contentious."[6] They concluded that the actual power possessed by the Accused must be carefully assessed on a case by case basis so as to ascertain whether he in reality had the power "to prevent the commission of the alleged crimes or to punish the perpetrators thereof."[7] As seen earlier, the Tokyo judgment does not concern itself with the reality of the *actual* (de facto) authority and control of military commanders or civilian superiors.

In one of the next cases decided at the ICTR, the Trial Chamber actually convicted the accused under a theory of civilian superior responsibility, citing the Tokyo judgment, and particularly the conviction of Hirota. Since the civilian in question, Albert Musema, was not a civilian official but rather the manager of a tea factory, the boundaries of civilian superior responsibility appeared to be expanding rapidly beyond the careful approach indicated by the Akayesu Case. The details of the Musema Case, and the related Kayishema Case, need not detain us here, for the future of the modern doctrine of superior/command responsibility was meanwhile being shaped at the ICTY.

In November 1998, a Trial Chamber of the ICTY convicted one of the civilian defendants in the so-called Celebici Case under a theory of superior responsibility.[8] The accused had held a position of authority in a detention camp in which the prisoners suffered severe mistreatment. The Celebici Trial Chamber embarked upon the most extensive review to date of the WWII jurisprudence on command responsibility. In regard to civilian superiors it particularly examined the conviction of Hirota by the IMTFE. It also extensively reviewed the disparate holdings of WWII tribunals on the required mental element for conviction under command responsibility, concluding that the "should have known" standard, as applied at Tokyo, was consistent with the "had reason to

---

[5] Akayesu Trial Judgment paragraph 490. Note here that Roeling appears to consider the theory of responsibility to be the "general principles of law" applying to omissions and not a theory of command responsibility,

[6] Akayesu Trial Judgment paragraph 491.

[7] Ibid. It should be understood that the "power to prevent or punish" referred to by the Trial Chamber is the basis of the definition of the superior–subordinate relations required under modern doctrine to convict a military or civilian superior. To establish the required element of a "superior–subordinate relationship" the prosecution must prove that the Accused had "effective control" of the individuals or formations that perpetrated the offense. The definition of "effective control" is the actual power to prevent the crimes or punish the perpetrators.

[8] The Celebici Case is officially *Prosecutor v. Zejail Delalic, et al.* (ICTY IT-96-21-T).

know" definition of the mental element in Article 7(3) of the ICTY Statute.[9] On appeal from the judgment of the Trial Chamber the legal elements of the theory of superior responsibility became one of the important issues facing the Appeals Chamber. In the Celebici Case the ICTY Appeals Chamber took the opportunity to establish authoritatively the required elements of this doctrine. The Celebici Appeals judgment became the leading case on this issue for both the ICTR and the ICTY, and for this reason, and because of its consideration of the Tokyo judgment, deserves our further attention.[10]

The Celebici Appeals Chamber, in its judgment of February 1998, holds that it is well established in international conventional and customary law that civilian as well as military superiors may be held "criminally responsible for acts of their subordinates."[11] In regard to the "reason to know" standard, the Appeals Chamber considers three questions: (1) whether a superior has a "duty to know" of the action of his subordinates and whether neglect of that duty gives rise to criminal liability; (2) whether "reason to know" means that the commander had information or that due to neglect of his duty he had no information; (3) whether international law distinguishes between military and civilian commanders in regard to the duty to be informed.

The Appeals Chamber resolves these issues by holding that: (1) The neglect of a duty imposed by national law will not result in a commander's liability under international law. There is no "duty to know" under international customary law.[12] The Appeals Chamber further holds, in flat contradiction of both the Yamashita Case and the IMTFE judgment, that a negligence standard is not recognized as a mental element sufficient to ground conviction under international law for breach of duty.[13] (2) The appropriate test under international law is whether information was available to a commander which would have put him on inquiry notice.[14] (3) International law makes no distinction between military and civilian superiors in regard to a duty to be properly informed of

---

[9] The Celebici Trial Chamber found that the conviction of Hirota was on the principle of command responsibility. Hirota, of course, possessed neither de facto authority or even the slightest power to influence, let alone to control, the actual military perpetrators in Nanjing. As the Appeals Chamber recognized, the Trial Chamber in Celebici was trying to "homogenize" all of the disparate command responsibility cases from WWII so that they could find that there was fundamental agreement in these cases, which, as the Appeals Chamber points out, there quite obviously was not.

[10] It should be understood that the ICTY and ICTR share the same Appeals Chamber, so the Celebici Appeals Judgment is authoritative for both tribunals.

[11] Celebici Appeals Judgment (ICTY IT-96-21-A) paragraph 195; see also paras. 222 and 225 on responsibility predicated upon the acts of the subordinates.

[12] Paragraph 224.

[13] Paragraph 226.

[14] Paragraph 241.

misconduct by subordinates, because international law recognized no such affirmative duty for either category of superior.[15]

In its arguments on appeal the prosecution extensively relied upon the conviction of Mutō and Hirota. The prosecution cited the conviction of Mutō for the proposition, considered by the Musema Trial Chamber, that "substantial influence" is sufficient to establish a superior-subordinate relationship. This position is based on the IMTFE finding that because Mutō could "influence policy" as chief of staff under Yamashita he became liable for the crimes committed by troops under Yamashita's command. The Appeals Chamber, recognizing the vagueness and incoherence of the IMTFE finding against Mutō, responded that the basis of the IMTFE conviction of Muto is not clear, for:

> It is difficult to ascertain from the Judgment in that case whether his conviction on Count 55 for his failure to take adequate steps to ensure the observance of the laws of war reflected his participation in the making of that policy or was linked to his conviction on Count 54, which alleged that he 'ordered, authorized, and permitted' the commission of conventional war crimes. It is possible the conviction on Count 54 led to the conviction on Count 55.[16]

The Appeals Chamber then notes that the conviction of Mutō on this point is directly contrary to the explicit finding in the NMT Hostage Case that a chief of staff is not liable under command responsibility because he holds no command authority. He can only be held liable for his participation in the execution of the crimes in question.[17]

The Appeals Chamber next turns to the prosecution's citation of Hirota for the proposition that his conviction was based upon "powers of persuasion" rather formal authority to "order action to be taken." The Appeals Chamber rejects this standard, and finds that the Trial Chamber was correct in finding that the weight of international customary law did not support it. As seen here, the Celebici Appeals Judgment rejects the mens rea standard of "should have known" applied by the IMTFE as a negligent failure to acquire information.

The Appeals Chamber affirmed this position in the Blaskic Appeals Judgment and the Baglishema Appeals Judgment.[18] While holding that the doctrine of superior responsibility applies to both military and civilian superiors, the established elements of the doctrine as applied by the ICTY in post-Celebici jurisprudence bear little resemblance to the Pacific theater jurisprudence of

---

[15] Paragraph 240. The Statue of the International Criminal Court, Article 28, however, articulates different standards for civilian and military superiors.
[16] Paragraph 259.
[17] Paragraph 260.
[18] Baglishema Appeals Judgment (*Prosecutor v. Ignace Baglishema*, ICTR-95-1A-A) paragraphs 34–35. *Prosecutor v. Tihomir Blaskic*, ICTY IT-95-14-A.

the Tokyo Trial, the Yamashita Case, or the Australian command responsibility cases.[19] In general, the direction of modern jurisprudence on the responsibility of military superiors follows the direction laid out by the High Command and Hostage Cases in the European theater.

In regard to civilian superiors, on the one hand the IMTFE did not actually convict civilian officials under this theory, and on the other hand the grounds on which the convictions were based would scarcely meet the more stringent standards based on the ICTY and ICTR statutes. In general, the ICTY has greatly restricted the importance of the doctrine of superior responsibility as applied to civilian civil authorities and political leaders. The International Criminal Court has gone even further in this direction because its Statute has a much stricter requirement of proof for the prosecution in establishing the mental element against civilian and opposed to military superiors.[20]

Apart from cases that occasionally cite the IMTFE judgment, the later, post-Celebici, jurisprudence of the ICTY makes relatively little reference to the Tokyo judgment, or to WWII cases in general, for two reasons. On the one hand, the tribunal developed its own jurisprudence based upon the authoritative decisions of its own Appeals Chamber, of course shaped in part by the WWII legacy. On the other hand, the doctrine of superior responsibility assumed a secondary role because of the ascendancy of the doctrine of joint criminal enterprise (JCE) as the preferred theory of liability relied upon by the prosecution, particularly at the ICTY (as well as other tribunals in Cambodia and Sierra Leone). Although the prosecution continued to advance both superior responsibility and JCE as alternative theories of liability, the ICTY judgments came to recognize JCE as a form of individual responsibility under Article 7(1) as primary and hence did not also convict on superior responsibility.[21] Where it appeared that an accused did in fact bear superior responsibility for the crimes committed this was taken into account as an aggravating factor in sentencing decisions.[22] At the ICTR on the other hand, superior responsibility continued to play an important role as a central theory of liability, for example in the "Military Case" (Bagesora Case) where leading commanders were prosecuted for their role in the Rwandan genocide.[23] In the lengthy consideration of superior responsibility in the Trial and Appeals Chamber Judgments in that

---

[19] On the Australian cases, see Totani, *Justice in Asia and the Pacific Region, 1945–1952*, chapter 4, and also Fitzpatrick, McCormack, and Morris, eds., *Australia's War Crimes Trials 1945–51*.

[20] ICC Statute Article 28.

[21] The reasoning by which the ICTY cases have refrained from making findings on superior responsibility under Article 7(3) of their Statute when findings have been made on JCE under Article 7(1) of the Statute have most recently been summarized in the Trial Judgment of the Mladic Case (*Prosecutor v. Ratko Mladic* ICTY IT-09-92-T) pp. 2454–5.

[22] Ibid.

[23] *Prosecutor v. Theoneste Bagesora*, ICTR-98-41-T pp. 510–30. See also the Bagesora Appeals Judgment, ICTR-98-41-A pp. 147–82, 221–40.

case, however, one finds no reference to any of the WWII jurisprudence. By the time of the Appeals Chamber Judgment in December 2011 the core elements of superior responsibility no longer required juristic elaboration for which it might have been necessary to consider the IMTFE or other cases. The underlying issue of linking high-level commanders and civilian superiors to mass atrocity crimes, however, remains at the core of the challenge of establishing accountability for such criminal conduct. The legacy of the IMTFE's findings of liability of leaders like Hirota and Tojo for war crimes is represented in the continuing quest for international justice and accountability.

# References

## Archives

Archief Ministerie van Buitenlandse Zaken, Den Haag (ABZ).
Australian War Memorial, Canberra.
Hoover Library & Archives, Stanford University, CA.
Kaikō bunko, Yasukuni Shrine, Tokyo, Japan.
National Archives, Kew, Surrey, Richmond, UK.
National Archives and Records Administration, College Park, MD.
National Archives of Australia, Canberra.
National Archives of the Netherlands, Den Haag (which houses the former Archive B.V.A. Roeling, of the now defunct Polemologisch Instituut Groningen, located under the number 2.21.273).
National Diet Library, Tokyo, Japan.
University of Virginia School of Law Library, VA.

## Online Sources

The Avalon Project: Documents in Law, History and Diplomacy, Yale Law School, Lillian Goldman Law Library http://avalon.law.yale.edu
Bangalore Principle of Judicial Conduct www.un.org/ruleoflaw/blog/document/the-bangalore-principles-of-judicial-conduct
Database of the Tokyo Trials Literature www.tokyotrial.cn
European Court of Human Rights www.echr.coe.int/Pages/home.aspx?p=home
Extraordinary Chambers in the Courts of Cambodia https://eccc.gov.kh/en
Harry S. Truman Library & Museum www.trumanlibrary.org
History of Australian Diplomacy, Department of Foreign Affairs and Trade, Australian Government http://dfat.gov.au/about-us/history-of-australian-diplomacy/Pages/documents-on-australian-foreign-policy.aspx
International Committee of the Red Cross www.icrc.org
International Criminal Court Legal Tools www.icc-cpi.int/en_menus/icc/Pages/defaut/aspx
International Criminal Tribunal for the Former Yugoslavia www.icty.org
The Japan Center for Asian Historical Records, National Archives of Japan www.jacar.go.jp
Military Legal Resources, Library of Congress www.loc.gov/rr/frd/Military_Law/Nuremberg_trials.html

Model Penal Code http://home.heinonline.org/titles/American-Law-Institute-Library/Model-Penal-Code/?letter=M
National Archives of Australia http://naa.gov.au/
National Diet Library www.ndl.go.jp/en/index.html
Office of the Historian, The Department of State, The United States of America https://history.state.gov/historicaldocuments
Organization for Security and Co-operation in Europe www.osce.org/odihr/94214
Special Court for Sierra Leone, Residual Special Court for Sierra Leone http://rscsl.org/
The Tokyo War Crimes Trial, Digital Collection, University of Virginia School of Law Library http://imtfe.law.virginia.edu/
Treaty of Peace with Japan www.taiwandocuments.org/sanfrancisco01.htm
United Nations and the Rule of Law www.un.org/ruleoflaw
United Nations Human Rights Office of the High Commissioner www.ohchr.org/Documents/ProfessionalInterest/ccpr.pdf
United Nations Mechanism for International Criminal Tribunals, Legacy Website of the International Criminal Tribunal for Rwanda http://unictr.unmict.org/
US Supreme Court Center http://supreme.justia.com

## Published Primary Sources – Microfilms

M1668: Records of the Chief Prosecutor Relating to Preparation for and Conduct of Cases Tried at the International Military Tribunal for the Far East, 1946–1948. 18 rolls. College Park, MD: National Archives and Records Administration.

M1727: Records of Trials of Accused Japanese War Criminals Tried at Manila, Philippines, by a Military Commission Convened by the Commanding General of the United States Army in the Western Pacific, 1945–1947. 33 rolls. College Park, MD: National Archives and Records Administration.

T918: Court Papers, Journals, Exhibits, and Judgments of the International Military Tribunal for the Far East. 62 rolls. College Park, MD: National Archives and Records Administration.

## Published Primary Sources – Book Format

*The Department of State Bulletin*. Office of Media Services, Department of State, United States, 1939–89.

*Documents on Australian Foreign Policy, 1937–1949*, 16 Vols. Canberra: Australian Government Publishing Service, 1975–2001.

*Documents on New Zealand External Relations, Vol. II: The Surrender and Occupation of Japan*. New Zealand: P. D. Hasselberg, Government Printer, 1982.

*Documents on the Tokyo International Military Tribunal: Charter, Indictment, and Judgments*. Edited by Neil Boister and Robert Cryer. Oxford University Press, 2008.

*Foreign Relations of the United States*. US Department of State. Washington, DC: US Government Printing Office. https://history.state.gov/historicaldocuments/about-frus

*Kokusai kensatsu kyoku (IPS) jinmon chōsho* [The records of interrogations by the International Prosecution Section (IPS)]. 52 Vols. Edited by Awaya Kentarō and Yoshida Yutaka. Tokyo: Nihon tosho sentā, 1993.

*Kyokutō kokusai gunji saiban kiroku mokuroku* [The catalog of the record of the International Military Tribunal for the Far East]. 3 Vols. Edited by Tōkyō daigaku shakai kagaku kenkyūjo [The Institute of Social Science, the University of Tokyo]. Tokyo: Tōkyō daigaku shakai kagaku kenkyūjo "Nihon kindaika" kenkyū soshiki, 1971–3.

*Kyokutō kokusai gunji saiban kiroku: Mokuroku oyobi sakuin* [The record of the International Military Tribunal for the Far East: The catalog and index]. Edited by Asahi shinbunsha chōsa kenkyūshitsu [The Asahi Newspaper investigation and research room]. Tokyo: Asahi shinbun chōsa kenkyū shitsu, 1953.

*Kyokutō kokusai gunji saiban sokkiroki* [Transcripts of court proceedings of the International Military Tribunal for the Far East]. 10 Vols. Tokyo: Yūshōdō shoten, 1968.

*The Law of War: A Documentary History.* 2 Vols. Edited by Leon Friedman with a Foreword by Telford Taylor. New York: Random House, 1972.

*Shinbun shiryō ni miru Tōkyō saiban, BC-kyū saiban* [The Tokyo Trial and Class BC trials seen in newspaper sources]. 2 Vols. Edited by Nagai Hitoshi and Utsumi Aiko. Tokyo: Gendai shiryō shuppan, 2000.

*Shiryō Nihon senryō: 1. Tennōsei* [Sources on the occupation of Japan: 1. The emperor system]. Edited by Yamagiwa Akira, Nakamura Masanori, and Okada Ryōnosuke. Tokyo: Ōtsuki shoten, 1990.

*Sūmitsuin kaigi gijiroku* [Records of the Proceedings of the Privy Council Meetings], 96 Vols. Tōkyō daigaku shuppankai, 1984–96.

*The Thailand-Burma Railway, 1942–1946: Documents and Selected Writings.* 6 Vols. Edited by Paul H. Kratoska. London, New York: Routledge, 2006.

*The Tokyo Judgment: The International Military Tribunal for the Far East (I.M.T.F.E.), 29 April 1946–12 November 1948.* Edited by V. B. A. Röling and C. F. Rüter. Amsterdam: APA-University Press, 1977.

*Tōkyō saiban e no michi: Kokusai kensatsu-kyoku, seisaku kettei kankei bunsho* [The road to the Tokyo Trial: Records relative to the International Prosecution Section's policy making]. 5 Vols. Edited by Awaya Kentarō, Nagai Hitoshi, and Toyoda Masayuki. Tokyo: Gendai shiryō shuppan, 1999.

*Tōkyō saiban hanketsu: Kyokutō kokusai gunji saibansho hanketsubun* [The judgment at the Tokyo Trial: The decision by the International Military Tribunal for the Far East]. Tokyo: Mainichi shinbun, 1949.

*Tōkyō saiban shiryō: Kido Kōichi jinmon chōsho* [Sources of the Tokyo Trial: The records of Kido Kōichi's interrogation]. Edited by Awaya Kentarō, Adachi Hiroaki, and Kobayshi Motohiro. Translated by Okada Nobuhiro. Tokyo: Ōtsuki shoten, 1987.

*Tōkyō saiban shiryō: Tanaka Ryūkichi jinmon chōsho* [Sources of the Tokyo Trial: The records of Tanaka Ryūkichi's interrogation]. Edited by Awaya Kentarō, Ikō Toshiya, Okada Nobuhiro, and Otabe Yūji. Translated by Okada Ryōnosuke. Tokyo: Ōtsuki shoten, 1994.

*Tōkyō saiban to kokusai kensatsu kyoku: Kaitei kara hanketsu made* [The Tokyo Trial and the International Prosecution Section: From the opening of the court to the judgment]. 5 vols. Edited by Awaya Kentarō, Herbert Bix, and Toyoda Masayuki. Tokyo: Gendai shiryō shuppan, 2000.

*The Tokyo War Crimes Trial.* 22 Vols. Annotated, compiled, and edited by R. John Pritchard and Sonia Magbanua Zaide. New York and London: Garland, 1981.

*The Tokyo War Crimes Trial: The Comprehensive Index and Guide to the Proceedings of the International Military Tribunal for the Far East in Five Volumes.* 5 Vols.

Annotated, compiled, and edited by R. John Pritchard, Sonia Magbanua Zaide, and Donald Cameron Watt. New York and London: Garland, 1981–7.

*Trial of the Major War Criminals before the International Military Tribunal: Nuremberg, 14 November 1945–1 October 1946*. 42 Vols. Nuremberg, Germany, 1947–9. *Trial of Sumida Haruzo and Twenty Others (The "Double Tenth" Trial)*, War Crimes Trials Series, Vol. 8. Edited by Colin Sleeman and S. C. Silkin. London: William Hodge, 1951.

*Trials of War Criminals Before the Nuernberg Military Tribunals Under Control Council Law No. 10, October 1946–April 1949*. 15 Vols. Washington, DC: US Government Printing Office, 1949–53.

## Secondary Literature

Ajia minshū hōtei junbikai [The association for the preparation of the Asian people's trial], ed. *Toinaosu Tōkyō saiban* [Questioning the Tokyo Trial afresh]. Tokyo: Ryokufū shuppan, 1995.

Asahi shinbun hōtei kishadan [The Asahi Newspaper court reporters], ed. *Tōkyō saiban* [The Tokyo Trial]. 3 Vols. Tokyo: Tōkyō saiban kankō kai, 1962.

Awaya Kentarō. *Tōkyō saiban ron* [A treatise on the Tokyo Trial]. Tokyo: Ōtsuki shoten, 1989.

*Tōkyō saiban e no michi* [The road to the Tokyo Trial]. 2 Vols. Tokyo: Kōdansha, 2006.

*Tōkyō saiban e no michi* [The road to the Tokyo Trial]. Tokyo: Kōdansha, 2013.

Beevor, Antony. *Stalingrad: The Fateful Siege: 1942–1943*. New York: Viking, 1998.

*The Fall of Berlin, 1945*. New York: Viking, 2002.

Bergerud, Eric. *Touched with Fire: The Land War in the South Pacific*. New York: Penguin Books, 1996.

Blakeslee, George Hubbard. *The Far Eastern Commission: A Study in International Cooperation: 1945 to 1952*. Washington, DC: Department of State, 1953.

Bōeichō bōei kensyūjo sensishitsu (Military History Room, Defense Research Institute, Defense Agency), ed. *Senshi sōsho* [The war history series]. 102 Vols. Tokyo: Asagumo shinbunsha, 1966–80.

Boister, Neil, and Robert Cryer. *The Tokyo International Military Tribunal: A Reappraisal*. Oxford University Press, 2008.

Brackman, Arnold C. *The Other Nuremberg: The Untold Story of the Tokyo War Crimes Trials*. New York: William Morrow and Company, 1987.

Brook, Timothy. "The Tokyo Judgment and the Rape of Nanking." *The Journal of Asian Studies*, Vol. 60, No. 3 (August 2001): 673–700.

Chadani Seiichi. *Shōwa senzenki no kyūchū seiryoku to seiji* [The power of the court's inner circle and politics in the prewar Shōwa period]. Tokyo: Yoshikawa kōbunkan, 2009.

Cheah, Wui Ling. "Post-World War II British 'Hell-Ship' Trials in Singapore: Omissions and the Attribution of Responsibility." *Journal of International Criminal Justice*, Vol. 8 (2010): 1035–58.

Cohen, David. "Beyond Nuremberg: Individual Responsibility for War Crimes." In *Human Rights in Political Transitions: Gettysburg to Bosnia*. Edited by Carla Hesse and Robert Post. New York: Zone Books, 1999, pp. 53–92.

"Military Justice from WWII to Guantanamo: Fair Trials, Judicial Murder, and International Standards in WWII War Crimes Trials in Asia." In *Summa Dieter Simon zum 70. Gebeurtstag*. Edited by Rainer Maria Kiesow, Regina Ogorek, and Spiros Simitis. Frankfurt am Main: Vittorio Klostermann, 2005, pp. 59–80.

"The Singapore War Crimes Trials and Their Relevance Today." *Singapore Law Review*, Vol. 31 (2013): 1–38.

"The Historiography of the Historical Foundations of Theories of Responsibility in International Criminal Law." In *Historical Origins of International Criminal Law*, Vol. 1. Edited by Morten Bergsmo, Cheah Wui Ling, and Yi Ping. New York: Torkel Opsahl Academic EPublisher, 2014, pp. 23–83.

Cryer, Robert. "Roeling in Tokyo: A Dignified Dissenter." *Journal of International Criminal Justice*, Vol. 8 (2010): 1109–26.

Dandō Shigemitsu. "Sensō hanzai no rironteki kaibō" [The theoretical anatomy of war crimes]. In *Keihō no kindaiteki tenkai*. [The modern development of criminal law]. Edited by Shigemitsu Dandō. Tokyo: Kōbundō, 1948, pp. 159–84.

Esmein, Jean. "Le juge Henri Bernard au procès de Tôkyô." *Vingtième Siècle. Revue d'histoire Année*, Vol. 59 (1998): 3–14.

Fitzpatrick, Georgina, Tim McCormack, and Narrelle Morris, eds. *Australia's War Crimes Trials 1945–51*. Leiden: Brill Nijhoff, 2016.

Frank, Richard. *Downfall: The End of Imperial Japanese Empire*. New York: Penguin Books, 1999.

Fujita Hisakazu. "Tōkyō saiban no konnichiteki imi" [The present-day significance of the Tokyo Trial]. *Hōritsu jihō* [Law reports] Vol. 61, No. 9 (1989): 24–30.

*Sensō hanzai to wa nani ka* [What is a war crime?]. Tokyo: Iwanami shoten, 1995.

*Kokusai jindō hō* [International Humanitarian Law]. Tokyo: Yūshindō kōbunsha, 2000.

Furuya Hisatsuna. *Système représentatif au Japon*. Bruxelles: H. Lamertin, 1899.

Futamura, Madoka. *War Crimes Tribunals and Transitional Justice: The Tokyo Trial and the Nuremberg Legacy*. London; New York: Routledge, 2008.

Harris, Sheldon H. *Factories of Death: Japanese Biological Warfare 1932–45 and the American Cover-up*. London; New York: Routledge, 1994.

Harries, Meirion, and Susie Harries. *Sheathing the Sword: The Demilitarization of Postwar Japan*. New York: Macmillan, 1987.

Hayashi Hirofumi. *Sabakareta sensō hanzai: Igirisu no tai-Nichi senpan saiban* [War crimes tried: The British war crimes trials against the Japanese]. Tokyo: Iwanami shoten, 1998. https://apjjf.org/-Hayashi-Hirofumi/3187/article.html

"The Battle of Singapore, the Massacre of Chinese and Understanding of the Issue in Postwar Japan." *The Asia-Pacific Journal*, Vol. 7, Issue 28, No. 4 (July 13, 2009): 1–20.

*Shingapōru kakyō shukusei: Nihongun wa Shingapōru de nani o shitanoka* [The purge of Chinese in Singapore: What did the Japanese military do in Singapore?]. Tokyo: Kōbunken, 2007.

Higurashi Yoshinobu. "Kyokutō kokusai gunji saibansho kōseikoku no jōken: Indo saibankan ninmei mondai o megutte" [The conditions for becoming a member of the International Military Tribunal for the Far East: Concerning the appointment of the Indian judge]. *Kokusai seiji*, No. 95 (October 1990): 151–66.

"Paru hanketsu saikō: Tōkyō saiban ni okeru bekko iken no kokusai kankyō" [Rethinking Pal's Judgment: The international environment surrounding the separate opinion at the Tokyo Trial]. In *Nihon kindaishi no saikō⁻chiku* [Reconstruction of modern

Japanese history]. Edited by Itō Takashi. Tokyo: Yamakawa shuppansha, 1993, pp. 384–411.

*Tōkyō saiban no kokusai kankei: kokusai seiji ni okeru kenryoku to kihan* [International relations of the Tokyo Trial: power and norm in international politics]. Tokyo: Bokutakusha, 2002.

*Tōkyō saiban* [The Tokyo Trial]. Tokyo: Kōdansha, 2008.

Hilberg, Raul. *The Destruction of the European Jews*, Student Edition. New York: Holmes & Meier, 1985.

Honjō Shigeru. *Honjō nikki* [The Honjō diary]. Tokyo: Hara shobō, 1967.

Horiba Kazuo. *Shina jihen sensō shido shi* [The history of the directing of the war during the China Incident]. Tokyo: Jiji tsūshinsha, 1962.

Horwitz, Solis. "The Tokyo Trial." *International Conciliation*, No. 465 (November 1950): 473–584.

Hosoya Chihiro, Andō Nisuke, and Ōnuma Yasuaki. *Kokusai shinpojiumu: Tōkyō saiban o tou* [An International Symposium: Questioning the Tokyo Trial]. Tokyo: Kōdansha, 1984.

*The Tokyo War Crimes Trial: An International Symposium*. Tokyo: Kodansha, 1986.

Irie Keishirō. "Tōkyō hanketsu no yōryō to sono shōkai" [A summary and explanation of the Tokyo Judgment]. *Hōritsu jihō* [Law reports], Vol. 21, No. 2 (1949): 29–45, 12.

Ishii Itarō. *Gaikōkan no isshō: tai-Chūgoku gaikō no kaisō* [The life of a diplomat: Reminiscences of diplomacy with China]. Tokyo: Taihei shuppansha, 1972.

*Ishi Itarō nikki* [The diary of Ishii Itarō]. Tokyo: Chūō kōronsha, 1993.

Itō, Hirobumi. *Commentaries on the Constitution of the Empire*. Translated by Miyoji Itō. Tokyo: Igirisu-hōritsu gakkō, 1889.

Jackson, Robert H. *Report of Robert H. Jackson United States Representative to the International Conference on Military Trials*. Department of State Publication, 3080. Washington, DC: U.S. Government Printing Office, February 1949.

Jescheck, Hans-Heinrich. *Die Verantwortlichkeit der Staatsorgane nach Voelkerstrafrecht: Eine Studie zu der Nuernberger Prozessen*. Bonn: Roehrscheid, 1952.

"The General Principles of International Law as Set Out in Nuremberg, as mirrored in the ICC Statute." *Journal of International Criminal Justice* (2004) 2: 38–55.

Joerges, Christian, and Navraj Singh Ghaleigh, eds. *Darker Legacies of Law in Europe: The Shadow of National Socialism and Fascism Over Europe and Its Legal Traditions*. Oxford; Portland, OR: Hart, 2003.

Kainō Michitaka. "Sensō saiban no hōritsu riron" [Legal theory of a war trial]. *Rekishi hyōron*, Vol. 3, No. 6 (1948): 13–24.

"Kyokutō saiban" [The Far Eastern Trial]. In *Nihon shihonshugi kōza 1* [Lectures on Japanese capitalism, Vol. 1]. Edited by Michitaka Kainō. Tokyo: Iwanami shoten, 1953, pp. 385–96.

"Kyokutō saiban: sono go" [The Far Eastern Trial: Afterwards]. In *Kainō Michitaka chosakushū 3. saiban* [Kainō Michitaka's writings, Vol. 3. trials]. Edited and annotated by Shiomi Toshitaka. Tokyo: Nihon hyōronsha, 1977, pp. 275–84.

"Hōtei gijutsu" [Court techniques]. In *Kainō Michitaka chosakushū 3. saiban* [Kainō Michitaka's writings, Vol. 3. trials]. Edited and annotated by Shiomi Toshitaka. Tokyo: Nihon hyōronsha, 1977, pp. 3–116.

Kajii Sumihiro. "Tōkyō saiban ni okeru 'BC-kyū hanzai' tsuikyū" [The pursuit of Class BC war crimes at the Tokyo Trial]. *Ritsumeikan hōgaku gakusei ronshū (bessatsu)* [The compilation of law students' essays at Ritsumeikan University (the extra issue)], No. 42 (1996): 492–531.

Kido Kōichi. *Heiwa e no doryoku: Kido Kōichi nikki, Tōkyō saibanki* [The Kido Kōichi diary, The record of the Tokyo Trial]. Tokyo: Tōkyō daigaku shuppankai, 1980.

Konoe Fumimaro. *Heiwa e no doryoku: Konoe Fumimaro shuki* [An endeavor toward peace: A personal record of Konoe Fumimaro]. Tokyo: Nihon denpō tūshinsha, 1946.

Kopelman, Elizabeth. "Ideology and International Law: The Dissent of the Indian Justice at the Tokyo War Crimes Trial." *New York University International Law and Politics*, Vol. 23, No. 2 (Winter 1991): 373–444.

Lebra, Joyce C. *Jungle Alliance: Japan and the Indian National Army.* Singapore: Donald Moore for Asia Pacific Press, 1971.

Linton, Suzannah, ed. *Hong Kong's War Crimes Trials.* Oxford: Oxford University Press, 2013.

Lord Wright. "War Crimes and International Law." *International Law Review*, Vol. 62, No. 1 (January 1946): 40–52.

Maga, Tim. *Judgment at Tokyo: The Japanese War Crimes Trials.* Lexington, KY: University Press of Kentucky, 2001.

Matsumoto Naotoshi, ed. *Tōkyō saiban shinri yōmoku* [The summary of proceedings at the Tokyo Trial]. Tokyo: Yūshōdō shuppan, 2010.

Minear, Richard H. *Victor's Justice: The Tokyo War Crimes Trial.* Princeton, NJ: Princeton University Press, 1971. Reprinted in 2001.

Morimura Seiichi. *Akuma no hōshoku: "Kantōgun saikin butai"* [Devil's Gluttony: "The bacteriological unit of the Kwantung Army"]. Tokyo: Kobunsha, 1981.

Mouralis, Guillaume. "The Rejection of International Criminal Law in Germany after the Second World War." In *History, Memory and Politics in Central and Eastern Europe: Memory Games*. Edited by Georges Mink and Laure Neumayer. London: Palgrave MacMillan, 2013, pp. 226–41.

Nagai Hitoshi, ed. *Sensō hanzai chōsa shiryō: furyo chōsa chūō iinkai chōsa hōkokusho tsuzuri* [Sources on war crimes investigations: The compilation of investigation reports by the central committee for investigations concerning prisoners of war]. Tokyo: Higashi shuppan, 1995.

*Firipin to tai-Nichi senpan saiban, 1945–1953* [The Philippines and war crimes trials against the Japanese, 1945–1953]. Tokyo: Iwanami shoten, 2010.

"Wasurerareta Tōkyō saiban Firipin hanji: Derufin Haranīrya hanji no shōgai" [The forgotten Philippine justice at the Tokyo Trial: The life of Delfin Jaranilla]. In *Kingendai Nihon no sensō to heiwa* [War and peace in modern Japan]. Edited by Awaya Kentarō. Tokyo: Gendai shiryō shuppan, 2011, pp. 303–66.

Nakajima Takeshi. "The Tokyo Tribunal, Justice Pal and the Revisionist Distortion of History." *The Asia-Pacific Journal Japan*, Vol. 9, Issue 33, No. 3 (October 2011): 1–20.

Nakano, Tomio. *The Ordinance Power of the Japanese Emperor.* Baltimore, MD: Johns Hopkins Press, 1923.

Nakazato, Nariaki. *Neonationalist Mythology in Postwar Japan: Pal's Dissenting Judgment at the Tokyo War Crimes Tribunal.* Lanham, Boulder, New York, and London: Lexington Books, 2016.

Nandy, Ashis. "The Other Within: The Strange Case of Radhabinod Pal's Judgment on Culpability." *New Literary History*, Vol. 23, No. 1 (Winter 1992): 45–67.
Nichigai Associates, ed. *Taiheiyō sensō tosho mokuroku 1945–1994* [The Pacific War books, 1945–1994: A catalog]. Tokyo: Kinokuniya shoten, 1995.
  ed. *Taiheiyō sensō tosho mokuroku: 1995–2004* [The Pacific War books, 1995–2005: A catalog]. Tokyo: Kinokuniya shoten, 2005.
  ed. *Taiheiyō sensō tosho mokuroku: 2005–2015* [The Pacific War books, 2005–2015: A catalog]. Tokyo: Kinokuniya shoten, 2016.
Okinawa taimusu sha [The Okinawan Times], ed. Tetsu no bōfū [The iron storm]. Tokyo: Asahi shinbunsha, 1950.
Okuhara Toshio. "Tōkyō saiban ni okeru kyōdō bōgi riron" [The theory of conspiracy at the Tokyo Trial]. 3 installments. *Kokushikan daigaku seikei ronsō* [Kokushikan University, political economy debate series], no. 5 (September 1966), 155–92; no. 7 (January 1968), 387–413; and no. 12 (June 1970), 181–204.
Ōnuma Yasuaki. *Sensō sekinin josetsu: "heiwa ni taisuru tsumi" no keisei katei ni okeru ideologī-sei to kōsoku-sei* [The introduction to war responsibility: Ideological features and constraints in the formation of "crimes against peace"]. Tokyo: Tōkyō daigaku shuppankai, 1975.
  *Tōkyō saiban kara sengo sekinin no shisō e: zōhoban* [From the Tokyo Trial to the concept of postwar responsibility, expanded edition]. Tokyo: Tōshindō, 1987.
Ōoka Yūichirō. *Tōkyō saiban: Furansujin hanji no muzairon* [The Tokyo Trial: The not-guilty thesis by the French justice]. Tokyo: Bungei shunjū, 2012.
Oppenheim, L. *International Law: A Treatise*. 6th edn. 2 Vols. Edited by H. Lauterpacht. London, New York, and Toronto: Longmans, Green and Co., 1940.
  *International Law: A Treatise*. 7th edn. 2 Vols. Edited by H. Lauterpacht. London, New York, and Toronto: Longmans, Green and Co., 1951.
Osten, Philipp. "Tōkyō saiban ni okeru hanzai kōsei yōken no saihō: shoki kokusai keihōshi no ichi danmen no sobyō" [Revisiting the elements of crimes at the Tokyo Trial: Sketches of an aspect in the early phase of the history of international criminal law]. *Hōgaku kenkyū: hōritsu, seiji, shakai* [Journal of law, politics, and sociology], Vol. 82, No. 1 (January 2009): 315–38.
Overy, Richard. *The Bombers and the Bombs: Allied Air War Over Europe, 1940–1945*. New York: Viking Penguin, 2013.
Ozaki, Yukio. *The Voice of Japanese Democracy: Being an Essay on Constitutional Loyalty*. Translated by J. E. De Becker. Yokohama: Kelly and Walsh, 1918.
Pal, Radhabinod. *Zen'yaku, Nihon muzairon: Kyokutō kokusai gunji saiban Indo daihyō hanji R. Pāru jutsu* [The complete translation: The Japan-Is-Not Guilty view: Written by Justice R. Pal, the Indian member of the International Military Tribunal for the Far East]. Tokyo: Nihon shobō, 1952.
Powell, John. "Japan's Germ Warfare: The U.S. Cover-Up of a War Crimes." *Bulletin of Concerned Asian Scholars*, Vol. 12, No. 4 (October–December 1980): 2–17.
  "A Hidden Chapter in History." *Bulletin of the Atomic Scientists*, Vol. 37, No. 8 (October 1981): 44–53.
Radbruch, Gustav. *Rechtsphilosophie*. 4th edn. Stuttgart: Koehler, 1950.
Radbruch, G. "Fuenf Minuten Rechtsphilosophie." In Gesamtausgabe Radbruch. Edited by Arthur Kaufmann, Vol. 3. 1990, pp. 78–82.

Reel, A. Frank. *The Case of General Yamashita*. Chicago, IL: University of Chicago Press, 1949.

Röling, B. V. A., and Antonio Cassese. *The Tokyo Trial and Beyond: Reflections of a Peacemonger*. Cambridge, UK: Polity Press, 1993.

Russell, Edward F. L. *The Knights of Bushido: A Short History of Japanese War Crimes*. London: Cassell, 1958.

Ryan, Allan A. *Yamashita's Ghost: War Crimes, MacArthur's Justice, and Command Accountability*. Lawrence, KS: University of Kansas Press, 2012.

Satō Kenryō. *Tōjō Hideki to Taiheiyō sensō* [Tōjō Hideki and the Pacific War]. Tokyo: Bungei shunjū shinsha, 1960.

Sellars, Kirsten. "The Legacy of the Tokyo Dissents on 'Crimes against Peace'." In *The Crime of Aggression: A Commentary*. Edited by Claus Kress and Stefan Barriga. Cambridge, UK: Cambridge University Press, 2016.

Shigemitsu Mamoru. *Sugamo nikki* [The Sugamo diary]. Tokyo: Bungei shunjū, 1953.

Sissons, D. C. S. "Australian War Crimes Trials and Investigations (1942–1951)." Available at the University of California–Berkeley War Crimes Studies Center website. www.ocf.berkeley.edu/~changmin/documents/Sissons%20Final%20War%20Crimes%20Text%2018-3-06.pdf

Sugawara Yutaka. *Tōkyō saiban no shōtai* [The true character of the Tokyo Trial]. Tokyo: Jiji tsūshinsha, 1961.

Sumitani Takeshi. "Sensō hanzai saiban ron, sensō seknin ron no dōkō: Bunken shōkai o chūshin ni" [Trends in the debates on war crimes trials and war responsibility: Centering on the introduction of historical literature]. *Shisō* [Idea] No. 719 (May 1984): 123–31.

Sumitani Takeshi, Utsumi Aiko, and Akazawa Shirō. "Tōkyō saiban, BC-kyū sensō hanzai, sensō sekinin kankei shuyō bunken mokuroku" [The bibliographic catalog to major literature on the Tokyo Trial, Class BC war crimes, war responsibility]. *Shisō* [Idea] No. 719 (May 1984): appendix (28 pages).

Takeda Kiyoko. *Tennō kan no sōkoku: 1945-nen zengo* [Competing views concerning the emperor: Around the year 1945]. Tokyo: Iwanami shoten, 1978.

*The Dual-Image of the Japanese Emperor*. New York: New York University Press, 1988.

Takeda, Kayoko. *Interpreting the Tokyo War Crimes Tribunal: A Sociopolitical Analysis*. Ottawa: University of Ottawa Press, 2010.

Tanaka Masaaki, ed. *Pāru hakase jutsu, shinri no sabaki, Nihon muzai ron* [The judgment of truth, as told by Dr. Pal: The Japan-Is-Not Guilty view]. Tokyo: Taiheiyō shuppansha, 1952.

*Pāru hakase no Nihon muzai ron* [Japan Is Not Guilty: The view propounded by Dr. Pal]. Kanagawa: Keibunsha, 1963, reprinted in 1992. Also available in a new edition by Shōgakukan, 2001.

Tanaka, Yuki, Timothy L. H. McCormack, and Gerry Simpson, eds. *The Tokyo War Crimes Trial Revisited*. International Humanitarian Law Series. Leiden, The Netherlands: Martinus Nijhoff, 2010.

Taylor, Telford. *The Anatomy of the Nuremberg Trials: A Personal Memoir*. New York: Alfred A. Knopf, 1992.

Terasaki Hidenari. *Shōwa tennō dokuhakuroku: Terasaki Hidenari goyōgakari nikki* [Emperor Showa's monologue: The diary of an imperial assistant, Terasaki Hidenari]. Tokyo: Bungei shunjū, 1991.

Tōkyō saiban kenkyūkai [The Tokyo Trial research group], ed. *Kyōdō kenkyū: Paru hanketsusho* [Collaborative research on Pal's Judgment]. Tokyo: Tōkyō saiban kankōkai, 1966. Reprint in 2 Vols. Tokyo: Kōdansha gakujutsu bunko, 1984.

Totani, Yuma. *The Tokyo War Crimes Trial: The Pursuit of Justice in the Wake of World War II*. Cambridge, MA: Harvard University Asia Center, 2008.

*Justice in Asia and the Pacific Region, 1945–1952: Allied War Crimes Prosecutions*. New York: Cambridge University Press, 2015.

"Zhanfan shenpan yanjiu de lishi yiyi: Cong Dongjing shenpan dao geguo shenpan de yanshen" [The historical significance of the studies of war crimes trials: From the Tokyo Trial to the national trials]. Translated by Chen Aiguo. ed. Center for the Tokyo Trial Studies. In *Donjing shenpan zai taolun* [The restudy of the Tokyo Trial]. Shanghai: Shanghai jiaotong daxue chubanshe, 2016, pp. 30–63.

Uchida Rikizō. "Kyokutō saiban no hōrironteki igi: Shu to shite Eibei hōgaku no tachiba kara" [The significance of the Far Eastern Trial in legal theory: Primarily from the viewpoint of the field of Anglo-American Law]. *Chōryū* [Current]. Vol. 3, No. 8 (September 1948): 22–30.

Udagawa Kōta. "Tōkyō saiban to Nihon kaigun: shinri katei to bengogawa no saiban taisaku ni chakumoku shite" [The Tokyo Trial and the Imperial Japanese Navy: Focusing on the court proceedings and the defense policy on the trial]. *Nihonshi kenkyū* [Studies of Japanese history], No. 609 (May 2013): 1–25.

United Nations War Crimes Commission, comp. *History of the United Nations War Crimes Commission and the Development of the Laws of War*. London: His Majesty's Stationery Office, 1948.

ed. *Law Reports of Trials of War Criminals*. 15 Vols. London: His Majesty's Stationery Office, 1947–9.

Ushimura, Kei. "Pal's 'Dissentient Judgment' Reconsidered: Some Notes on Postwar Japan's Responses to the Opinion." *Japan Review*, Vol. 19 (2007): 215–23.

Van der Wilt, Harmen. "A Valiant Champion of Equity and Humaneness: The Legacy of Bert Röling for International Criminal Law." *Journal of International Criminal Justice*, Vol. 8, No. 4 (September 2010): 1127–40.

Van Poelgeest, L. *Tōkyō saiban to Oranda* [The Tokyo Trial and the Netherlands]. Translated by Mizushima Jirō and Tsukahara Tōgo. Annotated by Awaya Kentarō. Tokyo: Misuzu shobō, 1997.

*Nederland en het Tribunaal van Tokio: Volkenrechtelijke polemiek en internationale politiek rond de berechting en gratiëring van de Japanse oorlogsmisdadigers*. Arnhem: Gouda Quint, 1989.

Welch, Jeanie M., ed. *The Tokyo Trial: A Bibliographic Guide to English-Language Sources*. Westport, CT: Greenwood Press, 2002.

Werrell, Kenneth P. *Blankets of Fire*. Washington, DC: Smithsonian Institution Press, 1996.

Yamada Akira. *Gunbi kakuchō no kindaishi: Nihongun no bōchō to hōkai* [The modern history of armament: expansion and dissolution of the Japanese Army]. Tokyo: Yoshikawa kōbunkan, 1997.

*Shōwa tennō no gunji shisō to senryaku* [The military thought and strategy of Emperor Shōwa]. Tokyo: Azekura shobō, 2002.

*Rikugun Noborito kenkyūjo: Inpeisareta bōryaku himitsu heiki kaihatsu* [The Noborito Army Research Institute: Cover-up of the development of conspiratorial secrete weapons]. Tokyo: Aoki shoten, 2003.

Yokota Kisaburō. *Sensō hanzai ron* [A treatise on war crimes]. Tokyo: Yūhikaku, 1947; expanded edition, 1949.

"Sekai no shinpan: jiei ron o funsai" [The verdict of the world; The doctrine of self-defense destroyed]. Published in *Mainichi shinbun* [Mainichi newspaper] on 13 November 1948. Reproduced in *Shinbun shiryō ni miru Tōkyō saiban, BC-kyū saiban 1: Tōkyō saiban* [The Tokyo Trial and Class BC trials seen in newspaper sources, Vol. 1: The Tokyo Trial]. Edited by Nagai Hitoshi and Utsumi Aiko. Tokyo: Gendai shiryō shuppan, 2000, p. 346.

"Tōkyō hanketsu to jiei ron" [The Tokyo Judgment and the doctrine of self-defense]. *Hroītsu jihō*, Vol. 21, No. 2 (1949): 5–12.

Yoshida Yutaka. *Shōwa tennō no shūsenshi* [Emperor Shōwa's history in the termination of the war]. Tokyo: Iwanami shoten, 1992.

"Haisen go ni okeru kōbunsho no shōkyaku to intoku" [The burning and concealment of government records at the time of defeat]. In *Gendai rekishigaku to sensō sekinin* [Studies of modern history and the issues of responsibility for the war]. Edited by Yoshida Yutaka. Tokyo: Aoki shoten, 1997, pp. 127–41.

"Gunji kankei shiryō no sengoshi: jōhō kōkai hō no shikō to Nihon kindaishi kenkyū" [The postwar history of military-related historical records: The implementation of the Freedom of Information Act and the research of the modern Japanese history]. In *Ākaibuzu no kagaku: 1. kiroku shiryō to bunsho kan* [The archival science. Vol. 1. Historical documents and records offices]. Edited by Kokubungaku kenkyū shiryōkan shiryōkan [The national literature research archives and the historical records offices]. Tokyo: Kashiwa shobō, 2003, pp. 262–75.

Yoshimi Yoshiaki. *Jūgun ianfu* [Military comfort women]. Tokyo: Iwanami shoten, 1995.

*Comfort Women: Sexual Slavery in the Japanese Military during World War II*. Translated by Suzanne O'Brien. New York: Columbia University Press, 2000.

"Sensō no kioku, sensō no kiroku: 'jūgun ianfu' kankei kiroku no mondai o rei to shite" [War memory and war records: In the case of the issues on the records relating to "military comfort women]. In *Ākaibuzu no kagaku: 1. kiroku shiryō to bunsho kan* [The archival science. Vol. 1. Historical documents and records offices]. Edited by Kokubungaku kenkyū shiryōkan shiryōkan [The national literature research archives and the historical records offices] Tokyo: Kashiwa shobō, 2003, pp. 276–96.

Yui Masaomi, ed. *Sūmitsuin no kenkyū* [Studies of the Privy Council]. Tokyo: Yoshikawa kōbunkan, 2003.

# Index

abduction of women, 18, 214
Abe Genki, 186
Act of State doctrine, 15, 90, 98, 314, 315, 441, 442, 489, 500–501, 501
admissibility, 54, 55, 56, 67
affidavit evidence, 57–58
aggressive war. *See* crimes against peace
Akayesu Case, 516–17
Allied Council for Japan, 42
Andaman and Nicobar Islands, 206, 358, 467
Anti-Comintern Pact, 31, 83, 121
Araki Sadao, 158, 284–85, 389, 424
Arimura Tsunemichi, 491
Arita Hachirō, 281, 282
Atlee, Clement, 36
atom bombing, 434, 447–49, 456–57, 469, 470, 478–79, 480, 493, 494, 495, 499, 501, 502–5
Australia
  on the Japanese Emperor, 36, 42, 140, 379, 401, 512
  war crimes investigations by, 49, 306, 375
Awaya Kentarō, 18, 19
Ayabe Kijutsu, 241, 384

B-29, 31–32, 33
Baba Eiichi, 281, 282
bacteriological weapons, 202
Bagesora Case, 520
Baglishema Case, 519
bandits, 156, 157
Bangalore Principles of Judicial Conduct, 79
Banka Island, 206, 216
Basic Principle of National Policy, 161, 163–66, 175, 178, 179, 423
Bataan Death Marches, 216, 221, 480, 491, 494, 500, 509
Batavia, 65
Bates, Miner S., 212
Bauman, Zygmunt, 373

Beiping, 161, 162, 167, 168, 169, 212
Berendson, Sir Carl, 43
Berlin, 31, 331, 383
Bernard Opinion, 391–430, 403, 431, 466, 495. *See also* Bernard, Henri
Bernard, Henri, 44, 51, 142, 287, 354, 433, 435, 438, 439, 443, 507
Blaskic Case, 519
Boister, Neil, 2, 5, 21, 22, 255
Borneo, 63, 206, 238, 239, 356, 358, 467
Boshin War, 106
Bosnia, 372, 373
Boxer Protocol, 162
Brabner-Smith, John W., 76, 77, 78
Brackman, Arnold, 1, 435
Bulgaria, 476, 477
burden of proof, 7, 13, 19, 24, 197, 202, 204, 207, 231, 250, 257, 303, 321, 327, 359, 361, 362, 373, 388, 396, 461, 512
Burma, 206, 238, 239, 240, 361, 386, 466, 489
Burma-Siam Death Railway, 204, 216, 219, 350, 351, 360, 374, 386, 475, 489, 491, 493–94

cabinet responsibility, 13–14, 199, 200, 204, 209, 212–13, 224, 230–31, 245, 247, 248–50, 250–52, 320, 340, 341–48, 350, 351, 365–69, 371, 379–80, 379–80, 381–83, 383, 385, 388, 389, 417, 429, 461, 475, 480, 486, 490, 492, 515
Cairo Declaration, 29–30, 33, 86, 412
Cambodia, 57, 373, 513, 520. *See also* Extraordinary Chambers in the Courts of Cambodia
Celebici Case, 518, 517–19, 519, 520

535

Changsha, 472
Charter of the United Nations, 157
Chiang Kai-shek, 125, 169, 173, 180, 183, 185, 326, 327, 336, 423, 425, 428
Chifley, J. B., 36
China Incident, 171, 172, 173, 183, 215, 234, 328, 332
China, Republic of. *See* Chiang Kai-shek
Ching-Dohihara Agreement, 162
Chisholm, James, 217
Churchill, Winston, 36, 412
Class A, 38, 40, 42, 48, 53, 65, 66, 69, 399
comfort women, 233, 354
command responsibility, 189, 198, 234, 255, 343, 345, 347, 358, 514, 515, 516, 517, 518, 519, 520
*Commentaries on the Constitution of the Empire of Japan*, 117
Comyns-Carr, Arthur S., 77
Concerning the Instruction and Control of the Speeches and Actions of the Army Unites and Units and Army Men Returned from the China Incident Area, 234–35, 359
conspiracy, 14, 37, 69, 71, 73, 72–79, 79, 80, 82, 83, 84, 90, 92–93, 99–100, 101, 128, 129, 130, 143–187, 190, 193, 194, 195–96, 196, 199, 260, 262, 265–66, 266, 267, 266–68, 268–70, 271–84, 284–92, 292–93, 293–95, 295, 301, 296–304, 307, 316–18, 320, 321, 328, 329, 331, 332, 334, 335, 338, 340, 349, 365, 390, 392, 395, 399, 400, 437, 438–39, 440, 442, 450, 455, 452–58, 464, 496, 510, 511
Constitution of the Empire of Japan, 103–5, 106, 112, 113, 114, 115–16, 117–18, 138
Corregidor, 221
Covenant of the League of Nations, 80, 156
Covenant of the League of Nations' Charter, 157
Cramer, Myron C., 50, 51, 263, 287, 355, 380
crime-base evidence, 205, 225, 236, 374
crimes against humanity, 6, 38, 40, 65, 71, 73, 84, 97, 101, 190, 192–93, 194, 203, 268, 315–16, 346, 389, 401, 408, 496, 505, 511
crimes against peace, 69–100, 143–187, 255–338, 391–458, 496–512
criminal organizations, 41
cross-examination, 46, 55, 57, 60–61
Cryer, Robert, 2, 5, 21, 22, 255

Damste, Sinninge, J. S., 207
Dandō Shigemitsu, 12, 13
deportation, 37, 38, 192, 194, 201, 214, 346, 374
destruction of property, 38, 201, 206, 207, 208, 209, 212
Dohihara Kenji, 50, 155, 160, 217, 238, 239, 240, 296–97, 297, 318–20, 356–57, 357, 358, 359–60, 360, 384, 424
Doolittle Flyers, 10, 220, 384
Double Tenth Trial, 465

Einsatzgruppen, 345
enslavement, 30, 38, 192, 194, 201, 315
European Convention on Human Rights, 497
ex post facto, 10, 11, 12–13, 15, 24, 88, 94, 188, 190, 191, 192, 256, 265, 313, 317, 318, 393, 400, 414, 415, 443, 499, 500
execution of Allied air crew, 492–93, 500
extermination, 38, 192, 194, 315, 323, 366, 367, 372, 381, 488
Extraordinary Chambers in the Courts of Cambodia, 55, 505

fair-trial protection, 6, 7, 46, 48, 53–61, 140, 258, 311, 392, 398–99, 420, 450, 497–98, 504
Far Eastern Commission, 42–44
February 26 Incident, 164, 285
FEC 007/3, 42, 43, 44
flying balloons, 504
forced labor, 34, 207, 214, 483–84, 484
forced prostitution, 18, 214, 354, 467. *See also* comfort women
Formosa. *See* Taiwan
Four-Power reply, 34, 35, 36
Freedom and People's Rights Movement, 106
French Indochina, 65, 83, 179, 181, 185, 206, 239, 298
Frick, Wilhelm, 462
Fritzsche, Hans, 256, 309
Fujita Hisakazu, 14, 20
Fundamental Policy for the Disposition of the China Incident, 171–73
Funk, Walter, 463
Fuwa Hiroshi, 240

Gauss, C. E., 212, 213
Geneva Conventions, 1929, 24, 200–201, 205, 219, 330, 348, 351, 382, 397, 436, 476, 478, 480, 481, 483–85, 485, 488
German-Soviet Non-Aggression Pact, 121

Germany. *See also* Tripartite Pact
  compared with the Allied Powers, 432, 434, 447–48, 448, 469–70
  unconditional surrender by, 9, 94–95, 95, 393
  victor's justice views in, 7–8, 8, 11, 256, 498
Glueck, Sheldon, 411, 439
Goette, John, 329
Gotovina Case, 374
government responsibility, 200, 209, 225, 231, 248, 249, 250–52. *See also* cabinet responsibility
Great Britain
  on the Japanese Emperor, 35–36, 36, 42, 400
Grew, Joseph, 212
Guam, 216
Guangdong, 471
Guilin, 354, 472

habeas corpus, 52, 352, 355, 362
Hague Conventions, 1907, 11, 24, 89, 201, 200–201, 214, 219, 341, 348, 351, 395, 397, 436, 463, 476, 477, 476–78, 485, 486, 488, 499
Hainan Island, 206
Hamaguchi Osachi, 150
Hankou, 212, 213, 232, 377, 425
Hara Teizō, 467
Hara Yoshimichi, 183
Harada Kumao, 66, 67, 132
Hashimoto Kingorō, 151, 256, 297–98, 299, 320–21, 424
Hata Shunroku, 50, 121–22, 122, 214, 232, 298–99, 321–22, 357–58, 359, 360, 361, 384–85, 386, 424, 425–26
Hayashi Kyūjirō, 152
Hayashi Senjūrō, 154, 186
Hazeyama Tetsuo, 240, 241
Hell Ships, 216, 490
Heydrich, Reinhard, 372
Hidaka Shunrokurō, 226, 229
High Command Case, 6, 228, 240, 241, 242, 248, 347, 357, 363, 436, 460, 463, 468, 478, 489, 514, 520
Higurashi Yoshinobu, 19
Hilberg, Raul, 373
Hiranuma Kiichirō, 50, 53, 114, 115, 116, 121, 122, 159, 186, 287–88, 299–300, 323, 322–24, 327, 365–67, 367, 368, 375, 381, 383, 389, 424, 488

Hirohito, 18, 26, 29, 35, 36, 39, 42, 66, 67, 87, 122, 129, 131, 132, 133, 134, 135, 138, 139, 142, 150, 153, 154, 157, 158, 159, 160, 164, 169, 174, 179, 182, 183, 184, 185, 186, 187, 220, 249, 259, 287, 288, 299, 310, 323, 335, 341, 379, 380, 398, 400, 482, 512
  clean-slate order by, 139, 184
  monologue by, 40, 160
  non-prosecution of, 10, 17, 18, 43, 44, 106, 141, 142, 392, 398, 399, 401
Hirota Kōki, 3, 14, 50, 116, 123, 161, 164–66, 167–68, 169–70, 172–73, 174, 175, 178, 186, 187, 210, 211–13, 228–31, 249, 280–84, 285, 286, 299–300, 324–28, 332, 337, 344, 367, 368, 377, 379, 389, 402, 403, 418–24, 424, 425–30, 460, 516–18, 519
Hitler, Adolf, 10, 31, 157, 293, 309, 323, 334, 370, 372, 378, 382, 412, 421
Hokkaid, 34
Honjō Shigeru, 155, 164
Honma Masaharu, 52, 216, 229, 345, 479, 480, 494
Horinouchi Kensuke, 167, 168, 169
Horwitz, Solis, 103, 135
Hoshino Naoki, 46, 47, 50, 124, 424
Hostage Case, 460, 463, 468, 514, 519, 520
Ho-Umezu Agreement, 162
Hull, Cordell, 185

Ichigaya, 44, 48
Ikejiri Satoshi, 240
incident (*jihen*), 148, 149, 157, 214, 215, 320, 323, 326, 328, 371, 422. *See also* China Incident, Lukouchiao, Mukden, Manchuria
Indian National Army, 509
Instrument of Surrender, 35, 86, 95, 96, 309, 310, 497
International Committee for the Nanjing Safety Zone, 209, 212
International Committee of the Red Cross, 56, 201, 237
International Covenant on Civil and Political Rights (ICCPR), 497, 504
International Criminal Court (ICC), 520. *See also* Rome Statute of the International Criminal Court

538    Index

International Criminal Tribunal for Rwanda (ICTR), 258, 505, 513–521
International Criminal Tribunal for the former Yugoslavia (ICTY), 55, 264, 505, 513–521
International Military Tribunal (IMT)
 Charter, 7, 8, 9, 38, 45, 69, 86–87, 87, 88, 90, 94–95, 192, 193, 199, 315, 453, 477, 501, 502. *See also* London Agreement
 Indictment, 73, 77, 79, 188, 189, 190, 192, 193, 194, 195, 202
 Judgment, 70, 87, 88–89, 90, 94, 99–100, 256, 262, 263, 265, 266, 268–70, 293, 296, 309, 310, 311, 314–16, 345, 363, 370, 392, 393, 406–7, 407, 409, 439, 440–41, 453–54, 454, 462, 477, 478, 489, 502, 507, 510, 514
International Military Tribunal for the Far East (IMTFE)
 Charter, 8, 9, 10, 41, 42, 40–42, 51, 53–56, 69, 72, 76, 79, 86, 88, 94, 96, 163, 192, 193, 194, 199, 263, 264, 268, 270, 274, 301, 309–10, 310, 311, 315, 317–18, 393–94, 399, 400, 403, 405, 407, 408, 413, 405–16, 419, 427, 429, 438, 443, 453, 454, 496, 497, 501, 502, 505–7, 510, 511
 defense counsel, 13, 46–47
 Indictment, 10, 48, 49, 50, 52, 65, 66, 70–86, 101, 103, 108, 123, 128, 136, 143, 144, 146, 176, 187, 188–202, 208, 209, 217, 225, 231, 234, 249, 255, 263, 265–70, 271, 276, 278, 292, 293, 295, 299, 320, 332, 348, 360, 365, 369, 373, 376, 381, 392, 432, 443, 444, 452, 453, 459, 462, 463, 469, 474, 494, 496, 498, 500, 503, 506, 511, 512, 515
 International Prosecution Section, 22, 45–46
 Judgment, 15, 21, 50–52. *See also* Majority Judgment, *individual separate opinions, and* Webb's draft judgment
 rules of procedure, 42, 53–61
interpretation, 56–57, 57
Inukai Tsuyoshi, 284
IPS Document No. 0006, 54–55, 57–61
Irie Keishirō, 14
Ishii Itarō, 168, 229, 230, 231, 249, 367
Isono Yūzō, 62
Itagaki Seishirō, 121, 152, 155, 157–58, 160, 179, 218, 234, 238, 239, 240, 241, 287, 323, 358, 359, 358–60, 360, 378, 384, 385, 424

Italy, 37, 81, 83, 177, 184, 476, 477. *See also* Tripartite Pact
Itō Hirobumi, 107, 117, 118, 119
Itō Nobufumi, 212
Iwo Jima, 31

Jackson, Robert H., 441, 445, 446, 447, 452
Japan
 10th Army, 226, 228
 14th Area Army, 189, 238, 239, 242
 25th Army, 241
 7th Area Army, 239, 240–41, 356, 359, 384
 Army General Staff, 44, 62–63, 107, 110, 154, 155, 166–68, 170–71, 172, 173–75, 177, 178, 229, 267, 287, 293, 326, 342
 Board of Marshals and Fleet Admirals, 107
 Burma Area Army, 239, 240–41, 331, 360, 386
 Cabinet, 66, 85, 93, 105, 106, 109, 110–11, 112, 113, 114, 115–20, 115–20, 122, 123, 125–27, 127, 128, 129, 130, 133, 134, 139, 140–41, 148, 276, 280–82, 282–83, 284–91, 294, 303–4, 336–38. *See also specific Cabinets by the name of prime minister*
 Central China Area Army, 208, 209, 210, 211, 215, 226–28, 242
 Central China Expeditionary Army, 232, 358
 Central Committee for Investigations Concerning Prisoners of War, 215
 chief aide-de-camp to the emperor, 107
 China Affairs Board, 124–25, 125
 China Expeditionary Force, 215, 232
 China Garrison Army, 162, 167
 Conference for the Supreme Direction of the War, 112, 127, 129, 133, 134, 135, 247, 249, 367
 Eastern District Army, 217, 384
 Eighth Submarine Squadron, 243
 Emperor, 29, 35, 34–36, 38–40, 42–44, 44, 65, 66, 96, 101–142, 109, 177–78, 276, 289, 109, 379–80, 381, 382, 383, 385, 389, 391, 399, 400–401, 460, 511–12, 512. *See also and* Hirohito
 First Submarine Force, 378
 Five Minister Conference, 110, 125, 127, 161, 164, 423
 Four Minister Conference, 110, 127
 General Affairs Board of the Government of Manchukuo, 124
 *genrō*, 66, 107–8. *See also* Saionji Kinmochi

Index

Imperial Conference, 85, 109, 110, 111–12, 127, 130–35, 139, 140–41, 142, 171–73, 174, 179, 180–87, 187, 326, 329, 330, 335, 337, 371
Imperial Diet, 66, 105, 106, 112–14, 322, 323, 325, 326, 331, 332, 366, 371, 381, 388, 423, 425, 488
Imperial Headquarters, 34, 35, 110, 130, 169, 170, 182, 230, 280–82, 491, 492
Imperial Headquarters Conference, 112, 127, 129, 130
Imperial Guards Division, 164, 239, 241, 361. *See also* Second Imperial Guards Division
*jūshiin* (ex-premiers), 186
*jūshin* (ex-premiers), 85, 108, 133, 179, 186, 299
Korea Army, 63, 155, 154–55, 167, 218
Kwantung Army, 123, 124, 149–56, 157, 158, 160, 162, 167, 319, 321, 330, 383
Liaison Conference, 85, 110–12, 127, 128–29, 130, 131, 132, 133, 134, 135, 140–41, 170, 172, 174, 173–75, 179, 230, 288–89, 290, 323, 329, 332, 337, 363, 367, 377
Lord Keeper of the Privy Seal, 66, 67, 108, 122, 132, 133, 140, 153, 164. *See also* Kido Kōichi
Manchurian Affairs Board, 124
Military Affairs Bureau, 110, 214, 216, 217, 221, 223–24, 230, 301, 330, 331, 332, 362, 364, 377, 387, 388, 389
Ministry of Colonial Affairs, 126, 224
Ministry of Foreign Affairs, 62, 123, 126, 122–27, 211–12, 220–21, 223–24, 227, 228–31, 247, 287, 335, 367, 377, 382, 388, 413
Ministry of Greater East Asia, 125–27, 224
Ministry of Imperial Household, 66, 108, 131
Ministry of the Army, 44, 63, 123, 168, 216–17, 217, 220–24, 230, 233, 243, 247, 250, 281, 300, 331, 354, 377, 381, 386. *See also* Military Affairs Bureau
Ministry of the Navy, 224, 230, 244, 247, 250, 281. *See also* Naval Affairs Bureau
Naval Affairs Bureau, 110, 219, 224, 243, 244, 363–64, 363–65, 388
Navy General Staff, 48, 107, 110, 132, 182, 243, 342
Planning Board, 125, 245, 246
Prisoner-of-War Administration Section, 245, 387

Prisoner-of-War Information Bureau, 214, 216, 217, 220, 221, 223, 224, 248, 484
Privy Council, 66, 105, 106, 111, 112, 113, 114–15, 115, 116, 133, 140, 159–60, 183, 276, 290, 323, 342, 365, 381
Second Imperial Guards Division, 239
Shanghai Expeditionary Army, 226, 228
Southern Army, 238, 241, 491
Supreme War Council, 85, 107, 320
Japan-Manchukuo Protocol, 158, 159, 160
Jaranilla Opinion, 496–512. *See also* Jaranilla, Delfin
Jaranilla, Delfin, 51, 263, 353, 355
Java, 63, 206, 238, 239, 356, 358, 466
Jescheck, Hans-Heinrich, 8, 11
joint criminal enterprise, 73, 264–65, 267, 520

Kainō Michitaka, 12
Karadzic Case, 265
Kawabe Torashirō, 62, 63, 154, 371
Kaya Okinori, 244, 245, 246, 280, 281, 286, 300, 328–29, 389, 424
Kayishema Case, 517
Keenan, Joseph B., 45, 71, 76, 77, 140, 144, 145, 146, 190
Kellogg-Briand Pact. *See* Pact of Paris
Kelsen, Hans, 397, 411, 439
Kenpeitai, 207, 354, 379, 460, 465, 466
Kharkov, 10
*Kido Diary*, 66–67, 87, 121, 122, 133, 134, 153, 154, 157, 182, 183, 184, 185, 186, 187, 287, 324
Kido Kōichi, 45, 47, 66–67, 87, 108, 121, 122, 133, 134, 138, 139, 140, 153, 158, 170–71, 173, 182, 184, 186, 280, 281, 310, 367–68, 368, 418, 419, 422, 424, 426
Kimura Heitarō, 50, 218, 219, 220, 238, 239, 240, 300–301, 301, 329–31, 358, 360–61, 378, 382, 385–86, 424
Kiyose Ichirō, 44, 78
Koiso Kuniaki, 14, 53, 129–30, 245, 246, 248, 327, 367, 375, 381, 382–83, 424
Konoe Fumimaro, 122, 132, 167, 168, 170, 174, 182, 183, 184, 186, 283, 286, 289, 322, 422
Korea, 17, 30, 63, 154, 218, 235, 330, 358, 385, 386, 434, 447
Kosovo, 373
Kumegawa Yoshiharu, 242
Kuril Islands, 34
Kursk, 31
Kuwashima Kazue, 155, 319
Kwajalein, 216, 218, 243

## Index

Kwantung Leased Territory, 123, 124, 148, 149

Lake Khasan, 179, 333
Lauterpacht, H., 310, 312, 411, 439, 449, 478
League of Nations, 80, 81, 123, 148, 156, 168, 311, 409, 410, 411, 445, 446
Lebensraum, 447, 454
Leningrad, 31
Liebert, John G., 328
linkage evidence, 203, 204, 205, 216, 225, 374
London Agreement, 86–87, 95, 407, 412
looting, 206, 208, 209, 227. *See also* plunder
Lord Lytton, 156
Lord Patrick, 51, 309, 405
Lord Wright, 98, 439
Lukouchiao, 128, 161, 162, 163, 166–68, 168, 169, 171, 179, 326
Lytton Report, 148, 149, 156

MacArthur, Douglas, 35, 39, 40, 43, 44, 52, 96, 190, 191, 192, 193, 198, 305
Majority Judgment, 2, 4, 5, 15, 16, 20, 49, 50–52, 60, 71, 74, 79, 80, 81, 85, 87, 88, 93, 102, 109, 115, 121, 142, 144, 146, 154, 176, 187, 188, 189, 190, 193, 194, 198, 199, 200, 203, 207, 213, 217, 240, 255–304, 305–6, 307–9, 309, 311, 313–14, 314, 316, 317, 318, 320, 324, 325, 328, 331, 332, 333, 339–369, 370, 374, 378–79, 384, 389, 390, 391, 393, 395, 400, 401, 406, 427, 431–32, 433, 435, 437, 439, 453, 460, 480, 495, 496, 502, 504, 509, 510, 511, 513
Majority justices, 51
Makino Nobuaki, 164, 445
Malaya, 63, 206, 238, 239, 356, 358, 465, 509
Manchukuo, 24, 31, 33, 34, 105, 123, 124, 148, 157, 158–60, 161, 165, 170, 171, 172, 179, 224, 284, 325, 327, 328, 330, 333, 335, 383, 418, 423, 434
Manila, 10, 52, 189, 216, 352, 387, 388, 470, 473–75, 479, 494, 500, 509
Mansfield, Alan J., 58, 59, 204, 205, 206, 207
March Incident, 150
Matsui Iwane, 208, 209, 210–11, 215, 226–28, 229, 361, 387, 389, 424, 474
Matsuo Denzō, 164
Matsuoka Yōsuke, 48, 181, 500
McCoy, Frank R., 43
McDougall, E. S., 51
Mei Ruao, 51, 267, 297, 305, 353, 354, 355, 362, 392, 437
Meiji Constitution. *See* Constitution of the Empire of Japan

Meiji Emperor, 103, 119, 139
Meiji Restoration, 104, 106
*Mein Kampf*, 99
mens rea, 93, 196, 199, 295, 519
mental element, 93, 196, 199, 271, 291, 295, 301, 320, 321, 356, 359, 361, 362, 379, 460, 514, 517, 518, 520. *See also* mens rea
Minami Jirō, 124, 151, 153, 154, 155, 424
Minear, Richard, 1, 16, 17
Ministries Case, 345, 382, 403, 460, 461, 463, 468
Morishima Morito, 152
Moscow Declaration, 30, 412
Mukden, 37, 63, 152, 153, 155, 297, 319
Musema Case, 517, 519
Mutō Akira, 209, 210, 211, 214, 217, 238, 239, 241–43, 361–63, 364, 386–89, 424, 519
Mutsuhito. *See* Meiji Emperor

*Nacht und Nebel*, 372
Nagano Osami, 48, 182, 219, 335
Nakahara, Jirō, 243
Nakayama Yasuto, 214, 226, 227
Nanjing, 3, 123, 125, 162, 163, 166, 169, 206–7, 208–13, 213, 215, 225–31, 233, 234, 361, 367–68, 377, 387–88, 389, 419, 425, 429, 464, 466, 469, 470–71, 475
Naoetsu, 217, 221, 384
National General Mobilization Law, 103
national sovereignty, principle of, 169, 409, 410, 411, 418, 500
New Zealand, 43, 44, 47, 65
Nine-Power Treaty, 81–82, 82, 148, 159, 319, 322
Nolan, Henry G., 103
Nomonhan, 174, 179
Nomura Kichisaburō, 336
Northcroft, E. H., 44, 45, 47, 51, 274, 305, 349, 352
*nullem crimen sine lege*, 94, 414
Nuremberg Judgment. *See* International Military Tribunal (IMT), Judgment
Nuremberg Principles, 7, 8
Nuremberg Subsequent Proceedings, 6, 9, 343, 345, 403, 438, 460, 463, 477, 485, 501

October Incident, 157
Ōhira Hideo, 241
Oka Takazumi, 219, 243–44, 302, 362, 363–65, 388, 389, 424
Okada Keisuke, 148, 150, 164, 186, 285
Okada Ryōhei, 159, 160

Ōkawa Shūmei, 48, 151, 195, 292–93
Okinawa, 32
Okuhara Toshio, 14
Ōmori, 221
Ōnuma Yasuaki, 14
Oppenheim, L., 91, 98, 310, 312, 411, 439, 478
Ōshima Hiroshi, 176–78, 218, 378, 383, 424, 433
Ott, Eugene, 331
Ōyama Ayao, 233, 234, 492
Ozaki Yukio, 118

Pact of Paris, 80–81, 88–89, 91, 98, 148, 159, 311, 312, 313, 314–15, 315, 317, 394, 409, 410–11, 411, 414
Pal Opinion, 2, 5, 89, 157, 259, 260–61, 261, 264, 270, 306, 314, 324, 333, 337, 373–74, 379, 390, 391–92, 403, 431–395, 496, 500–501. *See also* Pal, Radhabinod
Pal, Radhabinod, 1, 5, 7, 9, 15–17, 51, 70, 78–79, 92, 98, 306, 313, 315, 372, 373, 374, 379, 382, 393, 395, 396, 402, 404, 414, 420, 431, 496, 498–99, 499, 500, 502, 503, 504–7, 507, 509
Peace Preservation Law, 103
Pearl Harbor, 5, 128, 129, 191, 299
Perisic Case, 374
permitting, 190, 191, 195, 196–98, 199, 208, 350, 351, 352, 354–55, 359, 361, 366, 367, 378, 469, 474, 488, 515, 519
Philippines
  battles in, 189, 238, 362, 479
  war crimes in, 238, 350, 378, 386, 388, 465, 470, 473–75, 501, 509
plunder, 38, 214, 235, 387, 442, 472
poison gas, 201, 202
Poland, 121, 157, 309, 346, 372, 382
Potsdam Declaration, 9, 29, 32–35, 36, 39, 61, 86–87, 95–97, 133, 134, 309, 310, 408
Prince Fushimi, 131
Prince Kan'in, 154, 170, 179
Prince Takamatsu, 186
Prisoner-of-War Convention. *See* Geneva Conventions, 1929
Pritchard, R. John, 21
Pu Yi, 148, 155

Quilliam, R. H., 47, 65, 71, 77

Radbruch, Gustav, 394
Rangoon, 240, 378
rape, 18, 201, 206, 207, 208, 209, 211, 214, 227, 233–34, 234, 235, 350, 354, 361, 374, 376, 377, 387, 429, 442, 464, 470, 471, 472, 473–75, 494, 509, 516

Red-Cross Convention. *See* Geneva Conventions, 1929
Ridgway, Matthew, 44
Roeling Opinion, 26, 92, 97, 259, 261, 264, 270, 324, 333, 335, 337, 368, 391–430, 431, 438, 466, 495. *See also* Roeling, B. V. A.
Roeling, B. V. A., 10, 20, 21, 51, 70, 98, 191, 261, 283, 325, 333, 350, 351, 353, 376, 382, 391, 433, 435, 438, 439, 440, 443, 447, 458, 461, 498, 500, 502, 505, 506, 507, 509, 516, 517
Rome Statute of the International Criminal Court, 256, 313, 505, 519
Roosevelt, Franklin D., 412
Rules of Procedure of the International Military Tribunal for the Far East, 53–54
RuSHA Case, 477
Russo-Japanese War, 123, 173, 179
Rwanda, 57, 373, 516, 520. *See also* International Criminal Tribunal for Rwanda (ICTR)

Saionji Kinmochi, 66, 67, 107, 132, 153
*Saionji-Harada Memoirs*, 66–67, 173, 174, 177, 179, 325, 326
Saipan, 31
Saitō Makoto, 164, 284, 285
Saitō Seiei, 240, 241
Sakhalin, 34
San Francisco Peace Treaty, 53
Sandakan Death Marches, 216, 350
Satō Kenryō, 50, 217, 239, 301, 302, 331–32, 362, 364, 388–89, 424
Satsuma Rebellion, 106
Schacht, Hjalmar, 256, 309, 370, 421
self-defense, 2, 90–92, 98, 146, 156–57, 157, 163, 181, 311–13, 332, 337
sexual violence. *See specific types of sexual violence*
Shanghai, 162, 168, 169, 210, 212, 226, 227, 229, 326, 498
Shidehara Kijūrō, 148, 151, 152, 155
Shigemitsu Mamoru, 14, 35, 45, 50, 52, 53, 129, 204, 218, 224, 245, 246–50, 293, 302–3, 303, 304, 332–34, 367, 368–69, 375, 378, 382, 383, 389, 402, 403, 418, 419, 424, 426, 430, 516
Shimada Shigetarō, 126, 186, 219, 243–44, 301–2, 334–35, 364, 424
Shiratori Toshio, 53, 176, 195, 424
Shōwa Emperor. *See* Hirohito
Siberia, 34, 325, 327
Sierra Leone, 520. *See also* Special Court for Sierra Leone

Singapore, 206, 216, 218, 238, 241, 384, 465, 466, 467, 479, 480, 491
slave labor, 37, 463, 479, 484, 491. *See also* forced labor
Southern Manchurian Railway, 149, 152
Special Court for Sierra Leone, 408
Speer, Albert, 463
Stalin, Josef, 31, 33, 412
Stanisic Case, 374
Strugar Case, 516
submarine atrocities, 201, 218–19, 243, 244, 378
Sugamo, 48, 53
Sugiyama Hajime, 182, 220, 230, 330, 429
Sumatra, 206, 239, 241, 356, 358, 361
superior responsibility, 343, 375, 513, 514, 516, 517–18, 519, 520–21
Supreme Commander for the Allied Powers (SCAP), 34–35, 35, 37, 39, 38–40, 41, 42, 43, 44, 45, 51, 52, 87, 96–97, 134, 190, 192, 309–10, 506. *See also* MacArthur, Douglas
Suzuki Kantarō, 33, 134, 164
Suzuki Tadakatsu, 223, 224, 246, 247, 248, 249, 367, 377
Suzuki Teiichi, 125, 126, 186, 245, 246, 290, 424
SWNCC 57/3, 36–38, 40, 41, 42
synopsis method, 58–60, 205, 215

Tada Hayao, 170, 173, 174, 175
Tadic Case, 264–65
Taiwan, 17, 63, 206, 235, 330, 434, 447
Takahashi Korekiyo, 164
Tanaka Giichi, 149, 150, 294
Tanaka Ryūkichi, 217, 321, 483, 484
Tanaka Shin'ichi, 169, 330
Tanaka Takeo, 129
Tangku Truce, 161–63
Tani Masayuki, 126
Tarawa, 29
Tavenner, Frank S. Jr., 77
Tazumi Genzō, 240
Terauchi Hisaichi, 241
The President's Judgment. *See* Webb's draft judgment
Tianjin, 155, 160, 161, 162, 167, 168, 319
Tōgō Shigenori, 52, 53, 123–27, 128, 185, 218, 224, 246, 303–4, 335–38, 383, 418, 419, 424, 426
Tōjō Hideki, 116, 126, 138, 139–40, 183, 184, 186, 187, 205, 218, 219–22, 223, 225, 239, 246, 301, 322, 324, 329, 330, 334, 336, 338, 365, 377, 383, 389, 424, 475, 480, 484, 485, 487, 489, 516

*Tōkyō saiban*, 49
Tomioka Sadatoshi, 243
torture, 201, 207, 209, 214, 234, 235, 354, 361, 362, 374, 465, 492
toture, 207
Toyoda Trial, 228, 399
Trainin, A. N., 439
translation, 55, 56, 57, 58–59, 66, 67, 68, 185, 187, 223, 503. *See also* interpretation
Tripartite Pact, 31, 176, 179, 333, 423
Truk, 218
Truman, Harry S., 35, 96
Tsukada Osamu, 211
Tsukamoto Kōji, 226
Twenty-One Demands, 149

Uchida Rikizō, 13
Uemura Mikio, 484
Umezu Yoshijirō, 35, 50, 53, 162, 424
unconditional surrender, 9, 16, 30, 33, 34, 35, 87, 94–97, 393, 418, 497
United Nations, 157, 258, 501
United Nations War Crimes Commission, 30, 42, 98, 213
United States
 Joint Chiefs of Staff, 38–40, 43
 State-War-Navy Coordinating Committee (SWNCC), 36
 Supreme Court, 52–53, 355
Uzawa Sōmei, 78

victor's justice, 7–11, 12, 14–20, 22, 188, 258, 307, 311, 324, 332, 392, 496–99, 513
Von Dirksen, Herbert, 169, 170, 172
Von Neurath, Konstantin, 172, 336
Von Papen, Franz, 256
Von Ribbentrop, Joachim, 345, 403
Von Weiszaecker, Ernst, 382, 345, 403

Wachi Takeji, 221
Wakamatsu Tadakazu, 220
Wakatsuki Reijirō, 148, 150, 151, 152, 153, 154, 155, 157, 186, 284, 324
Wake Island, 243
Wang Jingwei, 125, 214, 298
Wannsee Conference, 372
war crimes, 188–252, 339–430, 459–512. *See specific types of war crimes*
Watanabe Yasuji, 238
waterboarding ("water cure"), 207, 354
Webb Separate Opinion, 51, 257, 496–512. *See also* Webb, Sir William F.

Webb, Sir Wlliam F., 4, 8, 44, 48–49, 50,
  51, 57, 59, 60, 61, 78, 80, 89, 98,
  139–40, 142, 187, 204–5, 213, 217,
  232, 237, 238–39, 250, 261, 265, 274,
  275, 283, 299, 304, 394, 403–4, 405,
  408, 409, 413–14, 419, 420–21, 428,
  429, 430, 432, 433, 435, 438, 439,
  454, 460, 466, 498, 500, 501,
  502, 509
Webb's draft judgment, 100, 261, 273,
  278, 279, 282, 283, 287, 295,
  305–338, 341, 349, 356, 364, 365,
  370–390, 392, 393, 396, 401, 418, 422,
  428, 453, 513. *See also* Webb,
  Sir William F.
Williams, G. C., 46, 47

Yamamoto Chikao, 243
Yamamoto Kumaichi, 126, 128
Yamamoto Yoshio, 243
Yamashita Trial, 10, 22, 52, 188–89, 193,
  196–99, 200, 216, 238, 343, 345, 352,
  355, 362, 378, 494, 514, 518, 520
Yamawaki Masataka, 234, 359
Yamazaki Shigeru, 216, 217, 387
Yokota Kisaburō, 12, 13
Yonai Mitsumasa, 324
Yoshibashi Kaizō, 232, 233
Yuasa Kurahei, 132

Zaryanov, Ivan M., 51, 433
Zhang Tsolin, 149, 150, 151, 158
Zhang Xueliang, 158

For EU product safety concerns, contact us at Calle de José Abascal, 56–1°,
28003 Madrid, Spain or eugpsr@cambridge.org.

www.ingramcontent.com/pod-product-compliance
Ingram Content Group UK Ltd.
Pitfield, Milton Keynes, MK11 3LW, UK
UKHW020348060825
461487UK00008B/570